THE PENAL SYSTEM

THE PENAL SYSTEM

An Introduction

Fourth edition

Michael Cavadino and
James Dignan

Los Angeles | London | New Delhi
Singapore | Washington DC

SAGE Publications Ltd
1 Oliver's Yard
55 City Road
London EC1Y 1SP

SAGE Publications Inc
2455 Teller Road
Thousand Oaks, California 91320

SAGE Publications India Pvt Ltd
B 1/I1 Mohan Cooperative Industrial Area
Mathura Road
New Delhi 110 044

SAGE Publications Asia-Pacific Pte Ltd
33 Pekin Street #02-01
Far East Square
Singapore 048763

Library of Congress Control Number Available

British Library Cataloguing in Publication data

A catalogue record for this book is available from the British
Library.

ISBN 978-1-4129-2946-2
ISBN 978-1-4129-2947-9

Typeset by C&M Digitals (P) Ltd., Chennai, India
Printed in Great Britain by Ashford Colour Press Ltd, Gosport, Hampshire

Contents

Preface to the Fourth Edition

It's all happening, isn't it? Since the third edition of this 'essential text . . . indispensable resource' (as the reviewers say) came out in 2002, we have had the highly eventful Home Secretaryships of David Blunkett and Charles Clarke and the brief but even more dramatic reign of John Reid. Law and order remains high up the political agenda, with Tony Blair's 'Respect Agenda' setting much of the pace and tone, at least for the moment. The framework for sentencing has been completely revised (at least until the next time) by the Criminal Justice Act 2003. Oh, and the penal system continues to lurch alarmingly through what seems now to be a never-ending crisis, with record and ever-rising numbers of prisoners combining with shrill 'law and order' attitudes to make the situation more difficult and dangerous than ever.

So of course all students of the penal system of England and Wales will need this book. Which is now more useful than ever, because along with our suggestions for useful websites in the 'self-study guide' at the end we now also provide a **companion website** to this book itself, on which you can find summaries of recent legislation, official reports and proposals, and other updates and supplementary information (with appropriate weblinks) so that, no matter what the pace of penal change before the next edition, this is the product that will keep you fully informed and abreast of the penal system and all the dramatic developments which (we confidently predict) are still to come. The website's address is www.sagepub.co.uk/thepenalsystem

Also available in all good bookshops (and not to be confused with this book) is our companion work to this volume, *Penal Systems: A Comparative Approach* (Cavadino and Dignan, 2006), in which we compare penal systems in 12 different countries. We refer to this other work here and there in what follows, but serious students will need to study it separately to fully discover what we can learn from other countries, and in particular why it is that they do not all suffer from a penal crisis like England's.

Our thanks are due to our colleagues in the Centre for Criminological and Legal Research and the Faculty of Law at Sheffield (especially Gwen Robinson and Estella Baker), to Mick's new colleagues in the Lancashire Law School and Centre for Criminology and Criminal Justice at the University of Central Lancashire, to the various kind souls who praised the third edition and encouraged us to keep going, and to other colleagues in the wider criminological community, who are either too numerous or too embarrassingly few to mention individually (you guess which). We again have to thank the team at Sage, especially Caroline Porter, who have been as helpful as ever. Thanks also, as always, to Lucille Cavadino and Angela Dignan for their understanding, tolerance, patience and loving support during the writing of this book.

Introduction

This book is about the penal system – the system that exists to deal with people who have (usually)[1] been convicted of a criminal offence: the system that delivers official punishment for those who have broken the law.[2] More precisely, we are centrally concerned with the 'English' penal system, by which we mean the system in England and Wales (Scotland and Northern Ireland have separate systems). However, much of what we say (especially about penal philosophy and penal sociology in Chapters 2 and 3) is of relevance to more than one country; and at times we will be referring to other penal systems to help illuminate the English (and Welsh) experience.[3] While we have tried to be factually correct, to outline differing viewpoints and to be as comprehensive as is possible in a book of this size, we have not felt any need to be shy about expressing our own opinions. In a nutshell, these are that the English penal system is unjustly and irrationally harsh, and that our penal practices and attitudes towards punishment require radical revision.

The Criminal Justice System

I.1 The penal system is part of a larger entity known as the *criminal justice system*, a term covering all those institutions that respond officially to the commission of offences, notably the police, prosecution authorities and courts. It is often misleading or unsatisfactory to examine the penal system in isolation from the larger criminal justice system. Consequently at times in this book – for example in Chapters 9 and 10 – we deal with the criminal justice system as a whole.

There now follows a very brief and basic guide to the criminal justice system as a whole, to assist readers who may not be familiar with the system or its terminology. Figure I.1 is a simplified diagram of the criminal justice system up to the point where an offender is sentenced by a court, which is the moment when the offender enters the *penal* system.

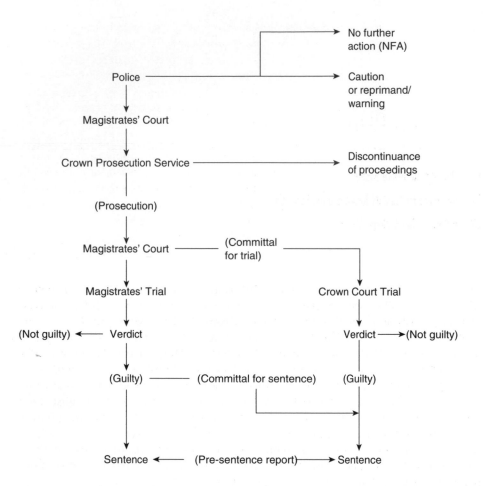

Figure I.1   *The criminal justice system in England and Wales, up to the point of sentence*

In many cases when a crime is committed – indeed, in most cases – the agencies of criminal justice never respond at all. For the criminal justice process normally starts to operate only when a crime is reported to the police, and fewer than half of all crimes are reported. In 2004/5 only 43 per cent of all the crimes uncovered by the official British Crime Survey were reported to the police, and only 32 per cent were officially recorded as crimes by the police (Nicholas et al., 2005: 36). If an alleged offence is reported, or otherwise comes to the attention of the police, the police may then investigate it. The police have a wide range of powers (notably those contained in the Police and Criminal Evidence Act 1984) to carry out searches and to arrest and question suspects in pursuit of their investigations. If there appears to be sufficient evidence to put a suspect on trial, the police may *charge* an arrested suspect with the offence. This is the first stage in the prosecution process, and it is now the Crown Prosecution Service (CPS) – a state agency independent of the police – who instruct the police as to whether suspects should be charged in most cases.[4] The police then normally take the suspect before the local magistrates' court, where the prosecution is conducted by the CPS.

An alternative procedure (used for about two-thirds of all prosecutions) is at present known as the *summons*. Under this procedure the police apply to a magistrate for a summons, which is an order to attend court, but the suspect remains at liberty for the time being. (Under provisions of the Criminal Justice Act 2003 which have not yet been implemented, the existing 'charge' and 'summons' will be replaced by a single procedure known as a 'written charge', which can be made by either the police or the CPS.) Another possible alternative[5] is to dispense with prosecution entirely and for the police instead to administer an official warning. In the case of an offender of 18 or over, this is known as a *caution*. A caution should not be given unless the offender admits guilt. No formal punishment ensues, but the caution will form part of the offender's official criminal record. A variant is a 'conditional caution', where the caution is accompanied by specific conditions which the offender must comply with.[6] Young offenders under 18 receive not 'cautions' but *'reprimands'* and *'warnings'* (also known as 'final warnings'), which are explained more fully in Chapter 9. In 2005, 38 per cent of known offenders[7] were 'diverted from court' by being cautioned, reprimanded or warned rather than prosecuted. Yet another possibility, of increasing importance, is a *fixed penalty notice* (or 'spot fine'), which can be imposed by police officers and certain other specified officials for a widening variety of minor offences.[8]

When the alleged offender reaches the magistrates' court (and becomes a 'defendant'), the court may have to decide whether to grant the defendant *bail* (conditional release prior to the actual trial) or whether the defendant should be *remanded in custody* for the time being. (See further Chapter 4, section 4.2.) Custodial remands are usually to prison, or to a remand centre (a type of prison reserved for remandees).[9]

Criminal offences fall into three categories: indictable only, summary only, and triable either way.[10] This categorization determines at which court – magistrates' court or Crown Court – the trial will be held. Offences which are indictable only (for example, murder, rape and robbery) must be tried at the Crown Court before a judge, with a jury of 12 randomly selected lay people to decide on the verdict if the defendant pleads not guilty. In these cases the magistrates' court sends the case to the Crown Court for trial 'on indictment'. Offences that are summary only (for example, common assault, minor criminal damage and most motoring offences) must be tried 'summarily' at the magistrates' court before at least two and normally three lay justices of the peace or a single district judge (a professional judge, formerly known as a 'stipendiary magistrate'). Offences that are 'triable either way' include theft, arson and most burglaries. If a defendant charged with one of these offences pleads guilty, the case will stay in the magistrates' court at least for the time being.[11] But if the defendant pleads not guilty, the magistrates then decide whether to 'commit' the defendant to be tried in the Crown Court trial or whether the case may be tried in the magistrates' court. A defendant who intends to plead not guilty has the right to insist on a Crown Court trial for an offence which is triable either way. In practice the great majority of triable either way offences are dealt with in the magistrates' court. (For more on 'mode of trial', see Chapter 4, section 4.3.)

Defendants have the choice of pleading either guilty or not guilty in either the magistrates' court or the Crown Court. If the plea is not guilty, the burden rests on the prosecution to prove to the magistrates or jury that the defendant is guilty 'beyond reasonable doubt'. But the great majority of defendants plead guilty: around 90 per cent in the magistrates' court and over 60 per cent at the Crown Court.

If the defendant pleads guilty or is found guilty (in other words, is *convicted* of the offence), the magistrates or judge then pass *sentence*. The sentence is the punishment (or other order of the court) which is imposed upon the defendant as a consequence of committing the crime. A few offences have mandatory or semi-mandatory penalties attached, as explained in Chapter 4. Most offences, however, have a statutory maximum penalty – for example, seven years' imprisonment for theft – but no statutory minimum. The magistrates' court also has statutory limits on its sentencing powers: it cannot sentence an offender to more than six months in prison for a single offence or to more than 12 months in total, nor can it normally impose a fine of more than £5,000. (These maxima will be increased to 12 months and 65 weeks when sections 154–5 of the Criminal Justice Act 2003 are brought into force.) However, a magistrates' court can commit an offender it has convicted to the Crown Court for sentence if it feels that its sentencing powers are inadequate. As long as the statutory maxima are not exceeded, the court usually has a wide range of sentences to choose from. These include the *custodial* sentences of imprisonment (for adults), detention in a young offender institution (at present, for offenders aged 18 to 20) and detention and training orders (for young offenders under 18). *Non-custodial* penalties (to which we devote Chapter 5) include suspended prison sentences, fines, community orders (including what used to be known as probation and community service orders[12]), and absolute and conditional discharges. The court may be assisted in its choice of sentence by a pre-sentence report (PSR), usually prepared by a probation officer (or, in the case of juvenile offenders, by a member of the youth offending team: see Chapter 9). Pre-sentence reports provide the sentencer with information about the offender's behaviour and social and family background, and normally include a proposal for what the sentence should be.

Convicted defendants may appeal to a higher court either against their conviction or against the sentence which has been passed, or both. The Attorney General (a 'government law officer' who is both a member of the government and its chief legal adviser) additionally has the power to refer certain sentences passed by the Crown Court to the Court of Appeal on the grounds that they are too lenient (see Chapter 4 for details).

A sentence of imprisonment means that the offender is allocated to a prison by the Prison Service. (We examine prisons and imprisonment in Chapters 6 and 7.) Under present arrangements, prisoners do not usually serve the full term of the sentence pronounced by the court. For example, an offender sentenced to two years' imprisonment will normally be released after one year, and at the discretion of the prison authorities may be released up to four and a half months earlier still under a 'home detention curfew'. Shorter-term prisoners are released automatically at a certain point of their sentence, but for longer-term prisoners and for those who it is considered may pose a special risk, early release may be at the discretion of the Parole Board. For most prisoners, early release is combined with compulsory supervision by a probation officer in the community, and released prisoners can under certain circumstances be returned to prison to serve the unexpired portion of the sentence. Early release under the home detention curfew scheme involves both supervision and a home curfew enforced by electronic monitoring or 'tagging' of the offender. (For fuller details of the system of early release from prison sentences, see Chapter 8.)

Non-custodial sentences (see Chapter 5) usually require the offender to carry out some action, such as pay a fine or compensation or perform unpaid work (community service). Alternatively, the offender may be required to *refrain* from acting in certain ways, in particular to avoid reoffending within a given time limit (for example, if the sentence is a conditional discharge or a suspended sentence). Offenders who 'breach' the terms of their sentences either by disobeying their requirements or by reoffending can be brought back to court as a result, and the court will then have a range of sanctions available. These sanctions often include the power to pass custodial sentences, which may be additional (or 'consecutive') to any custodial sentence imposed for a fresh offence.

Punishment in both prison and in the community is administered by NOMS (the National Offender Management Service). NOMS, which combines the Prison and Probation Services, was created in 2004 in response to a recommendation in the Carter Report (2003). Its first Chief Executive (2004–5) was Martin Narey, previously Director General of the Prison Service. The Chief Executive of NOMS is (from May 2007)[13] answerable to the Secretary of State for Justice.

Importantly, the whole of the criminal justice system is subject to the provisions of the Human Rights Act 1998, which incorporates the European Convention on Human Rights into English law. Before the Human Rights Act, the United Kingdom government was bound by treaty to respect and defend the human rights set out in the Convention – such as the rights to life, liberty, security, respect for private and family life, freedoms of thought and expression and the right not to be subject to inhuman or degrading treatment – but the Convention was not directly binding in domestic law. Those who considered that their human rights had been violated could only gain redress by the long drawn-out procedure of petitioning the European Court of Human Rights in Strasbourg. If the Court found that UK law was incompatible with the Convention, a duty lay on the government to introduce legislation through Parliament to rectify domestic law. (This arrangement sometimes had important effects on English penal law, for example in altering arrangements for early release – see Chapter 8.) Under the 1998 Act, all public bodies – including criminal justice agencies such as the police and NOMS – are under a legal duty to act in accordance with the Convention. Furthermore, English courts are bound *where possible* to interpret English Acts of Parliament so that they are compatible with the Convention. If the court decides that English law is unequivocally incompatible with the Convention, it must make a formal declaration to this effect; the government then has the power to 'fast-track' legislation through Parliament to remove the incompatibility.

Strategies for Criminal Justice and the Penal Crisis

1.2 This book is largely concerned with the 'crisis' in the English penal system and the policies which governments have developed in response to this crisis. We introduce the penal crisis in general terms in Chapter 1. In Chapter 11 we provide a history of the strategies adopted by national governments up to the present day, but a brief summary is appropriate here to set the scene.

We find it helpful to use a general, threefold categorization of criminal justice policies which we call *Strategies A, B and C* (based on Rutherford, 1993; see also Cavadino et al., 1999). Strategy A is a *highly punitive* approach embodying what we call 'law and order ideology' (see Chapter 1): the attitude that offenders should be dealt with as severely as possible. A governmental strategy based on this attitude would involve making criminal justice harsher and more punitive at every stage and in every respect. Strategy A embodies an *'exclusionary'* approach to offenders, tending to reject them as members of the community (see Cavadino et al., 1999: 48–50). The *'managerialist'* Strategy B seeks to apply administrative and bureaucratic mechanisms to criminal justice in an attempt to make the system as smooth-running and cost-effective as possible. Strategy C seeks to protect and uphold the *human rights* of offenders, victims and potential victims of crime. It seeks to minimize punishment and to ensure fairness and humane treatment within the criminal justice system, and is *'inclusive'*, seeking to maintain offenders within the community and reintegrate them as law-abiding citizens. Proponents of Strategy C are not all of one mind: some favour measures to rehabilitate and reform offenders, while others advocate *'restorative justice'* measures that seek to ensure that offenders perform reparation to their victims and to the community (see Chapters 2, 5 and 9). Others again, while still being motivated by humanitarianism and a wish to lessen the harshness of punishment in general, propound the view that offenders should be punished in proportion to the seriousness of their offences, according to their *'just deserts'* (see Chapter 2).

In the early 1980s, the Conservative government of Margaret Thatcher injected a heavy dose of Strategy A into penal policy. This meant being deliberately harsher in punishing offenders (although as we shall see, especially in Chapters 9 and 11, this was by no means entirely the case across the board). From around 1987 onwards, however – a period we refer to as 'the Hurd era', after Home Secretary Douglas Hurd (1985–89) – the Thatcher government's penal policy became less dogmatic and more pragmatic, although still tinged with punitive 'law and order' rhetoric. The centrepiece of this new strategy was the Criminal Justice Act 1991, which represented the most radical legislative reform to the penal system since the Second World War. This Act combined elements of all three strategies, but importantly it was hoped that it would reduce the prison population and make it more easily manageable (a Strategy B aim). The idea was that more offenders than hitherto should undergo *'punishment in the community'* rather than being sent to prison; additionally, most offenders (with some significant exceptions) were to receive punishments that were in proportion to the seriousness of the crime ('just deserts'). However, within months of the Act's implementation in 1992, the Conservative government (now headed by Mrs Thatcher's successor, John Major) had abandoned the strategy embodied by the Act. From 1993 to 1997, in a development we call *'the law and order counter-reformation'*, the Conservative government – especially in the person of Michael Howard, Home Secretary from 1993 to 1997– pursued ever harsher Strategy A policies, marked by Mr Howard's famous declaration to the Conservative Party Conference in October 1993 that *'prison works'*. Thus did we enter a phase which has been termed 'the new punitiveness' (Pratt et al., 2005; see also Chapter 3, section 3.6).

Following their victory in the General Election of 1997, the New Labour government of Tony Blair – and his Home Secretaries Jack Straw (1997–2001), David Blunkett (2001–4), Charles Clarke (2004–6) and John Reid (2006–07) – sought to implement its famous campaign promise to be 'tough on crime and tough on the causes of crime' by pursuing a mixture of policies with elements of all three Strategies A, B and C. This has included introducing some new measures based on 'restorative justice' (see especially Chapter 9) – in line with one version of Strategy C – and an emphasis on assessing the effectiveness and cost-effectiveness of penal measures (which fits with the managerialism of Strategy B). Strategy A was also well represented in the New Labour policy mix, as the government favoured the increased use of imprisonment for persistent offenders and pursued policies of 'zero tolerance' (see Cavadino et al., 1999: 28–30) towards various categories of wrongdoing. (A term we will be employing for this hybrid approach – especially in Chapter 9, where it is more fully explained – is *'neo-correctionalism'*.) The most important recent developments – the Criminal Justice Act of 2003 and the Carter Report (2003) – will be explained and discussed in the chapters that follow.

Chapter 1 introduces the 'penal crisis', and we then go on to discuss facets of this crisis and the responses to it throughout this book. Chapters 2 and 3 are heavily theoretical, but unashamedly so, for they are also intimately connected to the crisis theme. Chapter 3's exploration of penal sociology underpins our analysis of how the crisis should be explained, while our investigation of the philosophy of punishment in Chapter 2 should contribute to an understanding of why the penal system suffers from its crucial 'crisis of legitimacy'. Chapters 4 to 10 deal with various aspects of the system and its crisis. Chapter 4 identifies the decisions of courts – in particular their sentencing decisions, but also their actions in relation to bail and mode of trial – as the crux of the crisis. Chapter 6 investigates the troubled prison system, while Chapters 5, 7 and 8 deal with three developments which have so far had less than total success in relieving pressure on the system: the proliferation of non-custodial penalties, the policy of privatization, and the mechanisms for early release of prisoners. Chapter 9 examines the parallel system of youth justice, equally prone to its own parallel crisis or 'system disaster', and for similar reasons. Chapter 10 investigates the burning issue of bias within the criminal justice system. Finally, in Chapter 11 we discuss whether the crisis is likely to be solved, and put forward our own agenda for change.

A Note on Terminology: 'System'

1.3 Perhaps the title of this book is misleading. Arguably, one of the salient features of the English penal and criminal justice *'systems'* – at least until recently – has been their highly *unsystematic* nature. For many years a number of disparate relatively autonomous agencies have worked in relative isolation from each other, exercising wide and unaccountable discretionary powers, and subject to no overall coordination or strategic control (or 'joined-up thinking', to use a New Labour phrase). Some writers have even described criminal justice as a 'non-system'. Whether that description is still an accurate one is one of the issues we will be considering in the light of recent attempts at reform: see in particular Chapters 4, 5 and 9. In any event, we do have penal and criminal justice 'systems' in the sense that they are composed of different agencies which are *interdependent*: their activities intimately affect each other and they need to be studied within this context of interdependency (see, for example, Feeney, 1985). We see this kind of 'systems analysis' as an important tool in understanding the penal system and attempting to bring about positive modifications (this is a particular theme of Chapter 9).

Notes

1 There is one very important exception to this. The prison system – part of the penal system – houses many *remand prisoners,* who accounted for 17 per cent of the total prison population on 31 October 2006. Most of these are prisoners who have been remanded in custody while awaiting trial; a minority have already been convicted and are awaiting sentence. We say more about remand in Chapter 4, section 4.2.

2 We use the term 'punishment' to mean any measure that is imposed on an offender in response to an offence, whether or not it is intended to be 'punitive'. See further Chapter 2, note 1.

3 The subject of 'comparative penology' is explored more fully in Cavadino and Dignan (2006).

4 A policy announced in the White Paper *Justice for All* (Home Office et al., 2002: 3.31).

5 In addition, it is possible for police officers and certain other specified officials to issue 'fixed penalty notices' ('spot fines') for a variety of minor offences.

6 Introduced on a statutory basis by the Criminal Justice Act 2003 (ss. 22–27; in force from April 2004). It is the responsibility of the CPS to decide if a conditional caution is

appropriate, but they are administered by the police. The offender must agree to the conditional caution. Section 17 of the Police and Justice Act 2006 (not yet in force) provides that the caution may come with a condition that the offender pay a financial penalty of up to £250 for a range of offences yet to be specified.

7   I.e. all those who receive a conviction, caution, reprimand or warning for an *indictable only* or *triable either way* offence (see paragraph after next and note 10 below).

8   Fixed penalty notices (FPNs, currently of up to £80) were introduced by the Criminal Justice and Police Act 2001 and extended nationally in 2004. They can be used for a number of minor offences, notably relating to anti-social behaviour in public, but now also including shoplifting up to the value of £200. People issued with FPNs can choose to pay the penalty, or if they contest their guilt they may be prosecuted in the magistrates' court in the traditional manner.

9   Remand prisoners may also be held in cells in police stations because of prison overcrowding. This was common for many years until 1995, when the practice was discontinued. However, it was revived from July to November 2002, in October 2005, and then again in October 2006. Police cells were still being used in this way at the time of writing.

10   Unless otherwise stated, statistics for offences and offenders which we present in this book normally relate to indictable offences, i.e. offences that are either 'indictable only' or triable either way.

11   As we shall see, however, it is still possible for the defendant to be committed to the Crown Court for sentence. See further Chapter 4, section 4.3.

12   Under the Criminal Justice Act 2003, courts may now pass 'community orders' which may contain requirements to be supervised by a probation officer, to carry out unpaid work to benefit the community and/or a wide variety of other requirements (including curfews enforced by electronic tagging: see Chapter 5).

13   The Ministry of Justice was created in May 2007. Its responsibilities include NOMS, criminal justice reform, youth justice and sentencing policy (all previously dealt with by the Home Office), together with the courts and legal system generally. The Home Office remains responsible for crime, policing, security, anti-terrorism and policy on drugs and anti-social behaviour. See further Chapter 4, section 4.1.

1 Crisis? What Crisis?

Is There a Crisis?

1.1 On 5 May 2006, Home Secretary Charles Clarke – holder of one of the highest offices in the British government – lost his job. The main reason was the deep political embarrassment caused by the revelation that over 1,000 foreign prisoners had been mistakenly released from prisons in England and Wales without being considered for deportation. His successor, John Reid, took over declaring that the Home Office – the government department with responsibility for criminal justice and immigration – was 'not fit for purpose' (*BBC News Online*, 23 May 2006).

The penal system for which Dr Reid assumed responsibility contained a record number of prisoners, a figure which continued to grow at an alarming rate and threatened to exceed the upper limits of the prison system's capacity. The Director of the new and troubled National Offender Management Service (NOMS), Martin Narey, had unexpectedly resigned a few months earlier. A spate of cases came to light in which offenders released on licence from prison or under probation supervision had committed very serious crimes, including some horrific murders. An outcry against an allegedly lenient sentence passed on a paedophile[1] caused an intra-governmental dispute between Dr Reid and the Attorney General Lord Goldsmith. The Lord Chief Justice weighed in with a wide-ranging critique of the penal system and especially of overcrowding in prisons, and the Director of the Prison Reform Trust said that the prison system was facing its worst crisis for 15 years (*Guardian*, 30 May 2006). The Prison Officers' Association held a ballot on national strike action. In October, Dr Reid announced that some prisoners would have to be held in police cells, and by January 2007 they were also spilling over into court cells.

At times like this, it might not seem controversial to claim that the penal system is in a state of crisis. Nor would most people in Britain imagine that this 'penal crisis' is either new or sudden. For many years, media reports have acquainted everyone with the notion that rocketing prison populations, overcrowding, unrest among staff and inmates, escapes and riots and disorder in prisons add up to a severe and deepening penal crisis. The term 'crisis' has been common currency in both media and academic accounts of the penal system for well over 20 years; the word recurs in newspaper headlines and in the titles of academic books and articles (for example, Bottoms and Preston, 1980; Rutherford, 1988; see also Ramsbotham, 2005).[2] Evidence for the existence of a crisis seems to be constantly in the news. Recent years have seen – to mention just a few out of many possible illustrations – embarrassing escapes from two high-security prisons in 1994 and 1995; the dramatic sacking of Prison Service Director General Derek Lewis by Home Secretary Michael Howard in 1995; the jailing in 2000 and 2001 of six prison officers from Wormwood Scrubs for planned and sustained attacks on inmates; the disturbing racist murder of Zahid Mubarek by a fellow inmate in Feltham Young Offender Institution in March 2000; plus the list of scandals and embarrassments with which we commenced this chapter. All this comes against the background of a prison population scaling ever higher, all-time record levels and a continuing deep malaise running through the penal system as a whole.

Yet is it really a 'crisis'? A cynic could be forgiven for finding the penal crisis uncannily reminiscent of the supposed 'crisis of capitalism', which some Marxists used constantly to insist was real, severe, ever-worsening and likely to prove terminal in the near future. Yet both capitalism and the penal system seem to keep going somehow, unlike those regimes, parties and theories that were founded on Marxism. Perhaps few would dispute that the penal system has serious problems – but is it really in a state of *crisis*? Then again, how long can a crisis last while remaining a crisis rather than business as usual? Surely there is something paradoxical in claims that the crisis has lasted for decades, or even that the system has been 'in a perpetual state of crisis since the Gladstone Committee report of 1895' (Fitzgerald and Sim, 1982: 3).

If to be in crisis means that the whole system is on the brink of total collapse or explosion, then we probably do not have a crisis. (Although it should not be forgotten that when systems do collapse or explode – like the communist system in Eastern Europe in the late 1980s and early 1990s, or the system of order within Strangeways Prison immediately before the historic riot of April 1990 – they can do so very suddenly.) But it can be validly claimed that there is a crisis in at least two senses, identified by Morris (1989: 125). First, we have 'a state of affairs that is so acute as to constitute a danger' – and, we would add, a moral challenge of a scale which makes it one of the most pressing social issues of the day. Second, we may be at a *critical juncture*, much as a seriously ill person may reach a 'turning point at which the patient either begins to improve or sinks into a fatal decline'. In other words, either the present situation could be used as an opportunity to reform the system into something more rational and humane, or else it will deteriorate into something much worse even than the present. In this book we will be using the 'C-word' in these senses to refer to the present penal situation in England and Wales, albeit with slight embarrassment and the worry that it has been used so often and for so long that there is a danger that it may be losing its dramatic impact.

Whether or not we choose to use the word 'crisis', what are the causes of the state the penal system is in, and how do its different problems relate to each other?

The Orthodox Account of the Crisis

1.2 The *orthodox account* of the penal crisis is probably still the kind of analysis most often encountered in the mass media. At least until Lord Justice Woolf's[3] 1991 report into the Strangeways riot (Woolf and Tumim, 1991), versions of it were also regularly found in official reports purporting to explain phenomena such as prison disturbances. It is well summarized by the following extract from a newspaper article entitled 'Why the Prisons Could Explode' (Humphry and May, 1977):

Explosive problems remain in many of Britain's prisons – a higher number of lifers ... who have nothing left to lose; overcrowding which forces men to sleep three to a cell and understaffing which weakens security. Prisons, too, are forced to handle men with profound psychiatric problems in conditions which are totally unsuitable.

This passage gives us almost all the components of the 'orthodox account' of the penal crisis. The crisis is seen as being located very specifically within the *prison* system – it is not seen as a crisis of the whole *penal* system, or of the criminal justice system, let alone as a crisis of society as a whole. The immediate cause of the crisis is seen as the combination of different types of difficult prisoners – what has been called the 'toxic mix' of prisoners (Home Office, 1984a: para. 124) – in physically poor and insecure conditions which could give rise to an 'explosion'.

The orthodox account points to the following factors as implicated in the crisis:

1   the high prison population (or the 'numbers crisis');
2   overcrowding;
3   bad conditions within prison (for both inmates and prison officers);
4   understaffing;
5   unrest among the staff;
6   poor security;
7   the 'toxic mix' of long-term and life-sentence prisoners and mentally disturbed inmates;
8   riots and other breakdowns of control over prisoners.

These factors are seen as linked, with number 8 – riots and disorder – being the end product that epitomizes the state of crisis. Figure 1.1 shows how the different factors interact according to the orthodox account. The high prison population is held responsible for overcrowding and understaffing in prisons, both of which exacerbate the bad physical conditions within prison. The combination of poor conditions and inadequate staffing have an adverse effect on staff morale, causing unrest which (through industrial action, for example) serves to worsen conditions still further. The four factors of bad conditions, overcrowding, understaffing and staff unrest are blamed for poor security, which is another factor contributing to the unstable prison environment. Finally, the combination of the 'toxic mix' of prisoners with these deteriorating conditions within which they are contained is thought to trigger off the periodic riots and disturbances to which the prison system is increasingly prone.

We do not believe that the orthodox account provides a satisfactory explanation of the crisis, for reasons we shall be giving shortly. But most of the factors identified by this account are real and important, as we shall now detail.

The High Prison Population (the 'Numbers Crisis')

It is widely agreed – although perhaps not by all politicians – that the number of prisoners in England and Wales is alarmingly high. It is also rapidly rising. Table 1.1 shows how (despite occasional dips),[4] the prison population has doubled to over 80,000 from under 40,000 in 1975, a year in which prison numbers were already causing serious concern. The prison population reached its highest ever peak so far in October 2006 when it breached 80,000 for the first time. But only so far: official Home Office projections estimate that by 2013 the prison population could be over 106,000 if current trends continue (de Silva et al., 2006). So the

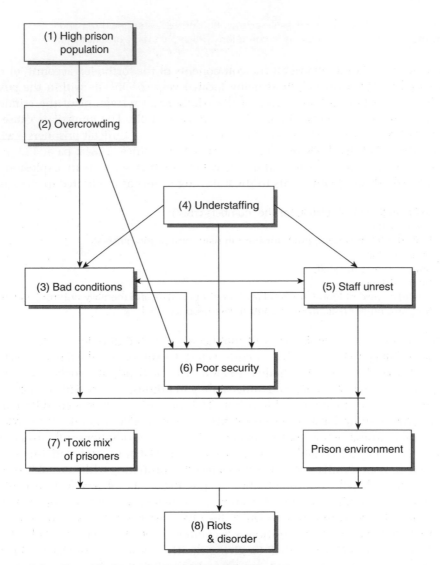

Figure 1.1 *The orthodox account of the penal crisis*

figures are set to continue regularly breaking all-time records, as they have since 1995. Although John Reid announced in July 2006 that an extra 8,000 prison places were to be created by 2012, at this rate the Prison Service could be over 20,000 places short by then. Already in November 2006 the prison population was just 317 below the system's absolute maximum capacity (*Guardian*, 30 November 2006).

There are several factors involved in this increase in prison numbers in recent years. In Chapter 4 we discuss the relationship between some of these factors, and conclude that the most crucial is the pattern of decisions by the courts. The most important of these is *the sentencing decision* – whether convicted offenders should be sent to custody and, if so, for how long – which we call 'the crux of the crisis'.

Table 1.1 The prison population of England and Wales, 1975–2006

1975	39,820
1980	43,109
1985	46,278
1986	46,889
1987	48,963
1988	49,949
1989	48,610
1990	45,636
1991	45,897
1992	45,817
1993	44,566
1994	48,794
1995	51,047
1996	55,281
1997	61,114
1998	65,298
1999	64,770
2000	64,602
2001	66,301
2002	70,861
2003	73,038
2004	74,657
2005 (31 October)	78,284
2006 (31 October)	80,306

Sources: Home Office and NOMS statistics; 1975–2004 figures are daily average populations.[5]

Also important, however, are decisions about which courts defendants should be tried in and whether they should be remanded in custody in the meantime.

These court decisions can in their turn be greatly influenced by government policies, actions and rhetoric. For a long time both Conservative and Labour governments generally attempted to keep the size of the prison population under control by a mixture of legislation, executive action and exhortations to courts. However, from 1993 onwards John Major's Conservative administration reversed this stand and pursued policies whose explicit aim was to increase the numbers of people in prison. Most notable was Home Secretary Michael Howard's declaration at the Conservative Party Conference in October 1993 that *'prison works'* and that he did not flinch from measures that would increase the prison population. The New Labour administration of Tony Blair which took power in 1997 may have dropped the slogan 'prison works',[6] but has shown little interest in trying to reduce custodial sentences. Indeed, Labour Home Secretaries have repeatedly called for tougher sentences for a wide range of offenders.[7] Not surprisingly, therefore, the rise in the prison population has shown little sign of abating under New Labour.

For many years now, England and Wales have consistently had one of the highest proportionate prison populations in Western Europe. Table 1.2 shows that in 2003–5

Table 1.2 Prison Populations in Western Europe, 2003–5

Country	Total prison population	No. of prisoners per 100,000 pop.
Luxembourg	655	144
ENGLAND AND WALES	75,320	142
Spain	59,899	140
Scotland	6,742	132
Portugal	13,498	128
The Netherlands	19,999	123
Austria	8,700	106
Italy	57,046	98
Germany	79,329	96
Turkey	67,772	95
France	55,028	91
Belgium	9,245	88
Ireland	3,417	85
Switzerland	6,021	81
Greece	8,760	82
Sweden	6,755	75
Northern Ireland	1,275	72
Finland	3,719	71
Denmark	3,774	70
Norway	2,975	65
Cyprus	355	50
Iceland	115	39

Source: Walmsley (2005)

the English prison population (in proportion to the total number of people in the country as a whole[8]) was second only to Luxembourg, with Scotland not far behind. It is true that proportionate prison populations are even higher in some countries outside Western Europe: indeed, the United States has over five times as many prisoners relative to its population as do England and Wales.[9] Nevertheless, within the Western European frame of reference, Britain does seem to be strikingly punitive, having maintained a position high in the prison population league table for many years now. This relatively high prison population does not seem to be because the UK has more crime, or more serious crime, than comparable countries.[10] Rather, it is because more offenders are sent to custody, and for longer periods, in the UK than elsewhere in Western Europe (see, for example, Barclay and Tavares, 2000; NACRO, 1998; Pease, 1992).

There should be little doubt, then, that the present and predicted future size of the prison population is a major problem. If drastic steps are not taken to reduce prison numbers – and there is currently no sign of any such steps being taken by the government – they seem almost certain to grow even more alarmingly in the coming years.

Overcrowding

On 31 October 2006, English and Welsh prisons[11] officially had adequate space for 70,832 inmates, but actually contained 80,306, making the system as a whole overcrowded by a factor of 13 per cent (NOMS, 2006d). By 'adequate space' we mean the official figure for the 'in use certified normal accommodation' (or 'uncrowded capacity'[12]) of all prisons in total. The Prison Service also identifies a higher figure, the 'operational capacity', defined as 'the total number of prisoners that an establishment can hold taking into account control, security and the proper operation of the planned regime'. Adding the operational capacity of all prisons together and deducting a safety margin of 1,700 yields a total 'usable operational capacity' – informally known as the 'bust limit' – for the system as a whole. This 'bust limit' was actually exceeded in April 2004, and currently the prison population is hovering perilously close to it, with just 317 places to spare in November 2006 (*Guardian*, 30 November 2006).

Even these overall figures do not do justice to the overcrowding problem because prisoners are not spread evenly throughout the system. High security prisons (see Chapter 6) are frequently not filled to capacity, while overcrowding is concentrated in local prisons (which predominantly house remand prisoners and those on short-term sentences) (see HM Prison Service, 2006a: 89). At the end of October 2006, 62 per cent of prisons were overcrowded, with 12 prisons containing more than half as many prisoners again as they should (Shrewsbury Prison had 90 per cent more). As a result of overcrowding, currently around 18,000 prisoners (22 per cent of the prison population) are sleeping two to a cell designed for a single inmate, or otherwise housed in overcrowded cells,[13] while others are being kept in cells in police stations and courthouses. The situation has been worsening for some time – in 1995 the system was 'only' overcrowded by 2 per cent, with 8,700 inmates sharing cells – and is obviously likely to deteriorate further in the immediate future if the current expansion in the prison population continues. Independent monitors of prison conditions have expressed concerns that such overcrowding is likely to threaten safety and have multiple other serious adverse effects on prison conditions and regimes (Prison Reform Trust, 2006b: 7–8; see also Chapter 6, section 5).

Bad Conditions

Overcrowding, of course, contributes to bad physical conditions in prisons. (It has also led in recent years – and again currently as we write – to hundreds of remand prisoners being kept in even more inadequate conditions in police cells.) But there are other causes of bad conditions as well as overcrowding: many prisons are old and decaying, and newer prisons have often turned out to be so badly designed that they are not a noticeable improvement.

The particular issue of inadequate sanitary facilities in prison is something of a cliché. The fact that many prisoners routinely had to spend long periods in their cells without access to a toilet, having to use chamber pots and queue up to 'slop out', was a potent symbol of the squalor of British prisons. Perhaps it was this symbolic importance which led the then Home Secretary Kenneth Baker, when responding to the Woolf Report in February 1991, to announce a programme to provide all prisoners with access to toilet facilities. This project was officially completed in April 1996, although it seems clear that some prisoners still do not have adequate 24 hour per day access to toilets (see Chapter 6, section 6.5 for details).

In any event, the problem of prison conditions is hardly limited to slopping out. As we shall see in Chapter 6, other elements of prison life are equally important, such as the amount of time prisoners are kept cooped up in cells and the lack of opportunities for activities of all kinds. In these respects, there has been a general and continuing decline in prison conditions over a long period of time (King and McDermott, 1989). The poor conditions in prisons affect staff as well as inmates, contributing to low staff morale and unrest.

Understaffing

It is a constant complaint on the part of prison staff that they are overstretched, especially with the ever-rising prison population. Following cuts to the Prison Service budget in the closing years of the previous Conservative administration, the New Labour government substantially increased prison funding for a time after 1997 – although of course any extra resources have to go around a fast-rising number of prisoners. More recently the Prison Service has been operating within a standstill budget, which seems likely to remain the case for the foreseeable future. Consequently, there is constant pressure on prisons to keep staff numbers to a minimum: state-run prisons increasingly have to justify their spending levels in comparison with privately run prisons, which limit their own running costs by economizing on staff (see Chapter 7).

If prisons are understaffed (or if those running the prison believe they are understaffed), this affects conditions and regimes. Prisoners may be left locked in their cells for longer, because there is not the staff to supervise out-of-cell activities or to escort them from place to place. Visits to prisoners may be restricted or cancelled. And prison staff may become restless.

Staff Unrest

For many years the relationship between prison staff and the Home Office has rarely been better than one of simmering discontent. Local and national industrial action by prison officers has been a recurrent event. In 1978 widespread disruptive action led to the setting up of the May Inquiry into the Prison Service (May, 1979). But May's report and the government's response to it failed to satisfy the Prison Officers' Association (POA); 1986 saw the most alarming disruption ever, as protest action including a national overtime ban by prison officers over the issue of staffing levels sparked off the worst sequence of riots by inmates that had occurred up to that date. Industrial action over staffing arrangements continued, most notably at Wandsworth Prison in 1989, when police officers were drafted in to replace prison officers. Conservative legislation placed severe legal restrictions on the ability of prison officers to undertake industrial action, although this did not put an end to protest actions of varying degrees of legality and illegality. Under New Labour the relationship between the government and the POA seemed to improve for a while, and the statutory restrictions on industrial action were lifted in 2005, to be replaced by a no-strike agreement. However, by the summer of 2006 the POA were considering national industrial action over salary levels. Staff unrest never seems far away from the prison system, and is always likely to be exacerbated by increasing workloads due to rising numbers of prisoners, or other threatening developments such as prison privatization (see Chapters 6 and 7).

Security

S ecurity lapses always seem to have the potential to create more public uproar than almost any other event surrounding the penal system. This was well exemplified by the ructions which followed the breakouts from two high-security prisons, Whitemoor and Parkhurst, in 1994 and 1995. Two official reports (Woodcock, 1994; Learmont, 1995) exposed 'a chapter of errors at every level' (Learmont, 1995: para. 2.257) which had facilitated these escapes. The Parkhurst breakout led eventually to the Home Secretary sacking the Director General of the Prison Service and a furious political row in October 1995.

Yet despite the air of moral panic which surrounds such incidents, it remains the case that since the 1960s the English penal system has not had a bad record overall for security, in the sense of managing to keep prisoners inside prison. Escapes are currently neither common nor increasing: indeed, they have decreased in recent years, and the level of escapes in 2005/6 was the lowest since records began (HM Prison Service, 2006a; see further Chapter 6, section 6.5). Breakouts from high-security prisons had been extremely rare prior to the Whitemoor escape, and no top-security 'Category A' prisoner has escaped since 1995.

The word 'security' is often used in a different sense, to mean the adequate exercise of *control* over inmates inside prison – for example, preventing them from assaulting the staff or each other (see Chapter 6, section 6.5). Prison staff often complain that understaffing (combined sometimes with other deficiencies in material resources) reduces 'security' in prisons, making assaults, breakdowns in control and even escapes more likely. It is often 'security considerations' – *fears* about security and control – which exacerbate the physical conditions of prisoners; for example, they may be kept locked in their cells almost all day because they are not trusted to be let out without a high degree of staff-intensive supervision. In the wake of the Woodcock and Learmont inquiries into the Whitemoor and Parkhurst escapes in the mid-1990s, there was a noticeable and damaging shift of emphasis towards security (see Chapter 6). Such shifts have the natural tendency of diverting resources towards ensuring 'security' and changing staff practices in ways that adversely affect prison conditions and regimes still further.

'Toxic Mix' of Prisoners

W e can agree with the orthodox account on many details concerning the component factors of the crisis. But the notion of a 'toxic mix' of prisoners is an issue on which we definitely part company. We do not deny that some characteristics of prison inmates may make them more or less likely to cause problems – if the prisons predominantly housed old people or nuns rather than young men with a record of anti-social behaviour, they would doubtless experience fewer riots. But there are several difficulties with 'toxic mix theory'.

It is often said that one important constituent of the so-called 'toxic mix' is *lifers* – prisoners serving sentences of life imprisonment. Such prisoners are often said to have 'nothing left to lose' (for example, Humphry and May, 1977). Yet although there are more lifers than there used to be (see Chapter 8, section 8.5) – together with growing numbers of other prisoners serving the new indeterminate sentence of 'imprisonment for public protection' (see Chapters 4 and 8) – most of them have a great deal to lose. A 'life sentence' does not usually mean that the prisoner is kept in prison until he or she dies (although it may: about a dozen lifers die in prison each year), but lifers are only released at the discretion of the Parole Board (see Chapter 8). Few things jeopardize a prisoner's parole chances more than misbehaviour within prison, and especially participation in riots and protests. (Similar logic applies to other prisoners who are serving long 'fixed-term' sentences but who are eligible for early release.) Yet ironically, some recent policy developments have threatened to create a situation whereby some lifers and other long-term prisoners do have relatively little to lose. For example, there are now some lifers who have been told that they can never receive parole (see Chapter 8). If provision for early release becomes less generous, it becomes all the more likely that prisoners serving long sentences will feel that they have rather less to lose.

There is widespread agreement that there are many *mentally disturbed* people in prison who would be better off in hospital. Various surveys over the years have estimated that up to 90 per cent of prisoners could be categorized as having some form of mental disorder (see for example, Singleton et al, 1998; Gunn et al., 1991; Prison Reform Trust, 2006b: 26–7). The surveys that find the highest incidence of mental disorder among prisoners tend to include not only mental illness but also diagnoses over which some scepticism is arguably warranted, such as 'personality disorder' and alcohol and drug misuse. Even discounting such categories, it is clear that many prisoners suffer a disproportionate amount of mental distress and disturbance. And it is equally clear that the quality of psychiatric services for mentally ill prisoners is woefully inadequate (Reed and Lyne, 2000; Prison Reform Trust, 2006: 27–8). As human beings, we are suitably horrified by this state of affairs; but as penologists we wonder cynically how great a contribution this factor really makes to the penal crisis. Despite popular stereotypes, much mental illness makes the sufferers if anything more amenable to control rather than less, and mentally ill prisoners have not been prominent in organizing riots.

One interesting feature of the Woolf Report into the Strangeways and other riots of 1990 (Woolf and Tumim, 1991) was its implicit rejection of the 'toxic mix' theory.[14] We believe Woolf was right on this point. Apart from the difficulties we have already noted with the theory, we shall see shortly that the 'toxic mix' cannot always be implicated in causing riots, for it is often simply not present in prisons that experience disorder.

Riots and Disorder

To the general public, one of the most noticeable symptoms of the penal crisis – along with the occasional spectacular escape – is the prison riot. Apart from a riot at Parkhurst in 1969, disturbances were comparatively infrequent in British prisons until the year of 1972, which saw a major wave of rooftop demonstrations in many prisons. Subsequently – just to select some of the outstanding incidents – there were major riots at Hull in 1976, Gartree in 1978 and Albany in 1983. In 1986, as we have seen, a national overtime ban by prison officers sparked off riots in 18 prisons. April 1990 saw the worst ever series of prison riots, including a 25-day riot and siege at Strangeways Prison, Manchester. More riots have occurred in the years since Strangeways, for example at Full Sutton in 1997 and 1998, at Portland and Feltham Young Offender Institutions in 2000 and at Lincoln in 2002. Like staff unrest, inmate disorder shows no sign of disappearing from the scene.

Criticisms of the Orthodox Account

Generally speaking, then, most of the factors emphasized by the orthodox account are genuine enough (with the notable exception, in our opinion, of the 'toxic mix' idea). Where we believe the orthodox account to be seriously misleading is in the *causal relationships* it postulates between the different factors, and especially its explanation of prison riots.

One problem with the orthodox account is that it simply does not square with the facts about prison riots – and in particular, about where in the prison system they occur. If riots are caused by overcrowding, understaffing, bad physical conditions and poor security, one would expect them to occur exclusively in the local prisons and remand centres which are the most overcrowded and understaffed, where conditions are worse and security less tight than in many longer-stay establishments. Yet prior to the 1986 riots, major disorder was almost entirely confined to 'dispersal prisons' (now referred to as 'high-security prisons'; see section 6.3) – prisons that house prisoners on long sentences, that are not overcrowded or understaffed, where conditions are relatively good, and where security is at a maximum. After 1986 the pattern was largely reversed, with most major disorders occurring in local prisons (such as Strangeways), remand centres and lower-security establishments. But these riots are not satisfactorily explained by the orthodox account either, for such institutions lack the particular 'toxic mix' of prisoners which is supposed to be an important causative factor in inmate disorder. In a nutshell, the worst conditions and the supposedly most toxic mixes simply do not coexist in the same prisons. Then again, the prisons that experienced riots in 1986, 1990 and subsequently were not all overcrowded (for example, Northeye in 1986 and Dartmoor in 1990) or the worst in terms of physical conditions (Wymott and Wayland in 1986).[15]

The very phrase 'toxic mix', with its pseudo-scientific ring, indicates a more fundamental deficiency in the orthodox account. As we have portrayed it in Figure 1.1, the whole process of the crisis on this account seems very mechanistic (or *'positivistic'*, a term explained in Chapter 2). One thing leads automatically to another: prisoners and prison staff both seem to react to conditions in a mindless manner. The prisoners in particular seem to behave like molecules in a test tube: place such a combination in such a physical environment, agitate, increase the pressure, and an explosion is the automatic result.[16] We do not believe that people are like that. Rioting is not mindless behaviour; it is meaningful human action. Lord Scarman said in his famous report on inner-city riots that 'public disorder usually arises *out of a sense of injustice*' (Scarman, 1986: xiii; our italics), and as the Woolf Report (Woolf and Tumim, 1991) rightly recognized, this is as true in prisons as it is in the inner city. And this crucial sense of injustice is not a mindless automatic reaction, but an active interpretation of a situation. So for an adequate description and explanation of the penal crisis, we need to explore why there is this perception of injustice, and even to ask whether this perception is correct. In our opinion this is the main flaw in the orthodox account, and one we hope to go some way towards rectifying.

Improving on the Orthodox Account

1.3 We think a more adequate account of the penal crisis can be developed by taking on board and integrating into our explanation the insights of a variety of penal commentators. In what follows we draw in particular upon the Woolf Report (Woolf and Tumim, 1991); the radical account furnished by Mike Fitzgerald and Joe Sim in their book *British Prisons* (1982); the contributions of Tony Bottoms (1980, 1983, 1995; Bottoms and Stevenson, 1992); and Stuart Hall's work on the politics of law and order (1979, 1980; Hall et al., 1978). To begin with, we shall highlight certain aspects of the crisis which the orthodox account either ignores or fails to address adequately.

The Crisis of Penological Resources

It is implicit in the orthodox account that there is a problem of limited resources such as space within prisons and numbers of prison officers. But the problem is wider and deeper than that. Tony Bottoms (1980) identified a general *crisis of penological resources*, affecting not only prisons (to which the orthodox account is limited) but extending to the entire penal system. This includes the probation service, which provides and runs non-custodial penalties (see Chapter 5) and what might be called 'post-custodial' provision such as parole supervision (see Chapter 8).[17] 'This crisis takes two forms: the size of the prison population' (combined with the lack of prison places and the running expenses of locking up and catering for such a large number of prisoners) 'and the demands on the probation and after-care service' (Bottoms, 1980: 5). This twofold crisis of resources generates an imperative to limit the numbers in prison and to deal with more offenders outside the prison 'in the community', but without overloading the probation service. Another aspect of this crisis presumably is the lack of resources to keep prison officers sufficiently materially satisfied to defuse industrial relations problems within prisons, and to provide prison inmates with constructive and fulfilling ways of occupying their time.

This *material* aspect of the crisis – the ever-present issue of scarce material resources like buildings, staff, equipment and money – is one that always needs to be borne in mind when seeking to understand the state of the penal system. As we shall see, however, this is only one side of the picture.

The Crisis of Visibility

Perhaps the crisis of visibility (so named by Fitzgerald and Sim, 1982: 6–11) does not deserve its own heading, but it is an interesting example of an aspect of the crisis which the orthodox account fails to encompass. It concerns the secrecy that has for many years shrouded prisons and what goes on inside them. Developments in recent years have meant that 'slowly, but surely, the secrecy behind the prison walls is being breached, as alternative sources of information about the prisons are more securely established' (Fitzgerald and Sim, 1982: 11; see further Chapter 6).

Fitzgerald and Sim seem to see the *existence* of secrecy as a 'crisis' in itself. Morally speaking, we have no doubt that it has been; but again reverting to our cynical sociological standpoint, we suspect that on the contrary it is often the *dispelling* of secrecy that causes problems for the system and exacerbates the crisis. For if we assume that there is much in prisons that will not bear being exposed (and if not, why keep it secret?), then opening up the prison is likely to decrease the legitimacy of the system. If 'knowledge is power'[18] then there is a danger that the system will lose much of its power if it loses control of information about itself. (It may also increase staff unrest by leading prison officers to feel that their authority is being threatened.) On the other hand, however, it is noticeable that many incidents of prison disorder – especially the popular form of demonstration on the prison rooftop – are clearly motivated by the very desire to make prisoners' grievances and allegations *visible* in a way that would never normally happen. And if greater visibility should lead to prisoners being better treated (for fear of abuse being exposed), then visibility rather than secrecy could help to defuse the crisis. So, while we have no doubt that it is right that prison secrecy should be dispelled, it seems as if (paradoxically) both secrecy *and* openness can contribute to the crisis – as long as there are secrets to hide.

The problem with secrecy is that the secret information is often of a discreditable nature which, if it gets out, can damage 'legitimacy'. This means that the 'crisis of visibility' is only a part of what has justly been termed 'the final and most crucial aspect of the crisis in British prisons' (Fitzgerald and Sim, 1982: 23), and to which we now turn.

The Crisis of Legitimacy[19]

Whereas the crisis of penological resources is a *material* crisis, the crisis of legitimacy is *ideological* in nature: it exists in the minds of human beings. Sociologists use the term 'legitimacy' to mean *power that is perceived as morally justified*. The penal system wields power over its subjects, but its moral right to do so can be contested. Fitzgerald and Sim, who gave the 'crisis of legitimacy' its name, related it to 'calls for the abolition of imprisonment' and to 'a more fundamental political crisis which transcends the prison walls' (1982: 23–4). There may have been an element of revolutionary wishful thinking here: if all the system had to worry about was the minority of people who seriously call for the abolition of prisons or the prospect of the imminent overthrow of capitalism, there would not be much of a crisis.[20] Nevertheless, even among non-abolitionists (and across much of the political spectrum) there has been grave disquiet about the state of the prisons. Even conservative commentators can regard the conditions within some prisons as morally intolerable to a civilized community (some examples are given by Stern, 1993: 2, 4). The squalor produced by prison overcrowding is perhaps the issue which most scandalizes the public conscience, but there are others. These include the high incidence of suicides among prisoners (see Chapter 6); the presence in prisons (as noted previously) of large numbers of people with mental health problems; the over-representation within prisons of members of ethnic minorities; and the issue of racism in prisons (see Chapter 10).

Tony Bottoms (1980) also saw the penal system as suffering from a crisis of legitimacy (though he did not use the term), as well as from the crisis of resources discussed earlier. He identified as an important cause of the crisis of legitimacy *the collapse of the rehabilitative ideal.* Prior to the 1970s, the penal system could plausibly legitimate itself by claiming as its *raison d'être* the rehabilitation of offenders: the provision of training and treatment which would cure them of their criminality, benefiting both them and society as a whole. As we shall see in Chapter 2, this claim subsequently became less plausible and less acceptable, with a general belief arising that 'nothing works' in the treatment of offenders. This undermined the legitimacy of the penal system: not only of the prisons (whose claim to be providing effective rehabilitation was always shaky in many eyes) but equally for other components of the penal system. A notable example is the probation service, which has for many years now been demoralized and uncertain about what its proper rationale and direction should be (see Chapter 5). The system has found itself in dire need of new ways of legitimating itself, and this need has given rise to a variety of responses. We discuss these further in the following section; but they have included, most potently, the rise of what we shall be calling 'law and order ideology'.

It is not only the system's legitimacy with outside observers and the general public which is important. The system will also suffer severe difficulties if it lacks legitimacy for its own employees, including prison staff and probation officers. Perhaps most important of all is *the legitimacy of the system for those who are its subjects* – in our opinion, the crucial factor in the genesis of prison riots and of many of the system's other problems. After all, a penal system can only run with the acquiescence of offenders. No prison could run for long if not for the fact that most prisoners most of the time are prepared simply to cooperate with the staff and 'do their bird'. This is not to say that they normally have no sense of injustice. They may bear grievances about the fact that they are locked up in prison, perhaps for longer than they feel they deserve or for longer than other offenders whom they regard as comparable. (We shall see in Chapters 2, 4 and 10 that they may well have good grounds for this belief.) They may have other grievances concerning the prison regime, e.g. early release, the behaviour of prison staff and the prison disciplinary system (see Chapters 6, 7 and 8). Even so, prisoners do not normally riot unless this sense of injustice has been somehow inflamed beyond its normal simmering state.

Prisoners' sense of injustice was highlighted by the Woolf Report (Woolf and Tumim, 1991) on the prison riots of April 1990, which became established as a historic and classically liberal account of what is wrong with English prisons, what causes prison riots and what should be done to prevent them. Woolf's central finding was that

> there are three requirements which must be met if the prison system is to be stable: they are *security, control and justice* ... 'security' refers to the obligations of the Prison Service to prevent prisoners escaping. 'Control' deals with the obligation of the Prison Service to prevent prisoners being disruptive. 'Justice' refers to the obligation of the Prison Service to treat prisoners with humanity and fairness, and to prepare them for their return to the community in a way which makes it less likely that they will reoffend. (paras. 9.19–9.20; our italics)

'Security' and 'control' are hardly novel concepts, figuring significantly in the orthodox account. Woolf also acknowledged as relevant factors such as overcrowding and insanitary physical conditions, but did not regard these as crucial. Their significance for Woolf was in contributing to the prisoners' sense of injustice.

Woolf did not use the word 'legitimacy', but it is clearly the prison's lack of *legitimacy with inmates* which he saw as of central importance. He showed a keen awareness that, on the one hand, legitimacy is in the mind; but on the other hand what is in people's minds usually depends on the external reality:

> It is not possible for the Inquiry to form any judgment on whether the specific grievances of these prisoners were or were not well-founded. What is clear is that the Prison Service had failed to persuade these prisoners that it was treating them fairly. (para. 9.25)

Despite not committing himself about specific grievances, Woolf believed that genuine injustice contributes to a lack of legitimacy, which in turn makes disorder more likely. A substantial number of prisoners participated in the riots

> at least in part, because of the conditions in which they were held and the way in which they were treated. If a proper level of justice is provided in prisons, then it is less likely that prisoners will behave in this way. Justice, therefore, contributes to the maintenance of security and control. (para. 1.151)

Woolf's humanistic attention to the subjective *interpretation by prisoners of their situation* marks a distinct departure from the orthodox account.

While talking about the need to keep security, control and justice in 'balance', Woolf appeared to emphasize the importance of justice, and the imbalance he was most concerned about was the prospect of security and control measures exacerbating prisoners' sense of injustice. Although Woolf stated that 'there is no single cause of riots' (para. 9.23), it may not be too great a distortion to say that he saw the lack of legitimacy of the prison for its inmates as the key factor in explaining the disorders. For this reason he stressed in his recommendations not only measures to improve prison conditions but also reforms of grievance and disciplinary procedures (see Chapter 6) which might both improve the objective standard of justice within prisons and be seen as fairer by prisoners.

The penal system's legitimacy problems are – of course – by no means all related to feelings that the system is excessively harsh and inhumane. Rather more common among the general public is the perception (regularly encouraged by tabloid newspapers and many politicians) that the penal system is on the contrary overlenient, lax and insecure. It is bound to be difficult for the system to achieve legitimacy with all its different audiences – public, press, politicians, penal practitioners and penal subjects – under these circumstances.

Responses to the Crisis

1.4 How have governments responded to the penal crisis? And not only governments, but other actors in the penal arena, such as practitioners, commentators, Home Office civil servants and Opposition politicians? Their responses can be roughly split into two categories: *ideological* (or philosophical) responses to the crisis of legitimacy in particular; and *practical* responses to the management problems caused by the material crisis of resources.

On the *ideological* side, Tony Bottoms (1980) listed a number of varying responses to the collapse of the rehabilitative ideal and the consequent dire need for the penal system to find new ways of legitimating itself. These responses included the revival of the philosophy of 'just deserts' (see Chapter 2) between the 1970s and 1990s. But the most prominent ideological response, amounting to a massive shift in penal ideology, has been *'the new punitiveness'* (see Chapter 3, section 3.6): the rise and rise of what we call *'law and order ideology'* – the appeal to a harsh, Strategy A programme of 'toughness' which is represented as being an effective remedy for crime. (See the Introduction and Chapter 11 for further explanation and discussion of Strategies A, B and C.) In the sense in which we use the phrase, law and order ideology is more than just the unexceptionable beliefs that society should be governed by law, and that crime should be effectively controlled. It is a complex if naïve set of attitudes, including the beliefs that human beings have free will, that they must be strictly disciplined by restrictive rules, and that they should be harshly punished if they break the rules or fail to respect authority. Such an ideology naturally leads its adherents to favour a Strategy A approach to criminal justice policy. (The phrase *'populist punitiveness'*, coined by Bottoms (1995a), means much the same thing.)

The ideology of law and order was notably and provocatively analysed in the late 1970s and early 1980s by the Marxist theorist Stuart Hall (1979, 1980; Hall et al., 1978). Hall saw law and order ideology as an important component of what he called 'authoritarian populism', which in turn constituted an important strand in the political phenomenon of 'Thatcherism'. However, not only did the 'drift into a law and order society' in Britain begin well before the accession to power of the Conservative Party under Mrs Thatcher in 1979 – although that was something of a defining moment – but it accelerated significantly under her Conservative successor John Major. It has to a great extent persisted under the New Labour government that has been in power since 1997 (see Chapter 11). For Hall, law and order ideology forms part of a pro-ruling-class response to a wider crisis of social order whose roots lie partly in the problems of the British economy and of Britain's declining role in the world.

This is far from a full explanation, however. It does not account for similar developments in other countries,[21] or for the reinvigoration of law and order ideology since early 1993, at a time when Britain's role in the world may have continued to decline but her economy was not getting any worse. Other long-term social and political developments have led to a greater degree of 'populism' in politics, in Britain and elsewhere, especially in respect of criminal justice policy. One likely partial explanation for this is that the decline of traditional communities has led to both an increase in crime and a general feeling of insecurity in the psyche of the modern individual. This in turn feeds into a fear of crime and a tendency to favour punitive fixes for the perceived threat it poses.[22] 'In such a context, a politician seeking popularity can reasonably easily tap into the electorate's insecurities by promising tough action on "villains"' (Bottoms, 1995a: 47). And modern politicians increasingly attune their policies according to the results of opinion polls and focus groups, which seek to identify policies that are (often very superficially) attractive to voters. It is largely along these lines – by reference to the quest of contemporary politicians for power – that we would explain the 'law and order counter-reformation' under John Major from 1993 to 1997 and the persistence of a high dose of 'toughness' in criminal justice policy under Labour since 1997. As Hall (1979: 15) says, law and order ideology is not an automatic 'reflection of the crisis: it is itself a *response* to the crisis'; in other words, it is created by human beings operating in their own real environments; which for politicians is the world of politics.

This does not necessarily mean that pursuing Strategy A will be a genuine recipe for political success; let alone that it will solve the problems of crime and punishment. The fate of John Major's government – defeated by a New Labour landslide in the General Election of 1997 – suggests that 'playing the law and order card' is by no means a sure ticket to electoral success. For one thing, although politicians currently tend to see law and order ideology as ruling public perceptions about criminal justice, and consequently calculate that it is to their own advantage to be perceived as being 'tough', research suggests that the public may be nowhere near as punitive-minded as is generally supposed (see, for example, Mattinson and Mirrlees-Black, 2000; and see further Chapter 11: section 11.2). And even assuming they were, there would be no way of satisfying constant media calls for ever tougher criminal justice policies. So – on the ideological side of things – Strategy A will not solve the crisis of legitimacy. Moreover, pursuing ever harsher policies and indulging in law and order rhetoric inevitably worsens the crisis of penological resources (on the material side of the equation). Recent history bears out what one would expect, that 'tough' policies and rhetoric have had the natural result of increasing the harshness of punishment – and consequently the size of the prison population and the scale of the penal crisis. Thus, Worrall and Pease (1986: 186), examining the steep rise in prison numbers in 1985, found that the most plausible explanation was that 'a general penal climate in Great Britain has permeated sentencing practice and made it harsher'. Other surges in the prison population, in 1991–2 and from early 1993 onwards, have also coincided with an increase in the intensity of law and order rhetoric emanating from government ministers (Travis, 1993; see also Hough et al., 2003).

For a long time – certainly until the Major government's 'law and order counter-reformation' of 1993 – it could be said that the overall response of the British state to the penal crisis had been mostly directed towards the material crisis of resources rather than the ideological crisis of legitimacy. The response largely took the form of *penological pragmatism*: responding to developments and attempting to manage the resources crisis 'with no clear or coherent philosophical or other theoretical basis' (Bottoms, 1980: 4). This pragmatism – which is still a vital strand in policy even in these more ideological times – has not been completely shapeless. One strong theme was identified and christened by Tony Bottoms in a highly prescient paper back in 1977: the strategy of *bifurcation* (Bottoms, 1977, 1980). 'Bifurcation' refers to a dual-edged (or twin-track) approach to punishment: differentiating between 'ordinary' or 'run of the mill' offenders with whom less severe measures can be taken on the one hand, and on the other hand 'exceptional', 'very serious' or 'dangerous' offenders who can be made subject to much tougher measures. In this way 'a bifurcated policy allows governments to get tough and soft simultaneously' (Pitts, 1988: 29). From the point of view of the resources crisis, bifurcation looks like a rational response: because there are so many more 'run of the mill' than 'serious' offenders, a bifurcated policy should save many more resources than it costs. In terms of legitimacy with the general public, such a strategy could also be effective, since the public can be reassured that the really 'serious' offenders about whom they are most concerned will be kept locked up for long periods. Bifurcation can thus be seen as a pragmatic response to the combined crises of legitimacy and resources, conditioned by law and order ideology. But in terms of *legitimacy for prisoners* – and in terms of preventing disorder in prisons – bifurcation runs the risk of proving seriously counter-productive since it seems so unfair to those who are singled out as the 'very serious' cases in what they may see as an arbitrary manner.[23]

As the politics of punishment have grown harsher, the other limb of bifurcation – being less harsh to less serious offenders – has come into conflict with law and order ideology. The Criminal Justice Act 1991 embodied what we have termed 'punitive bifurcation', a version in which even lesser offenders were to be treated with apparent 'toughness'. For under that Act's policy of 'punishment in the community', although more offenders were to be kept out of prison, they would be *punished* in the community; non-custodial penalties were to be more punitive and controlling than hitherto. But even this harsher version of bifurcation did not survive the law and order counter-reformation, and as Michael Howard declared that 'prison works' and that more rather than fewer offenders should go to prison, both pragmatism and bifurcation were sacrificed on the altar of ideology. More recently, New Labour Home Secretaries have persisted with bifurcatory policies of varying kinds, but – probably because of the greater emphasis that is placed on the 'tough' side of the coin – the results to date have been further increases in the prison population and in the crisis of resources (see further Chapter 11).

Another strand of the pragmatic approach to penal policy, which seems to keep growing in strength over the long term, is the element known as *managerialism*. This is what we call the Strategy B approach to criminal justice (Cavadino et al., 1999: 41–5). (It is related to the 'new penology' which we discuss in Chapter 3, section 3.6.) This approach is based on the notion that modern managerial techniques can be successfully applied to the problems of crime and punishment, both to control crime and to deploy penal resources effectively and efficiently. A particularly influential, right-wing version of managerialism (known as 'New Public Management' (see C. Hood, 1991; McLaughlin et al., 2001, and Chapter 7 below) sees private sector business techniques as the model for management and seeks to improve the public sector by introducing privatization, commercial competition and general 'marketization'. The influence of managerialism (of different varieties) can be observed in such diverse developments as the 'systems management' approach to dealing with young offenders (see Chapter 9), the creation of the National Offender Management Service or NOMS (see Chapter 5), and the current Labour government's interest in seeking and applying evidence of 'what works' to control crime and prevent criminals from reoffending (see Chapters 2 and 11). Above all, it can be seen in the Labour government's conversion and subsequent dogmatic attachment to the principle of private sector participation in the delivery of both custodial (see Chapter 7) and non-custodial (see Chapter 5) penal interventions. Managerialism – like penological pragmatism more generally – is primarily directed at the material crisis of resources rather than the crisis of legitimacy. Pragmatism and bureaucracy may have their place in the practical running of things, but they are hardly likely in themselves to inspire minds sufficiently to defuse the legitimacy problems of the penal system.

Eagle-eyed readers may have noticed that we have mentioned both Strategy A-type (harsh and punitive) and Strategy B-type (managerial) responses to the crisis, and wondered: have there been no Strategy C-type (humanitarian, human rights-based) responses? To be fair, there have – although in recent years they have tended to take a poor third place to the other two strategies. There has been a revival of interest in measures that can be taken to reform and rehabilitate offenders, which can be seen as a generally humanitarian approach as well as aiming at the efficient control of crime. And the current Labour government has shown much greater interest than any government hitherto in the idea of *restorative justice* (see Chapters 2, 5, 9 and 11), especially for young offenders. We will give more details about all these responses to the crisis throughout this book, and in Chapter 11 we return to provide a general overview and give our own opinions, setting out the kind of responses we ourselves favour.

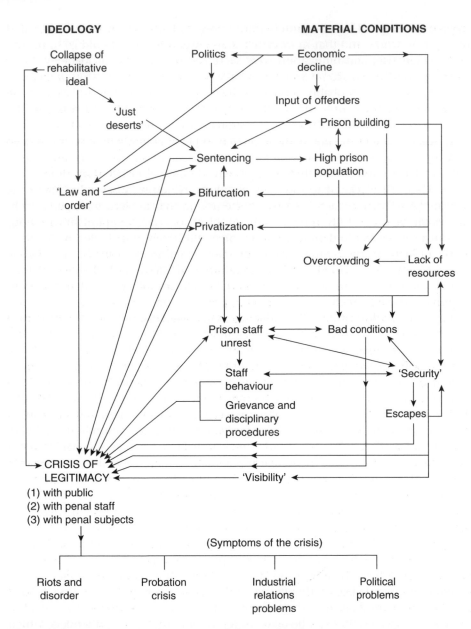

Figure 1.2 *A radical pluralist account of the penal crisis*

A Radical Pluralist Account of the Crisis

1.5

We said earlier that one problem with the orthodox account of the penal crisis is that it is *positivistic*: it sees the crisis in terms of mechanistic causes and effects and ignores the place of subjective human experience, perception, reflection and meaningful human action. It sees the crisis in overwhelmingly material terms – it recognizes the material crisis of resources but ignores the ideological crisis of legitimacy. In the previous two sections, by contrast, we have sought to emphasize that, although material circumstances are indeed of vital importance in explaining the penal crisis, they are only one side of the story. The other side, equally crucial, is the realm of ideas and ideology. Material and ideological factors interact with each other in a manner which could be described (in unfashionable Marxian terminology) as 'dialectical'.

In seeking to explain and understand the penal crisis, we wish to go further than just widening the orthodox account and adding the ideological dimension to it. We think the crisis can be analysed within the context of a general theoretical framework that is both intellectually respectable and useful, a theory we call *radical pluralism* (Cavadino, 1992). The nature of this theory will be explained in greater detail in Chapter 3, but it is a composite, compromise theory which is capable of incorporating those elements of the crisis which the orthodox account rightly identifies while also drawing upon the insights of commentators such as Fitzgerald and Sim, Bottoms, Hall and Lord Woolf.

The word 'pluralism' in the title of this theory means that we recognize that a large number of varied elements (including a variety of interest groups with greater or lesser power) are involved in the penal system and its crisis, and that these elements interact in a highly complex manner. We see a need to analyse the crisis in the context of the relationships between politics and economics, ideology and material conditions. We do not believe that this kind of analysis can be politically or morally neutral – and nor should it, for our understanding of the situation is that the penal system is morally indefensible and is in dire need of a programme of radical reform which would inevitably be highly political. On the other hand, the penal crisis is not simply a by-product of a 'crisis of capitalism', and it could be largely solved without a complete political and social revolution.

Our account is represented in diagrammatic form in Figure 1.2. The most striking feature of the diagram is its complexity; and yet Figure 1.2 is vastly oversimplified. An arrow in the diagram means that one factor affects (often this means 'exacerbates') another in the direction shown. Some of the connections pictured have already been discussed or mentioned. For example, we have already indicated how economic decline, political developments and the collapse of the rehabilitative ideal helped to give rise to a resurgence of 'law and order ideology'. Similarly, bifurcation can be seen as having been produced by a combination of law and order ideology and the practical need to do something about the high prison population in a situation of scarce penal resources and general economic stringency. Other factors and relationships will be dealt with in later chapters.

A few more points are worth stressing about this kind of account. First, it is crucial to emphasize again that the crisis is composed of both material and ideological elements, and we have consequently tried to organize Figure 1.2 accordingly. These two sides of the crisis interact in a complex fashion: indeed, certain features of the system, for example bifurcation, cannot be neatly placed on one side or the other of the (ultimately artificial) material/ideological divide since they are both ideologies and material practices at the same time.

The penal crisis is sometimes described as not one but several interlocking crises; for example, we ourselves talk about 'the crisis of resources' and 'the crisis of legitimacy' as if they were separate things. But ultimately it may be best to think of the penal system as one highly complex system and the penal crisis as a single entity – albeit with multiplex causation and a variety of symptoms. For there is a single unifying factor of the penal crisis, into which all the exacerbating elements flow and from which most of the symptoms of the crisis proceed (as Figure 1.2 shows). This key factor is the *crisis of legitimacy*, which is ignored by the orthodox account but which we see as crucial. Riots, staff unrest, the malaise in the probation service and the political problems caused by the penal system are not the direct results of a high prison population or a lack of money or of decent prison buildings (although these do contribute to the crisis). They result from what people believe and how they feel – from the *moral reactions* of people within and outside the penal system to the material situation. (In sociological jargon, the effects of the objective material conditions are 'mediated' through the subjective perceptions of human actors which are structured by ideology.)

The crisis of legitimacy, it is worth repeating, is at least threefold. The penal system needs to legitimate itself with different groups of people: with the public (including politicians, commentators etc.), with penal staff (including prison staff and probation officers) and with penal subjects (prisoners, probationers and others who are subject to penal treatment). Failing to satisfy the sense of justice of these different audiences leads to the alarming visible 'symptoms' of the crisis: political problems, industrial relations problems, malaise among prison and probation staff, and disorder amongst prisoners.

In saying that the crisis of legitimacy is central, we are saying that the penal crisis is in essence a *moral* crisis. By this we do not just mean that many people *believe* that the system is unjust. As we hope to make clear (especially in Chapter 2, but also throughout the whole of this book), the penal system is indeed in our opinion the source of very substantial injustice, and the crisis is unlikely to be solved unless this injustice is mitigated.

Finally, we are at pains to stress that, despite all the arrows in Figure 1.2, we do not believe that human actions and beliefs are mechanistically determined. For example, bifurcation was a policy which was *occasioned* and *encouraged* by the conjunction of overcrowding and lack of resources in an ideological atmosphere of 'law and order' and legitimacy crisis, but it was not inevitable: policy-makers could (and probably should) have decided to do something else instead. Nor were Michael Howard's law and order policies between 1993 and 1997 inexorably brought about by economic decline and the collapse of the rehabilitative ideal; nor are New Labour's current policies determined by iron laws of history. All of which means that the crisis was not inevitable and is not insoluble. But it cannot be solved unless we change people's ideas about punishment.

Notes

1   Craig Sweeney: see Chapter 4, section 4.5.

2   The use of 'the C-word' does wax and wane to some extent. In 2004 Liebling and Arnold (2004: 486) noted – perhaps prematurely – that 'we seem to have stopped hearing the word "crisis" in relation to prisons'.

3   The Woolf Report was co-authored by Her Majesty's Chief Inspector of Prisons, Judge Tumim. It is for convenience, and not out of any wish to disregard Judge Tumim's contribution, that we refer to 'Woolf' in the singular throughout this book.

4   For example, those which followed the implementation of the Criminal Justice Act 1991 and the introduction of 'home detention curfews' in 1999 (see Chapter 8, section 8.4).

5   The 'daily average' prison population is the figure for all prisons (including remand centres, institutions for young offenders and prisoners held in police cells) for an average day in the calendar year. The prison population fluctuates seasonally, and at times in the year the daily average population is significantly exceeded.

6   Home Secretary Jack Straw declared in October 1997 that he had 'no interest in chanting a simplistic mantra that prison works' (quoted in *Prison Report*, no. 41, Winter 1997, p. 3.) However, commentators described the package of measures launched by John Reid in July 2006 as a return to Mr Howard's 'prison works' policies (*Guardian*, 21 July 2006).

7   At the same time, however, there have been intermittent and (some would say) half-hearted efforts to encourage a lesser use of custody for *some* less serious offenders (see further Chapter 11).

8   In our opinion, this measure of a country's 'imprisonment rate' is a useful, if crude, yardstick of the relative punitiveness of different countries. See further Cavadino and Dignan (2006: 4–5).

9   The United States' two million prisoners give it the highest proportionate prison population in the world, with 714 people in prison out of every 100,000 people in the general population in 2003–5. (In joint second place were Russia, Belarus and Bermuda with 532: Walmsley, 2005.) The US, which contains 5 per cent of the planet's population, now accounts for 25 per cent of the world's prison inmates.

10 It is sometimes claimed that these figures can be explained by taking into account different countries' crime rates (for example, Barclay et al., 1995: 54; see also Pease, 1994). It is true that some recent international surveys of victims of crime (e.g. van Kesteren et al., 2001) do show the English rate for certain crimes to be higher than those of several other countries. However, the relatively high English prison population dates back to times when similar surveys (for example, Mayhew, 1994) found the level of crime in Britain to be similar to the European average for most offences.

11 Not counting (for purposes of this calculation) secure children's homes and secure training centres for young offenders.

12 For these various measures of prison capacity, see Chapter 6, section 6.5.

13 The figure at the end of November 2004 was 17,677 (Prison Reform Trust, 2006b: 7). In 2005/06 the figure for Prison Service accommodation was over 16,000 (calculated from HM Prison Service, 2006a).

14 Although some prison staff claimed to the Woolf Inquiry that there had been a worsening 'mix' of prisoners in their prisons prior to the disorders, Woolf's report did not say that this was a cause of the riots. He also recommended that most prisons should be 'community prisons' catering for a wide variety of prisoners from their locality (see further Chapter 6), a prescription which does not seem readily compatible with the notion that this sort of mixture is conducive to disorder.

15 One could try to modify the orthodox account to accommodate these factual discrepancies. See, for example, Sir James Hennessy's (1987) official report into the 1986 disturbances (which, as we shall see, contrasts interestingly with Lord Justice Woolf's report into the 1990 riots). Hennessy partly blamed the mix of offenders for the 1986 riots. But in doing so, he stood the traditional 'toxic mix' theory on its head by claiming that prison order was rendered unstable by young inmates serving *short* sentences, rather than long-term prisoners with 'nothing left to lose'. Even so, such an explanation could not of course account for the riots that have occurred in dispersal prisons at other times.

16 Hennessy (1987: para. 9.06) says almost exactly this in a passage which reads as not entirely metaphorical: 'It can perhaps be explained in terms of a chemical reaction. When a number of elements are brought together and a suitable catalyst is added, an explosion may result.'

17 Other penal agencies, such as Youth Offending Teams or 'YOTs' (see Chapter 9) are also affected by this crisis of penological resources.

18 This slight misquotation of Francis Bacon serves to paraphrase (also slightly inaccurately) Michel Foucault, whose ideas are discussed in Chapter 3, section 3.2.

19 For some discussions of the legitimacy of prisons, see Sparks (1994), Sparks and Bottoms (1995) and Sparks et al. (1996). See also Chapters 6, section 6.5 and Chapter 7, section 7.4.

20 See however Sim (1992, 1994), where he explains that 'abolition' does not entail a total end to the confinement of people however anti-social or dangerous they may be, but merely the abolition of the institution of prison as we know it. He also outlines the important part that 'abolitionists' have played in campaigns which have raised public awareness about the iniquities of the existing system.

21 There is a strong parallel between the rise to prominence of 'law and order' during the 'Thatcherite' period in Britain, and its similar rise under Ronald Reagan's presidency in the United States (1981–8). Other countries also provide partial parallels (see Cavadino and Dignan, 2006).

22 Cf. Garland (2001). We would also highlight the shift towards 'neo-liberal' economics as a factor in this process: see Chapter 3, section 3.6.

23 Indeed, bifurcatory changes in the parole system seem to have contributed to two riots in Scottish prisons in the 1980s: see Chapter 8, note 9.

2 Justifying Punishment

Is Punishment Unjust?

2.1 We need to ask the question: is punishment unjust? In Chapter 1 we argued that the most crucial factor in the current malaise in the penal system is the 'crisis of legitimacy'. A social institution is 'legitimate' if it is *perceived as morally justified*; the problem with the penal system is that this perception is lacking, and many people inside and outside the system believe that it is morally indefensible, or at least defective. We need to investigate whether such moral perceptions are accurate, if only to know what should be done about them. If they are inaccurate, then the obvious strategy would be to try to rectify the perceptions, by persuading people that the system is not unjust after all. But if the perceived injustices are real, then it is those injustices which should be rectified. This chapter accordingly deals with the moral philosophy of punishment and attempts to relate the philosophical issues to the reality of penal systems such as that of England and Wales today.

The basic moral question about punishment is an age-old one: 'What justifies the infliction of punishment[1] on people?' Punishing people certainly needs a justification, since it is almost always something that is harmful, painful or unpleasant to the recipient. Imprisonment, for example, causes physical discomfort, psychological suffering, indignity and general unhappiness along with a variety of other disadvantages (such as impaired prospects for employment and social life). Also, and not to be overlooked, punishments such as imprisonment typically inflict additional suffering on others, such as the offender's family, who have not even been found guilty of a crime (Codd, 1998). Deliberately inflicting suffering on people is at least prima facie immoral, and needs some special justification. It is true that in some cases the recipient does not find the punishment painful, or even welcomes it – for example, some offenders might find prison a refuge against the intolerable pressures of the outside world. And sometimes when we punish we are not trying to cause suffering: for example, when the punishment is mainly aimed at reforming the offender, or at ensuring that victims are benefited by reparation. But even in these cases, punishment is still something imposed: it is an intrusion on the liberty of the person punished, which also needs to be justified.

As well as having a *general justification* for having a system of punishment, we will also require morally valid *'principles of distribution'* for punishment, to determine how severe the punishment of individual offenders should be. This distinction (from Hart, 1968) will be of recurring importance in the following discussion.

The two most frequently cited justifications for punishment are *retribution* and what we call *reductivism* (Walker, 1972). Retributivism justifies punishment on the ground that it is *deserved* by the offender; reductivism justifies punishment on the ground that it helps to *reduce the incidence of crime*. We begin with reductivism.

Reductivism

2.2 Reductivism is a forward-looking (or 'consequentialist') theory: it seeks to justify punishment by its alleged *future consequences*. Punishment is justified because, it is claimed, it helps to control crime. If punishment is inflicted, there will be less crime committed thereafter than there would be if no penalty were imposed. Reductivist arguments can be supported by the form of moral reasoning known as *utilitarianism*. This is the general moral theory first systematically expounded by Jeremy Bentham (1748–1832) (an important figure in penal thought and history), which says that moral actions are those that produce 'the greatest happiness of the greatest number' of people. If punishment does indeed reduce the future incidence of crime, then the pain and unhappiness caused to the offender may be outweighed by the unpleasantness to other people in the future which is prevented – thus making punishment morally right from a utilitarian point of view. But it is not necessary to be a utilitarian to be a reductivist. Indeed, at the end of this chapter we shall be arguing an alternative position (based on human rights) which, although non-utilitarian, nevertheless takes account of the possible reductivist effects of punishment.

How is it claimed that punishment reduces crime? There are several alleged mechanisms of reduction, which we shall discuss in turn.

Deterrence

Essentially, deterrence is the simple idea that the incidence of crime is reduced because of people's fear or apprehension of the punishment they may receive if they offend – that, in the words of Home Secretary Michael Howard addressing the Conservative Party conference in 1993, 'Prison works ... It makes many who are tempted to commit crime think twice.' There are two kinds of deterrence, known as 'individual' and 'general' deterrence.

Individual deterrence occurs when someone commits a crime, is punished for it, and finds the punishment so unpleasant or frightening that the offence is never repeated for fear of more of the same treatment, or worse. This sounds a plausible theory, but unfortunately it seems not to work too well in practice. If individual deterrence did work as the theory suggests, we would expect that if we introduced a new kind of harsh punishment designed to deter, the offenders who suffered the new punishment would be measurably less likely to reoffend than similar offenders who underwent a more lenient penalty. However, as was found with the 'short, sharp shock' detention centre regime for young offenders introduced in the early 1980s, this simply does not seem to work.[2] Indeed, there is some research that indicates – quite contrary to what the theory of individual deterrence suggests – that offenders who suffer more severe or punitive penalties (including penalties specifically aimed at deterrence) are *more* (not less) likely to reoffend (West, 1982: 109; Brody, 1976: 14–16; Lipsey, 1992: 139; Lipsey, 1995: 74). And one particularly thorough research study on boys growing up in London seemed to find that if a boy offends, the best way to prevent him from offending repeatedly is *not to catch him* in the first place (West, 1982: 104–11)!

This research evidence seems contrary to common sense, but such findings are not as incomprehensible as they look at first sight. They do not show that punishment has no deterrent effect on offenders, or that no offender is ever deterred. But they suggest that punishment has other effects which may cancel out and even outweigh its deterrent effects. These anti-deterrent effects of punishment are known as *'labelling effects'*. 'Labelling theory' in criminology claims (and is supported by research studies such as those just mentioned) that catching and punishing offenders 'labels' them as criminals, stigmatizing them, and that this process can in various ways make it more difficult for them to conform to a law-abiding life in future. They may find respectable society and lawful opportunities closed to them while unlawful ones are opened up (custodial institutions are notoriously 'schools for crime' where offenders can meet each other, learn criminal techniques and enter into a criminal subculture), and their self-image may change from that of a law-abiding person to that of a deviant. Harsher penalties in particular could help to foster a tough, 'macho' criminal self-image in the young men who predominate in the criminal statistics. (For a fuller discussion of labelling theory, see I. Taylor et al., 1973: ch. 5.)

So the notion of individual deterrence seems to be of little value in justifying our penal practices. But there is another, perhaps more promising category of deterrent effect: *general deterrence*. This is the idea that offenders are punished, not to deter the offenders themselves, but *pour encourager les autres*.[3] General deterrence theory is often cited to justify punishments, including those imposed on particular offenders. One faintly ludicrous example is a 1983 case[4] where the Court of Appeal said that a particular sentence would 'indicate to other people who might be minded to set fire to armchairs in the middle of a domestic row that if they do, they were likely to go to prison for as long as two years'.

Now, there can be little doubt that the existence of a *system of punishment* has some general deterrent effect. When during the Second World War, the German occupiers deported the entire Danish police force for several months, recorded rates of theft and robbery (though not of sexual offences) rose spectacularly (Christiansen, 1975; Beyleveld, 1980: 159). And if, for instance, on-the-spot execution were to be introduced for parking on a double yellow line, there might well be a significant reduction in the rate of illegal parking. But short of such extreme situations, it seems that *what punishments are actually inflicted* on offenders makes little difference to general deterrence. For example, in Birmingham in 1973 a young mugger was sentenced to a draconian 20 years' detention amid enormous publicity, and yet this sentence made no difference to the incidence of mugging offences in Birmingham or in other areas (Baxter and Nuttall, 1975; Beyleveld, 1980: 157). Similarly, studies have found little if any evidence that jurisdictions with harsh levels of sentencing benefit as a result from reduced crime rates (von Hirsch et al., 1999: ch. 6).[5]

This does not mean that deterrence never works, but it does mean that its effects are limited and easy to overestimate. There are several reasons for this. First, most people most of the time obey the law out of moral considerations rather than for selfish instrumental reasons (Tyler, 1990; Paternoster et al., 1983). Second, people are more likely to be deterred by the likely moral reactions of those close to them than by the threat of formal punishment (Willcock and Stokes, 1968). Again, potential offenders may well be ignorant of the likely penalty, or believe they will never get caught. Research has found that bank robbers tend to be dismissive of their chances of being caught even when they already have been caught and sent to prison, and as a result most do not think twice about the kind of sentence they might get (Gill, 2000). Much the same seems to be true of burglars (Bennett and Wright, 1984: ch. 6). Or the offender may commit the crime while in a thought-less, angry or drunken state. There is some good evidence that general deterrence can be improved if potential offenders' *perceived likelihood of detection* can be increased,[6] but little to suggest that severer punishments deter any better than more lenient ones (see Bottoms, 2004: 63–6).

These truths were officially recognized by the then Conservative government in 1990 (before Mr Howard's announcement that 'prison works'). The 1990 White Paper *Crime, Justice and Protecting the Public* (Home Office, 1990a: para. 2.8) stated:

> There are doubtless some criminals who carefully calculate the possible gains and risks. But much crime is committed on impulse, given the opportunity presented by an open window or unlocked door, and it is committed by offenders who live from moment to moment; their crimes are as impulsive as the rest of their feckless, sad or pathetic lives. It is unrealistic to construct sentencing arrangements on the assumption that most offenders will weigh up the possibilities in advance and base their conduct on rational calculation. Often they do not.

All of this suggests that, while general deterrence might form the basis of a plausible *general justification* for having a *system* of punishment, it is more difficult to argue that the *amount of punishment imposed* by our system can be justified in this way. In terms of its deterrent effects, it seems almost certain that the English penal system is engaging in a massive amount of 'overkill'. As we saw in Chapter 1 (especially Table 1.2), England has more prisoners proportionate to its population than any other country in Western Europe (apart, currently, from Luxembourg). For example, con-trast England with Finland, which in 2004 had 71 prisoners per 100,000 population compared with England and Wales's 141. Unlike England, Finland from the mid-1970s onwards has as a deliberate matter of policy sought to reduce its prison popu-lation (Törnudd, 1993; Cavadino and Dignan, 2006: 160–7), and has succeeded in doing so without noticeably poor effects on its crime rate (which has risen at a sim-ilar rate to that of other European countries). Similarly, a significant reduction in the West German prison population in the 1980s did not lead to an increase in major crime or make the streets less safe (Feest, 1988; Flynn, 1995).

A utilitarian deterrence theorist ought to conclude from this that the English penal system is an immoral one. Jeremy Bentham (1970: 179) himself propounded the principle of 'frugality', more often referred to as *'parsimony'* in punishment, which states that penalties should be no more severe than they need to be to pro-duce a utilitarian quantity of deterrence. 'Overkill' causes unnecessary suffering to the offender, and all suffering is bad unless it prevents a greater amount of suffering or brings about a greater quantity of pleasure.[7] So although utilitarian deterrence might justify having a penal system, it does not justify the one we actually have. We shall argue later that the same is true for our preferred approach based on human rights.

Incapacitation

P rison works, according to Conservative Home Secretary Michael Howard in 1993, not only by deterrence, but also because 'it ensures that we are protected from murderers, muggers and rapists' – a reference to the reductivist mechanism known as 'incapacitation'. Incapacitation simply means that the offender is (usually physically) prevented from reoffending by the punishment imposed, either temporarily or permanently. The practice in some societies of chopping off the hands of thieves incapacitates in this way (as well as possibly deterring theft). Similarly, one of the few obviously valid arguments in favour of capital punishment is that executed offenders never reoffend afterwards. Lesser penalties can also have some incapacitatory effects. Disqualification from driving may do something to prevent motoring offenders from repeating their crimes. Attendance centres can be used to keep hooligans away from football matches. And imprisonment normally ensures that the offender is deprived of the opportunity to commit at least some kinds of offence for the duration. Not all crimes, by any means: many thefts and assaults (on staff and other inmates) take place in prison, as do drug offences, while headlines such as 'Bootlegger ran £23m empire from prison' (*Guardian*, 2 December 1999) exemplify some of the other criminal opportunities open to the incarcerated felon. But it is true that offences such as domestic burglary and car theft become somewhat more difficult when you are locked up in prison.

Life imprisonment is one sentence which is specifically used in many cases for the purposes of incapacitation. A 'life imprisonment' sentence would be more precisely described as a *potentially* lifelong prison sentence, since most 'lifers' are eventually released; but the life sentence means that they will not be released as long as it is believed that they pose an unacceptable risk or serious reoffending (see Chapter 8). Life sentences may be imposed, and lifers kept in prison, even though this exceeds what would be a normal length sentence proportionate to the seriousness of the offence. The sentences of 'imprisonment for public protection' and the 'extended sentences' created by the Criminal Justice Act 2003 (see Chapters 4 and 8) are also aimed at incapacitating offenders.

It is certainly a plausible claim that incapacitation could be a justification (or partial justification) for punishments such as disqualification from driving and attendance centre orders. As to whether and how far incapacitation can serve to justify imprisonment, one key issue is the factual question of how effectively prison reduces crime in this way. Although only rough estimates are possible, the best calculations suggest that the incapacitation effects of imprisonment are only modest. This is largely because most 'criminal careers' are relatively short, so that by the time offenders are locked away they may be about to give up crime or reduce their offending anyway.[8] Moreover, supporters of incapacitation (see, for example, Green et al., 2005) tend to overlook the fact that offenders who are locked up are often replaced by a new generation of criminals. One authoritative estimate, by the former head of the Home Office Research and Planning Unit, Roger Tarling (1993: 154), is that 'a change in the use of custody of the order of 25 per cent would be needed to produce a 1 per cent change in the level of crime'.[9] On the other hand, the prison population could be substantially *reduced* without creating a massive crime wave: if the numbers in prison were cut by 40 per cent, this could be expected to lead to an increase in criminal convictions of only 1.6 per cent (Brody and Tarling, 1980).

Nor is there much evidence that incapacitatory sentences can be targeted with any great success or efficiency on more selected groups of repeat offenders who are especially likely to reoffend.[10] Nor can we accurately predict which offenders are likely to commit particularly serious crimes if they do reoffend (Ashworth, 2005: 206–7, 215–16): our powers of prediction are simply not up to the job, whether we use impressionistic guesswork, psychological testing, statistical prediction techniques or any other method. If we do try to pick out individuals in any of these ways and subject them to extra-long sentences on the basis of our predictions, we will be imprisoning a large number of people who would not in fact reoffend; typically at least twice as many as those who actually would offend again. And even if it were possible to target potential recidivists or those likely to commit grave crimes, this would run into the ethical objection that we were punishing people not for what they have done but for what they *might* do in the future – punishment for imaginary crimes in the future rather than real ones in the past – which might not be fundamentally wrong in principle to a utilitarian, but is a serious objection for most moral codes, including retributivism and human rights theory.

It seems unlikely, then, that incapacitation can provide a general justification for our present practice of imprisonment, let alone justify increasing our use of imprisonment, or introducing any new incapacitatory measures.[11] Nevertheless, the current trend in both England and the United States is for governments to create new sentences explicitly aimed at achieving incapacitation, even if the punishment inflicted is out of all proportion to the offence committed.[12] Most US jurisdictions now have so-called 'three strikes and you're out' laws, whereby repeat offenders are automatically jailed for life for a third offence. Under these laws, people have literally been sent to prison for life for offences such as stealing a slice of pizza, which was the third offence of the unfortunate Jerry Williams in California in 1995 (*Guardian*, 13 October 1995). Since 1997 England has also adopted the 'three strikes and you're out' principle, with various mandatory prison sentences for burglars, drug dealers and those convicted of unlawful possession of firearms, as well as introducing new extended and indefinite sentences to protect the public from offenders who are thought to be dangerous (see Chapter 4).

Reform

Reform (or 'rehabilitation')[13] is the idea that punishment can reduce the incidence of crime by taking a form which will improve the individual offender's character or behaviour and make him or her less likely to reoffend in future. Reform as the central aim of the penal system was a highly popular notion in the 1950s and 1960s, when penological thought was dominated by 'the rehabilitative ideal'. Some proponents of reform (of a kind known as 'positivists': see later in this chapter) have favoured a particularly strong version of this ideal called the 'treatment model'. This viewed criminal behaviour not as freely willed action but (either metaphorically or literally) as a symptom of some kind of mental illness which should not be punished but 'treated' like an illness.

For some advocates of rehabilitation, optimism about reforming offenders has extended to the sentence of imprisonment, with incarceration being seen not so much as a retributive or deterrent punishment but as an opportunity to provide effective reformative training and treatment. For most rehabilitationists, however, the conventional wisdom has long been that 'prison doesn't work' in reforming offenders, and so cannot be justified in these terms.[14] Figures showing high rates of reoffending following release from custody are often quoted as bearing this out; for example, 66 per cent of offenders released from prison in 2003 (and 76 per cent of males aged 18 to 20 released from custody) were reconvicted within two years (Shepherd and Whiting, 2006: 19). After seven years, 73 per cent of released prisoners are reconvicted (Kershaw, 1999: 11).[15] Statistics such as these led the government to famously state in the White Paper which preceded the Criminal Justice Act 1991 that imprisonment 'can be *an expensive way of making bad people worse*' (Home Office, 1990a: para. 2.7; our italics).

Although once dominant in penal discourse, the ideal of reform became discredited in the early 1970s, a development known as the *'collapse of the rehabilitative ideal'* (Bottoms, 1980). This was partly due to research results which suggested that penal measures intended to reform offenders were no more effective in preventing recidivism than were punitive measures. The received wisdom about reform came to be that *'nothing works'*, that 'whatever you do to offenders makes no difference', although this was always an exaggeration. It is true that in the 1970s extensive reviews of research in the United States (Lipton et al., 1975) and in Britain (Brody, 1976) found it to be generally the case that different penal measures had equally unimpressive outcomes in terms of reoffending. Similarly, recent studies[16] have found that, when account is taken of the differing characteristics of offenders[17] sentenced to custody and various types of community sentence, the type of sentence they receive seems to make no discernible difference to whether they reoffend or not. However, studies from the 1970s onwards – including those most often quoted as evidence that 'nothing works' – have also found examples of reformative programmes which seem to work to some extent with certain groups of offenders (see Palmer, 1975). The generalized conclusion (associated with the American Robert Martinson)[18] that `nothing works' became widely accepted – not so much because it had been shown to be true, but more because the disappointment of the high hopes invested in reform led to an overreaction against the rehabilitative ideal.

In recent years (since the early 1990s in Britain) there has been something of a revival of the reformative approach. The new attitude – sometimes associated with the managerialist Strategy B approach to criminal justice (see the Introduction) – has been that *'something* works': that systematic experimentation, research and monitoring can identify effective methods of dealing with offenders and are already doing so. The current New Labour government accepts this new conventional wisdom, and an important strand of its criminal justice policy is to elicit evidence as to *'what works'* to reduce offending and apply the results of research evidence in practice: an *'evidence-based'* policy of trying to increase the effectiveness of the criminal justice system. (Although as we shall see, especially in Chapter 11, it is arguable that government policy is still based more upon ideological and political considerations than upon any dispassionate consideration of the evidence.)

The claims that are now made for the effectiveness of reformative measures are usually more modest than those that were put forward during the period of rehabilitative optimism. Few nowadays hold to the 'medical' or 'treatment' models of punishment, or claim that science can provide a cure for all criminality. Reform tends now to be seen not as 'treatment' which is imagined to work independently of the will of the offender, but as measures that enable or assist rather than force offenders to improve their behaviour – what has been called 'facilitated change' rather than 'coerced cure' (Morris, 1974: 13–20). Many currently popular programmes are based on the *'cognitive behavioural'* approach,[19] which attempts to change how offenders think by improving their cognitive and reasoning skills, often by confronting them with the consequences and social unacceptability of their offending in the hope that they will as a result decide to change their attitudes towards breaking the law. Cognitive behavioural training also seeks to teach offenders skills and techniques for altering and controlling their behaviour. ('Anger management' is one kind of training that is based on cognitive behavioural principles.) Claims have been made that programmes based on the cognitive behavioural approach can reduce reoffending by around 10–15 per cent, and by more if they are effectively targeted on those offenders who can best benefit from them. Some of the same researchers also maintain that punishments that are designed as deterrents can be shown to *increase* delinquency.[20] The cognitive behavioural approach has won official backing, and accreditation processes were set up both within the Prison Service (in 1996) and in the probation service (in 1998) to ensure that training programmes are in accordance with its principles (Debidin and Lovbakke, 2005: 32).

This kind of approach does not deny the offender's free will, rather it appeals to it, aiming to better enable offenders to do what they really want to do. It follows that reform can never be guaranteed to work (as of course research well and truly confirms). But it may still be well worth trying, even though we retain a degree of scepticism about some of the more enthusiastic claims for the effectiveness of reformative programmes. The empirical evidence may have destroyed the reformative aim as a plausible *general justification of the penal system*, but reform remains a reductivist aim which it may well be right to pursue *within* a system of punishment – provided we can find some other general justification.

Retributivism

2.3 The retributivist principle – that wrongdoers should be punished because they deserve it – is in some ways the complete antithesis of reductivism. Where reductivism is forward-looking, retributivism looks backwards in time, to the offence. It is the fact that the offender has committed a wrongful act which deserves punishment, not the future consequences of the punishment, that is important to the retributivist. Retributivism claims that it is in some way morally right to return evil for evil, that two wrongs can somehow make a right.

If people are to be punished because they deserve it, it is natural to say that they should also be punished as severely as they deserve – that they should get their *just deserts*. Retributivism thus advocates what is known as a *tariff*, a set of punishments of varying severity which are matched to crimes of differing seriousness: minor punishments for minor crimes, more severe punishments for more serious offences.[21] The punishment should fit the crime in the sense of being in proportion to the moral culpability shown by the offender in committing the crime. The Old Testament *lex talionis* (an eye for an eye, a life for a life, etc.) is one example of such a tariff, but only one: a retributive tariff could be considerably more lenient than this, as long as the proportionate relationship between crimes and punishments was retained.

This is a point that needs stressing, because it is a common mistake – certainly among our own students – to assume that retributivists are those who advocate the harshest punishments, and to equate retributivism with a draconian, Strategy A approach to criminal justice. In fact, it is often the case that retributivists (for example, those who follow the 'justice model' of punishment we discuss in section 2.5) favour relatively lenient punishment. (But punishment that is ultimately justified by the fact that it is deserved and proportionate.) On the other hand, some notable exponents of Strategy A – such as Michael Howard, Conservative Home Secretary from 1992 to 1997 – have attempted to justify their harsh penal policies by appeals to their supposed effectiveness in controlling crime by reductivist mechanisms such as deterrence and incapacitation. The mistake is understandable, and there may be a certain psychological truth behind it. Maybe, whatever their proclaimed motives, many advocates of Strategy A are primarily motivated more by a hatred of criminals and a wish to see them 'get what they deserve' than by a desire to pursue rational steps to reduce crime. But retributivism is not inherently harsher than other philosophies, and indeed it has certain attractive features to those of a humane disposition.

One of these attractive features is its consonance with what is generally acknowledged to be one fundamental principle of justice: that *like cases should be treated alike*. ('Like' for retributivists means alike in the intuitively appealing sense of 'similarly deserving'.)

Another attractive feature of retributivism is that there is a natural connection between the retributive approach and the idea that both offenders and victims have *rights*. Reductivist theory (at least in its utilitarian form) has always found it difficult to encompass the notion of rights, even when it comes to providing entirely innocent people with a right not to be punished. (For if we could achieve the desired reductive consequences by framing an innocent person, and if these effects are all that is needed to justify punishment, what would be wrong with punishing the innocent?) Retributivism has no such problem, since it follows automatically from the retributive principle that it must be wrong to punish non-offenders. Nor may we punish criminals to a greater extent than their crimes are felt to deserve (for example, in the hope of reforming or incapacitating them or deterring others): under the retributivist principle offenders have a right to go free once they have 'paid their debt to society'. Life imprisonment for stealing a pizza would be ruled out as disproportionate, for example. Retributivism thus fits in well with our common-sense intuitions which insist that it is indeed morally relevant whether the person punished has behaved well, badly or very badly. Probably for this reason, it has proved a remarkably resilient idea. For many years retributivism was regarded (at least in academic circles) as outmoded and even atavistic, but it enjoyed a major revival from the early 1970s onwards, notably in the form of the 'justice model' (see section 2.5 of this chapter) – though at the moment it is less fashionable again.

But retributivism is not without its own philosophical difficulties. One problem is how to justify the retributive principle itself. It may accord with some of our moral gut reactions, which seem to tell us that wrongdoers should be made to suffer. But maybe these reactions are merely irrational vindictive emotions (akin to vengeance) which, morally speaking, we ought to curb rather than indulge. A related objection is that it is not immediately clear how the retributivist principle relates to any general notion of what is right or wrong. At least utilitarian reductivism has the virtue that it can be derived from the general moral and political theory of utilitarianism.

Some theorists have attempted to counter these objections by reference to the 'social contract', a theory which provides a general account of political obligation (see especially Murphy, 1979). The idea is that all citizens are bound together in a sort of multilateral contract which defines our reciprocal rights and duties. The terms of this contract include the law of the land, which applies fairly and equally to all of us. The lawbreaker has disturbed this equilibrium of equality and gained an unfair advantage over those of us who have behaved well and abided by the rules. Retributive punishment restores the balance by cancelling out this advantage with a commensurate disadvantage. It thus ensures that wrongdoers do not profit from their wrongdoings, and is justified because if we failed to punish law-breakers it would be unfair to the law-abiding.

This 'modern retributivism' was highly influential for a time, although it was always far from universally accepted and it eventually became discredited even in the eyes of some of its foremost former advocates (Murphy, 1992: 24–5, 47–8; von Hirsch, 1986: ch. 5; von Hirsch, 1993: ch. 2). But even if we assume that it is sound at an abstract philosophical level, it would be extremely dubious to assert that this theory can justify our present practices of punishment or anything like them. One serious difficulty is that the theory only applies if our society is a just one in which all citizens are genuinely equal; otherwise there is no equilibrium of equality for punishment to restore. If – as appears to be the case – detected offenders typically start from a position of social disadvantage (which means that the obligation to obey the law weighs more heavily upon them than on others), then punishment will tend to increase inequality rather than do the opposite. In fact, this was exactly the conclusion once reached by the modern retributivist Jeffrie Murphy (1979: 95), who stated that 'modern societies largely lack the moral right to punish'.[22] Even if such a sweeping conclusion is not warranted, retributivists should be strongly critical of many aspects of our penal system. Not least among these are the lack of consistency in sentencing practices (see Chapter 4), and an increasing number of mandatory and incapacitatory sentences (see Chapters 4 and 8), which mean that offenders are to a great extent not dealt with in proportion to their just deserts. They should also disapprove strongly of the growing trend to concentrate more punishment on persistent offenders rather than those whose current offences are the most serious.[23] So despite its resilience and its various attractions, retributivism remains an implausible justification for our actual practices of punishment.

More promisingly, perhaps, retributivism is sometimes combined with reductivism to produce hybrid or 'compromise' theories (Honderich, 1984: ch. 6). Often these compromise theories state, in effect, that punishment is justified only if it is both deserved *and* likely to have reductivist effects on crime (for example, von Hirsch, 1976: chs 5 and 6). One such compromise theory is *'limiting retributivism'*. This theory states that punishment may be inflicted for forward-looking purposes such as the reduction of crime, but it is nevertheless wrong to punish anyone by more than they deserve. Thus the retributive principle limits the amount of punishment which may be imposed for reasons other than retribution. We shall return to this principle of limiting retributivism in section 2.7, and shall find reasons to approve of it – which are also, however, reasons to criticize many of the punishments that are actually inflicted within the penal system that we have.

Other Justifications

2.4 Reductivism and retributivism do not exhaust all the possible justifications for punishment, or the aims which it has been suggested punishment can rightly pursue. We now proceed to deal with two of these: denunciation and restorative justice, and the notions of reparation and reintegrative shaming with which restorative justice is associated.

Denunciation

Giving evidence to the Royal Commission on Capital Punishment in the 1950s, Lord Denning (Gowers, 1953: para. 53) made the following statement:

The punishment for grave crimes should adequately reflect the revulsion felt by the great majority of citizens for them. It is a mistake to consider the objects of punishment as being deterrent or reformative or preventive and nothing else ... The ultimate justification of punishment is not that it is a deterrent, but that it is the emphatic denunciation by the community of a crime.

The idea that punishment does and should demonstrate society's abhorrence of the offence, and that this in some way justifies punishment, is quite a popular one. It was explicitly cited as a rationale for the sentence in the 1981 case of Marcus Sarjeant, an unemployed teenager who fired blanks at the Queen during the Trooping the Colour ceremony. Sentencing Sarjeant to five years' imprisonment, Lord Lane (the Lord Chief Justice) said: 'The public sense of outrage must be marked. You must be punished for the wicked thing you did' (*The Times*, 15 September 1981). Similarly, a 1990 White Paper (Home Office, 1990a: para. 2.4) stated that 'punishment can effectively denounce criminal behaviour'.

Denunciation might be advocated for more than one reason. What we term *instrumental denunciation* is actually a form of reductivism (which we discuss at this stage for convenience). This is the idea that denunciation can help to reduce the incidence of crime – a notion which may at first seem somewhat obscure, but which has a distinguished intellectual pedigree. Émile Durkheim (1960: vol. 1, ch. 2; see below, Chapter 3, section 3.3) argued that one function of the criminal law and punishment was to reinforce the *conscience collective* of society and thereby ensure that members of society continued to refrain from crime. Punishment, Durkheim thought, has an educative effect. It not only teaches people to obey the law out of fear and prudence (which is deterrence); it also sends a symbolic moral message that the offender's action is socially abhorred, and therefore wrong.

As with general deterrence, it is difficult on the evidence to make very strong claims about the effectiveness of denunciation. Research suggests that members of the public are not influenced in their moral attitudes towards offences by the punishments that are imposed (or which they believe are imposed). People seem to have sufficient *respect for the law* to disapprove more strongly of an action when a law is passed against it, but they do not have sufficient *respect for the criminal justice system* to be influenced by the severity of punishment inflicted (Walker and Marsh, 1984; cf. Tyler, 1990: 44–7). This suggests that (like general deterrence) instrumental denunciation cannot justify any particular level of severity of punishment; nor can the penal system (as is sometimes fondly imagined)[24] 'give a lead' to public opinion about the rights and wrongs of how people should behave.

A different version of denunciation theory (and the one we suspect Lords Denning and Lane subscribe to) is what we term *expressive denunciation*. This is the (non-forward-looking) notion that punishment is justified *simply* because it is the expression of society's abhorrence of crime. Sometimes this is explained in terms of the community showing its recognition of and commitment to its own values (for example, Lacey, 1988).

The claim is therefore that denunciatory punishment is justified *even if it has no good consequences* such as educating the public conscience and thereby reducing the amount of crime. When posed in such stark but accurate terms it becomes difficult to see why this is supposed to amount to a distinct moral justification for punishment. It looks suspiciously like knee-jerk retributivism, spuriously ennobled by

appropriate way of responding to it. The three most important 'restorative justice processes' which have been used in this country are *victim/offender mediation, conferencing* and *citizen panels*. Of these, only mediation actually requires the victim to participate, whether directly (involving face-to-face dialogue between victim and offender in the presence of a neutral mediator) or indirectly (where the mediator acts as a go-between). People other than the direct victim – including the families of both victim and offender, and representatives of the local community – may also be 'stakeholders' with an interest in how the offence is resolved, and other restorative justice processes such as conferencing provide a forum within which they too may participate. 'Police-led conferencing', as the name suggests, is convened and facilitated by the police, whereas in 'family group conferencing' the facilitator is more likely to be a government official. Citizen panels provide an informal forum in which lay people may deliberate with offenders, family members and others (possibly including victims) about the offence and its impact with a view to negotiating a 'contract' with the offender who undertakes to make amends in agreed ways. (See further Chapters 5 and 9.)

Restorative justice's aim of communicating with the offender about the wrongfulness of the crime has clear affinities with Antony Duff's 'communicative theory' discussed briefly under the previous heading. Two other aims of restorative justice, which we now proceed to discuss, are 'reparation' and 'reintegrative shaming'.

Reparation is the notion that people who have offended should do something to 'repair' the wrong they have done. This can take the form of compensating the victim of the offence or doing something else to assist the victim. If there is no individual or identifiable victim (or if the victim is unwilling to accept it), reparation can be made to the community as a whole by performing community service or paying a fine into public funds. 'Symbolic reparation' can also occur, for example, in the form of an apology for having committed the offence. Reparation is a sound and valid principle which we strongly favour (Dignan, 1994; Dignan and Cavadino, 1996; Cavadino and Dignan, 1997b); one of its virtues is that it could be of great value in assisting the 'reintegration' of offenders, as we discuss shortly. Reparation can be seen either as a desirable aim in its own right, or as a valuable but secondary aim which may be pursued when imposing punishment which is justified on other grounds (such as reductivism). If punishment is to be inflicted, it is surely better that the punishment should directly benefit the victim or society than that it should merely hurt or restrict the offender.

Restorative justice has also increasingly been linked to and underpinned by a general theory of crime and punishment propounded by John Braithwaite (1989). Braithwaite claims that successful societal responses to crime are those that bring about the *reintegrative shaming* of the offender. Offenders should be dealt with in a manner that shames them before other members of their community. But the shaming should not be of a 'stigmatizing' nature, which will tend to exclude them from being accepted members of the community; this (as the 'labelling theory' we mentioned in section 2.2 suggests) will be counter-productive, as it will make reoffending much more likely. Instead, the shaming should be of a kind which serves to reintegrate offenders, by getting them to accept that they have done wrong while encouraging others to readmit them to society. The measures and processes associated with restorative justice are particularly suitable for pursuing reintegrative shaming (Dignan, 1994), for the performance of reparation shames the offender symbolically while seeking to set matters right between the offender, the victim and the community. If such a strategy were to be an effective one – and the jury is still out on this,[26] although it seems a promising idea – then reintegrative shaming would be a valuable method of reforming offenders, which we see as a valid reductivist aim which could be pursued within a morally defensible penal system.

Even if restorative justice is no more effective in controlling crime than the traditional criminal justice system, it is in our opinion a preferable approach wherever it can feasibly be applied. (We shall return to this in Chapter 11.) It is obvious, however, that the principles and aims of restorative justice cannot begin to justify the penal system that we have, since most punishments (and most notably imprisonment) contain little or no restorative element, and may even make it difficult or impossible for the offender to make amends. But if restoration were more consistently pursued, we should have a much more civilized and morally acceptable penal system than the present one.

Schools of Penal Thought

2.5 The various justifications for punishment we have outlined have waxed and waned in relative popularity over time. In this section we provide a brief history of the development of penal thought in the West to show how different combinations of penal justifications have found favour in different eras.

The Classical School: Deterrence and the Tariff

The year 1764 saw the publication of one of the most influential works of penal philosophy of all time – *Dei Delitti e delle Pene* [On Crimes and Punishments] by the Italian, Cesare Beccaria (Beccaria, 1963). This book, the seminal work of the 'classical' schools of criminal law and penology, provided a thoroughgoing critique of the criminal justice systems of eighteenth-century Europe along with a blueprint for reform along more rational and humane lines.

To understand the classicists, it helps to have some understanding of what they were reacting against. Punishment under the *ancien regime* of eighteenth-century Europe was both arbitrary and harshly retributive, dominated by capital and corporal penalties. Moreover, 'due process' in the form of effective legal safeguards against wrongful conviction was all but absent in the criminal justice system of the time, and even the laws that defined which actions were criminal were vague and extremely wide. On the other hand, the existence of wide discretion in the hands of judges and of the sovereign (notably in the form of the pardon, which was extensively used) meant that the guilty were as likely to go unpunished as were the innocent to be wrongly convicted and harshly dealt with. The classicists claimed that such a system was not only inhumane and unfair, but profoundly irrational and inefficient for the task of controlling crime.

Beccaria's blueprint called for clarity in the law and due process in criminal procedure combined with certainty and regularity of punishment. There should be a definite, fixed penalty for every offence, laid down in advance by the legislature in a strict tariff. These penalties should be proportionate to the gravity of the offence but as mild as possible, in contrast to the 'useless prodigality of torments' which characterized the existing system. Once an offender was found guilty, however, the sentence should follow automatically; in the strict classicism of Beccaria there was no room for clemency by way of pardons, reduction of sentences because of mitigating circumstances, or early release from the punishment laid down. All people were to be treated as fully responsible for their own actions, including their own offences.

The intellectual influence of classicism, and of Beccaria in particular, was enormous. Its principles were praised by reforming monarchs such as Frederick II of Prussia, Maria Theresa of Austria and Catherine the Great of Russia; the French Code introduced by the revolutionary regime in 1791 was an attempt at direct implementation of his plan for a rigid tariff of punishments; and Beccaria also greatly influenced such English jurists as Romilly and Blackstone. Its greatest impact was, however, on the framing of codes of criminal law rather than on penal systems. Beccaria's blueprint was never implemented in full.

Classicism grew out of the Enlightenment, the eighteenth-century philosophical movement which stressed the importance of human reason and which undertook the critical reappraisal of existing ideas and social institutions. Beccaria made particular use of the Enlightenment notion of the 'social contract' as the source of legitimate political authority. He argued that rational people drawing up a just social contract would only be willing to grant governments the power to punish to the extent that was necessary to protect themselves from the crimes of others. It followed that punishments should be no harsher than was necessary to achieve reductivist ends by means of deterrence. From this he derived his proposal for a tariff of fixed, certain penalties, proportionate to the offence but relatively mild by the standards of his own day. (Thus, like retributivists, he advocated a proportionate tariff, although he was himself a reductivist.) Beccaria opposed capital punishment as being cruel and inefficient as a deterrent. Punishments should, he said, be public and of a kind appropriate to the type of offence: corporal punishments for crimes of violence, public humiliation for 'crimes founded on pride' and so on. This would, he thought, assist in deterrence because 'in crude, vulgar minds, the seductive picture of a particularly advantageous crime should immediately call up the associated idea of punishment' (Beccaria, 1963: 57).

In general, Beccaria's philosophy exhibits what could be regarded as a curious combination of concern with the rights of the individual under the social contract on the one hand, and utilitarian reductivism on the other – curious because rights theory and utilitarianism are often thought to be philosophically incompatible. Yet he explicitly appeals to both concepts. (Indeed, not only did Beccaria use the concept of utility, but Bentham himself acknowledged his intellectual debt to Beccaria in the most fulsome terms and is even believed to have first encountered the phrase 'the greatest happiness of the greatest number' in Beccaria's master work: see Beccaria, 1963: x–xi, 8.) This intriguingly attractive blend of rights theory with forward-looking reductivism is one of the features that make Beccaria a continually fascinating and influential penal thinker even today.

Bentham and Neo-Classicism: Deterrence and Reform

The Englishman Jeremy Bentham (1748–1832), the main founder of the utilitarian philosophy, was also a major penal thinker and reformer. His penal thinking was an application of his general philosophy that law and government should pursue 'the greatest happiness of the greatest number'. This logically led him to espouse a purely reductivist approach to punishment, with no place for retributivism of any description. Despite the intellectual debt he acknowledged to Beccaria, his ideas differed from those of his Italian predecessor in several respects. At a philosophical level he had no time for notions of the social contract or human rights (he famously described the idea of natural rights as 'nonsense upon stilts'). Like Beccaria, he regarded clarity and due process in the criminal law as desirable, but from a purely utilitarian point of view. Similarly, he followed Beccaria in advocating a proportionate tariff of punishments for offences. Like Beccaria, he said that punishment should be primarily justified because of its deterrent effects, but he also proclaimed that punishment of the right kind could serve a further reductivist aim: that of reform.

His model of utilitarian punishment was exemplified most famously in the Panopticon – a prison he designed and narrowly failed to persuade the British government to let him build. The Panopticon was designed in such a way that prisoners were under constant surveillance by inspectors in a central observation tower. Prisoners were to be made to perform productive work within the prison in a consistent and regular manner in order that they should acquire rational work habits which they would retain after release instead of returning to crime. Thus, whereas classicism's image of human nature portrayed all human beings as being fully responsible for their own actions, Bentham saw criminals as having limited rationality and responsibility, but thought that they could be made more rational by the correct application of reformative techniques in his 'mill for grinding rogues honest', as he called the Panopticon. His thinking also took account of limited human rationality on the question of responsibility for offences; unlike Beccaria, he allowed for mitigating circumstances such as duress, infancy and insanity to reduce or even remove an individual's liability to punishment.

Beccaria's ideas had been fated to win great praise but achieve less by way of practical influence in the running of penal systems. Bentham's success was greater but far from total. Utilitarian reductivism became a prominent rationale for punishment but never displaced retributivism entirely. Criminal justice systems in the nineteenth century developed along *neo-classical* lines. This meant that criminal laws were clarified and in some countries codified, as both Beccaria and Bentham advocated, but leaving a greater degree of flexibility and judicial discretion than either would have found congenial. For example, the highly Beccarian French Code of 1791 was soon revised to reintroduce recognition of mitigating circumstances, judicial discretion in sentencing and the prerogative of mercy.

The Benthamite approach had its greatest impact in respect of one of its greatest points of difference from Beccarian classicism: the *form* punishment should take. Beccaria's scheme had no place for imprisonment as a punishment. (He only discussed imprisonment as the temporary incarceration of a suspect before trial, and while he did advocate penal servitude as a punishment for certain offences, this was not to be served in prison.) Bentham by contrast saw prison, in the shape of the Panopticon, as a useful method of dealing with offenders. Although the Panopticon was never built exactly as he designed it (a modified version was constructed at Millbank on the Thames and opened, with extremely poor results, in 1817), imprisonment rapidly became the pre-eminent method of punishment. As Foucault (1977) famously observed, the end of the eighteenth century and the early nineteenth century saw a massive shift (which Foucault (1977: 15) called 'the great transformation') from *corporal* to *carceral* punishment (see further Chapter 5). Moreover, this was a new form of imprisonment, the aims of which were not confined to containing offenders for a period and deterring the populace from crime. It also set out to retrain (or 'discipline' to use Foucault's word) the inmates, along the kind of lines Bentham advocated. As Foucault (1977: 16) put it, punishment no longer addressed itself to the body of the criminal, but to the soul.

Positivism: The Rehabilitative Ideal

A century after Cesare Beccaria's *Dei Delitti e delle Pene* saw the light of day, there came the publication of another work by an Italian called Cesare, equally seminal and revolutionary but in most respects diametrically opposed to Beccaria's way of thinking. This was Cesare Lombroso's *L'Uomo Delinquente* [The Criminal Man] (1876). Lombroso is best known for his theory, an extension of Charles Darwin's ideas, that criminals were atavistic throwbacks to an earlier stage of evolution. But more important than this particular theory (which he was later to modify substantially) was Lombroso's role as the founder of the *positive school of criminology*. The positivist view is that crime, along with all other natural and social phenomena, is *caused* by factors and processes which can be discovered by scientific investigation. These causes are not necessarily genetic, but may include environmental factors such as family upbringing, social conditioning and so on. Positivists believe in the doctrine of *determinism*: the belief that human beings, including criminals, do not act from their own free will but are impelled to act by forces beyond their control. Thus, where Beccaria's vision of human nature had been one of untrammelled free will and while Bentham had admitted that the responsibility of some humans was limited, positivism denies responsibility altogether.

It follows (for the positivist) that it is wrong to hold people responsible for their crimes and punish them in ways that imply that their crimes are their own fault. Criminality is no more the fault of the offender than illness is the fault of the invalid, and both require treatment not blame. So retributivism is clearly excluded as a justification for punishment. Positivism is also typically sceptical about deterrence, on the grounds that empirical evidence scientifically assessed demonstrates that punishment is ineffective as a deterrent. The reductivist methods favoured by positivism are incapacitation, and especially reform. Criminological science should be able to predict which offenders (and perhaps even which people who have not yet offended) are likely to commit further crimes. Such people should be diagnosed by experts and given appropriate treatment which will prevent them from reoffending; if necessary they can be detained to incapacitate them in the meantime and ensure that they are available to be treated.

Positivism in its purest form rejects two important doctrines common to both classicism and neo-classicism, namely due process and proportionality. Due process is not appropriate in the diagnosis and treatment of crime any more than it is in medicine, since the scientific investigative process does not and should not proceed along legalistic lines. Proportionality is similarly seen as a mistaken notion, since there is no reason why the treatment needed by the offender should be in proportion to the gravity of the offence. Instead of the punishment fitting the crime, the treatment should fit the individual criminal. (For this reason the positivistic approach is sometimes referred to as the *'individualized treatment model'*.) Positivism particularly favours the *indeterminate sentence*: it is premature to decide at the time of sentence how long the offender should be detained for, since this may depend on how quickly the treatment works; ideally, therefore, the release decision should be left in the hands of treatment experts to take at a later date.

Positivism, and the *rehabilitative ideal* associated with it, gradually came to dominate criminological thinking and rhetoric, reaching its zenith in the 1950s and 1960s, especially in the United States. For example, indeterminate and semi-indeterminate sentences (such as 'one year to life') became more and more common in the USA, with release dates dependent not upon the sentence passed at the trial but upon the parole process. This was a time of 'rehabilitative optimism': there was a widespread belief that criminology and other behavioural sciences would progressively discover the causes of crime and the way to cure all offenders of their criminality. In the 1970s, however, the positivist approach was dealt a series of severe blows which led to the collapse of the rehabilitative ideal. One of these blows (mentioned under 'Reform' in section 2.2 above) was cruelly self-inflicted: positivistic criminological research, far from demonstrating the effectiveness of treatment measures, seemed instead to show that treatment did not work. At much the same time, positivism came under a powerful and sustained political and theoretical critique associated with the 'justice model'.

The Justice Model: Just Deserts and Due Process

The justice model (Bottomley, 1980; Hudson, 1987) first emerged in the US as a critique of the positivistic 'individualized treatment model'.[27] The first book-length statement of the justice model in the 1970s was the American Friends Service Committee's report *Struggle for Justice*, published in 1971. The authors claimed that the treatment model was 'theoretically faulty, systematically discriminatory in administration, and inconsistent with some of our most basic concepts of justice' (American Friends Service Committee, 1971: 12). Theoretically faulty, because the individualized treatment model identified the cause of crime as a pathology within the individual, whereas the authors saw the true causes of crime as structural, resulting from the way in which society is organized. Systematically discriminatory, because the wide discretion which positivism vested in supposed experts within the criminal justice system operated in practice to disadvantage offenders from poorer sections of society. And inconsistent with justice, because the lack of due process and proportionality in the treatment model offends our moral intuitions about the rights of the individual and the unfairness of treating offences of similar gravity in possibly widely varying ways. It was also felt that the positivistic notion that offenders were not rational and responsible agents, and that they should be reprogrammed until they conform to society, was a profound insult to human dignity.

The justice model asserts two central principles, both of which hark back to the classicism of Beccaria. The first is due process in procedure, and the general limitation of official discretion within the criminal justice system. The second is proportionality of punishments to the gravity of offences – or in other words, that offenders should receive their *just deserts*.[28] Disproportionate sentences with the alleged purpose of reforming the offender are to be rejected. This is so whether the reformative sentence would be disproportionately long or disproportionately short, although most adherents of the justice model in the 1970s (who tended to be liberal or moderately radical in political persuasion) wanted a just deserts system which would punish less harshly overall – again like Beccaria two centuries previously.

It is not only reform as an aim of punishment that the justice model eyes with suspicion. Justice model writers are also mostly sceptical of the effectiveness of deterrence and even more so of the validity of deriving a just tariff from deterrent considerations (as Beccaria and Bentham claimed to do). The justice model's philosophy consequently relies heavily on either retribution or denunciation as at least a partial justification for punishment. The most definitive justice model statement of the 1970s, the Committee for the Study of Incarceration's *Doing Justice* (von Hirsch, 1976: chs 5, and 6), adapted Jeffrie Murphy's (1979) modern retributivist theory and concluded that retribution and deterrence in combination provided the general justification for punishment. Subsequently, Andrew von Hirsch (1986: ch. 5, 1993: ch. 2) has claimed that punishment is justified on the two grounds of reductivism (which he calls 'the preventive function' of punishment) and denunciation (or 'the blaming function'), the latter being the basis for adopting proportionality as the principle for the distribution of punishment.[29]

The justice model made its impact on both sides of the Atlantic and elsewhere.[30] In the USA many states moved substantially away from indeterminate sentences and positivistic devices such as parole.[31] The high-water mark of the justice model's influence in Britain was the 'just deserts' strategy which was pursued by the British Conservative government prior to 1993 and which centred around the Criminal Justice Act 1991 (see the Introduction and Chapters 4 and 11). Although by no means representing the justice model in a pure form, the 1991 Act sought to establish 'just deserts' as the primary aim of sentencing (Home Office, 1990a: paras 2.1–2.4). But as we shall see in more detail in Chapters 4 and 11, both the 1991 Act and its just deserts principles were to come rapidly to grief.

From 'Just Deserts' to 'the New Punitiveness' – and Beyond?

It is sometimes said that the justice model, although originally proposed by liberals and radicals who wished to reduce the overall harshness of punishment, was 'co-opted' from the late 1970s onwards by the political Right (for example, Bottoms, 1980: 11; Hudson, 1987: 72). Whether or not this is the best way of describing the situation, it is true that some important strategies and approaches to punishment in this period combined aspects of the justice model with a generous dash of the populist, punitive ideology of 'law and order', which we discussed in Chapter 1 and which has gathered ever greater influence since the 1970s. Indeed, the 'just deserts' strategy in the Criminal Justice Act 1991 can be seen as a hybrid of this kind, for along with pursuing a greater proportionality in sentencing in general, the government insisted that community penalties should be made more toughly punitive ('punishment in the community') and that custodial sentences for violent and sexual offenders should be increased.

Other just deserts/law and order hybrid approaches have been considerably more punitive than this. It is possible to discern – for example, in the United States for much of the late 1970s and 1980s – a kind of 'right-wing just deserts' approach which shares with the liberal version a retributivist approach and a preference for proportionate, 'just deserts' punishments, but advocates *more severe* fixed-term sentences. Reformative measures are disfavoured by this approach not because they might be disproportionately harsh, but because they may be too soft. However, this approach departed from the liberal justice model markedly in its attitude to due process: if anything it disapproved of excessive procedural safeguards on the grounds that they are likely to act as an obstacle to ensuring offenders receive their just deserts.

From the vantage point of the present day, these more punitive versions of 'just deserts' assume the appearance of temporary staging posts on a rapid journey heading towards a 'new punitiveness' (see the Introduction and Chapter 3). In Britain, we have heard little about 'just deserts' – certainly from either Conservative or Labour politicians – since the 'law and order counter-reformation' of 1992–3. In terms of the philosophy of punishment, the Conservative government then abandoned 'just deserts' in favour of the assertion that 'prison works' by incapacitation and deterrence – although this was perhaps not so much philosophy as a rationalization designed to legitimate a populist set of 'tough' (Strategy A) penal policies. Arguably, the historical role of the justice model – entirely contrary to the intentions of its progenitors – was to pave the way for the transition to a more punitive penal system and a more authoritarian society. As we shall see throughout this book, much of this punitiveness lives on under the New Labour government first elected in May 1997, which remains little influenced by the philosophy of 'just deserts'.[32] One illustration of this is the government's insistence that the penalty of imprisonment is appropriate not only for serious offenders but also for persistent petty offenders, a policy which offends against the idea that the punishment should fit the crime.[33] More generally, the government justifies its policies not on the basis that they provide a fair amount of punishment for offenders, but because they are claimed to be effective in controlling crime – which is of course reductivism. For the moment at least, 'just deserts' is out of fashion with those who have most power to determine the shape of criminal justice. What reigns in its place at the moment is not simply 'law and order', but a combination of philosophies and strategies, as we shall see throughout this book.

Philosophies, Strategies and Attitudes

2.6 It is not as simple as one might imagine to relate these philosophies and schools of thought to the broad 'Strategies' (Strategies A, B and C) we detailed in the Introduction. (To recap briefly, Strategy A is harshly punitive, Strategy B is managerialist, and Strategy C is humane and rights-based.) Newcomers to the subject tend to assume that retributivism (with its traditional overtones of 'an eye for an eye') is the harshest philosophy and the one underlying the punitive Strategy A. It is indeed possible to espouse Strategy A and call for maximum punishment on the basis of a harsh interpretation of retributivism. But, as we have seen, some notable proponents of Strategy A (such as Michael Howard) have justified their policies on *reductivist* grounds, claiming for example, that 'prison works' to deter and incapacitate. On the other hand, the retributivist philosophy insists not only that punishment should be proportionate to the offence, but that it *should not be disproportionately severe because this would be undeserved*. This is, indeed, a central message of the justice model, most of whose proponents we would place under the heading of Strategy C, because they were concerned to minimize the violation of human rights involved in the infliction of excessively severe punishments.

So Strategy A can be based – although not necessarily with any great intellectual coherence – on either retributivism or reductivism (or indeed on the theory of denunciation). Proponents of the lenient, human rights-based Strategy C can also draw on any of these philosophies and justifications for punishment. Those whose humanitarianism takes the form of advocating reformative measures invoke reductivism (and the belief that reformative treatment can help reduce future crime); while, as we have seen, proponents of the justice model can appeal to either retributivism or denunciation, typically combined with reductivism in a hybrid justification for punishment. Those who favour restorative justice may be reductivists (believing that this kind of justice is the most effective at controlling crime) or may appeal to the desirability of reparation as an independent aim in its own right.

There is therefore no simple equation between the *philosophies* of punishment and what we term *strategies*. Both reductivism and retributivism can be either harsh or humane. However, when it comes to Strategy B – the managerialist strategy – there is one general philosophy which fits it very neatly. This is the philosophy of *utilitarianism,* the notion that one should always act in the interests of the 'greatest number' of people. The emphasis that managerialism places on effectiveness and cost-efficiency has a decidedly utilitarian tinge. So does the way in which managerialism is not greatly concerned about the human rights of individual offenders or about ensuring that offenders get their 'just deserts' (however much or little that is conceived to be). It follows that a proponent of Strategy B should, if consistent, espouse utilitarian *reductivism* as the basic aim of punishment. And indeed, the rise of managerialism in criminal justice has occurred in conjunction with an increasing interest in 'what works' to reduce crime (by both general crime prevention measures and penal sanctions aimed at reducing recidivism, including reformative treatments) – and, significantly, what works most efficiently and cost-effectively. This utilitarian (Strategy B) agenda is currently very prominent in New Labour's criminal justice policies, combined with a strong streak of (Strategy A) new punitiveness and a slight dash of Strategy C, notably in the introduction of 'restorative justice' measures for some young offenders (see Chapter 9).

Underlying much of the conflict between different penal philosophies and strategies, we can perhaps discern a very general tension between what could be termed two fundamentally different attitudes towards offenders. This is the contrast between *exclusive* and *inclusive* attitudes. The exclusive attitude rejects offenders as members of the community and seeks to shut them out of mainstream society by measures such as imprisonment. This attitude is allied to notions of deterrence, incapacitation and an illiberal version of retributivism. The inclusive attitude, on the other hand, seeks to maintain offenders within the community and reintegrate them into mainstream society. It can be found embodied in notions and practices of reform, resocialization, restorative justice and more liberal versions of retributivism (such as the 'justice model'). (See further Cavadino et al., 1999: 48–50.) Strategy A is clearly aligned with the exclusive attitude and Strategy C with the inclusive; Strategy B, however, is essentially indifferent to the inclusion/exclusion dimension, and would favour whichever approach happens to work best in practice. We can see this conflict between inclusion and exclusion of the offender being played out throughout this book, including the philosophical debates covered in this chapter.

Conclusions: Punishment And Human Rights

2.7 This chapter has been a complex one, but it has nevertheless been an exercise in oversimplification. As well as reducing some sophisticated philosophies down to some relatively crude statements, we have probably also given the impression that penal systems 'in the real world' at different stages in history possess a consistency and coherence that is in fact largely lacking. The philosophies we have described do exert a very real influence on the shaping of penal systems and penal practices, but none of the various schools of thought has ever been totally dominant, even at the height of its popularity. No penal system has ever been entirely retributivist, or entirely reductivist, or thoroughly Beccarian. This impurity of the real world can be seen in the existing English system: the legally accepted justifications for punishment include retribution, deterrence, incapacitation, denunciation, reform and reparation in a promiscuously eclectic mixture.[34] Government policies have been similarly eclectic, as a variety of penal aims and philosophies have been cited (often simultaneously) to justify policies whether harsh or relatively lenient. Reductivism rather than retributivism is currently in the ascendancy as a general principle, but with deterrence, incapacitation, reform and reparation all finding favour to various degrees.

Given this confusing welter of competing and combining philosophies, can we reach any valid conclusions about the rightness or otherwise of punishment? We think we can, although any such conclusions (which we can only sketch out here) will inevitably be inherently controversial.

Any verdict we pass on punishment must be soundly based on an acceptable general moral philosophy. This does not necessarily mean that a diversity of penal aims is ruled out, but each of the different aims must be justified by the same general philosophy if our position is to be coherent. Our preferred philosophical basis is *human rights theory* rather than utilitarianism. Along with theorists such as Ronald Dworkin (1978) and Alan Gewirth (1978), we hold that each individual human being has certain fundamental rights which we possess equally by virtue of being human. These fundamental rights are variously described and vindicated by a variety of philosophical arguments to which we cannot do justice here. Suffice it to say that we think that at least one important human right can be described as a right – belonging equally to each human individual – to maximum 'positive freedom', by which we mean the ability of people to make effective choices about their lives.[35]

If there is a right to positive freedom, then punishment (which reduces the freedom of the person punished) is prima facie wrong and requires special moral justification. It is difficult to see how punishment could be justified on purely retributivist grounds consistently with the positive freedom principle, and the same would seem to go for expressive denunciation as a general justification of the system. For if retribution and denunciation were all that punishment achieved, the criminal's freedom would be gratuitously diminished without this doing anything to improve anyone's prospects for exercising choice. However, rights theory allows for one person's prima facie right to be overridden in the interests of other individuals' more important 'competing rights' (see Dworkin, 1978). The relevant competing rights here are those of the potential victims of crime in the future. The commission of crimes against them will have the effect of diminishing their positive freedom, to which they also have a right. For example, crimes of injurious violence reduce the victims' freedom to operate physically free from pain, while property offences will deprive them of resources and thereby remove their freedom to choose to act in ways that require the use of those resources.[36] *The general justification for having a system of punishment must therefore be forward-looking and primarily[37] reductivist*, based on the claim that punishment does something to reduce the incidence of crime, and thereby prevents the diminution of some other people's positive freedom. The most plausible mechanism by which reference to the 'community'. Perhaps it is right that the official institutions of a community should express moral judgements on behalf of its law-abiding members – but why should it have to take the form of punishment? Why – unless perhaps we are closet retributivists or reductivists – should not offenders simply be formally denounced with words and ceremony and then set free? Unless we care nothing for human freedom and are impervious to human suffering, denunciation seems an implausible *general justification* for a system which deliberately inflicts punishment on people.

Nevertheless, there may be something to be said for the notion of denunciation. Whether or not things could be otherwise in a radically different society, as things are, the conviction and punishment of an offender necessarily carry a moral, condemnatory message and are seen as so doing. Perhaps, as we have seen, members of the public are currently not greatly influenced by such messages; but there is still something morally wrong about making incorrect moral statements (cf. von Hirsch, 1986: ch. 5). It follows that it is wrong to convict and punish someone who has done nothing morally wrong. And if it makes sense to punish at all, there is some point in trying to punish offenders at least roughly in proportion to the moral gravity of their offences. Denunciation may not on its own provide a general justification for having a penal system, but it may help provide us with one[25] acceptable *principle of distribution* for punishment.

A theory that resembles denunciation (but which also contains elements of reform and reintegrative shaming) is the 'communicative theory' of punishment put forward by Antony Duff (1986). Duff sees punishment as an attempt at moral dialogue with offenders, censuring their actions and hoping to secure their 'contrition', with the result that they mend their ways. We doubt whether this theory can on its own provide an adequate justification for punishment, let alone for our current practices. But the idea that penal practices can and should be designed to foster this kind of moral dialogue is an attractive one. It fits in well with the 'cognitive behavioural' approach to reforming offenders (see above, section 2.2), and with the ideas and practices we discuss under the next heading.

Restorative Justice: Reparation and Reintegration

The idea of *restorative justice* is an approach to offending and how we should respond to it which has come very much to the fore in recent years, including finding a degree of favour with the current New Labour government (Home Office, 2003b), although it has made only limited inroads into criminal justice practice (see generally Dignan, 2005a). Restorative justice seeks to restore or repair the relations between the offender, the victim and the community that have been damaged by the commission of the crime. To put things right, the offender is encouraged to accept responsibility for having committed the crime, to acknowledge its wrongfulness, and to make amends to those who have been hurt or harmed by the crime.

This restoration may be pursued by a variety of methods, which seek to provide an opportunity for those affected by the offence to deliberate together on the most punishment may be thought to achieve this aim is general deterrence, although other reductivist effects such as instrumental denunciation and incapacitation may make a secondary contribution.

The reductivist aim must, however, be pursued in a manner consistent with the human rights of the offender (or suspected offender). We think that retributivists and denunciationists are right to insist that there is no justification for punishing someone who has not deliberately and wrongfully broken a just law and thereby exercised a freedom to which they are not entitled (because to do so has diminished other people's freedom or has threatened to do so). Rights theory therefore provides a basis for a principled compromise between reductivism and retributivism. It also follows that, although offenders do forfeit some portion of the rights citizens should normally enjoy, they still retain the status of human beings and therefore retain important human rights (Richardson, 1985) – a point on which we are closer to some retributivist thinkers than to classical utilitarianism.

We further agree with retributivists, denunciationists and justice model theorists that one valid general principle for the *distribution* of punishment is that offenders should be punished at least roughly in proportion to the moral gravity of their offences. Our main reason[38] for this is an argument we referred to when discussing denunciation: that to punish disproportionately is to convey incorrect moral messages about the relative gravity of offences. But this principle – called by Hart (1968: 9) 'retribution in distribution' – is only one valid principle among others,[39] and is hardly inviolate in every single instance. We would take some convincing that it can be right to depart from it by punishing more harshly than an offender 'deserves' on a standard tariff, for example, by sentencing an offender to an exceptionally long custodial sentence for purposes of reform or incapacitation.[40] But we see no reason why it should not be acceptable (and consistent with our human rights philosophy) for aims such as reform,[41] reparation and reintegration to be considered and pursued when it has to be decided what punishment (if any) should be allocated to individual offenders, as long as this does not have the result of making the punishment harsher. The operative principle should therefore be a *limiting retributivism*, or a *'retributive maximum'* (as advocated by Norval Morris, 1974: 75). An offender may be punished up to the level indicated by the tariff, but no more harshly; and there is no obligation to exact punishment of this severity if other valid considerations indicate that a more lenient course will be more constructive or humane. As Morris says, 'deserved justice and a discriminating clemency are not irreconcilable'.

This human rights-based approach leads, naturally enough, to the 'inclusive attitude' towards offenders and to a Strategy C-type approach to criminal justice: one, indeed, that incorporates the concerns of the different varieties of Strategy C which we have identified. There is a place in this approach for proportionality in punishment ('just deserts') – as explained in the previous paragraph – and also for reformative and restorative measures where it is possible and appropriate to apply them (cf. Cavadino, 1997b: chs 2 and 3; Cavadino and Dignan, 1997b). We particularly favour the restorative justice approach, for a variety of reasons. For example, one virtue of many reparation schemes is that they afford both offender and victim a say in determining the nature of the offender's punishment. This increases the positive freedom of the victim as well as the offender, a consideration which should normally justify a downwards departure from the proportionate tariff. (See further Cavadino and Dignan, 1997b; Dignan, 2003.)

Strategy A is, as one would expect, anathema to this human rights approach for at least two reasons. First, it leads to punishments – such as 'three strikes and you're out' sentences – which are unfair to individual offenders because they are disproportionate, exceeding the offender's 'just deserts' for the crime committed. And second, the general levels of punishment called for by Strategy A are also grossly excessive because of the 'overkill' involved: the suffering and loss of liberty caused is outweighed by the relatively small amount of crime which is prevented by such heavy penalties compared with a more lenient regime (Cavadino et al., 1999: 37–41). There is, however, room in our approach for Strategy B-type managerial techniques, provided these are used in the pursuit of human rights-based aims (Cavadino et al., 1999: ch. 2). For example, there is nothing wrong with using techniques such as research and monitoring to discover and apply 'what works' to reform offenders or help secure reparation for victims, and indeed we strongly favour such an evidence-based approach.

If our rights-based theory is the correct moral framework for punishment, how should we judge our current penal practices? Our own judgement is a severely negative one, and for one central reason: *we punish too much* – and in particular, we imprison far too much. For the 'principle of parsimony' applies as much to our forward-looking human rights theory as it does to utilitarianism: offenders have a right not to have their freedom gratuitously diminished to a degree greater than is necessary to produce the desired reductivist results. We would go so far as to argue that a thoroughgoing application of the principle of parsimony means that imprisonment should be used very sparingly indeed. It should be reserved for offenders who represent a serious danger to others and need to be 'incapacitated', and perhaps also – for very brief periods only – for offenders who intransigently refuse to cooperate with non-custodial measures. Otherwise, there is no morally legitimate aim of punishment which cannot be achieved just as well and more humanely by the use of non-custodial punishment (Cavadino et al., 1999: 117–20). But it is not necessary to follow us as far as this to accept the evidence that – as we saw under the heading of deterrence in section 2.2 – the penal system is engaging in a massive 'overkill' operation. This amounts to a scandalous infringement of the human rights of those who are punished excessively. And as punishment levels continue to increase, so does the immorality of our penal practices.

It is not necessary to subscribe to human rights philosophy to agree with this conclusion. Indeed, we find it impossible to imagine a plausible and consistent moral philosophy which could justify our present penal practices or anything like them. (We have already seen that utilitarians and retributivists should also condemn our existing system.) It is difficult to resist the implication that our penal system is morally unjustifiable – morally bankrupt might not be too strong a phrase. Of course, not everyone is well versed in moral philosophy. But this is hardly necessary in order to make valid observations about how the penal system treats people unfairly, causes unnecessary suffering, does little to reduce crime, and fails to punish offenders in accordance with their moral deserts. So perhaps it is no wonder that we are not the only ones who perceive the system as unjust, and that it finds itself with a crisis of legitimacy on its hands.

Notes

1 By '*punishment*' we mean any measure that is imposed on an offender in response to an offence, even if it is intended to help the offender (or victim) rather than to hurt or harm. However – and for want of a better word – we use the word '*punitive*' in this book as an adjective referring to measures whose primary purpose is to confine offenders or otherwise make their lives less pleasant, for purposes such as retribution or deterrence. Thus, in our terminology there are 'punitive punishments' such as imprisonment and 'non-punitive punishments' which have aims such as the reformation of the offender or providing reparation to victims. Both types of punishment require a moral justification.
2 Home Office (1984b). See further Chapter 9, section 9.3.
3 This famous phrase is from Voltaire's *Candide* (1947: 111), in which the hero witnesses the execution of the luckless English Admiral Byng who lost Minorca to France in a sea battle. An Englishman explains to Candide that 'in this country we find it pays to shoot an admiral from time to time to encourage the others'.
4 *R. v. Fairman* [1983] *Criminal Law Review* 197. It is quite possible that the court's tongue may have been in its collective judicial cheek.
5 Incidentally, there is no good evidence that capital punishment is a more effective deterrent than alternative penalties for murder, and for all we know it could even be less effective. See, e.g., Fagan (2005), or evidence collected at http://www.deathpenaltyinfo.org
6 See Beyleveld (1980: 147–9, 209–11); von Hirsch et al. (1999: 13, 45). It is the offenders' subjective *perception* of the risk of detection which counts. It is often difficult to affect this perception even by increasing the real risk (Maguire, 1982: 88). On the other hand, it is sometimes possible to deter people by merely increasing the *apparent* risk, as when the Copenhagen police claimed to have reduced speeding offences by 33 per cent by placing cardboard cut-out policemen by the side of the road (*Guardian*, 9 February 1988). Similar results have been claimed for devices such as plastic cut-out police cars positioned beside roads and on flyovers (*Guardian*, 6 May 1992).
7 Nor should the utilitarian overlook the economic cost of punishments such as imprisonment. On average it cost around £40,000 to keep a prisoner in custody for a year (see Chapter 6, note 1), whereas the estimated average annual costs of probation and community service orders are about £3,000 and £2,000 respectively (Coulsfield, 2004: 21). So each unnecessary inmate represents significant resources which could have been deployed for any number of more utilitarian purposes such as health or education.
8 There is also evidence that non-custodial measures can often be equally effective at preventing or at least postponing reoffending at much lower cost than imprisonment (See, for example, Ashworth, 1983: 32; Raynor, 1988: 111).
9 In 2003 it was estimated (on the basis of unpublished research by the Prime Minister's Strategy Unit) that a 22 per cent increase in the prison population since 1997 had reduced crime by around 5 per cent during a period when overall crime fell by 30 per cent (Carter, 2003: 16). The contribution to the reduction brought about by the increasing use of imprisonment during this period was thus relatively small and achieved at enormous expense. Carter went on to state that there was 'no convincing evidence that further increases in the use of imprisonment would significantly reduce crime' (2003: 30) See further Bottoms (2004: 66–71).

10 Ashworth (2005: 80–1); Tarling (1993: 154–160); Hagell and Newburn (1994). We return to the question of 'targeting persistent offenders' in Chapter 11.

11 The Halliday Report (2001: 10) agreed that 'the available evidence does not suggest a case for changing the [sentencing] framework in any particular direction for the sole purpose of increasing an "incapacitation" effect', as did the 2004 Carter Report (see note 9 above).

12 'Three strikes and you're out' sentences have also been defended on the grounds that they enhance deterrence; potential offenders are supposedly deterred by the knowledge that if caught and convicted they will receive an automatic prison sentence. Given what we have already said about deterrence, this seems unlikely. In any event, studies of 'three strikes' laws have demonstrated that, like so much else in criminal justice, they make no measurable difference to crime rates (Stolzenberg and D'Allessio, 1997; Zimring et al., 2001) whether by deterring or incapacitating.

13 We use the words 'reform' and 'rehabilitation' interchangeably, although some writers have defined them in different ways (for example, Bean, 1981: 46).

14 However, while it may not be justifiable to imprison offenders *in order to* reform them, it does not necessarily follow that it cannot be worthwhile to offer rehabilitative training to those whom we do imprison (perhaps for other reasons). Research on the effectiveness of rehabilitative programmes suggests that well-designed programmes can make a difference to reoffending rates whether they take place in prison or in the community (although they work better in the community: Andrews et al., 1990: 382, 384).

15 It is not clear that imprisonment performs any worse in this respect than ordinary non-custodial penalties. Kershaw et al. (1999) found that 58 per cent of prisoners released in 1995 were reconvicted within two years compared with 56 per cent of those sentenced to 'community penalties' (probation and/or community service), an insignificant difference when all possible relevant factors were taken into account. However, since non-custodial penalties fare *no worse* than imprisonment, it can be forcibly argued that they should be preferred because they are both cheaper (see above, note 7) and more humane than custody.

16 For example, Kershaw et al. (1999): see previous note.

17 This adjustment needs to be made because offenders who are sentenced to custody are usually more likely to have those characteristics (especially extensive previous records of offending) which make reoffending more likely in any event.

18 In fact Martinson (1974) never said '*nothing* works', and he later (1979: 244) revised his views and asserted that 'some treatment programs *do* have an appreciable effect on recidivism'.

19 For example, Ross et al. (1989). As the name suggests, this approach is based on a synthesis of methods drawn from behavioural and cognitive psychology (Hollin, 1990; Meichenbaum, 1977).

20 See Lipsey (1992, 1995), Vennard et al. (1997: 15) and more generally McGuire (1995, 2002). However, the results of recent evaluations of the effects of cognitive behavioural programmes (summarized in Debidin and Lovbakke, 2005) have been variable. The Halliday Report (2001: para. 1.49) advised the government that the correct national application of offending behaviour programmes of this kind could be expected to reduce offenders' reconviction rates by between 5 and 15 per cent – a claim that was (for various reasons) always rash, and was not borne out by subsequent events (Bottoms, 2004: 61–3).

21 Standard retributivist theory leads to the logical conclusion that there should be an '*offence-based tariff*': punishment should be in proportion to the seriousness of the *current offence*, and therefore it is generally wrong to increase a sentence on the grounds of the offender's past record of previous convictions (for offences for which the offender has already been punished). In practice, however, courts tend to operate two tariffs in

tandem: an *'offence-based tariff'*, and an *'offender-based tariff'* which punishes recidivists more severely. (See further Cavadino, 1997b: 35–40.) This distinction between the two kinds of tariff will become important in Chapter 4.

22   However, Murphy suggested (1979: 107) that retributivism might justify punishing some offenders, for example business executives who commit tax fraud, who start off in a position of equality or better. It is also arguable that criminals who offend against victims who are less well off than themselves, or whose actions leave their victims in a situation of severe disadvantage, could have their punishments justified in a similar manner.

23   See above, note 21.

24   See, for example, *R. v. Sargeant* (1974) 60 Cr App Rep 74, where Lord Justice Lawton said that 'society, through the courts, must show its abhorrence of particular types of crime, and the only way in which courts can show this is by the sentences they pass … Perhaps the main duty of the court is to lead public opinion.' (The Sargeant in this case was not the Marcus Sarjeant who shot blanks at the Queen, but an over-enthusiastic disco bouncer.)

25   The 'justice model' theorist Andrew von Hirsch (1993: ch. 2) argues in effect that what he calls 'the blaming function of punishment' requires that punishments should in general be *strictly* proportionate to the gravity of the offence, so that proportionality is not just one, but the only or paramount principle of distribution. In our opinion this approach is both over-rigid in practice and unjustified in principle (Cavadino and Dignan, 1997b).

26   The results of evaluations of restorative justice schemes have varied as regards their reformative effectiveness: see e.g. Halliday (2001: 132); Wilcox et al. (2004).

27   Critics included not only liberal academics and penal administrators, but prisoners themselves: the rôle of prisoners' protests in the rise of the justice model is often unjustly overlooked (see Cavadino and Dignan, 2006: 61n).

28   For justice model theorists, this usually means that there should essentially be an offence-based rather than an offender-based tariff (see note 21 above), although they are not always entirely consistent on this point (see, e.g., von Hirsch, 1976).

29   See above, note 25.

30   Other countries where similar developments occurred include Canada, Australia, New Zealand, Sweden and Finland. For the latter four countries, see Cavadino and Dignan (2006).

31   However, many of these American developments, although moving towards more predictable and often fixed-term sentences, did not adhere to the 'just deserts' principle of proportionality between offence gravity and sentence severity (see von Hirsch, 1993: ch. 10). Thus, in our terms, these developments can be seen as owing more to 'law and order ideology' than to the justice model.

32   Jack Straw (New Labour Home Secretary 1997–2001) said explicitly that he wanted to end the just deserts philosophy underlying the 1991 Criminal Justice Act and that it was time to make the sentence fit the offender rather than the offence (*Guardian*, 1 February 2000).

33   The idea that there should be progression in the sentencing of petty offenders (see further Chapter 4, section 4.4) so that persistent offending will earn them custody means espousing the kind of 'offender-based tariff' (see note 21 above) which offends against just deserts philosophy.

34   Criminal Justice Act 2003, s. 142; see Chapter 4, section 4.5.

35   This 'positive freedom principle' is discussed more fully in Cavadino (1983; 1989: ch. 10; 1997a). Some rights theorists, including Dworkin (1978), justify rights on the relativistic ground that people in our society happen to accept that such rights exist. We find more interesting the non-relativistic argument of Alan Gewirth (1978) to the effect that

human reason can establish that human beings in any society possess certain definable fundamental rights. A similar argument for the positive freedom principle is put forward by Cavadino (1983, 1997a).

36 Not all crimes have individual victims; but many crimes that do not have indirect effects that threaten to reduce the positive freedom of (perhaps many) individuals. For example, defrauding the Inland Revenue depletes the public purse, which may have the effect of reducing public provision and thereby removing choices of various kinds from members of the public. Punishment cannot be justified on this basis if the law that the offender has broken itself violates the positive freedom principle. The law should not forbid harmless actions which do nothing to reduce anyone's positive freedom, however indirectly. More generally, if society is to be just, it should be organized so as to uphold everyone's equal right to positive freedom. The less just society is in these terms, the less just its penal system will tend to be.

37 The aims of restorative justice, which include reparation and the promotion of cohesive communities, can be seen as independent, auxiliary justifications for the appropriate kind of restorative measures.

38 The principle of justice that like cases should be treated alike is also relevant here.

39 See further Cavadino and Dignan (1997b).

40 In the case of 'protective sentences' – exceptionally long custodial sentences for the purpose of incapacitating supposedly dangerous offenders – we would adopt the rights-based reasoning of Bottoms and Brownsword (1983). This rules out protective sentences for all but the most 'vividly dangerous' offenders.

41 Not all methods of attempted reform are acceptable, however. To be consistent with the positive freedom principle, reform must take the shape of 'facilitated change' rather than 'coerced cure' (Morris, N., 1974: 13 20). Coerced cure is inconsistent with the offender's right to freedom.

3 Explaining Punishment

The Sociology Of Punishment

3.1 Why do we have a penal system? Why does punishment take different forms in different societies and at different stages in history? Why, for example, have penal ideas and practices altered over time in the West in the ways described in section 2.5 of the previous chapter?

The *sociology of punishment* is the area of inquiry that seeks to answer questions like these. The answers put forward are often controversial. Like many areas of sociology, the sociology of punishment lends itself to (often radically) differing approaches which provide rival explanations of penality. (We use the word 'penality' to include *ideas* about punishment as well as concrete penal practices; cf. Garland and Young, 1983a; Garland, 1990a.) Again like other fields of sociology, these approaches can be conveniently located within competing traditions which each owe their orientation to one of the three great 'founding fathers' of the discipline of sociology: Karl Marx, Émile Durkheim and Max Weber. It is equally convenient for us to divide this chapter accordingly.

The Marxist Tradition

3.2 Karl Marx (1818–83) was not only the founder of modern communism but also the originator of one of the most influential traditions in sociology. His message was that societies had to be understood in terms of their economic structures, and in particular their social relations of production and the conflicts between the different economic classes which exist as a result of those relations. He claimed that capitalist society was polarizing 'into two great hostile camps, into two great classes directly facing each other: Bourgeoisie and Proletariat' (Marx, 1977: 222). The bourgeoisie or capitalist class (the ruling class under capitalism) comprises those people who own the means of production (including factories, industrial machinery, etc. in an industrialized society), while the proletariat or working class comprises those who need to sell their 'labour power' (their ability to work) to the capitalists in order to live. The struggle between these two classes was for Marx the key to understanding modern society and its future, which he envisaged as the revolutionary overthrow of capitalism by the proletariat leading ultimately to a classless communist society. In a key passage, Marx wrote (1977: 389):

> The sum total of these relations of production constitutes the economic structure of society, the real foundation, on which rises a legal and political superstructure and to which correspond definite forms of social consciousness. The mode of production of material life conditions the social, political, and intellectual life process in general. It is not the consciousness of men that determines their being, but, on the contrary, their social being that determines their consciousness.

This passage is the source for one of the most debated features of Marxist social theory, known as the '*base and superstructure* metaphor': the idea that the economic 'material base' of society determines developments in the 'superstructural' realms of law, of politics and of people's ideas generally. Marx described the consciousness of people in a situation of class conflict as *ideological*, meaning that although they might represent and believe their ideas to be objective and of universal validity, in reality these ideas express and serve class interests. In particular, Marx claimed that 'the ruling ideas of each age have ever been the ideas of its ruling class' (1977: 236).

Marxist penology applies this method of analysis (known as 'historical materialism') to the study of penality. It relates punishment to the economic structure of the society in which it takes place and to the class interests furthered by penal practices and ideologies. A general point is that punishment is inflicted by the state for breaches of the law. Marxists see both state and law as operating in the interests of the ruling class rather than society as a whole. Punishing people for disobeying the existing laws – which maintain the status quo and the position of the ruling class – functions to reinforce the power and privilege of that class.

Historical materialism can also be used to explain the history of penal thought sketched in the previous chapter. For example, it has often been observed (by no means only by Marxists) that the ideas of Beccaria – and the Enlightenment generally – were linked to the interests of the bourgeois class who were gaining in economic and political power at the time but still needed legal protection against the old ruling class, the landowning aristocracy who retained a corrupt control of the levers of state power (Beccaria, 1963: xxi; Taylor et al., 1973: ch. 1). Similarly, Bentham's penology – and utilitarianism generally – were functional to the interests of the bourgeoisie at a slightly later historical stage (Ignatieff, 1978; Hogg, 1979). Positivism in turn can be seen as a set of ideas tending to reinforce the ideological domination (or 'hegemony') of the bourgeois class at a yet later stage when it had become the ruling class in Europe: if criminal actions can be described as the result of mindless pathology rather than rational choice, this both absolves capitalism of any blame for crime and helps to delegitimize protest against the existing order (Taylor et al., 1973: ch. 2). Conventional histories of punishment tend to represent these developments in thought and practice as rational, progressive, scientific and humane; Marxists are sceptical of such claims and see the furtherance of class interests as of prime importance. When we come nearer the present with the rise of 'law and order ideology' in recent decades, Marxists are likely to have little difficulty perceiving whose interests are being served by the notion that crime is entirely the fault of individual, predominantly working-class offenders who should be punished as severely as possible (Hall et al., 1978; Hall, 1979, 1980).

While much of the above would probably be unobjectionable to most Marxists, there are some important fissures within the Marxist tradition itself, especially in relation to the 'base and superstructure metaphor', which have an important bearing on the nature of the explanations of punishment offered by different kinds of Marxists. It will be instructive therefore to examine some of these different strands within Marxism.

Economic Determinism: Rusche and Kirchheimer

In the minds of many people, Marxism means simple economic determinism: the idea that economics determines everything, that the 'superstructure' of law, politics and ideology merely reflects the state of the economic 'base'. Few Marxists today believe this (and certainly Marx himself never believed anything so crude), but the misconception is understandable since this simplified version of Marx's message was communist orthodoxy for a long time. The 'economic determinist' approach produced one classic, pioneering work of Marxist penology: Georg Rusche and Otto Kirchheimer's *Punishment and Social Structure* (1939).

Rusche and Kirchheimer attempted to demonstrate that penal practices in any society were directly connected to the mode of production. 'Every system of production tends to discover punishments which correspond to its productive relationships' (1939: 5). For example, 'it is self-evident that enslavement as a form of punishment is impossible without a slave economy; that prison labour is impossible without manufacture or industry, that monetary fines for all classes of society are impossible without a monetary economy'. Moreover, 'If a slave economy finds the supply of slaves meagre and the demand pressing' it will be likely to introduce penal slavery. But once society had advanced from a slave economy to feudalism, penal slavery was no longer an option. Nor were fines an option for punishing the majority of (thoroughly impoverished) offenders, so feudalism relied instead on capital and corporal punishments (1939: 6).

A similar economic explanation was offered for the rise of the 'house of correction' (the forerunner of the modern prison) from the end of the sixteenth century onwards. Early capitalism needed more labour power, so it became uneconomic to kill and mutilate offenders. It was better for capitalism that offenders should be incarcerated and set to productive work (whose profits would, naturally, be pocketed by the capitalist class in the usual manner). Punishment could therefore be used to 'fill out the gaps in the labour market' (1939: 7). Even where this was not the case, Rusche and Kirchheimer argued that the choice of methods of punishment is largely influenced by fiscal interests, such as how much a punishment costs to administer.

This analysis of punishment is inadequate for at least two reasons. First, it fails to explain the mechanisms linking an economic imperative with a penal practice. Capitalism needed the house of correction, and somehow it magically came into being as a result. Unless the capitalist class was engaged in a conspiracy which was simultaneously crudely self-interested, brilliantly well hidden and (remarkably) informed by economic analyses of a kind which had never been published at the time, it is hard to see how and why this occurred. It is also hard to see in this theory any picture of real human beings (capitalist or otherwise) operating with limited rationality and knowledge in a recognizably real world. Or to put it another way, the analysis lacks both humanism and a theory of ideology – a theory about why people have the ideas they have, and what effects they have.

A second problem is that the theory embarrassingly fails to fit the facts of history. Rusche and Kirchheimer themselves admit (1939: 102) that imprisonment became the standard method of punishment at a time when the demand for prison labour had *fallen* as a result of technological and other developments. Again, a theory of ideology seems necessary to explain this seeming disjuncture between base and superstructure (Garland and Young, 1983b: 25).

This is not to say that economic imperatives play no part in penal developments. For example, it seems very likely that pragmatic considerations including essentially economic ones (concerning stretched penal resources) have played their part in the expansion of the parole system (see Chapter 8). It has also been argued strongly, especially by Andrew Scull (1977), that the move towards creating 'alternatives to custody' in the 1960s and 1970s was primarily a product of fiscal calculation (see Chapter 5). And the current 'crisis of resources' in the penal system is an economic reality which certainly has had its effects on penal policy. But economics do not determine penal practices in a simple and direct manner; if they did we should hardly have the extremely wasteful penal system that exists in this country today, with its needlessly and expensively high prison population. Economic considerations are mediated through the minds of human beings who live in a social world, which means that the impact of economics is crucially conditioned by ideology – a notion which has been explored and expanded by the Marxist theorists to whom we now turn.

Ideology and Hegemony: The Legacy of Gramsci

Antonio Gramsci (1891–1937) was not a penologist – but he was, famously, a prisoner. Imprisoned by the Italian fascists for his communist affiliation and activities from 1926 until his death, his contribution to Marxist theory was written inside prison (Gramsci, 1971).

Gramsci's writings marked a major shift away from the one-sided economic determinism of writers such as Rusche and Kirchheimer. For Gramsci, the 'superstructure' of ideology, law and politics was of great significance in the revolutionary struggle in an advanced capitalist society. Central to his ideas was the notion of *hegemony* – the ideological domination exercised throughout society by a successful ruling class. Hegemony meant that one class has persuaded the other classes to accept its own moral, political and cultural values. This was important because the ruling class (and the state which was its instrument) did not merely rule by coercion – which for our purposes means in particular by punishing people for breaking its laws. Equally important was the ideological factor of *consent*: in a situation of hegemony, subordinate classes 'consent' to the existing social relations because they are effectively represented as being universally beneficial. The production of this consent is one vital task for the state, and one necessary component of the continual reproduction of existing social relations.

Thus ideology and the superstructure are not merely reflections of the material economic base, but interact with it in a two-way relationship. The economics of the base could not explain everything that existed or occurred in the superstructure; as Marx's collaborator Engels had suggested, the economy was only the mainspring of history 'in the last analysis' (Gramsci, 1971: 162). And the superstructure could make a difference to the base. If consent were not successfully produced and reproduced, this could ultimately affect the condition and prospects of the economic base, not least by making a great deal of difference to the likely success of the revolutionary struggle.

Importantly, Gramsci did not believe that consent was produced as the result of a ruling-class conspiracy to hoax the workers; for him, ideologies arose out of the material realities within which human beings live and work. Or, as Marx said, people's consciousness was determined by their social being (albeit not entirely determined by their *economic* position). Nor was hegemony an inevitable or universal phenomenon, and conscious efforts to combat it at the ideological level were a necessary part of the socialist project. (These ideas of Gramsci's have been notably developed and applied to modern criminal justice policy by Stuart Hall (1980; Hall et al., 1978), whose account of 'law and order ideology' we touched on in Chapter 1.)

There is much more to Gramsci than this: for example, Marxist theory is indebted to his pioneering use of concepts such as 'praxis', 'civil society', 'class fractions' and the 'historical bloc' and his analysis of the nature, role and composition of the state in class societies. Perhaps above all, Gramsci injected a sense of humanism into Marxism: for him, history was made by human beings. He believed that socialism would not come about as the inevitable result of impersonal laws of economic development but would have to be built by active human beings working purposively and creatively. However, it is in his treatment of ideology that Gramsci's legacy has been most pervasive and where he is the unmistakeable precursor of all the Marxist and post-Marxist theorists we now proceed to discuss.

'Structuralist Marxism' and Althusser

The French philosopher Louis Althusser (1918–90) created a sophisticated reinterpretation of Marxism often referred to as 'structuralist Marxism'. Although Althusser himself disclaimed the label 'structuralist', it is at least loosely apt to describe his ideas, since he regarded the structure of the social system (and in particular the relationships between its different 'levels' or 'instances') as central to the task of understanding society.[1] Among the important features of Althusser's 'structuralism' is a rejection of humanism as a valid element in Marxism. He claimed to detect an 'epistemological break' in the writings of Marx in the year 1845, discarding Marx's (undoubtably humanist) early works as juvenilia and constructing a non-humanistic, 'scientific' Marxism on the basis of his later works only (Althusser, 1969). History, according to Althusser, is not made by freely acting human beings but by 'structural causality'.

Society, according to Althusser, is a complex unity of different, unevenly related 'levels' or 'instances'. The economy is the ultimately determining instance, but the superstructural instances of ideology and politics are not mere reflections of it: they possess a 'relative autonomy' (Althusser, 1969: 111, 240; 1971: 135). Indeed, the different instances are mutually determining: there is a reciprocal action of the superstructure on the base (Althusser, 1971: 135), and the ideological and political instances are part of the essential conditions of existence of the entire social formation. It is still the case that the economy is determining 'in the last instance', but the economy never functions in isolation from the other instances. As Althusser put it (1969: 113): 'the economic dialectic is never active *in the pure state*; in History, these instances, the superstructures, etc. – are never seen to step respectfully aside when their work is done … From the first moment to the last, the lonely hour of the "last instance" never comes.'

It is difficult to see how, on this account, the economy is supposed to retain its ultimately determining role. Since the political and ideological instances are just as necessary for the existence of a social formation, they seem to be equally determining, and the economic base no longer looks to be especially basic. Perhaps Althusser was unwilling to acknowledge this outright, because to do so would be to run the risk of departing from the fundamental Marxist doctrine which asserts the primacy of economics in social explanation. Consequently, Althusser denied the logical conclusion of his own theory by continuing to invoke 'economic determination in the last instance' as a dogmatic but essentially metaphysical, almost religious assertion.

Be that as it may, it is clear that ideology was at least as important to Althusser as it was to Gramsci. All societies (not only class societies, according to Althusser) need ideology as part of their conditions of existence. And a society's ideology must be constantly reproduced if the society is to survive, just as (for example) an industrial society must continually renovate and update its machinery and ensure that the next generation of workers is produced, kept alive and prepared for productive labour. For production could not continue unless the proletariat were ideologically conditioned in each generation to submit to the rules of the established order within which production occurs.

Althusser stressed the role in this reproductive process of what he called Ideological State Apparatuses (ISAs) (Althusser, 1971: 127–84). Among these he included the educational system and also many institutions that are not usually thought of as part of the state, such as the family, churches, the media, trade unions and political parties.[2] These ISAs were to be distinguished from the more instantly recognizable Repressive State Apparatus (RSA), consisting of 'the Government, the Administration, the Army, the Police, the Courts, the Prisons, etc.' As the names suggest, the RSA functions predominantly by overt coercion to ensure that the conditions of production are maintained, while ISAs function predominantly to reproduce existing ideology, which is the ideology of the ruling class.

For our purposes, it is interesting that although Althusser locates the penal system logically enough within the Repressive State Apparatus, he also makes it clear that there is no such thing as a purely repressive apparatus, and that the RSA also functions (if only secondarily) by ideology. (Similarly, he identifies the law as both an ISA and part of the RSA since it functions both to coerce and to reproduce ruling-class values.) This provokes the consideration that the penal system may perform a dual function in the reproduction of the social formation. On the one hand, and most obviously, it comprises a set of repressive practices which among other things may help to preserve the conditions of production by deterring crime.

But it may also function ideologically, by conveying conservative moral messages. For example, retributive punishment might help inculcate law-abiding ideology in the populace by telling them that breaking the law is wicked and deserves punishment. Reformative punishment could assure people that the existing state was effectively combating crime to the benefit of all, including even the offender – disguising the truth that the capitalist state in fact operates for the benefit of the ruling class. A Marxist approach which takes the role of ideology seriously needs to analyse punishment in terms such as these.

In the last analysis (as it were), we doubt whether Althusser's theory represents a significant advance on the work of Gramsci. In some important respects – particularly Althusser's dogmatism, determinism and anti-humanism – we think it represents a definite step in the wrong direction. But aspects of his work, especially his insistence on the importance of ideology, were a positive influence on modern Marxism and on some Marxist studies of crime and punishment. For example, Stuart Hall's analysis of 'law and order' owed much to Althusser as well as to Gramsci. Fitzgerald and Sim's *British Prisons* (1982) was another example of radical analysis which paid at least as much attention to ideology as to economics. Whatever the overall balance sheet, Althusser's impact has been undeniable.

Post-Structuralism, Discipline and Power: Michel Foucault

Michel Foucault (1926–84), who studied under Althusser, took the step his teacher never did and distanced himself from Marxism while remaining politically radical. Perhaps even more than Althusser, Foucault represents a decisive move away from economic determinism. Like Althusser, Foucault was once called a structuralist, but although he showed great interest in structures (including the structures of thought and of 'discourse' in different ages) he differed significantly from both Althusser and other structuralists, often being described consequently as 'post-structuralist' (and also as 'post-Marxist' and 'post-modernist'). He shared structuralism's anti-humanism, but had a much more dynamic conception of structures. The structuralist account portrayed structures as relatively unchanging and self-reproducing; the post-structuralism of Foucault discerned and investigated a continual flux and change in society and in structures themselves. As Alan Sheridan (1980: 90) says, 'there is a sense in which his work is profoundly anti-Structuralist. Far from wishing to "freeze" the movement of history in structures, his whole work has been an examination of the nature of historical change.'

For penology, Foucault's most important examination of historical change is his great work *Discipline and Punish: The Birth of the Prison* (1977). In this book Foucault investigated the massive shift or 'great transformation' (mentioned in Chapter 2) from 'corporal' to 'carceral' punishment between the late eighteenth and mid-nineteenth centuries (see also Chapter 5). His explanation for the coming of the prison at that time was that this was 'the moment when it became understood that it was more efficient and profitable in terms of the economy of power to place people under surveillance than to subject them to some exemplary penalty' (Foucault, 1980: 38). The new industrial social order required new techniques of power and new institutions to control the subordinate classes. The prison was one of these new institutions, along with the factory, asylum, school and workhouse, all of which shared certain common features with the prison.

Two central concepts here are *discipline* and *power*. Discipline was the new feature of the Benthamesque, industrial-age prison, whereby the inmate was 'normalized' or schooled into conformity by constant surveillance and the imposition of a highly regulated physical routine, including repetitive forced labour. Where the earlier forms of corporal punishment were directed at the body of the convict, disciplinary punishment aimed, via the body, at the 'soul' of the offender. Not that 'prison worked' in its intended goal of reforming criminals; on the contrary its failure in this respect was almost immediately apparent. But the prison was (and is) paradoxically successful in a different way precisely because of this. It successfully *produces delinquents*, creating a criminal section of the population and thereby dividing the subordinate classes into mutually antagonistic fractions. The criminals created by prison could be used by the bourgeoisie for a variety of political purposes, for example as informers, *agents provocateurs* and strike breakers (Foucault, 1977: 264–92; 1980: 40–2) – essentially a 'divide and rule' strategy.

The concept of *power* for Foucault is intimately connected with that of 'knowledge', which in turn is not a matter of objective truth separable from power relations. 'Power and knowledge directly imply each other … there is no power relation without the correlative constitution of a field of knowledge, nor any knowledge that does not presuppose and constitute at the same time power relations' (Foucault, 1977: 27). Thus, the disciplinary surveillance of the prison created a new kind of 'knowledge' of the convict's body, which created a new kind of power. However, power for Foucault is not merely exercised in a simple manner by the state or by one class over others via punishment and other mechanisms, but is a ubiquitous and many-sided phenomenon; there exists a 'multiplicity of power relations' in society which are the constant focus of negotiation and struggle. It follows that punishment – or indeed any social phenomenon – is an inevitably highly complex phenomenon which should require extremely subtle analysis. Ironically, however, one criticism of Foucault is that his penology is actually too crude and simple, reducing the complex phenomenon of penality to questions of power and little else, and postulating what looks suspiciously like an old-fashioned class conspiracy theory to explain the advent and historical persistence of the prison (Garland, 1990a: ch. 6; 1990b).

Foucault's cryptic style leaves the nature of his theory obscure in many respects. The traditional Marxist 'base and superstructure' is conspicuous by its absence in Foucault, but it is less clear what he thought is the role of economics in social and penal change. As Stan Cohen (1985: 24) remarks, Foucault 'veers between a materialist connection between prison and emerging capitalism and an idealist obsession with the power of ideas'. Clearly though, he was more concerned with the ideological genesis and effects of punishment than with its relationship with economics.

Foucault has been much analysed, and criticized by some on both theoretical and historical grounds (Ignatieff, 1981; Garland, 1985, 1990a: ch. 7; 1990b) – although even his critics in the field of penal sociology have been profoundly influenced by Foucault. Foucauldian concepts such as 'normalization' and 'discipline' have become standard tools of analysis; for example, there is one major debate (discussed in Chapter 5) as to whether we are witnessing a 'dispersal of discipline' emanating from the prison and spreading throughout society (Cohen, 1979; Bottoms, 1983). Foucault's contribution has certainly transformed the sociology of punishment.

Humanistic Materialism: The Case of E.P. Thompson

The English historian E.P. Thompson (1924–93) represents a humanistic current of Marxism far removed from either Althusser's structuralism or Foucault's post-structuralism. He contributed not only to general Marxist theory, but also directly to penology in *Whigs and Hunters* (1977), his painstaking historical study of the passing of the 'Black Act' of 1723, a penal statute of extraordinary scope and ferocity.

Thompson's *The Poverty of Theory* (1978) is an extended polemic against Althusser and his disciples. Above all, Thompson insisted that history is made, not by the inevitable operation of impersonal structures, but by the actions of real human beings. 'For all these "instances" and "levels" are in fact human activities, institutions, and ideas. We are talking about men and women, in their material life, in their determinate relationships, in their experience of these, and in their self-consciousness of this experience' (1978: 289).

He also accused Althusser of covert 'idealism' in that his structuralism in effect denies the genuine role of the economy in constraining legal and ideological forms. Thompson claimed, for instance, that when he was researching *Whigs and Hunters*, 'on several occasions, while I was actually watching, the lonely hour of the last instance *actually came*' (1978: 288). A change in the mode of production from feudalism to agrarian capitalism required and forced the emergence of new forms of law and punishment appropriate to the new economy, such as Enclosure Acts and laws to penalize poor foresters who attempted to exercise their customary rights of grazing and timber-cutting in the forests.

Thompson had much to say about law. He accepted that law is 'relatively autonomous' of the economy, but he found little use for the 'base/superstructure metaphor', rejecting what he saw as Althusser's rigid division of social formations into different 'instances' or 'levels'. Law, he said, is to be found 'at *every* bloody level'.[3] Law can function ideologically, to legitimate the existing order and 'mystify' subordinate classes into acquiescence (what Gramsci called 'consent'). However,

> people are not as stupid as some structuralist philosophers suppose them to be. They will not be mystified by the first man who puts on a wig ... If the law is evidently partial and unjust, then it will mask nothing, legitimize nothing, contribute nothing to any class's hegemony. (Thompson, 1977: 262–3)

So law was never the exclusive possession of the ruling class; rather it provided 'an arena for class struggle, within which alternative notions of law were fought out'

(Thompson, 1978: 288). The foresters' view that customary law vindicated their rights to use the forest conflicted with an emerging capitalist version of law under which these customary rights were extinguished; thus a class battle was fought in the forum of legal debate.

Much of what Thompson said about law can also (we think usefully) be applied to punishment. Penality can also be found 'at every bloody level', although it can perhaps be roughly divided into (material) penal *practices* and (ideological) penal *rhetoric*. The relationship between the two is not necessarily straightforward; for example, penal rhetoric might be predominantly positivistic at a time when actual penal practice is predominantly classicistic and deterrent. (Arguably this was the case in the English penal system during the supposed reign of the 'rehabilitative ideal'.) Yet such discrepancies are not caused by the logic of structures but by the messy and often far from inevitable ways in which people come to understand the world around them and their own practices. Again, like law, punishment and ideas about punishment can serve to mystify and legitimate oppression, but can also afford 'an arena for class struggle'; and as we suggested earlier in this chapter, the history of penal thought can be fruitfully viewed in these terms. Readers will doubtless have already gathered that, if forced to choose a version of Marxism, we would favour one similar to Thompson's.

The Durkheimian Tradition

3.3 Émile Durkheim (1858–1917) addressed himself directly to the question of punishment to a much greater extent than either Marx or Weber ever did. He did this especially in two works: *The Division of Labor in Society* (1960, first published 1893) and the article 'Two Laws of Penal Evolution' (1973, first published 1900).

The Division of Labor expounds Durkheim's theory about the development of specialized work in society. Durkheim distinguishes between simple, pre-industrial societies in which there is little division of labour (sometimes referred to as *Gemeinschaft* societies) and more advanced (*Gesellschaft*) societies in which people perform specialized jobs. The central question for Durkheim was *social solidarity*, or 'the bonds which unite men one with another' (cited in Lukes, 1975: 139). This solidarity took different forms in the two different kinds of society, but in each case Durkheim saw punishment as playing an important role in the creation and maintenance of the solidarity which was a necessary condition for social order and the continued existence of society.

Durkheim said that simple societies were held together by 'mechanical solidarity through likeness': people were united by the similarity in the labour and the general social roles they performed, which also gave rise to a homogeneous *conscience collective*. 'Conscience collective' is variously translatable as 'collective conscience' or 'collective consciousness', and means 'the totality of beliefs and sentiments common to average members of the same society'. Crime, for Durkheim, could be defined in terms of the *conscience collective*: 'an act is criminal when it offends strong and defined states of the collective conscience' (Durkheim, 1960: 79–80). Criminal acts call forth a collective hostile response in the shape of punishment, and the punishment serves to restore and reinforce the outraged *conscience collective*. So punishment is not primarily deterrent or reformative; it is produced by collective *retributive* emotions and has a useful *denunciatory* effect. 'Its true function is to maintain social cohesion intact.' The *conscience collective* 'would necessarily lose its energy, if an emotional reaction of the community did not come to compensate its loss, and it would result in a breakdown of social solidarity' (1960: 108).

In *The Division of Labor*, Durkheim claimed that the *conscience collective* played only a small part in maintaining social cohesion in more advanced, industrial societies. Differentiated labour meant that people now differed from each other to a much greater extent, including in their consciences. Social solidarity was now 'organic', deriving from the interdependence of people who were no longer largely self-sufficient as a result of their own labour alone. The *conscience collective* became weaker, vaguer, less religious and more humanistic in character. Punishment would consequently also dwindle in importance as the division of labour progressed, and punitive law would come to be replaced by 'restitutive law' which requires lawbreakers to make reparation to their victims rather than suffer retributive punishment.[4]

By the time Durkheim came to write 'Two Laws of Penal Evolution', he had modified his theory about the decline in importance of the *conscience collective* (a phrase he ceased to use) and had come to believe that 'collective sentiments' were a crucial factor in any society. However, he still held that the nature of these collective sentiments differed at different stages of society's development, being of a predominantly religious character in simple societies but becoming much more secular, humanistic and individualistic in industrial societies.

His first 'law of penal evolution' was a two-pronged 'law of quantitative change': 'The intensity of punishment is the greater the more closely societies approximate to a less developed type – and the more the central power assumes an absolute character' (Durkheim, 1973: 285). The first part of this law he explains as follows. In simple societies, whose collective sentiments are based on religion, all crimes (even crimes such as murder) are essentially 'religious criminality': they are seen as offences against God or the gods. Consequently punishments tend to be severe because any sympathy for the offender is overwhelmed by the need to appease God. But as collective sentiments change, it is 'human criminality', comprising only offences against other people, which shocks collective sentiments and attracts a punitive response. The shock value, however, is less.

> The offence of man against man cannot arouse the same indignation as an offence of man against God. At the same time, the sentiments of pity which he who suffers punishment evokes in us can no longer be so easily nor so completely extinguished by the sentiments he has offended and which react against him; for both are of the same nature. (Durkheim, 1973: 303)

The same humanistic sympathy which causes crimes against people to be criminalized also serves to mitigate the punishment; so in general the severity of punishment should diminish as societies develop. But this progression will not continue indefinitely until punishment disappears; on the contrary, Durkheim predicted that the tendency would reverse, and less serious crimes against the person would come to be criminalized.

A second, independent factor affecting the severity of punishment is the degree of absolutism in government. Where government takes the form of absolute power, 'the one who controls it appears to the people as a divinity ... this religiosity cannot fail to have its usual effects on punishment' (1973: 305). Hence punishment is more severe than one would expect for a society of the same level of development but with a less absolute government. For Durkheim, this explained the harshness of punishment in the seventeenth and eighteenth centuries, when absolute monarchy was at its height.

Durkheim's second 'law' was: 'Deprivations of liberty, and of liberty alone, varying in time according to the seriousness of the crime, tend to become more and more the normal means of social control' (1973: 294). Durkheim saw the centrality of the prison as largely brought about by the operation of the first part of his first law: prison was a milder penalty than capital and corporal punishments and so became adopted as collective sentiments became more sympathetic to the criminal's suffering. (This account stands in marked contrast to Foucault's explanation of the same historical phenomenon, discussed previously. What Foucault saw as a self-interested, indeed cruel strategy for exercising power, Durkheim saw as motivated by sympathy for the criminal; see Garland, 1990b.)

Durkheim's social theory differs sharply from Marxism in several respects. One of these is the role of economics. Although Durkheim did not see economic developments as unimportant, for him they were in no way basic. The most important determining social force to Durkheim was collective sentiments, and especially religion – a factor which some would describe as 'cultural' and Marxists tend to characterize as 'ideological'. In this respect, the more recent Marxist theories which give greater explanatory weight to ideology have narrowed (but far from closed) the gap between Durkheim and Marxism.

Another difference from Marxism is the stress Durkheim places on the existence of *consensus* and the need for order in society (and for change to be of a peaceful and evolutionary nature), where Marxism stresses the centrality of class conflict and the necessity of revolution. To some extent, this can be seen as a matter of political temperament determining which side of the coin one emphasizes. Even a Marxist like Gramsci, who spoke of the 'consent' of the subordinate classes, saw consensus as false consciousness and hoped for revolutionary change. On the other hand Durkheim, a reformist socialist of sorts, was passionately opposed to violent revolution and agitation, and was concerned to identify and encourage the social consensus that made possible a peaceful social order for the benefit of everyone.

One of Durkheim's main legacies is the sociological tradition known as *functionalism*. Functionalism analyses social phenomena in terms of their functions – that is, their positive effects in helping the entire social system to continue operating. (The two most eminent functionalists to follow Durkheim were Robert Merton (1968) and the 'structural-functionalist' Talcott Parsons (1937, 1951).) Like Durkheim, functionalists assume that a certain degree of order is necessary for societies to survive, and see shared social values as vital in securing this order. They see society and human action as being structured by social rules and values, and portray social systems as reproducing themselves via socialization – the transmission of social values to new generations through the family, the educational system and so on. Another functionalist concept, present in Durkheim's work and elaborated by his successors, is *social control*, a term which encompasses all the methods whereby society keeps its members obedient to its rules.

Although functionalism has often been attacked as a conservative sociological tradition, some of its terminology and aspects of its mode of analysis have been appropriated by Marxist and radical theorists. Clearly, for example, Althusserian structuralism has at times a quite tangible functionalist flavour, especially in its account of the reproduction of capitalist relations of production. Most notably, the concept of 'social control' has been taken over wholesale by radical criminologists with little apparent sense of embarrassment (see Cohen, 1985) – but for radicals, 'social control' is usually a term of abuse denoting capitalist repression.[5]

The Durkheimian tradition remains a source of influence for non-Marxist penologists as well. Tony Bottoms (1977) used Durkheim's 'two laws of penal evolution' to offer an explanation of the trend towards 'bifurcation' in British penal policy, whereby (at that time) policy-makers attempted to combine less severe punishments for the majority of offenders with harsher measures for the minority of really serious offenders (see Chapter 1). The trend towards greater leniency for most offenders could be explained by the operation of the first part of Durkheim's first law, which postulates increasing leniency as collective sentiments become more secular. On the other hand, Bottoms saw the central power of the British state as having become more absolute in recent years, which part two of law one says should lead to harsher punishment. This duly transpires, but only for the more serious offenders. The concentration of punitive attention on more serious and violent offenders is an 'attempt to reassert an agreed *conscience collective*, or other kind of consensus, in a time of great social and moral doubt and confusion. Such a reassertion will, in the criminal field, result in the attempt to create consensus at any rate around the crimes which we almost all abhor, such as serious violence' (Bottoms, 1977: 90). Whether or not Bottoms' analysis was correct – and clearly it would need some modifying to explain later shifts away from this kind of bifurcation with the rise of law and order ideology – the Durkheimian concern with shared social values and sentiments as an explanatory factor remains highly relevant to sociology, and to the explanation of punishment in particular.

The Weberian Tradition

3.4 Despite being one of the major streams of modern sociological thought, the theoretical tradition founded by Max Weber (1864–1920) has produced relatively little explicitly Weberian penology.[6] But this probably reflects negatively on penology and penologists rather than on Weber and his thought. We shall concentrate briefly on those aspects of Weber's sociology which have the most obvious relevance to penology.

Weber's sociology is sometimes described as 'a debate with the ghost of Marx' (MacRae, 1974: 52). Weber recognized the importance of economics in shaping social reality, but was concerned to demonstrate that culture and religion influenced economic development just as much as economics influenced culture. He explored this theme most famously in *The Protestant Ethic and the Spirit of Capitalism* (Weber, 1930) and related works, arguing that Calvinistic Protestantism's individualistic ethos and positive attitude to the accumulation of private wealth provided the key to understanding why capitalism first arose in the West rather than in Asia where the economic conditions for capitalist development existed to at least an equal extent. But he also accepted that economics in turn influenced culture; it was the version of Marxism which saw culture as a mere 'reflection' of the economic base that Weber was concerned to refute. The difference between Weber's position and the more sophisticated Marxisms that see culture as relatively autonomous and interacting with the economy in a reciprocal (or 'dialectical') relationship is perhaps not great.

Another important contribution of Weber's was his analysis of different kinds of power in society (Weber, 1968: chs. 1 and 3). He distinguished between simple *power* (the ability to make one's will prevail against the resistance of others), *domination* (enduring power associated with a habit of obedience on the part of the subordinate person or group) and *legitimacy* (power which exists and endures because those subject to it believe it is morally right to obey). All governments and powerful groups seek to acquire legitimacy, for the very good reason that it is the most efficient and stable basis for exercising power. As we saw was true of Durkheim, much of this analysis and terminology of Weber's has been adopted by radical and Marxist theorists; thus we find radicals such as Fitzgerald and Sim (1982) identifying a 'crisis of legitimacy' in the penal system (see Chapter 1).[7]

Weber went on to distinguish three types of legitimate authority: traditional authority, charismatic authority and 'legal authority'. He saw legal authority as characteristic of modern Western societies. A person who wields authority in such a society does not do so typically by virtue of traditional rules (about kingship or hereditary authority, for example) or because of that person's supposed special charismatic qualities, but as a result of an impersonal rule which has been consciously created by a rational legislative process, Weber says that the appropriate administrative form for a system of legal authority – because it is the most efficient form – is *bureaucracy* (Weber, 1968: chs. 3 and 11). Characteristics of bureaucracy include impersonality, the interchangeability of officials, routinization of procedure and a dependency on the existence of recorded information.

In Weberian vein, Kamenka and Tay (1975) suggest that advanced capitalist societies tend to develop 'bureaucratic-administrative law' which increasingly regulates human activities for impersonal collective purposes such as general economic efficiency. Tony Bottoms (1983) suggests that this analysis may explain some recent developments in penal systems, such as the rise in importance of relatively impersonal and standardized penalties such as the fine. Other penal developments can also be seen in this light. Obvious examples are the emergence of fixed penalties for certain motoring offences, the (highly bureaucratic) parole system (see Chapter 8), the move towards standardization in sentencing by such means as sentencing guidelines (see Chapter 4), and the general trend towards 'managerialism' and Strategy B in criminal justice (see Introduction and Chapters 1, 5 and 6). One manifestation may have been the 'blizzard of paper' which the Learmont Report (1995: para. 3.125) complained had been engulfing a Prison Service 'strangled by bureaucracy'.

Finally we should mention Weber's general importance in the development of humanism in sociology. For Weber, the sociologist needed to understand (*verstehen*) the subjective experience of 'ideal-typical' human individuals located within particular societies, classes and cultures – not, of course, denying that social forces shape and influence individuals, but insisting that individual human beings and the meanings they use to interpret their social world are of prime importance in understanding society. This must be as valid an insight in the penal field as in any other.

Pluralism And Radical Pluralism

3.5 In our opinion, the most satisfactory framework for explaining penal phenomena is one that draws on several different sociological traditions.[8] We call this a *radical pluralist* position,[9] since it represents a compromise between Marxism and the pluralist tradition in sociology.

Pluralism (for example, Dahl, 1961) holds that, at least in modern Western democracies, power is not monopolized by a single ruling class but is distributed between a plurality of interest groups of different kinds, which are represented in the political arena by a variety of organizations including political parties. Politics is a process of competition, bargaining and compromise between the different interest groups in which the state plays an impartial and independent role as 'honest broker' between the various parties. This vision of society contrasts with that of Marxism, which sees power in capitalist society as concentrated in the hands of the (bourgeois) ruling class, and society as primarily divided into two great opposing classes rather than a motley collection of interacting interest groups. Similarly, the state for Marxists is by no means neutral and independent but is, in the words of Marx and Engels, 'but a committee for managing the common affairs of the whole bourgeoisie' (Marx, 1977: 223). Although the state might operate as an honest broker between different sections of the ruling class and may seek to give the appearance of neutrality to mystify its class nature and role, it will never be neutral as between the general interests of the bourgeoisie and the proletariat.

Neither traditional Marxism nor conventional pluralism seems adequate to us. Marxism's main flaw is its insistence on economics and the economic category of class as the one fundamental explanatory factor. This has meant, for example, that despite some valiant efforts, Marxism has been ultimately unable to deal with other important social dimensions such as race and gender differences without reducing them to a mere aspect of class oppression and class struggle. We are not convinced that the penal realities concerning race and gender outlined in Chapter 10 can be satisfactorily explained in this manner.

Nor can all the groups involved in penal developments and penal conflicts and struggles be easily defined in terms of economic classes (although an attempt could perhaps be made to analyse them as representing 'alliances of class fractions'). We might mention non-state

> groups like PROP, the prisoners' group which for many years campaigned for prisoners' rights ... Radical Alternatives to Prison (RAP) which successfully campaigned against control units [see Chapter 6] ... Women in Prison (WIP) which explored conditions in Durham's maximum security wing as well as drawing attention to the high incidence of self-injury among female offenders ... [or] Inquest which has bullied the Prison Department into setting up a suicide prevention unit. (Ryan, 1993: 401; see also Ryan, 1978; Sim, 1994)

A recent development has been the rise of populist non-state groupings such as the Victims of Crime Trust, which campaign for harsher penal policies.

Again, as devotees of the classic BBC television comedy *Yes, Minister* may recall, the state bureaucracies and their members have their own organizational and personal interests to pursue which are often at variance with those of their supposed political masters, which in turn are not invariably identical with those of either the electorate or of any coalition of interest groups.[10] This would appear to be true for example of the Home Office, which for many years (at least prior to the advent of Michael Howard as Home Secretary) was largely successful in getting its strategy of 'penological pragmatism' implemented (see Chapters 1 and 11; Bottoms, 1980; Fitzgerald and Sim, 1980). Joanna Shapland (1988) has shrewdly likened both non-state groups and the state agencies involved in the criminal justice system (such as the police and the courts) to feudal 'fiefdoms'. While, of course, we do not live in a feudal society, this analogy is in some ways highly apt: such fiefdoms represent partially autonomous concentrations of power and interest not readily reducible to class analysis.

Pluralism, on the other hand, is unembarrassed by the existence of a plurality of important social divisions. But conventional pluralism has its own defects, chiefly its 'honest broker' conception of the state. It seems clear, at least to us, that the state is by no means fully independent of, and impartial between, all groups and classes in society. ('Relative autonomy' is not perhaps a bad description.) For one thing, the personnel of the state are members of some of these interest groups themselves, and the more powerful state personnel will tend to be members of, or sympathetic to – or sharing the ideologies of – the more powerful and entrenched classes and groups. In the penal field, certain kinds of (more respectable) interest and pressure groups have at times been allowed a degree of influence on official policy,[11] while others – especially those that challenge ruling ideologies – have had to struggle much harder to make an impact (Ryan, 1978).

However, the chasm between the pluralist and Marxist views has narrowed encouragingly in recent years (McLennan, 1989). Marxists have discovered the state to be relatively autonomous and classes to be composed of 'class fractions' which seem to interact in a manner curiously reminiscent of the pluralist account.

(They have also recognized the political virtues of pluralistic multi-party democracy, which pluralism appeared to celebrate while Marxists previously derided it as 'bourgeois democracy', which merely served to mystify the reality of class oppression.) The modified Marxism of E.P. Thompson approaches even closer to pluralism. For Thompson (1978: 298–9), classes are not the inevitable creation of economic relations, but 'arise because men and women, in determinate productive relations, identify their antagonistic interests, and come to struggle, to think, and to value in class ways'. Furthermore, law and the state afford 'an arena for class struggle' (1978: 288) in which victory for the ruling class is not necessarily assured. If this is true of classes, why should it not also be true of other interest groups, and what ultimately differentiates this from pluralism? Especially since there has been convergence from the pluralist side as well. Some pluralist writers have accepted that class division and class competition are pervasive factors in modern society, and that not all interest groups are equal in power or equally able to compete in the political arena (for example, Dahl, 1985).

Radical pluralism can build on the common ground that has emerged between these two traditions. It can also incorporate some features of the Weberian and Durkheimian traditions – and perhaps not only the ones that, as we have seen, have already been purloined by Marxism – and can equally avail itself of the insights of other modes of sociological analysis. There are some who would object on philosophical grounds to this kind of synthesizing approach. Different theoretical traditions, it is sometimes claimed, belong to 'incommensurable paradigms' (Kuhn, 1962); one can work within only one of them at a time. But there is no good reason, philosophical or otherwise, why a synthesis of different theories should not be sought, as long as the assembled components do not actually contradict each other. (It would be incoherent, for example, to amalgamate wholesale the theories of E.P. Thompson and Michel Foucault since the humanism of the former is incompatible with the anti-humanism of the latter.)

We think that a coherent radical pluralism can be constructed on the basis of a humanism which accepts, as Marx put it, that human beings 'make their own history, but they do not make it just as they please; they do not make it under circumstances chosen by themselves' (Marx, 1977: 300). These constraining circumstances on human agency include the economic, political, cultural and ideological factors which shape our social world, but neither economics nor ideology is 'basic'. The economic situation may set limits on what is socially possible but (as Weber for one insisted) this is equally true of the prevailing ideological situation. Economics and ideology are thus both 'determining' in a weak sense and they interact with each other, but neither makes a single future inevitable. Indeed, much of what happens in human affairs, including the realm of penality, depends on the 'swarming circumstances' (Garland, 1990a: 285) that hold sway at any particular moment, and on how the people subject to those circumstances make sense of them and respond to them.

As we said in Chapter 1, we think that the current 'penal crisis' should be seen in terms such as these. Material factors such as the shortage of penal resources) interact with ideological developments (such as 'law and order ideology' and the all-important 'crisis of legitimacy') in a complex and sometimes unpredictable manner. Much of this complexity and unpredictability is precisely because the intersection between the material and the ideological occurs in the practices of living human beings: offenders, sentencers, employees of the penal system, politicians, penal campaigners and members of the public. This vital human element makes the study of penality a complex and uncertain business. But it also means that people can, by their efforts, have a positive (or, of course, a negative) effect on the reality of punishment.

We now proceed to consider some of the ways in which punishment has varied – both over time and between different societies at the same time – to see how penal sociology might be applied to help explain these variations.

Applying Penal Sociology

The New Penology and the New Punitiveness

3.6 Punishment in many countries has changed significantly in recent decades, and a number of very noticeable penal trends have been categorized and variously named 'the new penology' (Feeley and Simon, 2002), 'the new punitiveness' (Pratt et al., 2005) and 'postmodern penality' (Pratt, 2000). The most notable international trend has been a 'new punitiveness': a general increase in the harshness of punishment. One measure of the severity of punishment is the 'imprisonment rate': the number of prisoners a country has per 100,000 of its general population. In recent years nearly three-quarters of all the countries in the world have seen increased imprisonment rates (Walmsley, 2005). In many respects, this new harshness has been led by the United States, whose prison population and imprisonment rates are the highest in the world[12] and where numbers of prisoners have quintupled since the early 1970s. (The US has also in effect reintroduced and massively expanded its use of capital punishment since 1977, despite having carried out no executions between 1967 and 1977.) England, along with other nations, has followed this trend for a 'new punitiveness', if not to anything like the same extent, as we saw in Chapter 1. Associated with this punitiveness has been the 'law and order ideology' (or 'populist punitiveness') we discussed in Chapter 1, as public and media discourse about crime has increasingly taken the form of urging tougher punishment as the appropriate response to crime. The 'new punitiveness' is also very much bound up with what we term Strategy A (see the Introduction). Populist policies and slogans, such as 'three strikes and you're out' or 'zero tolerance', are manifestations of the new punitiveness.

There have been other significant international trends as well as this increasing severity. The 'new *penology*' is a rather different concept from the 'new *punitiveness*' – it relates to Strategy B rather than Strategy A. What has been called the 'new penology' is 'managerial rather than transformative' (Feeley and Simon, 1992: 452): it is not concerned with reforming and treating the offender (or indeed – unlike the 'new punitiveness' – with placing moral blame on the criminal). Instead 'it is concerned with techniques to identify, classify, and manage groupings sorted by dangerousness' (1992: 452). Such techniques include statistical methods of carrying out 'risk assessments' of offenders, and applying new tools of offender management (for example, electronic surveillance and monitoring) based on the outcome of such assessments. This managerial 'new penology' is one strong trend influencing the current government's penal strategy, which can be characterized as a 'neo-correctionalism' (see especially Chapter 9, sections 9.2 and 9.3), which combines elements of both the new punitiveness and the new penology.

Can the sociology of punishment – and our radical pluralist approach in particular – help to explain or elucidate developments such as these? We think that they can. First, the 'new penology': Of the sociological theories and traditions we have covered in this chapter, it is the Weberian tradition (assimilated into our radical pluralism) which would seem to provide the most appropriate tools to understand this phenomenon. The new penology is managerial, bureaucratic and impersonal, just as Weber theorized that administration in a developed and complex society would be. In other words, it is *'modernizing'*:[13] it represents an attempt to deal with crime and offenders in a rational and scientific manner untrammelled by traditional attitudes and practices, such as retributivism and a concentration on morally condemning offenders and making them suffer.

But although this Weberian analysis might explain the 'new penology', it can hardly account for the 'new punitiveness', which precisely *does* aim at making offenders suffer. To try to explain this paradox, we need to digress briefly into the fascinating realm of comparative penology.

Comparative Penology and the New Punitiveness

If we compare the practice of punishment across different countries (see Cavadino and Dignan, 2006), it is instantly noticeable that there are wide variations. Countries differ in the *methods* of punishment they employ: witness, for example, the use of capital punishment in the United States but not in Europe. They also differ in the general degree of *severity* with which they punish offenders. Again looking at 'imprisonment rates', these range from a high of 714 prisoners per 100,000 population in the United States of America to a low of 29 in India and Nepal (Walmsley, 2005). Even if we confine ourselves to developed 'Western' countries, the US imprisonment rate far exceeds that of England and Wales (142) and even more so those of (for example) Germany (96) and Finland (71). What is it about different societies which makes for such different rates of punishment?

It is possible to relate some important characteristics of a country's *political economy* – and in particular its welfare system – to the severity of its penal practices. Modern Western countries can be categorized as either 'neo-liberal', 'conservative corporatist' or 'social democratic' nations (Esping-Andersen, 1990; Lash and Urry, 1987, 1994).[14] *'Neo-liberalism'* refers to the (politically conservative) free-market capitalism exemplified by the United States, but also characterizing to a lesser extent countries such as Britain, Australia and New Zealand in recent decades. The general ethos – or the culture, or ideology – of neo-liberalism is one of individualism rather than communitarianism or collectivism. Under neo-liberalism, the welfare state is minimalist, consisting mainly of means-tested welfare benefits, entitlement to which is often heavily stigmatized. The economic system creates much material inequality, and this results in the social exclusion of many people who find themselves unable to participate to any great extent in civil, political and social life. Indeed, typically whole communities find themselves excluded in acutely deprived 'ghetto' areas.

In *'conservative corporatist'* countries (such as Germany and other nations in continental Western Europe), important national interest groups (notably organizations representing employers and workers) are integrated with the national state and are expected to act in accordance with a consensual 'national interest'. In return, members of these groups enjoy welfare benefits that are more generous than those found in neo-liberal countries. The ideology and culture of conservative corporatism is a communitarian one which seeks to include and integrate all citizens within the nation, via individuals' membership of interest groups. Conservative corporatist states offer their citizens greater protection against the vagaries of market forces and produce significantly less inequality than does neo-liberalism, but they are not strongly egalitarian. Their welfare states enshrine and perpetuate traditional class, status and economic divisions between different groups of citizens who are entitled to different levels of welfare benefits.

A third arrangement (on the political left) is the *'social democratic'* version of corporatism – more egalitarian than the conservative version – whose prime examples are Sweden and the other Nordic countries. These countries share the consensual, communitarian approach of conservative corporatism, but their welfare systems are more generous and more egalitarian, being based on universal benefits.

Table 3.1 shows the imprisonment rates of a sample of 11 countries, divided into these three categories. It also shows that currently there are almost watertight dividing lines between these different types of political economy as regards imprisonment rates in these countries. With one exception, all the neo-liberal countries have higher rates than all the conservative corporatist countries (the single exception being that the Netherlands' rate is currently higher than Australia's); while the Nordic social democracies[15] have the lowest imprisonment rates. But why should there be this relationship between political economy and rates of punishment?

One likely answer is that in these different kinds of political economy we find different *cultural attitudes* towards our deviant and marginalized fellow citizens. The neo-liberal society tends to exclude both those who fail in the economic marketplace and those who fail to abide by the law – in the latter case by means of imprisonment, or even more radically by execution. Both types of exclusion are associated with a highly individualistic social ethos – the attitude that, in Margaret Thatcher's famous words, 'there is no such thing as society'. Economic failure is seen as the fault of the individual, not the responsibility of society – hence the minimal safety-net welfare state. Crime is likewise seen as entirely the responsibility of the offending individual. The social soil is fertile ground for a harsh 'law and

TABLE 3.1 Political economy and imprisonment rates

	Imprisonment rate (per 100,000 population)	Year
NEO-LIBERAL COUNTRIES		
USA	714	2003
South Africa	413	2004
New Zealand	168	2004
England and Wales	142	2005
Australia	117	2004
CONSERVATIVE CORPORATIST COUNTRIES		
Netherlands	123	2004
Italy	98	2004
Germany	96	2004
France	91	2004
SOCIAL DEMOCRACIES		
Sweden	75	2003
Finland	71	2004

Source: Walmsley (2005)

order ideology'. On the other hand, corporatist societies like Germany – and to an even greater extent, social democratic ones like Sweden – have traditionally had a different culture and a different attitude towards the failing or deviant citizen. Corporatist and social democratic states offer their citizens a far greater degree of protection against the vicissitudes of market forces and seek to ensure that all citizens are looked after. Similarly, there is a more communitarian, less individualistic attitude towards the offender, who is regarded not as an isolated culpable individual who must be rejected and excluded from law-abiding society, but as a social being who is still the responsibility of the community as a whole. A more developed welfare state goes along with a less punitive penal culture. The most developed welfare states of all – the Nordic social democracies – also have the lowest imprisonment rates among these Western nations. (See further Cavadino and Dignan, 2006.)

This association between types of political economy and levels of punitiveness may also go a long way towards explaining the rise of the 'new punitiveness' of recent decades:[16] as neo-liberalism has advanced, so too has law and order ideology. It is no coincidence that the United States has since the 1970s been leading the world in the direction both of neo-liberalism and of the new punitiveness, for the two go together. And this also helps to explain why so many other countries have gone down the punitive road, for so many of them have adopted neo-liberalism to a greater or lesser extent.[17] Britain is very much a case in point, despite retaining a relatively well-developed welfare system compared with that of the US. The Conservative governments of 1979–97 moved Britain decisively towards neo-liberalism, a shift their New Labour successors have accepted and indeed in most respects embraced. And the 'new punitiveness' towards offenders has come along with it. At the same time, however – in a parallel and sometimes conflicting trend – there has also been a long-term move towards the more managerial 'new penology' we discussed under the previous heading.

The different sociological traditions covered in this chapter would view and explain this association between political economies and punitiveness in different ways. The Durkheimian approach (see, for example, Greenberg, 1999) would emphasize the culture and 'collective sentiments' of different societies, and might seek to explain both a country's welfare system and its penality by saying that they were *both produced by* the society's culture. For example, the individualistic culture of the United States made the nation inclined to adopt both a minimalist welfare state and severe penal policies. Marxists, on the other hand, would see economics rather than culture as basic, and might assert that it is the economic facts of a society's welfare system which conditions the ideology of its citizens in either an individualistic or communitarian (and in an egalitarian or inegalitarian) direction, leading to a harsh or lenient penality. More sophisticated Marxists would accept that it is not all one way, and that ideologies can have a 'reciprocal action' on the economic base, but (if they remain Marxists) they must assert the primacy of the latter.

We, and the radical pluralism that we favour, would take a view more akin to that of Weber: the realms of culture (or ideology) and of economics *interact* with each other, and although at times one might seem a more dominant determining factor, neither is basic. So it is true (as the Durkheimian approach suggests) that a society's cultural attitudes towards our deviant and marginalized fellow citizens affect both our penality and the economic system we adopt. But these attitudes are not only *embodied* in the economic system, they are also *embedded* in them, and the reality of living life in a society that is organized and runs on either individualistic lines or communitarian ones is likely to condition, reinforce and reproduce our attitudes towards others in society, thus (normally) helping to continue the existing system and culture, including the penal culture and the penal practices which that culture brings about.

These systems and cultures can of course change and evolve, in interaction with each other. And so it has been that in countries like Britain, the welfare state, the economic system and the general culture have all altered markedly in recent decades, as has the 'penal *Zeitgeist*'.[18] For now at least, in an age of neo-liberalism, the 'new punitiveness' predominates.

Notes

1   Althusser disclaimed the label 'structuralist' to distance himself from other theorists (notably the anthropologist Lévi-Strauss), for whom the structures of thought and language are determining. For Althusser, by contrast, it is the structure of the entire social formation, including the economic and political 'instances', which determines history.

2   Althusser's remarkably broad concept of the state relates to an important intra-Marxist debate which we cannot explore here. Many of the institutions which Althusser categorizes

as part of the state would be viewed by Gramsci as part of 'civil society'. For what it is worth, we prefer the Gramscian approach.

3　This may be unfair on Althusser, who as we have seen described law as both part of the Repressive State Apparatus and as an Ideological State Apparatus, and who said that the different instances never exist or function in a pure manner independent of each other.

4　Durkheim got his penal anthropology wrong on this point. Bottoms (1980a: 23n) notes that Durkheim was 'ignorant of the great extent of the role of restitution in primitive societies'. His thesis in *The Division of Labor* also seems inconsistent with his later prediction in 'Two Laws of Penal Evolution' that more and more offences against the person would come to be criminalized in the future.

5　One of us has argued elsewhere (Cavadino, 1989: ch. 2) that although social control is inherently conservative in the sense that it tends to preserve the existing state of society, this does not make all social control objectionable even from a radical's point of view, because there is much in existing society which radicals should want to preserve. (Durkheim would undoubtedly have agreed with this!)

6　However, Garland (1990a: ch. 8) argues convincingly that Weber has been a major influence on some significant penological work, including that of Foucault, often without receiving due acknowledgement.

7　We suspect that Fitzgerald and Sim borrowed the idea of a crisis of legitimacy from the German Marxist theorist Jürgen Habermas (1976), who in turn was profoundly influenced by Weber. We might also note that Gramsci's concept of hegemony has much in common with the notion of legitimacy.

8　Our position has much in common with that of David Garland (1990a, 1990b), who similarly wishes to synthesize the contributions to penology of the different traditions. However, Garland avoids making any attempt to link the sociology of punishment to any wider social theory, such as our radical pluralism. See further on this point Cavadino (1992: 13–14).

9　Unfortunately, there is no generally accepted term for such a position, nor is there a generally accepted meaning for 'radical pluralism'. For example, McLennan (1989) uses this term to refer to a position which is emphatically not ours, namely the 'postmodernist' philosophy which rejects any notion of universal reason. McLennan would call our position 'critical pluralism'.

10　Readers who are too young to remember this may find it useful to refer to Lynn and Jay (1981); see also Kellner and Crowther-Hunt (1980); Chapman (1978).

11　Victim Support is probably the most obvious example, which continues to wield a degree of influence that eludes more oppositional groups working in the same field such as the Rape Crisis Federation (or Rape Crisis Co-ordinating Group, as it is now known) or Women's Aid. However, in the recent climate of 'law and order', other respectable penal reform organizations (which include Nacro and the Howard League for Penal Reform) have found it more difficult to have much effect on policy-making.

12　With over two million prisoners and an imprisonment rate of 714 per 100,000 in 2003 (compared with 142 in England and Wales). Although the US contains only 5 per cent of the world's population, it accounts for nearly a quarter of its prisoners.

13　Consequently, like Garland (1995a) and unlike Pratt (2000) and Simon (1993), we do not see the new penology as being 'post-modern', but as being a development of 'late modernity'. The rehabilitative approach was also an attempt to be rational and modern, but the more recent downplaying of rehabilitation is not post-modern but equally modernist in a different way. See further Cavadino and Dignan (2006: 7–9).

14　In Cavadino and Dignan (2006) we identify a fourth variant – 'oriental corporatist' – exemplified by Japan, and explain how its political economy can likewise be related to its penal practices.

15 Denmark (70) and Norway (65) have similar imprisonment rates to Sweden and Finland.

16 There may well be other factors involved, such as an increase in sensationalist reporting about crime and punishment in the tabloid media and (associated with this) more 'penal populism' on the part of politicians (see generally Cavadino and Dignan, 2006). Another possibility is that the phenomenon of 'globalization' has contributed to the rise and spread of the new punitiveness: see Baker and Roberts (2005).

17 Neo-liberal developments can also be seen as exacerbating the decline of traditional communities, which we suggested in Chapter 1 (section 1.4) as a factor in the rise of the new punitiveness.

18 For which apt phrase we thank Hanns von Hofer.

4 Court Decisions: The Crux of the Crisis

The 'System'

4.1 There is nothing inevitable about the penal crisis that we described in Chapter 1. It has been brought about by decisions, made by people. In particular, the prison numbers crisis, along with many of the problems associated with it, is the result of a whole series of decisions taken by the people who staff the various institutions that make up the criminal justice system in this country (sketched out in the Introduction). The various stages of decision-making have been likened to a series of filters which between them determine who gets embroiled in the criminal justice system and for how long. For example, if the police do not act against an alleged offender or if the Crown Prosecution Service (CPS) declines to prosecute, the suspect will never reach court, let alone go to prison and contribute to the numbers crisis. Criminal justice agencies typically possess extensive *discretion* in how they make these decisions, and tend to make them under conditions of low visibility and subject to minimal restraint by other bodies. If we want to understand the current penal crisis, we need to examine how this discretion is exercised, its consequences for the rest of the penal system, and why over the years it has not been subjected to more effective and appropriate control.

Although the police and the CPS have a vital role in determining who will proceed to subsequent stages of the criminal process, the most direct and immediate impact on the penal system is exercised by judges and magistrates sitting in the courts, especially when they pass sentence on offenders (which we describe as 'the crux of the crisis'), but also when they make decisions about remand and mode of trial. In many respects the courts epitomize the *unsystematic* nature of the criminal justice system, which we referred to at the end of the Introduction. As we saw in the Introduction, responsibility for deciding how offenders should be dealt with is allocated to three different tiers of courts: magistrates' courts, Crown Courts and the Court of Appeal. Each court is staffed by different sets of judicial officials, and both the powers at their disposal and the parameters within which they choose to exercise them vary considerably. The criminal justice legislation that defines these powers is complex, and is frequently irrational and lacking coherence.

Indeed, confusion and irrationality extend to the heart of government and are reflected in the idiosyncratic arrangements allocating political responsibility for the different parts of the criminal justice system. Unlike many other countries, which have a unified Ministry of Justice, in England and Wales responsibility is shared between three separate government departments. Prior to May 2007, responsibility for the judiciary and the courts rested with the Department for Constitutional Affairs (DCA) presided over by the Lord Chancellor (formerly the Lord Chancellor's Department, prior to 2003), but the Home Office was responsible for drafting the criminal justice legislation which they had to apply, and also for the police, prisons and probation. The CPS, meanwhile, came and still comes under the remit of the Attorney General. However, in May 2007 these responsibilities were re-divided, with a new Ministry of Justice replacing the DCA and assuming responsibililty for NOMS (prisons and probation), youth justice, criminal law and sentencing policy – although the Home Secretary is to retain a 'core role' in the last two areas.[1] This still somewhat muddled set of constitutional arrangements has at best made for an absence of 'joined-up government' at the heart of criminal justice and penal administration. At worst it can result in an undignified turf war between contending criminal justice 'fiefdoms' (Shapland, 1988; see also Chapter 3 above). It also makes the task of reforming the 'system' much more difficult in the absence of a unified and integrated policy-making process.

In previous editions of this book, we summed up the picture that we paint in this chapter as one of a system out of control. We now have to modify that judgement. There is still a certain lack of control over the discretion that is enjoyed by all criminal justice agencies, including the courts, and a tendency for this discretion to be exercised without regard for the impact which decisions may have on other parts of the system. But our overall judgement now is that the English sentencing 'system' is best described as *inappropriately* controlled. Sentencers are subject to more formal controls than they were. However, some of these (notably new minimum and mandatory penalties) are the wrong kind of controls, while other controls are still too weak or ineffective to prevent sentencers using their discretion to pass inconsistent and excessively harsh sentences. This might not matter so much if judges and magistrates were not so inclined by their *sentencing culture* to impose such penalties – if the courts did not have a long-standing and indeed intensifying 'love affair with custody' (Travis, 2003) – and if they were not constantly encouraged in this infatuation by external pressures such as 'law and order' rhetoric from politicians.

In this chapter we examine in turn three sets of decisions for which the courts are responsible: *remand* decisions (whether accused persons are freed on bail or remanded in custody); *mode of trial* decisions (whether they are tried in the magistrates' court or committed for trial in the Crown Court); and – last and most crucially – *sentencing* decisions.[2] We will be saying something about the decision-makers themselves, describing the legal framework and organizational context in which they take their decisions, assessing their impact on the overall penal crisis, outlining the recent history of reforms to the system, and considering the prospects for the future.

The Remand Decision

'Please do not ask for bail as a refusal often offends.'[3]

4.2 People who are suspected of crimes or prosecuted for them are officially presumed innocent until proven guilty; but they can still find that their liberty is taken away, first by the police arresting and detaining them, and second by being remanded in custody by the courts. The courts also remand in custody some offenders who have been convicted, prior to passing sentence. Suspects who are detained by the police are normally kept in police stations, but those whom the courts remand in custody are detained in prisons and remand centres, adding to the prison population. Decisions to imprison defendants and unsentenced offenders can contribute to the penal crisis in two main ways. First, they can worsen both the prison numbers crisis and all the other problems – of conditions, control and so on – which are exacerbated by a high prison population. Currently, remand prisoners make up 17 per cent of the total prison population,[4] a figure which has risen as high as 26 per cent (in 1994: RDS NOMS, 2004: Table 8.1). Second, remand decisions can fuel the crisis of legitimacy if defendants are remanded in custody inappropriately or unjustly. The conditions of their custody are typically worse than those of many sentenced prisoners, since they are more likely to find themselves in overcrowded local prisons and remand centres, despite the fact that they are still supposed to be innocent in the eyes of the law, or (in the case of unsentenced convicts) have not yet been sentenced to imprisonment. Of particular concern is the enduring, chilling fact that remand prisoners are consistently and significantly more likely to take their own lives than are other prisoners.[5] Conversely, however, the legitimacy of the system may also suffer if courts are successfully portrayed as being too ready to set free suspects who may be popularly, if not officially, regarded as guilty.

In the early stages of the criminal process, the decision to keep suspects in custody or to release them either unconditionally or on bail (i.e. conditional freedom for the time being) rests with the police.[6] Once a case has reached the magistrates' court, responsibility for granting bail or remanding in custody is a matter for the court, after hearing representations from the defendant and from the Crown Prosecution Service. The CPS, whose information comes from the police, may decide to oppose the granting of bail at the court hearing. There are three main stages at which a court decision on bail may be needed. The first is where an adjournment is sought before or during the course of a trial. A second is at the 'committal stage', in cases that are to be tried in the Crown Court (see the following section). The third occurs after conviction, when the court may adjourn in order to obtain reports on the defendant and take time for deliberation before passing sentence.

The legal framework regulating the circumstances in which a person can be remanded in custody is provided by the Bail Act 1976 (as subsequently amended). This Act lays down a statutory presumption in favour of bail, but qualifies this by providing that bail can be refused if certain criteria are satisfied. A court may remand a defendant in custody where there are substantial grounds for believing that, if released on bail, the defendant would fail to appear for trial, would commit an offence while on bail, or would obstruct the course of justice. Bail may also be denied if the court thinks this is necessary for the defendant's own protection, if there has been insufficient time to enable the court to obtain enough information to reach a decision, or if the defendant has previously failed to answer bail. Conditions may be attached to the granting of bail,[7] for example requiring the bailee to live in a specified place, to report regularly to the police, or even to be subject to a curfew (which can be enforced by electronic monitoring of the kind discussed in Chapter 5).

There have been several legislative amendments to the Bail Act in recent years, generally having the effect of restricting defendants' entitlement to bail. Section 26 of the Criminal Justice and Public Order Act 1994 – introduced when Conservative Home Secretary Michael Howard was applying a concertedly Strategy A approach to criminal justice – removed the normal presumption in favour of bail from defendants who are charged with an indictable offence that appears to have been committed while they were on bail for an earlier alleged offence. This provision was in turn replaced by New Labour legislation providing that in future such a defendant '*may not* be granted bail unless the court is satisfied that there is no significant risk of his committing an offence'.[8] Similarly, defendants who have been released on bail and have been arrested for either absconding or for breach of their bail conditions are not now eligible for bail unless there is no significant risk of a further absconding.[9] Section 25 of Mr Howard's 1994 Act entirely forbade the granting of bail to persons charged with serious offences such as murder, manslaughter and rape who had previously been convicted of any such offence. In anticipation of a challenge under the Human Rights Act, this total ban was modified under the New Labour government with a provision that bail could be granted in such cases if the court decides that there are 'exceptional circumstances which justify it'.[10]

On the other hand, there have also been various attempts at different times to facilitate the granting of bail in appropriate cases. These have included *bail information schemes*, to ensure that courts are provided with sufficient background information on defendants to identify better those who will be 'good risks' if granted bail; *bail support schemes* (especially for young offenders) which provide a variety of interventions aimed at reducing reoffending while on bail; and *bail hostels* to accommodate homeless defendants who would otherwise be unlikely to receive bail.[11] Nevertheless, recent years have still seen an increase in the proportion of defendants remanded in custody: whereas in 1994 magistrates denied bail to 9 per cent of remanded defendants, in 2004 the figure was 11 per cent (Home Office, 2005e: Table 4.4).

Efforts have also been made to reduce the numbers imprisoned on remand at any one time by cutting down the time it takes to deal with cases in the courts. These include the introduction of statutory time limits under the Prosecution of Offences Act 1985, which limit the length of time for which a person may be held in custody awaiting trial.[12] New measures were also introduced following the Narey Report (1997) with the intention of speeding up criminal proceedings, which if successful should also have the effect of cutting the time spent on remand and therefore reducing the remand population. And, as we shall see in the following section, there have also been measures aimed at increasing the number of 'triable either way' cases which are tried in the magistrates' court instead of being committed to the Crown Court, thus avoiding the more lengthy period of remand involved in awaiting a Crown Court trial. There was for a while some progress on waiting times. Between 1989 and 1994 the average length of time spent in custody by defendants awaiting Crown Court trial increased from 10 to 13.5 weeks; by 1997 this had come down to 8.7 weeks; but in 2004 it was back up to 14 weeks[13] (Home Office, 2000a: 138; 2005e: Table 2B). As we have seen, the *proportion* of the total prison population made up of remandees has declined from a peak of 26 per cent in 1994 to 17 per cent in 2006. However, in absolute terms the 2006 figure of

13,067 is actually higher than the 1994 figure (12,533) – but it is 17 per cent of a much larger total prison population.

It is not just that these large numbers of remand prisoners contribute to the practical problems of the penal system. Nor is it merely that they are technically 'innocent until proven guilty'. Some are actually innocent. Of defendants who have been denied bail before trial in either the magistrates' or Crown Court, a disturbingly high proportion – over one in five – are acquitted altogether or have charges against them dropped.[14] Another one-third are convicted, but receive a non-custodial sentence. This means that – remarkably – only 48 per cent of those who are remanded in custody while officially innocent end up being sentenced to immediate imprisonment[15] (Home Office, 2005e: paras. 4.8, 4.10).[16] These statistics do not necessarily mean that bail was improperly denied in all these cases (see Ashworth, 1998: 219–23). However, they do cast serious doubt on the need and justification for pre-trial detention on the present scale.

Confidence in the decision-making process is not perhaps heightened by the finding that bail decisions in magistrates' courts take an average of six minutes (cited by Auld, 2001: 428). Concerns about the fairness of the decision-making process are also fuelled by evidence of persistent and widespread disparities in the rate of custodial remands in different parts of the country. For example, one study found a custodial remand rate as low as 5 per 1,000 indictable proceedings in Liverpool and as high as 698 in Lambeth (Gibson, 1987; see also Hucklesby, 1997). One obvious reason for this kind of disparity is the fact that the guidance contained in the 1976 Act affords massive scope for the differing exercise of discretion by magistrates, thereby enabling different policies to be pursued in individual court areas.

So far we have been concentrating on complaints that bail law and procedures afford inadequate protection to defendants, and that bail might often be wrongly refused. However, the law and practice of bail have been subject to intense criticism of the opposite kind in recent years, alleging that bail is granted too readily, allowing 'bail bandits' to abscond and offend while on bail. One example of such criticism formed part of a wide-ranging critique of the criminal justice system by the then Metropolitan Police Commissioner Sir John Stevens (2002), who claimed that 'it is not uncommon in London to have muggers released on bail eight or nine times before they face trial for their first attack'. How much truth is there in such claims? The proportion of defendants who *fail to appear* at court after being released on bail was 14 per cent in 2003 (Home Office, 2004a: 75). However, in some cases there may be legitimate reasons for failing to appear; and in many other cases the decision to grant bail on the information available at the time will no doubt have been entirely correct.

Rather more attention has been focused in recent years on the problem of *offending while on bail*. A survey of bailees in Northumbria and Greater Manchester in 1996 found that 24 per cent of them committed at least one offence while on bail (Brown, 1998). Offences were committed by 12 per cent of those bailed by the police and 15 per cent of those bailed – typically for rather longer periods of time – by the courts. However, there is no evidence that rates of offending on bail have increased in recent years, or that courts are making a habit of recklessly bailing defendants where the police and CPS oppose the grant of bail.[17] It needs to be borne in mind that many of the offences committed on bail are minor crimes which would not themselves attract a custodial sentence, so it is hard to see a justification for imprisoning someone in case they might commit such an act. Again, the research shows that juvenile bailees are more than twice as likely as adults to offend while on bail; yet juveniles are more likely to receive bail. For not only are there special statutory restrictions on the custodial remand of persons under 17, but magistrates are understandably often reluctant to remand in custody a young person who has never been imprisoned before and has not yet been convicted of an offence. It may be necessary and right to accept that there will inevitably always be a significant number of bailees who offend.

Although most of the political pressure recently has been to restrict the granting of bail further, more concern should arguably be focused on the violations of human rights which unnecessary remands in custody represent. Doubts have been raised as to whether several of the recent legal provisions restricting the right to bail are compatible with the European Convention on Human Rights.[18] There is a strong case for removing these restrictions, and also for further reforms including tightening the time limits for custodial remands and amending the Bail Act to prevent courts remanding in custody in cases where an eventual custodial sentence is unlikely (Penal Affairs Consortium, 2000).

The Mode of Trial Decision

4.3 The size of the remand prison population does not just depend on how many defendants are refused bail; it is also affected by how long it takes their cases to come to trial. One factor determining how long this wait will be is where the trial will be held: in the magistrates' court or the Crown Court. For although delays are far from negligible even in magistrates' courts, the problem is particularly acute in relation to Crown Courts, where the average waiting time for those denied bail is currently 14 weeks from committal to trial (Home Office, 2005e: para. 2.23). So any alteration in the proportions of defendants who are dealt with in the two courts is likely to have significant repercussions for the remand population. So too will any increase in the proportion of Crown Court defendants who are remanded in custody prior to their trials.[19] Where cases are tried also has implications for the size of the rest of the prison population – those sentenced to prison. For offenders tried and sentenced in the Crown Court are in general likely to receive considerably more severe sentences[20] than those tried in the magistrates' court (Hedderman and Moxon, 1992); thus the more cases tried in the Crown Court, the higher the prison population is likely to be. Decisions about the venue of trials can also have major practical and financial effects on the administration of justice, with more Crown Court trials meaning more delay and greater expense[21] in processing cases. They may also influence perceptions of the fairness of criminal justice, especially since trial by jury is widely regarded as the fairest system of deciding guilt or innocence; so they may have an important bearing on the wider crisis of legitimacy that affects the criminal justice system as a whole.

As we saw in the Introduction, where a case will be tried depends on whether the alleged offence is categorized as 'indictable only', 'summary only' or 'triable either way'. The most serious offences, such as murder, rape and robbery, are 'indictable only', meaning that they must be tried in the Crown Court. A much more numerous group of offences, the least serious, are 'summary only' and can only be tried in the magistrates' court. A third category comprises offences including theft, handling stolen goods and burglary, crimes of an intermediate or variable degree of seriousness, and these are 'triable either way'. These 'triable either way cases' commence in the magistrates' court. Before it is decided where the actual trial should take place, defendants are invited to indicate whether they will be pleading guilty or not guilty. (This system of 'plea before venue' was introduced in 1997;[22] previously 'venue' decisions were made before any indication of plea.) If the defendant indicates an intention to plead guilty, the case must be tried (and the defendant convicted) in the magistrates' court. (However, the magistrates may subsequently decide that their powers of sentencing are insufficient, in which case they can still commit the defendant to the Crown Court not for trial but for sentence.) If, however, the defendant indicates an intention to plead not guilty (or gives no indication either way), a decision needs to be taken as to whether the case will be heard by the magistrates or by the Crown Court.

The next stage is for the magistrates to decide which trial venue would in their opinion be more appropriate. As with bail decisions, the magistrates receive representations from the CPS and the defence before deciding. Among the factors that magistrates are required to take into account in reaching a decision are the seriousness of the offence, and whether their own powers of punishment would be adequate if the defendant were to be convicted.[23] Further guidance for magistrates has hitherto been contained in National Mode of Trial Guidelines.[24] Following the Criminal Justice Act 2003, the Sentencing Guidelines Council (or SGC; see below, sections 4.4 and 4.5) now has responsibility for issuing National Allocation Guidelines; the Council issued draft guidelines in February 2006 which as we write are subject to consultation. If the magistrates decide that a Crown Court trial is called for, they commit the case there and the defendant has no say in the matter. If, however, the magistrates decide that the case can most appropriately be tried summarily, this is not the end of the matter: the defendant must now be offered the choice between the two venues.[25] Consequently, in these 'triable either way' cases, defendants can always insist on having their guilt or innocence decided by a jury in the Crown Court, while the magistrates can also insist that the case goes to the higher court.

Around 90 per cent of triable either way cases are tried in the magistrates' court, with the remaining 10 per cent being committed to the Crown Court (Auld, 2001: 677). Most of the cases which are committed – 70 per cent according to Auld (2001: 193, 677) – go to the Crown Court as a result of the decision of the magistrates, not at the insistence of defendants. The great majority of defendants – around

95 per cent – who are given a choice of court choose to be tried in the magistrates' court.[26] Those defendants who do opt for Crown Court trial typically do so because they wish to plead not guilty and believe, usually on the advice of their lawyers, that a trial by jury affords them a better chance of acquittal (Hedderman and Moxon, 1992) – a judgment which, it seems, will very often be perfectly correct.[27]

Magistrates' committal decisions appear to be heavily influenced by the recommendations they receive from the CPS. Indeed, studies have found magistrates agreeing with these recommendations 96–98 per cent of the time (Riley and Vennard, 1988; Herbert, 2004: 73).[28] As with bail applications, there is again plenty of evidence of 'justice by geography', in that committal rates are found to vary wildly from place to place, for no apparently good reason. For example, Herbert (2004) – studying just three magistrates' courts – found committal rates for triable either way cases ranging from 18 to 45 per cent. (See also Riley and Vennard, 1988.)

In the 1980s there was a dramatic increase in the number of committals to the Crown Court for trial, rising from 55,300 in 1979 to 113,500 in 1988 (Home Office, 1980. Table 4.5, 1993. Table 8.8), causing the criminal justice system serious administrative and financial problems. In response, four 'either way' offences were reclassified as 'summary only' by the Criminal Justice Act 1988; and the National Mode of Trial Guidelines were introduced in 1990, in the hope that they would not only bring about greater consistency in committal decisions, but also lead to fewer committals. By 1993 the numbers committed to the Crown Court had dropped to 85,800. Nevertheless, in that year the Royal Commission on Criminal Justice (1993: 88) recommended, largely for managerial and economic reasons, that defendants should lose their right to insist on a Crown Court trial in triable either way cases. Thus, if the magistrates' court decided (after hearing representations) that a case should be heard summarily, that decision could not be overridden by the defendant electing to go to the Crown Court. This controversial recommendation to remove rights to jury trial was echoed by both Martin Narey's (1997) review of delay in the criminal justice system and Sir Robin Auld's (2001: 197) review of the criminal courts. The New Labour government, despite having previously opposed the idea, attempted to implement it in two parliamentary Bills in 1999 and 2000.[29] Both Bills were defeated in the House of Lords, and in the face of continuing opposition government plans to introduce a third similar Bill were finally dropped in 2002.

An attempt along different lines to reduce the number of Crown Court cases was the 'plea before venue' system, which came into force on 1 October 1997.[30] Under this system, magistrates cannot commit to Crown Court *for trial* defendants charged with an 'either way' offence who indicate an intention to plead guilty; but they can still subsequently commit them *for sentence*. The immediate effect of the new system was to cut the number of committals to the Crown Court for trial from 87,700 in 1997 to 70,200 in 2000 (Home Office, 2004a: 74). However, at the same time the number of defendants committed to the Crown Court for sentence increased, albeit by a lesser amount, from 7,300 in 1997 to 20,400 in 1999 (Home Office, 2000a: 137).[31] After 2000 the figures went into partial reverse, with committals for trial climbing back to stand at 78,400 in 2004 and committals for sentence falling back to 16,900 (Home Office, 2005e: para. 2.17).

If the aim is to reduce the number of committals, it might be most fruitful to concentrate, not on the decisions of defendants to exercise their right to jury trial, but on the decisions of magistrates. After all, 70 per cent of committals occur because the magistrates, not the defendant, have insisted on a Crown Court trial (Auld, 2001: 193, 677), and the great majority of defendants in these cases would have preferred a summary trial (see Hedderman and Moxon, 1992). Research has also found that most of those committed to the Crown Court by the magistrates' decision end up receiving sentences which the magistrates could themselves have passed (Hedderman and Moxon, 1992; Auld, 2001: 678), which strongly suggests that a great many committals are simply unnecessary.

An important prospective change to the whole system is contained in section 154 of the Criminal Justice Act 2003. If and when this is implemented, it will double the sentencing powers of magistrates, from a maximum of six months' imprisonment for a single offence to a maximum of 12 months – although as we shall see later, implementation (originally planned for the autumn of 2006) has been delayed and thrown into doubt. (Under the Act's general scheme, sentences of imprisonment up to 12 months should in future be new 'custody plus' sentences, explained in section 4.5 below.) In theory, these enhanced sentencing powers should encourage magistrates to keep more cases in their own court, where previously they might have felt their powers were inadequate. In practice, however, this may not work as intended. A recent study of magistrates found that they believed existing committal rates were appropriate and resented being encouraged to make fewer committals. Other court participants doubted whether increased sentencing powers would lead to fewer committals, saying, for example: 'they might increase existing sentences rather than keep additional work', or 'magistrates would give longer sentences, but still wouldn't touch more serious matters' (Herbert, 2003: 322). In other words, the result could be just as many committals, along with longer sentences for many of those *not* committed to the Crown Court – and an overall increase in the prison population, further fuelling the penal crisis.

The 2003 Act did create another opportunity for reducing committals to the Crown Court by magistrates. As we mentioned previously, the National Mode of Trial Guidelines are now to be replaced by National Allocation Guidelines issued by the Sentencing Guidelines Council. It would in principle be possible for the SGC to revise and tighten the guidelines in conjunction with new sentencing guidelines in a manner designed to ensure that more cases not only stay in the magistrates' court but also receive less harsh sentences. At the same time, administrative means could be used to require the CPS to make more appropriate recommendations that are consistent from place to place (but with the aim of levelling committal rates down rather than up). This seems unlikely to happen in the near future, however. The draft guidelines issued by the SGC in February 2006,[32] although stating that 'as many cases as possible should be dealt with in a magistrates' court', then immediately go on to contradict this by saying that: 'where any uncertainty remains in relation to the adequacy of the sentencing powers available it should be resolved in favour of the case being dealt with in the Crown Court' (para. 3.6.1). Excessive and inconsistent committals seem likely to continue, with negative consequences for the prison population and the penal crisis.

The Sentencing Decision

The Crux of the Crisis

4.4 Sentencing is 'the crux of the penal crisis'. It is sentencing decisions that mainly determine the size of the prison numbers crisis and the more general crisis of penal resources, and thereby also determine the size of many other penal problems such as overcrowding and impoverished prison regimes and conditions. They are also a potent source of perceived injustices fuelling the crisis of legitimacy.

Not, of course, that sentencing is the only factor contributing to the crisis. Simply on the issue of the prison population, we saw earlier in this chapter that remand and mode of trial decisions also play their part in determining how many remand (unsentenced) prisoners the system has to deal with. The mechanisms for early release from prison sentences (see Chapter 8; also Hough et al., 2003: 18–19) also affect how many prisoners there are at any one time, as will the number of offenders who are brought before the courts for sentencing in the first place. However, it is historically and statistically true that in England the sentencing practice of the courts (and especially of the Crown Court[33]) has had by far the greatest effect on prison numbers. This is particularly noticeable regarding the last decade or so, when increasingly severe sentencing has been the main cause of the rocketing prison population (Halliday, 2001: 79–81; Carter, 2003: 9–12). It has not been caused by an increase in crime – indeed, crime generally (as recorded by the British Crime Survey) *decreased* by no less than 44 per cent between 1995 and 2005 (Nicholas et al., 2005). Nor can it be attributed to the modest increase in the number of offenders coming before the courts;[34] nor has there been any increase in the seriousness of those offences which have been brought before the courts (Carter, 2003: 10; Hough et al., 2003: 10–11). But the proportion of persons found guilty of an indictable offence who received a custodial sentence rose from 15 per cent in 1991 and 21 per cent in 1996 to 25 per cent in 2001.[35] Moreover, the average *length* of custodial sentences has also risen substantially in the Crown Court, from 20 months in 1993 to 27 in 2003.[36] Overall, offenders who a decade ago might have received a fine are now likely to receive a more onerous community penalty, those who might have received community penalties are now more likely to be imprisoned, and those imprisoned face longer prison terms. (See generally Morgan, 2003; Hough et al., 2003: ch. 2.) The entire relationship between offences and sentences has been *'ratcheted up'* a gear. Responsibility for the massive increase in the prison population in recent years thus rests largely in the hands of sentencers, significantly aided and abetted by 'law and order' rhetoric, policy and legislation emanating from politicians.[37]

There is also evidence which strongly suggests that many English courts may be using custody excessively, because they use it to a greater extent than other courts to whom they may be compared. First, there appear to be marked differences in courts' use of imprisonment and the length of sentences passed between England and Wales and many other comparable countries, even when dealing with similar offences. For example, studies in which judges from different countries were asked to assess the range of sentences which should be imposed in respect of various offences (International Bar Association, 1990; NACRO, 1998) have found that the English response was more punitive than that of most other jurisdictions, and than almost any other European country involved in the studies. And it is this more severe sentencing which seems to account for England's high imprisonment rate compared with other Western European states (as seen in Table 1.2 in Chapter 1).[38]

Second, there is evidence of excessive use of sentences of imprisonment *by the Crown Court* in particular, obtained by comparing its sentencing practice with that of the magistrates' court. Research we mentioned earlier (Hedderman and Moxon, 1992) found in a sample of comparable (triable either way) cases that the Crown Court passed sentences of immediate custody almost three times as often as magistrates' courts, and such sentences were on average two and a half times as long in the Crown Court. Another study – carried out when sentencing was significantly less harsh than it currently is – found that where the Crown Court convicted a defendant of a minor property offence (involving property worth less than £200), as many as two-fifths received unsuspended custody, despite much concern expressed at the time about the need to restrict custody to only the most serious property offenders (Moxon, 1988: 15).

Third, there is also considerable *geographical* variation in sentencing. A succession of research studies over the years (commencing with Hood, 1962) has repeatedly demonstrated wide disparities in the sentencing practice of different magistrates' courts. Figures quoted by the Halliday Report (2001: 90) show that in 1999 one unnamed court sentenced half of its domestic burglars to immediate custody while another did so for only 13 per cent. The percentage of custodial sentences for actual bodily harm ranged from 2 to 53 per cent. An earlier study (Tarling et al., 1985) showed that similar variations could not fully be explained by differences in either the kind of offences with which each court had to deal or the offenders coming before them; in other words the disparities were real. Similar disparities in the sentencing practices of different Crown Courts have also been demonstrated: in 1998 the imprisonment rate for domestic burglars ranged from 56 per cent in the Newport (Isle of Wight) Crown Court to 92 per cent at the Old Bailey and 87 per cent in Carlisle, and average lengths of imprisonment from 12 months in Newport to 31 months in Woolwich (Halliday, 2001: 90–1). These figures suggest that those which make relatively heavy use of imprisonment 'frequently have no reason to do so if the experience of other courts is any criterion' (Hood, 1962: 122).

Such excessive and inconsistent sentencing does not merely fuel the crises of prison numbers and resources; it also diminishes the legitimacy of the penal system, not least for those who are on the receiving end of relatively harsh sentencing. Prisoners who owe their confinement to a sentence more severe than it needed to be, might be excused for experiencing a sense of injustice, especially if they rightly perceive that other similar offenders have been treated more leniently. Inconsistent sentencing violates the basic principle that like cases should be treated alike, and inevitably adds to the penal system's crucial crisis of legitimacy.

Who Are the Sentencers?

Within the English criminal justice system, the power to pass sentence is conferred on two completely different sets of sentencers – magistrates and Crown Court judges – who contrast not only in the powers at their disposal, but also in their social background, composition, mode of selection and training and much else besides. Around 95 per cent of all criminal cases are dealt with in the magistrates' courts. Offenders who are convicted here are normally sentenced by a bench of three 'lay' (unpaid, and largely untrained) magistrates (or 'justices of the peace', or 'JPs'). In the larger conurbations these lay benches are supplemented by full-time professional magistrates known as district judges (magistrates' courts) – formerly known as 'stipendiary magistrates',[39] who sit alone. Although magistrates are officially supposed to be broadly representative of the communities they serve, successive studies and surveys (notably Baldwin, 1976; see also Burney, 1979; Raine, 1989; Dignan and Wynne, 1997) have confirmed that this is far from the case; JPs are still overwhelmingly middle-aged and middle-class; for example, Dignan and Wynne (1997: 4–5) found over 80 per cent of their sample of magistrates to be aged 50 or more, with only 5 per cent being under 40 and just a quarter of male JPs being wage earners. Seven per cent of magistrates are of ethnic minority origin (Home Office, 2005b: 106) compared with around 9 per cent of the general population of England and Wales. However, women – formerly seriously under-represented on the bench – now account for 49 per cent of magistrates (Home Office, 2004b: 48). Magistrates tend to be 'middle-minded' (and significantly more likely to vote Conservative than the general population in their localities: see, for example, Dignan and Wynne, 1997: 8). Moreover, in the course of their training and induction onto the bench, they are imbued with a particular perception of their role (Parker et al., 1989), aspects of which we shall discuss shortly.

Magistrates are given a small amount of training, in which sentencing matters feature fairly prominently, and when sitting in court are assisted in the exercise of their powers by a legally qualified clerk.[40] However, studies (Hood, 1962, 1972; Parker et al., 1989) have shown that the chief formative influence on sentencing practice in magistrates' courts is not the law, their training or the advice they receive from other professionals, nor even the way similar cases have been decided by that particular court in the past. Instead the principal influence is the 'sentencing culture' of a particular bench, into which new recruits are gradually socialized by watching their more experienced colleagues at work. Their perception of their role as magistrates is based on an ideology – a set of shared ideas – embedded in the bench culture. This ideology holds, first, that every individual case is unique. This means that consistency in sentencing is not recognized as a virtue. Instead, each case is seen as requiring a special judgment 'on its individual merits', a judgment that only the magistrate is deemed qualified to make. Because sentencing is viewed by magistrates as a craft or mystery, whose rites are known only to initiates (as opposed to a rational enterprise dedicated to the pursuit of defined goals), this renders it both impervious to criticism from outside, and highly resistant to attempts at external control. Thus, magistrates subscribe to a strong notion of *magisterial independence*, essentially identical to the doctrine of judicial independence which we discuss in the next section.

Defendants in the Crown Court are sentenced by a Crown Court judge.[41] Crown Court judges differ from magistrates in a number of important respects (though it could be said that their ideologies are similar). One important difference between them is that judges are not only legally trained but have invariably spent most of their working lives as practising barristers (or, less often, solicitors). They receive little training for their role *as* judges, in contrast to most West European countries which have a professional career structure for judges who are recruited immediately on graduating from law school. In England, training for Crown Court judges is provided by the Judicial Studies Board, and consists of short induction courses for new recruits and continuation courses for more experienced judges. Although judicial attitudes towards training are becoming less dismissive than they were in the past, it remains the case that the main method of 'perfecting the art' of sentencing is by practising on actual offenders.

The fact that Crown Court judges are recruited almost exclusively from the ranks of successful practising barristers has also had the effect of narrowing considerably the background from which the judges are drawn, even in comparison with the far from representative magistracy. Judges who sit in the Crown Court tend to be slightly older than magistrates on average (around 60 for judges and 56 for lay justices). However, in contrast to magistrates, Crown Court judges are predominantly male: in 2002, only 12 per cent were women (Home Office, 2004c: 48). They are also more unrepresentative than magistrates in terms of race: in 2003, only 4 per cent of Crown Court judges were from ethnic minorities (Home Office, 2005b: 106).

As for the social composition of the judiciary, the many surveys that have been carried out in recent years show an overwhelming predominance of upper-class and upper-middle-class backgrounds among judges (see, for example, Griffith, 1997: 18; House of Commons Home Affairs Committee, 1995). Not only did around 80 per cent of the country's judges receive a public school education, with over three-quarters attending either Oxford or Cambridge universities, but this social profile has remained virtually unaltered over the last half century. Thus, there exists an enormous social gulf between those who pass sentence in the Crown Court and those on the receiving end. Even more importantly, this social profile helps to explain the uniqueness of English judicial culture compared with that elsewhere.[42] This judicial culture is founded on an ideology whose cornerstone is *the doctrine of judicial independence*, to which we now turn.

The Doctrine of Judicial Independence

The doctrine of judicial independence is not controversial in itself. It is generally accepted that the judiciary should be separate and independent from the legislature (Parliament) and the executive (the government of the day): this is part of the basic constitutional concept of the 'separation of powers'. Judicial independence is usually interpreted – in most countries and by most people – to mean, simply and uncontroversially, that governments must not be allowed to influence the decisions of the courts *in individual cases*[43] However, in England this principle has been curiously distorted and inflated by the judiciary into an 'extravagant version' of the doctrine: the claim that the sentencing discretion of judges should be left untouched, and that it is improper for government or Parliament even to lay down broad sentencing policies (Ashworth, 2000: 46–8; Ashworth, 2005: 50–4). This claim – which of course has the effect, attractive to judges, of maximizing their powers to sentence in any way they want – clearly has no basis in constitutional law and theory, not least because Parliament is entitled to legislate on sentencing as well as on anything else. Nevertheless, for a long time governments in practice accepted the extravagant version, largely doubtless for fear of provoking a confrontation with the judges. On the rare occasions that government and Parliament threatened to infringe the doctrine, the judiciary would typically protest loudly and end up getting its own way.

'Judicial independence' became a potent myth, which had the effect of perpetuating the largely untrammelled sentencing powers enjoyed by the courts in England, meaning that for many years sentencing was left not only out of control but in a policy vacuum. More recently, since the enactment of the Criminal Justice Act 1991, governments and judges have both moved in the direction of accepting the legitimacy of legislative intervention and governmental strategy in sentencing, but the extravagant version of the doctrine continues to cast a shadow.

We now need to consider what limits and constraints do exist on the discretion of sentencers in England and Wales.

Constraints on the Powers of Sentencers

In deciding what sentence to impose, sentencers – judges and magistrates – may take a variety of considerations into account. They include facts relating to the offence (including any aggravating or mitigating circumstances), facts relating to the offender, and the aims or purposes that the sentencer might hope to achieve in choosing a sentence. All sentencing decisions take place within a framework of legal rules, guidelines and other constraints, which we shall detail in due course. However, this framework leaves sentencers with a very broad discretion as to how, and how far, they allow themselves to be influenced by any of the factors just mentioned, and consequently with wide scope for different sentencing outcomes. As we saw above, it is these outcomes – the sentences actually passed – which very largely dictate the size of the prison population and the scale of the penal crisis.

The exercise of discretion, such as that enjoyed by judges and magistrates when deciding on sentences, can be controlled in three basic ways (Davis, 1969). Discretion can be *confined* by setting fixed limits on the decisions that can be made; it can be *checked* by allowing appeals and reviews after the decisions have been made; or it can be *structured* (or guided) by means of more flexible devices such as guidelines and codes of practice. Another useful preliminary distinction is that between *external control* over sentencing discretion on the one hand, and on the other *self–regulation* practised by sentencers themselves. For, as we shall see, one important effect of the extravagant conception of judicial independence over the years has been the extent to which sentencers have been left to police themselves according to their own lights and their own rules.

One manifestation of this has been that sentencers have not only generally been left free (within certain defined limits) to decide which specific sentence to choose out of the wide range available for any individual offender; they have also been free to decide for themselves *what their sentencing is supposed to be trying to achieve.* We saw in Chapter 2 that punishment can be seen as having a wide variety of aims and purported justifications, not all of them obviously consistent with each other, including retribution, deterrence, reform, incapacitation, denunciation and reparation. Traditionally, the sentencer has been free to decide for him or herself which of these aims is to be pursued in each individual case.[44] This eclectic tradition lives on in section 142 of the Criminal Justice Act 2003, which sets out the purposes of sentencing as being: '(a) the punishment of offenders [i.e. retribution and denunciation]; (b) the reduction of crime (including its reduction by deterrence); (c) the reform and rehabilitation of offenders; (d) the protection of the public [incapacitation]; and (e) the making of reparation by offenders to persons affected by their offences'. Although the section states that sentencers must 'have regard' to all these purposes, the effect is to allow sentencers to pick and choose their penal aims and philosophies as much as ever.

Confining Discretion

Compared with some other jurisdictions, relatively little attempt has been made in England and Wales to confine the exercise of sentencers' discretion by limiting the extent of their powers. Magistrates, it is true, only have limited powers: they cannot impose a custodial sentence that is longer than six months (although this may in future be increased to one year)[45] in respect of a single offence. Nor can they normally impose a fine of more than £5,000. Nevertheless, they enjoy a considerable degree of discretion within these upper limits. Crown Court judges have much more extensive powers. Each particular offence carries a statutory *maximum* penalty, but many of these maxima were set so long ago, and in such different circumstances, as to render them largely irrelevant for the control of judicial sentencing today. Moreover the tendency during the twentieth and twenty-first centuries has been to create broadly defined criminal offences (such as theft), with a sufficiently generous maximum to cater for the worst contingency.

There are still relatively few *mandatory* or *minimum* sentences. For a long time the only major exception was the mandatory life imprisonment sentence for murder. Even this is unpopular with the judiciary as an infringement on their discretion to do justice in individual cases, and there have been repeated calls for its abolition (for example, Nathan et al., 1989; Lane, 1993; Blom–Cooper and Morris, 2004). (As we shall see more fully in Chapter 8, the nature of this mandatory life sentence has changed over time and the sentencing judge now has much more say over how long a convicted murderer remains in prison.) There is also a 'semi-mandatory' sentence of disqualification from driving for the offence of driving with excess alcohol in the blood; 'semi-mandatory' meaning that the sentence is required unless the court finds that there are exceptional circumstances in the individual case. A number of new semi-mandatory and minimum sentences were introduced by the Crime (Sentences) Act 1997 and the Criminal Justice Act 2003, as we shall see below, some of them based on American[46] 'three strikes and you're out' sentences. But apart from these limited inroads, little attempt has been made to confine the discretion of sentencers by statute.[47]

Checking Discretion: Appeals

People who are convicted and sentenced by the courts can appeal against their convictions, against their sentences, or both. Those tried at the magistrates' court normally appeal to the Crown Court; those tried in the Crown Court may take their case to the Court of Appeal. Since 1988 it also possible for the prosecution (in the form of the Attorney General[48]) to appeal to the Court of Appeal against the passing of a Crown Court sentence which is alleged to be unduly lenient, although this procedure is only available for a limited number of relatively serious offences and only happens in a few score cases each year.

Although there is no such thing as a 'correct' sentence (except where mandatory penalties apply), there exists a fairly vague and impressionistic notional scale of penalties familiarly known as the *'tariff'*, which is based on the normal range of sentences that have been passed by courts on similar offenders in the past. This 'normal range' is in turn based largely on the notion that the severity of a sentence should be proportionate to the seriousness of the offence – in other words, that offenders should receive their 'just deserts' (see Chapter 2). Sentences can also be varied to reflect any aggravating and mitigating circumstances relating either to the offence or to the offender as a person. In particular, a sentence will typically be more severe if the offender has previous convictions: the worse the offender's record, the more severe the sentence.[49] If a court imposes a sentence that clearly exceeds the normal tariff, it may be reduced on appeal. However, appeal courts will often be slow to interfere with a lower court's decision unless either it is clearly well out of line or new information is available on appeal. Again, sentencers have a legal duty to give reasons (albeit only 'in general terms', and 'in ordinary language') for the sentences they pass (Criminal Justice Act 2003, s. 174), and in theory a sentence could be quashed if the reasons given are inadequate; but it seems unlikely in practice that this would ever occur. And of course, all of this depends on the offender (or Attorney General) taking the case to appeal in the first place. Consequently the retrospective checking of sentencing decisions via the appeal process provides only a limited amount of control over sentencers' discretion.

Another difficulty with the tariff is the fact that there are probably at least as many different tariffs in practice as there are levels of court (Court of Appeal, Crown Court and magistrates' court).[50] As we noted earlier, when sentences for similar cases tried in the Crown Court and the magistrates' court are compared, it has been found that those sentenced in the Crown Court are almost three times as likely to receive a custodial sentence, and that the Crown Court's custodial sentences are on average two and a half times as long (Hedderman and Moxon, 1992).[51] Similarly, the sentences imposed by the Court of Appeal seem likely to be in general more severe than those typically passed by the Crown Court. For the Court of Appeal normally hears appeals by defendants against Crown Court sentences they consider too severe, and hence usually only comes to hear about relatively harsh Crown Court sentences (and never about sentences passed in the magistrates' court) shaping and distorting its perceptions about what the 'going rate' actually is in practice.

One illustration of this was the 1980 case of *R. v. McCann*,[52] in which the Court of Appeal reduced the sentence for a relatively minor burglary by an offender who had only one distant previous conviction, from two years' imprisonment to nine months. Even this reduced sentence considerably exceeded the maximum penalty that could have been imposed in a magistrates' court (which is where the majority of burglars of this type would normally have been tried). And indeed in the magistrates' court in 1980, less than a one-third of such cases would have received a custodial penalty at all (Home Office, 1981a). Thus, it seems highly likely that a sentence which is genuinely much more severe than the general 'going rate' in the Crown Court (let alone the magistrates' court) may easily be wrongly perceived by the Court of Appeal as quite normal, and will be confirmed.

Structuring and Guiding Discretion

Sentencers' exercise of their discretion can be guided in various ways. One that we will mention here is the provision of information and advice to judges and magistrates by means of *reports* which may be supplied to the court. One such is the statement known as 'the antecedents' provided by the prosecution and containing brief details of the offender's previous convictions, sentences and cautions. In the case of offenders who appear to be mentally disordered, the court may receive a medical report from a psychiatrist. In some cases there may be 'victim personal statements', whereby victims of the crime can explain the effect it has had on them.[53]

One particularly important source of information and guidance consists of the *pre-sentence report* (or PSR, formerly known as the social inquiry report), which is prepared for the court by probation officers, or in the case of young offenders by members of the local youth offending team (see Chapter 9). As well as providing factual information about offenders and their backgrounds and histories, PSRs can make proposals as to what the sentence should be. In some cases a shortened form of PSR, known as a 'specific sentence report', can be used by courts when contemplating the imposition of a reparation or action plan order on a young offender (see Chapter 9). Sentencers are normally required to consider a PSR before imposing either a custodial sentence or one of the more restrictive 'community sentences' (see Chapter 5). However, there is a wide 'get-out clause': for adult offenders: sentencers may dispense with a PSR 'if, in the circumstances of the case, the court is of the opinion that it is unnecessary to obtain a pre-sentence report'.[54] It has been found that around 15 per cent of adult offenders are given custodial sentences without the benefit of a PSR, but community sentences are rarely imposed in the absence of such a report (Charles et al., 1997). The proposals for sentences contained in PSRs have become more severe over recent years: between 1990 and 2000 explicit proposals for custody doubled from 2–3 per cent to 5–6 per cent, while proposals for fines and discharges halved. Thus probation officers – who have faced long-standing pressure to make more 'realistic' proposals – have responded accordingly, thereby playing their own part in the 'ratcheting up' of sentencing (Morgan, 2003: 15).

Apart from the kind of guidance which can be obtained from such reports, there are various methods of *structuring* sentencing discretion. One is the setting out of relatively broad rules and principles (in statute and elsewhere) about the aims to be pursued in sentencing and criteria that must be considered before imposing particular penalties (such as imprisonment) and deciding how severe the penalty should be. Such principles and criteria may be expressed in Acts of Parliament or in the pronouncements of judges, or both, and can take a variety of forms. For example, there is a general principle which has found expression in differing ways in various statutory provisions,[55] but is also a principle which sentencers regularly claim to be following as a matter of custom and conscience:[56] the *principle of last resort,* the idea that imprisonment should only be used if no lesser sentence can be considered appropriate. A related principle is one we mentioned in Chapter 2 in connection with Jeremy Bentham's utilitarianism: the principle of *parsimony,* that punishment (especially custodial punishment) should be used as sparingly as possible. Another general principle[57] is that of *proportionality* or *just deserts*, the idea that the severity of the punishment should be in proportion to the seriousness of the offence. Yet another principle is one that competes and conflicts with proportionality: the *principle of progression*[58] (see, for example, Straw, 1996; or the 'principle of persistence'), according to which offenders should be punished more severely the more they reoffend.

It is principles such as these which underlie the notion of the sentencing 'tariff', briefly explained previously, and which does guide sentencing to a degree but (as we have seen) only a limited degree, due to its inherent vagueness and other factors. One perennially controversial issue, arguably still unresolved, is to what extent sentences, and the tariff, should reflect the offender's past criminality. Should the tariff be – as the principle of proportionality and the theory of 'just deserts' would suggest, and as we would prefer[59] – primarily *'offence-based'*, with sentences in proportion to the current offences? Or should it follow the principle of progression and be more *'offender-based'*, so that – for example – petty persistent offenders can be imprisoned even though their latest offence taken in isolation would not warrant this? We return to this question in section 4.5 of this chapter.

Another method of structuring sentencing discretion, which has been gaining in favour in a number of countries in recent decades, consists of published *guidelines* for courts to follow when sentencing. What guidelines do is to prescribe in advance, with varying degrees of precision, the appropriate penalty for a whole range of combinations of offence and offender. They can take various forms.[60] By providing sentencers with one set of criteria relating to the circumstances of the offence in question, and a different range of criteria taking into account relevant characteristics of the offender, guidelines can operate rather like a road mileage chart, enabling the appropriate penalty to be simply 'read off' from a grid or matrix. Or they can be less mechanical than this, simply providing a range of standard sentences for different kinds of typical offence, along with guidance on roughly how much to adjust the standard sentence in the light of common aggravating and mitigating circumstances. This is the form that sentencing guidelines have taken in England. In either case, guidelines normally only provide a 'presumptive sentence' or starting point, from which the sentencer is free to depart if this is thought appropriate in an individual case, provided reasons are given for doing so.

Guidelines potentially allow a tighter and more consistent control of sentencing than could ever be achieved just by retrospectively checking individual sentencing decisions on appeal. In theory they could help attain greater consistency in sentencing, helping to avoid unjust and delegitimizing disparities, and could also be designed to pursue other aims such as a reduction in the general level of sentencing (and hence in the prison population). Moreover, sentencers seem to respond better and more willingly to the structuring of their discretion by guidelines than to having it confined by maximum, minimum and mandatory sentences. They resent the latter, which constrain their power to do justice as they see it in individual cases. But sentencers often welcome external guidance as to how they should make their (often difficult, sometimes agonizing) sentencing decisions, whether this comes from official guidelines or the informal sentencing culture of the bench or advice from more experienced colleagues.

In England, sentencing guidelines originally began to develop as an extension of the checking function of the Court of Appeal, which (once its sentencing decisions came to be regularly reported) occasionally took the opportunity when hearing appeals in individual cases to lay down general principles for lower courts to apply in similar cases in the future. From the mid-1970s onwards, the Court of Appeal increasingly sought to provide more systematic guidance for sentencers by laying down 'guideline judgments'. These go beyond the immediate issues raised by a particular case and spell out, for example, the range of penalties felt to be appropriate for varying degrees of seriousness within a given offence category. Thus, for instance, in *R. v. Billam*[61] the Court laid down a series of 'starting points' for sentences for rape, ranging from five years' imprisonment for 'rape committed by an adult without any aggravating or mitigating features' to life imprisonment for cases where the offender is likely to remain a danger for an indefinite time. In the early 1980s the Court of Appeal also sought to formulate more general guidance by attempting to 'talk down' the level of custodial sentencing for relatively minor offences.[62]

This 'self-regulation' of the judiciary by the Court of Appeal had a number of serious limitations as a control on sentencing practice. First, the tariff laid down by these guideline judgments is inherently vague. The guidelines do not provide a cut-and-dried list of appropriate penalties, merely a rough guide to the general sentencing levels that the Court of Appeal feels is appropriate. Moreover, if a sentencing judge in the Crown Court passes a sentence that seems to breach the guidelines, the Court of Appeal will still allow the judge considerable latitude before interfering with the sentence. Nor has the Court of Appeal been entirely consistent in its own pronouncements: for example, there were conflicting declarations[63] on the fundamental issue of whether sentencing should be primarily based on the seriousness of the current offence (an 'offence-based tariff'), or whether courts could rightfully pay principal heed to the offender's previous record (an 'offender-based tariff') and thus give petty persistent offenders punishments quite out of proportion to the offences for which they are being sentenced. Another problem related to the likelihood, discussed previously, of the Court of Appeal being out of touch with the tariffs normally applied in the lower courts when it laid down its guidelines. The likely effect of this would be guidelines more severe than previous lower court practice, which if followed would serve to ratchet up general sentencing levels (see Hough et al., 2003: 25).

A further limitation of Court of Appeal guidelines as a method of control of general sentencing practice was its failure for a long time to provide any real guidance at all in respect of many common offences such as theft and burglary.[64] Nor was the Court of Appeal even in a position to issue guidelines covering summary offences, which never come before the Court of Appeal in any event.[65] However, these gaps were to some extent filled when in 1989 the Magistrates' Association began issuing its own sentencing guidelines for use in magistrates' courts. [66]

The Court of Appeal's role in issuing guidelines was – albeit briefly and temporarily – extended and made more proactive by the New Labour government's Crime and Disorder Act 1998. Section 80 of this Act gave the Court a duty, whenever hearing an appeal against sentence, to consider whether it should take the opportunity to issue a new sentencing guideline. Section 81 of the Act established a new body, the Sentencing Advisory Panel (SAP), chaired by law professor Martin Wasik,[67] with responsibility for advising and assisting the Court of Appeal on the issuing of sentencing guidelines. The Court at this time again made some attempts to encourage restraint in the use of custody for relatively minor non-violent offences, but with little noticeable impact on sentencing levels.

The Criminal Justice Act 2003 (ss. 167–73) took the history of sentencing guidelines a stage further, by removing the task of framing and issuing guidelines away from the Court of Appeal and bestowing it on a new body, the Sentencing Guidelines Council (SGC).[68] In theory at least, this represents a substantial step away from the self-regulation of the judiciary in matters of sentencing and the imposition of external control by a government-appointed quango. However, the SGC (which came into existence in March 2004) is chaired by the Lord Chief Justice (the senior judge who presides over the Court of Appeal), and contains seven other judicial members (appointed by the Lord Chancellor) plus four non-judges (appointed by the Secretary of State).[69] The SAP remains in being to advise the SGC. Either the SAP or the Justice Secretary may take the initiative and propose that the SGC should frame or revise guidelines for particular categories of offence. When a topic is being considered for a guideline, the SGC commissions the SAP to advise it. The SAP then consults widely and submits its advice to the SGC; this advice will include information concerning the current level of sentencing for such offences and about how expensive or effective the available sentences are. The SGC then produces a draft guideline, which may be considered by the Justice Secretary, Parliament and anyone else the SGC sees fit to consult. Finally, the SGC issues a definitive guideline. When framing these, the SGC is required to have regard to the need to promote consistency in sentencing; to the sentences currently imposed for offences in this category; to the cost of different sentences and their relative effects in preventing reoffending; and to the need to promote public confidence in the criminal justice system (Criminal Justice Act 2003, s. 170(5)). Under sections 172 and 174 of the Act, any court passing a sentence covered by a guideline must have regard to it, and the court must give reasons if it departs from the normal range of sentences which the guideline indicates. The first sets of final guidelines were issued by the SGC in December 2004. The intention is eventually to create comprehensive sentencing guidelines covering all offences (and both the Crown Court and magistrates' court) (Home Office, 2002a: 89). We shall return to the SGC towards the end of this chapter.

The Criminal Justice Act 2003 also introduced a new set of *statutory* guidelines – contained in the Act itself (Schedule 21) – to cover one specialized area of sentencing, namely the setting of the 'tariff' element of the sentence for those convicted of murder (i.e. the minimum period of the mandatory life sentence that must be served before the murderer can be released on parole). These will be discussed and explained in greater detail in Chapter 8.

A Brief, Tangled Recent History Of Sentencing

1991: From the Strategy of Encouragement to a New Sentencing Framework

4.5 For many years following the Second World War, successive governments deferred to the judiciary and allowed them the 'judicial independence' in sentencing that they desired. This virtual abdication of government responsibility for developing a coherent sentencing policy left the courts with wide discretion which was only marginally constrained by guidance from the Court of Appeal. Very few attempts were made by governments during this time to fill the policy-making vacuum, and even these were met by implacable and almost invariably successful opposition from the judiciary.[70] The main response of successive governments to the growing prison numbers crisis from the 1960s to the 1980s was what we call *'the strategy of encouragement'*. Parliament provided a wider range of non-custodial penalties, such as community service and suspended sentences (see Chapter 5) and then, out of deference to the principle of judicial independence, the government relied on exhortation[71] rather than legislative control in an attempt to encourage the courts to use these 'alternatives to imprisonment'. In the early 1980s Home Office ministers and the Lord Chief Justice worked together to press the case for restraint in the use of custody, but with only very temporary and limited effect.[72] The prison population continued to rise in the 1980s, and record prison numbers helped to persuade the Conservative government of the day that something more than encouragement was needed.

The government's approach changed around 1987 when Douglas Hurd was Home Secretary.[73] The government began to discuss punishment, and especially imprisonment, in a strikingly different way. A Green Paper[74] published in 1988 (Home Office, 1988a: para. 1.8) stated bluntly that 'imprisonment is not the most effective punishment for most crime. Custody should be reserved for very serious offences, especially when the offender is violent and a continuing risk to the public'. A 1990 White Paper famously stated that imprisonment 'can be an expensive way of making bad people worse' (Home Office, 1990a: para. 2.7). The attitude towards judicial independence was also much changed. The White Paper stated: 'The independence of the judiciary is rightly regarded as a cornerstone of our liberties. But sentencing principles and sentencing practice are matters of legitimate concern to Government' (Home Office, 1990a: para. 2.1). The government was now prepared to risk the wrath of the judges by setting out a framework for sentencing which would give much clearer guidance and instruction to sentencers than at any time in the past. The keystone of the government's strategy was the Criminal Justice Act of 1991, whose principal features were as follows.

Just deserts   The 1991 Act sought to rationalize sentencing as an enterprise with coherent purposes, of which the primary purpose was *'just deserts'*. Whereas previously courts had been left free to decide not only upon the sentence for the individual case but also what sentencing aims and philosophies to pursue, the White Paper stated: 'Punishment in proportion to the seriousness of the crime has long been accepted as *one of many* objectives in sentencing. It should be the *principal* focus for sentencing decisions' (Home Office, 1990a: para. 2.2; our italics).

In line with this approach, the Act instituted *a three-tier sentencing framework,* which sought to structure the sentencing discretion of the courts in line with the principles of proportionality and last resort. Offenders should receive custodial sentences only if the current offence was 'so serious that only such a sentence can be justified for the offence' (s. 1(2)(a)). Below this 'custody threshold' determined by offence seriousness, an offender could qualify for a second tier of sentences – the more onerous 'community sentences', including probation, community service orders and curfew orders – if the current offence was 'serious enough to warrant such a sentence' (s. 6(1)). Below this second threshold of seriousness, offenders could receive lesser (third tier) penalties such as fines (which would now be 'unit fines', tied more closely to the offender's own means), compensation orders and conditional discharges.

The Act also laid down that the lengths of custodial sentences and the restrictions on liberty represented by community sentences should in general be 'commensurate with the seriousness of the offence'.[75] Sentencing aims other than 'just deserts' were still allowed a place, however: for example, in the case of violent and sexual offences, the Act allowed prison sentences to be longer than the period commensurate with the offence if the court deemed this necessary to protect the public by 'incapacitating' the offender from committing further crimes.[76] In general, however, 'just deserts' was to be the guiding principle. Furthermore, it was made clear that the sentencing tariff should be primarily 'offence-based' rather than 'offender-based'. Section 29(1) of the Act laid down that offences should not be regarded as more serious 'by reason of any previous convictions of the offender'. Although this section did not in fact prevent more persistent offenders from receiving heavier sentences than first-timers,[77] it was to prove one of the Act's most controversial (and short-lived) provisions.

Punishment in the community   The intention behind the Act was to engineer a shift in sentencing patterns so that more offenders than previously could be dealt with in the community. Part of the strategy was the creation of yet more new alternatives to imprisonment in the form of combination and curfew orders (see Chapter 5). Importantly, although the objective of reforming offenders by means of non-custodial disposals such as probation was far from abandoned, the emphasis was to be on *punishment* in the community along 'just deserts' lines, of a severity in proportion to the seriousness of the offence. Penalties such as community service were 'toughened up' by national guidance and took on a more punitive aura. The idea was that community sentences should no longer be seen as 'soft options' or 'let-offs', so that courts would be encouraged to use them in place of shorter prison sentences.

Bifurcation   The Act continued the existing trend of 'bifurcation' (or 'twin-track policy'), whereby lesser offenders could receive more lenient punishments than hitherto (in the community – albeit in the form of 'toughened-up' measures – rather than in custody), while on the other hand it was intended that more serious violent and sexual offenders would receive more severe sentences than previously (Home Office, 1990a: para. 2.15).[78]

Partnership between the legislature and the judiciary   The statutory framework for sentencing contained in the 1991 Act was not one that tightly constricted the judiciary. The Act's strategy was to provide statutory *structuring* of the courts' sentencing discretion by laying down the principle of commensuracy and the seriousness thresholds for custody and community sentences in the most general terms only, providing only minimal encroachment on the courts' 'judicial independence'. It was left up to the courts to decide how these principles should be interpreted and applied in individual cases, and to the Court of Appeal to develop more detailed guidance.

****

The weakness of the controls which the 1991 Act exerted over sentencers (compounded by some opaque drafting) meant that in many ways it failed to work as intended. For example, the Court of Appeal proved reluctant to take the lead envisaged for it in developing clear guidance for the lower courts, especially in relation to the 'custody threshold'. Despite the Act's clear intention that imprisonment should only be used as a last resort in cases of genuine seriousness, the Court of Appeal in many cases upheld custodial sentences for relatively minor thefts.[79] Nevertheless, the Act (implemented in October 1992) did at least initially achieve some of its aims (Cavadino et al., 1999: 68–9), most notably in bringing about an immediate reduction in custodial sentences for minor offenders and a consequential fall in the prison population from around 47,000 earlier in the year to 40,600 in December 1992. But it was not to last.

1992–1997: the Law and Order Counter-Reformation

The 1991 reform strategy all began to unravel in spectacular fashion from late 1992 onwards in what has been described (Ashworth and Gibson, 1994: 101) as 'one of the most remarkable *voltes face* in the history of penal policy in England and Wales'. We discuss this dramatic U-turn further in Chapter 11, but we note here that one factor (though probably a relatively minor one) was a public and judicial backlash against some aspects of the 1991 Criminal Justice Act, particularly section 29 (discussed earlier) and the unit fine system (see Chapter 5).

The response from John Major's Conservative government was 'the law and order counter-reformation': a conscious policy decision to 'play the law and order card' for all it was worth. Hastily prepared amendments were added to the Criminal Justice Act 1993 to reverse some of the effects of the 1991 Act. One of these was the total abolition of the new unit fine system (see Chapter 5). Another was a rewriting of section 29. As we have seen, this originally stated that offences were not to be regarded as more serious by reason of the offender's previous convictions; the new section gave sentencers a free hand 'to take into account any previous convictions of the offender or any failure of his to respond to previous sentences' – in effect allowing open season on petty persistent offenders. Even more important than these legislative amendments, however, were the drastic changes in political rhetoric which accompanied them, the most notable instance being Home Secretary Michael Howard's speech to the 1993 Conservative Party Conference. In this speech, Mr Howard declared that *'prison works'* and that he would not flinch from policies which increased the prison population. Law and order ideology and Strategy A policies predominated. The government now stridently renounced the principles underlying the 1991 reforms, such as using custody only as a last resort and the preference for punishment in the community for minor offenders. The result of this 'counter-reformation' was a marked increase in both the proportionate use of custody and also the average length of prison sentences (as we saw in section 4.4 of this chapter).

The 'law and order counter-reformation' reached its climax in the Crime (Sentences) Act 1997, which introduced three new (semi-)mandatory and minimum sentences, based on the American 'three strikes and you're out' model.[80] The 1997 Act required the imposition of a life sentence when an offender was convicted of a second serious violent or sexual offence ('two strikes and you're out'), unless there were exceptional circumstances.[81] It also required a minimum sentence of at least seven years' imprisonment for an offender convicted of a Class A drug trafficking offence for the third time ('three strikes and you're out'), unless the court considered this to be 'unjust in all the circumstances'.[82] And courts were similarly required to impose a minimum sentence of at least three years on an offender who is convicted for a third offence of domestic burglary.[83] Although this Act was enacted by the outgoing Conservative administration, the Labour Party had been broadly supportive of the proposals while in opposition, and all three provisions were ultimately implemented by the New Labour government which took office in 1997 (although they subsequently repealed the 'two-strike' law when introducing their new sentencing framework in the Criminal Justice Act 2003).

Conservative and Labour support for these 'two-strike' and 'three-strike' penalties was not shared by the judiciary, who resented the intrusion on their sentencing discretion and felt that this would lead to injustice in many individual cases while proving ineffective as deterrents. (A reasonable view, since successive research studies in the United States have found that 'three-strike' sentences do nothing to lower crime rates: see, for example, Kovandzic et al., 2004). In 2000, the Court of Appeal succeeded in reinterpreting the meaning of 'exceptional circumstances' in the 'two-strike' penalty for serious offences, so that life sentences in such cases became in effect significantly less mandatory.[84] The 'three-strike' sentences have proved equally unpopular with sentencers, who in these cases already had the benefit of a wider 'get-out clause' in the original legislation, being empowered to pass a lighter sentence if the one prescribed seems 'unjust'. As a result, between 2000 and 2003 there were only 21 'three–strikes' sentences passed on domestic burglars, and only six persistent drug dealers received the 'mandatory' seven-year sentence (RDS NOMS, 2005a: Table 2.7). We saw previously how governments have failed to bend sentencers to their will when seeking to reduce sentencing levels. This episode shows that, although government rhetoric can successfully exhort the judiciary to sentence more harshly in general terms, they can also be resistant to legislation that removes their discretion to be *less* harsh than the government desires in cases where the merits of the individual case seem to them to warrant it.

New Labour, Mixed Messages

When New Labour came to power in 1997, its penal policy slogan was 'tough on crime and tough on the causes of crime'. The overall strategy has always been a more pragmatic and managerial one than was pursued when Michael Howard was the Conservative Home Secretary – more Strategy B, less Strategy A. However, New Labour has always been concerned not to appear 'soft' on law and order issues, and prominent players including Tony Blair and Home Secretaries Jack Straw (1997–2001), David Blunkett (2001–04) and John Reid (2006–07) have in any event often appeared to be more than sympathetic to populist calls for tougher sentencing. This Strategy A streak has led to ongoing tension between the government's much-vaunted 'toughness' and its desire to keep the prison population and the penal crisis within manageable proportions. In the realm of sentencing, as elsewhere, the message coming across from the government has been mixed, with its (higher volume) calls for toughness tending to drown out its more considered appeals for restraint. This was perhaps most noticeable when the Home Secretary was David Blunkett, who repeatedly berated judges for allegedly being 'out of touch' with ordinary people's desire for firm punishment (see, for example, *Guardian*, 15 May 2003), but who also joined with the Lord Chancellor and Lord Chief Justice to urge that prison should only be used as a last resort for minor non-violent crime.[85] Not surprisingly, perhaps, sentencing and prison population figures seemed to demonstrate that the former message was having a greater impact (Travis, 2003).

For certain types of offender, the New Labour government's message clearly was that there should be greater toughness. One of these was people who are responsible for low-level anti-social and disorderly behaviour, for whom the 'anti-social behaviour order' (or ASBO, discussed at greater length in Chapter 9) was introduced. Another category singled out for tougher measures was murderers and others regarded as dangerous. A third was the petty persistent offender. As we have seen, the previous Conservative government had rewritten section 29 of the Criminal Justice Act 1991 to encourage greater notice to be taken of offenders' past records. New Labour took this further, unambiguously rejecting the 'just deserts' approach (and its associated 'offence-based tariff') and insisting that prison is an appropriate punishment not only for serious offenders but also for those who persist in repeated petty crime. As well as this concern for 'progression' in sentencing, New Labour has also long expressed a desire for more *consistent* sentencing (see, for example, Straw, 1996), a desire which led to the (temporary) enhancement of the Court of Appeal's role in issuing guidelines and the creation of the Sentencing Advisory Panel by the Crime and Disorder Act 1998 and ultimately to the establishment of the Sentencing Guidelines Council by the Criminal Justice Act 2003 (see above, section 4.4).

In May 2000, Home Secretary Jack Straw commissioned a general review of the sentencing framework under the direction of Sir John Halliday, a senior civil servant. The terms of this commission made it clear that the government wanted a more 'progressive' sentencing system whereby repeat offenders would incur more severe penalties, and the Halliday Report (2001) did not disappoint the government on this score. With some modifications, the Halliday proposals found their way into the Criminal Justice Act 2003, which we shall now explain in some detail.

The Criminal Justice Act 2003: Another New Framework

The Criminal Justice Act 2003 represents yet another new legislative framework for sentencing, replacing the Criminal Justice Act 1991 (which had remained mostly in force despite the 'law and order counter-reformation' of 1992–3). The 2003 Act contains a wide range of measures relating to sentencing, including provisions to control sentencing by confining and structuring it in a variety of ways. Most of these provisions came into force in 2005.

Section 142 sets out the approved *purposes of sentencing*[86] as punishment (meaning presumably retribution and denunciation), the reduction of crime (via deterrence and reform of the offender), the protection of the public ('incapacitation'), and reparation. Echoing the Criminal Justice Act 1991, section 152(2) lays down a *'seriousness threshold'* for the use of custody: courts should not pass custodial sentences unless the current offences are 'so serious that neither a fine alone nor a community sentence can be justified for the offence'.[87] At first sight this might seem to reinstate the offence-based tariff of 1991. However, section 143(2) ensures that 'seriousness of the current offence' has a radically different meaning in this statute, as it states that courts should treat previous convictions as an aggravating factor increasing the 'seriousness' of the offence – thus instituting a tariff in which the offender's past record looms large, and giving courts a free hand (subject to guidelines, to be discussed shortly) to send petty offenders to prison provided they are sufficiently persistent.[88] Similarly, the length of a custodial sentence should be 'the shortest term ... commensurate with the seriousness of the offence' (s. 153(2)) – but with 'seriousness' again reckoned with regard to the offender's past record. A far cry from the 'just deserts' orientation of the 1991 Act, but a set of provisions which attempt to combine aspects of the principles of last resort, parsimony, proportionality and progression.

Another departure from the principles of just deserts took the form of specially severe sentences intended to protect the public from *violent or sexual offenders*. Sections 227–8 provided for 'extended sentences' in which a 'normal' prison sentence is augmented by an extra-long period of supervision in the community which the court *must* impose if it considers this necessary to protect the public from serious harm. [89] More drastically, section 225 also introduced a new indeterminate sentence of *'imprisonment for public protection'*. Like the sentence of life imprisonment (which continues to exist, and which is discussed in greater detail in Chapter 8), this is a fully indeterminate sentence, which can lead to offenders remaining in prison for the rest of their lives. It is available even for offences whose maximum penalty is less than life imprisonment, and whose seriousness does not justify indeterminate detention. Yet courts are *required* by the Act to impose this sentence on any offender over the age of 18 who is convicted of one of a number of specified serious offences if the court is of the opinion that there is 'a significant risk to members of the public of serious harm' from the offender committing further crimes. It is a *mandatory* sentence for such offenders, without even the usual 'get-out clause' for cases involving 'exceptional circumstances'. Between April 2005 (when this provision came into force) and July 2006, 1,120 of these new unlimited sentences were imposed by the courts (Home Office, 2006c: para. 2.20). (We shall be discussing sentences that are designed to protect the public from offenders deemed to be dangerous in Chapter 8, section 8.5.)

Another (semi-)mandatory provision is section 287, introduced in response to concern about rising levels of gun crime, which requires a minimum sentence of five years' imprisonment for various offences involving the unlawful possession of firearms. Although this section allows for a lighter sentence in cases of 'exceptional circumstances', reported cases so far do not show the courts stretching points to avoid the mandatory five-year sentences under this provision.[90] (Additionally, the 'three strikes and you're out' minimum sentence provisions for Class A drug traffickers and domestic burglars introduced by the Crime (Sentences) Act 1997 (see previous sub-section) remain in force.)

The Act also restructured both prison and community sentences. Prison sentences of up to 12 months are – or at least were – to be replaced by a new sentence called *'custody plus'* (sections 181–2), under which offenders would serve a maximum of three months in prison plus a period of at least six months' compulsory supervision in the community. (The introduction of this new penalty, which we discuss further in Chapter 5, was deferred indefinitely in July 2006.) Sections 177–80 created a new 'generic' non–custodial penalty called a *community order,* replacing probation, community service[91] and curfews with a single sentence which can contain and/or combine any or all of these along with other requirements (see further Chapter 5). New non-custodial and semi-custodial penalties (suspended sentence orders and intermittent custody; of which more in Chapter 5), were introduced. As previously mentioned, the intention was that the sentencing powers of magistrates' courts would increase.[92] And, perhaps most importantly of all, sections 167–73 of the 2003 Act introduced a new system for producing comprehensive sentencing guidelines, with the new Sentencing Guidelines Council ('SGC', advised by the Sentencing Advisory Panel or 'SAP') charged with the responsibility of framing the guidelines and keeping them under review, as explained in section 4.4 of this chapter. The Act also contains (in Schedule 21) specific statutory guidelines for the 'tariff' element of sentences for murder, as explained more fully in Chapter 8.

But how will all of this affect the *practice* of sentencing: how will sentencers henceforth operate *within* the legal framework provided by the 2003 Act? And what policy or strategy does the government have on this? We now need to turn to the Carter Report of 2003.

The Carter Report: Targeting Sentences

In March 2003, Home Secretary David Blunkett commissioned the businessman and 'government trouble shooter' Patrick Carter to carry out an independent review of correctional services. Carter reported in December 2003 (Carter, 2003); perhaps not surprisingly his report had a managerial (or Strategy B) flavour. He concluded that sentencing practice had become much more severe in recent years, with much greater use being made of prison and probation, but found little evidence to suggest that this increased severity of punishment was a significant deterrent to crime. Sentences, Carter proclaimed in a key phrase, were *poorly targeted,* with the increased use of prison being concentrated on first-time offenders rather than serious, dangerous and highly persistent offenders, leading to poor use of resources, prison overcrowding, excessive probation caseloads and associated difficulties. There was still great variation between sentencing practice in different areas, and sentencers lacked the information they needed to make the most effective use of prison and probation. A new vision was needed with a focus on managing offenders, to reduce crime and maintain public confidence.

Some of Carter's key proposals, including establishing a National Offender Management Service (NOMS) combining the prison and probation services and introducing competition between public and private providers in the penal system, will be dealt with in Chapters 5 and 7. On the sentencing front, Carter felt that what was needed was better *targeted* sentences (and in general, a reversal of the futile 'ratcheting up' of sentencing levels which had occurred in recent years). Sentences should reflect both the seriousness of the offence and the risk of reoffending, with more rigorous sanctions and efforts at rehabilitation being targeted upon serious, dangerous and persistent offenders. So very low-risk offenders should be diverted out of the court system altogether by using conditional cautions (see the Introduction). Other low-risk offenders should receive income-related 'day fines' (see Chapter 5). There should be three levels of community sentence, based on a risk assessment of offenders, within the framework of the 'generic' community order introduced by the Criminal Justice Act 2003 (see Chapter 5). Custody should be reserved for ('targeted' on) serious, dangerous and highly persistent offenders. Crucial to this strategy of targeted sentencing would be the new Sentencing Guidelines Council (SGC), which should quickly issue comprehensive sentencing guidelines and review them annually, informed by evidence on what reduces offending ('what works') and makes cost-effective use of existing resources.

When Carter reported, the prison population was projected to rise from around 74,000 in late 2003 to 93,000 in 2009, with 300,000 under supervision. Carter believed his proposals could cut these 2009 figures to 80,000 in custody and 240,000 under supervision.

The Prospects?

The Carter Report got several important things right.[93] Sentencing has become much harsher, and this harshness achieves little. If the penal crisis is to be contained, let alone solved, then sentencing must be reined in somehow. The most promising mechanism for attempting this is comprehensive sentencing guidelines, carefully designed and framed by a body such as the SGC with expert advice from the SAP. If well framed, such guidelines could potentially have the positive effects of reducing inconsistency in sentencing, and – if carefully pitched at the right level, and if followed by the sentencers – of reducing the prison population. All of which could be achieved, not by removing or confining sentencers' powers, but by guiding and structuring their use.

But will such a strategy actually be implemented, and if so will it succeed? The government's initial response to Carter (Blunkett, 2004) was extremely positive in almost all respects, including accepting the aim of 'capping' the prison population at a figure of 80,000. However, in September 2005, Home Secretary Charles Clarke indicated that the government was abandoning this proposed target (*Guardian*, 19 September 2005) (which was subsequently to be duly breached in November 2006). At the same time Mr Clarke indicated that the previous (Carteresque)[94] proposal to place a legal obligation on the SGC to have regard to penal resources including the prison population when framing their guidelines[95] was also to be dropped; in both cases these policy reversals followed persistent Conservative criticism that attempting to restrict prison numbers in these ways amounted to being 'soft on crime'. As we write, the government's commitment to the Carter strategy on sentencing is looking extremely doubtful.

But even if the Carter strategy were to be assiduously implemented, there are a variety of ways in which it might fail to work. The SGC could fail to produce sufficiently clear or comprehensive guidelines. Or it could easily produce the wrong guidelines, which when followed had the effect of increasing the prison population rather than reducing it; indeed, many practitioners believe that this has been the general effect of sentencing guidelines to date in this country.[96] (There has certainly been a tendency to date in this country for guidelines to become harsher over time: Carter, 2003: 12.) Again, the provisions of the 2003 Act for the production of guidelines – which require the SGC to consult the Secretary of State and Parliament before issuing final versions of guidelines – are almost designed to encourage populist politics to influence the content of guidelines by making them harsher,[97] and certainly to inhibit the SGC and the SAP from suggesting anything that could be represented as over-lenient. On the other hand, the SAP's role in advising the Council about the empirical realities of present sentencing levels and the cost-effectiveness of different sentences (on which score custodial sentences tend to come out poorly) and the SGC's statutory duties to take account of all such matters represent (at least in theory) positive encouragements to produce guidelines that prescribe a more parsimonious use of custody.

The SGC is presented with a particular problem in producing guidelines that are both parsimonious and equitable thanks to the special guidelines which are enshrined on the statute book, contained in the Criminal Justice Act 2003 itself (Schedule 21), relating to the sentencing of murderers. As we shall see in Chapter 8, these guidelines seem designed to increase substantially the length of time that many murderers spend in prison. If sentences for lesser violent offences are to be kept in proportion to sentences for murder, this would seem to point to guidelines for such offences which would inflate rather than decrease the prison population.[98]

Another possibility is that the SGC could come out with excellent guidelines, but that these might not be adequately followed by the sentencers themselves,[99] who have become used to sentencing harshly and will not easily be guided out of their old ways. And a final danger is that, like the Criminal Justice Act 1991 (Cavadino et al., 1999: 68–73), the new system might fail politically: it could be attacked by sections of the media, judiciary and politicians, with the result that the system is abandoned or heavily modified, and sentencers revert to their old ways or worse.

Despite these dire possibilities, we remain of the view that a sentencing guidelines system of the kind instituted by the 2003 Act represents the best prospect of achieving a degree of appropriate control over the discretion of sentencers – but making it work as it should will require an enormous amount of political wisdom, skill and goodwill from politicians and judiciary as well as the SGC and SAP. As we write, the SGC has issued seven sets of final guidelines (between December 2004 and December 2006), covering: the reduction of sentences in return for pleas of guilty; how to assess the seriousness of offences; the new sentences introduced by the Criminal Justice Act 2003; manslaughter by reason of provocation, robbery and domestic violence.[100] Noteworthy features of these first guidelines include the following. The guideline on assessing 'seriousness' only attempts to give very general guidance, but does state that 'the culpability of the offender ... should be the initial factor in determining the seriousness of the offence'. It thus (in line with 'just deserts' thinking: see Cavadino, 1997b: 29–35) prioritizes the culpability or 'blameworthiness' of the offender above the harm that has actually resulted from the criminal act, and apparently also above the offender's previous criminal record.[101]

Thus – despite the government's longstanding preference for 'progression' in sentencing – the SGC's approach to interpreting and applying the 2003 Act seems to be tilting towards an 'offence-based' rather than an 'offender-based' tariff. The SGC similarly did not attempt any detailed definition of when the 2003 Act's 'custody threshold' is passed in relation to different offences, but was nevertheless at pains to point out that section 152's clear intention 'is to reserve prison as a punishment for the most serious offences'. Even more strikingly, when advising on implementing the new sentences provided by the 2003 Act, the SGC took the view that if prison sentences continued to be passed as before, this would represent an unwarranted increase in the sentence actually served (whether in prison or in the community following early release – for details see Chapter 8). As a result, the SGC recommended as a general guide that custodial sentences of 12 months or more should be reduced by 15 per cent. Thus, the SGC's guidelines so far bespeak a general desire to bring down the level of custodial sentencing, but whether their (relatively vague[102]) admonitions will have the desired effect on sentencers who have become used to dealing out more severe penalties is a moot point.

Other provisions of the 2003 Act have also given rise to concern. In April 2005, just after many of the Act's provisions were brought into force, several senior judges (interviewed anonymously) expressed fears that the Act, and in particular its mandatory sentencing provisions such as the new indeterminate 'imprisonment for public protection', could lead to 'an explosion in the prison population' and to judges being forced to impose many unfair sentences (*Guardian*, 26 April 2005). The continued rocketing of the prison population thereafter seems to be confirming such fears. Whether or not this carries on into the future is likely to depend crucially on the work of the SGC and the ensuing response of sentencers. It can certainly not be taken for granted that sentencers will dutifully implement the principles of parsimony and last resort which are indeed to be found in the 2003 Act (although to some the phrase 'lip service' may spring to mind). After all, the pre-existing legal framework dating from 1991 embodied similar principles. And yet in 2002 the courts sent 3,000 people to prison for minor thefts (such as shoplifting and theft of bicycles) despite their having no previous convictions.[103] Clearly, some sentencers are relatively quick to convince themselves that they have reached the 'last resort' stage.

Ultimately we need to recognize that formal and legal controls on sentencing, however well designed, are fairly blunt instruments. If sentencers resent the controls, they can undermine and avoid them in a variety of ways (as indeed history has often shown). Arguably more important than these formal controls is the *sentencing culture* of the judiciary (see Cavadino and Dignan, 2006: 338) – and it is not always easy to influence a culture from the outside. Political leadership and rhetoric can play a part. But for would-be penal reformers, the depressing pattern has been that exhortations to sentencers to 'get tough' have often been effective (Worrall and Pease, 1986: 186; Travis, 1993) while encouragement to use custody less has often fallen on deaf ears (Travis, 2003).

As we write, most of the pressure on sentencing – from both politicians and the media – is in the reverse direction, towards greater harshness. Thus, for example, in autumn 2005 the SGC published draft guidelines for robbery cases, which made it clear that the starting point for sentencers should almost always be a custodial sentence; however, for young first-time offenders who used minimal force or threat of force, a community order might be appropriate. One tabloid responded with the headline: 'RIDICULOUS: Muggers must not be sent to prison says the Lord Chief Justice' (Sentencing Guidelines Council and Sentencing Advisory Panel, 2006: 2). In August 2006 a consultation paper from the Sentencing Advisory Panel suggested that ordinary shoplifting should not attract a custodial sentence (unless perhaps the offender was 'seriously persistent'). Although broadly in line with current sentencing practice, this attracted a scathing attack from the British Retail Consortium, who said that it sent 'entirely the wrong message to would-be thieves' (*Guardian*, 25 August 2006).

Even greater attention was lavished on the case of Craig Sweeney, a paedophile offender sentenced in June 2006 for abducting and assaulting a 3-year old girl. Sweeney was sentenced to life imprisonment with a 'tariff' period – the absolute minimum of time he must serve before becoming eligible to apply for parole[104] – of five years and 108 days. Despite his life sentence and the fact that Sweeney was never likely to be released until much longer than five years had elapsed, the case caused an uproar. Home Secretary John Reid criticized the sentence within hours of its being passed and said he would ask the Attorney General to consider appealing against it to the Court of Appeal. Embarrassingly, Lord Goldsmith refused (*Guardian*, 11 July 2006) as the sentence was clearly within existing guidelines, notably the principle that a discount of one third should be applied where the offender has pleaded guilty at the first opportunity. Dr Reid's further response was to ask the SGC to consider amending the guideline so that the discount could be removed or reduced in cases where the evidence is overwhelming (Home Office, 2006d: 10). The government was now keen to increase the discretion of sentencers – but only, it seemed, their discretion to sentence more harshly.

Despite the escalating prison numbers crisis, the government is still as willing as ever to follow the media's enthusiastic campaign for a 'tougher' approach, which is bound to limit the effectiveness of any efforts the SGC may make to exercise restraint on sentencing. Ending the courts' 'love affair with custody' was never going to be an easy task, and it is all the more daunting when both the media and the government share their passion for imprisonment.

Notes

1 Plans for a Ministry of Justice bringing together sections of the Home Office, Lord Chancellor's Department and Attorney General's office were reportedly proposed and favoured by sections within the government and Civil Service previously in the early 2000s, but were successfully resisted by Home Secretary David Blunkett. The untidy result was the creation of the Department for Constitutional Affairs as part of a ministerial reshuffle in June 2003, leaving the responsibilities of the Home Office essentially intact (*Guardian*, 12 June 2003).

2 The other major decision for which the criminal courts are also responsible – determining the guilt or innocence of a defendant – lies outside the scope of this book. It is worth pointing out, however, that continuing doubts over the courts' ability to deliver justice fairly and consistently when trying defendants contribute to the wider crisis of legitimacy that suffuses the entire criminal justice system.

3 Notice reputed to have hung in the gaoler's office of a London magistrates' court (Corre and Wolchover, 1999: 1).

4 On 30 June 2006, there were 13,067 remand prisoners, 17 per cent of the total prison population (NOMS, 2006a). Of these, 8,064 (62 per cent) were untried and 5,003 (38 per cent) were convicted but unsentenced.

5 Between 1995 and 2004 remand prisoners accounted for 55 per cent of all prison suicides despite comprising only around one-fifth of the prison population (Howard League for Penal Reform press release, 5 July 2005).

6 The police may grant bail to an arrested suspect as an alternative to continued detention in the police station before or after charge (Police and Criminal Evidence Act 1984, ss. 37, 38). They may attach conditions to bail similar to those a court may impose (Police and Criminal Evidence Act 1984, s. 47 (1A), inserted by Criminal Justice and Public Order Act 1994, s. 27). Since January 2004 they have also had the power to grant 'street bail' to suspects who have been arrested but not taken to a police station (Criminal Justice Act 2003, s. 4).

7 Under section 3 of the Bail Act. The traditional requirement of a 'surety' – some other person who undertakes to forfeit a specified sum of money if the defendant fails to surrender to custody – is still possible, but now rarely imposed in England. The court can also require a 'security' – a forfeitable sum – to be provided by or on behalf of the defendant.

8 Criminal Justice Act 2003, section 14 (not yet in force as we write).

9 Criminal Justice Act 2003, section 15. Additionally, section 19 specifies that bail should be refused to defendants who have tested positive for Class A drugs and who refuse to be assessed for drug dependency unless there is no significant risk of their reoffending while on bail.

10 Crime and Disorder Act 1998, section 56.

11 See Cavadino and Dignan (2002: 86–7) for discussion of bail hostels and bail information and support schemes.

12 For indictable cases, the custody time limit in magistrates' courts is normally 70 days between first appearance and the start of the trial or committal proceedings, while for summary offences the limit is 56 days. Where the accused is committed for Crown Court trial, the time limit is 112 days before the start of the trial, or 182 days for 'indictable only' offences. (See the Prosecution of Offences (Custody Time Limit) Regulations 1987 (SI 299) as amended by SI 1991/1515, SI 1995/555, SI 1999/2744 and SI 2000/3284.) Under section 43 of the Crime and Disorder Act 1998, different time limits may now be set for different types of cases.

13 Part – but only a relatively small part – of this later rise in average waiting times is due to the introduction of 'plea before venue' (see following section) as from October 1997,

which for the next couple of years reduced the number of defendants pleading guilty tried in the Crown Court. Since guilty plea cases are likely to experience less delay, this caused an *increase* in the *average* waiting time for Crown Court trial immediately following 1997. But this change cannot account for the increase from 9.6 weeks in 1999 to 14 in 2004.

14 This is despite the fact that being remanded in custody is likely to make it much more difficult to prepare a defence, as borne out by statistical evidence that defendants remanded in custody are significantly more likely to be convicted (see Cavadino and Dignan, 2002: 85).

15 'Immediate imprisonment' means a sentence of imprisonment which is not suspended (see Chapter 5).

16 Ironically, a defendant who is remanded in custody and who *does* receive custodial sentence may not suffer overall as a result, since time already spent in custody while on remand will usually be deducted from their prison sentence. On the other hand, *acquitted* defendants only rarely receive any compensation for their wrongful detention (see Machover, 2002).

17 Studies indicate that CPS recommendations exercise a significant influence over magistrates' remand decisions. see, e.g., Hucklesby (1997: 133 5) who found that magistrates agreed with 99 per cent of CPS recommendations for bail and 86 per cent of their recommendations for remands in custody.

18 Law Commission (1999). However, the Law Commission (2001) ultimately concluded that the current law as amended by the Criminal Justice Act 2003 could be applied in a manner that complies with the Convention.

19 In 1994, 23 per cent of those committed for Crown Court trial were remanded in custody. In 2004 the figure was 30 per cent. These percentages represent 20,300 persons held in custody in 1994 and 23,600 in 2004 (Home Office, 2005e: Table 4.6).

20 Mode of trial can also affect a defendant's chance of acquittal: it is quite well established that defendants generally have a better chance of being acquitted by a jury in the Crown Court than by a magistrates' court (see Vennard, 1985).

21 It was estimated in 1998 that the average cost of a trial with a 'not guilty' plea in the Crown Court was £13,500, compared with £2,500 in the magistrates' court (*Guardian*, 29 July 1998). To this may be added the saving in 'custody costs' (relating both to remand and sentenced prisoners) if cases are kept away from the Crown Court.

22 By the Criminal Procedure and Investigations Act 1996, s. 49.

23 Magistrates' Courts Act 1980, s.19. Currently, a magistrates' court can only impose a maximum of six months' imprisonment for a single offence and cannot normally impose a fine greater than £5,000. The six-month maximum is to be doubled under the Criminal Justice Act 2003, s. 154: see note 45 below.

24 National Mode of Trial Guidelines were first issued in 1990. The most recent (1995) version can be found in the Consolidated Criminal Practice Direction, available online at http://www.hmcourts-service.gov.uk/cms/files/consolidated_criminal_practice_direction_060328.pdf.

25 Under the provisions of the Criminal Justice Act 2003, Schedule 3, in future a defendant will at this stage, before deciding which venue to choose, be able to request an 'indication of sentence', i.e. an indication of whether a custodial or non-custodial sentence would be more likely were the defendant to plead guilty (and thereby accept a summary trial) at this stage. (If the court indicates a non-custodial sentence, this will be binding on the court provided the defendant does change plea immediately.)

26 Calculated from figures provided by Auld (2001: 677–8), although Auld himself says that less than 4 per cent chose the Crown Court.

27 See above, note 20.

28   Impressive figures, if not perhaps quite as dramatic as they sound. Herbert (2003: 321; 2004: 72–5) found that court participants regarded up to three-quarters of mode of trial decisions as obvious; that the CPS did not always make a recommendation in borderline cases; that mode of trial was only genuinely contested in some 5 per cent of cases; and that most venue decisions were effectively agreed beforehand between the prosecution and defence, in the light of the general pattern of decisions made by the local magistrates. But he also found substantial evidence from interviews with magistrates to the effect that they generally deferred to the CPS view.

29   Criminal Justice (Mode of Trial) Bills 1999 and 2000. Home Secretary Jack Straw had previously (when in opposition) described the proposal as 'not only wrong, but short-sighted, and likely to prove ineffective' (*The Times*, 28 February 1997).

30   Introduced by the Criminal Procedure and Investigations Act 1996 (s. 49.)

31   This was to be expected, as under 'plea before venue' many defendants whom the magistrates' court would have committed for trial under the previous system will now plead guilty and be convicted in the magistrates' court, but the magistrates will then decide that the seriousness of the offence requires the greater sentencing powers of the Crown Court.

32   Available online at http://www.sentencing-guidelines.gov.uk/docs/allocation_draft_guideline_160206.pdf.

33   Only around 10 per cent of the sentenced prison population at any one time are serving sentences of 6 months' imprisonment or less (NOMS, 2005b), which is currently the normal maximum the magistrates' court can pass. Although very many more offenders are sentenced for indictable offences in magistrates' courts than in the Crown Court (260,000 and 73,000 respectively in 2003: RDS NOMS, 2005a: Tables 2.1 and 2.2), the proportionate use of custody is very much lower in magistrates' courts (14 compared with 60 per cent in 2003). And since the custodial sentences imposed by Crown Courts also tend to be longer than those passed by magistrates' courts (average 27 months as against 3 months), the sentencing practice of the Crown Court is always going to be a much more potent factor in generating the prison numbers crisis.

34   There was a 9 per cent increase in the numbers sentenced for indictable offences between 1993 and 2003 (calculated from figures in RDS NOMS, 2005a), during which period the prison population rose by 65 per cent.

35   Carter (2003: 11). The figure was still 25 per cent in the second quarter of 2005 (NOMS, 2005b: 3). Some further telling figures: the custody rate for indictable offences in the Crown Court rose from 49 per cent in 1993 to 61 per cent in 2004, and in the magistrates' court from 6 to 15 per cent (RDS NOMS, 2005a and 2005b: Tables 2.2 and 2.1).

36   Average sentence lengths in the magistrates' court remained around 3 per cent over this period (RDS NOMS, 2005: Tables 2.1 and 2.2).

37   Some of the increased severity of sentencing can also be attributed to a tendency for sentencing guidelines (see below) to be made harsher over time: see note 66 below. There have also been other inflationary pressures, including a flow of new legislation from Parliament toughening the provisions of sentencing for particular offences, creating 'knock-on' effects as sentencers strive to maintain a proportionate relationship between their sentences for different offences (Hough et al., 2003: 24).

38   For the objection that geographical comparisons of this sort are not entirely compelling because of important differences between criminal justice systems and levels of crime in the countries concerned, see Chapter 1, note 10 and Cavadino and Dignan (2006: 4–5).

39   The change of name was brought about in August 2000, by section 78 of the Access to Justice Act 1999.

40   In theory the clerk's role is confined to advising magistrates on what sentences are available to them, rather than on which sentence to choose in individual cases, though in

practice this distinction is sometimes a difficult one to sustain. See further, Darbyshire (1999).

41 Three ranks of judge sit in the Crown Court: recorders (part-time judges), circuit judges (who also sit in the (civil) county courts), and High Court judges (who preside over the most serious cases).

42 See Downes (1988) for an interesting contrast in judicial cultures between England and the Netherlands in the 1980s.

43 The Constitutional Reform Act 2005 (s. 3) lays down that the government must 'uphold the continued independence of the judiciary', and in particular must not 'seek to influence particular judicial decisions through any special access to the judiciary'.

44 See *R. v. Sargeant* (1974) 60 Cr App R 74, where the Court of Appeal expressly endorsed retribution, deterrence, 'prevention' and reform as legitimate aims of sentencing.

45 Criminal Justice Act 2003, s. 154. (This proposed change is likely to be introduced if and when prison sentences of less than 12 months are replaced by the new sentence of 'custody plus'; see section 4.5 following.) If the offender is convicted of more than one offence, the maximum total sentence in the magistrates' court is 12 months (to be increased to 65 weeks by the Criminal Justice Act 2003, s. 155).

46 Most American states have 'three strikes and you're out' provisions. California led the way with what is still the best known example, a law adopted in 1994 which provides that certain offenders must receive a life imprisonment sentence with no parole for at least 25 years when they are convicted for a third time.

47 One notable (and short-lived) exception was a provision in the Criminal Justice Act 1967 compelling courts to suspend all sentences of imprisonment of up to six months. This provoked fierce opposition from the Magistrates' Association, which viewed it as an unwarranted attack on the independence of magistrates, and just five years later the measure was repealed.

48 The Attorney General is the member of the government with responsibility for the Crown Prosecution Service.

49 One important issue, discussed later in this chapter, is to what extent the tariff should be primarily *'offence-based'*, with sentences in proportion to the current offences, or *'offender-based'*, with sentences largely determined by the offender's previous criminal record.

50 There is also evidence that professional district judges (formerly known as stipendiary magistrates) sentence offenders more severely than their lay colleagues, even when other relevant factors affecting the types of cases dealt with are taken into account (Flood-Page and Mackie, 1998: 69).

51 See also the Justices' Clerks' Society (1982) whose comparative survey of the use of custody in the two levels of court for a selected range of offences revealed even greater differentials.

52 (1980) 71 Cr App R 381: see Ashworth (1983: 41).

53 The Victim Personal Statement Scheme was introduced in 2001 (see Edwards, 2002).

54 Criminal Justice Act 2003, s. 156. If the offender is under 18, a new PSR is required unless the court considers a previous PSR made in respect of the same young person.

55 Including section 1(2)(a) of the Criminal Justice Act 1991 and section 152 of the Criminal Justice Act 2003, for which see section 4.5 below.

56 See e.g. Hough et al. (2003: 35). It may be questioned how far sentencers typically apply this principle in practice: see, for example, the cases cited in note 79 below.

57 Enshrined in their differing fashions in sections 2(2)(a) and 6(2)(b) of the Criminal Justice Act 1991 and various sections of the Criminal Justice Act 2003: see section 4.5 below.

58 A principle which, as we shall see in section 4.5, is combined with the last resort, parsimony and proportionality principles in the Criminal Justice Act 2003.

59 See Cavadino (1997a: 35–40). In practice it is clear that both 'tariffs' greatly influence sentences (see e.g. Stafford and Hill, 1987; Halliday, 2001: 94), but the Carter Report (2003: 18) was doubtless right to conclude that sentencers generally 'appear to give greater emphasis to the seriousness of the offence rather than the number of previous convictions'.

60 See von Hirsch (1987) for details.

61 (1986) 8 Cr App R (S) 48. For some other examples of guideline judgments, see *R. v. Aramah* (1982) 4 Cr App R (S) 407 (importation of drugs); *R. v. Boswell* (1984) 6 Cr App R (S) 257 (causing death by dangerous driving); *R. v. Stewart* (1987) 9 Cr App R (S) (social security fraud).

62 See in particular the cases of *R. v. Upton* (1980) 71 Cr App R 102 and *R. v. Begum Bibi* (1980) 71 Cr App R 360.

63 Contrast *R. v. Queen* (1981) 3 Cr App R (S) 245 with *R. v. Gilbertson* (1980) 2 Cr App R (S).

64 For example, in *R. v. Mussell* (1990) 12 Cr App R (S) 607, the Court of Appeal declined to set proper guidelines for burglary, stating that 'each offence has to be judged individually'. However, guidelines for domestic burglary were eventually issued in *R. v. Brewster and Others* [1998] 1 Cr App R (S) 181.

65 Because, as explained above, appeals from the magistrates' court go to the Crown Court not the Court of Appeal, giving the Court of Appeal no opportunity to pronounce on the sentencing of such cases.

66 The latest (2004) version of these guidelines are available online at: http://www.jsboard.co.uk/magistrates/adult_court/index.htm. Analysis of the guidelines has shown that over one-third of them have become more severe since 1993 (Carter, 2003: 12).

67 The ten other members include academics, sentencers (magistrates and a Crown Court judge), those with knowledge of the criminal justice system (including prisons and probation) and independent members.

68 The SGC closely resembles the 'Sentencing Council' which many commentators – most notably and eminently Andrew Ashworth (1983, 2000: 358–9), but also including ourselves (Cavadino and Dignan, 1997a: 106–7) have advocated for many years. It was recommended (as one option) by the Halliday Report (2001) and adopted by the government in the White Paper *Justice for All* in 2002 (Home Office, 2002a: 89–90).

69 The judicial members include representatives from all levels of criminal court. Currently the non-judicial members include a chief constable, the Director of Public Prosecutions, a defence solicitor, and the head of policy of Victim Support. The chief executive of NOMS (see Chapter 5) and the Chairman of the SAP also sit in at meetings of the SGC.

70 See above, note 47.

71 See, for example, the Advisory Council on the Penal System's 1977 interim report, *The Length of Prison Sentences*, which invited judges to think about imposing shorter prison sentences as a contribution towards relieving the problem of prison overcrowding, a copy of which was sent to every judge and every bench of magistrates (Ashworth, 2000: 49).

72 Although the Lord Chief Justice's pronouncements in the cases of *Upton* and *Bibi* (see note 62 above) were followed by reductions in the average length of prison sentences in both the magistrates' court and the Crown Court, these were relatively modest and soon reversed.

73 Although Douglas Hurd was Home Secretary from 1985 to 1989, the 'Hurd era' and the 'Hurd approach' really cover the years 1987 to 1992.

74 A Green Paper is a consultation document issued by the government when it is considering legislation or major policy changes. A White Paper sets out the government's considered intentions for legislation.

75 Criminal Justice Act 1991, sections 2(2)(a) (regarding the length of custodial sentences) and 6(2)(b) (community sentences).

76 Criminal Justice Act 1991, section 2(2)(b). The government founded its adherence to the 'just deserts' principle on the notions of denunciation and retribution, which in combination should be 'the first objective for all sentences'. But additionally: 'Depending on the offence and the offender, the sentence may also aim to achieve public protection, reparation and reform of the offender, preferably in the community'. (Home Office, 1990a: 2.9). Deterrence, on the other hand, received little endorsement and was omitted from the White Paper's list of approved objectives of sentencing (2.8–2.9).

77 Because, although section 29 stated that a bad record is not to be treated as aggravating the seriousness of the current offence, a relatively *good* previous record could be treated as a *mitigating* factor (Ashworth, 2000: 169–70).

78 Home Office (1990a: 2.15). This was embodied in sections 1(2)(b) and 2(2)(b) of the Act, which permitted sentences for violent and sexual offenders who were regarded as dangerous which were more severe than the seriousness of the offence (and the offender's just deserts) would warrant.

79 See, for example *R. v. Costello* (1993) 15 Cr App R (S) 240; *R. v. Keogh* (1994) 15 Cr App R (S) 279 and *R. v McCormick* (1995) 16 Cr App R (S) 134.

80 See above, note 46.

81 Crime (Sentences) Act, section 2, later section 109 of the Powers of Criminal Courts (Sentencing) Act 2000, and eventually repealed by the Criminal Justice Act 2003.

82 Originally section 3 of the Crime (Sentences) Act 1997. See now Powers of Criminal Courts (Sentencing) Act 2000, s. 110.

83 Originally section 4 of the Crime (Sentences) Act 1997; see now Powers of Criminal Courts (Sentencing) Act 2000, s. 111.

84 *R. v. Offen* [2001] 2 Cr App R (S) 10. Nevertheless, between 2000 and 2003, 200 life sentences were passed under the 'two-strike' provision (RDS NOMS, 2005a: Table 2.7).

85 Lord Chancellor's Department Press Release, 14 June 2002, in which Mr Blunkett and the Lord Chancellor welcomed guidance from the Lord Chief Justice in cases such as *R. v. Kefford* [2002] EWCA Crim 519 that prison should be used as a last resort and for no longer than necessary, guidance which was attacked by sections of the media. Mr Blunkett was probably not being inconsistent. His general position seemed to be that there should be more *bifurcation* in sentencing – with heavier sentences for more serious offenders but less use of custody for minor offenders – but the message was never clearly received. Civil servants resorted to showing disbelieving magistrates film clips of Mr Blunkett's Commons statements to try to convince them that he favoured non-custodial penalties over short prison sentences (*Guardian*, 17 November 2004).

86 For adults: for young offenders the principal aim was stated as being 'to prevent offending by children and young persons' by section 37 of the Crime and Disorder Act 1998 (see Chapter 9).

87 A custodial sentence may also be passed if the offender fails to agree to the terms of a proposed community sentence, or fails to comply with an order for a pre-sentence drug test (s. 152(3)).

88 See, however, the Sentencing Guidelines Council's guideline on 'Overarching Principles: Seriousness' (December 2004), discussed in the final subsection in this chapter, which downplays the importance of previous convictions as opposed to the seriousness of the current offence.

89 The offender will first serve an 'appropriate custodial term', which is the shortest term commensurate with the seriousness of the offence, augmented by his or her previous criminal record, unless the normal sentence would have been less than 12 months, in which case the 'appropriate custodial term' will be 12 months. Unlike other prisoners, those on extended sentences are not normally automatically released halfway through

this term, but only if the Parole Board so recommends (section 247). Post-release supervision may be extended by order of the court by up to five years for a violent offence or eight years for a sexual offence.

90 See for example the following cases, in all of which it was decided that 'exceptional circumstances' did not apply: *R.v. Jordan* [2005] *Criminal Law Review* 312 (offenders pleaded guilty; one believed the gun to be a replica and had no ammunition for it); *R.v. McEneaney* [2005] *Criminal Law Review* 579 (offender was suffering from mental illness); *R.v. Walker* (*Guardian*, 14 July 2005; offender drunkenly shot himself in the testicles with an illegal shotgun). Generally see *R.v Rehman; R.v Wood* [2005] *Criminal Law Review* 878.

91 Or, to give them what were their official titles between 2001 and 2005 (under the Criminal Justice and Court Services Act 2000), community rehabilitation and community punishment orders.

92 Sections 154–5 (not yet in force as we write).

93 Things it might have got wrong included the desirability of restructuring correctional services under the new all–encompassing NOMS (National Offender Management Service) and of introducing a greater level of privatization into the penal system (see Chapters 5 and 7).

94 See Carter (2003: 31).

95 Contained in the Management of Offenders and Sentencing Bill 2005, which fell with the 2005 General Election.

96 Wasik (2004a: 293). Martin Wasik (2004b: 250–2) discusses some of the reasons why guidelines could easily encourage an upward drift in sentencing – which at least shows that the chair of the Sentencing Advisory Panel is aware of the dangers. Guidelines do not necessarily have this kind of inflationary effect, and indeed have at times been effective in restraining sentencing in a number of American states (Tonry, 2004).

97 This has already occurred. Draft guidelines on discounts in sentences for pleas of guilty issued by the SGC in September 2004 proposed that murderers should be able to receive up to a third off the 'tariff' component of their life sentences (see Chapter 8) for a timely guilty plea. Following strident pressure by Home Secretary David Blunkett, this was reduced to one-sixth in the final version of the guideline issued in December 2004.

98 There are already signs of the murder guidelines beginning to have this kind of impact. In *R. v. Ford* [2005] *Criminal Law Review* 807 the Court of Appeal accepted that the level of sentence for particularly serious *attempted* murders should now be generally higher following the introduction of the 2003 guidelines.

99 See Tarling (2006), who found that the promulgation of the very detailed Magistrates' Association guidelines did not appear to have brought about any greater uniformity in magistrates' sentencing between 1975 and 2000. Tarling suggests that, as well as the guidelines themselves, there is a need for the Sentencing Guidelines Council to monitor their usage and ensure that they are followed by the courts.

100 The guidelines are available on the SGC's website (http://www.sentencing-guidelines.gov.uk/).

101 The guideline ('Overarching Principles: Seriousness', December 2004) mentions previous record as an aggravating factor of which account must be taken, but only as one in a long list of such factors.

102 And arguably impractical: it is difficult to imagine sentencers conscientiously reducing each prison term by 15 per cent, particularly since this is a far from straightforward calculation.

103 Cited by Martin Narey, House of Commons Select Committee on Education and Skills Minutes of Evidence, 17 November 2004. See also the cases cited in note 79, above.

104 For a fuller explanation, see Chapter 8, section 8.5.

5 Administering Punishment in the Community

Community punishment in a rapidly changing penal landscape

5.1 The brief period since the turn of the millennium has witnessed an unprecedented transformation of the context within which community punishment is administered. As we shall see in this chapter, there have been important changes in the modalities of community punishment. By 'modalities' we mean the various *types* of punishment (probation supervision, community service, the fine, etc.), the *forms* that punishment takes (e.g. supervision, surveillance, the levying of penalties on the offender's money or time) and the *methods* by which it is delivered (e.g. by state agency or by the private or voluntary sectors). The two key agencies that have in the past been responsible for administering the delivery of punishment – the probation and the prison services – have effectively been merged and the entire basis on which they each operate is in the process of radical restructuring. Indeed, at an even more fundamental conceptual level, the long-standing assumption of a mutually exclusive binary division *between* community punishment and custodial punishment has itself been undermined by the introduction of new 'hybrid' penalties that combine elements of both. And even the traditional division of labour between judges and those responsible for delivering community punishment is showing distinct signs of unravelling.

Periods of seismic upheaval are often marked by confusion and uncertainty as familiar landmarks are overturned and new formations have yet to be mapped in detail. The same can also be said of the state of community punishment in England and Wales following the radical reforms of the past few years. In this chapter we will begin the mapping exercise by setting out the current legal framework that shows the various non-custodial[1] (or semi-custodial) options that are available to the courts. This will pave the way for an overview of the changing modalities of community punishment in which we begin by briefly tracing the historical development of the main forms of non-custodial punishment and identify the various strategies governments adopted to try to influence their use by the courts. Next, we turn to some important operational issues including the way community penalties are enforced, their effectiveness and also the emerging concept of 'sentence management' that appears to herald a significant change in the traditional role of the judiciary. In section 5.5 we examine two important recent changes in the way community punishment is administered. The first of these relates to the merging of the prison and probation services into the National Offender Management Service in 2004. The second involves recent moves towards setting up a market economy for the commissioning and delivery of community punishment. In the penultimate section we will critically examine three rival theories that offer contrasting interpretations of the significance of some of these developments for the future of social control systems, before drawing our own conclusions.

CUSTODIAL SENTENCES

Immediate imprisonment

[Custody plus - not yet implemented]

Intermittent custody

Suspended sentence

CUSTODY THRESHOLD

Criterion: offence is 'so serious' that neither a fine alone nor a community sentence can be justified - s. 152(2) Criminal Justice Act 2003

COMMUNITY ORDERS

Community orders may comprise one or more of the following elements:-

	(Derived/Descended from:)
Exclusion requirement	(exclusion order)
Curfew requirement	(curfew order)
Residence requirement	(probation with conditions)
Mental health requirement	(probation with conditions)
Drug rehabilitation requirement	(probation with conditions)
Alcohol requirement	(probation with conditions)
Unpaid work requirement	(community service/community punishment order)
Programme requirement	(probation with conditions)
Activity requirement, e.g. reparation	(attendance at probation day centre)
Prohibited activity requirement	(probation with conditions)
Attendance centre requirement	(attendance centre order)
Supervision requirement	(probation/community rehabilitation order)

COMMUNITY ORDER THRESHOLD

Criterion: offence is 'serious enough' to warrant such a sentence - s. 148(1) CJA 2003
AND
the constituent requirements are in the opinion of the court the 'most suitable' for the offender and also 'commensurate with the seriousness of the offence' - s. 148(2) CJA 2003

FINANCIAL PENALTIES

Compensation Order   Fine

ADMONITORY PENALTIES

Conditional discharge   Bind-over

NOMINAL PENALTY

Absolute discharge

Figure 5.1 *The sentencing framework for adult offenders established by the Criminal Justice Act 2003*

Non-custodial punishment and the current sentencing framework

5.2 The current sentencing framework is set out in Figure 5.1, which places the various penalties broadly in terms of ascending severity from purely nominal measures at the bottom of the chart to a series of 'hybrid' penalties combining elements of custody and community punishment at the top. This framework was established by the Criminal Justice Act 2003[2] and replaces an earlier version that was introduced by the Criminal Justice Act 1991 (see Cavadino and Dignan, 2002: 124). Although several of the measures remain relatively unchanged – notably those we refer to as 'nominal' and 'admonitory' (or warning) penalties and compensation orders – many have been radically restructured, particularly in the case of community orders and the new semi-custodial measures. In this section we provide an overview of the legal framework within which sentencers operate before examining the evolution of some of the main types of non-custodial punishment and the penal strategies that have helped to shape them.

Nominal and admonitory penalties

Where a court is satisfied that it would be 'inexpedient to inflict punishment',[3] it may *discharge* the offender instead. This discharge can take one of two forms. The first is an *absolute discharge*, which is the most lenient response a court can make following a conviction, since it requires nothing from an offender and entails no restrictions on future conduct. Absolute discharges are rarely used, and account for only around 1 per cent of court disposals. In part this may be because cases that are likely to be dealt with by means of a purely nominal penalty tend to be discontinued or dealt with by means of a caution instead of being prosecuted, so never reach court at all.

Most discharges are *conditional*, which means that the offender is required not to commit a further offence within a specified period that may be up to three years in duration. If this condition is breached, the offender may be dealt with not only for the fresh offence but also in respect of the one for which the conditional discharge was originally imposed. In essence, the conditional discharge represents both a reprimand or admonishment to the offender – hence the term 'admonitory penalty' – and a threat, or warning, of future punishment, so the sentencing aims with which it is most closely associated are denunciation and (especially) deterrence (see Chapter 2).

Another 'admonitory' measure that is also available to sentencers is the ancient common law power to '*bind over*' the offender. Its use is not restricted to convicted offenders: indeed, a Law Commission survey undertaken in 1987 indicated that nearly three-quarters of bind-overs were directed against non-offenders, including witnesses, complainants or anyone else involved in the proceedings. A bind-over is in effect a suspended fine since the offender stands to forfeit a specified sum of money unless he or she abides by an undertaking to be of good behaviour and keep the peace. Although the Law Commission (1994) recommended the abolition of this increasingly anachronistic power, its flexibility and popularity with magistrates[4] may yet ensure its survival for a while longer.

Finally, a much more recent (and controversial) form of admonitory penalty is the quasi-criminal anti-social behaviour order (ASBO) that was introduced by the 1998 Crime and Disorder Act. ASBOs are predominantly invoked in respect of younger offenders,[5] and hence will be dealt with more fully in Chapter 9, though they may also be imposed on adult offenders whose behaviour has caused or has threatened to cause 'harassment, alarm or distress' to others. ASBOs are flexible civil orders and may entail a variety of prohibitions that are felt to be necessary in order to protect people living in an area from further anti-social acts committed by the defendant. Failure to comply with these admonitory requirements is a criminal offence, and in the case of adults can result in a prison sentence of up to five years.

Financial penalties

The chief difference between the two main types of financial penalties is that the compensation order requires the offender to pay the victim a specified compensatory sum, whereas a fine is paid to the state itself. Although the needs of victims were for many years seriously neglected by the criminal justice system, courts were given the power to award compensation for the first time in 1972 in cases involving injury, loss or damage.[6] Initially it could only be ordered as an 'ancillary' measure alongside some other form of punishment. Ten years later, however, courts were given the power to award compensation in its own right, and since the 1982 Criminal Justice Act, they have been ordered to prioritize compensation at the expense of the fine in cases where the offender cannot afford to pay both.[7] Courts are now also obliged by law to consider compensation in every case where there has been loss or damage to personal property or personal injury and to give reasons for not making an order.[8]

Fines may be imposed in respect of almost all offences irrespective of the type of court, and there is no upper limit on the amount a Crown Court can impose,[9] though magistrates' courts are restricted to a maximum of £5,000 in most cases. The general principle is that the level of a fine should reflect the seriousness of an offence (Criminal Justice Act 2003, s. 164). However, the court also has to take into account the financial circumstances of the offender (Criminal Justice Act 2003, s. 164(3)), and in order to do that, it is required to investigate these (Criminal Justice Act 2003, s. 164(1)).[10] The fluctuating fortunes of the fine and the problems associated with its use are discussed in the following section.

Community penalties

Prior to the introduction of the sentencing framework contained in the Criminal Justice Act 2003, the range of non-custodial sentences available to English courts was probably unparalleled anywhere in the world and included no fewer than ten mid-range 'community orders'[11] (see Cavadino and Dignan, 2002: 136ff.). These have now been replaced by a single 'generic' sentence known as a 'community order',[12] which can be 'customized' to suit each individual offender by selecting one or more requirements from a menu of 12 possible options. These are set out in Figure 5.1 in roughly ascending order of severity, with the names of the older orders from which they are derived shown in parenthesis. Before describing the various requirements themselves, however, it is necessary to consider the 'threshold' criteria that have to be satisfied before a court may impose a community order.

A community order can only be imposed if one of two sets of conditions is satisfied. The first and principal one[13] is where a court takes the view that the offence is 'serious enough' to warrant such a sentence, and also that the requirements it imposes are the most suitable for the offender and commensurate with the seriousness of the offence. The second, alternative condition for imposing a community order applies to those relatively minor offenders who have previously been dealt with solely by means of a fine in respect of three or more previous convictions and whose current offence would not normally satisfy the 'seriousness' test. The court can nevertheless impose a community order in such cases where it considers that a community order is 'in the interests of justice' (Criminal Justice Act 2003, s. 151). The Sentencing Guidelines Council has urged sentencers to exercise restraint when applying both of these conditions, stressing the need to avoid disproportionate responses to relative minor offences (Sentencing Guidelines Council, 2004), though it remains to be seen what impact if any these will have on sentencing practice.

We turn now to detail each of the main requirements that may form part of a community order, in the light of past and current developments.

The *supervision requirement* is descended from the traditional probation order[14] and, as such, is likely to continue to be routinely used as one of the most prevalent elements of the new-style generic community orders, either alone or in combination with one or more of the other requirements.[15] Section 213 of the Act links it, unequivocally if unsurprisingly, to the sentencing aim of promoting the offender's rehabilitation and spells out the key obligation, which is for the offender to attend appointments with the responsible officer as required. The frequency and intensity of supervision can vary considerably according to the perceived requirements of the offender. Intensive Supervision and Monitoring (ISM) schemes (or 'Prolific and other Priority Offender schemes' as they are now known) have been devised for persistent adult offenders providing fast access to services and support for rehabilitation backed up by swift enforcement action and penalties for non-compliance. These schemes are delivered by police and probation services working in collaboration with partner agencies providing housing and employment services, education and training, leisure facilities and treatment programmes for alcohol and drug abuse.[16]

The *attendance centre requirement* is available for offenders up to the age of 25,[17] who are obliged to attend a local attendance centre (if available[18]) for specified periods totalling not more than 36 hours (24 in the case of those under 16). In the past, offenders were typically obliged to attend such a centre on a Saturday afternoon for a three-hour session run by the police and involving physical training and constructive work.

The *prohibited activity requirement* is one of a number of elements that are derived from more intensive forms of probation, which combined straightforward supervision with additional positive of negative obligations. Under section 203, an offender can be required to refrain from engaging in specified activities – for example carrying a firearm, driving a car or mixing with named individuals – for a specified period or on specific days, though the court is obliged to consult a probation officer before doing so.

Conversely, the *activity requirement* requires offenders to attend a specified place such as a 'community rehabilitation centre' (formerly known as probation centres) for up to 60 days (s. 201). While there, they are obliged to engage in such activities as are directed, which may include reparative tasks[19] as well as those aimed at rehabilitating offenders such as improving their social and communication skills etc.

A *programme requirement* also obliges offenders to participate in specific activities which, in this case, take the form of accredited programmes that are devised with the requirements of particular groups of offenders in mind. Examples include programmes for treating sex offenders, anger management, cognitive reasoning and programmes catering for drink drivers. These are also clearly aimed at the rehabilitation of offenders but may only be imposed on the recommendation of a probation officer and are subject to local availability (s. 202).

The *unpaid work requirement* is similar to the old community service order[20] and requires an offender to perform a specified number of hours (between 40 and 300)[21] of unpaid work as directed by a responsible officer (ss. 199 and 200). The work has to be completed within 12 months, and the court has to be satisfied that the offender is a suitable person to undertake it.

As its name suggests, the *alcohol treatment requirement* is aimed at offenders who are dependent on alcohol. (Prior to the Criminal Justice Act 2003, such a requirement was only available as part of a probation order.) Before imposing it, the court has to be satisfied that the offender's dependency is susceptible to treatment, that such treatment is available and that the offender consents to it (s. 212).

The *drug rehabilitation requirement* (ss. 209–11) is similar, though it differs in two important respects. First, it requires an offender to submit to regular testing, as well as treatment, for a period of at least six months. And second, there are provisions authorizing the court to review periodically the offender's progress during the course of the order in hearings that the offender may be required to attend, and to modify the terms of the requirement accordingly. These latter aspects of the requirement resemble the 'drug courts' that originated in the United States (see Bean, 1996). The treatment itself is mostly administered by multi-agency teams that may draw on the services of probation officers, community psychiatric nurses, psychiatrists, psychologists, drug workers and GPs. The immediate forerunner of this requirement was the drug treatment and testing order (DTTO), first introduced by the Crime and Disorder Act 1998 (ss. 61–4).

This trio of treatment-oriented measures is completed by the *mental health treatment requirement*, which requires an offender to submit to treatment either as an in-patient or out-patient with a view to improving their medical condition (ss. 207 and 208). Similar requirements had long been available as conditions contained within probation orders.

The *residence requirement* is likewise a reformulation of a long-standing additional condition that could be attached to a probation order, whereby an offender can be required to reside at a specified place such as a probation hostel, at the offender's own home or with a relative (s. 206).

The *curfew requirement* reconstitutes the pre-existing (free-standing) curfew order. It obliges the offender to remain for specified periods of not less than two hours or more than 12 hours at a place designated in the order, normally the offender's own home (s. 204). The maximum duration of such an order is six months. There is a presumption (see s. 177(3)) that any curfew requirement will be accompanied by an additional *electronic monitoring requirement* (see below). Curfews with electronic monitoring requirements may also be imposed alongside most of the other requirements available under a community order.

Finally, an *exclusion requirement* prohibits an offender from entering (either totally or at particular times) a place that is designated in the order for a specified period of up to two years (s. 205). As with curfews, there is a presumption that such an order will be accompanied by an electronic monitoring requirement.

One of the criticisms levelled at the pre-2003 system of community sentences was that sentencers were confused as to the place of the various penalties on the sentencing 'tariff' (see Chapter 4, section 4.4) in the absence of any method for comparing their relative severity (their 'penal weight': Halliday, 2001: paras. 6.2–6.5). In the wake of the 2003 Act, the Sentencing Guidelines Council (2004: paras. 1.1.25–1.1.32) has published guidelines that graduate the various requirements on the basis of a threefold scale of severity that is intended to help sentencers determine that the restrictions that they impose are commensurate with the seriousness of the offence (as required by s.148(2) of the 2003 Act).[22] The following restrictions are seen as suitable for less serious offences:[23] 40–80 hours of unpaid work; a curfew requirement of up to 12 hours a day 'for a few weeks'; an exclusion requirement (without electronic monitoring) of a few months; a prohibited activity requirement; or an attendance centre requirement. For offences of medium seriousness,[24] the guidelines propose an increased amount of unpaid work (80–150 hours); an activity requirement of 20–30 days; a prohibited activity requirement; a curfew requirement lasting 2–3 months; or an exclusion requirement of around six months. For more serious offences (for example, first-time domestic burglary) the guidelines' suggestions include 150–300 hours of unpaid work, activity requirements up to the 60 day maximum; or curfew orders lasting four to six months.

Semi-custodial penalties

Sentences of immediate imprisonment fall outside the scope of this chapter, but it is nevertheless appropriate to deal here with three *semi-custodial* penalties since they combine elements of community punishment with the imposition or threatened imposition of a term of imprisonment. All custodial penalties, as we have seen, are subject to a 'threshold' test: they can only be imposed if the court is satisfied that the offence is so serious that neither a fine alone nor a community sentence would be justified (Criminal Justice Act 2003, s. 152(2)).

The Criminal Justice Act 2003 introduces a new *suspended sentence order* that allows a suspended prison sentence of between 28 and 51 weeks to be combined with one or more of the requirements that can form part of a community order (ss. 189–192).[25] These requirements have to be completed within the 'operational period' (which can be between six months and two years) during which the prison sentence is suspended. There are also provisions for the order to be reviewed peri-odically, giving the court a chance to monitor the offender's progress. If, during this operational period, the offender commits a further imprisonable offence, the court is obliged to send the offender to prison, unless it considers that it would be unjust to do so (Schedule 12).

A second new semi-custodial penalty which was introduced by the 2003 Act (but abandoned by the government in November 2006) was *intermittent custody.* This provision would have enabled a court to pass a sentence requiring an offender to serve a specified number of days (between 14 and 90) in prison over a period of between 28 and 51 weeks. The rest of the sentence was to be served in the com-munity on a 'licence', which could also include other requirements.

Finally, the Criminal Justice Act 2003 envisaged that all prison sentences of up to 12 months would ultimately take the form of *custody plus,* which would com-bine a relatively short custodial portion (between 2 and 13 weeks) with a longer period (at least six months) under supervision in the community. During this period the offender could again be ordered to comply with requirements that are available under a community order. (The government had planned to implement 'custody plus' in November 2006, but this plan was cancelled by Home Secretary John Reid in July 2006.) The 'hybridization' of community and custodial punish-ment represented by suspended sentence orders, intermittent custody and 'custody plus' is of interest for both theoretical and practical reasons, and we will be dis-cussing it further in later sections of this chapter.

The Changing Modalities of Non-Custodial Punishment

5.3 Non-custodial punishments may assume a variety of forms and are capable of being used in various ways and with varying levels of enthu-siasm. In discussing the impact of the various non-custodial options that are available to the courts, particularly with regard to the prison population, we shall be referring to Table 5.1, below, which indicates their changing pattern of usage over the last 60 years.[26] Table 5.1 is also helpful in assessing the influence of the various penal strategies that have helped to shape the development of non-custodial and, more specifically, community punishment over the years.

A brief history of non-custodial punishment

Warning penalties

The use of *warning penalties* such as the conditional discharge has fluctuated over time, and the way they are viewed by policy-makers has also wavered confusingly. As can be seen from Table 5.1, after experiencing a sharp decline after the war, the proportionate use of the conditional discharge for adult offenders increased

Table 5.1 Adult indictable offenders: types of sentence*

Type of sentence	Percentage of offenders						
	1938	1959	1975	1989	1994	1999	2004
Imprisonment	33.3	29.1	13.4	17.5	18.2	26.0	28.6
Supervisory penalties							
Probation	15.1	11.9	7.0	9.0	12.0	12.7	12.0
Community service	N/A	N/A	0.5	5.4	10.7	8.8	8.6
Combination order	N/A	N/A	N/A	N/A	2.4	3.4	2.3
Curfew order	N/A	N/A	N/A	N/A	N/A	0.2	2.0
DTTO**	–	–	–	–	–	–	3.2
Total	**15.1**	**11.9**	**7.5**	**14.4**	**25.1**	**25.1**	**28.1**
Non-supervisory penalties							
Suspended sentence	N/A	N/A	11.2	10.5	1.1	1.1	0.9
Fine	27.2	44.8	55.3	41.4	34.9	29.5	22.7
Discharge	23.4	13.1	12.0	14.1	18.2	15.1	15.2
Other penalties	1.0	1.1	0.6	2.1	2.4	3.2	4.3
Total	**51.6**	**59.0**	**79.1**	**68.1**	**56.6**	**48.9**	**43.1**
Number	38,896	75,358	209,709	216,400	215,500	229,900	223,600

*The table is based on Table 8.1 in Bottoms (1983: 167) and Table 1 in Bottoms (1980: 6), updated in the light of the relevant volumes of the Criminal Statistics for England and Wales for 1989 (Home Office, 1990c), 1994 (Home Office, 1995b) and 1999 (Home Office, 2000a). These statistics are no longer published in the current Sentencing Statistics published by RDS NOMS (2005b). However, the relevant statistics for 2004 on which the calculations shown in the table were based were very kindly provided by the Home Office Research, Development and Statistics Department.
**DTTO = 'drug treatment and testing order'

steadily during the 1980s[27] but began to fall back again in the mid-1990s. The sentencing aim of deterrence, with which it is most closely associated, sat awkwardly with the 'desert-based' philosophy that underpinned the 1991 Criminal Justice Act and had been disparaged in the White Paper that preceded it (Home Office, 1990a: para. 2.8). The Halliday Report (2001: para. 6.19) was much more supportive, commenting favourably on its lower than predicted reconviction rates. However, the New Labour government has been more hostile towards it, forbidding its use in respect of certain young offenders (see Chapter 9, below) and also when dealing with those who breach anti-social behaviour orders, not deeming it sufficiently 'controlling' in these cases.[28] Somewhat surprisingly, as Mair (2004: 139) points out, there has been virtually no research on this particular measure, in marked contrast to most of the other disposals available to the courts.

Financial penalties

The performance of *financial penalties* such as the fine has been even more erratic over the decades.[29] As can be seen from Table 5.1, the post-war years coincided with a dramatic expansion in its usage, culminating in a 'market share' of over half of all sentences imposed on adult indictable offenders by the mid-1970s. Thereafter its decline has been equally precipitous, falling steadily to just 23 per cent in 2004, which puts it below the pre-war figure for the first time.

The sentencing philosophy on which the fine is based has been described as straightforwardly punitive (Ashworth, 2005: 303), thus fitting the aims of retribution, denunciation and deterrence. However, it can also be seen as reparative: the offender literally pays back something to the community to make amends for the offence. The fine is also flexible, non-intrusive, does not require the intervention of a penal agent, and is relatively easy to adjust in accordance with an offender's desert or personal circumstances. Unusually, it is also one of the few penal measures to raise revenue as opposed to consuming scarce penal resources. Moreover, reconviction rates for the fine in general compare favourably with those for other penalties (Home Office, 1964; Softley, 1978; House of Commons Home Affairs Committee, 1998). All of these attributes help to explain the post-war popularity of the fine – particularly for straightforward, run-of-the-mill offenders who lacked any obvious social problems that might warrant the assistance of a probation officer during an era of near full-employment. Moreover, unlike probation, the fine did not become tarnished by association with the discredited treatment model (see below).

During the 1980s and 1990s, however, the fine steadily lost much of its attraction for sentencers during a period of rising unemployment levels, growing competition from other sentencing disposals and an increasingly punitive penal climate. In particular, sentencers were constrained by both the law and conscience from imposing large fines on the unemployed people who constituted the majority of offenders. Attempts were made to halt its decline, most notably by introducing a new system of *'unit fines'* into the magistrates' courts as part of the 'just deserts in sentencing' reform programme that culminated in the Criminal Justice Act of 1991. Unit fines made it possible to relate the size of the fine more accurately to the means of the offender, and thereby not only promoted greater fairness in fining but also encouraged sentencers to use fines for a wider range of offenders irrespective of their income levels. Unit fines were derived from the 'day fine' principle that is employed in other countries (notably Germany and Sweden) as a means of ensuring 'equal impact' on offenders by fining them so many days' pay rather than a fixed amount. The English unit fine system involved two sets of calculations: the first involved a judicial assessment of the seriousness of the offence on a scale from 1 to 50 units, with magistrates sentencing the offender to a fine of 'x units'. The second involved an assessment of the offender's income and was used to determine the monetary 'value' of each unit for any given offender; the actual amount of the fine being calculated by multiplying the number of units imposed by the offender's weekly disposable income.

Despite being a relatively unusual penological success story – since the downward slide in magistrates' use of the fine was reversed in the period immediately following its implementation, and its use for unemployed offenders increased sharply[30] – it also proved to be a political failure, and this led to its early demise. It failed politically mainly because it resulted in hitherto uncharacteristically high fines being imposed on relatively well-off, middle-class motoring offenders (and on some people who refused to declare their means[31]), whose cause was vigorously championed by sections of the media at a time when the government was deeply unpopular for other reasons. Although there were some teething problems associated with the unit fine system,[32] these could almost certainly have been overcome without too much difficulty (Mair, 2004: 143). However, a politically enfeebled government decided instead to abolish it peremptorily in the summer of 1993, in an astonishing *volte face* that until then had few parallels in the history of the English criminal justice system.[33] Following the demise of the unit fine, the use of fines resumed its downward trajectory and research indicated a resumption of disparity in fining decisions as magistrates' courts adopted different strategies for taking account of an offender's financial circumstances (Charman et al., 1996).

Another problem that may also have contributed to the fine's continuing decline relates to the 'desert-based' approach underpinning the 1991 sentencing framework. For, as the Halliday Report (2001: para. 6.15) suggests, by assigning it to the lowest of the three tiers of penalties created by the 1991 Criminal Justice Act (see Chapter 4, section 4.5), the impression may have been conveyed that it should be reserved for only the least serious of offenders. Halliday's proposed solution to the problem was, in effect, to dissolve the 'serious enough' threshold that separated the fine from community punishment tiers and to allow fines to be imposed – either alone or in combination with other penalties – in any of the tiers. Halliday's diagnosis was corroborated by Morgan (2003), who demonstrated that offenders who would previously have been fined were now being given mid-range community sentences such as probation, thereby pushing them up the tariff and clogging up the probation service with minor offenders who did not require supervision. The Carter Report (2003) also called for a rejuvenation of the fine by introducing a 'day fine' system similar to the short-lived unit fines[34] for less serious offenders.[35] In its response to Carter, the Home Office (2004e) undertook to consider the introduction of day fines, and provision for it was included in the Management of Offenders and Sentencing Bill 2004–5, which however fell due to the 2005 General Election. Day fines featured in the government's five-year strategy published in February 2006 (Home Office, 2006b), but were not mentioned in the later document of July 2006 (Home Office, 2006c) after John Reid had replaced Charles Clarke as Home Secretary.[36] However, it is difficult to see how the fine can be successfully revitalized as a penalty for any but the pettiest offenders without a wholesale ratcheting down of the existing scale of penalties to reverse the remorseless escalation in severity that Morgan identified.

Currently an increasing number of financial penalties are being levied not by the courts but by the police, under the 'fixed penalty notice' scheme explained in the Introduction. This scheme serves to 'widen the net' of those subject to punishment (without the trappings and safeguards of traditional due process), and indeed is intended so to do (see the discussion of the government's 'Respect Agenda' in Chapter 11). The development is also notable in that the scheme of *fixed* penalties is of course the very reverse of the means-related approach to financial penalties embodied by the 'unit fine' and 'day fine' systems. In future, prosecutors will also be allowed to impose financial penalties: section 17 of the Police and Justice Act 2006 (not yet in force) provides that a conditional caution (see Introduction) may come with a condition that the offender pay a financial penalty of up to £250 for a range of offences yet to be specified.

Compensatory penalties

Ironically, in view of the fact that requiring offenders to make reparation to those affected by their offences has now been acknowledged as an official aim of sentencing,[37] the use of *compensation orders* by the courts has also declined sharply in recent years, at least for relatively serious offenders. Thus, the proportion of indictable offenders who were ordered to pay compensation in the Crown Court was just 7 per cent in 2004, compared with 21 per cent in 1990, while in the magistrates' courts the figure was 16 per cent compared with 29 per cent in 1990.[38] One possible reason for the decline relates to the steady growth in the use of custody over the same period, since the Court of Appeal generally discourages combining a compensation order with a sentence of imprisonment.[39] A Home Office study (Flood-Page and Mackie, 1998: 62, 111) found that one reason sentencers themselves gave for not awarding compensation was that the offender lacked the means to pay, and some felt reluctant to award compensation if the amount that could be afforded would appear too derisory. (As with fines, courts are obliged to relate the amount of any compensation awarded to the offender's means.) Sentencers also complained that information about the value of the loss or harm caused is often lacking.[40]

Victims who are awarded compensation from their offenders may have to wait up to two or three years for this to be paid (always assuming the offender pays up and does not default). This is an added source of frustration that could have been avoided had the government accepted a proposal that the court should immediately pay the victim the amount awarded in full and then recover it from the offender in the normal way.[41] As a matter of principle, however, even this proposal does not in our view go far enough. For it hardly seems fair that a victim's entitlement to court-ordered compensation should depend entirely on an offender's ability and willingness to pay while the state profits handsomely from fines that are imposed on offenders. We would therefore favour a scheme in which the revenue from fines is used to fund a reformed criminal compensation scheme that would not be subject to the vagaries of the offender's financial circumstances and willingness to pay up. Indeed, this could form an important part of a more radical reformulation of our existing system of punishments in which the elements of reparation for victims and the reintegration of offenders are given far greater prominence (see Chapter 11).

In the meantime, other urgent reforms are required to ensure that sentencers start to take more seriously their legal responsibilities to prioritize victims' entitlement to compensation, instead of relegating this to a subordinate consideration, as so often seems to happen. For example, compensation is commonly withheld or reduced in amount, not because the offender lacks the means to pay, but simply because courts insist on imposing fines or awarding costs against offenders, despite clear legislative directions to give precedence to compensation in such circumstances (Flood-Page and Mackie, 1998: 127). Likewise, the statutory obligation to give reasons for not awarding compensation is ignored altogether in over 70 per cent of cases (1998: 60–4). This may be an area that is ripe for review under the Human Rights Act, since current practice arguably infringes the right to a fair trial guaranteed by the European Convention on Human Rights.

Even if the existing compensation system were to be reformed along the lines we have suggested, it would remain inherently limited in scope, however.[42] For one thing, it only affords one limited form of redress for victims, since it is restricted to financial compensation for material loss or damage. However welcome this may be,[43] it may do little to repair any harm that may have been done to the victim's mental or psychological sense of well-being, or to restore the social or moral relationships that may have been damaged by an offence (Watson et al., 1989: 214).[44] Moreover, neither victims nor offenders are likely to feel greatly empowered by an award of compensation since they are not directly involved in the decision-making process and have no control over its outcome.

Reparative penalties

Reparation can in principle take a variety of other forms apart from financial compensation. For example, it can also include offenders apologizing to victims; making amends in other ways by doing things for or on behalf of victims; or combining an undertaking to change their behaviour with constructive steps to facilitate this. Where these reparative outcomes are negotiated by victims and offenders themselves in the course of a fair process that provides appropriate safeguards for all who participate, this is likely to be more empowering than a conventional court hearing. Conceivably it could also help them come to terms with what has happened and move beyond it. These are the basic premises on which a variety of *restorative justice* (see Chapter 2, section 2.4) procedures have been developed in recent years, the best-known of which involve some form of mediation or 'conferencing'.[45] *'Victim offender mediation'* generally involves a neutral third party facilitating dialogue between offenders and their victims. This may entail a face-to-face discussion between the protagonists, though it often involves an indirect form of communication in which the mediator acts as a conduit, relaying questions, answers, information or sentiments between them. *Conferencing* generally entails a more elaborate procedure that may involve a variety of other participants, including supporters of either party, those who have been indirectly affected by the offence, members of the wider community and, possibly, some who are involved in a more official capacity.

Conventional criminal justice systems tend to afford very limited scope for these more interactive restorative justice processes and the more flexible forms of reparation that they make possible.[46] Where officials are allowed sufficient discretion, however, it may sometimes be possible for them to be accommodated within existing procedures. During the mid-1980s, for example, a number of experimental 'victim offender mediation and reparation schemes' were established (some of which had government funding; see Marshall and Merry (1990) for details). Some of these operated at the pre-court stage and aimed to divert offenders away from prosecution by referring them instead to a reparation/diversion bureau with a view to negotiating an appropriate form of reparation that might also involve a meeting with the victim. Most such schemes were aimed at juvenile offenders and were criticized for neglecting the interests of victims in order to improve the chances of diverting offenders from prosecution (Davis et al., 1988, 1989). However, one scheme that was aimed at adult offenders (operated by the Kettering Adult Reparation Bureau) demonstrated that it was possible to pursue a philosophy of even-handed reparation. A three-year evaluation showed that it was possible to combine diversion for offenders with acceptable reparation for victims in a reasonably high proportion of cases to the satisfaction of both parties (Dignan, 1991, 1992). Schemes such as this helped pave the way for the introduction of conditional cautioning (see the Introduction).

Other schemes operated at the point of sentence or immediately prior to sentence, when the court referred a case to the probation service for a pre-sentence report. The possibility of mediation leading to some form of reparation was then explored, and, if the parties agreed, a proposal might then be presented to the court as part of a package involving some form of non-custodial sentence instead of imprisonment. Many of these schemes were only concerned with less serious, 'low-tariff' offences, in which case their potential to divert offenders from custody was obviously limited (since few of these offenders would have been imprisoned in any event). A notable exception, however, was the very ambitious Leeds Mediation and Reparation Service, which deliberately targeted 'high-tariff' offenders, including adults, with the aim of providing an alternative to custody (Wynne, 1996).

More recently, the Home Office has funded a number of pilot projects to test the scope for restorative justice approaches to be used in connection with more serious and relatively 'high-volume' offences such as robberies, burglaries and grievous bodily harm, and also with adult offenders. Three separate sets of projects have been funded, each of which is quite distinct in terms of the type of restorative justice interventions on offer (though they include both mediation and conferencing processes) and also the stage in the criminal justice process at which they are available. The three schemes are being independently evaluated, a process that will not be completed until the end of 2007, though two interim reports have been produced (Shapland et al., 2004, 2006).

Restorative justice schemes of this kind potentially offer a way of combining diversion from prosecution with constructive reparation for victims. Indeed, experience elsewhere (notably in New Zealand and Australia)[47] gives ground for cautious optimism that this kind of approach might assist in the development of a more restorative system of criminal justice in general, with the potential to ameliorate many aspects of the current penal crisis (see also Dignan, 2002). Although the development of restorative justice measures in England and Wales has been slower and more cautious,[48] some progress has nevertheless been made since the early experimental schemes in the 1980s. Some initiatives – for example, the introduction of conditional cautioning for adult offenders and the current Home Office pilot projects – we have mentioned already. Other initiatives that have also been influenced in part by the philosophy of restorative justice – notably with regard to the introduction of reparation orders, action plan orders and referral orders – involve young offenders exclusively and these will be examined more closely in Chapter 9.

Supervisory penalties and the changing role of the probation service

For many years the probation order provided the only major alternative to a custodial sentence apart from a fine or warning penalty; indeed, for offenders with personal or social problems, it was the only disposal offering any form of assistance or guidance. This helps to account for its early popularity with sentencers though, as Table 5.1 indicates, it suffered a sharp decline in popularity during the early post-war period followed by a modest revival during the last two decades of the twentieth century.

Until relatively recently, the history of penal supervision has been inextricably bound up with the often turbulent history of the probation service. This has experienced a number of profound transformations between its official inception in 1907 and concerns over its possible effective demise just under a century later when it was subsumed into the National Offender Management Service (NOMS). Figure 5.2, below, summarizes in simplified form[49] some of the key shifts that have taken place with regard to the underlying ethos and structural organization of the service and the consequential changes these have wrought on relationships with offenders, courts and the wider criminal justice system.

The origins of the English probation service can be traced back to the activities of a disparate collection of well-meaning amateur reformers inspired by an evangelical belief in the possibility of redemption, many of whom belonged to the Church of England Temperance Society. Towards the end of the nineteenth century, these philanthropic missionaries began offering their services to local police courts to take responsibility for the moral reform of offenders, particularly in the case of alcohol-related offences. Sentencing magistrates – many of whom presumably came from similar backgrounds to the reformers and shared with them a public service ethos – would release suitable offenders under their informal supervision as an alternative to punishment to see if they could 'prove' themselves. The 1907 Probation of Offenders Act formalized this practice and thereby initiated the gradual development of a comprehensive service staffed by professional officers employed by local probation authorities.

As the probation service sought during the inter-war period to develop a more professional bureaucratic form of organization combined with a regular career structure, it adopted a more secular and scientific ethos based on the importation of an American-style 'casework' approach (McWilliams, 1981: 100; Pease, 1999). The relationship between probation officers and their 'clients' also metamorphosed from one based on personal befriending and mentoring to a psychotherapeutic relationship in which the officer would seek to diagnose the client's underlying needs and

Era	Ethos	Relationship with offenders	Relationship with court	Relations with criminal justice system	Organization
'The early years' 1907–1920s	Evangelical philanthropism	Personal befriending	Like-minded 'friends'	Independent adjunct	Local voluntary associations
'The golden era' 1930s–1970s	Secular scientific rationalism	Expert-client 'caseworker' approach	Professional 'acquaintances'	Detached co-workers	Autonomous local professional associations
'Winds of change' 1980s	Punitive managerialism	Penal control agent offering alternatives to imprisonment	Executors of community sentences	Integrated partner	Centralized criminal justice agency
'Beginning of the end' for the Probation Service? 1990s–2006	Public protection and crime reduction	Risk-managers and deliverers or commissioners of supervisory and other programmes	Regulatory partners in the management of sentences	Non-monopolistic provider of specific programmes in competition with others	National Probation Service set up; then subsumed into a unified corrections agency (NOMS)

Figure 5.2 A schematic history of the Probation Service in England and Wales, 1907–2006

motivations and assist in the 'readjustment of the culprit' (Radzinowicz, 1958). Another victim of these changes was the previously close relationships based on a common sense of purpose between probation officers and the courts they ostensibly served. As the language used by probation officers became more technical and abstract and as their growing responsibilities reduced the amount of time they spent in court,[50] probation officers progressed from being like-minded 'friends of the court' to mere (professional) acquaintances. McWilliams' (1981) astute analysis of this process offers one possible explanation for the otherwise unexpectedly early post-war decline in the use of probation (see Table 5.1 above), given that this pre-dated the introduction of other alternatives and growing doubts about the effectiveness of rehabilitation during the 1970s. With regard to the rest of the criminal justice system, the probation service at this time operated in a somewhat detached manner while retaining a high level of local autonomy.

By the end of the 1970s, the collapse of the rehabilitative ideal (see Chapter 2, section 2.5) had left the probation service without a clear philosophical rationale and this rendered it increasingly vulnerable to enforced change in the face of both external and internal pressures.[51] For a time its ambitions became more modest as the aim of 'treating' and 'improving' offenders gave way to the more prosaic goal of avoiding harm by providing an alternative to custody that would help avoid the damage inflicted by unnecessary incarceration. The election of a Conservative government in 1979 served to unleash a revolution that was to have profound implications for just about every aspect of the probation service. The Conservatives' agenda was more punitive than its Labour predecessor, but equally importantly, it sought to impose a new *managerialism* on the probation service.

An early manifestation of this managerial approach took the form of a Statement of National Objectives and Priorities, which was issued by the Home Office (1984b). This urged local probation committees and chief officers to ensure that probation resources were managed 'efficiently and effectively' in pursuit of clear objectives with a view to delivering value for money to the taxpayer. It was rapidly augmented by a barrage of initiatives intended to ensure that local probation services attained the targets that were set for them. However, this was merely the first indication that the old *laissez-faire* approach to probation policy, which placed a high value on the professional autonomy of individual caseworkers and on the independence of local probation services, was about to be replaced by a much more assertive form of centralized control.

A second key aim of the government's managerialist strategy was to integrate the probation service much more closely into the wider penal system. This aim was clearly spelt out in a Green Paper which characterized the probation service as a criminal justice agency whose primary role was to complement the work of the police, prisons and courts rather than to function as a separate social work agency (Home Office, 1990c). This change in role was closely bound up with a third key aim which was directed at changing both the ethos of the probation service and also the nature of its work with offenders. Henceforth, the aim of probation was redefined in terms of 'punishment and control' as opposed to the pursuit of welfare objectives (Home Office, 1988a). The 1991 Criminal Justice Act gave added legal bite to this change of emphasis by converting the probation order into a 'sentence of the court' or formal punishment for the first time.[52] Within the context of the 1991 Act, probation was initially expected to play an important part in developing and delivering 'credible' community penalties to the courts as part of the drive to limit the use of custody for less serious offences.

Such attempts to convert probation officers unambiguously into penal control agents also inevitably affected their relationships both with offenders and the courts. Increasingly, courts had been granted powers to augment the straightforward supervision that a probation order entails with a variety of additional requirements, such as requirements to attend probation day centres or engage in offender training programmes. (Many of these additional requirements, or equivalents, can now be incorporated in the new generic community order that was described in section 5.2 above). These greatly increased the scope for the control and discipline of offenders as well as providing the basis for special programmes aimed at preventing or reducing re-offending. They also increased the demands placed upon offenders who were given probation orders, thereby multiplying the risks of non-compliance. This in turn added to the responsibilities placed on probation officers, as they were expected to execute and enforce the increasingly detailed commands that were likely to be embodied in probation orders.

The 'law and order counter-reformation' that took hold under the Conservative government of the early 1990s precipitated a further cycle of profound upheaval for the probation service. By this stage a further radical change had taken place in the ethos that underpins both the criminal justice system in general and the probation service in particular, which was now increasingly expressed in the language of 'public protection'. As a direct result of the law and order counter-reformation, previous attempts to curb the use of imprisonment had been abandoned and sentencers were being encouraged instead to ensure that even those given community sentences would be dealt with ever more punitively (Home Office, 1995a).

Under New Labour, there has been some shift of emphasis back towards rehabilitation (notably in the shape of 'doing what works' to confront and change offenders' attitudes towards crime. However, the stress on 'protection of the public' via firm control of offenders is as strong as ever. In 2000, the probation officer's historic statutory obligation to 'advise, assist and befriend' the offender (first enacted in the Probation of Offenders Act 1907) was finally abolished and replaced with a new set of aims in which protection of the public was given pride of place, and which included 'the proper punishment of offenders'.[53]

One important consequence of all this for the probation service is that it has found itself dealing with a set of clients who tend to have fewer previous convictions,[54] who are less likely to re-offend, and who are therefore arguably less in need of the more intensive forms of supervision. At the same time the service has also been required to assume responsibility for larger numbers of other groups of offenders, such as those released from prison on licence, many of whom have committed much more serious offences, have much worse previous records, and are much more likely to re-offend. Unsurprisingly, perhaps, the probation service responded to the predicament in which it found itself – which was exacerbated by the continuing scarcity of penal resources – by seeking to ration its input according to the perceived 'risk' of the individual offender. Robinson (1999, 2002) has described how, as a result, the probation service increasingly defined its own role during the 1990s in terms of risk management, commenting in addition on the techniques it deployed for this purpose and the consequences for its relations with both offenders and the courts.

Two tendencies are particularly noteworthy (Robinson, 1999: 429; Oldfield, 1998; Underdown, 1998). The first is a gradual (though by no means universal) shift from the traditional concept of a 'caseworker' to that of 'case manager'. In the casework model, the tasks of assessing and supervising offenders and enforcing compliance with community orders tend to be vested in a single 'generic' probation officer who is personally known to the offender – a holistic approach. In the case management model, the tasks of planning, arranging, coordinating and reviewing probation supervision are likely to be undertaken by a qualified probation officer who will not necessarily deliver the supervision or associated interventions personally. Indeed, such tasks may often be delegated to unqualified staff.

The second, closely related tendency involves the augmentation and partial (but again by no means universal) displacement of generic probation practitioners who were personally involved in most if not all aspects of an offender's supervision by a more specialist model of practice. Under this model, different probation (and other) staff tend to specialize in particular aspects of the supervision process. Thus, some may concentrate on assessment and the writing of pre-sentence reports, while others are involved in programme delivery, and still others may specialize further by supervising particular categories of offenders such as those at high risk of harming others (Robinson and Dignan, 2004: 319).[55] Here, the rationing exercise referred to above frequently results in certain lower-key elements of the supervisory process or work with lower-risk offenders being allocated to unqualified probation staff. Indeed, some functions may even be contracted out to other agencies, in a move that could have far-reaching, longer-term implications for the probation service as a whole, as we shall discuss further in section 5.5 below.

As for relations between the probation service and the courts, these are likely to be influenced by two further sets of developments. The first involves the substitution of a single community order that may comprise multiple components for the wide variety of community sentences prior to the 2003 Criminal Justice Act (see section 5.2 above). One likely consequence of this shift will be to involve sentencers much more closely in specifying an offender's particular punitive obligations, as opposed to simply selecting an 'off-the-peg' penalty as in the past. The second development relates to the growing tendency to confer on courts a continuing responsibility to monitor and review the progress of certain offenders while they are subject to community orders (see section 5.4 below) and even to adjust the terms of the penalty itself accordingly. One possible longer-term result of these developments could be to encourage a much closer partnership between sentencers and those who responsible for delivering community orders, since they will almost certainly require much more detailed feedback relating to the offender's performance while subject to the order.

Last, but by no means least, the probation service has just undergone not one but two radical structural reorganizations in quick succession. In April 2001, the 54 separate and partly autonomous local probation services were replaced by a single National Probation Service[56] with a single national Director, directly accountable to the Home Secretary. The Criminal Justice and Court Services Act 2000, which set out the new structure, also spelt out the aims of the new service: to protect the public, reduce offending and provide for the proper punishment of offending, as well as the rehabilitation of offenders.[57] This was followed by the publication – by the new Director of the service – of a new integrated management strategy (National Probation Service, 2001).

Almost before the ink was dry on this document, however, the government-commissioned Carter Report on the correctional services (2003) recommended that the delivery of custodial and non-custodial penalties be brought together under the auspices of a new organization to be known as the National Offender Management Service (NOMS). Five years previously, a review commissioned by the then newly elected Labour government had rejected a full-scale merger between the probation and prison services (Home Office, 1998). This time, however, the government unreservedly accepted Carter's proposal, and NOMS came into existence in June 2004. The government also accepted an approach suggested by Carter which, if implemented in full, would entail the effective demise of the probation service in anything like its current form. This involved the introduction of a 'purchaser–provider split' for the delivery of non-custodial services,[58] whereby NOMS (the purchaser) would identify the services needed in its different regions and would buy them from a range of different 'providers'. This 'contestability' would require the probation service to compete with private commercial or voluntary sector rivals for contracts to deliver non-custodial services. These might include contracts to supervise particular groups of offenders within a given area, to deliver specified training programmes, or to deliver any of the other requirements that might form part of a community order. We shall return to this radical reform programme and its implications for the probation service in a later section.

Currently the morale and public image of the probation service are at a low ebb. The effects of the disruptive and demoralizing developments we have outlined have been exacerbated by a spate of high-profile cases in which offenders who were subject to supervision by the service committed serious offences, including rape and murder. One of these cases – the killing of London financier John Monckton in 2004 – was said by the Chief Inspector of Probation to have exposed a 'collective failure' in supervision by the probation service (HM Inspectorate of Probation, 2006a).

Unpaid work ('community service')

Powers to impose an obligation to undertake unpaid work in the community date back to the introduction of the Community Service Order (CSO) by the Criminal Justice Act 1972. The CSO was an independent court order, but the provision of community service was made the responsibility of the probation service. As can be seen from Table 5.1, the measure swiftly established itself and thereafter maintained a reasonably consistent level of popularity among sentencers.

Part of its initial popularity probably derived from its appeal to a range of different sentencing philosophies, since it combines elements of reparation, rehabilitation and retribution. The *reparative* element in unpaid work penalties requires the offender to makes amends to the community as a whole rather than to the individual victim, and thus – contrary to the ethos of restorative justice – is often imposed on an offender who has no choice in the matter.[59] The type of work to be undertaken is decided by the probation service in consultation with relevant agencies, many of which operate in the voluntary sector, who offer work placements that are approved by the probation service as being suitable. However, in principle there is no reason why offenders should not agree to undertake unpaid work of a particular kind in the context of a restorative justice process such as mediation or conferencing. Antony Duff (2001) has argued that community service fits well with his communicative theory of punishment (see Chapter 2, section 2.4). Others (for example, Walgrave, 1999; Dignan, 2002: 184) have also spoken of its potential if the criminal justice system were to be reformed in accordance with restorative justice precepts.

There is some evidence to support claims of community service's *rehabilitative* potential, since offenders in receipt of this sentence have been shown to have lower reconviction rates than would have been predicted on the basis of their age, criminal history and other relevant characteristics (Lloyd et al., 1995). In addition, May (1999) found that offenders who were given community service had lower reconviction rates than would have been expected when social factors such as unemployment or drug use were taken into account. There is also evidence that the rehabilitative potential of community service might be enhanced by improving the quality of the work undertaken by offenders. McIvor (1998), for example, found that community service placements which were viewed by offenders as most rewarding were associated with reductions in recidivism, while Killias et al. (2000) found that offenders who perceived their sentence as fair had lower than expected reconviction rates.

However, it is also possible to conceptualize community service in an unambiguously punitive manner, as a 'fine on an offender's time', particularly where the offender is required to perform tasks that are pointless, demeaning or unrelated to the crime (Bottoms, 2000). In recent years there has been a tendency to prioritize this aspect of the penalty at the expense of the other two aims. Thus, the National Standards that were published in 2000 stressed that work placements should 'occupy offenders fully and be physically, emotionally or mentally demanding' (Home Office et al., 2000: D16). In similar vein, the maximum number of hours that can be imposed was increased from 240 to 300 by the Criminal Justice Act 2003 (s. 199). The evidence referred to above suggests that a government that was interested in penal effectiveness as opposed to penal posturing would do better to focus on the reintegrative and rehabilitative aspects of the penalty instead of being punitive for its own sake.[60]

Most recently, the government has sought to 'rebrand' unpaid work with the label 'Community Payback' (a term suggestive of both retribution and reparation). The government said that it should be 'at the heart of community sentences', an aspiration that was central to the five-year strategy published by Home Secretary Charles Clarke in February 2006 (Home Office, 2006b: 3.16). This strategy aimed to double the number of hours of unpaid work carried out from 5 million hours in 2005 to 10 million. 'Community Payback' was to emphasize 'visible reparation' to the community, with offenders being garbed in distinctively coloured uniforms[61] while performing their tasks. As such, it was to feature both in an expansion of community orders (for lesser offenders as an alternative to custody) and in the proposed new 'custody plus' sentence (see below). Whatever the prospects of 'custody plus', it seems that the expanded 'community payback' scheme is set to go ahead (*Guardian*, 29 September 2006).

Penalties involving surveillance and restrictions on movement: curfews, electronic monitoring, etc.

They may sound similar, but the concepts of 'supervision' and 'surveillance' imply two fundamentally different modalities of social control that have radically different implications for offenders and, indeed, the penal system as a whole. 'Supervision' is a more 'holistic' and humanistic concept: it implies the existence of a personal relationship based on periodic contact between supervisor and supervisee and entails a degree of watchfulness combined with the possibility of guidance on the part of the supervisor, but ultimately depends on the supervisee acting in a trustworthy manner. 'Surveillance', on the other hand, implies the existence of a form of impersonal technology that offers the prospect (although not always the reality) of monitoring a person's whereabouts and movements. It gives the appearance of being backed by a more intensive and ostensibly more reliable enforcement regime that is less dependent on the trustworthiness of the offender. Even before the development of advanced technological monitoring systems, attempts were made to regulate the movement of offenders; for example, by imposing residence requirements, by means of more intensive reporting or 'tracking' requirements linked with probation supervision, or by imposing curfews. But in the absence of a reliable enforcement mechanism, these tended to lack credibility. The advent of a new form of electronic surveillance during the 1980s[62] laid the foundations for a new and controversial form of social control.

Electronic monitoring (or 'tagging') was first used in England on an experimental basis, initially as a means of enforcing bail restrictions in 1989–90 and then as a means of enforcing a free-standing curfew order (introduced by the Criminal Justice Act 1991). In 1999 curfews with electronic monitoring were made available nation-wide and the same technology was also used in conjunction with the introduction of home detention curfews for certain categories of prison inmates who were deemed suitable for early release (see Chapter 8). Electronic monitoring is also used on young offenders who are placed on Intensive Supervision and Surveillance

Programmes (ISSPs; see Chapter 9). As we have seen, under the 2003 Criminal Justice Act (s. 177), a curfew enforced by electronic monitoring can now be included in a generic community order, either on its own or in combination with one or more of the other 11 possible components of such an order. Moreover, the court can now also order electronic monitoring to be used as a means of enforcing any other requirement of a community order.

In its original (and still by far commonest) guise, electronic monitoring takes the form of an electronic device attached to the offender's ankle or wrist, which is in radio contact with a device on the offender's domestic telephone. This can confirm or deny that the offender is abiding by a curfew, which (if part of a community order) restricts the offender to his or her home for at least two and at most 12 hours per day. However, technological developments offer the prospect of developing more sophisticated methods of keeping offenders under surveillance. They include the use of voice verification technology, which make it possible to monitor an offender's presence at multiple locations, and satellite-based global positioning systems which allow the 'tracking' of an offender's movements. The latter development also makes it possible to monitor compliance with specific restrictions on the offender's movements contained in an 'exclusion requirement' in a community order or post-release licence.[63] One distinctive feature of this emergent social control technique, at least in England and Wales, is its reliance on *private* security firms rather than the probation service – which was initially ideologically strongly opposed to the new technology – in order to monitor compliance.[64]

The use of curfew orders for indictable offences registered a sharp increase of 60 per cent to 8,300 in 2004, which constituted 7 per cent of the community sentences handed down for such offences (RDS NOMS, 2005b). The fact that electronic monitoring is now available as a means of enforcing compliance with *any* community order, and not just a curfew, is likely to consolidate still further England's position as world leader in the proportionate use of electronic monitoring (Nellis, 2003: 245).[65] Although the use of electronic monitoring has been credited with contributing to significant reductions in the use of imprisonment in Sweden (Carlsson, 2003; Olkiewicz, 2003), this does not appear to be the case in England and Wales. Research commissioned by the Home Office found that the curfew order was used as an alternative to imprisonment in only around 20 per cent of cases, whereas it replaced a fine or a discharge in nearly 45 per cent of cases and some other community penalty in just under 33 per cent of cases (Walters, 2002: 40). Nellis (2003: 253ff.) has suggested, plausibly, that one possible explanation for this could have to do with people's acclimatization to a growing 'surveillance culture'. As the notion of personal surveillance and 'locatability' becomes more entrenched as a result of developments in CCTV technology and mobile phone ownership, the monitoring of offenders' whereabouts is seen as being qualitatively little different from people's everyday experience. Consequently, the fact that offenders' movements may theoretically be subjected even to constant monitoring is considered to be insufficiently punitive to count as a serious alternative to prison.[66]

The penalty that could be most seriously threatened by the spread of electronic monitoring is the more traditional form of supervision conducted by the probation service. Its vulnerability was heightened by a growing sense of moral panic during the spring of 2006, following a number of high-visibility failures (mentioned above) in which offenders who were supposedly under supervision in the community went on to commit other serious offences.[67] One of the attractions of electronic monitoring stems from the fact that it *appears* to improve the enforceability of community penalties without having to rely on the trustworthiness of offenders and the limitations of their human supervisors. However, reciprocal concerns have been voiced by probation staff about the number of violations involving offenders who are subject to electronic monitoring before they are breached, and the fact that – unlike probation supervision – there is no routine monitoring of violations (National Association of Probation Officers, 2005).[68] Indeed, some recent cases could be seen as demonstrating the limitations of electronic monitoring as a means of effective control over offenders. In one such case, a young tagged offender (released on home detention curfew: see Chapter 8) called Peter Williams was convicted of assisting the murder of Nottingham jeweller Marian Bates in 2003. Williams had repeatedly breached his curfew order and removed his tag, but little was done to control him (*Guardian*, 19 September 2005).

Nevertheless, it is difficult to deny that the image of 'automated enforcement', even if not matched in reality, has helped to shore up the political credibility of electronic monitoring at a time when confidence in more personalized forms of supervision appears to be rapidly waning (Nellis, 2004: 239). When these developments are set in the context of a decisive shift in the direction of greater private sector involvement in the administration of community punishment under the guise of 'contestability' (see section 5.5, below), the prospects for more traditional forms of probation-linked supervision look even more insecure.

Quasi- and semi-custodial 'hybrid' penalties

Historically, there was a sharp dichotomy between custodial and non-custodial forms of punishment which manifested itself conceptually, institutionally and also experientially for those convicted offenders who were sentenced to either one or the other, but never both at the same time. In recent years, however, the previously watertight boundaries between them have become increasingly permeable with the emergence of various quasi- or semi-custodial penalties that now combine elements of both forms of punishment.

The history of this new generation of 'hybrid' penalties in England and Wales dates back to the introduction of the *suspended sentence* in 1967, one of the first initiatives to be adopted in the post-war era as a means of restraining the rapidly expanding prison population.[69] Sentences of imprisonment of up to two years could be suspended for an 'operational period' of from one to two years; if the offender committed a further imprisonable offence in this time, the suspended sentence would normally be activated by the court reconvicting the offender. In this original guise, the suspended sentence of imprisonment imposed no constraints or obligations on an offender beyond the requirement not to re-offend during the operational period.[70] Despite its popularity with sentencers over many years (see Figure 5.1), the suspended sentence was a penological failure in as much as it failed to reduce or even curb the increase in the prison population. This was largely because – although supposedly a direct alternative to custody – it was often seen and used by sentencers as an alternative to other non-custodial penalties rather than a substitute for imprisonment (the phenomenon known as 'net-widening'). This in turn may have had an inflationary effect on prison numbers, as those who re-offended were far more likely to go to prison, and for longer periods, than if they had received an alternative sentence.

Courts were discouraged from using the suspended sentence by the Criminal Justice Act 1991, which restricted its availability to cases involving 'exceptional circumstances', and this had a dramatic effect on its usage, as can also be seen from Figure 5.1. The Criminal Justice Act 2003 (ss. 189–94) went further and replaced the old suspended sentence with a completely new version known as the 'suspended sentence order'.[71] This allows the court to pass a sentence of imprisonment for a fixed term (between 28 and 51 weeks), which may be suspended for an operational period of between six months and two years. The new suspended sentence order differs from its predecessor in two important respects.

First, the court passing the suspended sentence order can additionally order the offender to comply with one or more of the 12 requirements that are available as part of the new generic community sentence (see above). These requirements take effect during a specified 'supervision period' (which cannot be longer than the operational period). This feature may be seen as a response to the oft-voiced criticism that the original suspended sentence consisted of a 'let-off' in as much as it entailed no serious consequences for an offender – provided, of course, that there was no further offence. Second, the order may provide for the suspended sentence to be reviewed periodically by the court,[72] which allows it to amend the requirements at a later stage, either by strengthening them where an offender's compliance may be in doubt, or relaxing them if the offender is making satisfactory progress. This aspect of the sentence is another example of a potentially radical change in the role of the court, which is no longer confined to simply pronouncing a sentence, but increasingly can also entail a 'sentence management' function (see below).

Both aspects of the new suspended sentence order give it added 'punitive bite' and accentuate its position as a 'high tariff' measure. The suspended sentence order is subject to the 'custody threshold' set out in s. 152(2) of the Criminal Justice Act 2003: the requirement that the offence is 'so serious that neither a fine alone nor a community sentence can be justified for the offence'. Moreover, the Sentencing Guidelines Council (2004: para. 2.2.11) has issued guidelines that are intended to reinforce this requirement. The SGC has also stipulated that courts should be careful not to make the 'community punishment' requirements of the sentence too onerous (2004: para. 2.2.14). It remains to be seen, however, whether these measures will successfully avoid the malfunctions associated with the old-style suspended sentence. In Canada, the introduction of a similar provision known as the conditional sentence did contribute to a reduction in prison numbers without endangering public safety (Roberts, 2003, 2004).[73] However, much will depend on the willingness of the English courts to apply the custody threshold strictly and comply with the SGC guidelines. Given the courts' track record in the past, this remains a cause for concern. Moreover, offenders serving new-style suspended sentences are liable to have them activated not only if they re-offend during the operational period, but also if they fail to comply with the community punishment requirements during the supervisory period.[74] So, although the new-style suspended sentence has the potential to ease some of the pressure on the prison population if used properly, like its predecessor it is also vulnerable to misuse and malfunction, which could have the reverse effect.

A second type of 'hybrid' penalty which existed briefly in two areas was the sentence of *intermittent custody*. This was also introduced in the Criminal Justice Act 2003 (s. 183) and resembled the new suspended sentence order in terms of sentence length (between 28 and 51 weeks). It enabled a court to prescribe a number of days – between 14 and 90 – that had to be served in custody, though they could be served intermittently rather than as a continuous term. This might enable offenders to maintain jobs or caring responsibilities during the week and submit to custody only at weekends, for example (or indeed vice versa), which could in theory alleviate some of the damaging exclusionary consequences of a conventional custody penalty. The rest of the sentence was to be served on a licence, which could specify certain requirements akin to those contained in community orders. The new sentence was tried out in two prisons from April 2004. It always seemed improbable that intermittent custody could achieve much worthwhile – being at least as likely to 'widen the net' and give many offenders a 'taste of custody' who might otherwise have been given a fully non-custodial sentence as to divert others from full-time imprisonment. Moreover, it was practically inevitable that it would waste scarce prison cells, and so it proved. A Prisons Inspectorate report on Kirkham Prison in June 2005 found that a 39-place intermittent custody unit contained only one prisoner during the week, and had never had more than three (HM Chief Inspector of Prisons 2005d: 8.80; *Guardian*, 3 June 2005.) In November 2006 intermittent custody was summarily abolished, with the government pleading the need to prioritize protecting the public from more serious offenders (BBC News, 2 November 2006).

The 2003 Act's trio of new 'hybrid' semi-custodial penalties was meant to be completed by a penalty known as *'custody plus'* (ss. 181–2). This was intended as a replacement for all custodial sentences of less than 12 months (except those that take the form of suspended sentences or intermittent custody), but its prospects are unclear as we write. The Halliday Report (2001) identified a number of serious shortcomings associated with existing short prison sentences. The fact that offenders were liable to be automatically released at the halfway stage or even earlier under the home detention curfew scheme (see Chapter 8) meant that the custodial period was normally too short to enable any constructive programmes to be undertaken while in prison. The fact that offenders were automatically and unconditionally released on licence meant that no conditions could be attached or support provided during this period. Moreover, the fact that many of those receiving short custodial sentences were persistent offenders with multiple social problems whose risk of reoffending was extremely high meant that the public received little protection from them.

Custody plus was proposed by Halliday as a solution to these problems by combining a short period of custody with a period on licence during which offenders would be expected to comply with 'community punishment' requirements that would meet their needs while addressing the factors responsible for their offending behaviour. Both components of the sentence are subject to restrictions on length. The custodial element may be as short as two weeks and cannot exceed 13 weeks for a single offence, which is equivalent to a six-month sentence when an offender's entitlement to automatic release at the halfway stage is taken into account. The minimum licence period is set at 26 weeks to enable an offender to take part in meaningful rehabilitation or treatment programmes. Taking account of both components, the overall minimum sentence is 28 weeks (2 weeks' custody followed by 26 weeks on licence) while the maximum is 51 weeks (for example, 13 weeks in prison followed by 38 weeks on licence, or 2 weeks in custody and 49 weeks on licence).[75] Custody plus[76] was prominent in Charles Clarke's 'Five Year Strategy' published in February 2006; at this stage the plan was to bring in custody plus in the autumn of 2006. However, in July 2006 its implementation was shelved by incoming Home Secretary John Reid in the wake of an increasingly vitriolic debate over sentencing levels following a number of high-profile incidents involving offences committed by offenders serving community penalties or while on licence.

Of the three measures we have been examining in this section, custody plus could have the greatest potential to influence the size of the prison population. In the third quarter of 2005, two-thirds of all male and three quarters of all female entrants to the prison system were given sentences of less than 12 months (NOMS, 2006). However, the great majority of these (around 90 per cent in each case) were given sentences of six months or less, which obviously limits the scope for massive reductions in sentence length. Moreover, the risks of a major malfunction could be very high if and when custody plus is implemented.

One obvious problem is that 'custody plus' could appear to offer the 'best of both worlds' (Ashworth and Player, 2005: 832) to sentencers who wish to combine the rehabilitative prospects of a community penalty with a spell of imprisonment. This could result in the new penalty 'widening the net' – being used for offenders who in the past would have received a non-custodial option. A second problem is that sentencers might resent the government's attempt to reduce the amount of time offenders are kept in custody[77] and might respond by increasing the length of the custodial element, or even seek to circumvent the constraints altogether by imposing a sentence of more than 12 months. A third problem is that the success of the measure would depend crucially on the ability of community intervention programmes to succeed with one of the most challenging groups of offenders of all: socially disadvantaged, dislocated and disorganized petty persistent offenders. Moreover, the scale of the challenge is likely to be compounded by concerns over the level of resources available, organizational disruption following yet another major institutional upheaval (the creation of NOMS) and the effects on probation staff morale of anxiety over the threat of privatization. If, for whatever reason, community intervention programmes fail to deliver their intended benefits, this is likely to trigger a fourth problem. For as offenders – who are now subject to lengthier and more intrusive and demanding forms of community punishment – breach the requirements of that punishment, they are liable to end up in custody for longer periods than in the past.

Community Punishment: Strategic Issues

Changing penal strategies[78] and their impact on the use of imprisonment and community punishment

5.4 The quest for alternatives to imprisonment dates back over a century, with the introduction of probation and an expansion in the use of the fine. During the 1960s and 1970s, however, it became apparent that these traditional 'alternatives to custody' were unable to contain the prison numbers crisis. It was in this context that suspended sentences of imprisonment and community service orders were introduced (in 1967 and 1972 respectively), steps were taken to encourage the use of compensation orders, and new forms of probation were introduced (notably in 1982). However, the prevailing strategy was still heavily influenced by continuing deference on the part of governments towards the 'extravagant version' of the doctrine of judicial independence, resulting in a 'strategy of encouragement' regarding the use of non-custodial penalties instead of custody (see Chapter 4). This deferential approach was also reflected in a lack of clear guidance to sentencers as to how the new measures should be used. By 1991, it was clear that the policy of widening the sentencers' repertoire of non custodial sanctions had notably failed to alleviate the prison numbers crisis (except perhaps in the realm of juvenile justice: see Chapter 9). The general tendency was for non-custodial alternatives to supplement, rather than supplant, existing custodial measures and to function as alternatives to one another as much as to custody. Indeed, empirical evidence suggested that even when touted as direct alternatives to custody, new non-custodial penalties such as the CSO or suspended sentence usually replaced other non-custodial penalties at least half the time (Bottoms, 1981; Pease, 1985). Moreover, the proportionate use of custody by the courts actually increased significantly during much of the period in which the various new alternatives were made available, and this was reflected in a continued expansion in the size of the prison population. The penal and custodial 'nets' had widened to catch increasing numbers of offenders, not narrowed.

The failure of this *laissez-faire* approach, together with judicial concerns regarding the extent to which they were enforced, contributed to a radical shift in government policy towards the use of non-custodial penalties during the late 1980s. As we saw in Chapter 4 (section 4.5), this culminated in the introduction of a new sentencing framework in the Criminal Justice Act 1991. The new approach was symbolized by an important change in terminology, in which the terms 'punishment in the community' and 'community penalties' were substituted for the more traditional phrase 'alternatives to imprisonment'. The switch was intended to emphasize the government's initial desire that non-custodial measures should be seen as demanding penalties in their own right, and therefore appropriate for all but the most serious of offences. Efforts were also made to give substance to this tougher image for community penalties by greatly intensifying the restrictions they impose on the liberty of offenders, and also by tightening up on the way they were enforced (see below). This, too, was intended to make them more attractive to sentencers for the less serious offenders whom the government at that time wished to see being diverted from custody. We call this a policy of *'punitive bifurcation'* since it was based on a differentiation between serious and not-so-serious offenders (bifurcation), but also involved a more overtly punitive approach across the whole range of punishments. But in spite of the attempt to structure the decision-making processes of sentencers in the 1991 Act (see Chapter 4, section 4.5), the Act still relied heavily on the strategy of encouragement, since sentencers' discretion remained wide and was therefore capable of being exercised in widely varying ways. Indeed, the scope which the Act afforded sentencers was to prove capable of accommodating itself to further and more punitive shifts in the penal policy agenda.

The penal policy U-turn associated with 'the law and order counter-reformation' of the early 1990s ushered in a far more punitive climate as the 1991 Act's emphasis on 'just deserts' and 'punishment in the community' gave way to a different set of concerns centred around the newly emergent priorities of public protection and risk reduction.[79] This in turn helped to shape a new generation of community penalties that sought to harness a variety of strategies: managerialist techniques, technological controls, closer collaboration between agencies and attempts to relate restrictions on liberty to perceived risks of reoffending (rather than what the offender 'deserved'). The effect of this strategic shift can be seen in Table 5.1. This shows that the proportionate use of community penalties *which involve some form of supervision or surveillance*[80] almost doubled for adult indictable offenders from 14.4 to 28.1 per cent between 1989 and 2004. This sharp increase was not gained at the expense of custody, which also increased its 'market share' over the same period (from 17.5 per cent to 18.6 per cent). The penalties that lost out most spectacularly were the least intrusive and punitive measures such as the fine and the (old-style) suspended sentence in particular. Rod Morgan (2003: 17) demonstrated that at the end of this period, offenders who would previously have been fined were receiving 'community penalties' such as probation and community service. Meanwhile those who might previously have been given lower-level community punishments were now receiving more intrusive penalties, or being sent to custody.

As for the future, it is too soon to be able to predict with any certainty the likely consequences of the latest shift involving the adoption of a single generic community order together with a package of 'hybrid' penalties that combine short periods in custody with community punishment interventions. It is, however, a high-risk strategy that could all too easily backfire, particularly if the overall penal climate retains (or even intensifies) its current punitive orientation. One obvious danger with generic-style community orders is that courts might adopt an 'aggregative' approach when dealing with relatively minor persistent offenders. For example, they might seek to address a range of 'risk factors' simultaneously by imposing a combination of measures instead of, as in the past, progressively applying a range of different community penalties before finally resorting to custody. This could easily result in community sentences becoming even harsher than they are already. It could increase the likelihood of an offender being imprisoned for breaching some element of the package, or 'shorten the penal ladder' of different sentences which offenders typically climb before the decision is taken to impose a custodial sentence. If so, the overall effect on the prison population could well be inflationary rather than deflationary. Moreover, the risk of inflationary consequences would be further heightened by any tendency on the part of sentencers to resort too readily to one of the new semi-custodial penalties such as intermittent custody and custody plus. The fact that sentencing reforms have often malfunctioned badly in the past should serve as a warning.

Enforcement of community sentences: sticks or carrots?

If offenders breach the conditions of their community punishments, they can be returned to court ('breached') as a result. The court can then impose one of a range of sanctions (see below), which can include imprisoning the offender. For many years, decisions about enforcement of conditions were left to the discretion of local professionals (notably, individual probation officers). In recent years, however, enforcement policy has been more and more regulated by increasingly prescriptive National Standards (see, for example, Home Office, 2002b) and legislative requirements. Schedule 8 of the 2003 Criminal Justice Act requires a probation officer either to issue a warning or to initiate breach proceedings when dealing with a first breach of a community order requirement where there is no reasonable excuse. A second such breach *must* be dealt with by commencing breach proceedings and returning an offender to court.

Sanctions which can be imposed by the court for breach include the power to amend the terms of a community order with a view to imposing 'more onerous requirements' or to revoke the order and deal with the offender for the original offence (paras. 9 and 10 of Schedule 8). If the court considers that an offender has 'wilfully and persistently failed to comply with the requirements of an order', it may[81] impose a prison sentence of up to 51 weeks, even in cases where the original offence may not have been imprisonable.[82] However, the Sentencing Guidelines Council (2004: para. 1.1.47) has issued guidelines instructing courts that their primary objective should be to ensure compliance with the requirements of the sentence, and to reserve custody as a last resort for cases of deliberate and repeated breach where all reasonable efforts to ensure compliance have failed.

The adoption of a much tougher enforcement strategy in recent years dramatically increased the number of offenders jailed for breaching their community sentences from 5,364 in 1994 to 7,018 in 2004, only one-quarter of whom faced a further charge (*Guardian*, 31 August 2006). The largest proportion of those recalled for breaching community punishment orders (30 per cent) were considered 'out of touch', 18 per cent were breached for problems with their behaviour, 8 per cent for non-compliance with residence requirements, and 18 per cent for 'other reasons'. Government plans to introduce a new national enforcement service by 2007/8, announced in July 2006, appear to herald a further intensification of the existing 'get tough' enforcement strategy and seem likely to result in more offenders being sent to prison for breaching community sentences (Home Office, 2006c).

The rationale for adopting such a rigorous approach with breach proceedings is to maintain the credibility of community sentences in the eyes of sentencers (Hough et al., 2003: MORI, 2003). Whether this is the most effective way of ensuring that offenders comply with their orders is open to doubt, however. There is some research evidence that adopting appropriate enforcement action (by issuing warnings or initiating breach proceedings) may result in lower reconviction rates than overlooking non-compliance (May and Wadwell, 2001). However, another study, which compared enforcement practice in areas with different enforcement strategies, found that there was virtually no difference in terms of reconviction rates for offenders against whom breach proceedings were initiated between 'tough' and 'lenient' areas (Hearnden and Millie, 2003). Hedderman and Hough (2004) have argued that (despite some methodological flaws), this study indicates that strictness of enforcement appears to have little impact on overall reconviction rates, and that offenders appear to be relatively immune to the deterrent threats or practices of probation officers. Moreover, their contention that 'the "big stick" is neither the only nor the best way of securing offenders' compliance' (2000: 5), has been supported by a number of other commentators.

Ellis et al. (1996), for example, have suggested that more might be done to sustain an offender's engagement with community orders by such means as issuing appointment cards or coordinating appointments with signing-on days for the unemployed. (Reminder phone calls and text messages might also be helpful.) Others have taken on board Bottoms' (2001) observation that the punitive techniques of constraint and deterrence, which currently underpin official enforcement strategies, afford only one means of securing compliance and may be less effective than alternative approaches based on recognition and reward (Hedderman, 2003; Hedderman and Hough, 2004; Underdown, 2001). Teeside probation area's practice of providing breakfast to those attending final programme sessions provides one example of an alternative approach based on inducements rather than the threat of penalties. Another approach would be to relax the restrictions or reduce the demands imposed on an offender by the requirements of a community order as a reward for satisfactory compliance. This has only rarely been done up until now: only around 8 per cent of community rehabilitation (probation) orders were terminated early in response to good progress in 2002 (Home Office, 2004f). This could change, however, if courts were to be given a greater role in the oversight of community orders, which is an issue to which we now turn.

'Sentence management' and the changing role of the judiciary

The traditional image of the sentencer was aptly summed up by Zimmerman's reference (cited in Rottman and Casey, 1999: 13) to the 'dispassionate, disinterested magistrate', whose responsibility for influencing the offender's behaviour began and ended with the pronouncement of the sentence itself. This left the various tasks entailed in administering the penalty, including monitoring and enforcing an offender's compliance, for the most part in the hands of other criminal justice practitioners.

In recent years, this 'culture of 'compartmentalism' has been in retreat, and provisions authorizing the courts to monitor and review the progress of offenders have been attached to a number of penalties including, as we saw above, the new-style suspended sentence of imprisonment.[83] Review hearings also form an integral part of many community orders with drug rehabilitation requirements, an arrangement which implies a much more collaborative partnership between those responsible for administering the order and the sentencing court which is expected to actively monitor an offender's compliance with it. One prominent model for such a partnership is provided by American 'drug courts' (which have also been piloted in Scotland; see Eley et al., 2002). In these courts, sentencers are highly proactive, participate greatly in monitoring and reviewing sentences, and are noticeably more interested in securing compliance from offenders than in merely sanctioning them in the event of a breach. Judges in drug courts (who receive training in how to deal with substance abuse) often actively engage with offenders, with a view to motivating and encouraging them, and this may result in occasional lapses being overlooked, provided the offender is making genuine attempts to comply with the order. This kind of enforcement strategy comes much closer to the more constructive approach favoured by many critics of the current punitive mentality.

Recent tentative steps to encourage English judges to adopt a more proactive sentence management function fall a long way short of emulating these drug courts. Nevertheless, they represent a step in that direction. A possible pointer to the future is contained in the Criminal Justice Act 2003 (s. 178), which empowers the Secretary of State to direct all courts to make routine use of review hearings for the purpose of monitoring and reviewing the progress of offenders who are subject to community orders. If the traditional division of labour and responsibility between sentencers and those responsible for administering punishment are ultimately broken down, this will have major implications for the relationship between them, which will need to accommodate both their new responsibilities and also the need for new mechanisms of accountability. Or, as David Faulkner (2005: 39) has aptly put it: 'The old rules may no longer apply, but the new rules have not yet been written.'

Effectiveness of community sentences

We take the view that community sentences should always be used in preference to custodial punishment, unless the offender represents a serious risk to the safety of others, or (exceptionally and for brief periods only) where confinement is the only possible means of gaining the cooperation required to make the appropriate community sentence work. This opinion is founded on moral, rights-based considerations (see Chapter 2) rather than purely practical calculations. Nevertheless, whatever one's angle on the morality of punishment, we would also argue that community punishment is capable of serving almost all the purposes that are conventionally associated with imprisonment at least as effectively as custody itself, and in some cases more effectively (see further Cavadino et al., 1999: 117ff.)

The relative 'effectiveness' of penal sanctions (in terms of their success in reforming or individually deterring offenders) is conventionally measured by comparing reconviction rates, despite their well-known shortcomings as a measure of 'penal success'.[84] When the reconviction rates that are associated with custody and community penalties are compared – after allowing for factors that are known to influence the risk of reconviction (such as age at first offence, type of offence, criminal history and gender) – the differences between them are usually found to be negligible.[85] However, this may be because community penalties have not been living up to their potential. It has been claimed that community sentences that conform to certain principles – for example those focusing on social skills or utilizing cognitive behavioural methods – can have measurable positive effects on recidivism, whereas those with strong punitive effects can increase recidivism by some 25 per cent.[86] Research evidence also seems to show that comparable reformative programmes are more likely to be successful in community settings rather than in custody.[87]

Moreover, there is no reason in principle why community penalties should not also serve denunciatory or retributive ends, just as custody is supposed to. (For example, community punishments of differing onerousness (or 'penal weight') can be prescribed for offences of differing seriousness.) Indeed, community-based restorative justice processes such as mediation and conferencing have the added advantage, if conducted properly, of denouncing an offender's conduct without at the same time denigrating and stigmatizing the offender as a person, in the way that conventional penalties (and particularly custodial ones) do. As for the pursuit of other sentencing aims such as reparation and reintegrative shaming, it also seems highly probable that these are more likely to be successful where offenders are kept in the community, for fairly obvious reasons: it is hard to make amends to the community and become part of it again if you are locked away from it. This leaves, as the main apparent advantage that custody has over other penal measures, the 'public protection' effect it appears to offer by 'incapacitating' offenders from committing certain kinds of offences (see Chapter 2, section 2.2). We accept that there are some serious violent and sexual offenders who present such a clear and vivid threat to the safety and well-being of others that custodial incapacitation is both justifiable and right. For the great majority of less serious offenders who are routinely incarcerated, however, it is highly doubtful whether the temporary gain in public protection that custody appears to offer can be justified in view of the economic, social and personal costs that such an extreme sanction inflicts. The fact that community penalties appear to be at least as effective as custody in preventing reoffending, while at the same time affording greater opportunities for the needs of victims to be addressed, should in our view be conclusive.

The Carter Reforms and their Implications for the Probation Service

5.5 The controversial reform agenda emanating from the Carter Report of 2003 (see section 5.3) was unreservedly and almost immediately accepted by the government without any prior consultation and on the basis of only limited public discussion after the proposals had already been announced. It now forms part of an increasingly audacious 'modernization' agenda that seeks to transform the way the criminal justice system operates in order to meet the perceived new challenges it faces at the beginning of the twenty-first century. In this section we shall deal with the two most important aspects of the programme:

- the organizational changes that are intended to merge the work of the prison and probation services in the new era of 'seamless sentencing';[88] and
- the principle of 'contestability', which seems destined to transform the way offenders are managed with as yet unknown but potentially cataclysmic changes for the probation service on the eve of its centenary.

Organizational reform: the NOMS bombshell

The main rationale for merging the prison and probation services into a single correctional agency was based on the argument that they operated as two self-contained airtight 'silos' (Carter, 2003: 1), whose insularity inhibited the prospects of seamlessly 'managing' offenders throughout their sentence. Hence, Carter proposed to bring together the delivery of custodial and non-custodial punishment under the aegis of a single integrated body to be known as the National Offender Management Service (NOMS). This would entail the abolition of local probation boards and the appointment of ten NOMS Regional Offender Managers.[89] However, the proposals did not stop there for, as we saw in section 5.3, they also advocated the adoption of a 'purchaser–provider split' in the delivery of community penalties in order to facilitate the development a market-based approach (see below). Ultimately, Carter envisaged that the role of the Regional Offender Managers would be to identify the specific offender management services needed in their area and to 'commission' (i.e. purchase) them from service providers. These would include not only the public sector probation service, but also private sector companies and organizations operating in the voluntary and community sector, all of whom would be invited to tender on a competitive basis for the contract to deliver such services in their area. *'Contestability'* was the term used by Carter, and subsequently the government, for this competition to sell services to NOMS.

This entire reform agenda was as rudimentary in detail as it was radical in scope. The National Offender Management Service itself was established in June 2004 and National and Regional Offender Managers were also appointed. Thereafter, however, the implementation programme became increasingly shambolic as the first attempt to make the necessary legislative changes[90] was lost in the run-up to the

2005 General Election and then Martin Narey, who had recently been appointed as the first Chief Executive of NOMS, unexpectedly resigned in July 2005. Prior to this, the government's belated consultation document (Home Office, 2004g) had received a predictably hostile response (Rumgay, 2005) and for a while the most contentious aspects of the programme relating to the purchaser–provider split and 'contestability' proposals seemed to have been put on hold. However, a second consultation document (Home Office, 2005c) was published in October 2005, which signalled a more radical restructuring and a renewed commitment to press on with the contestability agenda despite the opposition to it. The local probation boards which oversee the probation service in their areas were to be abolished and replaced by 'probation trusts', described as 'smaller, more business-focused bodies' whose members need not have any connection with the locality. These trusts would compete with the private and voluntary sectors to sell probation services to the NOMS Regional Offender Manager. It was even envisaged that, in some areas, the public probation service might be left with no contracts and would cease to exist entirely (Travis, 2005). The whole reform process to date has been characterized by the sense of 'permanent revolution' (McLaughlin et al., 2001) that has been a hallmark of the government's approach to criminal justice reform (and much else besides) ever since the Crime and Disorder Act of 1998.[91]

Apart from the uncertainty this engenders, as old structures are torn down and new edifices hastily erected in their place, important questions have been raised concerning the need for and wisdom of such changes. While the logic of a more holistic approach to the treatment and supervision of offenders as they progress from prison to the community is widely accepted, Raynor and Maguire (2006: 21ff.) have pertinently questioned whether this necessitated yet another massively disruptive organizational upheaval. The consistent message from the research they review is that the key prerequisites for motivating offenders, supporting personal change and hence lowering the risk of reoffending depend on the quality of the supervisory relationships between practitioners and offenders. Yet it is not at all clear how this is going to be improved by a further potentially disruptive restructuring, which will result in the unitary process of offender management being arbitrarily split into three distinct elements: supervision, case management and administration. The risk of damaging fragmentation is likely to be increased if, as seems probable, these functions were carried out by two or three separate individuals. Indeed, the problems are likely to be compounded where staff are assigned to either the 'commissioning' or 'service delivery' side of the binary divide that underpins the entire concept of contestability. Already there is research evidence that the organizational dislocation brought about by the need to relocate and retrain staff has resulted in staff resistance and a loss of morale, role confusion and operational inefficiencies, together with communication problems and inhibitions about information sharing (PA Consultancy Group and MORI, 2005; see also Robinson and Burnett, forthcoming).

Another major problem associated with the restructuring is that it seems destined to remove the final vestiges of a probation service with strong local roots and a physical presence in local communities in favour of a supposedly more efficient but also more distant regional organization. The disbandment of local 'probation liaison committees' (linking probation services with the local bench of magistrates), which fell victim to the introduction of the National Probation Service in 2001, was already lamented by many magistrates and probation officers (Raine, 2006: 14). However, the proposed abolition of local probation boards and the possible extinction of some local probation services compounds the error. Quite how this will contribute to the twin aims of reducing reoffending while enhancing public confidence in the system of community punishment, particularly at a local level, is difficult to envisage. For, as Hough and Allen (2005/6: 30) also point out, the local dimension in probation work has been critically important in linking up with wider social policy initiatives to tackle social exclusion, regenerate communities and renew civil society. Ironically, these centralizing tendencies in the field of community punishment are proceeding apace at a time when the police seem to have rediscovered the value of strong community links.[92] Moreover, recent research conducted in Sheffield has highlighted the potential benefits to be derived by correctional agencies seeking to engage more creatively with local residents by demonstrating that the area's offenders are being dealt with constructively while showing sensitivity to their own genuine concerns (Bottoms and Wilson, 2004). Regrettably, there are no signs that such insights have registered with those responsible for the NOMS reforms.

Contestability: the 'marketization' of community punishment

Even more controversial than the NOMS-based organizational restructuring was Carter's total commitment to the principle of contestability, which Bottoms et al. (2004: 8) describe as 'arguably the dominant concept' in his report. Although the precise meaning of the term remains unclear and, indeed, is itself hotly 'contested', it is clearly about promoting greater involvement by the private and not-for-profit' sectors in the delivery of community interventions.[93] As Nellis (2006: 55) points out, this could mean little more than an extension of the principle of 'market testing' (see Chapter 7) to the sphere of community punishment as a mechanism for injecting better value-for-money and neutralizing opposition to modernizing reforms from hostile public sector trade unions. Or it could entail the deliberate introduction of a 'mixed economy' model in which the probation service would lose its former status as the near-monopoly provider of community interventions and become merely one declining player among several service providers operating in an increasingly competitive and uncertain environment. Initially the government (Home Office 2004e: 14) claimed to be 'not interested in using the private sector for its own sake'. By 2006, however, its five-year strategy document made no secret of its goal 'to harness the dynamism and talents of a much more diverse range of best-in-class public, private and not-for-profit providers, each with their own set of special skills and expertise' (Home Office, 2006b: 31).

As with the NOMS restructuring, this dogmatically driven strategy raises a number of major concerns. The first relates to an obvious tension between the government's desire to promote a more holistic and better integrated approach to the management of offenders and its apparent determination to engineer a massive proliferation in the number and range of players involved in the delivery of criminal justice interventions. This 'balkanization of the criminal justice system'[94] is likely to result in a further fragmentation. Indeed, if the experience of prison privatization is anything to go by, when the various service providers are operating in a competitive environment, the problems of communication, information-sharing and cooperating with one another are likely to grow rather than diminish.

A second problem has to do with the unknown consequences that are likely to ensue when the value-base that underpins the machinery for delivering community interventions shifts from the relatively disinterested, altruistic orientation of the traditional probation service to a more instrumental, commercially minded focus. This is likely to have major implications for the individual relationships between practitioners and offenders and also for relationships between those agencies that are responsible for delivering criminal justice interventions, the courts they serve and the wider public. As Liebling (2006: 75) has argued, it is disturbing that such fundamental issues do not seem to have received any serious consideration from those promoting the reforms, who seem quite content to press ahead in an evidential vacuum. For example, will the range of services to be contracted out extend to the preparation of pre-sentence reports, in which case what safeguards will be put in place to ensure that the recommendations are not coloured by commercial considerations? And even if they are not, can a probation service that operates in a commercially competitive environment be expected to provide the same kind of disinterested advice to the courts that it gave in the past?

Other difficult questions relate to the need for accountability and the added tensions that are likely to ensue between a service provider's accountability towards the court, the regional NOMS commissioning agency and its shareholders, and the need for political accountability at both local and national levels (Hough, 2006: 5). And finally, what will be the effect on the morale and operational effectiveness of the probation service itself? Mike Nellis (2006: 62) has correctly pointed out that the NOMS and contestability reforms are an expression of visionary 'blue skies thinking' at the heart of government. The problem with blue skies thinking is that it is, almost by definition, insufficiently grounded in empirical realities. Nellis is also right to warn (2006: 64) that, when attempts are made to actualize blue skies thinking without regard to those realities, 'the distance between blue skies and scorched earth is often far narrower than many contemporary modernisers would have us believe'.

Shifting Patterns of Penality: Theoretical Reflections

5.6   In this section we turn to the question of whether it is possible to make sense of the various developments (including the changing fortunes of the main sentencing disposals as depicted in Table 5.1) we have been examining so far. We shall also ask what light, if any, theories of penality can shed on such changes, and whether they have anything to tell us about the nature and future direction of social control mechanisms in general.

Although, as we shall see, there is considerable debate at present concerning the exact nature and significance of recent developments within the penal system, there is also much common ground between the various protagonists regarding the context within which these changes are said to be taking place. All are agreed that the starting point for the current debate lies in the so-called 'great transformation' of punishment which has been most notably chronicled by Foucault (1977) (see also Ignatieff, 1978; Rothman, 1971). This original 'transformation' was the major shift in the form of punishment from 'corporal' to 'carceral' punishment, which occurred around the end of the eighteenth and beginning of the nineteenth centuries (see Chapters 2 and 3).

There is also a broad measure of agreement on the part of contemporary penal commentators that a number of significant changes affecting the penal system have occurred since then, and particularly since the mid-1960s. But opinions differ as to whether these amount to a 'second transformation' and, if so, what form it is taking or how exactly it should be characterized.

Scull's 'Decarceration' Thesis

The opening shot in the present debate was fired by Andrew Scull in 1977 with the publication of his book *Decarceration: Community Treatment and the Deviant – A Radical View*. Although he has subsequently revised some of his ideas (Scull, 1984), Scull originally argued very strongly that we are now experiencing a major shift in the ideology and apparatus of social control that amounts to at least a partial reversal of the original 'great transformation'. Scull used the word *'decarceration'* to refer to 'the state-sponsored policy of closing down asylums, prisons and reformatories' (1984: 1).

The term thus encompasses two parallel tendencies. One is the so-called *'community corrections* movement', whereby offenders are increasingly dealt with in the 'community' instead of locking them up in custodial institutions. The other is the move towards *'community care'*, which extends the same principle to the treatment of people with mental disorders, and which results in the systematic closure of large-scale psychiatric institutions. Scull not only lumps together policies for dealing with the 'mad' and the 'bad' but he uses the same term – 'decarceration' – to cover both tendencies. He also illustrates his thesis with reference to both British and American developments, believing that the forces responsible for decarceration policies are at work throughout the contemporary capitalist system (see below).

According to Scull, the most potent of these forces are economic considerations, which now favour decarceration, whereas at the time of the original transformation of the penal system, a policy of incarceration made greater economic sense. In brief, by the turn of the nineteenth century the old 'poor law' system was quite unable to cope with the growing number of desperately poor people, many of whom were economically unproductive for much of the time and unable to provide for their own subsistence. Moreover, traditional methods of social control (based mainly on a feudal pattern of social obligations between rich and poor) were losing their effectiveness at this time. Consequently, the most economically efficient way of dealing with the problem of poverty and its attendant risk of social disorder was to move to a system of large-scale institutions within which the unproductive and the deviant could be provided for and controlled.

But by Scull's era (the late twentieth century), these economic and social considerations no longer applied. Instead, the cumulative effects of increased public expenditure over the years (on welfare, housing and industrial assistance programmes, among others) had plunged the state into a serious and worsening fiscal crisis, making it imperative for public expenditure to be drastically curbed. One way of doing this was by using welfare payments and social services to enable many of the so-called 'problem populations' (Scull, 1984: 135) who were previously incarcerated in institutions to be looked after and controlled in the community instead. From the state's point of view, it now seems much more expensive to keep people locked up in institutions than to subsidize others to look after them in the community. Scull is not convinced that community alternatives *are* necessarily cheaper to operate in practice than the institutions they displace – because of opposition from vested interests and the difficulty of achieving more than marginal cost-savings unless whole institutions can be closed down. But he does strongly maintain that decarceration has more to do with cost-saving imperatives than with the development of more effective forms of treatment, or any genuine commitment to humanitarian improvements in the lot of the incarcerated.

Indeed, far from being humane, he considers that decarceration is not in the interests either of all the deviants themselves, or of the community into which they are unceremoniously decanted. In the case of the elderly and the mentally ill, for example, he argues that such a policy results in many ex-inmates being herded into 'newly emerging "deviant ghettoes", sewers of human misery ... within which ... society's refuse may be repressively tolerated' (Scull, 1977: 153). As far as offenders are concerned, he speaks of 'burglars and muggers ... being left to walk the streets', and even 'the perpetrators of violent crime' as being 'turned loose under conditions which guarantee that they will receive little or no supervision'. As a result, he considers that decarceration 'forms yet one more burden heaped on the backs of those who are most obviously the victims of our society's inequities. And it places the deviant in those communities least able to care for or cope with him' (1977: 1–2).[95]

Scull is surely right to insist that we should look behind the façade of official rhetoric when examining the reasons for major penological change. But his thesis is vulnerable to three main lines of attack. It is theoretically shaky, since it is based on an over-simplistic form of economic determinism (see Chapter 3); it fails to fit the facts in a number of crucial respects; and Scull himself fails to probe sufficiently deeply behind the rhetoric of decarceration to expose the real consequences of the changes to which he refers. We shall now deal briefly with each of these charges in turn.

One major difficulty with Scull's 'fiscal crisis' argument is its rather simplistic assumption that because traditional methods of treating and controlling 'problem populations' are becoming relatively more expensive to operate, the state is obliged to adopt decarceration rather than seeking savings elsewhere, for example through cuts in welfare programmes. In fact, as critics such as Matthews (1979: 106) have noted, this is precisely what the state has done. Cuts in public expenditure during the late twentieth century were very selectively distributed, with the result that spending on law and order increased substantially during this period[96] at the expense of other public expenditure programmes, notably welfare spending. What the 'fiscal crisis' argument fails to take into account is that in any given period, penal policy is a product of the complex interplay between political and ideological pressures, in addition to the economic forces with which Scull was almost exclusively concerned.

Another serious problem that results from Scull's economic determinism is a tendency to over-generalize from the available data in a way that is not supported by the facts. Many commentators (see, for example, Cohen, 1979; Matthews, 1979; Burton, 1983; Hudson, 1984) agree that his thesis applies quite well to developments in mental health policy in recent years. However, he is almost universally criticized for assuming that because the same economic pressures presumably apply to the treatment of offenders as well, it follows that recent developments in penal policy must necessarily be part of the same phenomenon. In fact, as we shall see, this contention is fatally undermined by empirical evidence drawing on geographical, historical and contemporary data relating to trends in the use of imprisonment.

Geographically, the 'fiscal crisis' theory is seriously weakened by evidence relating to the Dutch experience following the Second World War. For although the Netherlands between the 1940s and mid-1970s provided almost a textbook example of decarceration in the penal sphere (Cavadino and Dignan, 2006: ch. 8), it spectacularly fails to conform to the fiscal crisis argument – in fact, quite the reverse. As Downes (1988: 58) has pointed out, the dramatic reduction in the Dutch prison population mostly occurred during a time of unprecedented prosperity which preceded the onset of the fiscal crisis to which Scull refers.[97] Conversely, a significant expansion of Dutch prison numbers coincided with a period of heightened economic uncertainty.[98]

Scull's decarceration thesis is also undermined by historical evidence relating to the use of imprisonment. This quickly dispels the notion that decarceration is a uniquely distinctive feature of post-war penal policy as it seeks to respond to novel economic constraints. For example, there was a remarkably rapid decline in the prison population from 1908 to 1918 (see Ruggles-Brise, 1921: ch. 17; Fox, 1934: ch. 17; Rutherford, 1986b: 122–31; Bottoms, 1987: 178–9). During this period – and against a background of steadily rising conviction and recorded crime rates (Rutherford, 1986b: 129) – the prison population more than halved from 22,029 to 9,196. By comparison, during the supposed post-war decarceration era that Scull refers to, his own figures show a near doubling of the prison and borstal population from 21,370 in 1951 to 38,382 in 1972.

It could be argued that such increases in the absolute number of people imprisoned are misleading unless account is taken of changes in the crime rate and, in particular, of the total number of convicted defendants (Bottoms, 1983: 183). When the *proportionate* use of imprisonment for all sentenced offenders is examined (see Table 5.1), it can be seen that there was indeed a fall in the proportion of the sentenced population that was sent to prison from 25 per cent in 1960 to 18 per cent in 1971. But thereafter it rose again and, in the case of adult male offenders, the rate of imprisonment almost doubled from 15 per cent in 1974 to 27.9 per cent in 1999. So even on this weaker definition of decarceration, Scull's thesis was not borne out by events, at least at the level of penal practice. Barbara Hudson (1984) has suggested that decarceration during this period occurred only at the level of rhetoric,[99] in official discourse about the use of imprisonment, and that Scull failed to probe behind this rhetoric to see what was really happening.

Scull's original assessment of the *consequences* of decarceration has also been criticized (see in particular Cohen, 1979: 361) for taking at face value claims that decarceration would lead to non-intervention (and not to intrusive control over offenders in the community), and for complaining that this would lead to a weakening of sanctions against offenders. In his more recent work (Scull, 1983, 1984), Scull acknowledged that the position was rather more complicated than this, and went on to claim that the community corrections movement had actually resulted in an undesirable *extension* of the state's social control apparatus. This he attributed to 'a strong conservative backlash against anything smacking of leniency towards crime and criminals', which he saw as the product of 'the accelerating volume of crime over the past quarter century' (1984: 175, 177).[100]

Even with these revisions, however, Scull's decarceration thesis is still defective. For example, no attempt is made to explain how the ideological factors favouring stronger control measures come to outweigh the economic imperatives favouring decarceration. Nor does he give sufficient weight to the influence of humanistic, inclusive penal ideologies in bringing about limited decarceration in those times when it did occur. Another major issue which the thesis fails to address fully is the debate about recent 'alternatives to custody' and how they relate to the 'extension of social control' argument. For an attempt to confront these issues, we turn now to a rival thesis which has been put forward by two very influential theorists of social control, Stanley Cohen and Thomas Mathiesen.

Cohen and Mathiesen: The 'Dispersal of Discipline' Thesis

In a series of works, especially his 1979 article 'The Punitive City' and his 1985 book *Visions of Social Control*, Stanley Cohen painted a nightmarish vision of the city of the future as being increasingly subjected to a sophisticated social control network. Unlike Scull, who initially described the community corrections movement as a reversal of the original 'great transformation', Cohen always considered it to be simply a continuation of the same 'disciplinary' project, albeit on a much more ambitious scale. Whereas the first transformation had the effect of concentrating the social control energies of the state on highly selected populations of deviants *inside* specially designated institutions like the prison and the asylum, he pointed out that this was no longer the case. Instead, recent penal developments associated with the community corrections movement demonstrate that the state is now spreading its tentacles of control ever more deeply into the tissues of society by significantly widening the reach and the scope of its social control apparatus.

Cohen described the key features of this second transformation in a memorable series of metaphors.[101] They include:

- **Widening the net.** This concept (which has already featured several times in this chapter) refers to the process whereby community programmes tend to 'capture' many who would not formerly have been subjected to the attentions of the criminal justice system. One example is when police cautioning is used not only as an alternative to prosecution but also for those who would otherwise have been informally dealt with. The end result is to 'increase rather than decrease the total *number* who get into the system in the first place' (Cohen, 1979: 347, italics in original).

- **Thinning the mesh.** Not only are more offenders brought into the system. Those who are dealt with by means of newer, more intensive community orders also experience a greater *degree of intervention* than would have been the case if a more traditional alternative to custody such as a fine, ordinary probation or conditional discharge had been used instead.

- **Blurring.** As a result of these and other developments – notably electronic monitoring and the introduction of seamless, semi-custodial penalties – there is a blurring of formerly rigid distinctions between institutional and non-institutional forms of control, or even between what is or is not regarded as punishment. Very presciently, Cohen foresaw a day when 'it will be impossible to determine who exactly is enmeshed in the social control system' (1979: 346).

- **Penetration.** The combined effect of these tendencies is that the whole (considerably enlarged) system of social control is now extending more and more deeply into the *informal* networks of society. Even more important, though, is the fact that these measures *augment* the existing prison system. They do not displace it; on the contrary, they enable the prison to reach out into the community. And so, as Downes (1988: 60) has put it, '[w]e end up with the worst of both worlds: an unreconstructed *ancien régime pénal* and a new-style carceral society'.

Cohen saw the whole of the community corrections movement as 'merely an extension of the overall pattern established in the nineteenth century' (1979: 359), whereby the mode of control founded on *discipline* is dispersed out of the big institutions in which it originated, and into the rest of society. ('Discipline' is the concept developed by Foucault (1977) to characterize the attempt to transform the 'soul' of the offender – see Chapter 3). Cohen cited (1979: 347, 357) community service (unpaid work) as just one obvious example of a form of punishment that penetrates deeply into the informal social networks of civil society by requiring offenders to undertake socially useful work in the community. Moreover, the fact that community service orders are often used in place of less intrusive penalties such as the fine is seen as evidence of its 'mesh-thinning' tendencies.

This 'dispersal of discipline' thesis was taken a stage further by the Norwegian criminologist, Thomas Mathiesen (1983). In a prediction which echoed the concerns voiced by Cohen, he too foresaw that 'the control system as a totality may *expand rather than shrink*' as a result of proposals to strengthen society's social control mechanisms by, among other things, developing 'crime care in the community'. But whereas Cohen's main concern was with crime control strategies that are individualistic in the sense that they still aim at 'a disciplining of the law-breakers 'one by one', Mathiesen (1983: 132) discerned in certain other recent developments the emergence of a new and complementary strategy that could 'move fully away from individualism, and focus on *control of whole groups and categories*' (1983: 139) by means of general surveillance. Mathiesen gave the following examples of the kind of social control techniques he had in mind:

> TV cameras on subway stations and in supermarkets, the development of advanced computer techniques in intelligence and surveillance, a general strengthening of the police, a general strengthening of the large privately-run security companies, as well as a whole range of other types of surveillance of whole categories of people – all of this is something we have begun to get, and have begun to get used to. (1983: 139)

Mathiesen believed that these new societal or collective forms of control would increasingly impinge on the everyday lives of groups and categories of people and that, as such, they represent a break with individualism as the archetypal form of social control.[102] Nevertheless, he still characterized them as 'disciplinary' measures and so they too were seen as extensions of the original carceral project, in which more efficient disciplinary social control measures are dispersed into the wider society. The difference for Mathiesen was that the new techniques he described involved 'a change *from open to hidden discipline* … The new control out there in society is either completely outside the individual's range of vision, or at least quite a bit less visible than the control forms of pure individual liberalism' (1983: 139).

While closed circuit television (CCTV) cameras of the kind mentioned by Mathiesen undoubtedly extend the range of surveillance, their impact is still partial and limited, since to date they normally either depend on the capacity and attentiveness of operatives who monitor the screens to identify those incidents meriting a response, or are only used retrospectively after an incident has occurred in order to obtain evidence and help identify an offender. As such, these relatively passive technologies at best represent a quantitative increase in the capacity of social control agencies to *detect* (and to some extent deter) law-breaking, whether by individuals or groups of individuals, rather than the exertion of constant control.

However, recent technological developments hold out the prospect of a further significant *qualitative* change in the nature of social control, which for some heralds the dawn of a new era of 'technocorrections' (Fabelo, 2000; see also Franko Aas, 2005; Haggerty, 2004; Jewkes, 2004/5). These developments include potential refinements in the capabilities of electronic monitoring as it switches from radio frequency to satellite tracking technology, the planned introduction of biometric identity cards and associated applications together with prospective advances in the development and utilization of DNA databases and gene therapy for crime control purposes. The crime control potential of these various developments is admittedly fairly embryonic at present, though it would be rash to imagine that this will always be the case. One highly plausible scenario might involve the immense capacity of computerized databases – drawn from a variety of official and commercial sources (such as loyalty cards) – being harnessed with the ability to undertake algorithmic analysis of digitized CCTV footage.[103] The effect of this kind of technological convergence – which Haggarty and Ericson (2000) refer to as a 'surveillant assemblage' – would add depth and intensity to the somewhat superficial capability of current systems. An even more sobering prospect would be a further synergization between the kind of general surveillance measures described by Mathiesen and high-tech versions of personalized crime control measures – perhaps utilizing satellite tracking technology linked with smart microchip implants – aimed at individual law-breakers. This would indeed conjure up a truly dystopian vision of a 'Panopticon society'[104] in which the authorities are able to exert near-total control over the lives of large groups of people or even entire populations.

Although these somewhat gloomy assessments of recent developments in social control may be in keeping with the spirit of the times – and while their Orwellian overtones fit the concerns of social control theorists speculating on the future – they are not without their critics. David Garland (1995b: 3), for example, has reminded us that, viewed sociologically, surveillance is and always has been an essential element of social control and, quite apart from being an inescapable adjunct of modernity, does have benevolent as well as repressive potential. Moreover, while technologies of the kind we have referred to above could be used to increase *detection* rates, there is no necessary connection between this and any increase (or indeed reduction) in the level of *penalties* for offenders once they are caught.[105] (This is not to belittle the important issues concerning civil liberties and privacy which undoubtedly do exist regarding the access to and use of the information which is gathered by way of these new technologies.)

More generally, Tony Bottoms (1983) – while finding much to commend in Cohen's and Mathiesen's analysis of specific control mechanisms – has questioned the way they analysed these developments in terms of the 'dispersal of discipline thesis'.[106] The central thrust of Bottoms' critique was that many of the new community control measures that are described by Cohen and Mathiesen are not in fact *disciplinary* measures; at least, not in the sense in which Foucault used the term. Bottoms argues persuasively (1983: 182) that Foucault's notion of discipline contains two key elements: one is *surveillance*, and the other involves the *'mechanics of a training'*, which aims to produce an obedient subject by repeatedly working on the offender's 'soul'. This, according to Foucault, was the fundamental objective of the original carceral project that emerged from the first great transformation of punishment. But if this is the case, then Mathiesen is mistaken to characterize the recent move towards a more collective form of social control as a dispersal of *discipline*. For the techniques he describes depend almost exclusively on the technique of surveillance alone, making use of advanced technological developments and improved methods of policing rather than any 'mechanics of a training'.

Of the more individualistic forms of control, community service was cited by both Cohen and Mathiesen as evidence of their contention that punishment is beginning to penetrate ever more deeply into the informal networks of society, and again this is depicted as an extension of *discipline*. Bottoms agreed that it appears to conform to some of the tendencies described by Cohen – mesh-thinning and community penetration in particular – but again he doubted whether this alone is sufficient to warrant the term 'discipline'. For although work can be, and indeed has been, used for disciplinary purposes ever since the birth of the carceral system, other aspects of community service – such as the element of reparation that it can entail – make it less congruent with the dispersal of discipline thesis.[107] Once again, much the same point could be made in respect of more recent surveillance and control measures, including those based on electronic monitoring, which by themselves do little or nothing to train offenders in habits of obedience.

Another serious charge against the 'dispersal of discipline' thesis in Bottoms' eyes was its neglect of certain other features of contemporary penal systems that are not at all consistent with the 'dispersal of discipline' thesis and which therefore cast some doubt on its universal applicability. Chief among these 'neglected features' of contemporary penal systems (at the time he developed his critique) was the dramatic post-war growth in the use of the fine, particularly in the period up to 1980. This was crucial to his argument for two main reasons. First, because the fine is manifestly *not* a disciplinary penalty in Foucault's sense of the word; and, second, because (as can be seen in Table 5.1) the fine did more to displace the use of imprisonment – at least during the early post-war period – than any of the more disciplinary penalties (such as probation).

This is not at all what one would expect of an emerging 'carceral society'. Rather, it chimes in with Bottoms' more general observation (1983: 169) that *'penalties not involving continuing supervision by a penal agent'* – that is, such non-disciplinary measures as the fine, and the suspended sentence – were at that time flourishing at the expense of more 'disciplinary' measures such as imprisonment and probation (see Table 5.1). Finally, Bottoms noted that the recent growth of concern for victims within the criminal justice system is another development that cannot be explained by the dispersal of discipline thesis.

For all these reasons, Bottoms concluded that the 'dispersal of discipline' thesis was not a particularly helpful way of characterizing contemporary penal developments. What was needed instead, he believed, was a thesis that could account for the relative *decline* in the significance of disciplinary punishments at that time within the total apparatus of social control. With this aim in mind, he tentatively advanced a third thesis which we call the *'juridical revival'* thesis.

Bottoms' 'Juridical Revival' Thesis

In developing his rival theory, Bottoms reminded us (1983: 176) that at the time of the original 'great transformation', there was a third model of punishment besides the traditional or *corporal* model (aimed at the body of the offender) and the *carceral* model (based on imprisonment) which displaced it. This third model, which Bottoms called the *juridical* system of punishment, was proposed by the classical reformers such as Beccaria (see Chapter 2) but ultimately exerted much less influence on forms of punishment at the time than did the disciplinary ideas of reformers like Bentham. Bottoms suggested (1983: 195), that the reason for this was because the social control techniques that were available at that time were largely ineffective in maintaining order. However, circumstances change, and the essence of Bottoms' thesis is that we may now be heading towards a second 'great transformation' from a carceral to a juridical system of punishment. The effect of this is seen – not in the dispersal of discipline throughout society, as Cohen and Mathiesen have argued – but as *diminishing* rather than increasing the role of punishment as a method of social control.

Unlike the carceral project which, as we have seen, was founded on reforming offenders through discipline, the juridical project aimed at 'requalifying individuals as subjects' (Bottoms, 1980: 21). This 'requalification' was to be achieved through the application of a standard set of penalties that were intended to be fixed in duration and proportionate to the seriousness of the offence. Once the punishment was completed, the offender would be readmitted to society as a full member with undiminished rights of citizenship. Most importantly, the preventive 'message' that the punishment was intended to represent was to be transmitted by the simple symbolic fact of punishment itself. Accordingly, there was no need for specific social control agencies designed to 'mould' offenders into obedient subjects (Bottoms, 1983: 176).

In the light of this analysis, Bottoms concluded that many of the penal developments to which he had drawn attention were more accurately characterized as embodying juridical rather than carceral tendencies. This was particularly true of the fine, which Bottoms correctly suggested is more of a 'classical' than a disciplinary punishment (1983: 178), but there were other pointers in the same direction. These included the general increase (at the time) in penalties not involving supervision by a penal agent, the increase in compensation payments by the courts, and also the recent growth of interest in the principle of reparation.

As for the reasons underlying these developments, Bottoms suggested (1983: 196) that the key to the debate lay in a more detailed appreciation of the nature of the transition from early to late capitalism than is to be found in any of the previous accounts. One strand in his proposed explanation was based on certain changes in the nature of law and social control that had occurred during this period (and in many ways have continued to develop since Bottoms wrote). These changes have been characterized by Kamenka and Tay (1975) in terms of a shift towards a 'bureaucratic-administrative' social and legal order in advanced capitalist societies (see Chapter 3). A key feature of this development was a shift in the locus of social control from the formal punishment system to other bureaucratic agencies, both public and private (for example, government departments, local authorities, television licensing authority, private security firms). Another aspect is the increased reliance on non-disciplinary forms of social control, based on a variety of techniques such as increased surveillance, negotiation and formal warnings.

Some aspects of Bottoms' analysis do not fit the penal scene of the twenty-first century as well as they did the early 1980s when he was writing. Most notably – as Table 5.1 dramatically demonstrates – the proportion of punishments that involve supervision or surveillance of some kind, following the decline which Bottoms charted, thereafter experienced an even more marked rise. Conversely, the (non-supervisory) penalties of fine and suspended sentence followed their previous steep rise with a steeper decline. One interpretation of this is that when Bottoms wrote, 'disciplinary' punishment was reaching a nadir, but has since recovered to record proportions. Is the 'punitive city' indeed upon us?

Conclusion: The Future of Punishment?

5.7 We have now examined three of the most important contributions to the recent debate about the nature of our contemporary social control system. Even at the time Scull wrote, there was little evidence to support his 'decarceration' thesis, except at the level of official rhetoric, and even that has now ended. However, the 1991 reforms did offer some support for both the other theories ('dispersal of discipline' and 'juridical revival'), suggesting a possible emerging bifurcatory approach whereby 'discipline' and 'juridical' measures would be applied to different groups of offenders (see Cavadino and Dignan, 1992: 197). Thus, at the time it seemed possible that the introduction of unit fines might herald a reinvigoration of this 'juridical-style' penalty, particularly for less serious but impoverished offenders who might previously have been imprisoned instead. Many developments in the treatment of younger offenders around that time were also more consistent with a 'juridical' rather than a 'disciplinary' approach.[108] However, other features of the 'just deserts' package suggested a strengthening of the disciplinary and control elements associated with community penalties such as probation and community service.

In the light of the punitive counter-reformation which took off in 1993 and continues to maintain a stranglehold in the minds of penal policymakers, there has been little prospect in recent years of an imminent resurgence in the use of 'juridical' penalties for any group of offenders.[109] Indeed, Table 5.1 shows a continuing increase in the proportionate use of supervisory community sentences (especially probation), and also custodial sentences, at the expense of non-supervisory penalties. The first of these tendencies is more consistent with the 'dispersal of discipline' thesis, though the net-widening potential of other recent developments – conditional cautions, fixed penalty notices and anti-social behaviour orders – might also be noted in this context. Ever-increasing government enthusiasm for electronic monitoring (both as a near-standard component of most community orders and also as a form of pre-release mechanism; see Chapter 8) and the advent of new hybrid semi-custodial penalties seem destined to 'blur' still further the distinction between institutional and non-institutional forms of social control (as also suggested by Cohen). Moreover, the government's clear preference for ultra-summary forms of 'justice' that enable formal penalties to be imposed by the police in respect of increasingly trivial forms of 'misbehaviour' with minimal legal safeguards or constraints shows how formal control mechanisms are penetrating ever deeper into society. On the other hand, the recent (and seemingly relentless) upsurge in the use of custody represents a clear change and, at the very least, a partial reverse in the direction of penal policy back towards custody and away from community punishments, at least for the time being.

Realistically, albeit reluctantly, we have to acknowledge that the recent track record strongly suggests that substantial decarceration is unlikely to occur in England and Wales at least in the foreseeable future. If it ever does occur, it will almost certainly not be brought about either as a result of a mere 'strategy of encouragement', nor from a revival of the old 'rehabilitative ideal'. Likewise, it seems improbable that pressures from advocates of 'just deserts' will succeed where these older strategies failed, despite the best endeavours of some, and occasional undoubted successes in some other countries (von Hirsch, 1993: 91–4). As for electronic monitoring, which has been credited with contributing to a reduction in the Swedish prison population (Cavadino and Dignan, 2006: 158), we agree with Nellis (2003: 256) that this is unlikely to happen in England and Wales where community orders with monitoring requirements are much more likely to be used to supplement or supplant other community penalties rather than be used as an alternative to imprisonment.[110] Moreover, we share his concerns (Nellis, 2005: 142) that growing government support for the measure signifies a disturbing shift from a predominantly humanistic 'low-tech' paradigm to a predominantly surveillant 'high-tech' paradigm in community supervision and punishment.

Any significant change in the direction of penal policy of the kind we are advocating is likely to require a much more prescriptive structuring of sentencing discretion (see Chapter 4) and/or a vigorous and well-supported application of systems management techniques (see Chapter 9). But neither of these is likely to come about without a radical change in the penal ideologies of sentencers, the public, other criminal justice practitioners and policy-makers and (especially) government politicians. Above all, we need a 'replacement discourse'[111] and a new ideology in which punishment in the community is seen as the paradigm of *normal punishment* and not as a 'let-off' in which criminals scandalously 'walk free'. Sentencers, politicians, media and public need to end their long-standing and passionate 'love affair with custody' (Travis, 2003). Could this happen?

Despite the rather gloomy short-term prognosis, we believe and hope that the longer-term future of penality remains open. We do not believe that there is any inexorable tendency at work in the evolution of penal policy, whether in the direction of increased use of custody, net-widening or an intensification of social control via 'high-tech' gadgetry. In spite of the many recent policy failures that we have recounted, we remain convinced that decarceration and diversion from custody are desirable and achievable goals. We are fortified in this conviction by the fact that genuine decarceration has occurred in other jurisdictions such as the Netherlands (Downes, 1988; Cavadino and Dignan, 2006: ch. 8), Ontario, Canada (McMahon, 1992), and Finland (Cavadino and Dignan, 2006: ch. 10; Törnudd, 1993) in the recent past. Indeed, it happened in England and Wales earlier this century, when the prison population was halved between the years 1908 and 1923 (Rutherford, 1986b: 123–31). A substantial decarceration also occurred with young offenders in England and Wales in the 1980s, as we shall recount in Chapter 9.

Moreover, we are reasonably hopeful that strategies could be devised to ensure that decarceration can be attained without widening the criminal justice net – or thinning its mesh – to an unacceptable extent. Several pieces of research (see, for example, Bottoms, 1995b: 10–11) confirm that it is possible for relatively intensive non-custodial penalties to be accurately 'targeted' so that they do not serve to 'thin the mesh' or 'up-tariff' offenders (see Chapter 9). McMahon (1992) also found that decarceration in Ontario was not accompanied by any general net-widening, except in the near-inevitable sense that if a supervisory sentence is used as a substitute for a short prison term, then the offender is likely to stay 'within the net' for longer. The experience of the Kettering Adult Reparation Board (Dignan, 1991) was that the introduction of a reparation scheme may have had some 'net-widening' and 'mesh-thinning' effects with a small proportion of offenders (although a higher proportion were diverted from prosecution altogether); however, we would regard these particular effects as acceptable, since one result was that victims were benefited by the reparation carried out as a result.

While it may be possible to envisage decarcerative strategies, and even to identify ones that have been successful either elsewhere or in the past, this is no guarantee that they are likely to happen in England and Wales in the near future. For example, some of the genuine decarceration documented by McMahon in Ontario happened because there was a strong prevailing belief in the rehabilitative ideal which is unlikely to return, at least in its previous form. Nevertheless, we believe that there are grounds for believing, cautiously, that moves towards decarceration could occur in the not-too-distant future. The reasons for our cautious optimism are based on a reading of the penality debate that differs in several key respects from the three accounts we have been considering.

In the first place, we are not convinced that the term 'carceral' is the best way of describing the original penal transformation that took place during the late eighteenth and early nineteenth centuries. For in reality the displacement of corporal and capital punishment during this period was accomplished by a variety of practices (including transportation for a time), in addition to the various non-custodial penalties that have subsequently been developed alongside the carceral system. In our view the change in the nature of penality that accompanied the original 'great transformation', and also those that have taken place thereafter, are more accurately characterized according to the functions they perform (or are intended to perform), as opposed to the precise institutional form they may take at any given time.[112]

In the early days of imprisonment, one of the main functions it was intended to perform was to 'transform' offenders[113] into obedient subjects by subjecting them to the disciplinary techniques to which Foucault (and later Bottoms) referred. Subsequently other, non-custodial penalties – notably probation – developed with similar 'transformatory' objectives in mind. Although the collapse of the rehabilitative ideal cast doubt on their transformatory potential, existing penal measures such as imprisonment and probation were not abandoned, though they were displaced to some extent by the introduction and expansion of alternative penal measures such as the fine, suspended sentence, community service and others. Following the collapse of the rehabilitative ideal, the justification for all penal measures came to rest on rather different philosophical foundations (see Chapter 2) which, in turn, were founded on the rather different functions that punishment can perform.

We shall examine the various aims and functions of imprisonment in Chapter 6. Here, we wish to emphasize that the various non-custodial penalties that have been introduced alongside imprisonment itself are likewise intended to perform a range of different functions. One function involves the application of some form of unpleasantness or *deprivation* on offenders for purposes of retribution, denunciation or deterrence. The 'commodity' of which the offender is deprived may take a number of different forms: liberty in the case of imprisonment; time and effort in the case of community service; and money in the case of fines. One of the most distinctive aspects of the 1991 reforms was their attempt to rank these different penal currencies in a comprehensive tariff covering the full range of offences from the most to the least serious.[114] However, deprivation is not a feature of all penalties. Some, such as the conditional discharge and the suspended sentence, are principally admonitory in the way they operate. Finally, it is worth noting that some non-custodial penalties may also be intended to perform preventive or incapacitative functions. For example, disqualification is intended to stop motoring offenders from driving, attendance centre orders may be used to keep football hooligans away from matches, and curfews backed by electronic monitoring can be used to prevent offenders being at large at times when they are thought most likely to offend.

Most contributors to the 'nature of penality' debate have tended to gloss over these differences in the functions performed by different forms of punishment and the way in which the importance that is attached to them has waxed and waned over time. They have also overlooked one feature that is shared by virtually all the conventional forms of punishment (including more recent innovations such as electronic monitoring) we have been considering up until now. This is the fact that they rely almost exclusively on the application of '*external*' as opposed to '*internal*' sanctions and, as such, are directed primarily *against* an offender.[115]

During the last few years, however, two rather different sets of penal responses have emerged which could, conceivably, contain the seeds of a distinctly different kind of penality. One set of responses seeks to engage offenders in a variety of processes that require them to reflect on the harm they have caused to others and encourages them to try to make amends for what they have done. Some of these processes involve some form of dialogue between victims and offenders (for example, mediation, family group or community conferencing, or circle sentencing) and are associated with the approach known as *restorative justice*. Others involve the use of cognitive behavioural techniques (see Chapter 2, section 2.2), which do not necessarily require the participation of a victim. One feature that both sets of processes have in common is that they rely on the use of *internal sanctions* which operate on the basis of an offender's conscience rather than the application of external sanctions of the kind that characterize most conventional forms of punishment.

A second set of penal responses seeks to identify and address the causes of a person's offending behaviour, with a view to reducing the likelihood that the person will reoffend in the future. Several aspects of the New Labour government's youth justice reform programme (see Chapter 9) typify this approach.[116] They include the use of action plan orders and youth offender contracts, which can be used to try to tackle school attendance problems in cases where offending is felt to be attributable to truanting. Likewise, the use of mentors has been adopted in cases where a young person is felt to have inappropriate peer-group relationships. Some restorative justice approaches (notably family group conferencing; see Chapter 2) also encourage young offenders and their families to devise 'action plans' that will deliver appropriate reparation for victims and at the same time seek to address factors that are felt to have precipitated an offence.

We are inclined to believe that the best chance of ending our 'love affair with custody' and achieving significant decarceration in the future could rest on the development of restorative and reintegrative techniques of the kind we have just described. At the very least, a comprehensive strategy that aimed wherever possible to combine appropriate reparation for victims with the reintegration of offenders back into the community would offer a coherent and humane basis for moving away from the prevailing obsession with imprisonment as a response to crime. We are encouraged by the rapid growth of interest in such techniques on the part of penal policy-makers in very many penal jurisdictions around the world. In our view, they offer the best prospect for the development of a 'replacement penal discourse' that could challenge and change the basic assumptions that inform the current debate about punishment and the form it should take. We shall return to these issues and to our own vision for a just and humane (and predominantly non-custodial) penal system in our final chapter.

Notes

1   We use the term 'non-custodial punishment' to refer to the full range of penalties that are available to the courts following a criminal conviction and which do not involve the imposition of a term of immediate imprisonment. The generic term 'community punishment' is used to encompass all court-imposed penalties or orders that entail restrictions on a person's liberty apart from those with a custodial element (whether immediate, intermittent or suspended). The terms 'community sentence', 'community penalty' and 'community order' are used inter-changeably when referring to specific forms of community punishment. This chapter is mainly concerned with court-ordered punishments. However, there has been a growing tendency in recent years to empower other agencies (notably the police) to impose non-custodial penalties on less serious offenders. Recent examples include the power to impose fixed penalty notices (akin to the fine) and also conditional cautions (akin to the unpaid work requirement of a community order). See also the Introduction.

2   Most of the provisions of the 2003 Criminal Justice Act came into force on 4 April 2005, but not all of them; one exception is the new custody plus sentence (see below).

3   Powers of Criminal Courts (Sentencing) Act 2000 (hereafter 'PCC(S)A 2000'), Section 12.

4   Over 20,000 people were bound over in 2001 (Home Office, 2003d).

5   A review of the measure conducted by Campbell (2002) showed that 58 per cent of those given ASBOs were under the age of 18, while 75 per cent were under the age of 21.

6   Some victims of *violent* crime are also entitled to receive compensation from a separate state-funded Criminal Injuries Compensation Scheme, but only where the injury sustained exceeds the minimum threshold of £1,000; see Dignan (2005a) for details.

7   PCC(S)A 2000 (s. 130(12)).

8   The legal framework relating to compensation orders is set out in sections 130–4 of the PCC(S)A 2000.

9   There are, however, maxima for particular offences: offences are graded according to seriousness in five bands that determine the maximum fine applicable.

10 Offenders may be ordered to furnish the court with any information it requires for this purpose (Criminal Justice Act 2003, s. 162).

11 As they were officially called under the Criminal Justice Act 1991 (s. 6).

12 Criminal Justice Act 2003, s. 177. The maximum length of such an order is three years (s. 177(5)).

13 As set out in Criminal Justice Act 2003 (s. 148).

14 Also known, briefly, as the community rehabilitation order, following a 'rebranding' exercise in 2000 (Criminal Justice and Court Services Act).

15 In December 2005 the most prevalent requirements attached to the community order were supervision (accounting for 37 per cent of all requirements given), followed by unpaid work (30 per cent) and accredited programmes (18 per cent) (RDS NOMS, 2006a: Table 3.3). Forty-eight per cent of community orders had one requirement, 35 per cent had two, 14 per cent had three and 2 per cent had four or more requirements (RDS NOMS, 2006a: Table 3.2).

16 ISM schemes are broadly comparable to the Intensive Supervision and Surveillance Programmes available for young offenders and the Intensive Change and Control Programmes available for young adult (18–20 year-old) offenders (see Chapter 9). The collaborative partnership arrangements for delivering the intervention also somewhat resembles the Youth Offender Team model adopted as part of the wide-ranging youth justice reform programme introduced after 1997. So far the ISM scheme initiative has been subject to a process evaluation (Homes et al., 2005), which was broadly positive, though the findings of an outcome evaluation were not yet available at the time of writing.

17 Criminal Justice Act 2003 (s. 214). In the past it was only available for offenders below the age of 21.

18 Restricted availability of such centres, which are heavily dependent on the goodwill and commitment of individual police officers, is a major limitation. (This problem also affects other community interventions (Raine, 2006: 14).)

19 The Act specifically states that this can include activities involving contact between offenders and victims provided the latter agree to this, which in theory at least could provide a way of routinely facilitating certain kinds of restorative justice interventions (see below).

20 Or community punishment order as it was known for a short time; see also note 14 above.

21 Prior to the 2003 Act, the maximum number of hours of unpaid work that could be imposed was 240 hours.

22 The Carter Report (2003) had previously proposed an alternative three-point scale based on the perceived risk posed by offenders, in which low-risk offenders would be dealt with by means of 'Level 1' penalties such as community service. Offenders with risk-assessed needs including education, drugs, thinking and behaviour would attract 'Level 2' penalties such as probation with additional requirements, while persistent offenders would be dealt with by measures involving greater control and surveillance including electronic monitoring and satellite tracking (see below).

23 For example, petty persistent shoplifting and minor public order offences.

24 Examples given include some handling of stolen goods offences (where the value is less than £1,000); some burglaries of commercial premises; and some cases of taking vehicles without consent.

25 See below for an account of the history of the suspended sentence.

26 It will be noted that the way offences are grouped together for the purpose of Table 5.1 is different from the way they are ranked within the current sentencing framework. The reason for this will become apparent when we refer back to this table in the penultimate section of this chapter.

27 This was an era in which practitioners were heavily influenced by the philosophy of 'minimum interventionism', particularly with regard to younger offenders (see Chapter 9), but also in respect of less serious adult offenders.

28 As Ashworth (2005: 297) points out, the introduction of the conditional caution for adult offenders (see below) might be expected to divert from the courts some offenders who would otherwise have been dealt with by means of a conditional discharge.

29 A more detailed account of the early history of the fine can be found in Cavadino and Dignan (2002: 126ff.).

30 The use of the fine for unemployed indictable offenders rose sharply from 30 per cent in the summer of 1992 to 43 per cent in 1993. Moreover the average fine for the unemployed decreased during this period (from £88 to £66), while it increased for those in employment (from £144 to £233) (Home Office, 1994b).

31 The most famous case being the '£1,200 crisp packet' littering case (see Cavadino et al., 1999: 165).

32 See Ashworth (2005: 305–6), Cavadino and Dignan (2002: 128–9) or Cavadino et al. (1999: 164–5) for details.

33 But since paralleled by John Reid's remarkably similar about-turn with regard to the Criminal Justice Act 2003. As we will see in Chapter 6, however, this is by no means the only example of penological *déjà vu*.

34 See also Moore (2003), who has called for a revised version of the unit fine in which the seriousness of the offence would be reflected in the duration over which a fine would need to be paid, while the amount would be based on the offender's spare income, subject to a fixed minimum and maximum amount.

35 Carter also recommended transferring responsibility for collecting fines from the courts to the National Offender Management Service (NOMS), but the government – somewhat illogically, given that the responsibility for administering all other court sentences is to be vested in NOMS in the future (see below) – rejected this proposal.

36 There have been some attempts to tackle problems with the *enforcement* of fines in recent years. For example, the number of fine defaulters who are sent to prison has been drastically reduced by promoting alternative enforcement mechanisms (see Ashworth, 2005: 311–12 for details). Moreover, various measures have been introduced to try to improve collection rates, including the use of private contractors and incentives for early payment (Courts Act 2003, Schedule 5). But ignorance about the reasons for default and the way fine enforcement works continue to bedevil further progress in this area (Mair, 2004: 154).

37 Section 142 of the Criminal Justice Act 2003; see also Chapters 2 and 4.

38 The proportionate use of compensation for *summary* (less serious) offences in the magistrates' courts more than doubled during the same period, but even after this increase, only 15 per cent of summary offenders were ordered to pay compensation in 2004.

39 *Jorge* [1999] 2 Cr App R (S) 1. However, the Court ruled in that case, that the principle does not apply to offenders with substantial assets (particularly if they take the form of proceeds of crime) or the prospect of a sufficiently large income on release to warrant such an order.

40   Even though the legislation makes it clear that compensation should be considered even
      in the absence of any application on the part of the victim, the Court of Appeal has
      advised sentencers against 'simply plucking a figure from the air' (*R. v. Oliver* (1989) 11
      Cr App R (S) 10). See also Moxon et al. (1992).

41   The proposal was first mooted in a Green Paper (Home Office, 1988: para. 3.10) but
      the government refused to adopt it because of its financial implications (Home Office,
      1990a: para. 4.25). The idea was revived in a 2001 policy document that mentioned
      the possibility of establishing a 'Victims Fund' to ensure the earlier payment of com-
      pensation for victims (Home Office, 2001: para. 3.118). From 1 April 2007, a £15 sur-
      charge was added to all fines, the proceeds to go towards funding a range of services
      for victims and witnesses (but not to compensate them financially).

42   Until recently, one obvious limitation was that victims were not eligible for compensa
      tion at all if their offender was cautioned as opposed to being prosecuted, though this
      anomaly has recently been addressed by the introduction of conditional cautions (see
      the Introduction).

43   Shapland et al. (1985) reported that victims value the payment of compensation by
      offenders even if their loss or damage is not compensated in full. This may be partly
      because such payments represent a symbolic acknowledgement by offenders of the
      important principle that they owe a moral obligation to do what they can to repair the
      harm they have inflicted on their victim.

44   On the needs of victims within the criminal justice system generally, see Christie (1978);
      Shapland (1984); Shapland et al. (1985); Marshall (1985); Zehr (1985); Blom-Cooper
      (1988), Dignan (2005a).

45   See Dignan (2005a), for a more detailed account of the different restorative justice vari-
      ants including the way they operate, their relationship with the regular criminal justice
      process and relevant empirical findings.

46   In principle it is possible for them to operate outside the regular criminal justice system
      altogether, often where the system itself is not fully operative for one reason or another;
      recent examples include apartheid South Africa and, closer to home, Northern Ireland.
      Elsewhere, fully independent processes tend in practice to encounter problems in
      'recruiting' cases to deal with, not least because of the risk of 'double punishment' if the
      regular criminal justice process runs its course as well.

47   See, for example, Morris et al. (1993); McElrea (1994); and, for an overview of these
      and other related developments, Dignan and Cavadino (1996); Dignan (2005a).

48   Progress – at least in respect of young offenders – has been much more dramatic in
      Northern Ireland, where a statutory scheme has been introduced which mandates the
      use of conferencing both as an alternative to prosecution and also in place of the tradi-
      tional sentencing process (see Dignan, 2006 for details).

49   For some fuller and more detailed accounts of this complex history, see McWilliams
      (1983, 1985, 1986, 1987); Nellis and Gelsthorpe (2003); Raynor (2002); also previous
      editions of this book.

50   A process that was exacerbated during the 1960s by the assumption of additional
      responsibilities for the supervision of prisoners following their release from imprison-
      ment (see Raynor, 1993; see also Chapter 8).

51   Internally, the collapse of the rehabilitative ideal prompted a debate over the nature
      of probation values as a rising generation of young probation officers questioned the
      individualized treatment approach and sought to promote an anti-discriminatory
      agenda. This probably helped to reinforce the dominant perception in the media
      and government that the service was overly politicized (Nellis and Gelsthorpe, 2003:
      228).

52   Previously, courts had made probation orders 'instead of sentencing' the offender
      (Powers of Criminal Courts Act 1973, s. 2(1)). Subsequently, the Crime (Sentences) Act

1997 removed the statutory requirement for the offender to give consent before a probation order could be made.

53 Criminal Justice and Court Services Act 2000 (s. 2) (The full set of aims is : '(a) the protection of the public, (b) the reduction of re-offending, (c) the proper punishment of offenders, (d) ensuring offenders' awareness of the effects of crime on the victims of crime and the public, (e) the rehabilitation of offenders'.)

54 Hough et al. (2003) point out that the proportion of offenders given community penalties who had no previous convictions increased dramatically between 1991 and 2001. For those given probation/community reparation orders, the figures rose from 11 per cent to 27 per cent. For those given community service/community punishment orders the figures rose from 14 per cent to 51 per cent. For those given combination orders/community punishment and rehabilitation orders the figures rose from 10 per cent in 1992, when the order was introduced, to 28 per cent in 2001. See also Home Office (2002: 25).

55 See also Holdaway et al. (2001), who encountered a similar tension between generalist and specialist models of offender management and service delivery when evaluating the introduction of youth offending teams.

56 Comprising 42 areas.

57 Section 2(2); another aim was 'ensuring offenders' awareness of the effects of crime on the victims of crime and the public'. See also n. 53 above.

58 A similar purchaser/provider split had previously been introduced as part of a reorganization of the National Health Service during the 1980s. Elsewhere, the Queensland government adopted a similar approach (where it was referred to as 'corporatization') for the reorganization of its correctional services in 1997. The merits of such a strategy were called into question just a few years later, however, by a critical report which concluded that the purchaser/provider split had created inefficiencies and called for the strategy to be overturned; see Cavadino and Dignan (2006: 310) for details.

59 Originally the offender's consent was required before a community service order could be made, but (as with probation orders) this prerequisite was removed by the Crime (Sentences) Act 1997.

60 In 2003 the National Probation Service launched an initiative known as 'enhanced community punishment' to augment the then-existing community punishment order by combining its punitive and reparative aspects with a rehabilitative element. All offenders subject to the order were expected to address their employment-related skills and thinking skills in addition to the work element. See HM Inspectorate of Probation (2006c).

61 This idea seemed to have survived the departure of Mr Clarke in May 2006. His successor John Reid was reported in July 2006 as being 'interested in increasing the visibility of unpaid work, e.g. through uniforms'. Such work 'would have to be portrayed as "penance and contrition" and to be seen by the public as genuinely paying back to the community' (*Guardian*, 26 July 2006).

62 The development of the technology was originally inspired by an episode in a Spider-Man comic in which the villain sought to track Spider-Man's movements by means of an electronic bracelet. A New Mexico judge who read the story approached computer companies and a monitoring device was developed based on patents taken out in the 1960s by a Harvard professor, Dr Ralph Schwitzgebel (NACRO, 1988: Nellis, 2004).

63 In September 2004 a pilot satellite tracking scheme was launched to enable the police and probation service in three separate areas to monitor released sex offenders' compliance with restrictions imposed on their movements 24 hours a day. See Nellis (2005) for details and also more generally on satellite tracking. The report of the evaluation was

due to be submitted at the end of March 2006 (Parliamentary Written Answer 21 July 2005; col. 2215W), but had not been published as we write.

64 Initially the responsibility for providing electronic monitoring services was shared between three such firms covering England and Wales and one for Scotland. One of the English firms lost its contract in November 2004, however, on the day that a tagged offender was jailed for murdering an elderly homeless woman in Devon (National Association of Probation Officers, 2005).

65 Paul Goggins, then Minister for Correctional Services, gave an insight into government thinking on the scope for further expansion in the use of electronic monitoring: 'We have to open the possibility of tagging to all adult offenders' (quoted in Graham, 2004).

66 This might be seen as a contemporary illustration of the 'less eligibility' principle that in a previous era required conditions in workhouses to be patently worse than those experienced by the poorest of the non-institutionalized poor.

67 There was a spate of such incidents in the spring of 2006 including the kidnap, rape and stabbing to death of a 16-year-old schoolgirl by a six-strong gang, several of whom were under supervision while serving community penalties. Another involved the killing of a London financier which was said by the Chief Inspector of Probation to have exposed a 'collective failure' in supervision by the probation service (HM Inspectorate of Probation, 2006a).

68 Another objection to electronic monitoring relates to its cost. A Home Office evaluation in 1997 estimated that a three-month curfew with electronic monitoring costs £1,900. This compares with an annual cost of £2,200 for a probation order and £1,700 for a community service order (Mortimer and May, 1997: 42). The National Association of Probation Officers (2005) has subsequently claimed that it costs twice as much to 'tag' an offender as it does for a probation officer to supervise them.

69 For a more detailed account of the origins and operational history of the measure, see Bottoms (1981) and also the previous edition of this book.

70 Courts could pass a 'suspended sentence supervision order', which combined a suspended sentence with a requirement of supervision, but no other additional requirements were possible.

71 As proposed by the Halliday Report (2001), which suggested that the new version should be known as 'custody minus', though in the event the old name was retained; possibly, as Wasik (2004a) has suggested, because the new name did not sound tough enough.

72 Criminal Justice Act 2003 (ss. 191–3).

73 Roberts (2004: 88) has suggested that, unlike the English legislation, Canadian judges are specifically required by law to be satisfied that a conditional sentence would be consistent with the purpose and principles of sentencing as set out in the criminal code.

74 The consequences for offenders who breach a suspended sentence are set out in detail in Schedule 12 of the 2003 Act, and will normally result in an offender being warned after an initial breach and then brought to court for any subsequent lapse. The court is expected to order the custodial term to take effect either in whole or in part, unless it considers it unjust to do so, in which case it has the power to amend the order (para. 8(2)).

75 Or a total of 65 weeks, of which the custodial period cannot exceed 26 weeks, when a court imposes two or more terms of imprisonment to be served consecutively.

76 Together with a strong emphasis on the use of unpaid work as a major feature of licence conditions for the community portion of the sentence.

77 Halliday's insistence that very short prison sentences are 'meaningless and ineffective' is also vulnerable on this score.

78 See Bottoms et al. (2004) for a fuller analysis of the shifts in penal strategy since the early twentieth century.

79 Both sets of concerns were reflected in the creation of Multi-Agency Public Protection Arrangements (MAPPA) under the 2000 Criminal Justice and Court Services Act. Under these arrangements, police, prison and probation authorities in each of the 42 criminal justice areas in England and Wales are now required to assess and manage the risks posed by serious violent and sexual offenders, including those on the Sex Offenders' Register. Other relevant agencies including social services, youth offending teams, housing and education authorities have a duty to cooperate with the Responsible Authority for each MAPPA area and reports are issued annually outlining the work that is being undertaken under the auspices of MAPPA.

80 See further, section 5.6 below.

81 Section 53 of the Criminal Justice and Court Services Act 2000 would have introduced a presumption that the court should imprison offenders who appeared before them for breach of community orders. However, the government presumably thought better of it and this section (which was never brought into force) was repealed by the Criminal Justice Act 2003.

82 An additional sanction that is available to the courts when dealing with offenders who have breached a community sentence comprises a reduction or removal of certain benefit entitlements. The measure was introduced under the Child Support, Pensions and Social Security Act 2000, and was piloted initially in four probation areas. A report of the pilot evaluation was conducted by Colin Roberts (2004), and a summary of the report is available on the Department of Work and Pensions website at the following url: http://www.dwp.gov.uk/mediacentre/pressreleases/2004/feb/iad0502-ecswbp.asp.

83 Similar powers are also available in respect of a number of disposals that are available for young offenders, including the action plan order and referral orders.

84 See, for example, Brody (1976); Maltz (1984) and Lloyd et al. (1994: 3–10).

85 See, for example, Lloyd et al. (1994), who compared the actual reconviction rate with the predicted rate for imprisonment, probation and community service. See also Mair (1997) for further discussion and Raynor (2004) for a recent overview of the major lessons from international research of the effectiveness of rehabilitative and reintegrative approaches.

86 McGuire and Priestley (1995). McIvor (1992) has also shown that offenders whose experience of community service is rewarding and worthwhile tend to have lower reconviction rates than those who find it unrewarding.

87 See, for example, Andrews (2001), Andrews et al. (1990: 384), Goldblatt and Lewis (1998: 104), Lipsey (1992: 138) and Vennard et al. (1997: 3).

88 The term 'seamless sentence' refers to any sentence that is served partly in custody and partly in the community, of the kind that were introduced in the 2003 Criminal Justice Act (see above, section 5.3).

89 Nine for England and one covering Wales.

90 Management of Offenders and Sentencing Bill 2004–5. A replacement Bill was expected to be published in May 2006 but still had not appeared at the time of writing, so the timetable for reform is still uncertain, even though the government's commitment to the changes remains unwavering.

91 David Faulkner (2006: 82) has pointed out that whereas in former times the vision underpinning a major reform programme and much of the detailed narrative might have been spelt out in a White Paper or the report of a Royal Commission or departmental committee, this now has to be created within government departments and virtually from scratch, following the pronouncements of ministers.

92 See, for example, the government's Neighbourhood Policing Initiative (Home Office, 2005d).

93 As such, the 'contestability' agenda represents a clear example of the New Public Management approach to which we referred in Chapter 1 (see section 1.4).

94 A '*mot juste*' that was coined by our colleague, Joanna Shapland.

95 Some of these concerns were subsequently echoed in relation to the policy of 'care in the community' for psychiatric patients, which was pursued in the 1980s, following incidents such as the stabbing of Jonathon Zito by Christopher Clunis in December 1992 (see Ritchie, 1994). But for a more sceptical view of the moral panics surrounding the 'scare in the community' phenomenon, see Cavadino (2002: 176–7).

96 In England during the period 1956–78, spending on the prison system increased at a rate two and a half times as great as for public expenditure generally (Rutherford, 1986b: 90; Shaw, 1980). During the period 1980–90, spending on public order showed a threefold increase compared with a two or two-and-a-half-fold increase on other public services such as education, health and social services (Central Statistical Office, 1991: Table 9.4).

97 McMahon's (1992) very careful analysis of post-war penal trends in the Canadian province of Ontario provides another telling counter-example to Scull's thesis (see also Cavadino, 1994). She demonstrates that decarceration also occurred in Ontario in the 1960s and early 1970s, at least in the sense that admissions to prison and numbers in prison declined relative to the total population of Ontario during this period. In contrast to Scull's economistic explanation for the decline, McMahon (like Downes, 1988 in the Dutch context – see also Cavadino and Dignan, 2002: ch. 8) attributes the decarceration that occurred during this period to the influence of the then-prevailing ideology of rehabilitation.

98 The Dutch experience also fails to conform to predictions based on Scull's fiscal crisis theory in relation to the mentally ill, for whom institutional care has survived to a much greater extent than in either England or the United States.

99 A Marxist, or post-Marxist, might see this gap between the 'rhetoric' (or ideological message conveyed by the 'discourse' of the penal system) and its material reality as significant. See Chapter 3 for a more detailed discussion of the idea that the penal system may form part of a state's 'Ideological State Apparatus'.

100 In itself a dubious linkage, given that (to take one example), England since the early 1990s has seen a significant fall in crime rates but a noticeable decrease in tolerance and sympathy for offenders, while at other times (as we have just seen), prison populations have fallen in spite of a rising crime rate. (See also Cavadino and Dignan, 2002: 37.)

101 McMahon (1992: 32) has criticized the simplistic use of such metaphors to arrive at the assumption that the creation and development of non-custodial penalties will *inevitably* lead to an inexorable expansion in the numbers of people who are subject to penal control together with an intensification of that control. She does so on two main grounds: first that it is not supported by the empirical data; and second for fostering a nihilistic attitude to the prospects for penal reform, by suggesting that any 'decarcerative' penal reform projects are doomed to failure.

102 Others have discerned in such developments the emergence of a 'new penology' (Feeley and Simon, 1992), in which the adoption of a 'managerialist' perspective is increasingly harnessed to the task of regulating levels of deviance by targeting categories and sub-populations rather than individual deviants. In recent years the groups that have been targeted in this way include squatters, new age travellers, road protesters, participants in raves, hunt saboteurs, animal rights protesters, nuisance neighbours and others engaging in 'anti-social behaviour'.

103 Sophisticated computer software enables digitized video images to be converted into numerical data that can then be analysed by means of complex algorithms (Norris, 1995). This makes it possible to automatically 'read' vehicle number plates or facial features, which can than be checked against large databases; see also Norris (2003).

104 Bentham's planned prison, in which the inmates would be under constant surveillance (see Chapter 2, section 5), serves as an apt metaphor for current technological developments in the fields of surveillance and social control.

105   Indeed, it can plausibly be argued that an increased probability of detection could enable punishments to be made more lenient, since as we saw in Chapter 2, deterrence is far more likely to be achieved by increasing the *perceived risk of detection* than by severer penalties.

106   Nor are they alone. More recently Jewkes (2004/5: 6) has suggested that '[I]t is via these advances in technology that the disciplinary gaze might be said to be stretching beyond the confines of closed and controlled environments such as the prison or the factory to encompass society as a whole (Foucault, 1977)'.

107   Bottoms was writing before the introduction of uniform standards, the introduction of a compulsory manual labour element and the relentless attempts to toughen this and other forms of 'community punishment'. He did, however, anticipate that the measure 'could yet be developed in a more disciplinary form' (Bottoms, 1983: 180), and might well have viewed the measure in a different light on the basis of these more recent developments.

108   The same might also be said of the attempt by the Criminal Justice Act 1991 to grade penalties according to 'just-desert' criteria.

109   The introduction of conditional cautioning and fixed penalty notices for less serious adult offenders (see the Introduction) and plans to (re-)introduce day fines (see above, section 5.3) could conceivably herald the first tentative signs of a revival, however.

110   As for home detention curfew, see Chapter 8.

111   See Ashworth (1997), Cavadino et al. (1999: 31) and Dignan (2003).

112   As we shall see in Chapter 6, a somewhat similar analytical-explanatory framework was originally devised by Thomas Mathiesen (1974, 1990) specifically in connection with the rise and continued existence of imprisonment as one of the dominant forms of punishment in late capitalist societies.

113   As opposed to changing *the way in which offenders are punished* – or the system and institutions of punishment – which is a rather different kind of 'transformation'.

114   We have explained elsewhere (Cavadino et al., 1999: 121) why we believe this attempt was ultimately doomed to failure since its principal effect was simply to confirm the status of imprisonment as setting the 'gold standard' with regard to punishment, compared with which all other measures are likely to be dismissed as 'base metal counterfeits'.

115   There have been exceptions, such as probation (at least in its early 'police court missionary' phase), and also the 'silent' penitentiary system. What is distinctive about the responses we are about to describe is their reliance on a form of normative or moralizing discourse with an offender. (As such, they fit well with Anthony Duff's 'communicative theory of punishment' mentioned in Chapter 2 above) This kind of approach can also be deployed within a custodial setting (see Chapter 6).

116   Another measure favoured by the government involves the use of parenting orders in cases where a young person's offending behaviour is felt to be attributable to poor or inappropriate parenting skills (see Chapter 9, section 9.7). Shorn of its compulsory and punitive aspects, better support and guidance for parents who find it difficult to cope with the behaviour of their children could also be helpful and might even be welcomed by both parents and young people (Holdaway et al., 2001: 105).

6 Prisons and the Penal Crisis

Overview

'The degree of civilization in a society can be judged by entering its prisons' (Dostoevsky, 1852)

6.1 Imprisonment is both the most important and also the most problematic of all punishments in terms of its impact on the rest of the English penal system. While other punishments may be imposed with greater frequency, imprisonment retains a symbolic dominance by virtue of its status in the eyes of politicians and public alike as the 'gold standard' measure of punishment. Nevertheless, as we shall see in this chapter, imprisonment spectacularly and persistently fails to achieve one of its primary avowed aims, which is to reduce the level of reoffending by those who have been punished in this way. Partly for this reason, the very purpose and rationale of imprisonment is also a matter of persistent debate and contention.

In addition, the high cost of imprisonment contributes massively to the 'crisis of penological resources' (see Chapter 1). It not only fuels the seemingly inexhaustible demand for more prison capacity but also ties up resources that might otherwise be used to assist and support victims of crime or to develop alternative ways of dealing with offenders more constructively, effectively and humanely in the community. The total average cost of each prison place in 2004–5 was £40,992.[1] Twenty thousand additional prison places have been provided since 1997[2] at an average cost of £99,839 per place.[3] The total budget allocated to the Prison Service[4] for 2006–7 was £1,861 million (HM Prison Service, 2006b).[5] This represents 16 per cent of the £14 billion total expenditure on the criminal justice system compared with just 4 per cent going to the probation service and only 1.6 per cent on compensation and victim services (Home Office, 1999a).

Above all, the prison system continues to be afflicted by a variety of seemingly intractable operational problems that help to perpetuate the image of a penal system that is forever teetering on the brink of a potentially devastating crisis. Serious policy failings by successive governments are responsible for many of these problems, so we will also provide a brief overview of some of the key developments in prison policy-making, with particular emphasis on the period since the 1990 Strangeways riot and associated prison disturbances.

As for the operational problems themselves, for the sake of clarity we shall focus on seven distinct aspects of the ongoing prisons crisis, though most of them are closely interrelated. We will begin by examining the many-stranded *managerial* crisis that continues to beset the prison system. With regard to the crisis of *security*, it may appear as if the imminent threat of high-profile prison escapes has receded. As we shall see, however, the actions taken in response to this particular crisis continue to have serious ramifications for the rest of the prison system and in this sense the crisis is far from being resolved, quite apart from continuing concerns over the security and well-being of prison inmates. Next we shall deal with the *prison numbers* crisis and the associated problems of prison overcrowding. In discussing the crisis of *conditions*, the main emphasis will be on the physical environment and facilities that are available to prisoners. Relationships between inmates and with prison staff are discussed in the context of the broader crises of *control* and *authority*, which also encompass the various formal and informal responses to indiscipline and other forms of collective disobedience by prison inmates. The handling of inmate grievances by prison authorities and the operation of the various monitoring mechanisms are examined as aspects of the crisis of *accountability*. Last, but by no means least, we shall discuss the ongoing crisis of *legitimacy*, with particular emphasis on the action that will be needed if it is to be effectively tackled.

The Aims and Functions of Imprisonment

Official Aims of Imprisonment

6.2 In the early nineteenth century, the chief official aims of imprisonment were the imposition of deterrent and retributive justice on offenders, while not ruling out the possibility of reform and a return to society. By the turn of the century, the twin imperatives of deterrence and reformation had been adopted as official policy, and the subsequent ascendancy of the 'treatment model' was soon enshrined in the Prison Rules themselves.[6] By 1964 the following classic formulation had been given pride of place as Prison Rule Number 1: 'The purpose of the training and treatment of convicted prisoners shall be to encourage and assist them to lead a good and useful life.' Following the collapse of the rehabilitative ideal in the 1970s (see Chapters 1 and 2), various attempts were made to come up with an alternative formulation (see previous editions of this book for details). These attempts to fill the 'moral vacuum' created by the demise of the treatment model proved insuperable, however, and the original formulation still appears in the latest edition of the Prison Rules, though it has now been relegated to Rule Number 3.

As part of its current statement of purpose, the Prison Service sets out three rather more prosaic objectives: to hold prisoners securely; reduce the risk of reoffending; and provide safe, well-ordered establishments in which prisoners are treated humanely, decently and lawfully.[7] With regard to the second of these aims, the Prison Service's record in preventing reoffending is truly lamentable, and has in fact deteriorated in recent years. Thus, figures published by the Home Office in 2006 showed that two-thirds (65.8 per cent) of all prisoners are reconvicted within two years of being released, and for young men aged 18–20, the figure is 74.8 per cent (Shepherd and Whiting, 2006). This compares poorly with the situation just over a decade ago: of inmates who were discharged from prison in 1994, 56 per cent of males and 45 per cent of females were reconvicted within two years, while the figure for offenders under the age of 21 was 70 per cent (Home Office, 1999b).

As for the third of the above aims, we will be assessing the Prison Service's record later in the chapter; but the underlying message is that there is a very long way to go before it can claim to be providing safe, well-ordered establishments in which prisoners are treated humanely, decently and lawfully.

Even with regard to the first aim – holding prisoners securely – the record is extremely uneven. As we shall see, until recently escapes from custody were periodically a source of acute embarrassment to both the Prison Service and government ministers. Although concerns over the level of absconding have subsided in recent years, this improvement has come at a cost that has to be measured not only in financial terms but also in respect to the many adverse consequences that flow from the excessive preoccupation with external security matters. Again we shall examine these issues in more detail later in the chapter. Holding prisoners securely should mean more than simply preventing them from escaping, however, since they also need to be kept safe and free from danger. When we come to examine the Prison Service's performance with regard to preventing suicides and keeping inmates safe from assaults and free from anxiety, it will become apparent that its performance is far less impressive and continues to give rise to serious concern.

One obvious question that is prompted by this rather dismal track record concerns the rationale for what appears to be a 'chronically failing institution'. Another is how we can account for its longevity and apparent resilience despite its continuing inability to achieve its stated objectives. In order to answer both questions, it is necessary to probe behind the official rhetoric and examine the hidden social functions that prisons may continue to perform in modern societies even though they seem incapable of achieving their more instrumental crime control objectives.

The Social Functions of Imprisonment

Historically, the birth of the modern prison was part of a much broader movement – described by Foucault (1967: ch. 2) as the 'great confinement' – in which 'institutions' of various kinds came to be adopted as the solution to a wide range of social problems. The start of this process can be traced back to the 1600s, though the replacement of physical suffering by imprisonment as the *dominant* form of punishment (a process that Foucault (1977: 15) termed the 'great transformation') did not occur until the end of the eighteenth and beginning of the nineteenth centuries. This coincided with the emergence of industrial capitalism as the dominant mode of production in all the large European countries.

In Chapters 3 and 5 we discussed some of the sociological explanations which have been put forward for the birth of the prison (see also Matthews, 1999). An interesting radical explanation for the continued existence of the prison has been put forward by Norwegian penologist Thomas Mathiesen (1974, 1990, 2000). Mathiesen suggests that the reason why imprisonment remains the dominant mode of punishment has to do with the important social functions which it performs within advanced capitalist societies.

The first of these he terms *'the expurgatory function'*. Those who are both unproductive and disruptive of the normal processes of production are liable to find themselves being 'siphoned off' and 'contained' in prison where they can do least damage. When we come to examine the demographic profile of the prison population in the next section, it will become apparent that many of those in custody could, at least from a rather crude functionalist perspective, be described in this way. Or, as Pat Carlen (2006: 6) has more recently put it: 'Today, the prison still fulfils its age-old function of catering for the homeless, the mentally ill, the stranger, the non-complaint poor, the abused and the excluded.'

The second social function performed by prisons Mathiesen calls *the 'power-draining function'*. By this he means that those who are contained in this way are not only prevented from interfering with the normal processes of production but are also denied the opportunity to exercise responsibility. For the institution in which they are detained is designed to function on the basis of minimal practical contributions from the prisoners themselves. Once again this rings true with much of the literature on prison life, though quite how it helps inmates to lead a good and useful life on release is less easy to appreciate.

A third, 'symbolic' function refers to the *stigmatizing* effect of imprisonment, which enables those on the outside to distance themselves, in terms of their own moral self-perceptions, from those who have been publicly labelled in this way.

This is closely related to a fourth function, the *'diverting function'* of imprisonment. Here Mathiesen draws attention to the fact that the commission of socially harmful acts is by no means the prerogative of one particular section of society. Rather, he suggests that 'socially dangerous acts are increasingly being committed by individuals and classes with power in society' even though they are most unlikely to be punished for their transgressions (1974: 78). This is because the 'ultimate sanction' of imprisonment tends to be reserved for a highly selected group of offenders, drawn mainly from the lower working class who are most likely to commit a fairly narrow band of offences (for example, personal violence, and relatively petty property offences). Consequently, concern in the media and in the population at large tends to focus almost exclusively on transgressions of this kind. Mathiesen suggests that this has the effect of diverting public attention away from much more serious forms of social harm: those resulting from the destruction of entire eco-systems, major acts of pollution, or deaths and injuries resulting from the deliberate compromise of safety standards in the pursuit of profit, for example.[8] Those who are responsible for such harms are generally not seen as appropriate subjects for the ultimate sanction of imprisonment. This is partly because the harms themselves are committed by, or on behalf, of powerful corporations that have the legal power to act as a 'natural person', but are rarely subject to the same legal constraints and penalties. Moreover, those natural persons who take the decisions within such corporations are not only powerful individuals in their own right, but are themselves also actively engaged in the process of production at a high level.

Finally, Mathiesen identified (1990: 138) a fifth social function of imprisonment, which he called the *'action function'*. Because prison has the highest profile of any sanction in common use in our kind of society, it plays an important part in reassuring people that 'something is being done' about the problem of law and order, and the social threats which they are persuaded to take most seriously.[9]

Perhaps, however, imprisonment is not so functional to modern capitalism as Mathiesen suggests. For there is also a heavy price to be paid, not only in terms of resources and human suffering, but also in managing the increasing tensions that are associated with the steadily enduring penal crisis, as we shall see.

David Garland (1990a) has also highlighted the need to look beyond the prison's overt crime control functions, and to appreciate its more social and symbolic purposes, albeit in rather more Durkheimian terms than Mathiesen has used. Like Mathiesen, he sees the prison as a mechanism for enhancing solidarities and emphasizing divisions within communities (1990a: 284), but he also sees it as a social institution that reflects a community's cultural values including the pursuit of 'justice, tolerance, decency, humanity and civility' (1990a: 292). Drawing attention to the more subtle symbolic functions of the modern prison can help us to understand the resilience of the modern prison despite its instrumental failings. However, it does not absolve us of the responsibility to put its rhetorical aspirations to the test and to *critically assess* its conformity with the moral values it professes. This is what we shall be doing in the second half of this chapter.[10]

Anatomy of the prison system

People in Prison: Who Are They?

6.3 In October 2006, the prison population[11] in England and Wales stood at a record level of 80,306. The most recent demographic information that is available[12] relates to the approximately 75,000 inmates who were held in custody at the end of December 2005. Ninety-four per cent of these were men, though at 6 per cent, the proportion of female inmates was almost twice as high as in 1987 (3.6 per cent). While adults accounted for the vast majority of those in custody (85.5 per cent), those under the age of 18 (who are still technically children) made up 3.5 per cent of the total, the remaining 11 per cent consisting of young adults (aged 18 to 20).

The custodial population is not only heavily skewed in terms of gender and age but also in respect of its racial composition and social profile (see also Chapter 10). One-quarter of the prison population of the prison population at the end of 2005 was non-white in composition (15 per cent black, 6 per cent Asian, 3 per cent Mixed and 1 per cent Chinese or Other). The proportion of prisoners from ethnic minority backgrounds is nearly three times that of the general population. Part of this over-representation stems from the fact that foreign nationals make up 13.5 per cent of the total prison population and they exhibit an even greater ethnic imbalance (43 per cent black and 17 per cent Asian, with just 29 per cent white).

In terms of its social composition, data compiled by the Social Exclusion Unit (2002) paint a depressing picture of a prison population that is disproportionately drawn from marginalized and disadvantaged sectors of the community. Moreover, many prisoners lack even the basic life skills that are required in order to subsist and cope with the demands of everyday life (calling to mind Mathiesen's reference to the 'expurgatory role' of the prison; see above).

In terms of family background, almost half of all prisoners ran away as a child (compared with 11 per cent of the general population) and over one-quarter were taken into care (27 per cent compared with 2 per cent overall). Forty-three per cent came from a family one of whose members had been convicted of a criminal offence (compared with 16 per cent overall). In terms of their educational experience, nearly half of all male offenders and one third of female offenders had been excluded from school (compared with 2 per cent overall) and 30 per cent regularly truanted (ten times the national average). Just over half of all male offenders and 71 per cent of female offenders had no educational qualifications compared with 15 per cent overall and levels of innumeracy and illiteracy were also extremely high. Perhaps unsurprisingly, over two-thirds of all prison inmates were unemployed at the time they entered custody; 72 per cent were in receipt of benefits (compared with 13.7 per cent of the working age population) and just under half had a history of debt. Levels of homelessness were also high (32 per cent compared with under 1 per cent of the general population).

Prisoners also suffer from much poorer mental and physical health than the general population. On one estimate, at least 70 per cent of sentenced inmates suffer from two or more mental disorders,[13] while levels of hepatitis and HIV are also significantly higher among prison inmates than in the general population.

In short, prison inmates are disproportionately likely to be drawn from disadvantaged, indeed multiply disadvantaged, sections of the community. The most obvious question this prompts is whether prisons are the most appropriate institutions in which to deal with those whose serious and often acute personal and social handicaps are all too likely to have contributed to their offending behaviour. An equally pertinent question is what effect imprisonment itself is likely to have on such prisoners.

The literature on the effects of imprisonment (for an overview see Liebling and Maruna, 2005) highlights a range of damaging consequences that are highly likely to reduce rather than improve the prospects for a crime-free existence once they are released. Thus, imprisonment can itself impair the physical and mental health of inmates and can also induce post-traumatic stress. It is known to disrupt the very social ties that can help to reduce the likelihood of reoffending. For example, up to one-third of prison inmates are deprived of their housing as a result of being imprisoned (Social Exclusion Unit, 2002), often as a result of the way the Housing Benefit scheme operates. Two-thirds of those who are employed at the time of sentencing are known to lose their jobs. Family relationships are often difficult to maintain while a person is in prison and even where this is not the case, the imprisonment of a family member often imposes additional hardships on the rest of the family. The well-known 'institutionalizing' effects of imprisonment – whereby inmates become habituated to prison life and simultaneously less able to cope with life outside – are liable to exacerbate rather than ameliorate an inmate's deficiencies in life skills.

Factors such as these help to explain the lamentable reconviction figures that we referred to earlier. Equally disturbing is the fact that over 50 ex-prisoners are known to commit suicide each year shortly after release (Howard League, 2002). These 'pains of imprisonment' (Christie, 1981: 16) are the cause of real human suffering on a massive scale. If, as seems plausible, imprisonment increases the likelihood of further offending on release, the suffering of future victims represents an additional pain that is no less real for being impossible to quantify. In purely financial terms, however, the Social Exclusion Unit (2002: 5) has estimated that the cost of reoffending by ex-prisoners amounts to £11 billion per year.

One additional aspect of the profile of prison inmates needs to be mentioned. Of those in prison in 2006, 17 per cent were on remand. Most of these remand prisoners are not yet convicted and legally therefore should not be treated as offenders. Almost inevitably, however, they are exposed to many of the above 'pains of imprisonment'. Indeed, in some respects their predicament is even worse than that of sentenced prisoners. For they are not only liable to be detained in some of the worst prison establishments (see below) but may also find it more difficult to defend themselves against the charges they face, even when innocent, than if they were remanded on bail (see also Chapter 4).

Of the sentenced prison population at the end of 2005 (60,474), 25 per cent had been convicted of offences involving violence against the person (which includes murder but also encompasses a wide variety of less serious physical assaults and woundings). A further 10.5 per cent had been sentenced for sexual offences. Robbery accounted for 13.5 per cent of the total, and burglary for 13 per cent. Drug offences made up 17 per cent, theft 6 per cent and fraud and forgery a further 3 per cent of the total.

The Prison Estate

At the time of writing, there are 142 prisons in England and Wales. For many years the various prisons were organized into distinct categories according to the type of prisoners for whom they catered and also the functions they were intended to perform. It is still the case that adult males are generally held separately from adult female inmates,[14] and that young offenders are likewise held in separate institutions.[15] The four main functional categories comprised high-security prisons, closed training prisons, local prisons and open or semi-open prisons. High-security prisons (formerly known as 'dispersal prisons'; see section 6.5 below) were intended to hold those high-risk inmates whose escape would be dangerous. Closed training prisons were intended to offer education, training and work opportunities for medium-risk inmates serving reasonably lengthy sentences. Local prisons, many of which are located in inner-city areas, are generally very large, and were originally designed for remand inmates, those newly sentenced and those serving short sentences. Finally, open or semi-open prisons were intended for relatively low-risk inmates who could safely be housed in less secure establishments. In addition, a small number of prisons were designated as 'resettlement prisons' to meet the needs of longer-sentenced prisoners who were nearing release by providing them with work opportunities in the community under closely monitored conditions.

This functional categorization of the prison estate was not only highly complex from a managerial perspective, but its relative inflexibility also caused major operational problems when seeking to 'place' a particular inmate in the appropriate type of prison accommodation. In recent years, however, the relentless increase in the size of the prison population combined with the need to utilize every available space (see section 6.5 below) has rendered the old functional segmentation of the prison estate largely unworkable. As a result, the way prisons are currently categorized has become much more amorphous, and many prisons now perform more than one function.

Key phases in recent prison policy-making

6.4 In this section we provide a brief descriptive overview of some of the key phases in the tortuous development of recent prison policy in order to set out the historical context in which these particular issues have come to prominence (see also Liebling and Arnold, 2004: ch. 1).

1991–1995: The Woolf Reform Agenda and Its Legacy

Following the riot at Strangeways Prison, Manchester and other prison disturbances in April 1990, Lord Woolf's magisterial report not only provided a cogent diagnosis of the factors that precipitated these events but also set out a comprehensive and ambitious blueprint for reform (Woolf and Tumim, 1991). One of the key themes in the report was the need to ensure an appropriate balance between the three essential elements of security, control and justice (para. 9.19). Woolf made no attempt to hide his strong belief that an excessive preoccupation with the first two concerns at the expense of justice over many years had put the balance out of kilter. The only way of restoring it, in his view, would be to place far greater emphasis on the need to treat prisoners with humanity and fairness. This liberal, humanitarian ethos underpinned many of his proposals, most notably with regard to the need for radical reform of the prison system's disciplinary and grievance procedures. However, his reform agenda also encompassed the need for managerial reform, action to address prison overcrowding, better physical conditions, greater clarity with regard to prisoners' entitlements and responsibilities, and even a reconfiguration of the entire prison estate.

In terms of his influence on official prison policy-making, however, the impact of Woolf's reform agenda was less far-reaching and durable than might have been expected given the widespread acclaim with which it was greeted. The government responded by publishing a White Paper entitled *Custody, Care and Justice* (Home Office, 1991) which purported to set out a strategy for delivering the Woolf reform agenda, though without specifying an implementation plan, a timetable or any commitment to resourcing the changes. In the event, however, the government adopted a classic 'cherry-picking' response to the recommendations by moving to end 'slopping out' (see also Chapter 1) and a package of measures to enable prisoners to maintain better links with the outside world while quietly shelving the rest.

Within the Prison Service itself, Woolf's impact was far more pervasive, at least for a while, as the newly appointed Director General of the Prison Service, Joe Pilling (1992), set out to articulate the implications of Woolf's emphasis on justice for reforming relationships between prison staff and inmates. He did so by emphasizing the need for respect, fairness, individuality, care and openness. Encouragingly, prison staff in both public and private prisons responded by striving to develop and deliver more constructive and balanced regimes (Liebling and Arnold, 2004: 13; see also James et al., 1997). Even within the prison system, however, Woolf's legacy was soon to be overthrown by an abrupt reversion to more traditional prison priorities. (This process may have been assisted by the fact that in 1993 Joe Pilling was replaced as Director General by Derek Lewis, a candidate from outside both the Prison Service and the Civil Service, as the Prison Service was transformed into an 'executive agency' (see below, section 6.5).)

1995–1999: Post-Woolf Backlash – the Security and Control Agenda

Instead of delivering the promised panacea of a safe, stable and secure prison system, the post-Woolf era was rocked by a series of extremely embarrassing high-profile escapes from maximum security prisons and mounting concern over the level of disorderly conduct throughout the system. Both sets of incidents are described more fully in section 6.5 below. Here, it is sufficient to note that the first escape, in September 1994, involved six extremely high-risk inmates, including five IRA terrorists, who broke out of a supposedly escape-proof Special Security Unit at Whitemoor Prison. Although the men were swiftly recaptured, the government's embarrassment was heightened by the discovery of Semtex explosive and detonators at the prison, and also by allegations that prison staff undertook errands for inmates. Less than six months later, three high-security life sentence prisoners escaped from Parkhurst Prison on the Isle of Wight in January 1995, and remained at liberty for five days before being recaptured.

Meanwhile, concerns were being voiced – although with little hard evidence – that the Prison Service's attempts to improve relationships between staff and inmates, far from encouraging compliance and defusing tensions, had resulted in lax regimes that were characterized by lethargy on the part of many inmates, and disturbingly high levels of bullying and drug-taking.

By this stage, Michael Howard had taken over as Home Secretary (in 1993), and the 'law and order counter-reformation' was already in full swing (see Introduction and Chapter 11). His immediate response to the security lapses was to commission two reports, one focusing on the Whitemoor incident (Woodcock, 1994), while the second was a more general inquiry into prison security that also took account of the Parkhurst episode (Learmont, 1995). The government unquestioningly accepted their conclusions that the fault lay with over-permissive regimes in which effective power and control lay with inmates rather than prison staff, and resolved to return power unequivocally to prison officers and management by adopting a 'decent but austere' regime. Policy changes included an increase in internal and perimeter security, restrictions on temporary release, the introduction of dedicated search teams, mandatory drug testing, restrictions on personal possessions,[16] and a new 'sticks and carrots' regime of incentives and earned privileges (see section 6.5, below; also Creighton and King, 2000: 136). The consequences for prisoners were immediate and profound since they emerged with fewer privileges, less personal property and were subject to far more frequent and thorough searches than before (Liebling, 2001). Practices were adopted that were widely perceived as dehumanizing if not barbaric, such as the shackling of pregnant female prisoners as they gave birth in civilian hospitals, and a resurgence of staff violence against prisoners. As early as 1996, the Chief Inspector of Prisons had expressed anxiety about the illegal use of force against inmates in the segregation unit at Wormwood Scrubs. Then, on 6 September 2000, three prison officers had the dubious distinction of becoming the first in modern English penal history to be imprisoned for acts of brutality against prisoners (HM Chief Inspector of Prisons, 1999c). Between 1 January and 30 June 1999, a total of 44 prison officers (including those at Wormwood Scrubs) were suspended in prisons in England and Wales for a variety of alleged assaults against prisoners.

1999–2002: The 'Decency Agenda' and the 'Effectiveness Credo' – the quest for a 'Balanced' Approach

The preoccupation with security matters lasted until 1999, by which time there had been a change of government and yet another change in the Prison Service's senior management (see section 6.5 below). In the face of the escalating threat to the legitimacy of the Prison Service and its tactics, Martin Narey took over as Director General in 1999 and signalled a dramatic change of emphasis by invoking moral principles rather than security concerns when articulating the service's priorities (Narey, 1999). In a speech[17] whose bitter eloquence was born out of personal knowledge, he complained of a 'litany of failure and moral neglect', lamented the 'very immorality of our treatment of some prisoners and the degradation of some establishments', and admitted that for too long the Prison Service 'used to tolerate inhumanity'. With equal frankness, he also appeared to acknowledge the monumental scale of the task and strength of cultural resistance from within the service by threatening to leave his post unless he received the support he required in order to push through the radical changes he believed were needed. This new approach has come to be known as the '*decency agenda*' (Liebling and Arnold, 2004: 33), which involves treating prisoners fairly and with dignity while nevertheless effectively challenging their offending behaviour.

As Narey's address also made clear, however, the quest for decency was to be pursued as part of a broader attempt to modernize the Prison Service in a bid to extirpate some of the shameful and unacceptable attitudes and practices of the past and improve its performance. 'Failing prisons' would no longer be tolerated and all prisons would be expected to embrace a new working credo of effectiveness (Liebling and Arnold, 2004: 34ff.) dedicated to the reduction of reoffending and protection of the public. The means by which these goals were to be pursued were overtly managerialist and included the promulgation of acceptable standards, the use of accreditation procedures to monitor prison programmes and regimes, improved links with other agencies and, underpinning all of these, an emphasis on 'best value'. Another important aspect of this 'effectiveness credo' (to which we shall return in Chapter 7) is its implicit belief in the superiority of private sector methods and the value of competition as a means for driving up standards, overcoming obstructionist attitudes and ensuring the efficient use of resources.

2002–2006: Keeping the Lid on – Pragmatism Reasserts Itself

Martin Narey relinquished responsibility for English prisons to become Chief Executive of the children's charity Barnado's in 2005. But outwardly at least, the Prison Service retains its commitment both to Narey's decency agenda and also to the effectiveness ethos as the surest way of pursuing it. The former is reflected in the Prison Service business plan for 2006–7 (HM Prison Service, 2006b), which lists the decency agenda as second only to the reduction of reoffending among its list of main priorities or 'deliverables' for 2006–7. Likewise, the effectiveness ethos is reflected in the various key performance indicators that are listed in Appendix 2 of the plan. Unfortunately, however, the rediscovery of the importance of moral principles as the lodestar for Prison Service reform has coincided with a period of unprecedented growth in the size of the prison population which threatens to render many of its worthy aspirations unattainable (Liebling and Arnold, 2004: 40). An equally inevitable consequence of the relentless rise in the number of prison inmates is that prison staff will find it increasingly difficult to attain many of their targets, as the service itself admits (HM Prison Service, 2006b: 6). Those relating to the reduction of overcrowding, curbing the rate of self-inflicted deaths and providing constructive educational training or employment opportunities prior to release are likely to be particularly difficult to achieve in such circumstances. Consequently, the main priority for the Prison Service for the foreseeable future is likely to be the much more prosaic and pragmatic one of simply trying to accommodate the ever-growing number of inmates within a system that is almost literally creaking at the seams.

2006: A Five-Year Strategy – New Beginning or False Dawn?

In February 2006, Home Secretary Charles Clarke published a *Five Year Strategy for Protecting the Public and Reducing Reoffending*. This was of interest in the present context for two main reasons. First, it reiterated that prison should be reserved for the most dangerous, violent and seriously persistent offenders (Home Office, 2006b: 22). It also reaffirmed (at page 21) the government's commitment to implementing the 'custody plus' provisions that were intended to reduce the length of time that many less serious offenders served in custody (see Chapters 4 and 5). Second, it announced an ambitious plan to reconfigure the prison estate by developing a network of community prisons that would make it easier for less serious prisoners to be housed closer to where they live. This in turn would enable them to maintain closer links with their families and communities to assist with the process of reintegration on release. Fifteen years earlier, the Woolf Report had also favoured the development of a network of community prisons by dividing up many of the larger inner-city prisons into a series of smaller living units. Woolf had also proposed that within these units, different kinds of specialist regimes could be made available for meeting the requirements of different categories of prisoners.

Just three months later, a new Home Secretary – John Reid – was in post, and plans had been announced for the construction of an additional 8,000 prison places, but the 'Vision for Community Prisons' that was due to have been published in spring 2006 had still not materialized. Indeed, the future prospects of the Five-Year strategy itself were also plunged into doubt following the announcement of a further wide-ranging review of the criminal justice system, the pledge of further reforms, and the indefinite postponement of the 'custody plus' sentence. This rapid turnover of the most senior and powerful prison policy-makers and the accompanying volatility in the direction of prison policy is symptomatic of a much deeper managerial crisis that pervades the Prison Service at all levels. In the next section we examine the various crises to which the prison system appears to be congenitally prone, starting with this debilitating managerial crisis.

The prison system and its crises

6.5 The problems that beset the English prison system can be described in terms of a set of interlocking crises – over numbers and overcrowding, security, conditions and regimes, the maintenance of order and control, and the lack of effective accountability mechanisms or grievance procedures. Many of these individual crises are related to a general *crisis of resources*, which has intensified as the prison population has continued to grow to ever-higher record levels. All the individual 'crises' have contributed to a deep-seated *crisis of legitimacy* within prisons. In recent years there has been an air of almost permanent crisis management throughout the Prison Service, but this is compounded by the fact that senior government policy-makers of whatever political party have lacked the vision and courage to take effective action to tackle the underlying causes of the crisis. We begin this section by examining the ongoing managerial crisis that will have to be resolved if the remaining crises are also to be effectively addressed.

Managerial Crisis

Shortly after becoming Home Secretary in May 2006, John Reid famously declared – in a phrase that seems destined to haunt him and his successors for some time to come – that his new department was 'not fit for purpose' (*Guardian*, 24 May 2006). This characteristically blunt epithet was nevertheless apt, not only in respect of the Home Office's complex organizational structure – for many years it had also been responsible for internal security matters and immigration as well as prisons – but also with regard to the way it had administered the prisons. However, the malaise extends beyond these administrative failings to encompass a long-running failure of political leadership. Successive Home Secretaries and Home Office ministers have failed to provide the Prison Service with appropriate strategic direction, whether in terms of defining the purposes of imprisonment or formulating sensible criteria to ensure that its use is not allowed to exceed the resources that the government chooses to make available. Instead, as a former Chief Inspector of Prisons has made clear in a trenchant critique, ministers have persistently failed to ameliorate the 'competing burdens of unrelieved overcrowding and remorseless resource constraints' that continue to bedevil the Prison Service and deflect it from pursuing its primary aims (Ramsbotham, 2005: 216).

In addition to these pivotal political failings, the Prison Service also suffers from acute organizational weaknesses. As Andrew Coyle (2005a: 180) observes, the Prison Service is just about the only major organization that is totally under central government control, despite its enormous size – 142 prisons and 40,000 staff who are responsible for nearly 80,000 inmates – and labyrinthine complexity. The organizational crisis within the Prison Service was cruelly exposed by the Strangeways riot of April 1990. At that time the Prison Service formed an integral part (the Prison Department) of the Home Office and was characterized by a 'top down' structure with a very high level of central control (Prison Reform Trust, 1991). This caused particular problems for the Strangeways governor at the time of the riots, who was required throughout to consult his superiors within the Prison Department, many of whom had no operational experience. The organizational problems confronting the Prison Service had long been recognized. The Woolf Report spoke scathingly of the gulf that existed between Home Office ministers, Prison Headquarters staff and those working in the service itself, and of the deep 'dissension, division and distrust' that existed at all levels of the service (Woolf and Tumim, 1991: para. 12.1–12.4). Woolf's primary concern was the need for 'clear and visible leadership' of the service by someone recruited internally. His call for a much less directive 'hands-off' approach by ministers which would leave the Director General free to manage and be publicly answerable for the performance of the service was also echoed at around the same time by an independent review of Prison Service management (Lygo, 1991).

The Prison Service became an executive agency in April 1993. In theory, the aim of 'agency status' is to allow the Prison Service to operate at arm's length from central government. 'Operational' matters are the responsibility of the Director General, who works to a policy and resources framework set by the Secretary of State. Meanwhile, much responsibility and authority for implementing policy are supposed to be devolved from headquarters to individual governors. In practice, however, the new management structure has signally failed to give the Prison Service greater freedom from political interference in the day-to-day running of prisons. The clearest illustration of this failure came in the wake of the security debacle that culminated in the embarrassing prison escapes at Whitemoor in 1994 and Parkhurst Prison in 1995 (see section 6.4, above). The Director General, Derek Lewis, swiftly found himself embroiled in an unseemly and unprecedented fracas with a politically embattled Home Secretary – Michael Howard – over who was responsible for the escapes. The extraordinary struggle culminated first in the removal of the Parkhurst governor, amid allegations that he was being made a scapegoat for policy failings at a higher level.[18] This was followed, shortly afterwards, by the very public sacking of the Director General himself, who subsequently succeeded in his legal action against the Home Office for wrongful dismissal (Jenkins, 1995; Lewis, 1997: ch. 13).

Since the General Election of 1997, the Prison Service has experienced further organizational upheaval accompanied by several changes of personnel. Agency status was confirmed in 1999 (HM Prison Service, 1999) following a quinquennial review. A new area structure was adopted in April 2000, which was based on the same geographical and operational boundaries as other criminal justice agencies such as the police and probation. Subsequently, and much more fundamentally, a new National Offender Management Service (NOMS) has been set up, as we saw in Chapter 5. The effect of this latest change is to incorporate the prison and probation services within a unified service under the direction of a single Chief Executive, the National Offender Manager, who is to be accountable to Ministers 'for punishing offenders and reducing reoffending'. In Chapter 5 we discussed this new system in terms of its implications for the non-custodial treatment of offenders, while in Chapter 7 we shall discuss it in relation to the privatization of penal services. What else does it mean for the running of the prison system?

At first glance the new NOMS structure (which had been proposed by the 2003 Carter report) appeared to address the concerns of those who had called for a statutory separation of the Prison Service from the Home Office whereby operational responsibility would be devolved from Whitehall control to a completely independent agency. Advocates of such an approach included official government reports on the management of the Prison Service (Laming, 2000), the former Director General of the Prison Service, Derek Lewis (1996) and the former Chief Inspector of Prisons, David Ramsbotham (2005). Likewise the appointment of ten Regional Offender Managers appears to meet the concerns of these and other critics who have complained of an over-centralized Prison Service that would benefit from the delegation of specific responsibilities to more manageable geographical areas.

On closer inspection, however, the way the changes have been implemented seems likely to disappoint those calling for a systemic break with the past. One problem has to do with the personnel and occupational background of those who have been appointed to oversee the reforms. Following the sacking of Derek Lewis, who was the first external appointment to the post of Director General, Richard Tilt became the first former prison governor to occupy the post. In 1999 he was succeeded by Martin Narey, a former career civil servant from the Home Office, initially as Director General and subsequently as the first Chief Executive of the newly established NOMS. Alison Liebling has described this development as a clear break from the 'independent chief executive' model and a reversion to Whitehall control (Liebling and Arnold, 2004: 33). By this stage it had also become clear that, although the Carter Report was originally commissioned by the Prime Minister as well as the Home Secretary, responsibility for its implementation had been very firmly wrested back by the Home Office (Ramsbotham, 2005: 256ff.). Instead of

publishing the report and allowing adequate time for consultations before responding to the recommendations, the Home Office preferred instead to issue its own blueprint for change simultaneously with the Carter report itself. Such precipitate haste, combined with a reluctance to involve others in the reform process, heightened suspicions that the Home Office was more concerned with fending off perceived threats to its fiefdom than engaging in a dispassionate review of the most appropriate way of organizing and administering the Prison Service.

At the heart of this long-running saga is a still unresolved debate over the appropriate constitutional relationship between the politicians who are responsible for formulating the overall direction of prison policy and those officials who are charged with implementing that policy. At present the doctrine of ministerial responsibility perpetuates the constitutional fiction that the Home Secretary is responsible for everything that goes on within this massive department of over 70,000 officials, including those responsible for the prison system. The sad reality, as Derek Lewis (2006: 10) found to his cost, is that ministers continue to wield authority without responsibility, while the Prison Service has responsibility without authority. In principle, it should be possible to reformulate the doctrine of ministerial responsibility so that prison officials are made directly accountable for clearly defined operational matters while ministers are held responsible for their policy decisions, which include the allocation of resources (Lodge and Rogers, 2006). In its present unreformed state, however, the doctrine of ministerial responsibility remains a deeply flawed mechanism for securing the accountability of those whose actions and policies contribute to or exacerbate the continuing crises within the prison system: there is still no adequate safeguard against ministerial meddling. But this is far from being the only source of the managerial crisis within the prison system.

A second important aspect of the managerial crisis relates to very general, indeed all-pervading changes in the conduct of prison management *within* the prison system during the post-war era. Ditchfield (1990: 147–52) has characterized this in terms of a shift in the source of authority from a highly personalized form of power to a 'bureaucratic-lawful' model (Barak-Glantz, 1981), in which authority is increasingly derived from a more bureaucratic system of general rules and regulations.[19] Particularly since the late 1980s, this transition has come to be associated with the approach known as *'managerialism'*, whereby the management of organizations is conducted with reference to the need for strategic planning, performance targets, efficiency and value for money (McEvoy, 2001: 254–8). More specifically, it has been closely linked with the *'New Public Management'* approach (see Chapter 1) which regards the private sector as the repository of all managerial wisdom and efficiency. The appointment of Derek Lewis – a private business executive with no experience of prisons – as Director General of the Prison Service in 1993 greatly accelerated the move towards a more managerialist style of prison governance. His tenure was associated with the introduction of the Prison Service's first corporate plan which set out its aims over a three-year period, together with a business plan that focused on the programme of activities planned over the next twelve months (Coyle, 2005a: 48).

Two of the most distinctive techniques associated with managerialism involve the setting of targets for an organization and regular monitoring of its performance as a means of prompting compliance. The Prison Service currently has 14 Key Performance Indicators (KPIs) or targets with which it is expected to comply. These cover a variety of measures including prison escapes, drug testing and treatment programmes, overcrowding, self-inflicted deaths, offending behaviour programmes, assault rates, race equality measures, educational awards, staff sickness rates and resettlement measures.[20] Since 2003, this plethora of control measures has been further augmented by the adoption of a new 'benchmarking programme' through which prisons are now categorized into league tables depending on their level of performance (ranging from 1–4).

This headlong rush to embrace these managerialist techniques has not been universally welcomed, even though the substitution of written instructions and rules for personal supervision and leadership was evident long before the onset of managerialism. One of the fiercest criticisms in the Learmont (1995) Report on the escape from Parkhurst Prison was reserved for the avalanche of instructions and communications received daily from prison headquarters. Learmont estimated that, if extrapolated to all prisons for the length of the inquiry, they would amount to 47 tons of paper, which would produce a pile almost a mile high or 800 feet higher than Ben Nevis!

Coyle (2005a: 4) has pointed out that one of the distinguishing features of managerialism is its emphasis on process and the way things are done (outputs) rather than on outcomes and what is being achieved. This is often linked to the criticism that managerialism tends to concentrate somewhat arbitrarily on those measures that can easily be *counted* rather than those things that *ought to 'count'* in strategic terms. An oft-cited example relates to the KPI that focuses on the number of 'accredited offending behaviour training programmes' undertaken each year. However, this says nothing at all about how effective they are or how many of those who might benefit from them actually get on to them (Coyle, 2005a: 98; Ramsbotham, 2005: 84). Another problem with the use of targets is that those who are subject to them may become more adept at demonstrating that they have met the target than in improving the performance the target is intended to measure.[21] This is an example of a phenomenon sometimes referred to as 'Goodhart's Law' which states, in effect, that once a measure becomes a target, it ceases to be a useful measure.[22] From a more theoretical perspective, Sennett's (1998) telling critique argues that an emphasis on shallow, short-term flexible output measures may have a corrosive effect on deeper civic values such as trust, loyalty and commitment, to the detriment of individuals and, ultimately also, of the organizations for which they work.

A third important aspect of the managerial crisis has to do with the extremely poor industrial relations record of the prison system. Repeatedly, attempts by prison management to introduce changes that are perceived by the workforce to affect adversely their conditions of employment have been met by a willingness to resort to strikes and other forms of militant industrial action. Obduracy on the part of Prison Service managers may be partly responsible, but much of the blame for this state of affairs has also been ascribed to the Prison Officers' Association, which is widely portrayed as one of the last bastions of 'unreconstructed Trades Unionism' (Ramsbotham, 2005: 232; see also Laming, 2000). In 1994, the Conservative government of the day sought to resolve the problem by withdrawing the right to take strike action,[23] but this caused considerable resentment on the part of the Prison Officers' Association and, if anything, worsened the already bleak industrial relations climate.[24] In 2004, the Labour government lifted the strike ban[25] in return for a voluntary industrial relations protocol that amounted to a virtual 'no strike' agreement, since it obliged the union to give 12 months' notice of a strike. However, in September 2006 the Prison Officers' Association, having rejected a salary increase proposed by the Prison Service Pay Review Body, voted for strike action which was only averted at the last moment. Clearly, there is still no obvious solution in sight to the continuing problem of prison staff unrest.

A fourth and final aspect of the managerial crisis within the prison system concerns the state of relations between prison officers and inmates. Since this forms part of a wider crisis of authority and control, we shall return to this issue once we have dealt with the separate crises of security, prison numbers and conditions. We conclude and summarize this section by noting that the Prison Service suffers from an excess of inappropriate 'micro management' techniques and an absence of effective 'macro management' strategies, both of which have exacerbated the various other crises to which we now turn.

Crisis of Security

An important task of any prison system is to hold prisoners securely, and one important aspect of this is *containment* – preventing them from escaping. The record of the English prison system in this respect has been uneven, and is punctuated by periodic panics over prison security. The first major crisis of containment in the post-war English penal system occurred in the mid-1960s. Until then, security considerations had been low on the prison authorities' agenda. However, this was already beginning to alter as a result of changes in the composition of the prison population, due mainly to an increased willingness on the part of judges to pass very long terms of imprisonment for some offences they regarded as particularly serious. Growing official concern over security was brought to a head by a succession of highly publicized escapes including two of the 'Great Train Robbers' (Charlie Wilson in 1964, and Ronnie Biggs in 1965) and the spy George Blake in October 1966 – all of whom were serving unprecedentedly long sentences. But this was only the most visible tip of a steadily growing iceberg as the escape rate had been steadily increasing ever since the turn of the century (Thomas and Pooley, 1980: 32). With the appointment of Lord Mountbatten to inquire into prison security in 1966, the crisis of containment moved to the top of the political agenda. The responses adopted in the wake of Mountbatten's report did much to shape the prison system of today, with continuing repercussions for the contemporary penal crisis.

The Mountbatten Report (Home Office, 1966) identified a number of weaknesses, both in the physical security of prisons and in the way they were administered. One recommendation which was immediately adopted was to categorize convicted prisoners according to their security risk on reception into prison, and to use this categorization when determining the type of institution to which they would ultimately be allocated. As a result of this change, all other aims (including those of training and treatment, preparation for release and the maintenance of internal control) were subordinated at a stroke to the requirements of security. Under Mountbatten's classification system – which with certain refinements remains with us today – there are four security categories:

1 **Category A** consists of 'those whose escape would be highly dangerous to the public or the police or to the security of the state'.[26] Such inmates are invariably housed in 'maximum security' conditions.
2 **Category B** are 'those prisoners for whom the very highest conditions of security are not necessary, but for whom escape must be made very difficult'.[27] Such inmates are likely to be housed in 'closed' but not necessarily 'maximum security' conditions.
3 **Category C** comprises 'prisoners who cannot be trusted in open conditions, but who do not have the ability or resources to make a determined escape bid'.
4 **Category D** inmates are 'those who can reasonably be entrusted to serve their sentences in open conditions' where there is little physical security.[28]

In terms of physical security, Mountbatten believed that existing prisons were sadly deficient, and so he proposed that one new, 'escape-proof', top-security prison should be built on the Isle of Wight to house *all* Category A prisoners in 'as liberal and constructive a regime as possible'. This 'concentration policy', as it was dubbed, would have allowed lower security conditions to prevail throughout the rest of the prison system. Ultimately Mountbatten's proposal was rejected, however, partly because of fears that *control* would be difficult in a 'fortress prison' populated by many of the country's most desperate and difficult inmates. It was also feared that the regime would inevitably become repressive, despite Mountbatten's hopes for a liberal approach. There were also concerns over the problems posed by other inmates who, while they may not pose a threat to security, are nevertheless highly disruptive and present a challenge to the maintenance of order in the wider prison system (Coyle, 2005a: 141).

In the end a compromise policy was adopted, which is still in operation, along the lines suggested by the later Radzinowicz Report (Advisory Council on the Penal System, 1968). This sought to dilute the anticipated control problem by spreading the high-security prisoners among a small number of prisons and subjecting them to the same regime as the lower-security (Category B) inmates with whom they would be housed. Although this strategy came to be known as the 'dispersal policy', this is something of a misnomer as it entails a considerable degree of concentration within a few establishments – formerly called 'dispersal prisons' but now officially known as high-security prisons.[29] It also involved a drastic (and expensive) upgrading of the security arrangements in these prisons, despite the fact that many of their inmates were designated Category B. However, its most pervasive and, in many respects, most detrimental impact was on the configuration of the overall prison estate (see section 6.3 above), which became divided into several different types of penal establishments, each designated for a different category of inmate. This not only distorted the amount of money spent on the different types of prisons, but also rendered them much less flexible in the way they are used, particularly during periods of overcrowding (see below).

Within the high-security prisons themselves, the arrangements designed for a relatively small number of Category A prisoners[30] resulted in a much more restrictive custodial regime for the majority of prisoners who did not present a security risk. King and Morgan (1980: 74) have described how, following the introduction of dispersal prisons, security considerations permeated inwards from external defences[31] to focus on internal buildings and even the regime itself. As a result, surveillance was increased by the installation of closed-circuit television, freedom of movement and time spent on association were drastically curtailed, and communal dining was phased out in favour of solitary meals provided in cells. Although the effects were experienced most intensely within the dispersal prisons themselves, the rest of the prison system was not immune from the growing security syndrome. Perimeter security was strengthened throughout the closed prison system, even if the level of paranoia was not quite so acute. And all establishments were affected indirectly, first by the considerable diversion of resources required to upgrade security at the dispersal prisons;[32] and second, as we shall see, by a policy of avoiding overcrowding and undermanning within the dispersal system, thus concentrating these problems in other prisons.

As we have seen, Lord Woolf (1991) spoke in his report of the need to maintain a proper balance between security, control and justice in the prisons. In particular he warned (Woolf and Tumim, 1991: para. 9.40) that excessive security and control would be counter-productive, since they would foster genuine grievances and a sense of oppression. Unfortunately, these warnings went unheeded almost from the outset. The Woolf Report was published in February 1991; by the summer, security concerns were once again in the ascendancy following the escape of two IRA suspects from Brixton Prison.

In the ensuing White Paper, *Custody, Care and Justice* (Home Office, 1991), the government's sense of priorities was starkly reflected in the adoption (in effect) of a two-speed approach on implementing the Woolf proposals. In the fast lane was, most conspicuously, a package of measures to improve security and control, including the introduction of annual security audits and the installation of X-ray machines and metal detectors in the entrances to maximum security prisons. These were to be given first claim on the Prison Service's budget and were accompanied by the introduction (in the Prison Security Act 1992) of a new offence of prison mutiny, and increased penalties for those convicted of assisting prison escapers. In the slow lane – to be implemented only over a timescale of 20 to 25 years, and then only out of existing resources – were many of the reforms to which Woolf had attached particular importance (see below).

Then, almost exactly 30 years after its emergence as a paramount policy concern, the crisis of containment returned to the top of the political agenda during the mid-1990s following the series of highly embarrassing security lapses that we described in section 6.4 above. The government's predictable response was to set up an inquiry, headed by Sir John Learmont (1995),[33] who was asked to undertake a general review of prison security. Like his predecessor Lord Mountbatten, Learmont called for a new system of prisoners' classification, this time to be based on six separate security categories. The sense of penological *déjà vu* was heightened by a reopening of the 'concentration versus dispersal' policy debate (Penal Affairs Consortium, 1995b). Learmont doubted whether dispersal prisons could meet the requirements of the next century even after upgrading. He therefore proposed a single new high-security prison (a so-called 'super-max' prison) for the estimated 200 or so prisoners who would be assigned to his proposed new categories 1 ('exceptional security risk' inmates) or 2 ('high-security risk' inmates). The parallels with Mountbatten did not stop there, for Learmont also favoured a 'purposeful training regime', at least for the high-security prison, offering a wide range of facilities.

In the end the government decided not to proceed with Learmont's proposal for a single 'super-max', high-security prison. However, it did implement most of his other recommendations (118 out of 127), once again highlighting the continuing overwhelming influence of security on prison policy at the expense of justice and humanity. Inmates who are identified as constituting an 'exceptional escape risk' are currently held in two Special Security Units (SSUs),[34] which are effectively prisons within a prison. Within the SSU they are held in 'small group isolation' in conditions that were described as 'cramped' and 'claustrophobic' by a former Chief Medical Officer; and are denied many of the basic rights to which other prisoners are entitled including access to library, gymnasium and chapel. They are also subjected to 'closed' visits in which the inmate sits behind a glass barrier and communicates via a telephone or grill and, despite such intensive security, are also subjected to strip-searches before and after every visit, supplemented by occasional even more intimate (and humiliating) 'squat' searches. Human rights organizations (for example, Amnesty International, 1997) have complained that such conditions constitute cruel, inhuman or degrading treatment, and the government's own inquiry, carried out in 1996, concluded that conditions in the SSUs could lead to mental illness.[35] Similar concerns were echoed more recently by the European Committee for the Prevention of Torture and Inhuman or Degrading Treatment (2006) following an inspection of the treatment of terror suspects and detainees awaiting deportation in a number of prisons including Belmarsh, Full Sutton and Long Lartin. The unremitting emphasis on security at the expense of humanity in the Learmont Report was roundly condemned by the former Chief Inspector of Prisons, Judge Stephen Tumim, who described it as 'the road to the concentration camp' (*Guardian*, 28 October 1995).

As for the crisis of containment itself, the Prison Service regularly claims to have successfully abated it, citing in evidence that no Category A prisoner has escaped since 1995. It has also met its performance target of ensuring that the overall escape rate is lower than 0.05 per cent of the average prison population (HM Prison Service, 2006a: 10).[36] However, this 'success' has come at a considerable price, as we have seen, which has to be measured not only financially but also in terms of the impoverishment inflicted on prison regimes and consequent hardships experienced by prison inmates throughout the system. Moreover the escape statistics only provide part of a much bigger picture. For in addition to its responsibility to keep prison inmates locked up, the Prison Service also has a duty to keep them secure in the sense of keeping them *safe*; measured against this broader yardstick, its performance is far less impressive and continues to give rise to serious concern.

One disturbing barometer of the Prison Service's continuing failure to keep prison inmates safe is the rate of self-inflicted deaths by prisoners, which doubled during the 1970s, and doubled again in the 1980s (Shaw, 1992a: 162). The trend continued during the 1990s and the 76 prison suicides recorded in 1998 represented more than twice the figure recorded in 1982. Since then both the number of self-inflicted deaths among prison inmates and also the rate of suicides per 100,000 prisoners have fluctuated. A record number of prison suicides – 95 – was recorded in 2002, which was almost 50 per cent higher than in 1997, when 65 suicides occurred (Prison Reform Trust, 2006b: 11). Similar figures were recorded in each of the two subsequent years before falling back to 78 in 2005, the lowest figure since 1998. The highest rate of prison suicides per 100,000 inmates was 140 in 1999. Compared with the general population, adult male prisoners are five times more likely to kill themselves, but boys aged 15–17 are 18 times more likely to do so than those living in the community (Fazel et al., 2005; cited in Prison Reform Trust, 2006b: 11). Even allowing for their generally adverse psychiatric profile (see Chapter 1), this is unacceptably high.

Suicides are disproportionately high among remand inmates, who account for more than half the annual total, even though they make up barely one-fifth of the prison population (Howard League for Penal Reform, 2005). Not surprisingly, local prisons, which house most remand prisoners, have the highest rate of prison suicides of any category in prison. Suicide rates are also disproportionately high among young prisoners, mentally disordered prisoners and those beginning very long sentences (Prison Reform Trust, 1997b). Prison suicides are believed[37] to result from an interaction between a number of factors. They include a pre-custodial history of vulnerability, such as anxiety or depression; background stress factors, such as bullying; and situational triggers, such as changes of location or missed visits (see below). Compared with the general population, however, prison inmates who commit suicide are far *less* likely to have had a history of psychiatric illness or treatment (Liebling, 1997).

Alison Liebling has intriguingly sought to account for the fluctuating suicide statistics during the period 1995 and 2002 by postulating an inverse relationship between prison suicide rates and variables that purport to reflect levels of respect, humanity and the strength of staff–inmate relationships (Liebling and Arnold, 2004: 48). This period encompasses the era characterized by the security and control agenda (1995–9; see section 6.4, above), during which prison suicide rates rocketed to unprecedented levels (peaking at 140 per 100,000, as we have seen). It also embraces the era characterized by the decency agenda (1999–2002), during which suicide rates fell sharply back. Liebling then hypothesizes that since 2002, the relentless pressure of prison numbers and consequent overcrowding have swamped the humanizing tendencies and thus help to account for the resurgence in the prison suicide rate during 2003 and 2004. However, the sharp decline in the suicide rate during 2005[38] suggests that there may be other factors at work. One possibility is that, somewhat paradoxically, the doubling up of cell occupancy in response to worsening overcrowding may afford some protection for vulnerable inmates by ensuring closer levels of informal monitoring by cell-mates.[39]

The problem of prison suicides has long been recognized (HM Chief Inspector of Prisons, 1990a),[40] and a programme of suicide prevention measures was introduced in 1994. In 2004–5, the Prison Service set itself the target of reducing the suicide rate to below 112.8 per 100,000, but in contrast to its performance with regard to prison escapes, it badly failed to meet this particular objective. While the strategy may have been well conceived, the Chief Inspector of Prisons has blamed the continuing unacceptably high levels of prison suicides on a lack of commitment and defective implementation of the programme on the part of staff and senior management (HM Chief Inspector of Prisons, 1999b).

Another barometer of the Prison Service's continuing failure to keep prison inmates safe and secure relates to the level of violence that inmates experience at the hands of their fellow prisoners. It is very difficult to assess the scale of this particular problem since the statistics compiled by the Prison Service for official purposes (especially with regard to the rate of compliance with key performance indicators) are likely to under-record the true incidence rate. In one survey covering two adult male prisons and two male young offender institutions in 1994–5, victimization of inmates was found to be pervasive (O'Donnell and Edgar, 1996a, 1996b; see also Edgar et al., 2003). No fewer than 46 per cent of young offenders and 30 per cent of adult offenders reported that they had either been assaulted, robbed or threatened with violence in the preceding *month,* though most reported that they felt safe most of the time in spite of this very high level of victimization.

The Prison Numbers Crisis and the Problem of Overcrowding

Compared with the crisis of security, the ongoing prison numbers crisis – and the related problem of overcrowding – may appear less dramatic. However, it is just as insidious in terms of its impact both on the development of prison policy and also on the lives of inmates. Prison overcrowding is predominantly a post-war phenomenon and follows a sustained period of surplus capacity between 1908 and 1938, during which period the average daily prison population was halved from 22,000 to 11,000 and some 25 prisons were closed (Rutherford, 1986b: 130–1). The period since the war has been one of almost relentless expansion, however,[41] and even though periodic attempts have been made to expand the size of the prison estate, for most of the time these have been insufficient to stave off serious overcrowding in the system. As we mentioned previously, 20,000 additional prison places were created between 1997 and 2006, yet 2006 saw the prisons yet again bursting at the seams.

Unable to keep pace with the relentless growth in the size of the prison population, the Prison Service has been obliged to resort to overcrowding on a massive scale, though the official measures it uses mask the true extent of the problem. The most objective measure of overcrowding is with reference to the occupancy level for which prison cells were initially designed, which in the vast majority of cases is a single inmate. Measured in this way, a total of 15,769 prisoners – 22 per cent of the prison population – were held in overcrowded conditions at the end of December 2004.

Traditionally, however, the Prison Service uses a looser definition of overcrowding based on the number of prisoners for whom government-appointed inspectors in consultation with prison authorities certify that each prison has adequate space, even though many prisoners may be sharing accommodation designed for a single inmate. This figure – the 'certified normal accommodation' or 'CNA' – is potentially flexible since there is nothing to stop the CNA being revised upwards by determining that single occupancy cells are, in fact, capable of holding two inmates, as indeed happened during the 1990s when the pressure on prison accommodation became more acute (Coyle, 2005a: 108). Thus, by a stroke of the pen, a substantial degree of overcrowding was built into the system. Additionally, a second official measure of overcrowding was introduced, based on a higher figure than the CNA – the 'operational capacity' of the system. The operational capacity is defined as the maximum number of inmates the prison system can hold after allowing for 'a safe level of overcrowding'. Not all cell accommodation is useable, however. Some spare capacity is required to accommodate receptions and transfers, and also to allow for the fact that some cell accommodation may only be available for particular categories of inmates: determined by gender, age, security categorization, criminal justice status (convicted or remand) or geographical location. The Prison Service has determined that it requires an operating margin of 1,700 places[42] in order to allow for this unavoidable inflexibility within the system. This figure is subtracted from the total number of spaces available to provide the 'useable operational capacity' – or the 'bust limit' as it is informally known – beyond which even the Prison Service accepts that it is operating beyond its safe capacity level.[43] This 'bust limit' was actually exceeded in April 2004 (*Guardian*, 7 April 2004).

On 22 September 2006, the useable operational capacity was 79,968 at a time when the total prison population stood at 79,285 (NOMS, 2006a), prompting a frantic quest for emergency solutions to the problem. Measures considered included plans (seemingly vetoed by the Prime Minister – *Times Online*, 31 August 2006) to make emergency use of existing powers of administrative release for short-sentence prisoners (*Guardian*, 6 July 2006), and to convert other accommodation including a disused army barracks near Dover[44] and a wing of Ashworth secure hospital in Merseyside into prison cells (*Guardian*, 20 September 2006). In October 2006 the government sought to commission new prison ships as temporary holding accommodation, a practice which had been discontinued since the decommissioning of *HMS Weare* in August 2005 (*Observer*, 22 October 2006), and implemented emergency measures to use police cells[45] to house prisoners (*Guardian*, 21 October 2006)

Faced with these difficulties, it now seems almost incredible that in 1991, during a brief period in which the prison population was steadily falling, Lord Woolf felt sufficiently confident to predict that prison overcrowding could soon become a 'thing of the past' (Woolf and Tumim, 1991: para. 1.189). Likewise, his call for each prison to be given a maximum occupancy level based on its CNA (para. 11.141) now seems fanciful. Instead, the drastic increase in the size of the prison population over the last few years has put paid to any prospect of an early end to the crisis of overcrowding – and the air of crisis management with which it is associated – at least for the foreseeable future.

The corrosive effects of prison overcrowding, and its impact on penal policy, continue to make themselves felt, however. It obviously has an adverse effect on living conditions (see next section), and results in restricted regimes since there is neither the space, facilities nor resources to provide inmates with a full range of training, work and educational opportunities when there are too many prisoners to cope with. Relations between staff and inmates can also be adversely affected in such circumstances. Moreover, overcrowding frequently results in the postpone-ment of long-overdue and badly needed refurbishment programmes, thereby per-petuating squalor and dilapidation, even when it does not result in grossly inappropriate alternative accommodation being pressed into service, as has hap-pened in the past and seems destined to happen again. Another consequence of overcrowding is the need to transfer prisoners around the system in the quest for available accommodation. This is not only highly disruptive to prisoners and their families but also contributes to the sense of bitterness and hostility which Woolf identified as a factor increasing the likelihood of reoffending on release (Woolf and Tumim, 1991: para. 10.27). Finally, the increase in tension and frustration caused by overcrowding is widely believed to aggravate the crisis of control (see below) by increasing the risk of disturbances, such as the riot at Strangeways in 1990.

The Crisis of Conditions

The present crisis of conditions comprises several elements that, individually and collectively, help to influence the quality of life of those living and work-ing in the English prison system:

1 the sheer wretchedness of the physical accommodation in which the great majority of prisoners are housed;
2 the impoverished and repressive nature of the regimes to which most of them are routinely subjected; and
3 the difficulties inmates experience in maintaining relationships with family and friends and sustaining links with the wider community to which they belong.

The accommodation in which prisoners are held is obviously a key element in the quality of life they experience. In recent decades the state of that accommodation in some parts of the prison system has become a byword for squalor, as reports by the Chief Inspector of Prisons have repeatedly testified.[46] As Lord Woolf (1991: para. 10.19) observed, justice itself is compromised if prisoners are held in condi-tions that are 'inhumane or degrading, or are otherwise wholly inappropriate'. Perhaps the nadir for the Prison Service was a finding by the European Committee for the Prevention of Torture (1991) that a number of features found in three English local prisons[47] – including the overcrowding, lack of integral sanitation and inadequate regime activities – were inhuman and degrading.

For many years, inmates' lack of access to integral toilet facilities symbolized the decrepit condition of much of the contemporary prison estate. Following its condemnation by the Woolf Report, the government proudly proclaimed in April 1996 that the anachronistic practice of inmates 'slopping out' their overnight waste buckets was finally at an end, though even this belated announcement proved to be premature. Prison inspection reports confirm that even as recently as 2006, female inmates at Bullwood Hall Prison in Essex were still routinely enduring the degrading practice. Meanwhile, the pressures of overcrowding are such that it is no longer possible for the Prison Service to guarantee continuous access to toilet facilities even in other parts of the English prison estate (HM Chief Inspector of Prisons, 2004). In Scotland the scale of the problem is even worse, and in 2004 a prisoner successfully sued the Scottish Ministers responsible for Scottish Prison Service for breach of his human rights under Article 3 of the European Convention on Human Rights.[48]

However, the introduction of integral sanitation has made only a limited improvement to prisoners' quality of life since it involved the installation of a toilet and wash basin in an already cramped cell measuring between 6 and 8 square metres. As we have seen, this tiny space is frequently occupied by two inmates instead of the single occupant it was designed for. A lack of adequate screening round the toilet means that they not only lack privacy when using the cramped facilities but also have to eat their meals and sleep in the same unhygienic conditions (Shaw, 1992a: 169; HM Chief Inspector of Prisons, 2000a).

Basic guidelines for prison conditions and regimes are set out in the Council of Europe's European Prison Rules, first promulgated in 1973 and revised in 1987 and 2006.[49] The European rules emphasize the importance of exercise and recreation and, in particular, recommend that prisoners should have the opportunity of at least one hour of exercise every day in the open air (Rule 27.1). However, these rules have no legal force in England. For many years English prisoners were indeed allowed out into the 'fresh' air for an hour a day, although usually this just meant trudging around within the confines of a drab internal courtyard. But in 1998 even this minimum entitlement was withdrawn when a new order came into force which prescribed that prisoners should have daily exercise in the fresh air 'for such a period as may be reasonable in the circumstances' (Prison Service Order No. 4275, 1998). As a result, it is now not unknown for outdoor exercise to be confined to just half an hour each day, a practice that drew sharp condemnation from the European Committee for the Prevention of Torture (2005) following its inspections in 2001 and 2003.

As with so many other aspects of prison life, it is in the local prisons that the provision of facilities and constructive activities are particularly deplorable.[50] They are the most overcrowded, holding on average 26 per cent more inmates than their certified normal accommodation (HM Chief Inspector of Prisons, 1999b). Figures published by the Prison Reform Trust (2006b) showed that in January 2006 the ten most overcrowded prisons in England and Wales – each with an occupancy rate of more than 150 per cent – were all local. Yet these same institutions house many prisoners on remand who are awaiting trial and who have not been found guilty of any offence.[51] Logically, those still presumed innocent might expect better treatment than those proved guilty. But as the government's own Chief Inspector (2000a) has pointed out, the reality – despite all the evidence and repeated criticism – continues to defy this logic.

Deplorable as the physical conditions in most English prisons undoubtedly are, their effects on the inmates who have to endure them may be less damaging than the restrictive and repressive daily regimes to which many of them are routinely subjected.[52] Prison regimes are restrictive in many respects, but one of the most obvious of these is the serious lack of suitably constructive and purposive activities for inmates to engage in. European Prison Rule 25.1 states that '[t]he regime provided for all prisoners shall offer a balanced programme of activities'. In English prison parlance, the term 'purposeful activity' is used to encompass time spent at work, in education, training or physical recreation or participating in programmes such as those designed to tackle offending behaviour. Time spent 'in association' – mixing with other inmates – is not included in the term. In general the performance of the Prison Service over many years with regard to providing inmates with a balanced and adequate programme of activities has been abysmal. In the current climate of gross and worsening overcrowding, there is little or no realistic prospect of any improvement in this state of affairs, at least for the foreseeable future.

Until 2004 the Prison Service did at least aim to provide a minimum level of purposeful activity, even though the target it set itself was as woefully inadequate as it was purely aspirational. Until that date the key performance indicator for purposeful activity was an average of 24 hours per week, or just 3.4 hours per day, leaving the other 20.6 hours each day without any structured activity. Even this modest aspiration proved unattainable in seven out of the preceding eight years,[53] however, whereupon the KPI itself was simply and summarily abandoned by the Prison Service in 2004, in a tacit admission of defeat.[54] This episode also exposes the chronic limitations of a managerial culture that elevates the pursuit of whatever arbitrary, shifting and often meaningless targets it sets for itself over the need to identify, report and address the real challenges and impediments it faces.

With regard to work activities, Rule 26.2 of the European Prison Rules states that 'prison authorities shall strive to provide sufficient work of a useful nature'. Rule 26.7 states that 'the organisation and methods of work in the institutions shall resemble as closely as possible those of similar work in the community'. In reality, much of the work that has traditionally been provided in prison is dull, repetitive and demeaning, including as it does wing cleaning, maintenance and orderly work. Far from equipping prisoners with useful skills which might improve their prospects for employment on release, it seems only to reflect a narrow work ethic that approves of hard manual labour as an instrument of punishment in its own right. Some work is available in prison workshops that approximates more closely to the conditions experienced in workplaces in the community. However, they only employed around 10,000 prisoners (equating to 13 per cent of the total prison population) in 2003–4, each inmate working an average of 25 hours per week (House of Commons Home Affairs Committee, 2005: para. 143). Regrettably, the recent massive expansion in the size of the prison population has far outstripped the provision of workshop facilities. An internal review of prison industries concluded that it was 'indefensible' that the Prison Service 'cannot find enough work or purposeful activity for prisoners' (Prison Industries Review Team, 2003). The low priority that both government and Prison Service accord to prison work schemes seems all the more remarkable in view of the importance that is attached to resettlement initiatives of various other kinds.

On the subject of prison education, the European Prison Rules state that '[e]very prison shall seek to provide all prisoners with access to educational programmes which are as comprehensive as possible and which meet their individual needs while taking into account their aspirations' (Rule 28.1). Once again, however, the performance of the Prison Service in this respect has been decidedly mixed. In purely financial terms, more money than ever before is now being spent on prison education, funding for which nearly trebled from £47.5 million in 1999–2000 to £122 million in 2004–5 (House of Commons Education and Skills Committee, 2005). However, this major investment was preceded by more than a decade of chronic underfunding for prison education, and the average spending per prisoner on prison education of £1,185 in 2002–3 was less than half the amount spent on secondary school pupils per year (Braggins and Talbot, 2003). As for the content of prison education, considerable emphasis has been placed on the provision of basic skills such as literacy and numeracy. While it is true that very many inmates have extremely poor educational attainments (see section 6.3, above), this has skewed resources away from further and higher education programmes to the detriment of more able inmates (House of Commons Education and Skills Committee, 2005: para. 11). It also fails to take account of individual prisoners' needs and aspirations as enjoined by European Prison Rule 28.1.

A number of other fundamental failings in the prison education system have been highlighted in reports compiled by HM Chief Inspector of Prisons (1999c) and the House of Commons Home Affairs Committee (2005). One persistent failing relates to the huge disparity in the level of investment in different categories of prisons and between individual prisons,[55] which reflects a lack of unified prison education policy across the entire estate and results in disturbing variations in levels of access to education classes. A second shortcoming relates to the continual disruption of planned educational programmes, either as a result of inmates being moved to other establishments before completing a course, or because of alleged shortages of security staff for the purposes of supervision. A third problem relates to the narrowness of the core curriculum that is provided by the Prison Service.

Apart from the physical conditions and regimes within prisons, a third element that has an important bearing on the present crisis of conditions relates to the ease with which prisoners are able to sustain relationships with their families and communities. The European Prison Rules require prison authorities to assist prisoners in maintaining contact with the outside world and to provide them with the appropriate welfare support to do so (Rule 24.5). Inmates should be allowed to communicate as often as possible with families and others (Rule 24.1) and visits should be arranged in such a way as to allow prisoners to maintain family relationships in as normal a manner as possible (Rule 24.4). Unfortunately, the configuration and geographical location of the prison estate make it extremely difficult for family and community links to be sustained, while the relentless pressure of overcrowding causes further disruption and hardship for prison inmates and, more especially, their families.

At the end of February 2003, over 27,000 prisoners (more than one-third of the prison population) were located over 50 miles from the town in which they were committed for trial, and 12,500 (more than one-sixth) were held over 100 miles away (House of Commons Home Affairs Committee, 2005: para. 40). This inevitably causes major hardships for both inmates and their families, who are restricted to two-hourly visits in a general visiting room that is supervised by prison staff and monitored by high-definition, closed-circuit television cameras. Unlike other countries, which allow private visits of longer duration in a manner that is more compatible with the right to family life enshrined in Article 8 of the European Convention on Human Rights, the British government has always resisted such arrangements (Coyle, 2005a: 112). Moreover, the relentless pressure of prison numbers and associated problem of overcrowding have resulted in a massive increase in the number of prison transfers as prisoners are moved around the country in order to make full use of the limited space that is available. In 2003–4 there were over 100,000 prison transfers, compared with 60,000 in 2000–1 (House of Commons Home Affairs Committee, 2005: para. 40). This continual 'churn', as it is known, causes huge disruption not only for prison educational and rehabilitative programmes but also for the inmates and families whose lives are further disrupted.

One way of minimizing the inevitable dislocation of family and community ties would be to reconfigure the prison estate into a more flexible system of multi-functional '*community prisons*', situated where possible close to the main centres of population. This would make it very much easier for most prisoners irrespective of their security classification to maintain close links with family and community, and thus assist in the process of reintegration on release. It would also have the advantage of reducing or even eliminating altogether the practice of regularly transferring inmates, often at short notice and frequently to distant parts of the country, thereby removing another major source of grievance for prison inmates. As we saw earlier (section 6.4), Lord Woolf advocated just such a system as a means of radically improving prison conditions. But although the idea was resurrected in early 2006, it would be impossible to achieve without a massive financial investment and, almost certainly, a significant reduction in the size of the prison population. In any event, as we also saw earlier, the prospect of such a fundamental reconfiguration of the prison estate appears to have been dashed, at least for the moment, by a combination of the remorseless rise in prison numbers and the appointment of yet another new Home Secretary.

Even if it proves impossible to overcome the geographical barriers thrown up by an inflexible prison estate, there are other ways of enabling prisoners to maintain links with families by making it easier for them to communicate by telephone. Until recently, most prisons allowed inmates to purchase phone cards for the purpose, but because this system was open to abuse (in the form of trafficking in phone cards), most prisons have now moved to a PIN number system. This allows inmates to call pre-specified numbers only by keying in their own unique PIN number, the cost of the calls being automatically deducted from money earned while working in prison. Although such facilities provide some compensation for the lack of social contact, this form of communication is not completely unfettered as prison officers are liable to listen in on some conversations, and some may be tape-recorded.

In very general terms, the trend since the Woolf Report is that there have been some improvements in physical conditions, though the scope for further improvement is severely restricted by the continuing population pressure. There were some very significant deteriorations in prison regimes during the mid-1990s, as the Prison Service struggled to cope with a rapidly expanding prison population during a period of financial stringency and an officially endorsed policy of austerity towards inmates. Since 1997 there has been a significant investment in the development of more constructive prison regimes, with the aim of reducing the stubbornly high reconviction rates that are associated with the use of imprisonment. However, much of the emphasis has been on the introduction of specific high-profile treatment programmes in individual prisons rather than securing overall improvements in prison regimes as a whole. Some of the petty restrictions associated with the austerity regime of the mid-1990s, such as the blanket ban on televisions in cells, have also been relaxed. However, progress overall has been patchy to date, and it would be true to say that the crisis of conditions is still as intractable as ever. It is likely to remain so unless and until the fundamental problem of grossly excessive prison numbers is finally resolved. And yet the case for drastic improvement in prison conditions remains unanswerable not just on humanitarian grounds, but because it would also be likely to elicit a more positive attitude on the part of prisoners. It could even have a beneficial effect on the problem of control within the prisons, as we shall argue in the next section.[56]

The Crises of Control and Authority

Prisons are coercive institutions, housing people who have little or no control over where they are allocated, how they spend their time, with whom they have to associate, or the conditions in which they are kept. Many are resentful of their captive state, some have severe behavioural or personality problems, and many feel aggrieved – often understandably and justifiably – about the way they are dealt with by basic-grade officers and the prison authorities alike. Maintaining order and control in such an environment presents a massive challenge for everyone who is employed within the Prison Service and also for those who are responsible for prescribing the policies that will help to determine how this challenge is met. The scale of the challenge – devising firm and effective procedures that are also fair and humane – is daunting, and the persistent failure of the Prison Service over many years to rise to it has generated a pervasive and persistent crisis of control that is far from being resolved.

Prison riots are the most visible and spectacular symbols of a more deep-seated crisis of control within the prison system.[57] At a more mundane level, the problem of disruptive behaviour poses a predictable – but equally intractable – problem for prison authorities. Having briefly examined prison riots and the competing explanations of their causes in Chapter 1, we are more concerned in this section with the issue of day-to-day control and the responses that have been developed for dealing with disruptive inmates. It is important to differentiate at the outset between the formal disciplinary system, which is used to deal with offences against prison discipline, and the informal control system, which affords a wide range of strategies for dealing with disruptive behaviour. As we shall see, both of these regulatory systems have all too often proved counter-productive in practice, and have diverted attention away from the need to improve the quality of the regimes themselves, the most important aspect of which is the state of relations between staff and inmates.

The formal prison disciplinary system

The disciplinary procedures to which prisoners are subject can substantially increase their period of captivity or worsen its conditions, and yet until recently they lacked many of the safeguards that are normally associated with judicial processes. Consequently, the prison disciplinary system was generally perceived by prisoners as operating in an arbitrary and unjust manner and has long been a focus for discontent on the part of inmates.

Before 1992 there was a two-tier system for adjudicating alleged disciplinary offences in which responsibility rested either with the prison governor or the prison Board of Visitors[58] (see below), depending on the seriousness of the offence. Prison governors were responsible for carrying out a preliminary investigation into all cases, and also for dealing with the least serious of these (constituting the vast majority). More serious cases were adjudicated by the prison's Board of Visitors, but although these were nominally independent of the prison system, with many of their members being lay magistrates, they were generally viewed by prisoners as being not so much independent as part of the prison authority system. Both tiers exercised considerable disciplinary powers that were not matched by the kind of judicial safeguards available to those on trial for ordinary criminal offences, which heightened still further the suspicion felt by inmates (see Maguire et al., 1985; Prior, 1985: Appendix 11).

As part of its attempt to improve the standard of justice within prisons, the Woolf Report recommended that Boards of Visitors should no longer be involved in the adjudication of disciplinary proceedings, and that there should be a clear differentiation between disciplinary and criminal proceedings. These recommendations were implemented by the Prison (Amendment) Rules, 1992 (SI 1992/514). Under the reformed system, relatively minor disciplinary offences were dealt with by a governor or deputy governor, though their disciplinary powers were considerably enlarged. The penalties they could impose included cautions, the forfeiture of privileges (for up to 42 days), exclusion from associated work or activities (21 days), stoppage of earnings (42 days), cellular confinement (for up to 14 days), and the award of additional days of imprisonment (formerly known as loss of remission – see Chapter 8) of up to 42 days. However, they were expected to refer to the police more serious forms of indiscipline (such as assault or possession of drugs) that constitute offences under the ordinary criminal law as opposed to more minor infractions of the prison disciplinary rules.[59]

In the previous edition of this book, we pointed out that even the reformed prison disciplinary system fell far short in many respects of the normal judicial safeguards that would conventionally be associated with the imposition of such significant deprivations of liberty. We also suggested that it would appear to be highly vulnerable to a successful challenge under the Human Rights Act, and in particular Article 6 of the European Convention on Human Rights. This guarantees the right to a fair and public hearing by an independent tribunal established by law to anyone who is charged with a criminal offence or faces a determination of their civil rights (see also Quinn, 1993, 1995; Prison Reform Trust, 2000c). In 2002 the European Court of Human Rights duly ruled that the disciplinary hearings system did not constitute a fair hearing (*Ezeh and Connors v. UK* (2002) 35 EHRR 28), and consequently the Prison Rules were changed yet again. Under the current system, prison governors are authorized to impose 'loss of privileges', the most severe of which is 'cellular confinement', which amounts to virtual solitary confinement without any facilities for 23 hours a day for a period not exceeding 14 days. More severe penalties up to and including the imposition of up to 42 'additional days' can now only be imposed by a legally qualified 'independent adjudicator' during a hearing at which the accused inmate is entitled to legal representation (Rule 55, Prison (Amendment) Rules 2002).

In 2004 there were 108,389 offences against prison discipline, which yields a rate of 145 offences per 100 prisoners compared with 224 offences per 100 prisoners a decade earlier (NOMS, 2005f: Tables 9.1 and 9.3). The commonest offences were disobeying lawful orders, unauthorized transactions (drug offences and possession of unauthorized articles) and violence (fights and assaults) (Table 9.3). The most frequently imposed punishments were forfeiture of privileges (45 per cent of the total), stoppage or reduction of earnings (32 per cent), cellular confinement (12 per cent) and the imposition of additional days (5 per cent) (Table 9.4).

Another major complaint about the prison disciplinary system used to be that it lacked any appeal to an outside body. The only appeal procedure involved an application to Prison Service Headquarters for determination by an Area Manager, but the success rate for such actions was less than 10 per cent (Livingstone and Owen, 1993: 203). However, in 1994 a Prisons Ombudsman (see below under 'crisis of accountability') was appointed following a recommendation to that effect by Lord Woolf. The Prisons Ombudsman is available as a final avenue of appeal against disciplinary findings, but only after all internal appeal procedures have been exhausted. Moreover, the Ombudsman is heavily dependent on information provided by prison staff in reaching a decision. It is still hard to say how far the existence of the Prisons Ombudsman has managed to assuage inmates' concerns about the fairness of the prison disciplinary system.

The informal prison disciplinary system

The three principal informal methods of exerting control over inmates who are perceived to be disruptive involve the use of physical force or restraint, segregation and transfer. In the past, punishment or repression based on the use of physical force was the standard response for those who resisted 'good order and discipline' in prisons. The official punishments of flogging and birching fell into disuse after 1962, and corporal punishment was formally abolished in 1967 (Thomas, 1972: 201). However, the tradition of exercising control by force lives on in a variety of other ways.

The use of force has frequently been authorized, albeit often clandestinely, as a means of coping with prison disorder. As long ago as 1931, a mutiny in Dartmoor prison was suppressed by prison officers backed up by armed police (Coyle, 2005a: 32 and 149). During the prison riots of the 1970s, specially trained prison staff (known as the 'MUFTI' – 'Minimum Use of Force Tactical Intervention' – squad) served as 'in house' riot squads to quell disorder in a number of prisons including Gartree in 1978 and also at Hull, Styal and Wormwood Scrubs in 1979. It later emerged that no fewer than 54 prison inmates had sustained injuries at the hands of the squad during the incident at Wormwood Scrubs (Thomas and Pooley, 1980: 136; Adams, 1994: 180). This paramilitary approach was taken a stage further in Scotland, where a hostage-taking incident at Peterhead Prison in 1986 resulted in the SAS (Special Air Services) being brought in to undertake the first armed intervention in a British prison dispute (Scraton et al., 1991: 24ff.). Although this brought about the release of the hostage concerned, another was seized almost immediately at Perth Prison, suggesting that the only long-term outcome of this particular intervention was a further escalation in a depressing retaliatory spiral of violence.

When the dispersal system was adopted, it was erroneously assumed that the problem of control was just another aspect of the security problem, and that the most disruptive prisoners would be the high-security inmates and vice versa (King and Elliott, 1977; King and Morgan, 1980; King, 1985; Adams, 1994: 181).[60] Not only was this assumption soon to be disproved, but it also became apparent that the relatively relaxed regimes and undifferentiated interior space associated with the dispersal prisons posed enormous control problems within their high-security perimeters. When, almost from the outset, the dispersal prisons began to experience serious control problems, prison authorities resorted to a combination of physical force, segregation and reallocation, none of which was conspicuously successful in averting or even quelling disorder.

The use of force is currently authorized under Rule 47 of the 1999 Prison Rules, which prescribe that it should not be used unnecessarily, and then only as much as is necessary. Where it is necessary, only approved 'control and restraint' (C & R) techniques are supposed to be used 'unless this is impractical'. Although the C & R manuals that have been issued by the Prison Service are classified, the techniques are said to be based on the martial art known as Aikido (Leech, 1995: 264; see also Coyle, 2005a: 151 for a detailed account of the techniques used). Serious disturbances are likely to be dealt with by specially trained 'incident control teams' comprising negotiators and specialist control and restraint staff (Coyle, 2005a: 152). Other less sophisticated forms of physical restraint have also been used routinely in the recent past, including bodybelts, ratchet handcuffs, staves and batons.

In addition to these approved methods of force and physical restraint, prison staff are frequently alleged (Boyle, 1977: 174; Scraton et al., 1991: 19ff.),[61] and sometimes proved, to resort unofficially to unapproved and unlawful methods, including deliberate assaults or the use of excessive force in restraining troublesome inmates. For many years it was exceedingly rare for allegations of flagrant brutality on the part of prison officers to receive any official confirmation, so impenetrable was the shroud of secrecy surrounding the prison system. And even when this veil of concealment was occasionally pierced, those responsible were unlikely to be made fully accountable, or even identified. For example, following a disturbance at Hull Prison in 1976, several prison officers were ultimately convicted of conspiring to assault and beat prisoners but escaped prison sentences. Then in 1992 an inquest jury returned a verdict of unlawful killing on Barry Prosser, an inmate at Winson Green Prison, who was kicked to death by the staff who were being paid to look after him (Coggan and Walker, 1982). So powerful was the conspiracy of silence, however, that no one was convicted for his death despite the jury's verdict (Scraton et al., 1991: 133).

More recently, however, allegations of continuing staff brutality have received incontrovertible confirmation from several authoritative official sources, although the problem of holding those responsible to account remains as intractable as ever. In 1996 the Chief Inspector of Prisons expressed his disquiet over allegations concerning the illegal use of force against inmates in the segregation unit at Wormwood Scrubs, a prison he memorably described as a 'flagship dead in the water' (Ramsbotham, 2005: 104). Just over two years later a second, even more damning, report was published (HM Chief Inspector of Prisons, 1999a), deploring the fact that no action had been taken in the meantime and that the treatment of inmates appeared to have deteriorated still further. Then in September 2000, three prison officers had the dubious distinction of becoming the first in modern English penal history to be imprisoned for acts of brutality against prisoners (*Independent*, 7 September 2000). Between 1 January and 30 June 1999, a total of 44 prison officers (including those at Wormwood Scrubs) were suspended in prisons in England and Wales for a variety of alleged assaults against prisoners. However, the convictions of those who had been imprisoned for assault were subsequently overturned on appeal (Ramsbotham, 2005: 106). Nor is this just an isolated example. In January 2006, staff bullying and intimidation of inmates was alleged at Leeds Prison, in which excessive and inappropriate use was made of the segregation unit, which in turn was described as being run on 'in a militaristic fashion' (HM Chief Inspector of Prisons, 2005c). An internal report leaked to the press in November 2006 spoke of a nine-year reign of terror involving over 160 prison officers at Wormwood Scrubs between 1992 and 2001. Abuses were said to include savage beatings, death threats and sexual assault on inmates, while some managers turned a blind eye to the situation (*Guardian*, 13 November 2006).

Apart from the use of physical force, one of the commonest options adopted by the authorities when confronted with disruptive prisoners is the physical segregation of those responsible. Under Rule 45 of the 1999 Prison Rules, a prison governor has the power to order the 'removal from association' of a prisoner where this appears desirable 'for the maintenance of good order and discipline'.[62] Prisoners segregated in this way are held in 'special cells' located in a segregation unit (or 'punishment block'), where they are kept in virtual isolation for 23 hours per day, deprived of almost all opportunities for work, education, contact and recreation (Creighton and King, 2000: 117). In 2004, this form of restraint was used in respect of 1,979 male and 101 female prisoners (NOMS, 2005f: Table 12.2). In spite of the severe deprivations it entails – amounting to indefinite solitary confinement – removal from association is categorized as an administrative procedure rather than a disciplinary sanction. Its use can often make matters worse by fuelling discontent among prisoners, as we shall see.[63] Attempts to challenge the legality of the segregation procedure have proved unsuccessful in the past,[64] and it is by no means certain that that a renewed challenge under Article 3 of the European Convention on Human Rights would succeed unless the conditions were wholly exceptional (see below).

Segregation was often combined in the past with another administrative process – the temporary transfer procedure – whereby difficult or disruptive prisoners were reallocated from their original prison to the segregation unit of a local prison. Although intended to provide a temporary (one month) 'cooling off' respite before returning to the original prison, the governor there could meanwhile apply to the Prison Service to have the inmate transferred to yet another establishment. At the time of the Strangeways riot, a large number of inmates who were alleged to be especially disruptive were being shunted from one prison to another every few months. The procedure was known by a variety of nicknames including the 'magic roundabout' or 'merry-go-round'.

For a long time temporary transfers – sometimes as many as 100,000 each year – were authorized under Home Office Circular Instruction 10/74 (otherwise known as 'Rule Ten-Seventy-Four' or, in prison jargon, the 'Ghost Train'). Following recommendations contained in the Woolf Report, a new procedure for managing persistently disruptive inmates known as the 'Continuous Assessment Scheme' was introduced. This revised procedure still authorized the use of transfers in the interests of 'good order and discipline', but only as a last resort, and subject to a regime of safeguards. The current strategy is to house the great majority of disruptive inmates in special units known as 'close supervision centres', the first of which was set up in 1998. This has not by any means eliminated temporary transfers, which still occur on much the same scale as before, though now mostly for administrative reasons in order to utilize every available space in response to the prison numbers crisis.

The use of specially adapted segregation units for particularly disruptive prisoners who could not be controlled within the relatively liberal and constructive regime of the standard dispersal or high-security prison has a long and not very honourable or successful history. It began in 1974 with the introduction of a special 'control unit' at Wakefield Prison,[65] following widespread prison disturbances in 1972. Within the control unit, both the physical conditions and the regime were intentionally spartan, and any amelioration of the conditions had to be 'earned' by satisfactory behaviour over a prolonged period. Following the controversy surrounding its use,[66] the operation of the control units was suspended in 1975. Then in 1983 the government's own Control Review Committee accepted that this particular response to the problem of disorder within the prison system represented a blind alley (Home Office, 1984a: para. 52).

In its place, the Committee recommended the creation of a new system of small sized 'Special Units' (see Bottomley and Hay, 1991), which offered a variety of different non-punitive regimes as a way of coping with seriously disruptive prisoners. Within these units, the need for tight security was counterbalanced by a liberal and humane regime in which the emphasis was on the resocialization of violently disruptive and aggressive prisoners who have often proved extremely difficult to handle in the normal prison environment. Three such Special Units were operational at any one time.[67] However, the Special Units themselves fell victim to the more repressive penal climate that accompanied the security clamp-down of the mid-1990s, despite some evidence of success in coping with some of the most intractable prisoners in the prison system (Boag, 1988, 1989; Bottomley, 1990; Martin, 1991; Cooke, 1989).

In July 1995, the Prison Service established a project[68] to investigate the feasibility of introducing a new 'Strict Regime' unit, which in 1998 resulted in the creation of a radically different system of Close Supervision Centres (CSCs) based at Woodhill and Durham Prisons, though the latter was subsequently closed. Their operating philosophy owed far more to the discredited and unsuccessful Control Unit initiative of the 1970s than the rather more enlightened (and penologically better informed) approach that had been pioneered in the Special Units they replaced. In a depressing illustration of the tendency for English penal history – and particularly its mistakes – to repeat itself, the CSCS were founded on the notion of a 'progressive' or 'staged' system which incorporated a crude and mechanistic 'stick and carrot' approach to eliciting good behaviour. The 'stick' consisted of a restricted regime offering no association and 'basic' or minimal privileges.[69] The 'carrots' on offer consisted of a graded series of 'earned privileges' that were intended to operate as a reward for compliant behaviour. Thus, prisoners were expected to graduate initially to a so-called 'structured' regime providing some opportunity for participating in association, constructive activities and behaviour programmes and thence to an 'intervention' unit, in which privileges would reach the 'standard' level on offer in the rest of the high-security estate.

Unfortunately (but all too predictably), the early experience of the CSC system disclosed a number of extremely serious operational failings which exposed basic flaws in the assumptions on which it rested. A thorough evaluation of the system found that out of 51 prisoners housed during its first 28 months of operation, only 12 inmates 'progressed' from it and, of these, only four managed to settle 'on normal location' without any recurrence of their disruptive behaviour (Clare and Bottomley, 2001: 103). Although 30 prisoners were thought to show reduced levels of disruptive behaviour within the CSC compared with outside, six showed an increased level of assaultive behaviour. Moreover, a group of eight prisoners 'refused to cooperate with the system from the outset and embarked upon a persistent campaign of confrontation and challenge, involving dirty protests, violence and/or threats of violence against staff, as well as litigation against the system'. Noting that for several of these prisoners, their behaviour had deteriorated dramatically following their transfer to the CSC, the report authors noted laconically that 'it would be unwise to claim that the overall effect of CSCs on these prisoners had been anything other than very negative'. Liebling (2001: 156) suggested that several of these inmates became more violent (and more disturbed) than they had been at any stage during their prison careers. Her interviews with this group of inmates revealed a sense of injustice with regard to every aspect of the system's operation which 'gave every excuse they needed to vent all the anger, frustration and hatred they could muster against its staff' (2001: 159).

A thematic review of the CSC system undertaken by HM Chief Inspector of Prisons (1999d) complained that the majority of prisoners who failed to progress were consigned to varying degrees of restriction 'with a significant proportion experiencing open-ended, long-term segregation in conditions that equate with punishment'.[70] He was even more outspokenly critical of both the regime itself and also the absence of any effective monitoring and oversight of the system in a subsequent account he wrote of his experiences as Chief Inspector (Ramsbotham, 2005: ch. 6, esp. p. 126).

A similar though less extreme 'sticks and carrots' regime known as the 'Incentives and Earned Privileges (IEP) scheme[71] was also introduced to the rest of the prison system in July 1995, as part of the post-Learmont security clamp-down. A Home Office-funded evaluation of this scheme (Liebling et al., 1999) found that there had been no significant overall improvements to prisoner behaviour in the five establishments studied. Significantly, however, there were reductions (from relatively high levels) in favourable inmate perceptions of staff fairness, relations with staff, regime fairness, consistency of treatment and progress in prison.[72] Negative feelings such as these among inmates are known to be highly detrimental to the maintenance of order in prisons (Sparks and Bottoms, 1995; Sparks et al., 1996) even though, paradoxically, this was supposed to be the main aim of the IEP system itself. Thus, it appeared that perceptions of unfairness on the part of inmates offset and outweighed any beneficial effects of the new system. None of this should have come as any surprise in the wake of the Woolf Report. As it is, the entire episode serves to highlight the chronic inability of English penal policy-makers to learn from either the depressingly long litany of well-documented policy failures or the much shorter (and often unsung) paean of more constructive interventions.[73]

As for Woolf himself, his main strategy for tackling the control problem (as we shall see below) was to attend to the genuine sense of grievance that he accepted was primarily to blame for most of the disturbances. However, he also accepted the need for some improvements in the security and control apparatus to deal with the much smaller number of disruptive and difficult prisoners who would undoubtedly remain.[74] In order to tackle this residual control problem, Woolf's proposed solution was heavily influenced by recent American thinking on prison design. Instead of the large-scale, relatively inflexible, open-access wings of conventional prison design, he favoured the use of a rather different model that is often referred to as a *'new generation prison'*, based on a collection of small, self-contained decentralized units (Ditchfield, 1990: 84–7). The first such prison in England – Woodhill, near Milton Keynes – was opened in July 1992. The theory is that within such a system, a variety of regimes may be offered to cater for the specific requirements of different groups of prisoners under the one roof. Being smaller, such designs are said to offer better standards of surveillance and control and also better interpersonal relations between staff and inmates.

However, Andrew Rutherford (1985: 408), one of the few British observers to have examined the new generation prisons in operation in America, has cautioned that they should not be seen as a panacea for all the existing system's ills. While there are undoubtedly some very successful new generation prisons in operation,[75] there are also some not-so-successful ones that can be just as repressive and brutal as those they are designed to replace (see also Scraton et al., 1991: 138ff.). Rutherford's conclusion – that the key to success lies in the management approach that is adopted and the way prisoners are treated rather than in prison architecture – chimes in well with Woolf's general approach.

One sadly neglected response to the control problem in prisons is the need to develop an appropriate strategy to improve the generally very poor state of staff–inmate relations. Or, as the government's own Control Review Committee put it in 1984: 'relations between staff and prisoners are at the heart of the whole prison system and … control and security flow from getting that relationship right' (Home Office, 1984a: para. 16). Perhaps one reason for continuing neglect of this issue (including by Woolf) – is to do with a rather different crisis in which prison officers themselves are a central part of the problem. This is the long-standing *crisis of authority*, to which we now turn.

Part of the problem stems from a persistent ambivalence over the role of prison staff that is reflected in the way they are recruited, trained, managed and also in the tasks they are expected to undertake. Until the middle of the twentieth century, the role of mainstream prison officers was unambiguous enough and could be exclusively described in terms of their 'turnkey' functions. Their job was simply to lock and unlock prisoners in their custody and make sure they were where they were supposed to be and doing what they were supposed to be doing (Coyle, 2005a: 84). No formal skills or qualifications were expected of basic-grade officers, many of whom were recruited from the armed forces, as were many of their superiors. Prison officers (and indeed governors) were not expected to show any initiative in the discharge of their duties, nor were they encouraged to 'fraternize' with those in their charge, largely for fear of corruption. Even now the bulk of their training is devoted to the 'security' aspects of their job. The Prison Service was, and still is, a hierarchical organization with a rigidly centralized 'command structure' in which considerable emphasis is placed on the importance of obeying instructions. It is also characterized by mutual suspicion and hostility between all levels within the hierarchy, but particularly between basic-grade officers and senior management.

From the middle of the twentieth century, however, many of these traditional verities were undermined as the Prison Service began recruiting growing numbers of professionally trained specialist welfare staff – probation officers, educational workers and prison psychologists – to undertake the treatment and training functions associated with the ethic of rehabilitation. Their responsibilities not only required a much higher level of interaction with inmates than had previously been tolerated, but also generated growing resentment on the part of basic-grade officers. The new prison professionals enjoyed better pay and conditions of service by virtue of their qualifications than ordinary prison officers, but were considered to be usurping a role to which prison officers also aspired, however unsuited to it they might be by temperament, training or ideology. Growing tension between the various categories of prison workers was reflected in the findings of a survey into the attitudes of Scottish prison officers towards those with whom they worked. Many more of them expressed concern about relations with social workers, psychologists and psychiatrists in particular (28 per cent, 27 per cent and 43 per cent respectively) than they did about relations with prisoners (8 per cent) (Wozniak and McAllister, 1991). The survey also showed a high level of concern about relations with prison governors, who were blamed, among other things, for 'giving in' to prisoners and failing to offer staff sufficient support.

Much of the resentment expressed by prison officers stems from a feeling that they are undervalued for the necessary, and increasingly dangerous,[76] work they are expected to do. Moreover, as Fitzgerald and Sim point out (1982: 123), they are also concerned that their job itself is under attack. In addition to the vociferous (and increasingly violent) protests of prisoners, and the alleged insensitivity on the part of the authorities towards their own concerns must now be added the threat of privatization (see Chapter 7). This has already resulted in the loss of certain former functions, such as court escort duties, which used to provide welcome relief to an otherwise tedious routine, and is increasingly seen as a threat to the jobs and livelihood of many prison officers. Another major source of prison staff resentment is over the issue of prisoners' rights and conditions, efforts to improve which are likely to be equated with attempts to subvert their own legitimate authority. Such attitudes are linked to the widely shared perception that society cares more about prisoners than about prison staff.[77] The Woolf Report also referred to the deep sense of frustration on the part of prison officers that their efforts were not appreciated (Woolf and Tumim, 1991: para. 12.1). Faced with this threat to their jobs, pay and conditions, and frustrated by a management in which, often for understandable reasons, they have no confidence, prison officers have tended to look to their trade union – the Prison Officers' Association – for support. This in turn has fuelled the ongoing industrial relations crisis we discussed earlier, and for which senior politicians, Prison Service management and prison staff trade unions are equally culpable. Or, as a senior businessman who was asked to look into the management of the Prison Service concluded: '[d]ifficult unions fill the vacuum left by ineffective management and all managements are ineffective if they are not allowed to manage (Lygo, 1991: 6; as quoted by Coyle, 2005a: 88).

Woolf acknowledged that any substantial change in the way prisoners are treated would require a major contribution from prison officers and considered that the best way of ensuring this, given the poor state of Prison Service morale, would be through improved in-service training. Among the benefits that he anticipated were improvements in staff self-esteem, reductions in racial discrimination and improved relations with inmates, as increased skills enabled staff to offer training and advice. While such recommendations represented a step in the right direction, Woolf had surprisingly little to say about the basic role, attitudes and cultural values of the prison staff themselves, despite the critical importance of these to the nature of prison regimes. All too often in the past attempts by governors and others to liberalize the prison system have been obstructed and frustrated by the actions and prejudices of basic-grade officers fearful of losing their 'authority' and control.

The clearest assessment of the need for a fundamental cultural change on the part of all staff working in the prison system came from Martin Narey when he served as Director General of the Prison Service. In his 1999, speech, which marked the commencement of the 'decency agenda (see section 6.4 above), he complained of a 'litany of failure and moral neglect', of the 'very immorality of our treatment of some prisoners and the degradation of some establishments'. It is hard to imagine a clearer indication of the scale of the crisis of authority facing the Prison Service than for its own Director General to feel compelled to publicly challenge the stubbornly recalcitrant elements within that service and to threaten to resign unless his reforms were supported.

Crisis of Accountability

'Accountability' is the term used to describe the various mechanisms for ensuring that those who wield power or take decisions that affect the lives of others can be made answerable for them (Mulgan, 2000). We have already described one such device – the doctrine of ministerial responsibility – and noted that it constitutes a deeply flawed mechanism for securing the *political* accountability of those senior policy-makers, up to and including the Secretary of State, who have the power to determine how the prison system will operate. Fortunately, other forms of accountability exist, and some modest gains have been achieved by a variety of agencies in ensuring a degree of answerability for its conduct and decisions on the part of the Prison Service. However, it would be fair to say that their cumulative effect has been merely to ameliorate rather than resolve the ongoing crisis of accountability from which the Prison Service continues to suffer. In this section we shall focus mainly on various forms of *administrative* and *judicial* accountability mechanisms.

For most of the twentieth century, the world of the prison was a closed one, screened from public view under a cloak of protective legislation that was originally designed to safeguard national security. One symptom of this equation between prison security and national security can be seen in the scope of the Official Secrets Act, whose inhibiting effects on those working within the prison system was tellingly (and, naturally enough, anonymously) described in 1975 by two assistant governors in the following terms:

> This all-pervasive Act not only inhibits disclosures of injustices which inevitably occur in any system but also prevents open dialogue between those within and outside the Prison Service wishing to improve the quality of training in our prisons and borstals. The ruling that prison officers should not express a view publicly leads to frustration, sterility and inertia'. (cited in Briggs, 1975: 22)

Operating alongside this cloak of secrecy was a legal and regulatory framework whose main aim was not to set out the rights and entitlements of prisoners but rather to serve the administrative convenience of the prison authorities. It did so by conferring on them wide discretionary power that was for the most part impervious to scrutiny and challenge. The main piece of primary legislation – the Prison Act 1952 – was conceived of as an enabling Act, and was intended to confer as much discretion as possible on the Home Secretary (Livingstone and Owen, 1999: 5). The 1952 Act has been repeatedly condemned as anachronistic by penal reform groups (see, for example, Prison Reform Trust 1996). As it was a consolidation measure, many of its main sections date back almost unaltered to the nineteenth century. It thus takes no account of important subsequent national developments such as the introduction of the Prisons Ombudsman and the adoption of agency status. Nor of equally important international developments such as the European Prison Rules, to say nothing of the incorporation of the European Convention on Human Rights in the Human Rights Act 1998.

Much of the regulatory framework governing prison life is contained not in primary legislation but in the Prison Rules,[78] which take the form of delegated legislation drawn up and amended by the Secretary of State. Even these Prison Rules provide only an outline framework and, like the Prison Act itself, are designed to maximize the discretion conferred on the prison authorities. The Rules are, in turn, supplemented by Standing Orders (which cover all aspects of prison life) and Prison Service Orders and Instructions, none of which has the force of law (Creighton and King, 2000: 13–14). In short, a wholesale revision of existing prison law is long overdue. This does not mean that it is likely to happen, however, because – cynical but true – governments are aware that such reforms win few votes.

Despite its air of permanence, the prison system's façade of inscrutability is a relatively recent accretion. During the early part of the nineteenth century, at a time when prisons were locally managed, the government introduced a system of inspectors in 1835, to monitor them, report on what they found, and make recommendations for what needed to be done to put things right (Coyle, 2005a: 55). Once central government assumed control over the entire prison system,[79] this embryonic monitoring system became moribund as inspectors' reports were no longer published separately and lost their critical edge.

It was not until 1979, during an era of growing unease about recurrent allegations of prison disturbances and their brutal suppression, that an official committee of inquiry (May, 1979) called for the resurrection of an independent prison inspectorate. Despite strong opposition from the Home Office, this recommendation was accepted and the first Chief Inspector of Prisons was appointed in 1981. Since then (and especially since the appointment of Judge Stephen Tumim as Chief Inspector in 1987), the reports published by the prisons inspectorate – often expressed in trenchant terms – have shed valuable light on the workings of the Prison Service as well as the conditions to be found in individual prisons. In dispelling the air of secrecy and puncturing the aura of complacency that surrounded the Prison Service for so long, they have acquired a well-deserved reputation around the world as a model to be emulated.[80] As a watchdog and whistle-blower, the Prisons Inspectorate has undoubtedly performed an exemplary service. As an accountability mechanism, however, the Inspectorate lacks teeth, since neither the Prison Service nor Home Office ministers are in any meaningful sense answerable to it. The familiar response of prison governors to a critical report on their prison is to delay its publication and then proclaim, however implausibly, that all has been put in order since the last inspection. The problem at ministerial level is that almost invariably there is no response at all, even to the Chief Inspector's annual reports, causing one former incumbent of the office to doubt whether they had even been read by the various Home Secretaries to whom they were addressed (Ramsbotham, 2005: 214).

One obvious reform would be to require the responsible minister to produce a written annual response to the Chief Inspector's reports, commenting on its findings and outlining the government's reactions to each of the main recommendations, as currently happens in Western Australia (Ramsbotham, 2005: 247). Instead, the government announced in November 2005 that it was planning to merge the five separate criminal justice inspectorates – for prisons, probation, courts, crown prosecutors and police – into a single 'super inspectorate'. This proposal understandably raised concerns among penal reform groups that the government's hidden agenda was to muzzle one of its sharpest and most authoritative critics by blurring its commendably single-minded focus on the most crucial and controversial agency of them all.[81] For a time there again seemed to be a danger that history may be about to repeat itself as one of the few progressive developments in the administration of the Prison Service in recent years became threatened with emasculation by a lethal combination of political hypersensitivity and bureaucratic suppression. Fortunately, however, the threat appears to have receded, at least for the time being, as the government was soundly defeated when the matter was debated in the House of Lords in October 2006 during a debate on the Police and Justice Bill. After threatening to reintroduce the proposal when the Bill returned to the House of Commons, the government subsequently relented and announced the following week that it was dropping the measure (*Guardian*, 19 October 2006).

The prisons inspectorate is by no means the only body to exercise a watchdog role with regard to the Prison Service. Another monitoring body was established in 1878 when central government assumed responsibility for prisons and established visiting committees of local magistrates for each prison to ensure that they were being properly managed (Coyle, 2005a: 56). These became known as Boards of Visitors in 1898, when their composition was also broadened to include local community volunteers as well as magistrates. In 2003 they were renamed Independent Monitoring Boards. Compared with the Prisons Inspectorate, however, they lack the resources, status and perceived independence that is required to adequately discharge such a demanding role.[82]

If the effectiveness of an accountability mechanism is measured in terms of its ability to render those who wield power answerable to an independent body, then mention should also be made of the European Committee for the Prevention of Torture (CPT). Like the domestic prisons inspectorate, it too has the right of access to any place where people can be deprived of their liberty together with the power to inspect documents and conduct private interviews with inmates. This committee has produced a number of well-publicized reports that have been highly critical of aspects of the English prison system. Moreover, unlike the national Prisons Inspectorate, the government is expected to respond to the criticisms directed against it, though convention requires that the two documents are published simultaneously, which provides an opportunity to show that action has been taken. Valuable though the CPT monitoring regime undoubtedly is, its reports are less systematic, intensive and frequent than those of the domestic inspectorate, which has also developed a reputation for producing extremely thorough thematic reports. If the Prisons Inspectorate were to be emasculated, however, as once seemed probable, then the role of the CPT would assume still greater importance.

Another important aspect of accountability is that abuses of power should be rectified, legitimate grievances remedied, and improper decisions set aside. Before 1990 there was a complex and cumbersome internal grievance procedure through which prisoners with grievances were expected to make their complaints. Like the prison disciplinary procedure, however, this evoked precious little confidence among those it was intended to assist, largely because it lacked any provision for independent review, and reserved the sole power to remedy grievances to the governors and the Home Secretary. Moreover, some of the Prison Rules seemed to have been designed to intimidate and deter prisoners who might have a legitimate grievance from pursuing it. For example, before 1989 it was an offence against the Prison Rules to make a 'false and malicious' allegation against a prison officer, which meant that complainants ran the risk of being found guilty of a disciplinary offence unless they could be certain of proving the allegation.

Following widespread concern over the perceived inadequacies of the grievance procedure, the system was reviewed by the Chief Inspector of Prisons (HM Chief Inspector of Prisons, 1987), leading to a reform of the system in September 1990. However, the new procedure was only marginally less cumbersome than the old (Woolf and Tumim, 1991: paras 14.321–325) and still lacked an independent element. Prisoners had a number of avenues of complaint including to the prison governor, the Board of Visitors,[83] the Prison Service area manager, a Member of Parliament, the Home Secretary and also the courts, via an action for judicial review. However, none of these could be said to be effective in protecting prisoners from injustice and ill-treatment. Those procedures that were internal to the Prison Service were perceived by prisoners as unfair and ineffective, while those that involved recourse to outside bodies such as the courts were expensive, time-consuming and severely limited in their scope.

Woolf recommended that, as a matter of good practice, reasons should be given to prisoners for any decisions that might adversely affect them to any material extent. He anticipated that this might forestall a number of complaints under the grievance procedure by reducing the sense of injustice to which such decisions often give rise; and that it might also improve the quality of decision-making by deterring arbitrary decisions. Woolf also agreed that an independent element in the complaints procedure was not just an 'optional extra'. Accordingly, he recommended the appointment of what he called an independent Complaints Adjudicator, who would both act as the final avenue of appeal in disciplinary matters and also 'recommend, advise and conciliate' at the final stage of the grievance procedure (Woolf and Tumim, 1991: para. 14.349).

The government accepted the broad thrust of the Woolf proposals on this issue, and the first Prisons Ombudsman was eventually appointed in October 1994. (The current Ombudsman is Stephen Shaw, formerly the Director of the Prison Reform Trust, who was appointed in 1999.) The early years of the Prisons Ombudsman were marred by a series of serious and damaging disputes over his initial appointment and terms of reference, which cast doubt on the government's commitment to the principle of an independent Ombudsman. Since 1997, however, these concerns have subsided and indeed the Ombudsman's remit has been considerably extended. His main responsibility is to investigate complaints about prisoners' treatment in both public and privately run prisons including disciplinary decisions, but excluding complaints about convictions, sentence lengths and release dates. In September 2001, the Ombudsman's remit (and title) was extended to embrace the probation service as well, following the creation of the National Probation Service. Since April 2004, the Prisons and Probation Ombudsman has been responsible for investigating all fatalities in prison and further extensions – to cover the immigration service, near fatalities and post-release deaths – seem likely to follow. In addition, the Ombudsman has also been asked to conduct a number of special investigations including one into allegations of racism at an immigration reception centre at Oakhampton. Another special investigation examined the handling of a case by the National Probation Service involving a serious sex offender who committed further very serious offences while under supervision on licence following a lengthy sentence of imprisonment.

All internal procedures have to be exhausted before a complaint can be made to the Ombudsman, whose powers are in any event limited to making recommendations and do not extend to the award of compensation, although he may recommend an ex gratia payment. Each year the Prisons and Probation Ombudsman receives over 4,000 complaints (more than double the 2002 figure), the vast majority of which emanate from prisoners.[84] Most complaints relate to the handling of prisoners' property and cash (16 per cent of the total) and general conditions (13 per cent), followed by concerns over pre-release and release decisions (11 per cent) and security concerns (10 per cent of the total). Not all of these can be investigated, however, as many (60 per cent) are ineligible, often because of a failure to exhaust all internal procedures. Consequently, the number of completed investigations in 2005–6 was only around 1,500. As for the outcomes of these investigations, recent annual reports have been rather more circumspect than their predecessors, which reported that approximately one-half of all investigations resulted in a recommendation being made. Nor do they disclose what proportion of recommendations are accepted by the Prison (and Probation) Service, which was a cause for concern in the early years (Prisons Ombudsman, 1995). The 2005–6 report explains that this is because investigators now seek to resolve complaints informally, and suggests that, as a broad rule of thumb, around one-third of the matters they investigate result in a positive outcome for the inmate (Prisons and Probation Ombudsman, 2006: 11). Although an informal dispute resolution approach may well be more appropriate in such cases (Vagg, 1991: 153; Cavadino and Dignan, 2002: 212–13), the absence of any supporting statistics also means that it is no longer as easy to verify such claims as it once was.

The advent of the Prisons Ombudsman has at least rectified one outstanding defect that was long associated with the prison system's complaints procedures: the absence of any independent oversight. However, the system still suffers from a number of weaknesses that could serve to increase rather than alleviate prisoners' feelings of injustice. One relates to the legal status of the post of Ombudsman, which lacks any statutory backing. (Moreover, the fact that the post-holder is nominated and appointed by the Secretary of State could raise understandable concerns that the office is not sufficiently independent of the government of the day.[85]) The current incumbent has been calling for this position to be rectified ever since his appointment in 1999, but this now seems unlikely to happen before 2008 at the earliest (Prisons and Probation Ombudsman, 2006: 13).

A second weakness relates to the stipulation that all internal complaints procedures have to be satisfied before a complaint becomes eligible, which is still a matter of concern with regard to both the Prison Service and the probation service.[86] A third, related problem is that of delay in dealing with the complaints internally, which means that many complaints relate to events that are more than a year old. A fourth problem is that some prisons have been suspected of placing barriers in the way of prisoners who wish to make a complaint.[87] A fifth and final weakness relates to the adequacy of staffing levels within the Ombudsman's office itself – despite a fivefold increase since 2002[88] – particularly in view of the recent substantial increases in its remit. Ramsbotham (2005: 253) complained that a shortage of staff to investigate fatal incidents meant that, initially at least, the Ombudsman had to 'borrow' Prison Service staff for this purpose, which is clearly far from ideal since it meant that complaints against prison staff were still being investigated by prison staff. By 2006, however, 28 fatal incidents investigators were listed on the Ombudsman's website.

There are also some more general factors which may limit the effectiveness of grievance procedures such as the Ombudsman, however formally fair. One is the closed nature of prisons. If an action that is complained of is 'invisible', taking place behind closed doors, it may be impossible for a prisoner to establish that it has in fact occurred. Second, a successful complaint is only likely if it can be shown that a rule has been broken, or that specific entitlements have been denied. In other words, grievance procedures are of limited value where the rules themselves are defective or lack the full force of law: hence the importance of properly enforceable minimum standards and safeguards covering all aspects of prison life. A third and final limitation with grievance procedures generally is their relatively narrow focus (Vagg, 1991: 152ff.), since they are primarily intended to deal with individual complaints rather than collective issues affecting groups of prisoners or even the inmate population as a whole. And yet many of the issues about which prisoners feel most aggrieved (for example, regarding prison conditions and facilities, or the attitude or behaviour of members of staff) affect them collectively and not just as individuals.[89]

In addition to these administrative remedies, prison inmates also retain their rights to seek judicial redress[90] either in the domestic courts, for example by seeking judicial review, or by applying to the European Court of Human Rights in Strasbourg. The record of the courts in holding the authorities legally accountable for mistaken, arbitrary or oppressive use of their powers has also been variable, however, as we have seen in this chapter.[91] For many years the English courts appeared reluctant to challenge the authority of the executive which, as we have seen, was generally buttressed by exceedingly wide-ranging discretionary powers, though they have become far less deferential in recent years (see Lennon, 2003: 449; Livingstone et al., 2003: 76). The European Court of Human Rights adopted a more vigorous approach from the outset, and was the setting for a number of famous victories including prisoners' entitlement to correspond with their lawyers without interference from prison authorities[92] and their entitlement to legal representation in connection with disciplinary proceedings.[93]

Since 1998, the Human Rights Act has incorporated the European Convention on Human Rights (ECHR) into English law, which means that English judges also have to apply its provisions in reaching their decisions. This is unlikely to render the European Court of Human Rights redundant, however, and it has continued to uphold challenges brought by prison inmates against the British government on a number of occasions since 1998. One notable example was a case brought by the parents of a mentally ill, pre-trial inmate who had been kicked to death by his schizophrenic cell-mate in Chelmsford Prison in 1994. Eight years later, the European Court finally affirmed that the British government had violated their son's right to life under Article 2 of the Convention.[94] However, even a successful legal challenge does not necessarily guarantee that the authorities will be held accountable for their failure to uphold prisoners' rights. One notable example relates to the indiscriminate ban on the entitlement of convicted inmates to vote in elections. This was successfully challenged in Strasbourg on the ground that it violates Article 3 of the ECHR.[95] Nevertheless, the government responded to the European Court's judgment by making it clear it had no intention of completely lifting the ban irrespective of the seriousness of a prisoner's offence. So although there have been some improvements in the procedures for making prison authorities accountable in recent years, there is still a long way to go before they can be considered fully accountable.

The Crisis of Legitimacy

The English prison system continues to suffer from a long-running, chronic crisis of legitimacy that seems as far as ever from being resolved. This final crisis has four main aspects: the prison system is generally viewed – by its several 'audiences': the general public, by politicians and the media, by penal staff and by prison inmates themselves – as being simultaneously ineffective in controlling crime, inefficient in its use of resources, insensitive in dealing with prison staff at all levels and, all too often, downright inhumane in its treatment of offenders. We have already fully discussed most of these failings, and will be relatively brief here.

The prison system's failure to provide an effective means of controlling crime is reflected in the chronically poor reconviction rates we examined at the start of this chapter. By any objective measure, a reconviction rate of two out of every three prisoners within two years of their release and three out of four young offenders is indisputably a mark of failure. The fact that sections of the general public – supported and encouraged by parts of the media and by many politicians believe that we need to have even greater recourse to this failed institution and to intensify its harshness underscores the intractability of this particular aspect of the crisis. The Prison Service's crisis of legitimacy with regard to prison staff is closely bound up with the chronic state of industrial relations and the broader managerial crisis that we discussed at the start of section 6.5. But as we shall see in this final section, senior prison staff have also on occasion been treated by their superiors with extraordinary insensitivity.

As for the Prison Service's crisis of legitimacy with regard to the inmates in its charge, we have already commented on the disturbingly high suicide rate in England's prisons, the litany of well-documented instances of cruel or brutal treatment, and the disturbing official reports by inspectors on prison conditions. Concern over the treatment of prison inmates is not confined to prisoners themselves, but also horrifies many criminal justice practitioners, informed observers (see, for example, Department for Christian Responsibility and Citizenship, 2004) and ordinary members of the public. Another aspect of the crisis of legitimacy that we have not yet touched on relates to corruption on the part of prison staff, a longstanding problem to which blind eyes must often have been turned. However, in August 2006, a leaked report suggested that at least 1,000 prison officers are involved in smuggling contraband items such as drugs or mobile phones into prisons or accepting bribes in order to facilitate transfers to less secure institutions (*Guardian*, 1 August 2006).

How to tackle the crisis of legitimacy

The scale, depth and multi-faceted nature of the prison system's crisis of legitimacy seems all too apparent and yet at the same time all too intractable. One response would be to follow the agenda of prison 'abolitionists' (for example, Bianchi, 1994; de Haan, 1990; Hulsman, 1991; Sim, 1992, 1994; Wilson, 2006) and get rid of the institution altogether. But of course – however tellingly the rational case for abolitionism may be presented – this hardly seems politically plausible at the present time, especially since many politicians and ordinary members of the public appear to be in denial that some important aspects of the legitimacy crisis (notably justice and humanity for prisoners) even pose a problem. The fact that the crisis is multi-faceted suggests that it can only be tackled by dealing with its different dimensions and addressing their respective audiences.

Many of the legitimacy problems of prisons stem indirectly from the numbers crisis, which exacerbates poor conditions and regimes and is likely to thwart any efforts to make prisons better managed, more decent and less hopelessly ineffective at turning offenders away from crime. In view of the generally unsympathetic attitudes towards prison inmates on the part of many politicians and members of the public, the prison system's most vulnerable aspect is almost certainly its lack of effectiveness. This can be easily demonstrated, and one might think that a government that professes to favour an evidence-led approach would be persuaded to take steps to consign fewer people to an institution which 'can be an expensive way of making bad people worse' (Home Office, 1990a: para. 2.7). But government is proving largely impervious to such rational arguments. One reason for this may be that imprisonment also serves a number of symbolic functions (see section 6.2), even though, as we have explained elsewhere, many of its instrumental functions could be discharged equally effectively by community penalties (Cavadino et al., 1999: 120). Another is that governments appear to have calculated that there are more votes to be gained in pursuing a tough punitive policy, however ineffective it might be, provided it is popular with the electorate. This only makes sense as a political strategy, however, on the assumption that the electorate is homogeneous and united in its attitudes towards offenders, which is far from being the case. Public opinion surveys, for example, regularly show that attitudes towards offenders are far less punitive than they are portrayed by the media: (see Chapter 11, section 11.3). Demonstrating that the electorate is both less blinkered and more rationally sophisticated than politicians often assume, may therefore offer the most hopeful long-term strategy for weaning politicians off their fixation for custodial forms of punishment.

Turning now to the prisons' crisis of legitimacy with their own inmates, there is mounting evidence, both anecdotal and empirical, that the best way to create legitimacy with inmates is to treat prisoners justly, respecting their dignity and their rights, just as the Woolf Report urged. Fairer and better regimes are not only more popular with prisoners, they also encourage them to behave better (Cooke 1989, 1991; Bottoms et al., 1990: 91; Sparks and Bottoms, 1995; Liebling and Arnold, 2004). However, this is by no means simply a question of giving prisoners *formal* rights and *formally* fair procedures, important though these are, for there is always likely to be a significant gap between the provision of formal justice 'in the books' and substantive justice in practice. Moreover, this gap will almost inevitably be increased in an institution like the prison, which lacks visibility and legitimacy, where prisoners are relatively powerless and where relationships between different groups of inhabitants are in a poor state. Lip-service justice, however formally impressive on paper, will never deliver legitimacy. We need to create an atmosphere and ethos in which prisoners' rights are genuinely and effectively respected, and where they in return afford legitimacy to the institution and behave accordingly.

How is this to be achieved? In our view the conventional approach to regulating life within prisons suffers from many of the same defects as the approach that is typically adopted outside the prison walls: namely, that there is a disproportionate emphasis on *material* rewards and punishments. Liebling (2001: 159) has astutely pointed out that this 'rational choice' model – which is based on a rather crude form of 'instrumental reasoning' – is singularly inappropriate for a group of emotionally unstable and often brutalized individuals. Many prison inmates who pose the greatest 'control' problems have very little control over their own behaviour and most are probably habituated to high levels of material deprivation. Very many inmates suffer from chronic under-socialization, and exceptionally low levels of self-esteem. And yet almost all prisoners have a highly developed sense of fair and unfair treatment and, whatever their perceptions of their own esteem, are acutely aware when they are not accorded the respect to which they feel they are entitled. Not surprisingly, these often highly charged perceptions on the part of prisoners are shaped above all by their personal dealings and relationships with prison staff. When staff act 'unfairly' or unnecessarily punitively, this is likely to reinforce inmates' intuitive perception that they themselves are the unjustly wronged victims of a cruel and vindictive system.

Counter-intuitive as it might seem, moralistic forms of reasoning – in which prison staff not only treat inmates fairly and with respect but also seek constantly to engage and interact with them as fellow human beings – are likely to be more successful than the failed 'instrumentalist' (or 'carrot-and-stick') approaches of the past.[96] The approach we favour is best described as a 'relational' one in the sense that the fostering of constructive and respectful social relationships between staff and inmates should be accorded the highest priority.[97] For relationships not only provide the context in which prisoners' perceptions of the way they are being treated are fostered, but also afford the only context in which any kind of constructive dialogue, emotional engagement and behavioural or attitudinal change is likely to be possible.[98] This kind of approach is all too rare within the English prison system. Moreover, as we have seen, most recent attempts at reform have also sadly neglected the state of relations between staff and inmates. Nevertheless, the very few successful initiatives that have been developed in British prisons in recent years have all been founded on a 'relational' approach of the kind we have just outlined.

The best-known of these was the pioneering regime that evolved at the Special Unit that was set up in Barlinnie Prison in 1973 to house some of Scotland's most violent and disruptive prisoners. The regime that evolved at Barlinnie afforded considerable scope for prisoners to plan their own daily routines, and also to participate with others in the day-to-day running of the community (Whatmore, 1987). Although not entirely problem-free,[99] the unit appears to have been unusually successful in reducing the overall level of assaultive and disruptive behaviour on the part of inmates (Cooke, 1989: 133ff.); its most notable achievement involved the remarkable rehabilitation of Glasgow gangster Jimmy Boyle (see Boyle, 1977).[100]

The unit's regime had a number of distinctive features that undoubtedly contributed to its success, including a relatively high staff–prisoner ratio; an ethos encouraging much less authoritarian relationships between staff and inmates; and a regular 'community meeting'. This acted as a forum for the redress of grievances, release of tensions and the assertion of non-confrontational group norms. In addition, the unit's inmates enjoyed certain privileges not normally available in penal establishments, crucially including regular and frequent visiting arrangements enabling contact to be maintained with family and friends. However, in spite of its international acclaim as one of the very few success stories within the British prison system, the Barlinnie Special Unit closed in March 1995 (Bowden, 1995). The ending of this liberal Scottish experiment[101] marked a partial return to the failed policies of the past, and a revival of more austere isolation and control units, including the recommissioning of the notorious 'cage' cells at Inverness for prisoners who are considered to be particularly recalcitrant.

Exceptional though it was, the Barlinnie unit was not a unique outpost of enlightenment in Britain. Grendon Underwood Prison is also run on the lines of a therapeutic community for prisoners with personality disorders,[102] many of whom are among the most difficult and dangerous in the prison system. Selection for Grendon is unique, since prisoners must first have been recommended by a medical officer and are then interviewed by Grendon staff to see if they will fit in (Leech and Cheney, 1999: 298). No one is compelled to go there, and inmates are free to return to the general prison system at any time, or they may be returned without consent if they fail to comply with the exacting requirements that are expected of them. While at Grendon, prisoners are expected to take part in a group therapy process, which teaches them about responsibility and the effect their actions have on other people. They are called to account for their behaviour (by fellow inmates rather than staff), and have to explain their conduct to the community as a whole. Like Barlinnie, Grendon has achieved some notable success stories. They include a prisoner who, having spent time in the strip cells of Dartmoor, graduated from Grendon with 'a different (and far more successful) outlook on life', and ultimately went on to produce the highly acclaimed *Prisons Handbook* (Leech and Cheney, 1999: 102). Nor was Mark Leech's experience unique. A seven-year reconviction study showed significant reductions in levels of re-imprisonment and violent offences for those who stayed at Grendon for more than 18 months after controlling for risk and mode of leaving Grendon (Taylor, 2000).[103] In spite (or possibly because) of its unique nature within the prison system as a whole, Grendon Prison was for a long time engaged in a battle of survival, in which it was denied both adequate resources and appropriate support from Prison Service Headquarters (HM Chief Inspector of Prisons, 1998). This pariah status is now at an end, however, following the opening of another special therapeutic unit at Dovegate in Staffordshire, which is a new (private) prison for Category B and C prisoners.

A third 'beacon of enlightenment' within the British penal system in recent years, at least until May 2000, was Blantyre House, a Category C prison that provided a resettlement function for longer-term prisoners within a relatively open regime. The prison was almost unique in that for 13 years it had enabled prisoners to develop and pursue 'personal career plans', which were negotiated with management (Leech and Cheney, 1999: 40). Prisoners were encouraged to grow in self-reliance and self-respect, chiefly through their relations with staff, with each other and with people from the outside community. Indeed, they were expected to work in the community rather than in the prison workshops. Security systems had a very low profile, but escapes were almost unknown; violence, alcohol and drugs were not acceptable and resulted in instant transfer. The reconviction rate of those released from Blantyre was just 8 per cent after two years, compared with a rate of 57 per cent for those who left all other prisons in 1996 (Cullen and Minchin, 2000). Even allowing for the fact that Blantyre inmates were carefully selected and may thus have presented a lower risk of reoffending, these are impressive results, and a succession of official inspections by the prisons inspectorate and also the Home Affairs Select Committee attested to its achievements (Ramsbotham, 2005: ch. 9).

Not everyone was impressed by Blantyre House's performance, however, including the Prison Service Area Manager at the time, who was described by former Chief Inspector of Prisons David Ramsbotham (2005: 159) as being feared by staff in the prisons for which he was responsible. He disapproved of the prison's liberal ethos and led an ultimately successful campaign to terminate it, assisted by Prison Service Director General Martin Narey and the Prisons Minister Paul Boateng. Blantyre's governor was removed and demoted and a more compliant successor installed, who immediately requested a thorough search of the prison. This was accomplished on 5 May 2000 with the aid of 84 prison officers in full riot gear accompanied by sniffer dogs, causing £6,000 of damage in the process as doors were smashed down and drawers were forced open. On 16 May the Director General of the Prison Service solemnly reported that 'a quite frightening amount of contraband material' had been found, and in answer to a Parliamentary question on 25 May, Mr Boateng referred to '98 finds of unauthorized articles'. The actual haul was far less sensational and amounted to three ecstasy pills, a small amount of cannabis, three unauthorized mobile phones and some credit cards. None of the inmates tested positive for drugs when subjected to mandatory tests, nor were any charges brought against either prisoners or staff (Ramsbotham, 2005: 160).

A devastating report on the raid by the House of Commons Home Affairs Select Committee (2000) condemned the raid itself after hearing (and implicitly rejecting) oral evidence from Mr Narey and Mr Boateng. It was also highly critical of the attempts made by the Prison Service to mislead the Committee itself, the media and also the public as to the purpose of the raid and the significance of what was found. One clue as to the real motive that lay behind the raid may be contained in press reports suggesting that Mr Narey believed that the former governor 'had allowed the balance to slip between progressive methods ... and the need for security'.[104] The Blantyre House fiasco serves as another unwelcome reminder of the Prison Service's enduring capacity to snatch failure from the jaws of success, and its chronic inability to learn even from its own all-too-rare successes, let alone its much more numerous failures. Equally importantly, it also underlines the scale of the managerial crisis within the Prison Service which we discussed earlier. Defects in the governance of prisons resulted in the cynical and bullying behaviour of an area manager being condoned by the head of the Prison Service and senior politicians alike, while a successful and respected prison governor's career was effectively destroyed. The Blantyre House saga is by no means unique[105] but epitomizes much that is wrong with the way the Prison Service is managed. Unless and until senior managers and the politicians to whom they are accountable can act with more wisdom – one could even say integrity – than was shown on this occasion, the prospects for resolving this aspect of the crisis of legitimacy seem as distant as ever.

In conclusion, if we are to create legitimacy within prisons, we need to alter regime methods, atmospheres, attitudes and relationships as well as the formal entitlements of prisoners. And one additional, inescapable issue is that of resources. For example, one vital factor in the success of the Barlinnie Special Unit was its high staff/inmate ratio, which facilitated positive relationships while also maintaining necessary levels of security and control. More generally, it will be impossible to give prisoners effective entitlements to decent conditions without the material resources required. Consequently, there can be little chance of successfully implementing reforms in anything more than small pockets within the prison system while an acute crisis of penal resources prevails. At present this crisis is set to worsen further as the prison population continues to soar. This trend needs to be forcibly reversed if we are ever to progress towards the goal of just and legitimate confinement, rather than continuing to travel at an ever quickening pace (in Judge Tumim's words) along the road to the concentration camp.

Notes

1 Fiona Mactaggart, Parliamentary Written Answers for 18 April 2006, col. 294W. The Prison Service itself generally quotes a much lower average cost of £27,000 for each prisoner for 2005/6. The reason for the discrepancy is that the Prison Service figure only takes account of 'direct resource expenditure' and thus excludes indirect 'fixed costs' such as the expense of maintaining Prison Service headquarters, capital expenditure on Prison Service land and buildings plus depreciation costs. The latter costs cannot be disaggregated at the level of individual establishments, which is presumably why they are excluded from Prison Service calculations, despite the misleading impression this creates.
2 House of Commons Written Answers, 16 March 2005, column 124WH. Shortly after becoming Home Secretary in May 2006, John Reid committed himself to providing an additional 8,000 places though funding for these had not yet been agreed by the Treasury at the time of writing.
3 House of Commons Written Answers, 30 June 2005, column 1669W.
4 Prior to 1993, the prisons were run by the Prison Department of the Home Office. Since then, Her Majesty's Prison Service has been an 'executive agency' (see section 6.5 below). For convenience we refer to both the pre-1993 Prison Department and today's service as the 'Prison Service'.
5 This was appreciably less than the £2,593 million allocated for 2005–6 (HM Prison Service, 2005b), despite the relentless rise in prison numbers which shows no sign of stopping.

6   The Prison Rules form part of the regulatory framework for the treatment of prisoners in England and Wales. They have the status of delegated legislation and are issued by the Secretary of State in the form of Statutory Instruments made under the Prison Act 1952. The first set of Prison Rules was issued in 1964, though they have been regularly updated since then and have subsequently been replaced by a new set of rules issued in 1999 (SI 1999/728). The rules were revised and consolidated in January 2006. They can be accessed via the Prison Service website at: http://www.hmprisonservice.gov.uk/ resourcecentre/publicationsdocuments/index.asp?cat=86

7   See Prison Service website at: http://www.hmprisonservice.gov.uk/abouttheservice/ statementofpurpose

8   An American professor of business administration has calculated that even taking into account only those costs that have been properly quantified by authoritative studies, corporations in the United States were permitted in 1994 to inflict $2.6 trillion-worth of social and environmental damage, which amounted to five times their total profits (Estes, 1996).

9   This function of imprisonment has frequently been evident in recent years during periods in which governments – whether formed by the Conservative Party in the early 1990s or the Labour Party more recently – have sought to pre-empt a loss of public support by announcing 'tough' new law and order measures such as new prison building programmes, increased sentences of imprisonment and restrictions on the early release of inmates.

10 See also Liebling and Arnold's (2004) innovative attempt to assess the moral performance of prisons.

11 This figure includes remand centres, institutions for young offenders and prisoners held in police cells.

12 The statistics contained in this paragraph were calculated from data provided by the National Offender Management Service (RDS NOMS, 2006).

13 But see Chapter 10, notes 46 and 48.

14 Apart from Peterborough, which is the first purpose-built prison to house both men and women.

15 See Chapter 9. At present young offenders under 21 are kept separate from adult prisoners, but the intention is that the dividing line should soon move down to 18.

16 Achieved by a policy of 'volumetric control' which effectively restricted the number of possessions an inmate could keep in prison to what could be contained within a box of a standard size.

17 Narey (2001). The speech is worth reading in full for its frank assessment of the need for a root-and-branch change in the nature of Prison Service culture.

18 This event led to the famous television interview in which Mr Howard repeatedly failed to answer Jeremy Paxman's question as to whether he had threatened to overrule Derek Lewis to force him to remove the Parkhurst governor.

19 Cf. Kamenka and Tay (1975); see also the section on the Weberian sociological tradition in Chapter 3.4. This distinction closely resembles Max Weber's (1968; see also Chapter 3) threefold typology of traditional, charismatic and 'legal' authority.

20 See Liebling and Arnold (2004: 58–63) for a detailed account of the changing content of KPIs in response to shifting concerns and priorities on the part of government during the period 1994–2003. See also HM Prison Service (2006a) for the current performance figures as measured against these targets.

21 An example of the cynicism this can engender is provided by Ramsbotham (2005: 84). After noting that prisons are judged against targets requiring them to achieve annual reductions in the number of inmates who test positive following monthly 'random' drug tests, he recalls a conversation with a prison inmate. The latter explained that the reason he had nine negative drug test certificates on his cell wall was because he was

known not to use drugs, which meant that he was 'randomly' selected for testing every month.

22　The principle is named after Professor Charles Goodhart (1984: 96), a former Chief Adviser to the Bank of England, who stated that '[a]ny observed statistical regularity will tend to collapse once pressure is placed upon it for control purposes'.

23　Criminal Justice and Public Order Act 1994, section 127, which forbade anyone to induce prison officers to withhold their services or commit a 'breach of discipline'.

24　In January 1999 (unlawful) industrial action over pay was reported in two-thirds of prisons, and this situation only ceased when the Home Office obtained an injunction in the courts (Prison Reform Trust, 1999a: 3).

25　By the Regulatory Reform (Prison Officers) (Industrial Action) Order 2005 (SI 2005/908).

26　Category A status is the only one that can apply to all types of prisoners, whether male, female, juvenile, sentenced or remand. Following a helicopter escape from Gartree in 1988, Category A prisoners are now assigned to one of three further subcategories: 'standard risk', 'high risk' or 'exceptional risk'. In addition, prisoners who either have escaped, or have attempted to, or who are believed to be planning to escape, may be placed on a supplementary 'Escape' or 'E List', which will also affect the kind of prison in which they may be held (Fitzgerald and Sim, 1982: 46; Adams, 1994: 151; Creighton and King, 2000: 55).

27　Unsentenced prisoners are automatically assigned to the B category, unless provisionally placed in Category A. Sentenced male prisoners are first held in an observation, classification and allocation unit of a local prison or remand centre before being assigned to a category and allocated to an appropriate institution.

28　All prisoners who are held in open prisons have to be in Category D, though they account for less than 10 per cent of the total prison population.

29　Currently there are five high-security prisons, all of which house long-term convicted adult male prisoners. They are Frankland, Full Sutton, Long Lartin, Wakefield and Whitemoor. Another three male local prisons (Belmarsh, Manchester and Woodhill) are designated as being sufficiently secure to hold Category A remand prisoners.

30　In July 2006 there were approximately, 1000 Category A prisoners (Bennett and Hartley, 2006), which is roughly 1.3 per cent of the total prison population. However, the high-security establishments in which they are housed also contain approximately 4,500 other prisoners, most of whom are Category B.

31　These include double security fences, barbed wire, geophonic alarms, high-mast flood-lighting, perimeter defence forces, dog patrols, VHF radio systems, emergency control rooms and radio links with local police stations.

32　HM Chief Inspector of Prisons (1997a) expressed concern that the Prison Service was divided into two distinct parts: 'the "haves" of the dispersal estate ... and the "have nots" (all the other establishments), who have neither the same resources, nor the same dedicated functional direction and management'.

33　A previous inquiry had already been established to investigate the Whitemoor Prison escape in September 1994 (Woodcock, 1994).

34　Whitemoor SSU holds convicted exceptional-risk Category A prisoners, and a High Security Unit at Belmarsh holds remand prisoners who have provisionally been categorized as either high- or exceptional-security risks, plus a small number of convicted exceptional-risk prisoners who are on temporary transfer.

35　Acheson (1996: para. 4.6). The report was not published, but its main conclusions are reported in Creighton and King (2000: 44).

36　See also Liebling and Arnold (2004: 16), who present data showing that the number of prison escapes declined from a peak of 315 in 1991 to just 5 in 2002–3.

37　See Liebling (1992, 1997); Liebling and Krarup (1993); and Crighton and Towl (1997).

38   The figure of 78 suicides out of a prison population of 76,079 in 2005 equates to a suicide rate of 102.5 per 100,000, which is the lowest for over a decade.

39   However, there are also dangers with such a policy if care is not taken to assess the compatibility of inmates before forcing them to share the claustrophobic conditions of a single cell. They are graphically illustrated by the tragic deaths of Christopher Edwards at the hands of a mentally disturbed cell mate (see note 94 below), and of Zahid Mubarek at the hands of a violent racist cell mate (see Chapter 9, below).

40   In 2004, in an important ruling that was prompted partly by the Human Rights Act of 1998, the House of Lords decided that inquest juries would in future be allowed to add a rider to prison suicide verdicts attributing blame to failings or shortcomings in the prison system. See *R (on the application of Middleton) v. HM Coroner for the Western District of Somerset* [2004] UKHL 10; also *R (on the application of Sacker) v. HM Coroner for the County of West Yorkshire* [2004] UKHL 11.

41   Table 1.1 in Chapter 1 details the increase in the total prison population between 1975 and the present day.

42   This safety margin was officially cut by ministers from 2,000 to 1,700 in March 2004 when prison numbers were rapidly approaching the 'bust limit'.

43   The European Committee for the Prevention of Torture (2005a: para. 20; see also Coyle, 2005: 108) took the Prison Service to task for the way it defined the system's usable operational capacity. Following its 2003 inspection, it commented, 'In the CPT's opinion, the cell capacities approved by the Prison Service are too high; in particular, placing two persons in cells measuring as little as 6.5 m², including the sanitary facilities, cannot be considered acceptable.'

44   A plan abandoned in November 2006 (*Guardian*, 11 November 2006).

45   The practice of holding prisoners in police cells had been discontinued in 1995, but revived between July and December 2002 and again briefly in October 1995.

46   For example, in 2003 the Chief Inspector of Prisons Anne Owers described Wealstun Prison as being infested with rats, mould and drug-taking before condemning it as being unfit for human habitation (HM Chief Inspector of Prisons, 2003) More recently, she described a wing of Leeds Prison as being unfit for human habitation and called for its closure (HM Chief Inspector of Prisons, 2005c, 11). In both instances the problems were attributed to prison overcrowding.

47   Brixton, Wandsworth and Leeds.

48   *Napier v. The Scottish Ministers* [2004] UKHRR 881. The ruling was expected to cost the Scottish Prison Service up to £500,000 in compensation payments for the 1,500 or so Scottish inmates who were thought to have been affected by it.

49   The latest version is available on-line at: www.uncjin.org/Laws/prisrul.htm

50   In September 2006, for example, a report on Pentonville Prison described it as a dirty, vermin-infested institution where 40 per cent of inmates have been assaulted or insulted by staff and where new prisoners were told they should not expect to be given a pillow or a toothbrush (HM Chief Inspector of Prisons, 2006: 5).

51   Though 75 per cent of the local prison population comprises sentenced prisoners, including those serving short, medium, long and even life sentences (HM Chief Inspector of Prisons, 1999b).

52   As with prison conditions, it is impossible to generalize about English prison regimes since many operate constructive programmes that are delivered by committed and well-trained staff, while others are unrelentingly impoverished. Again, it tends to be the local prisons that suffer the worst forms of deprivation in terms of constructive activities, work or educational opportunities or even simply time spent out of the cell.

53   In 2003–4, the Prison Service only managed to provide an average of 23.2 hours per week for purposeful activities, though this masked a wide differential ranging from 18.8

hours a week at dispersal prisons and 18.9 hours at male local prisons to 43.8 hours at female open prisons (HM Prison Service, 2004). However, a diary exercise involving prison inmates that was conducted by the House of Commons Home Affairs Committee (2005: paras. 33–7) suggested that the situation could actually be even bleaker than the official figures suggest.

54 This is not of course how the Prison Service presented its plan to abandon the KPI. It claimed it had decided to focus on other indicators to measure the amount of work that aims to reduce reoffending, such as the number of prisoners achieving basic skills qualifications, participating in drug treatment programmes, or leaving prison with an education, training or employment place arranged (Solomon, 2004b: 11). The House of Commons Home Affairs Committee (2005: para. 38) was not persuaded by this argument, and commented that 'it is difficult to avoid the suspicion that the KPI has been dropped to avoid embarrassment arising from the Prison Service's continuing failure to meet the target'.

55 For example, amongst prisons holding lower security-risk (Category C) prisoners, the amount spent per head in 1999–2000 varied between £205 and £1,595 (Committee of Public Accounts, 2002: para. 8).

56 This appears to have been the case in France, for example, where a single improvement – the introduction of colour televisions in cells – has been credited with transforming both the attitudes of prisoners (by increasing their willingness to work, in order to pay for the hire of the sets) and also the problem of disorder (by helping to counter boredom and reduce the level of antagonism between inmates) (HM Chief Inspector of Prisons, 1990b). In England and Wales limited access to in-cell television is now available to certain prisoners as part of the Incentives and Earned Privileges Scheme (see below).

57 One of the more surprising aspects of the current prison scene is the relative paucity of serious rioting despite the resurgence of many of the factors – overcrowding, transfers and poor prison conditions – that were held partly to blame for the 1990s Strangeways riot. This relative quiescence on the part of prison inmates (since lower-level collective disorder remains a regular feature of prison life) presents a conundrum. One possibility is that greater access to in-cell television may have had a similarly tranquilizing effect as in France (see note 56, above). Another possibility is that a greater commitment to the 'decency agenda' may have neutralized another major source of antagonism for prison inmates, which would be consistent with the 'moral performance' thesis advanced by Liebling and Arnold (2004).

58 Boards of Visitors were the predecessors of Independent Monitoring Boards (see below under 'crisis of accountability'), which now perform an exclusively monitoring and 'watchdog' role, though prior to 1992 they also formed an important part of the prison disciplinary system.

59 See Rule 51 of the 1999 Prison Rules (SI 1999/728) for the full catalogue of offences against prison discipline. But see above, note 6.

60 Even Category C prisons experience control problems. See S. Marshall (1997) for a study of the methods used to deal with these.

61 See also the allegations of violence at issue in the case of *Weldon v Home Office* [1992] 1 AC 58.

62 Additionally, Rule 43 authorizes the removal of a prisoner from association where this appears desirable 'in his own interests', and is usually used for the protection of vulnerable inmates such as child or sex offenders with their agreement.

63 Reasons have to be given for the segregation, but may do little to allay a prisoner's sense of grievance since they may simply state that the inmate's behaviour posed a threat to the smooth running of the establishment.

64 For example in *R. v. Deputy Governor of Parkhurst Prison, ex p Hague; Weldon v. Home Office* [1992] 1 AC 58.

65 The control unit was modelled on austere segregation units known as punishment 'cages' at Peterhead and Inverness in Scotland, which are vividly described in Boyle (1977). A second control unit was planned but never used (Liebling, 2001: 128).

66 The unit was challenged in court by inmates, but the judge was not persuaded that the conditions amounted to 'cruel and unusual punishment'; *Williams v. Home Office (No. 2)* [1981] 1 All ER 1211. It would be surprising if the court's questionable insistence that conditions would need to be both cruel *and* unusual would have prevailed had the Human Rights Act been in force.

67 Liebling (2001: 133). The units were based at Parkhurst (opened in 1985), Lincoln (opened in 1987), Hull (opened in 1988) with Woodhill replacing Lincoln in 1993. Between them they housed around 22 prisoners in 1996, but a roughly equal number of inmates were deemed too disruptive even for these units and remained on indefinite 'Continuous Assessment Scheme' or 'merry-go-round' status (see above).

68 This culminated in the Spurr Report (HM Prison Service, 1996) which was not published, though its contents and assumptions are discussed perceptively and in detail in Liebling (2001).

69 In the post-Learmont era the list of privileges to which an inmate on the restricted regime was entitled was very limited indeed, as the following account illustrates: 'Prisoners were unlocked with an SO and five officers. They were entitled to one hour's exercise, which was taken in pairs, in separate yards. They were searched before and after, with their hands above their heads. They had few visits, which took place in closed conditions (except legal visits). They were fed through hatches. They had no access to education; and limited access to the library. They could send and receive letters (Liebling, 2001: 139).

70 See also critical commentaries by Stephen Shaw (1998, 1999a) before he became the Prisons Ombudsman.

71 The four main privileges are: access to private cash above the normal set amounts; extra or improved visits; eligibility to participate in enhanced earning schemes; and, for certain groups of prisoners, earned community visits.

72 Unsurprisingly, perhaps, the introduction of the new scheme in 1995 sparked off a protest by prisoners at Full Sutton Prison, which was only quelled with the aid of a prison officer 'riot squad' together with police and other emergency services (*Guardian*, 16 November 1995).

73 See also R. Sparks (2001: 166) on the history of penal politics and the 'repetition compulsion'.

74 Estimates vary as to the number of seriously and intractably disruptive inmates. HM Chief Inspector of Prisons (1999d: 2) spoke of 1,400 inmates who are allegedly dangerous and suffering from severe personality disorders. However, Liebling (2001) has suggested that the really difficult prisoners numbered no more than 40 (1.1 per cent) of the 3,500 who were then housed in the high-security estate, which represented 0.08 of the total prison population at the time.

75 They include Oak Park Heights in Minnesota, which was visited by the Woolf inquiry team.

76 In the survey of staff and prisoners' attitudes in Scottish prisons carried out by Wozniak and McAllister (1991), a majority of officers (60 per cent) expressed fears about their personal safety, and 48 per cent claimed to have been assaulted by a prisoner.

77 No less than 84 per cent of staff who were questioned in a 1983 attitude survey expressed such a view (see Home Office, 1985a: 57).

78 Currently the Prison Rules 1999 (SI 1999/728) as amended by the Prison (Amendment) Rules 2002 (SI 2002/2116) and the Prison (Amendment) Rules 2005 (SI 2005/869). See above note 6 for reference to the consolidated version published in January 2006.

79 In 1877; see Chapter 7, note 9.

80 For a more critical assessment of the role of the prisons inspectorate, see Morgan (1985) and Laming (2000: 22).

81 Not everyone – quite – is opposed to the idea of a 'super-inspectorate'. Rod Morgan, former Chairman of the Youth Justice Board and a long-time critic of the existing system of individual inspectorates (see note 80, above) once likened them to 'lumbering carthorses' that were apt to be out-manoeuvered by the 'racehorse' of the Audit Commission (Morgan, 2003: 87). In the eyes of its many critics, however, the creation of a super-inspectorate would be as likely to produce an even more ponderous and maladapted woolly mammoth as a racehorse. For the main problem is not the ineffectiveness of the prison inspectorate's communication systems, as Morgan alleges, so much as the imperviousness of its intended audience. Addressing this problem will require much more than the adoption of a more professional style of communication.

82 The Prison Reform Trust (1999a) complained that over half of all Boards of Visitors failed to publish their annual reports despite repeated encouragement from the Home Office to do so. See also Prison Reform Trust (1998a).

83 One of the primary responsibilities of Boards of Visitors/Independent Monitoring Boards (Prison Rule 77(4)), is to draw attention to any abuse of prisoners, but the way many Boards have discharged this responsibility has been severely criticized by the Chief Inspector or Prisons, Prisons Ombudsman and others.

84 4,466 complaints were received in 2005–6 (Prisons and Probation Ombudsman, 2006: 62), 93 per cent of which related to the Prison Service. The figures in this paragraph are derived from calculations based on the 2005–6 annual report.

85 For this reason, the Prisons and Probation Ombudsman is, somewhat embarrassingly, denied membership of the British and Irish Ombudsman Association.

86 Only 11 per cent of complaints relating to the probation service were ruled eligible in 2005–6 (Prisons and Probation Ombudsman, 2006: 63).

87 The Ombudsman has referred to at least one prison in which it is necessary to 'apply for a form for a form for a form'. He also lamented the under-representation of complaints from younger prisoners and women prisoners, pointing out that by 2000, not a single complaint had been received from at least two young offender institutions since the Prisons Ombudsman was established in 1994 (Prisons Ombudsman, 2000).

88 Just under 90 staff were employed in 2006 (Prison Ombudsman's website), compared with just 18 in 2002.

89 There is no intrinsic reason why this should be the case. Other jurisdictions, notably the United States, have developed procedures such as the 'class action', which enables similar cases to be dealt with as a single action with implications for all the members of the class in question. Courts in the United States have also been prepared to adopt a more activist approach in relation to complaints about prison life, in which they are prepared to consider complaints about, for example, prison conditions and their effects in the aggregate, and not just the impact of a grievance on an individual (Vagg, 1991: 153).

90 The House of Lords famously affirmed in the case of *Raymond v. Honey* [1983] 1 AC 1 that convicted prisoners retain all civil rights that are not expressly or by necessary implication removed from them by virtue of their imprisonment.

91 Compare the cases referred to at notes 40 and 48, for example, with those cited at notes 61 and 64, above.

92 See *Golder v. UK* (1975) 1EHRR 524, Series A No 18 and *Silver v. UK* [1983] 5 EHRR 347, Series A No. 61.

93 See *Campbell and Fell v. UK* (1985) 15 EHRR 137, Series A No. 80.

94 *Paul and Audrey Edwards v. UK* [2002] ECtHR, App No. 46477/99, Judgment of 14 March 2002, para. 69. See also Edwards (2002), which contains a detailed account by

the murdered prisoner's mother of the difficulties they encountered in holding the authorities accountable for their son's death.

95 *R. v Secretary of State for the Home Department ex parte Pearson and Martinez; Hirst* [2001] EWHC Admin 239.

96 Liebling (2001: 160) reaches very similar conclusions with regard to the most difficult and intractable group of prisoners who are housed in the close supervision centres we discussed above. We believe that the same also holds true of the great majority of prison inmates throughout the entire system, and Liebling's more recent research lends further weight to this argument (Liebling and Arnold, 2004).

97 This type of approach has much in common with the restorative justice approach that we have described elsewhere (see in particular Dignan, 2005a). Attempts to implement such an approach within the prison system are now underway, both in this country (see Stern, 2005) and abroad (Aertsen and Peters, 1998).

98 The approach also has an affinity with the kind of *'social crime prevention'* techniques (see Tremblay and Craig, 1995; Hope, 1995; Tonry and Farrington, 1995) that have been developed for use in schools; for example via personal and social education programmes.

99 The Unit experienced a number of political difficulties; however, most of these were fuelled by resentment towards it that emanated from other parts of the Scottish prison system.

100 See also the evaluation of a similar unit at Shotts Prison in Scotland, which was also based on the adoption of a similar therapeutic model (Bottomley et al., 1994).

101 The similar unit at Shotts Prison also merged with the rest of Shotts Prison in April 2000, as part of a 'rationalization' of the Scottish prison estate (Scottish Prison Service, 2000). Another relatively enlightened outpost within the English prison system, Parkhurst C wing, was also closed after it fell victim to the security clampdown following the 1995 prison breakouts.

102 Or, more precisely, five separate therapeutic communities within the one prison.

103 These findings, using a 'control group' methodology, broadly replicated those of an earlier four-year reconviction study at the same prison (S. Marshall, 1997). See also Genders and Player (1995).

104 *Independent*, 26 July 2000.

105 Ramsbotham (2005: 159) describes another episode involving the same Area Manager and the inappropriate restrictions he imposed on Ford open prison in the same year as the Blantyre House raid.

7 Prison Privatization: Panacea or Pandora's Box?

'I believe that people who are sentenced by the state to imprisonment should be deprived of their liberty, kept under lock and key by those who are accountable primarily and solely to the state.' (Blair, 1993)

During the late 1980s and early 1990s the seemingly relentless rise in prison numbers had the initial effect of tempering the Conservative government's instinctive law and order preferences with a much less dogmatic approach (see Chapter 11). The more pragmatic policies of this era included new measures intended to restrict the use of custody for less serious offenders and promote alternatives to imprisonment (see Chapter 5), and alterations to early release procedures (see Chapter 8, section 8.4). Around the same time, a new option began to take shape which not only appeared to offer a practical solution to many of the problems confronting the penal system, but also chimed in perfectly with the government's ideological predilections. The penal system's problems included a severe shortage of prison places, poor conditions in prisons, a perceived need for more flexible and accommodating working practices on the part of prison and probation staff, and the need for greater accountability from those responsible for running prison services. It was claimed that all these problems could be successfully tackled at substantially reduced costs simply by encouraging greater private sector involvement in the penal system, and this came increasingly to be seen[1] as a 'quick-fix' solution to many of the penal system's most pressing problems.

Since then the debate over prison privatization has been waged by commentators with contrasting ideological perspectives,[2] while others have sought to assess its potential from a more pragmatic standpoint[3] by seeking to compare the performance of public and private prisons with reference to empirical data. There are also those who argue that, whatever the merits or demerits of prison privatization from either perspective might be, as a matter of simple realpolitik, prison privatization is now a simple fact of penological life, a *'fait accompli'*, and that it is therefore no longer a live issue. In this chapter we shall of necessity be making reference to the general debate about the rights and wrongs of privatization, but our primary concern remains the penal crisis and whether prison privatization is likely to ameliorate or exacerbate it. In the sections that follow, we will begin by discussing the meaning of penal privatization and the various forms it can take. We shall then briefly sketch its recent resurgence in England and Wales and the factors that have contributed to it and consider the theoretical debate about privatization, before finally assessing its effect on the interconnecting penal crises we described in Chapters 1 and 6.

Meaning and Forms of Penal Privatization

7.1 Privatization involves a contractual process that 'shifts public functions, responsibilities and capital assets, in whole or in part, from the public to the private sector' (Austin and Coventry, 2001).[4] The first candidates for privatization under the Conservative administrations of 1979 to 1997 comprised previously nationalized industries that were involved in the manufacture of goods,[5] followed by some of the major public utilities (telecommunications, gas, electricity and water). It was not long before some on the right began calling for an extension of the policy into the social sphere, including the delivery of punishment (Adam Smith Institute, 1984; Young, 1987) and other aspects of the criminal justice system, including certain police functions and even some court services.

Private sector involvement in the penal system may take a variety of forms. In the case of prisons, it could in theory extend to selling off the entire prison system as a going concern, which was the approach adopted for many of the other formerly state-owned monopolies (Shaw, 1989: 56). In practice, however, the government has so far opted for a more limited form of private sector involvement, comprising the 'contracting-out'[6] of specific functions to private operators in relation to individual institutions. There are at least five distinct sets of functions relating to the activities of the prison service that could in principle be contracted out in this way.

First there are the various *ancillary services,* which do not form part of the 'core function' of detaining inmates in prison: activities such as catering, education, health care, prison workshops and farms, and also prison escort services. A great many prison ancillary services have now been contracted out both in the United Kingdom and elsewhere. A second function consists of the *design and construction* work for new prisons, which could also be contracted out rather than relying on in-house services as in the past, while the state continues to employ the custodial staff.[7] A third and rather more radical arrangement entails the contracting out of core management responsibilities – including *basic custodial functions* relating to security and control over inmates – to private sector companies while ownership of the prison buildings remains with the state. Fourth, the most far-reaching and controversial form of contracting out to date – and the currently favoured model of prison privatization – involves the private sector being given responsibility for the *design, construction, management and financing of* individual prisons (which are known as DCMF prisons). These are then run by the private company in return for a payment from the state per inmate per day for a predetermined period (usually 25 years). Finally, there is also a fifth possibility (so far only theoretical) that would entail the contracting-out not only of these various operational functions but also the more strategic responsibilities relating to the commissioning, monitoring and enforcement of prison service contracts.

Still with regard to prison privatization, a useful distinction is sometimes drawn regarding the depth of penetration by the private sector into the 'prisons market'. This refers to the *kind of institutions* that may be considered suitable for privatization. These vary considerably from so-called 'shallow-end' institutions – open prisons and those housing relatively low-security-risk inmates such as juveniles and remand prisoners – to those which operate at the 'deep-end', catering in the main for high-risk or even maximum-security adult prisoners. As we shall see in the next section, the initial tendency has been for privatization to involve mainly shallow-end institutions, though in England and Wales both the pace and depth of its immersion have increased rapidly after a somewhat hesitant start. Moreover, private sector involvement in the delivery of penal interventions is not necessarily confined to prison settings. For, as we saw in Chapter 5, a similar approach has now been adopted with regard to the delivery of non-custodial interventions, under the euphemistic label of 'contestability'. Although this chapter is mainly about private sector involvement in the construction and operation of prison facilities, many of the same arguments are equally applicable to these wider forms of privatization.

The History of Prison Privatization in England

7.2 Privately run prisons are not just a recent phenomenon. From the Middle Ages to the nineteenth century, the running of English prisons was frequently entrusted to private jail keepers, who received no official payment but were expected to charge fees from their captive 'customers' for the services they provided (Pugh, 1968). These included the provision of food, bedding and fuel, but fees were also charged for admission and discharge (Porter, 1990: 67), and were adjusted according to rank and ability to pay (McConville, 1981: 9). Jeremy Bentham's Panopticon prison proposal (see Chapter 2, section 2.5) was also envisaged as a privately run, profit-making concern, and one of the reasons for its failure to secure Parliamentary approval was a concern that it would rely too heavily on the exploitation of prison labour (Ryan and Ward, 1989a: 62a). The capacity for exploitation and extortion on the part of private jail keepers eventually became a target for penal reformers and contributed to the abolition of the fee system in 1815 (McConville, 1981: 247–8).

By this stage, however, private sector involvement in the penal system was beginning to assume a rather different form as a result of the rapid growth of penal transportation after 1788 (Shaw, 1966; Hughes, 1987; James et al., 1997: 10–11). Convict ships were operated by private contractors, but were regulated by highly detailed specifications set out in contracts drawn up by the British government. Responsibility for monitoring performance and enforcing the terms of the contract was entrusted to government-employed 'surgeon-superintendents' and naval agents, who accompanied each consignment of convicts.

The early history of prison privatization clearly foreshadows a number of more recent types of joint venture between governments and private enterprise in the operation of the penal system. Moreover, some (for example, Shichor, 1995: 43) have argued that the historical experience illuminates a number of potential defects relating to the policy of prison privatization that it would be unwise to ignore. They include, first, the potential for exploitation and mistreatment of inmates by contractors; second a lack of effective external oversight and accountability framework; and third the possibility of corruption between government officials, official inspectors, prison staff members and private contractors. As we shall see, the brief recent history of contracting out in England and Wales confirms the wisdom of taking all of these warnings very seriously in assessing whether privatization is capable of addressing any of the prison system's current problems. It also provides an instructive, if not particularly edifying, insight into the way that a major shift in penal policy, which has radical implications for the entire prison system, has been formulated and implemented.

The recent antecedents of prison privatization in England and Wales can be traced back to 1970 when the government entered into a contract with the private security firm, Securicor Ltd, to operate airport detention centres for suspected illegal immigrants.[8] This novel arrangement excited little interest at the time, even though by 1988 nearly half of all detained immigrants were held in such facilities (Joint Council for the Welfare of Immigrants, 1988: 13, quoting Green, 1989). The next tentative step towards prison privatization was a response to growing alarm over the use of police cells as temporary accommodation for remand prisoners, for whom no room could be found in the chronically overcrowded prisons of the late 1980s. One temporary expedient which the Home Office resorted to in May 1988 involved the use of the Alma Dettingen military barracks near Camberley. Although the prisoners were guarded by military police and troops, the catering service was contracted out to a small private company in what Shaw (1992b) described as 'virtually the first breach in the state monopoly of imprisonment since "nationalization" of the county gaols and recidivist prisons in the late 1870s'.[9]

The contracting out of prisons themselves was first advocated in England and Wales in a pamphlet published by the Adam Smith Institute (a right-wing think-tank) in 1984 but was not taken seriously in either government circles or the Home Office at the time. Indeed, in 1987 Home Secretary Douglas Hurd informed the House of Commons that: 'I do not think there is a case, and I do not believe that the House would accept a case, for auctioning or privatising the prisons or handing over the business of keeping prisoners safe to anyone other than government servants' (HC Deb. 16 July 1987, vol. 119, col. 1299).[10] By this stage, however, the cause of prison privatization had been taken up by a small number of Conservative backbench MPs and peers who began to promote it with almost evangelical zeal, backed by tireless and ultimately highly effective lobbying by the would-be providers of private prisons themselves. The activities of these 'policy entrepreneurs' (Jones and Newburn, 2005: 61) resulted in a policy U-turn, the scale and speed of which was only exceeded by the government's law and order 'counter-reformation' of 1993 (see Chapters 4 and 11).

Following a brief visit to a number of private prisons in the United States, the House of Commons Home Affairs Select Committee (1987) published a report calling for private sector involvement in the construction and management of custodial institutions in order to alleviate overcrowding in the remand sector in particular. Shortly afterwards its Chairman, Sir Edward Gardner, was recruited to serve as Chairman of Contract Prisons, a company founded 'to exploit the new opportunities' (Windlesham, 1993: 288), following his retirement from Parliament at the 1987 General Election. His appointment set in motion a 'revolving door' through which other senior Conservative politicians[11] were to pass, together with growing numbers of former senior prison service staff, senior civil servants and even members of the Prison Inspectorate (see below) as the momentum towards privatization gathered strength. Thus, a powerful combination of personal self-interest and corporate self-aggrandizement was another important factor in the early resurgence of prison privatization, reinforced by a close overlap between the political and commercial interests associated with senior members of the Conservative Party (Windlesham, 1993: 288–9).

In addition to the pragmatic rationale put forward by the Home Affairs Committee, the case for prison privatization was also argued on a much more ideologically partisan basis by Peter Young (1987) of the Adam Smith Institute. He championed the cause of prison privatization partly as a means of breaking the 'monopolistic provision' of imprisonment by the state but also, more specifically, to counter trade union influence on prison policy. As we shall see, such ideological considerations have proved crucial on more than one occasion in the campaign to promote the policy. The first real signs of a change in the government's attitude towards privatization came with the publication of a Green Paper in the autumn of 1988 (Home Office, 1988b). This specifically proposed the contracting out of court and escort duties that had hitherto been carried out by police and prison officers, and also recommended an experiment to assess the scope for greater involvement by the private sector in the management of remand prisons. The latter had experienced a disproportionate increase in inmate numbers over the previous decade,[12] and were felt to raise fewer operational difficulties or issues of principle than those holding sentenced prisoners. Management consultants were appointed to make detailed recommendations, and a legislative opportunity presented itself in the shape of the Criminal Justice Bill, which was being drafted to implement the government's 1991 reform programme.

By this stage, however, the largely pragmatic considerations favouring the introduction of contracting out with regard to remand prisons had become much less compelling following a fall in the overall remand population. Home Secretary David Waddington's initial inclination was thus to delete the provision of a power to contract out certain remand prisons since it would be unlikely to produce substantial savings (Windlesham, 1993: 297). However, when confirmation was sought from Prime Minister Margaret Thatcher, she personally insisted that the move towards privatization should go ahead.[13] Even so, the original wording of the Bill restricted the power to contract out: first, to remand centres; and second, only to those established after the implementation of the Act, thereby excluding existing remand centres and prisons housing sentenced prisoners. In the end, however, these restrictions were overturned by a 'sub-plot ... to which at least one Home Office junior minister was sympathetic, and which only came to light as the Bill progressed' (Windlesham, 1993: 420).

This involved a backbench Conservative MP tabling an amendment extending the power to contract out any type of prison, whether holding remand or sentenced prisoners, and whether new or existing. Connivance on the part of junior Home Office Minister Angela Rumbold ensured that the substance of the amendment was retained in section 84 of the 1991 Criminal Justice Act,[14] even though this went far beyond official government policy at the time. Despite her assurance that privatization of other parts of the prison service would only be allowed to proceed if the contracting-out of the first remand centre proved a success (HC Deb. vol. 186, col. 720, 7 Feb. 1991), further extensions of the policy soon followed. For in December 1991, even before the first remand centre to be contracted out – Wolds Prison – had received its first inmates (in April 1992), Home Secretary Kenneth Baker unexpectedly announced the contracting-out of Blakenhurst, which was to be another new prison catering for both remand and sentenced prisoners.[15] As Lord Windlesham pointed out (1993: 426): 'To claim that the tendering exercise had been a success in showing how much the private sector had to offer fell well short of fulfilling the undertaking to evaluate the actual experience of private sector management in practice.'[16]

Not long after this, the contracting-out policy was extended still further to embrace existing prisons when it was announced that the management of Strangeways Prison, rebuilt after the 1990 riot, would also be put up for tender, though in the event the in-house Prison Service bid was successful. The third private prison was Buckley Hall, near Rochdale. This had previously been a public sector prison which had been mothballed; it was then recommissioned and put out to tender, though it reverted to prison service management in 2000 when the tender came up for renewal. The next three private prisons (at Fazakerley, Bridgend and Salford) were the first DCMF prisons – designed, constructed, managed and financed by the private sector (see section 7.1 above) – which is the model that has subsequently been adopted for all new private prisons.

In September 1993, Home Secretary Michael Howard let it be known that the government was planning for around 10 per cent of English prisons (12) to be privately run during the initial phase of the privatization process. The aim was to create a sufficiently large private sector to provide sustained competition (HM Prison Service, 1993). The government also planned to contract out seven existing prisons, and a 'market-testing' programme to identify suitable candidates was launched, involving over 20 prisons. However, the entire programme was subsequently put in abeyance following a successful complaint in October 1994 by the Prison Officers' Association (POA) to the Central Arbitration Committee on the ground that it had not been properly consulted about the market-testing exercise.

Another major setback to government plans to contract out existing prisons was the realization that European Union laws designed to protect the jobs and conditions of workers affected by take-overs and mergers also applied to transfers from public to private sector employment. Under the European Commission's Acquired Rights Directive,[17] contractors are obliged to maintain existing jobs and conditions in respect of any contracts they win. Once the government was obliged to concede that the contracting-out of existing prisons was also covered by the directive,[18] this seriously undermined the economic rationale for the policy, which largely depends on contractors being able to reduce the size of both the workforce and the wage bill.[19]

In other respects, however, prison privatization proceeded at an even faster pace under the Conservative government. Thus, by May 1997 the process of contracting-out had been extended to include all prison – court escort services and a wide range of other ancillary services, such as education and some catering services. Of even greater long-term significance was the launch of the Private Finance Initiative in November 1992 (see further, section 7.4 below), a policy forbidding any new public expenditure from being agreed by the Treasury unless the use of private finance had first been considered and rejected. In May 1995, the Prison Service commissioned a report by a firm of management consultants, which concluded that there was considerable scope for the use of private finance projects to be extended. Among the examples cited were major refurbishment projects involving whole prisons, projects to replace or refurbish ancillary service functions (such as catering, prison industry workshops, health care, non-core administration and so on), and large-scale electronic projects such as the installation of CCTV, IT or communication systems.

For a brief period immediately after the 1997 General Election, the longer-term future of prison privatization in England and Wales appeared to be in doubt, since the victorious Labour Party had pledged repeatedly and unequivocally while in opposition, to take private prisons back into public ownership.[20] Shadow Home Secretary Jack Straw had even described prison privatization as 'morally repugnant'. However, this principled opposition began to melt away within days of the election victory. One week later Jack Straw, now the new Labour Home Secretary, announced that he would be prepared to sign contracts that were already in the pipeline if this proved to be the only way of providing new accommodation quickly. Just over one year later he confirmed[21] that a complete *volte face* had taken place when he announced that, in the wake of two internal (and secret) Prison Service reviews, all new prisons in England and Wales would be privately built and run.

The reviews were said to have concluded, first, that the option of using private finance to build new prisons while retaining the management function within the public sector was not affordable and did not offer value for money. If true, this is surprising, since just such an arrangement was subsequently proposed by another internal report. This one was commissioned by the Prison Service and undertaken by Patrick Carter (2002; see also Cavadino and Dignan, 2006: 316), the influential government adviser who later also authored a major review of correctional services (Carter, 2003; see above, Chapters 4 and 5). The second conclusion reached by the 1998 review was said to be that the immediate transfer of private prisons back to the public sector could not be justified, on similar grounds of cost-effectiveness. However, the failure to publish these reports casts serious doubt on the government's confidence in the cogency of their reasoning, and the conclusions themselves are hardly convincing, for the same reason.

By way of consolation for the public sector, the Prison Service was allowed to tender for private management contracts when these expired,[22] and over the next four years it secured three such contracts in the face of competition from the private sector.[23] These individual setbacks for the private sector did not, however, signal any weakening in the Labour government's new-found enthusiasm for the general policy of prison privatization. In July 1999 prisons minister Paul Boateng announced that Brixton Prison was to be market tested with a view to privatizing it after it was publicly labelled as a 'failing' prison – though somewhat embarrassingly for the government, not a single private sector bid was received. Undeterred by this setback, the government and prison service pressed ahead with the market-testing programme and announced plans to invite bids to operate three 'non-failing' public prisons on the Isle of Sheppey to be run as a cluster. However, in September 2005, NOMS suspended the plans as part of a review of its market-testing policy (Public Services International Research Unit, 2005a: 5).

By November 2006, a total of 11 prisons[24] were being contractually managed by private sector companies, all but two of them on a 'DCMF' basis.[25] The 2003 Carter review of correctional services had recommended the introduction of 'fixed term management contracts for *all* prisons, which would be open to competition at the end of the contract' (Carter, 2003: 37; our italics). Moreover, the government was now publicly committed to the creation of a 'vibrant mixed economy'[26] covering both the prison and probation service. While there is still some doubt over what precisely this might mean in practice, the policy of encouraging private sector involvement in the design, construction, financing and management of prisons in England and Wales now appears unassailable, at least for the foreseeable future.[27] This is especially so since the government, which from January 2004 to September 2005 was briefly committed to trying to hold the prison population below 80,000, had by the end of November 2006 allowed it to exceed this figure. Its promise to create at least another 8,000 prison places (Home Office, 2006c), envisaged that half would be provided by new private prisons (*Guardian*, 13 September 2006). Both government policy and legally binding contracts are currently locking the country ever more tightly into prison privatization.

Claims and Critique: The Theoretical Debate

7.3 The main philosophical justification for prison privatization derives from the *laissez-faire*, free-market economic theories originally championed by right-wing governments in the 1980s and 1990s and since adopted with equal enthusiasm by governments and parties that claim to represent the centre-left (notably New Labour). Various economic nostrums were invoked by 'true believers' in order to champion the case for privatizing areas of public provision. (See particularly, in relation to prison privatization, Young, 1987; Hutto, 1990; Logan, 1990). They included a reliance on free competition through the marketplace as the best spur to efficiency and quality of service, and also as the most effective scourge of restrictive practices and vested (trade union) interest. The case for privatization was also fuelled by a rhetorical belief in 'rolling back the frontiers of the state', at least to the extent of reducing its 'social role and responsibilities' (Kamerman and Kahn, 1989: 256).[28] In order to achieve this, it was necessary to engineer a split between the producers and purchasers of public services in order to establish an 'internal' or 'quasi-market'. To put it crudely, the seductive appeal of prison privatization is that it claims to offer more (prison capacity) and better (quality of service) for less. But perhaps the strongest selling point of privatization is the lamentable and all-too-obvious failings associated with the publicly run prison service which we documented in Chapter 6 – surely private prisons would have to be an improvement? Moreover, competition between private and public prisons could serve to drive up standards and efficiency across the board. Before examining the specific claims advanced on behalf of prison privatization, we wish to comment on these more basic arguments underpinning the programme.

First, whatever sentimental attachment some might feel towards a mythical bygone era in which a free and unregulated market supposedly delivered the best of all possible outcomes in response to the laws of supply and demand, today there is no such thing as free competition within an unregulated market. Moreover, such a model is singularly inappropriate with regard to the public sector in general and the sphere of penal policy in particular. For the size of the 'custodial market' itself, the nature of the services to be supplied, and also the terms on which this is to happen, including even (to some extent) the identities of the 'players', are all determined by the state. Indeed, the state is quite at liberty to forbid public sector institutions from submitting a bid should it choose to do so, which is precisely what happened with both the Wolds and Blakenhurst prison tenders. Not only that, the government also has it in its power to alter the balance of advantage between the public and private sectors. It can, if it chooses, simply starve publicly run prisons of the resources required to implement much-needed reforms, while investing lavishly in privately operated prisons in order to show the private sector off in the best light.[29] So much for the notion of free competition in an unregulated marketplace. One of those best qualified to pass judgement on the debate – Lord Browne, who chairs the British Petroleum management board – has publicly derided attempts by government to create what he pointedly refers to as 'pseudo-markets' in the public sector (*Financial Times*, 28 January 2005). He sees them as damaging to the professional ethos within public sector institutions such as the prisons, universities and hospitals and potentially counter-productive by alienating people against business in general.

Governments are not the only ones who are capable of 'rigging the market', however. For, as Sutherland (1956: 90) pointed out, 'big business does not like competition, and makes careful arrangements to reduce it and eliminate it'. This is most easily done where there are relatively few powerful corporations, the 'entry price' into the market is high, and opportunities for reallocating the contract are limited, all of which applies to the privatized prisons market. Despite an increase in the number of companies aspiring to join the 'corrections-commercial complex'[30] (Lilly and Knepper, 1990, 1992), the market itself is dominated by a small handful of multinational corporations or conglomerates for whom various mechanisms are open to limit competition. One is price-fixing; another is the taking over of rivals.[31] One danger is that once a government comes to depend on a small number of private companies, it may be 'held to ransom' and have little choice but to pay the higher prices charged to increase profitability. The risk would appear to be even greater where private operators are licensed not only to operate a particular institution but also to build, own and run it, as is now the case with all tenders in England and Wales. As we shall see in section 7.4, there are ample opportunities for correctional corporations to engage in market-rigging practices, and abundant evidence that they avail themselves of these opportunities to the full.

Although under the classical free market model, the laws of supply and demand are supposed to ensure responsiveness by the producer to the needs of the purchaser, it is extremely difficult to see how this is supposed to apply in the context of prison privatization (Shichor, 1995: 71–3). For instead of the traditional two-party relationship linking vendor and purchaser (or provider and client), with prison privatization there are three parties in the relationship. In addition to the private contractors, who build and operate the prisons, and the prison inmates who are the 'recipients' of the services they provide, there is also the state, which stipulates the type of facilities to be provided and pays the money. At the very least such an arrangement is likely to distort the normal operation of supply and demand mechanisms. Thus, the inmates who receive the contractor's services are self-evidently not free to shop around or 'take it or leave it' (Palumbo, 1986). Consequently, unlike typical recipients of services in a market, they have almost no power or leverage to affect the situation let alone dictate what contracts are made, particularly given their general political, economic and social impotence (Geis, 1987). Conversely, the service providers are much less dependent on the 'consumers' of their services for their economic success than they are on their primary customer or paying client, the government. Consequently, inmates may have even less control over their fate in a privatized prison system than in one being provided directly by the state itself. In short, it is not the inmates (or direct 'consumers' of prison services) whom the prison firms must satisfy, but the government as 'keeper of the purse'.

As for the argument that private prisons must be better because public ones are so bad, the deplorable state of the publicly run prison system clearly has to be acknowledged. At the same time, it is worth remembering that the main reason the state assumed responsibility for prisons in the first place (in the nineteenth century) was because of excesses and shortcomings associated with an earlier era of private provision. At the very least, this should warn us against accepting at face value simple dogmatic assertions that the private sector is inherently superior to the public sector in this sphere. Whether the private sector is in practice capable of delivering a superior performance for less money is in part an empirical question that we will address in passing in the next section. However, it is worth observing at the outset that the 'evidence base' on this issue remains grossly inadequate. One of the main reasons for this is because governments and private contractors seem strangely reluctant to commission the kind of rigorous analysis that is insisted on for other penal policy initiatives[32] or even to publish the available data that would help to provide more definitive answers to the question. In our view, though, the crucial question raised by prison privatization is not whether it is capable of 'delivering more for less', as it claims, but whether it is likely to alleviate or aggravate the various pressing crises that continue to confront the English prison system. It is to this primary set of questions that we mainly direct our attention in the next section.

Panacea or Pandora's Box? Prison Privatization and the Penal Crisis

The Crisis of Penological Resources

7.4

Prison privatization claims to be able to alleviate the crisis of penological resources in three main ways:

- by achieving efficiency gains that can significantly reduce operating costs;
- by enabling new prison buildings and facilities to be procured more efficiently and economically; and
- by providing governments with a fiscally advantageous method of investing in this new infrastructural capacity.

First, with regard to operating costs, imprisoning people is highly labour-intensive and staff costs account for 80 per cent of total running costs (National Audit Office, 2003). Savings might in principle be sought by taking on fewer staff, paying staff less, reducing the fringe benefits to which they are entitled, and withholding union recognition as a means of securing a more compliant workforce that is easier to pay and deploy efficiently. There is evidence that private prison operators have pursued most of these strategies as a means of reducing their operating costs, though other problems have often been encountered in doing so.

Thus, staffing levels are reported to be far lower at contracted-out prisons, which have 17 per cent fewer staff per prisoner than those in prisons operated by the public sector (Andrews, 2000). One way of reducing staff numbers is by investing instead in advanced technology electronic surveillance and security and control systems. However, several privately operated prisons that have done this have encountered serious operational difficulties. Both Doncaster and Blakenhurst, for example, experienced serious disturbances and were subsequently authorized to appoint large numbers of additional staff (Nathan, 1995b: 15), which may be seen as a tacit admission that the original staffing levels had been set much too low.[33] Most dramatically, a revolutionary new 'keyless' prison (Parc, near Bridgend in Wales) opened in 1997 with a system relying on computers and smartcards instead of keys. Within months the prison suffered serious disorder and two suicides, while the computer system proved so slow that keys had to be reintroduced (*Guardian*, 30 May 1998). So the scope for savings from such sources may be rather smaller than envisaged.

Pay and staff conditions for basic-grade prison officers[34] at privately run prisons also compare very unfavourably with those in the public sector. For example, the average starting salary in the public sector is 11 per cent higher than in the private sector, while the average basic pay rate is fully 41 per cent higher. The contracted working hours are longer in the private sector than in the public sector (41 and 39 hours respectively), pension provision is markedly inferior, and both overtime and annual leave arrangements are much less favourable.[35] Overall, private sector workers are estimated to spend 7 per cent more time at work than their public sector counterparts, which is one of the main reasons why contracted-out prisons can operate with fewer staff (Andrews, 2000). However, these differentials only apply to newly commissioned private prisons. For, as we explained earlier (see section 7.2), if an *existing* public sector prison were to be 'contracted out', for example under the 'market-testing' procedure, its employees' pay and conditions would be protected under the European Union's Acquired Rights Directive. This could be one reason why the private sector has shown much less interest in such tenders. As for union recognition, the main prison officers' union (the POA) has not been recognized for collective bargaining purposes in any of the privately managed prisons, despite a number of applications to the Central Arbitration Committee (Bach, 2002).[36]

Not surprisingly, the markedly inferior conditions of employment in private prisons are also reflected in very high levels of staff turnover compared with their public sector counterparts, which can give rise to serious problems. Staff turnover among private sector prison custody officers is 25 per cent, which is ten times greater than the 2.5 per cent turnover rate among public sector prison officers (DLA MCG Consulting, 2003; see also Sachdev, 2004: 23). Apart from the direct costs to the employers,[37] high turnover rates make it difficult for private prison contractors to meet the staffing levels stipulated in their contract bids and can have adverse consequences for the quality of facilities and services such as education that are provided for inmates (National Audit Office, 2003: 32).

In view of these marked differentials in terms of pay and conditions, it might be expected that the private sector's claim to be able to deliver significant operational savings would be unequivocally supported by convincing evidence but, perhaps surprisingly, this is not at all the case. In part this is due to technical problems in ensuring that 'like is being compared with like' across the two sectors.

One problem is that no new public sector prisons have been commissioned since Woodhill in 1992 and the vast majority are considerably older than that, with some such as Dartmoor dating back to the early nineteenth century. This is important because differences in age, design, composition of inmates and occupancy levels are all likely to have a significant bearing on operating costs.[38] Another problem is that the expenditure figures quoted by private prison operators may frequently under-represent the true costs by omitting ancillary costs such as the market-testing and contracting processes themselves.[39] Nor are they likely to acknowledge the costs of various 'hidden benefits' that may continue to be provided by the public sector. These may include the cost of utilities, repair of vandalism, and also the public support services that might be required in the event of a major disturbance or other difficulties (Shichor, 1995: 140). There is also a risk that private contractors may be tempted to put in unrealistically low bids at the outset, to establish a presence in the market,[40] after which they will seek to recoup lost profits once the government has come to depend (politically or economically) on their services. Confirmation from a somewhat unlikely source that such practices may have taken place is provided by the Confederation of British Industry (CBI) (2003: 42, also cited by

Sachdev, 2004: 23), which states that some private contractors may have 'engaged in aggressive competition to build market share', only to falter subsequently.[41]

Quite apart from these technical problems, attempts to compare public and private sector prison costs are bedevilled by a persistent refusal on the part of government and the private contractors themselves to disclose the necessary financial information on the grounds of 'commercial confidentiality'. For all these reasons, although various government-commissioned studies have claimed to find that the operating costs of privately operated prisons are between 11 to 15 per cent cheaper per prisoner per day (see, for example, Andrews, 2000; Park, 2000; Woodbridge, 1999), such findings should be viewed with considerable caution. In the absence of a rigorous, independently conducted comparison of costs, or the production of sufficiently detailed and reliable data to support them, such claims are at best premature, if not positively misleading. Moreover they are contradicted by conclusions based on several authoritative studies, including a number of published comparative evaluations in the US, which has a much longer experience with privatized prison institutions (see Shichor, 1995, chs 6 and 9 for details).

The United States General Accounting Office (1991, 1996) has thoroughly reviewed the evidence obtained from a variety of empirical studies. It concluded that these studies were so methodologically flawed that private prisons cannot be shown to have a clear advantage over public ones, and that no clear-cut recommendation in their favour can therefore be made. These findings are also supported by other more recent meta-analytical studies (Abt Associates, 1998; Pratt and Maahs, 1999). A similar line was taken by the US Department of Justice's Office of Justice Programmes, which reported that 'the cost benefits of privatization have not materialized to the extent promised by the private sector' (Austin and Coventry, 2001: 29). Moreover, a study in Colorado which factored in the 'hidden costs' to the state that are not reflected in the 'cost per prisoner per day' rate found that the 'real' costs were equal to or greater than those incurred by an equivalent state-run institution (Raher, 2002: 7). Yet the British government continues to invest heavily in prison privatization largely for dogmatic reasons, despite the lack of evidence of cost-effectiveness and the huge sums of public money that are involved. An equal cause for concern is that none of the bodies that are supposed to hold the government to account – Parliament and its Public Accounts and Home Affairs Committees, the National Audit Office and the Audit Commission – has challenged or criticized this state of affairs. We shall return to this lack of accountability later in the section.

Turning briefly to some of the ancillary services that have been contracted out, here too the promise that has been held out by advocates of privatization has frequently not been matched by its performance. One of the most striking illustrations of the gap between the two relates to the privatization in 1997 of the industrial functions of Coldingley Prison. This was established in the late 1960s as the first industrial training prison, but at the time that it was privatized, the industrial facilities were losing around £250,000 per year. Less than one year after privatization, the company concerned[42] had incurred losses estimated at £472,200 despite paying the 200 inmates at the prison only £7 per day to make road signs, clothes and engineering equipment (*Guardian*, 29 January 1999). In 1999 the scheme ignominiously became the first prison privatization project to revert to Prison Service control, when the five-year contract was rescinded and the staff once again became public sector employees. A scathing (but unpublished) internal audit report[43] accused the management at Coldingley of showing 'a total disregard for many of the fundamental tenets of government accounting and Prison Service financial policy' (Prison Reform Trust, 1999b).

Nor was this an isolated example. The high cost of the private catering contract at the (public sector) Woodhill Prison, for example, was criticized by the Chief Prisons Inspector for being 'far higher than that of employing prison officer caterers assisted by inmates' (Nathan, 1994: 15). Moreover, plans to contract out the prison escort service for the one remaining area in England and Wales received an embarrassing setback in December 1994, when all four private sector bids were found to be higher than the existing costs of providing the service (Nathan, 1995a: 16). Not that this stopped the privatization from ultimately going ahead.

A second major sphere in which it is claimed that private sector involvement can help to alleviate the crisis of resources is in respect of prison construction (as opposed to operating) costs. It is often simply assumed, even by those who are opposed to the privatization of operational and custodial functions (see, for example, Raher, 2002: 3), that it may well be cheaper to engage the private sector to undertake such major construction tasks. Once again, however, the evidence to support this contention is surprisingly thin and lacking in rigour. It is also difficult to disentangle this aspect from the debate over the method of financing such projects, even though there is no necessary connection between them. In the early days of the prison privatization debate, it was often claimed that the private sector could design, plan and build a prison inside a year, compared with around seven years for the public sector. The difference between the two sectors was, in reality, much more modest than this, however, largely because of the inevitable delays incurred at the planning stage. In any event, the National Audit Office reported in July 1994 that the average time taken to build a prison by conventional means had fallen from seven to just four years (Nathan, 1994: 18).

The third way in which it is claimed that privatization can alleviate the crisis of penological resources is in the financing of new prisons. Here, just as with the operational and construction costs, the comparative capabilities of the private and public sectors have never systematically been put to the test. Instead, as we have seen (in section 7.2), the Treasury simply decided in 1992 that its preferred method of procurement for any major new public spending projects would be for them to be privately financed. In the case of prisons, this effectively meant that they would all in future be designed, constructed, financed and managed by the private sector. The main attraction of this private finance initiative (PFI) to the Treasury is that it removes the need to borrow large sums of money 'up front' in order to defray the costs of building a prison several years before it is ready to take its first inmates. Instead, the government only starts to pay for the use of the facility – at a daily rate per prisoner – once the prison is ready to receive its first inmates. In technical parlance, the effect of the PFI is that major capital investments no longer count against the government's 'public sector borrowing requirement', which successive governments over the last quarter of a century have been at pains to reduce. Or, to put it another way, it has the effect of appearing to move major capital spending 'off balance-sheet'.

In reality, however, the benefit to the Treasury is just as illusory as the accountancy 'sleight of hand' that seems to magically convert capital into revenue spending. For exactly the same effect could be achieved just as easily – and far more transparently – by simply altering the Treasury's own self-imposed accounting rules themselves. One way of doing this, which has been proposed by the Centre for Public Services (2002: 61), would be for the government to employ the general government financial deficit (GGFD) as its measure for public sector current and capital expenditure accounting rather than the public sector borrowing requirement (or public sector net borrowing as it is now known). More importantly, it could enable public bodies to borrow money from the European Investment bank and European Investment Fund for capital investment projects without this counting as government borrowing.

Two other justifications are frequently cited in support of the PFI approach: that it represents better 'value for money' and that it enables the government to transfer the 'risk' involved in any major long-term capital project to the private sector. Neither of these arguments is convincing, however. With regard to the 'value for money' claim, governments (being the ultimate safe credit risk) can typically borrow money at significantly better rates than private sector concerns can. So while it is true that any state institution seeking capital investment for new projects is supposed to test the projected costs of PFI procurement approach against those procured by conventional state funding, the basis on which this is done has been called into question.[44]

The claim that PFI projects represent better value for money is further undermined by the bidding process itself, which bears little resemblance to the classical free-market competitive model enshrined in private enterprise rhetoric. The latter conjures up an image in which the government issues a detailed prospectus outlining in full the specification for the tender and launches an open competition between rival bidders who would each submit a fully costed tender document. This would enable the government to select the bid that comes closest to meeting its requirements including financial and other considerations as spelt out in its prospectus. The reality is very different, however, and involves the issue of an outline prospectus only, to which bidders are invited to respond merely by submitting outline tenders (Centre for Public Services, 2002: 21). These are then evaluated in order to select a 'preferred bidder', though another bidder may be held in reserve. It is at this point that the detailed negotiations begin between client and prospective contractor over the particular terms of the contract, including the actual specifications, allocation of risk and eventual price. All these discussions take place behind closed doors on a non-competitive basis during a lengthy process (6–18 months) in which the balance of advantage lies decidedly with the prospective contractor. As Monbiot (2002) points out, their consultants and advisers are well-placed to extract the best possible deal from the government effectively at public expense and with minimal risk to the contractor (Centre for Policy Studies, 2002: 21–1). Perhaps not surprisingly, it is not unknown for the projected costs of a project to rise two or three times between the allocation of preferred bidder status and the final allocation of a PFI contract.

As for the 'transfer of risk' argument, this is equally unconvincing. The theory is that the contractor bears all the risks of project failure including unanticipated cost overruns. In reality, however, private sector contractors seek to protect themselves by effectively setting up specific companies (known as 'special purpose vehicles') that are backed by limited equity reserves to undertake the project (Kochan, 2002). This has the effect of restricting liability if something should go wrong to the latter rather than the parent corporation itself. From the government's point of view, however, the supposed advantage of a PFI deal is once again illusory, as at the end of the day the state inevitably continues to bear both the political and financial risks of a project failure. Nor is this merely a hypothetical risk. In 2002 insurance companies refused to provide cover for two new private prisons after rioting led to the destruction by fire of a privately run Yarl's Wood asylum and immigration centre, thereby pressurizing the government to either meet the cost itself or at least accept part of the risk. Conversely, when the consortium that secured the contract for HMP Altcourse secured windfall profits that were 81 per cent higher than anticipated following a lucrative refinancing arrangement, they were under no obligation to share these gains with the Prison Service (Centre for Public Services, 2002: 34).[45]

The attractions of the PFI procurement policy for the private sector are self-evident. However, whether it holds any advantage for the state and for the public is much more questionable. After all, the public purse still has to pay the full economic cost of the facilities and services, as well as the needlessly inflated borrowing costs and the massive cost of the procurement process itself, plus whatever profit margin is necessary to attract private investment in the first place. The only apparent benefit is that capital-intensive projects can be funded on the basis of long-term revenue repayments that avoid the *appearance* (though not the reality) of contributing to government debt. Ordinary consumers are familiar with the advantages – and drawbacks – of such 'hire purchase' arrangements. But whereas companies providing hire purchase finance are obliged to spell out the full cost of the transaction, including the annual rate of interest, neither the government nor the contractors are under any obligation to provide such information to the taxpayer who ultimately has to foot the bill. So, far from alleviating the crisis of penological resources, private sector involvement in the penal system is all too likely to exacerbate it in the long run.

The Managerial Crisis

In Chapter 6 we outlined the following key components of the multi-stranded managerial crisis within the prison system: strategic shortcomings; organizational weaknesses; operational failings; and industrial relations problems. It is difficult to see how prison privatization could ameliorate any of these difficulties, and indeed there are strong grounds for believing that in each instance it is likely to make matters worse.

From a strategic perspective, the main charge against prison privatization is that it is likely to encourage a policy of toleration with regard to an expansion in prisoner numbers. One of the first consequences of the re-emergence of prison privatization as a credible policy option was to neutralize the economic and political constraints on governments that might have held them back from expanding the use of custody (Sparks, 1994: 25). A second consequence was to provide a political platform for an extremely influential lobby group representing the interests of large and powerful multinational corporations with a vested interest in promoting an expansionist prison policy (Shichor, 1995: 158). Ironically, the danger that this could have a distorting effect on penal policy was one that Tony Blair (1993) warned against in a public lecture while still in opposition, though he failed to heed the warning once he had gained office. A third consequence is that, once committed to the principle of prison privatization, the government has effectively stifled public debate on the subject by treating the matter as a *fait accompli*. By refusing to publish information or commission research that would enable the strategy to be properly evaluated, the government has compounded its abdication of strategic responsibility for addressing the real causes of the prisons crisis by diverting attention and efforts away from the key issues (Coyle, 2005b: 6). This democratic deficit is another adverse consequence of the government's 'evidence-light' prison privatization policy.

From an organizational perspective, the policy of prison privatization has helped to exacerbate the existing malaise in the penal system by encouraging yet another major structural reorganization of correctional services (NOMS) partly designed to facilitate the extension of a mixed economy 'contract culture' to other parts of the system. Ironically, however, the introduction of a contract culture within the prison system itself has resulted in a fragmentation of the Prison Service that contradicts the government's commitment to creating a 'joined-up' criminal justice system (Centre for Public Services, 2002: 6).

Indeed, from an operational and managerial perspective, it is difficult to see how the creation of a series of semi-autonomous private prisons can possibly improve the system's capacity for strategic planning and flexible deployment of accommodation within the entire prison estate. Not only is each individual private prison potentially under different ownership, with its own individual management structure and locked into a highly specific long-term contractual designation of its function and remit, but they are all to a greater or lesser extent at one remove from the rest of the prison system. One problem to which this can give rise was highlighted by the National Audit Office (2003: 6), which pointed out that prisons subject to PFI contracts may not be sufficiently flexible in design or operation to respond to changing penal priorities. The example it cited related to a switch in emphasis from workshop-based employment towards education and rehabilitation during the currency of some of the earlier PFI contracts. Having to negotiate changes to the contracts adds to the complexity (and expense) of the process. Likewise, the process of 're-roling' (or re-categorizing) prisons to cater for different types of inmates may be a much more complex and cumbersome exercise to undertake in respect of private sector prisons than it would be for those in the public sector.

Although prison privatization may not have been directly responsible for the extension of private sector managerialist attitudes and approaches throughout the prison system (see Chapter 6), it has given rise to further anomalies. One example is that public and private sector prisons may now be expected to comply with different sets of specifications and performance measures (Ramsbotham, 2005: 83). As a result, the experience of imprisonment may well differ markedly and also quite arbitrarily for different inmates depending on whether they are allocated to a public or a private sector prison.

Finally, from an industrial relations perspective, the already fraught relationship between prison service management and public sector prison staff has been further undermined by the advent of prison privatization. We have already noted the differences in pay and conditions between the two sectors and the hostile attitude of most private sector corporations towards the main prison service union. Fears for their jobs and associated benefits from the outset have contributed to a serious loss of morale and increased industrial unrest on the part of public sector prison staff at all levels almost from the outset. Government plans to subject existing public sector prisons to 'market testing' have provoked a particularly hostile response and were even held partly responsible for a series of disturbances at Everthorpe Prison in 1995. An internal inquiry into the causes concluded that the amount of time and effort devoted by prison managers in responding to the initiative in the run-up to the incidents had itself been a contributory factor (Nathan, 1995a: 15). More recently, the accelerating pace and scale of the market-testing programme has fuelled an upsurge of industrial unrest throughout the prison system. This culminated in a vote by members of the Prison Officers' Association in 2004 not to cooperate with the process, with the further threat of strike action if the government continued to press ahead with the programme (Burns, 2004; Prison Reform Trust, 2005b: 11).

With regard to the managerial crisis, therefore, it would be fair to say that the advent of prison privatization has had an unremittingly adverse impact in every respect. Most damaging of all, however, is the expansionary pressure it exerts on prison policy. This in turn has a direct bearing on the prison numbers crisis and the associated problem of prison overcrowding, to which we now turn.

The Prison Numbers Crisis and the Problem of Overcrowding

As we saw in section 7.2, prison privatization was initially advocated during the late 1980s, largely as a response to the problem of overcrowding in the remand sector of the English prison system. Indeed, the first private prison, Wolds, was initially commissioned as a prison catering exclusively for remand prisoners. The decision to press ahead with the policy even after this problem had abated, however, confirmed that the real impetus was ideological rather than operational. Once prison numbers began to rise again, during the mid-1990s, Wolds was recategorized to enable it to accept sentenced inmates and thus help to alleviate the chronic overcrowding problems then being experienced in the rest of the prison system. Indeed, it was not long before Wolds itself began to suffer from overcrowding (15 per cent according to its Board of Visitors, 1995), which necessitated some prisoners being housed three to a cell and resulted in an inevitable deterioration in standards.

Thereafter, as each new private prison came on-stream, provision was made from the outset in their operating contracts for a degree of overcrowding, despite the additional charges that become due when additional prisoners are admitted in excess of the Certified Normal Accommodation (CNA) figure. It quickly became clear that private prisons were no less immune to overcrowding than their public sector counterparts and might even be more susceptible to the scourge. Thus when a list of prisons that had exceeded even their safe maximum operational capacity was published in July 2005, three of the 15 prisons on the list – Altcourse, Forest Bank and Lowdham Grange – were privately operated (Prison Reform Trust, 2005c). This means that over one-quarter (27 per cent) of the privately managed prisons had exceeded their safe operational capacity compared with 9 per cent of those operated by the public sector. It is not at all clear why private prisons should be three times as likely to be operating at dangerously unsafe levels,[46] particularly in view of the additional cost to the public purse that this entails. What is abundantly clear, however, is that prison privatization is incapable of alleviating the prison numbers crisis and the scourge of overcrowding to which it gives rise.[47] Indeed, as we have argued, the policy is likely to seriously exacerbate the problem by removing the fiscal and financial constraints that once acted as a brake on the rampant expansion of prison numbers.

The Crises of Containment and Security

A s we explained in Chapter 6, the crises of containment and security encompass both the *physical security of prison establishments* in the sense of preventing escapes, and also the *personal safety of prison inmates* in the sense of preventing self-harm and violence from staff or other inmates. Once again we will deal with each aspect in turn.

At first it seemed unlikely that 'security issues' would pose much of a problem for contracted-out prisons, since it was originally intended that they would only house remand prisoners. Initially, as we have seen, the regime at Wolds Prison was designed specifically with this group of prisoners in mind.[48] Even after the policy of prison privatization was extended to cover sentenced prisoners, the first of the contracted-out prisons were initially intended to house mainly inmates who posed a relatively low security risk. However, they were by no means confined exclusively to 'shallow-end' institutions (see section 7.2 above) and by 2006, privately managed prisons encompassed a wide range of prison types. They included local and training prisons, one designated exclusively for female inmates (Bronzefield to the south west of London), one designated exclusively for young offenders (Ashfield, near Bristol) and one containing a 'Grendon-style' therapeutic community (see Chapter 6) (Dovegate in Staffordshire). The only major omission was high-security prisons, though Doncaster Prison started to become a Category A local prison during 1997–8, and had achieved full category A status by 1998–9 (Park, 2000: 5).

For a long time it was felt that it would be inappropriate for privatization to be extended to the dispersal or high-security sector of the prison estate, at least for the foreseeable future (see, for example, Learmont, 1995). However, the House of Commons Home Affairs Committee (1997) subsequently adopted a softer line, suggesting that 'while no absolute bar should be placed on the management of high risk prisons by private companies, progress toward this should follow a cautious, step-by-step approach'. Given the rate at which the policy has been extended across the rest of the prison estate, such a move cannot be ruled out in future, even though the need for very high levels of staff and security would presumably diminish still further the scope for privatization to bring any savings.

Although containment of prisoners is now much less of an issue than it was in the wake of the high-profile escapes of the mid-1990s, the private sector has had its share of security problems, albeit of a less dramatic nature. For example, the Independent Security Board for Parc Prison raised serious concerns about its security in the wake of an escape in October 2003, and noted that the prison was six places from the bottom of the Prison Service's performance standard weighted scorecard in February 2004 (PSIRU, 2004: 6). Moreover, the National Audit Office (2003: 24) reported that PFI prisons tended to perform less well overall in areas such as safety and security than their public sector counterparts, and singled out Ashfield Prison in particular, which received an unacceptable security rating from the Prisons Standards Audit Unit.

The overall escape rate is broadly comparable for both public and private prisons (National Audit Office, 2003: Figure 15), but when it comes to personal safety, there is a relatively high level of assaults in private prisons compared with their public sector counterparts. An early study conducted by the House of Commons Home Affairs Committee (1997) reported a significantly higher rate of assaults in all of the private prisons operating at the time compared with newly opened public sector prisons. Likewise, in 2001–2 no fewer than five out of seven PFI prisons had assault rates in the upper quartile for their category of prison (National Audit Office, 2003: Figure 14). In 2003–4 six out of nine private prisons failed to meet their targets on the number of serious assaults recorded against prisoners or staff expressed as a proportion of the prison population. Moreover, three of them – Dovegate, Parc and Wolds – were among the highest of any English prison (Prison Reform Trust, 2005b: 9). Low staffing levels and inexperienced staff are likely to be two of the contributory factors giving rise to such a consistently poor performance.

One private prison that has given rise to particular concern recently is Rye Hill, which was inspected in July 2005. The report noted that 'the prison had deteriorated to the extent that we considered that it was at that time an unsafe and unstable environment, both for prisoners and staff' (HM Chief Inspector of Prisons, 2005b: 5). In this instance the problems were specifically attributed to low staffing levels and a 40 per cent turnover of staff. A few months earlier one inmate had been stabbed to death by fellow inmates; and in a separate incident five staff were suspended and one arrested on suspicion of supplying controlled drugs after another inmate was found dead in his cell (*Guardian*, 20 April 2005).

Serious as it is, Rye Hill is not an isolated instance of a private prison seriously failing to protect the safety of inmates. Ashfield (England's first private young offender institution) was temporarily taken back under public sector management in 2002 amid fears for the safety of both inmates and staff. In February 2003, the Youth Justice Board announced a phased withdrawal of 172 sentenced young offenders from Ashfield after a scathing report by HM Chief Inspector of Prisons (2002), who accused the private prison operator of failing to provide 'the minimum requirements of a safe environment'. Concerns have also been expressed over the number of suicides recorded in private prisons. In the decade after the first private prison opened in 1992, there were no fewer than 30 suicides in such establishments, and between 2002 and 22 November 2006 a further 25 self-inflected deaths were recorded in privately managed prisons.[49]

In assessing the effect of private prisons on the crises of containment and security, it seems fair to say that the crisis of containment has substantially abated in recent years, though without any assistance from the introduction of private prisons, whose overall impact has been broadly neutral. But they appear to have had a distinctly negative impact on the physical security and well-being of prison inmates.

The Crisis of Conditions

When examining the crisis of conditions in Chapter 6, we focused on three main elements: physical conditions, regimes, and relationships with family and friends. Supporters of prison privatization claim that it is capable of delivering not only cheaper, but also better quality conditions and regimes than publicly run prisons. In this section we shall assess the evidence relating to these two issues (since we know of no claims that private prisons improve inmates' relationships with loved ones).

In terms of their physical conditions, there is undoubtedly a huge contrast between privately operated prisons, all of which are recently commissioned, and the older public sector prisons that house similar categories of inmates. However, there is much less to choose between the conditions and facilities in the *newer* prisons across the public–private sector divide, which provides a far more valid comparison. James et al. reported (1997: 135) that *all* the new prisons in their survey – public and private – provided markedly superior conditions and facilities than experienced elsewhere in the prison system. In general, they suggest that the overall balance sheet supports few definitive conclusions about the advantages or disadvantages associated with private sector as opposed to public sector prison management. Prisoners appeared to rate the physical conditions at Wolds (private) as rather better than those at Woodhill (public), particularly regarding the food. However, subsequent overcrowding at Wolds is known to have resulted in a deterioration in the standards available compared with when the prison first opened (James and Bottomley, 1998: 230). The same may well be true of other privately operated prisons, several of which, as we have seen, now contrast unfavourably with comparable public sector prisons in terms of overcrowding.

Confirmation of a marked deterioration in the quality of conditions provided in at least one English private prison is contained in the most recent inspection report for Doncaster Prison, the third private prison, which was opened in 1994 (HM Chief Inspector of Prisons, 2005a). The report described conditions as 'squalid' and accused the contractor of 'institutional meanness'. It criticized the failure to provide all inmates with basic necessities such as pillows, adequate mattresses, working televisions and even toilet seats. The problem was attributed to penny-pinching measures with regard to all areas that were not 'specifically mandated' in the contract, and warned of such failings becoming systemic during periods of financial stringency if contracts fail to prescribe sufficiently detailed standards. The report thus highlights the danger that competitive pressures may encourage private prisoner operators to make savings even in respect of basic commodities at the expense of powerless prison inmates. It also represents a marked shift from the generally positive assessments of private prison conditions in the first few years after they were introduced.

One distinctive feature of contracted-out prisons, at least in the early days, was that their operating contracts contained some very detailed specifications relating to their regimes and the way these were to be delivered. In many cases these compared very favourably with their public sector counterparts, notably with regard to the amount of time prisoners spent out of their cells. Over time, however, these early differentials between the two sectors decreased markedly, partly in response to the gradual spread of a 'performance culture' ethic throughout the Prison Service, and partly because of a gradual erosion of standards in privately operated prisons since their inception.

As we explained in Chapter 6, one measure of 'regime quality' that was in use until recently related to the amount of time inmates spend engaging in 'purposeful activities'. This is an area in which the overall performance of the Prison Service has been consistently low in recent years, persistently failing to meet even the modest target of 24 hours per week (Solomon, 2004b: 11). The performance of private prisons, while still modest, has been slightly better overall than that of public sector prisons, averaging 26.7 hours per week in 2003–4 (Prison Reform Trust, 2005b: 10). However, two private prisons (Doncaster and Forest Bank) fell considerably short of the overall performance target of 24 hours per week, and only one prison – Altcourse – managed to meet the admittedly somewhat higher specific target that is set for each private prison.

Out of the five constituent elements contributing to the crisis in the prison system which we have examined so far, this is the first area in which the private prison sector appears to be capable of out-performing the public sector, albeit not consistently and only by a relatively small margin. We cannot conclude from this that prison privatization helps to alleviate even this aspect of the prison crisis, however, partly because the level of performance varies so widely across both sectors. But partly also because it is likely to be affected by a range of other factors (including the level of resources provided and the size, age and category of the prisons) that have nothing to do with the sector in which they operate.

The Crises of Control and Authority

The evidence relating to the relative performance of public and private sector prisons in the spheres of authority and control is uneven and requires careful interpretation. On the one hand, private prison staff seem fairly consistently to score more highly than their public sector counterparts with regard to their attitudes and behaviour towards inmates, being much more likely to treat them with fairness and respect (Bottomley et al., 1996; Liebling and Arnold, 2002; Liebling and Arnold, 2004: 117; National Audit Office, 2003: 25; Prison Reform Trust, 2005b: 10). These findings are largely explained by the fact that private prison staff tend to be younger, and are far less often recruited from uniformed service backgrounds, making them far less likely to have authoritarian attitudes.

On the other hand, private prisons generally have a fairly dismal track record in maintaining control, securing compliance, and challenging inappropriate behaviour including bullying and aggression towards staff and other inmates (James et al., 1997: 70; James and Bottomley, 1998: 228; National Audit Office, 2003: 25; Prison Reform Trust, 2005b: 9). Virtually all privately managed prisons have experienced serious control problems, at least during the initial period after opening. In most cases, the problems appear to have been more severe, and more intractable, than would normally be expected in the case of a comparable newly commissioned public sector prison. They include: Wolds, which unsuccessfully pioneered a less restrictive style of control; Blakenhurst, which lost control of the prison after a disturbance shortly after opening; and Doncaster, where extra staff had to be appointed after a series of disruptive incidents over a nine-month period. Parc Prison experienced eight mini-riots and two hostage-taking incidents before its official opening in July 1998. Forest Bank experienced a riot shortly after opening in July 2000. Finally, and most spectacularly of all, as mentioned above, Ashfield Young Offender Institution was temporarily taken back under public sector management in 2002 due to safety concerns. Director General of the Prison Service, Martin Narey, described it as the worst prison in England and Wales 'by some measure' and threatened to take it back into permanent public ownership if performance did not improve.

Once again it is not too difficult to account for these failings, most of which are attributable to understaffing and high staff turnover, aggravated by inexperience and inadequate training on the part of private sector staff and management. Nor should this come as a surprise, since they are the predictable consequences of commercial undertakings seeking to reduce costs by minimizing staff numbers, wages and ancillary costs without sufficient regard to the probable consequences within a coercive and potentially unstable prison setting.

What policy consequences may be drawn from the experience of private prison involvement to date in this aspect of prison operations and management? In our view it confirms the feasibility of recruiting prison staff from a wider range of backgrounds and instilling in them a different, more humane and respectful ethos of the kind we were advocating in Chapter 6 (section 6.5). But it also confirms that respectful attitudes and relations by themselves are not sufficient to ensure that staff engage effectively with inmates to ensure that their needs are met, that regimes are improved, and that inmates are given the opportunity of engaging in purposeful activities without endangering themselves or others. What this also requires is proportionately more staff and fewer inmates – better staff–prisoner ratios in other words – which is only likely to happen if we can greatly reduce the prisoner population. It also requires much better trained and motivated staff, which, in turn, will necessitate far higher levels of investment in prison staff to ensure that they do work proactively and meaningfully with inmates. None of these core prerequisites are likely to be achieved by continuing down the road of private sector involvement in the running of prisons: indeed, we believe that the opposite is the case.

The Crisis of Accountability

In Chapter 6 (section 6.5) we examined various mechanisms – political, adminis- trative and judicial – for ensuring that those who wield power or take decisions that affect the lives of others can be made answerable for them within a prison con- text. In this section we focus on the extent to which private sector involvement in the operation and management of prisons is likely to ameliorate or exacerbate the current crisis of accountability.

It is first of all important to note that private sector involvement in the opera- tion and management of prisons raises a number of additional potentially prob- lematic accountability issues that do not apply to public sector prisons. One obvious example is that private corporations are accountable to their shareholders as well as to government funders and (to a very limited extent in practice) to the inmate recipients of the services they provide. However, the duty they owe to their shareholders could be said to take precedence over all their other responsibilities. This split set of loyalties creates a difficult tension between the duty – to maximize profits and dividends – that is owed to shareholders and the financial accountabil- ity that is owed to the public and their representatives by all those in receipt of public funds. In circumstances such as these, openness is an essential precondition of financial accountability and yet neither private prison corporations nor govern- ments have shown the degree of commitment to financial transparency that is required to allay well-founded concerns about the possible misuse of public money.

Right from the outset, as we have seen, the Home Office refused to publish any of the final contracts for private prisons on the grounds of 'commercial confiden- tiality' (although the concept does not operate in the United States, and indeed is 'wholly alien to the theory of perfect competition' (Nathan, 1993b: 13)). Some concessions were made subsequently in response to criticism from the Prison Reform Trust, which resulted in staffing details being published for the first time in the 1993 Prison Service Annual Report. This enabled some cost comparisons to be made,[50] though information relating to implied profit levels and penalty clauses continued to be withheld. Even though the veil of secrecy has been partially lifted with regard to certain aspects of the management of the public sector prisons, the cloak of commercial confidentiality is still used to suppress disclosures that are deemed to be 'sensitive' with regard to the contracted-out sector. For example, copies of a report by Scotland's Chief Inspector of Prisons disclosing that staffing levels at Kilmarnock Prison were between 30 and 50 per cent lower than in prisons run by the Scottish Prison Service were destroyed following threats of legal action by Premier Prison Services Ltd in 2000 (Nathan, 2000: 14). This paranoid attitude towards information that it seems clearly in the public interest to disclose is hard to defend in a democracy, particularly when the private corporations involved stand to benefit so handsomely from public largesse.

Because of their overriding commercial interests, there is a constant danger that the profit motive will override any commitment the private prison operators may have to the public interest. Critics of prison privatization have drawn attention to the potential threat to prisoners' civil liberties and well-being when the power to which they are subject is conferred on private corporations. Ryan and Ward (1989b), for example, warned that the disciplinary powers of prison governors could be abused by private prison operators, particularly since until 2002 these powers included the imposition of 'additional days' of imprisonment for misbehaviour, which would produce a direct financial benefit for the operator. Although prison governors no longer have the power to impose additional days, they can still affect the prisoners' release dates by determining whether they are granted early release subject to home detention curfew (HDC; explained in Chapter 8 below). Official figures for HDC releases between 28 January and 30 April 1999 showed some remarkable disparities in release rates between different prisons. While some public prisons managed to release all of those who were eligible for curfew, three broadly similar private prisons – Altcourse, Blakenhurst and Parc – managed release rates of just 15 per cent, 26 per cent and 5 per cent respectively (Hansard, Written Answers, 25 May 1999; see also Shaw, 1999b). The fact that it is clearly in the financial interest of the private firms who manage such prisons to prolong rather than curtail the length of time inmates stay in their prisons raises some important questions about the basis on which these decisions are taken. Unfortunately, data relating to release rates for different types of prisons are not routinely published (though the Home Office does compile them).[51] Without this information it is impossible to say whether such discrepancies were the result of a short-term aberration or could be indicative of systemic malpractice.

In an attempt to allay such concerns the Criminal Justice Act 1991 required the Home Secretary to appoint a controller for each private prison, in addition to the director, whose duties and functions broadly correspond to those of the governor in a state prison. Whereas the latter has the power to conduct disciplinary hearings and impose certain disciplinary penalties, in private prisons such powers are exercised instead by the controller. The controller's other duties are to keep under review the running of the relevant prison by the director, and to investigate and report on any allegations made against 'prisoner custody officers' (i.e. prison officers) in the performance of their duties. The division of functions within privatized prisons between the director, representing the company's interest, and the controller, representing the interests of the state, has occasionally been a source of friction. Clarification of the controller's role as the Home Office's representative on-site – especially in terms of monitoring performance – was called for by the Chief Inspector of Prisons in 1994 (HM Chief Inspector of Prisons, 1994). Critics (for example, Ryan, 1994) have called into question the controller's effectiveness as a safeguard, citing the ever-present risk of such monitors being 'captured' by the local management – in effect, co-opted onto the private firm's 'team' – when they operate permanently on-site.

Faced with the litany of serious concerns that we have reviewed in this chapter, few could doubt the need for additional accountability mechanisms of this kind, even though opinions might differ over their adequacy. The need was recently reinforced by the 2002 report of the influential European Committee for the Prevention of Torture, which specifically emphasized the importance of ongoing monitoring systems with regard to privately managed prisons, to ensure that the state remains in a position to discharge all its obligations to prisoners deprived of their liberty. It is all the more remarkable, therefore, that the government proposed in 2005 to transfer the remaining statutory powers of controllers to the contractors themselves, though without going so far as to abolish controllers altogether. This was not done in the light of any research commissioned into the operation of the mechanism. Indeed, the only justification cited – in an internal Prison Service document – was that private contractors were sufficiently mature and experienced that only contractual monitoring and the standard oversight mechanisms were now required (Prison Reform Trust, 2005b: 13). The proposal was contained in the Management of Offenders and Sentencing Bill that fell with the May 2005 General Election but a similar provision has since been reintroduced in the Offender Management Bill that was published in November 2006. Private prisons are operated by powerful and influential multinational conglomerates that are adept at securing and exploiting publicly funded market opportunities. By tamely agreeing to dismantle or dilute even the existing rudimentary accountability mechanisms, the government seems to be bearing out Hayward and Aspin's (2001: 15) contention (in an Australian context) that governments 'seem to have lost the power to monitor performance and to put in place effective accountability regimes'.

Turning now to the more general crisis of accountability, it is extremely difficult to imagine how this could be ameliorated by contracting out operational and managerial responsibilities to the private prison sector. Indeed, all the evidence to date points in the opposite direction. With regard to the need for effective *political accountability*, we have already drawn attention to the lack of effective Parliamentary scrutiny over the government's insistence on persisting with such a controversial and expensive policy in the absence of compelling evidence to support it. This was vividly illustrated by Jack Straw's decision within months of the 1997 General Election to overturn the Labour Party's long-standing opposition to the principle of private prisons – taken on the basis of internal Civil Service advice and in the absence of any public debate on the subject.

As for the need for effective *administrative accountability* mechanisms, advocates of privatization sometimes argue that the contractual relationship between the government and the prison firm means that private prisons are effectively more accountable than are public sector prisons, but this hardly seems to be borne out in reality. We have already raised doubts about the adequacy of the controller's role (even if this is not to be further diminished, as seems all too probable). The controller's ability to help to monitor a private prison's compliance with the terms of its contract even under existing arrangements was called into question by the remarkable disclosure that at Blakenhurst not even he was provided with a copy of the contract (HM Chief Inspector of Prisons, 1995). But in any event, as we have also seen, it is possible for a private prison contractor to comply meticulously with the strict terms of the contract and for inmates at Doncaster Prison still to be denied the most basic of necessities. Again, the recent highly critical report of Rye Hill Prison by the Chief Inspector of Prisons (mentioned earlier) noted that the issues to which she drew attention had all been raised in the previous year's National Audit Office report on contracted-out prisons.[52] This led her to query 'the effectiveness both of internal management systems within the prison, and of external monitoring and management' (HM Chief Inspector of Prisons, 2005b). Even more disturbingly, two privately run secure training centres for young offenders were reported to have refused access to an official Home Office inquiry team investigating their use of physical restraint techniques on teenage inmates following the death of a 15-year-old inmate at one of the centres (*Guardian*, 2 November 2005).

Turning, finally, to the need for effective *judicial accountability* mechanisms that are capable of remedying abuses when they do occur, once again the involvement of private sector corporations in the running of prisons and similar institutions raises further serious concerns. They are illustrated by the case of a former immigration detainee – John Quaquah – at a detention centre (Campsfield House) operated by Group 4 Security. Following a disturbance in 1997 that was prompted by a protest against conditions at the centre, a number of inmates were charged with a variety of offences. The case against the detainees collapsed and all were acquitted after video evidence produced at the trial showed conclusively that the testimony of Group 4 officers was simply not credible. When Mr Quaquah sought to sue the Home Office and the contractor for malicious prosecution, he was served with a deportation order that, had it taken effect, would have prevented him from seeking relief through the courts. He succeeded in challenging the deportation order. But his claim against the Home Office failed in the High Court on the ground that the government was not liable for wrongdoing on the part of a private contractor,[53] a decision that reinforces the view that prison privatization tends to undermine rather than strengthen existing public accountability mechanisms.

The Crisis of Legitimacy

Supporters of prison privatization (for example, Logan, 1990; McDonald, 1994) are apt to deny that it poses any special legitimation problems. They maintain that there is a sharp distinction between the *allocation* and the *delivery* of punishment. Most accept that the former should remain a function of the state and its public agencies – notably the courts – while arguing that the latter may properly be delegated, subject to appropriate safeguards, to any agency, public or private. As Sparks (1994: 22) points out, how that punishment is delivered, by whom, and on what terms, is then presented as a purely technical issue to be resolved by considering the comparative costs, quality and efficiency of the various contenders.

Critics of the policy (for example, Ryan and Ward, 1989a; Shichor, 1995) often argue that (in Jack Straw's words before the 1997 General Election) prison privization is inherently 'morally repugnant', typically on the ground that punishment is properly a matter for the state alone as it has a monopoly on the use of coercive force. Radzinowicz (1988) articulated this objection in the following terms:

> [I]n a democracy grounded on the rule of law and public accountability the enforcement of penal legislation, which includes prisoners deprived of their liberty while awaiting trial, should be the undiluted responsibility of the State. It is one thing for private companies to provide services for the prison system but it is altogether a different matter for bodies whose motivation is primarily commercial to have coercive powers over prisoners.

Whatever its intrinsic merits, this objection is unlikely to persuade supporters of privatization, many of whom are in any event ideologically committed to 'rolling back the frontiers of the state'. Moreover, it has to be conceded that people's views regarding the 'proper role of the state' have changed in the past, and are liable to change again over time. Nevertheless we would argue that prison privatization does raise a number of special legitimation problems of its own that are not so easily dismissed.

The first is that any delegation of coercive power carries with it the very real danger that this will be used 'to further private rather than public interests' (Lawrence, 1986: 662). The most obvious of these 'private ends' is the pursuit of profit and the extension of corporate hegemony, but it extends also to the promotion of personal self-interest, and even the pursuit of private vendettas. While it is true that public sector prisons are susceptible to a variety of abusive practices (including the use of unauthorized violence, neglect, waste and ineptitude), they are not nearly so prone to the potential additional problems of corporate or personal greed that private prisons are (Shichor, 1995: 179). The brief history of prison privatization in England and Wales to date provides plenty of ammunition for critics in these respects.

During the early days of prison privatization, concerns were raised over the enhanced opportunities which the policy provides for the promotion of personal self-interest and self-advancement. Many politicians who were involved in the policy-making process, for example, benefited subsequently by being offered positions within private prison firms, a phenomenon often referred to as the 'revolving door syndrome'.[54] Likewise, a number of senior civil servants, including some who were likely to have had inside knowledge or contacts that would be valuable to prospective commercial rivals, were also recruited into senior management positions within such firms.[55] Particular concern was expressed at Group 4's recruitment in 1992 of a member of the tender evaluation panel within the Home Office's Remands Contracts Unit nine months after the contract to run Wolds

Prison had been awarded to Group 4. Further questions were raised about the allocation of the contract when it was learned, first, that the successful tender was £2 million more than that submitted by rival firms; and second that the value of the contract then escalated still further from £4.4 million to £5.9 million a year (Nathan, 1994: 14). The House of Commons Public Accounts Committee recommended that 'to avoid any question of impropriety, detailed reasons should always be recorded whenever a contract is not awarded to a tenderer who submits the lowest bid, and who is judged capable of meeting the key performance criteria' (Nathan, 1995a: 15).[56]

Where the profit motive overrides the public interest in a prison context it is not only financial considerations that are at stake since the rights and safety of prison inmates may also be directly at risk. We will cite just a few instances, though they are by no means unique. The first involved a custody officer at privately run Blakenhurst Prison, who was jailed for 18 months in May 1994 after plotting to arrange the beating up of two prisoners whom he suspected of putting drugs in his coffee (Nathan, 1995b: 13). He was alleged to have offered to disguise two other prisoners and leave their cell doors unlocked in order to facilitate a night-time revenge attack against the pair he suspected, but the plan was foiled when details of the scheme were leaked. The officer was then said to have attempted to bribe the intended attackers – by offering one of them 28 days off a three-year sentence, and the other a move to an open prison – to allow the matter to be dealt with internally by the prison. They refused to go along with this, and went on hunger strike to ensure that the police and Home Office mounted an investigation. Even more disturbingly, they also alleged that Blakenhurst staff were given £50 'backhanders' to keep silent about a riot in February 1994, though this was denied by the prison firm UKDS, who claimed that the payments were made to staff in recognition of the way they handled the riot. Whatever the explanation for these particular payments might be, it is clear that private firms have a lot at stake in such situations, including the possibility of a substantial fine, or reduced prospects in future tender applications. In circumstances such as these, there is an increased risk that firms might encourage their staff, possibly by pressure or inducements, to be 'economical with the truth'.

A second incident that raised concerns about the illegitimate use of coercion by private prison staff was the death in 1995 of Alton Manning, a black prisoner at Blakenhurst. In March 1998 a coroner's jury returned a unanimous verdict that Manning was unlawfully killed by staff while he was being restrained during a fruitless search for drugs (Prison Reform Trust, 1998a: 13; 1998b: 16). Seven prison custody officers were suspended pending criminal investigations, and two of the most senior staff involved in the incident claimed to be ignorant of Home Office guidance warning of the dangers involve in the restraint technique they were using.

The third example relates to the Scottish private prison at Kilmarnock, which was the subject of a damning undercover television documentary in March 2005.[57] Among the allegations reported were claims that staff were encouraged not to be too meticulous in reporting rule infringements such as possession of heroin or assaults on staff or inmates, since these were liable to incur financial penalties for the prison that could result in its being closed down. Equally disturbing, in a prison that had experienced seven suicides in six years of operation, were reports that staff shortages led to records of suicide watches[58] being ignored, or in some instances falsified by completing them in advance.

In view of these shortcomings, it is clear that private prisons are subject to a number of special legitimation problems for which there currently do not appear to be any effective safeguards. Accordingly, there is little realistic prospect that the policy may be capable of addressing the broader crisis of legitimacy that we examined in Chapter 6. In short, prison privatization offers no panacea or cure-all for this or any other aspect of the current penal crisis. And while it may not be responsible for all that ails the English prison system, it probably makes a significant net contribution to the overall malaise – perhaps especially exacerbating the crisis of legitimacy and the numbers crisis (by encouraging a continuous reckless expansion of the prison population). Indeed, unless and until the policy is reversed, we find it difficult to see how any of the constituent elements of the penal crisis can be satisfactorily resolved. Reversing such a deeply entrenched policy would not be easy and could not be swift (which is yet another problem with the policy), although this has happened in other countries once the shortcomings of the policy have been exposed and opened up for public discussion.[59] The issues that we have raised in this chapter demonstrate the need for a serious debate over the future of the policy in England and Wales that takes into account its profoundly negative impact on the current penal crisis. Such a debate is now long overdue.

Notes

1 Initially, privatization found favour particularly among those on the right wing of the Conservative Party, while the Labour Party was strongly opposed to it, as our opening quotation makes clear. More recently, however, as we shall see, this opposition has faded, and prison privatization now forms an increasingly important part of New Labour's 'modernizing' agenda. Among the academic criminologists to have advocated privatization, see in particular McConville and Williams (1985) and Taylor and Pease (1989).
2 See, for example, Coyle et al. (2003); Harding (1997); Hutto (1990); Logan (1990); McDonald (1990); Matthews (1989); Posen (2003); Ryan and Ward (1989a, 1989b); and Shichor (1995).
3 See, for example, Gaes et al. (2004); James et al. (1997); Liebling and Arnold (2004).
4 We use the terms 'private sector' and 'privatization' to refer to the commercial (profit-making) sector, as distinct from the 'voluntary sector' (charities etc.) and the 'informal sector' of active but unpaid citizens. Various 'not-for-profit' organizations (e.g. Crime Concern, NACRO and SOVA) are actively involved in the delivery of various interventions on behalf of youth offender teams. Within the criminal justice system as a whole, certain activities have also been transferred to what has been described as the informal sector, as in the case of 'neighbourhood watch' (see Mawby, 1989; Nellis, 1989).
5 Rolls Royce, British Steel, British Shipbuilding, British Leyland and British Aerospace were among the first government-owned concerns to be privatized.

6   Technically, the government does not regard this as 'privatization', which may result in misleading answers being given to Parliamentary questions on the subject unless they are very carefully phrased (Nathan, 1995a: 18).

7   This arrangement is sometimes referred to as 'semi-privatization' and is the dominant form in some continental European countries such as France (see Cavadino and Dignan, 2006: 321–4).

8   See McDonald (1994), citing Green (1989) and Rutherford (1990). (Immigration detention centres are not strictly speaking part of the prison system, although immigration detainees may sometimes be detained in prisons.) Interestingly, an increase in the number of illegal immigrants during the 1970s, combined with a lack of funding for new facilities to house them, has also been linked to the development of privatization in the corrections sphere in the United States (Windlesham, 1993: 281).

9   Such prisons were originally a local responsibility, but they were brought under national administration in 1877.

10   Mr Hurd was, however, willing to accept that the private sector might have a more limited role to play in helping to accelerate the delivery of the government's prison-building programme. Both the Comptroller and the Auditor General and also the House of Commons Public Accounts Committee had expressed concerns regarding the pace of progress with regard to this programme (Windlesham, 1993: 279).

11   Most notably, Conservative Party Chairman Sir Norman Fowler, who was a non-executive director of Group 4 until he resigned in September 1993, following an outcry over his dual role. In addition, Sir John Wheeler MP, who succeeded Sir Edward Gardner as Chairman of the Home Affairs Committee was a former Chairman of the British Security Industries Association, many of whose members have also bid for contracts.

12   In the ten-year period between 1979 and 1988, the remand population increased by 76 per cent from 6,629 to 11,667, compared with a much more modest rate of increase (18 per cent) in the overall size of the prison population (James and Bottomley, 1998: 223).

13   The episode sheds interesting light on Mrs. Thatcher's approach to criminal justice policy, which appears not to have been particularly interventionist at this time. However, this did not stop her from giving free rein to her ideological instincts in response to a specific enquiry, without reference to Cabinet Committee or even other Home Office ministers (Windlesham, 1993: 298).

14   Subsequently, the legislative scope for prison privatization was extended still further by section 96 of the Criminal Justice and Public Order Act 1994, which allows for the contracting out of *parts* of public sector prisons. Moreover, section 99 authorizes the contracting out of any functions or activities at state-run prisons, which raises the prospect of private sector prison staff being brought in to undertake duties in prisons that have not themselves (yet) been privatized, though this has not happened as yet.

15   Wolds Prison was itself recategorized as a prison catering for both remand and sentenced prisoners in 1995.

16   In the event, the evaluation of Wolds Prison (by Professor Keith Bottomley of Hull University), which was supposed to have been successfully completed before any other parts of the prison service were privatized, did not appear until April 1996, and then only in summary form (Bottomley et al., 1996).

17   Directive (77/187), which was implemented in the UK in 1981 by the Transfer of Undertakings (Protection of Employment) Regulations (TUPE) (Crabbe, 1993: 34–5).

18   The High Court ruled in 1993 (*Kenny v. South Manchester College* [1993] IRLR 265) that Prison Service education lecturers' pay and conditions should remain as they were before the service was put out to tender (Nathan, 1993c: 14). Moreover the government was forced to concede (after taking legal advice) that existing staff contracts and

conditions of employment at Strangeways would be honoured even if a private operator were to secure the contract (Nathan, 1993a: 12).

19 Subsequently, the Labour government has altered the term of the Private Finance Initiative (see below) to ensure that it complies with the Directive (*Guardian,* 14 March 2000).

20 Both John Prescott (who was to become Deputy Prime Minister) and Jack Straw (who was to become Home Secretary) had reiterated the party's clearly stated opposition to the policy of prison privatization in speeches to the annual conference of the Prison Officers' Association (in 1994 and 1996 respectively). See Prison Reform Trust (1998b:1).

21 In a speech delivered, ironically, at another annual conference of the Prison Officers' Association on 18 May 1998 (Prison Reform Trust, 1998b:1).

22 The Prison Service had not been allowed to bid for the Wolds and Blakenhurst tenders.

23 The first of these – Buckley Hall – had previously been managed by Group 4 since it reopened in 1994 but in October 1999 it became the first privately operated prison to revert to public sector control. Then in January 2001 the Prison Service was named as the successful bidder to take over the management of Blakenhurst Prison from United Kingdom Detention Services (UKDS). The third successful public sector bid was to continue running Manchester (formerly known as Strangeways) Prison when its contract came up for renewal, also in January 2001.

24 In addition, there are four privately run secure training centres for young offenders (see Chapter 9): Medway, Hassockfield, Rainsbrook and Oakhill.

25 They were Altcourse, Ashfield, Bronzefield (Britain's first DCMF prison for women, located in Ashford, Middlesex), Doncaster, Dovegate, Forest Bank, Lowdham Grange, Parc, Peterborough, Rye Hill and Wolds. All apart from Doncaster and Wolds (which were financed and built by traditional procurement methods but are privately operated) are DCMF prisons.

26 A term used by former Home Secretary Charles Clarke in a speech to the Prison Reform Trust on 19 September 2005 (Public Services International Research Unit (2005c: 3). Such sentiments are almost indistinguishable from those associated with one of his predecessors, Michael Howard.

27 In marked contrast to the position in other jurisdictions such as New Zealand, which in 2004 became the first state to legislate against private prisons (Cavadino and Dignan, 2006: 318). The Australian state of Victoria has also reversed its former prison privatization policy (2006: p. 310). In April 2006, the government of Ontario in Canada announced that it, too, plans to transfer the operation of a privately run correctional centre to the public sector following a five-year performance review (Public Services International Research Unit (2006: 1).

28 It has often been observed that the attitude of the new right towards the role of the state is not consistent, since the Conservative agenda in relation to crime control has generally been to extend the reach of the law and extend the power of the state to enforce it while cutting back on its responsibilities for health, welfare and other social programmes (Shichor, 1995: 59).

29 Such criticisms have been voiced in respect of certain privately run correctional institutions in the United States, particularly the Silverdale Detention Centre in Tennessee, operated by 'market leaders' Corrections Corporation of America, and described as 'the most researched correctional facility in the United States (Shichor, 1995: 177).

30 Various terms have been coined to express the same idea, including 'criminal justice-industrial complex' (Quinney, 1977; Maghan, 1991; Shichor, 1995) and 'correctional industrial complex' (Bronstein, 1993/4).

31 The murky world of corporate corrections conglomerates is full of examples of takeovers, mergers and divestments in order to circumvent legislative restraints on business

monopolies. For example, in July 2005 it was reported that the GEO group was seeking to acquire its rival Correctional Services Corporation in a $62 million deal that would combine two of the largest private prison operators in the United States (Public Services International Research Unit, 2005b: 1).

32 The contrast with restorative justice is an instructive one. Although some tentative initiatives have been undertaken (see Dignan, 2006) and a 'strategy document' published (Home Office, 2003b), the government has refused to contemplate any further developments until the outcome of an extremely rigorous randomized control evaluation has been published. (See for interim reports Shapland et al., 2004, 2006). No such constraints have been placed on the rapid introduction of the far more radical and controversial – and expensive – prison privatization programme.

33 Staff at Blakenhurst also expressed concern about staffing levels (HM Chief Inspector of Prisons, 1995) following a serious disturbance in February 1994, and similar concerns have been voiced in relation to Doncaster (*Guardian*, 1 February 1995 and 8 September 1995).

34 At more senior levels, pay rates are higher in the private sector (up to 4 per cent in the case of middle managers and as much as 33 per cent for private sector directors as opposed to public sector prison governors: DLA MCG Consulting, 2005: Table ES2).

35 When pension and holiday entitlements are taken into account, Prison Service staff lead their private sector counterparts by 65 per cent based on hourly rates (DLA MCG Consulting, 2005: Table ES3).

36 However, Group 4 recognizes the GMB at its prisons and Premier has recognized a small breakaway union, the Prison Services Union (Confederation of British Industry, 2003).

37 Sachdev (2004: 23) points out that the average turnover cost per employee for low paid and low sector employees in 2000 was £3,933.

38 To give just one example, cells may be temporarily out of commission as a result of refurbishing, resulting in a reduction in the number of inmates held, which is more likely to affect older public sector prisons than new private sector facilities. It is all the more surprising, therefore, to find the inclusion of public prisons such as Chelmsford (1830), Lewes (1853), Pentonville (1842) and Swansea (1861) among a list of 'comparators' against which to assess the performance of a clutch of private prisons, none of them more than ten years old, in a study conducted by the National Audit Office (2003).

39 A study of competitive tendering by the Centre for Public Services (2002: 26) concluded that the government was heavily subsidizing the tendering process.

40 A practice referred to as 'lowballing' in the United States (Shichor, 1995: 160).

41 There was also a substantial 'cost-overrun' at Wolds Prison, where the estimated costs increased from £21.5million over five years to more than £28million. The additional costs (which related to bigger than expected expenditure on external visits and a failure to allow for utility costs) were made good at the taxpayer's expense (Nathan, 1994).

42 Wackenhut (UK) Ltd, which already had contracts for the management of prison escort services and an immigration detention centre, and which claimed extensive experience overseas.

43 The fact that this report was not published illustrates the point that the doctrine of commercial confidentiality can easily lead to the squandering of public money being covered up.

44 For example, Jeremy Colman, who is the Deputy Comptroller and Auditor-General at the National Audit Office, has accused government departments of relying on spurious figures to demonstrate that PFI projects offer value for money (quoted in Kochan, 2002). Likewise, the Centre for Public Services (2002: 21) is also critical of the use of 'public sector comparators' on the grounds that they do not provide appropriate benchmarks against which to assess the merits and defects of PFI projects. Nevertheless,

if somewhat cynically, public service managers know that PFI procurement is the preferred option for the Treasury, so there is little point in arguing that a conventional form of public sector procurement would be the best method of financing projects they put forward for consideration.

45 A deal between the Prison Service and consortium was eventually negotiated and, in the wake of an investigation into the controversy by the National Audit Office, it was announced that future contracts would make provision for refinancing benefits to be shared with the Prison Service. However, the underlying issue of excess profit-taking by PFI contractors was not addressed in the NAO report (Centre for Public Services, 2002: 34).

46 Prisons that exceed their 'safe overcrowding limit' (or 'usable operational capacity' as the Prison Service terms it) are, on the Prison Service's own assessment, jeopardizing 'control, security and the planned regime'. According to Juliet Lyon, Director of the Prison Reform Trust (2005c), 'This level of overcrowding poses a real and serious danger to prison and public safety'.

47 In the United States also, the study by Abt Associates (1998) noted (in respect of Texas, Florida and Oklahoma) that 'contracting for management services alone does not seem to have relieved overcrowding any faster than would have happened if the state built and then operated the facilities.'

48 One of the key concepts influencing the design of the Wolds Prison environment was that of 'normalization', which was intended to reflect the legally innocent status of the intended population (James and Bottomley, 1998: 225).

49 Figures supplied by the National Offenders Management Service in response to a request by the authors under the Freedom of Information Act. N.B. the Prison Service's definition of self-inflicted deaths is broader than the legal verdict of suicide and takes account of the fact that inquest verdicts may often not be available for some years after a death.

50 See Woodbridge (1999) and Park (2000).

51 Information relating to HDC release rates for all prisons – public and private – covering the period 2002–2006 inclusive was finally obtained under the Freedom of Information Act just as the book was going to press. Although the overall pattern is somewhat mixed, three private prisons – Bronzefield, Forest Bank and Parc – have release rates that are consistently below the overall average and far lower than might be expected in view of the type of inmates they house.

52 The Prisons Ombudsman (1995) has also noted the lack of eligible complaints from inmates in private prisons.

53 *Quaquah v. Group 4 (Total Security) and the Home Office* [2001] WL 542173.

54 See above, note 11.

55 In 1997 a team leader left the Prisons Inspectorate to work for Group 4 shortly after writing a highly favourable report on Buckley Hall – run by none other than Group 4 (Nathan, 1999: 13). Nevertheless, the group lost the Buckley Hall contract when it was retendered in October 1999.

56 Similar concerns were expressed by the National Audit Office (1994). HM Chief Inspector of Prisons (1993) criticized the lack of effective monitoring of the financial arrangements between Group 4 and the Prison Service, concluding that it was 'impossible to determine' whether value for money was provided.

57 *Prison Undercover: The Real Story*. BBC1 9 March 2005. See http//news.bbc.co.uk/1/hi/programmes/reas_story/default.stm

58 Suicide watch forms are intended to ensure that vulnerable prisoners are kept under regular observation and should be filled in every half hour.

59 In New Zealand, Victoria and Ontario: see note 27 above.

8 Early Release: The Penal System's Safety Valve

Early Release: Useful, Controversial, Troublesome

8.1

We saw in Chapter 4 that sentencing can be viewed as the 'crux of the crisis'. Changing metaphors, it is sentencing practice that stokes up both the prison population and much of the overall penal crisis. Given that there has been little success to date in turning down the heat and restraining sentencing, whether by governmental encouragement, legislation, initiatives by the senior judiciary or the use of sentencing guidelines (see Chapters 4 and 5), an attractive alternative tactic has been to provide a 'safety valve' to prevent the prisons from boiling over or even exploding. That safety valve has taken the form of the 'early release' of prisoners before the end of their sentences.

From the government's point of view, one great advantage of early release is that it can be operated *administratively* rather than judicially, and can thus serve the government's managerial ends rather than being subject to the outcome of relatively unregulated judicial discretion. One problem is, however, that the more extensively early release is used, the more tenuous becomes the relationship between the original sentence of the court and the sentence actually served. Another is that – precisely because they are administrative rather than judicial – early release schemes can seem lacking in legitimacy, since it may be felt that vital decisions concerning the liberty of the individual and the protection of the public are not being taken in a fair and proper way. As a result, the system of early release has always been vulnerable to criticism from commentators, penal reformers and sentencers alike, and has also contributed to cynicism and bitterness on the part of many prisoners, as well as being a potential source of outrage when released prisoners reoffend.

The whole concept of early release is difficult to justify from a variety of value positions, and in principle many would prefer a system where *'what you get is what you serve'* – in other words, the sentence pronounced by the judge specifies the exact length of time to be spent in prison. This is variously known as *'real time sentencing'*, *'honesty in sentencing'* and *'truth in sentencing'*. Those who favour a punitive Strategy A approach to criminal justice tend to dislike early release because it lets prisoners off with a lesser punishment than the 'law and order' mentality deems to be appropriate, which is less than the judge pronounced in court and which (it is argued) leaves the public dangerously vulnerable to crimes committed by offenders released early. The traditional, 'classicist' legal view which informs the justice model (see Chapter 2) has a different objection. It holds that early release offends against due process and the rule of law, because it means that the amount of punishment undergone for the crime is not determined by a judge following a hearing in open court. A judicial procedure would ensure that offenders had the full rights of natural justice, rights to hear all the evidence, present evidence, argue their case, be legally represented, have the decision justified by reasons and have rights of appeal; but instead the length of their punishment is determined by a discretionary administrative process which may be both secretive and unaccountable. It may also lead to unfair disproportionality, with offences of similar seriousness ultimately being punished by very different penalties (or vice versa).

Such classicist arguments tend to appeal to judges, whose power to determine offenders' punishments is infringed by early release schemes, and who have consequently often opposed and obstructed proposals to extend such schemes. Objections founded on 'natural justice' grounds resonate with prisoners, who may feel that the vital question of when they will be released is governed by a cruelly opaque and arbitrary process.[1] Most supporters of the human rights-oriented Strategy C are also repelled by the defects in due process and proportionality that are associated with early release procedures. On the other hand, they also believe that prison terms should be humanely short, at least for inmates who pose no serious threat to the safety of the public. Consequently, they insist that early release should as far as possible be automatic; but where it is discretionary, the discretion should be exercised within procedures that maximize due process and natural justice. Ideally, decisions to grant or withhold parole should be made by a court, or at least by a process which mimics court procedures as far as possible, with judicial-style hearings, reasons for decisions, rights to legal representation and appeal, and so on. As we shall see, such arguments have borne fruit over the years, and there has been something of a trend towards the '*judicialization*' of parole.[2]

On the other hand, support for a highly discretionary early release system comes from two quarters. The first of these is the traditional positivist 'individualized treatment model' (see Chapter 2), according to which it is only right that experts should make administrative decisions about when release occurs, since they are in the best position to judge when the offender is fit to be released. However, even though modern-day advocates of rehabilitation for offenders may still favour retaining early release, they tend to agree with other proponents of Strategy C that discretion should be limited by considerations of due process and fairness. The strongest support for discretionary early release comes from Strategy B – such a system is ideal for the practical, managerial task of regulating the size of the prison population both flexibly and cheaply. But such a strategy runs into the highly practical problem of legitimacy, since principled opposition to the system makes it difficult to implement with long-term political success. An even bigger weakness with a penal management strategy dependent on early release is its failure to address the main root cause of prison overcrowding, namely the sentencing practices of the courts – the real 'crux of the crisis'. As the Carlisle Committee pointedly said in 1988: 'Expediting the release of prisoners while doing nothing to stem the flow of admissions is like bailing water from a boat without repairing the gaping hole in its bottom' (1988: para. 236). Consequently, as experience has repeatedly shown, such a strategy can do no more than temporarily contain the crisis.

Various administrative mechanisms exist which allow the early release of prisoners. For example, the Secretary of State has a discretionary power under section 248 of the Criminal Justice Act 2003 to release any prisoner on licence on compassionate grounds in exceptional circumstances.[3] There is also a further power – although it has never been used[4] – under section 32 of the Criminal Justice Act 1982 to let out defined categories of offenders up to six months early. But the most important of these mechanisms are *automatic* early release, traditionally known as *remission*, and *discretionary* early release, traditionally known as *parole*. In 1999 these were augmented by *'home detention curfew'*, a scheme that allows short-term prisoners to be released early subject to a home curfew enforced by electronic monitoring. We shall begin with historical accounts[5] of the development of remission and parole, and then proceed to consider the system of early release now in place under the Criminal Justice Act 2003.

From Remission (The Original Safety Valve) to Automatic Early Release

8.2 The practice of early release from sentences has a long history. One of the earliest systems was introduced in the eighteenth century for offenders who were sentenced to transportation, and consisted of a 'ticket of leave' which was issued as a reward for good conduct. A similar scheme was extended to ordinary sentences of imprisonment under the Prison Act 1898. Prisoners had no right to have their sentences remitted: they had to earn it under an elaborate system of 'marks' which were awarded for 'industry and good conduct'. Because of this, remission was seen as an instrument for controlling the behaviour of prison inmates. Over time, however, remission was increasingly used primarily to control the size of the prison population. Although it remained in theory a reward for good behaviour while in prison, in practice remission of a set fraction of the prison sentence became automatic unless some or all of it was lost for breaches of prison rules or discipline. Various changes were introduced to the system of remission over the years, all of which were intended to reduce pressure on prison numbers and had little to do with maintaining discipline inside prisons. For example, in 1940 the remission period was increased from one-sixth to one-third of a prison sentence, and in 1987 it was further increased to one-half for sentences of 12 months or less.[6]

This system of remission (and the word itself) was abolished by the Criminal Justice Act 1991. But as we shall see, most prisoners are still normally released automatically before the end of their nominal sentence if they have not already received discretionary early release. This automatic early release, unlike the old remission system, now comes augmented with a 'licence' to which conditions including compulsory supervision can be attached, and prisoners can be recalled to custody during the period of their licence. Prisoners' release dates can still be delayed if they misbehave in prison, as up to 42 *'additional days'* (as 'loss of remission' is now called) may be awarded for offences against prison discipline. Until 2002 these 'additional days' could be awarded by a prison governor presiding over internal disciplinary hearings. However, as we saw in Chapter 6, the system was changed following a ruling of the European Court of Human Rights.[7] This ruling meant that governors lost the power to award additional days, and now have to refer more serious disciplinary cases to an independent adjudicator. District judges (see the Introduction) act as independent adjudicators, and it is only they who can now award additional days.[8] Prisoners are entitled to be legally represented before the independent adjudicator.

Parole 1967–1992: from principle to pragmatism (and bifurcation)

8.3 Whereas 'remission' over the years became more or less automatic unless forfeited for bad behaviour (which now needs to be formally and fairly proven), parole developed as a mechanism for release – at an earlier stage in the sentence – which was granted at the discretion of the administrative authorities, and which was revocable at any time. Thus, parole is traditionally regarded as a privilege rather than an entitlement. Release on parole was and is 'on licence': parolees are subject to compulsory supervision by a probation officer, and other conditions can be inserted into the parole 'licence'.

Parole was first introduced to England and Wales by the Criminal Justice Act 1967, which allowed prisoners to be paroled once they had served at least one-third of their sentences or 12 months, whichever was the longer, with the parole licence and compulsory supervision lasting until the date at which the prisoner would have been released with remission (then normally the two-thirds point of the sentence). The introduction of parole in England – imported from other jurisdictions such as the USA, where it was long established – has been variously described both as a manifestation of the positivistic 'rehabilitative ideal' prevailing at the time (Morgan, 1983: 137) and also as a product of 'penological pragmatism' (Bottomley, 1984: 25). In truth, *both* strands – ideological and practical – contributed to the origins and subsequent development of parole, though the weight of their respective contributions has altered over the years. The general trend may be described as a shift from principle (or ideology) to pragmatism.

Certainly when it was first introduced, the parole system was highly influenced and shaped by the ideology of positivism. As we saw in Chapter 2, the positivistic 'treatment model' favours the kind of indeterminacy and discretion which parole gives to punishment: offenders are 'treated' in custody until they are sufficiently reformed, at which point (whenever that is) they are released, with further treatment being provided after release in the form of compulsory supervision. Until the experts deem the prisoner to be sufficiently reformed, however, he or she remains in prison in order to protect the public and facilitate further treatment. Thus, the White Paper which announced the government's intention to introduce parole asserted (without any actual evidence) that a 'considerable number of long-term prisoners reach a recognisable peak in their training at which they may respond to generous treatment, but after which, if kept in prison, they may go downhill' (Home Office, 1965: para. 5). Parole was meant to enable this 'peak' to be fully utilized by releasing prisoners at just the right time, with their rehabilitation further assisted by compulsory supervision and support after release. In equally positivistic vein, release decisions were to depend to a great extent on the scientific assessment of the risk of future offending by the prisoner if released.

So the introduction of parole was by no means entirely driven by a pragmatic desire to cut down the prison population. Indeed, at first, certain features of parole meant that it was not particularly well designed for this practical task. One of these was concerned with the structure of decision-making. The government had originally envisaged an explicitly administrative procedure which would have vested considerable discretion in the Home Secretary, but parliamentary opposition resulted in the compromise adoption of a cumbersome three-stage process. First, inmates who applied for parole were considered by their prison's Local Review Committee (LRC), which recommended prisoners for consideration by the independent Parole Board. If the Board then recommended parole, the case passed to the Home Secretary, who took the final decision. So in effect the Home Secretary could veto the parole of individual prisoners, but could not parole anyone unless both the LRC and the Parole Board made positive recommendations. Combined with an understandable desire to 'play safe' this made for a very modest parole rate in the early days: in 1969, the system's first full year of operation, just 27 per cent of those eligible were paroled. And many prisoners were not even eligible, not having served at least 12 months *and* a third of their sentences (which meant that no one sentenced to three years or less could ever be paroled). But things were to change from the early 1970s onwards.

The early 1970s saw the collapse of rehabilitative optimism (see Chapters 1 and 2), which seriously undermined parole's original positivistic rationale. But parole survived – indeed, the numbers of prisoners paroled expanded dramatically – because it was seen as too useful a 'safety valve' for the practical purpose of reducing the numbers of people in prison. As a result, the development of the parole system over the next two decades was shaped much more by pragmatic considerations than by rehabilitative ideology. Some of the changes to parole during the period 1972–81 represented a shift in the balance of power between Home Office and Parole Board in favour of the former – which was important if parole was to be used as a practical instrument of government policy. Thus in 1972 the Home Secretary was given the power to determine certain categories of prisoner who might then be released by him *without* reference to the Parole Board, provided they had received a unanimously favourable recommendation from the LRC. In 1975 Home Secretary Roy Jenkins explicitly encouraged both the Parole Board and LRCs to grant parole much more readily, especially to relatively minor property offenders. As a result of these changes, by 1981 parole was being granted at double the rate it had been a decade earlier – in 55 per cent of cases considered compared with 27 per cent in 1969. But even this was not sufficient to abate the prison numbers crisis.

In 1981 came a more radical Home Office proposal (Home Office, 1981b) to release short-term prisoners (serving between six months and three years, and hitherto not eligible for parole at all) *automatically* after one-third of their sentences – a move again mainly motivated by a desire to reduce the prison population. But this time the government faced revolt: it was reaching the limits to which a policy of ever-increasing administrative pragmatism could be taken without incurring severe problems of legitimacy. The proposal was dropped, partly as a result of strong opposition from the judiciary, who regarded it as an unacceptable interference with the sentence passed by the court, and partly due to Home Secretary William Whitelaw's hostile reception at the 1981 Conservative Party Conference for law and order policies which were perceived as being too soft.

Following this setback, the government adopted an alternative approach: *bifurcation* (see Chapter 1). A package of measures formally introduced by Home Secretary Leon Brittan in 1983 aimed at increasing the availability of parole for shorter-term prisoners while simultaneously reducing it for some more serious offenders. At the lower end, the threshold of eligibility for parole was reduced from 12 to six months; but those serving sentences for certain serious offences would as a matter of policy be denied parole for longer. In this way, the government hoped to relieve the problem of prison overcrowding while appeasing those who demanded tough law and order policies. The new 'twin-track' policy did have the desired effect of increasing the overall rate of early release (with 11,886 prisoners receiving parole in 1984 compared with 5,346 in 1983). But the changes also contributed to a growing sense of unease about the way the entire parole process was operating.

After two decades of almost continuous modification, the scope and importance of the parole system had changed beyond recognition. Between 1969 and 1989, the number of parole applications granted went up more than sevenfold (from 1,833 to 13,751). Equally noteworthy, however, was a marked decline in the parole rate for long-term prisoners following the introduction of Mr Brittan's restrictions on parole: whereas in 1983, 33.5 per cent of prisoners serving more than five years whose cases were considered received parole, this figure slumped to 20 per cent in 1984. By contrast, the equivalent 1984 figure for prisoners serving less than two years was 76 per cent. So short-term prisoners were much more likely to be granted parole than those serving longer sentences, and the difference between the two types of prisoner had widened considerably. In other words, parole was serving to *increase the differentials* between different offenders' sentences. This bifurcatory tendency had two consequences. One was to contribute to the relentless build-up in the long-term prison population, virtually wiping out the gains that had been secured by extending parole to short-term prisoners (Carlisle, 1988: para. 38). The second consequence was to generate unrest about parole within prisons, exacerbating the already serious crisis of legitimacy. The policy of bifurcation was widely seen as unfair, repressive and discriminatory, and in the case of long-term prisoners it was seen as removing any incentive to behave well in prison.[9]

Another fiercely criticized aspect of the parole system – which had caused widespread resentment among prisoners from the very beginning – concerned the decision-making process itself, and its failure to comply with even the most elementary requirements of natural justice and due process. Not only was the procedure highly discretionary, it was also highly secretive. There was no 'hearing' as such: prisoners were excluded from the deliberations of the LRC and the Parole Board, nor were they represented at them (although they were interviewed by a LRC member). Consequently, there was no way of challenging any of the evidence on which the parole decision was based, even though much of it was said to be subjective and anecdotal (Cohen and Taylor, 1978: 90). No reasons were given where parole was not granted, and there was no right of appeal against a refusal of parole, nor any effective way to review or question the decision-making process. This lack of fairness and natural justice was all of a piece with the generally pragmatic nature of parole policies over the years – political and administrative expediency ruled at the expense of principle and justice.

Further problems included the sheer volume of cases to be dealt with. For long-term inmates this led to serious delays in the processing of applications for parole – it was even happening that prisoners' dates for release on parole were passing before they were informed of the decision. Shorter-sentenced prisoners, on the other hand, were being hurriedly granted parole on the basis of minimal scrutiny, thereby fuelling criticism by judges that in effect they were being given automatic early release, thus reviving the policy which they had seemed to defeat in 1981. All things considered, parole was seen as being in urgent need of review. In the 'Hurd era', this came to pass.

Early Release 1991–2003: Reform and the Threat of Near-Abolition (Lifted by New Labour)

The 1991 Reforms

8.4 In 1987 the government announced a comprehensive review of parole under the chairmanship of Lord Carlisle, who reported in November 1988. The Carlisle Committee strongly backed two key principles: first, the idea of *parsimony* in the use of custody, and second, the notion of '*real-time* custodial sentencing' (Carlisle, 1988: paras. 210, 217ff., 232), in which 'what you get is what you serve' (also known as 'honesty in sentencing' or 'truth in sentencing'). But – sentencing being outside their terms of reference – the Committee was (clearly reluctantly) unable to recommend significant reductions in the lengths of sentences passed by judges, which meant that Carlisle's two principles inevitably clashed with each other. So the Committee accepted a continuing need for early release mechanisms, which would inevitably mean that time spent in custody ('what you serve') would be appreciably less than the sentence pronounced by the judge ('what you get'). However, in order to restore at least some meaning to the full sentence passed, it recommended a rather uneasy compromise, which came into being with the passing of the Criminal Justice Act 1991.

Under the 1991 Act, those sentenced to imprisonment for less than four years were normally released *automatically* (without compulsory supervision) after serving half of their sentence. The unexpired portion of the sentence was held in suspense, and could be reactivated by a court if the offender was reconvicted of an offence committed before the end of the original full term. For those sentenced to 12 months or more but less than four years, there was a compulsory period of supervision 'on licence', normally from the point of release until three-quarters of the original term had elapsed. Other conditions, such as conditions of residence, could also be imposed during the licence period. Those sentenced to four years or more (but not life imprisonment) were not automatically released at the halfway point of the sentence, but could apply to the Parole Board for 'discretionary conditional release' (or 'parole') after serving one-half of their sentence. Paroled prisoners were released on licence with compulsory supervision until three-quarters of the original sentence had elapsed. If not granted discretionary release, these prisoners would still normally be released after serving two-thirds of the sentence (subject to delays for misbehaviour in prison). Again, the unexpired portion of a sentence could still be reactivated by a court if the prisoner was reconvicted, and the Home Secretary had the power to recall to prison during the licence period even if there had been no reconviction or breach of the licence conditions. (Provisions relating to sentences of life imprisonment are discussed in section 8.5 below.)

This revised early release system represented a shift in the direction of 'real-time sentencing', since no prisoners would normally now be released before serving half their sentences (whereas previously parole was a possibility for some after one-third). Licences now normally lasted until the three-quarters point, rather than the two-thirds mark. The 1991 Act also meant that the final portion of a sentence was always liable to be reactivated (and added on to a further sentence) in the event of a reconviction at any time up to the end of the original sentence, where under the old system this was not the case during the final, remitted third of the sentence. The natural consequence of these changes would be to increase the prison population. If this were to be avoided, sentencers would have to reduce the levels of their sentences to compensate. Consequently, the Carlisle Committee had recommended 'a thorough reassessment of present sentencing levels' and 'a determined attempt on the part of the Government and the judiciary to secure a corresponding reduction in sentencing at all levels' (1988: para. 295). But this did not happen. In 1992 the Lord Chief Justice[10] urged sentencers to take into account the new arrangements for early release and the actual period likely to be served in custody as a result. If this had any effect at all, it was only very temporary, for since then there has been a sharp increase rather than a reduction in the overall level of sentencing,[11] despite the fact that most prisoners now have to serve a larger proportion of their sentences in custody than before. It has been estimated that the 1991 reform added about 1,000 prisoners to the total prison population (Hood and Shute, 1996: 86).

Reforms around this time also introduced some important changes in the *procedures* for deciding on discretionary early release. The original three-tier structure of Local Review Committees, Parole Board and Home Secretary was ended by the 1991 Act, which abolished the Local Review Committees. The Carlisle Committee (1988: para. 313) would have gone further by removing the Home Secretary from the picture and giving the final say on all discretionary release decisions to the Parole Board rather than the Home Secretary. Instead, however, the Home Secretary's veto was retained in respect of those serving sentences of seven years or more (amended to 15 years in 1998). Certain procedural improvements to the discretionary release system were introduced in 1992, representing a move towards a less administrative and more judicialized system. All applicants for parole were now to be interviewed by a member of the Parole Board and were allowed to see the dossier of reports on which the Parole Board's decision was made. The Parole Board now had to give reasons for its decisions, but still sat in private to decide whether to grant parole. There was still no right to an oral hearing, and no right of appeal from the Parole Board's decision.

1995–1997: Threatened Near-Abolition

We saw previously that the Strategy A, 'law and order' mindset regards almost any early release as abhorrent because it lets criminals off too lightly. It was only logical, then, that the Conservative government's wholehearted adoption of Strategy A between 1993 and 1997 placed the whole system of early release in jeopardy. Home Secretary Michael Howard informed the Conservative Party Conference in October 1995 that he intended 'to get honesty back into sentencing'. Prisoners would lose any prospect of early release whatsoever, with the sole exception that 'model prisoners should get a little time off for good behaviour'.[12] This proposal found its way into the Crime (Sentences) Act 1997, passed shortly before the 1997 General Election, which provided that no prisoner could be released before the five-sixths point of the sentence. It was calculated (Penal Affairs Consortium, 1995) that this extra massive shift in the direction of 'real-time sentencing' would have increased the prison population by 24,000. But these drastic proposals were never implemented. Although the Act was passed, the relevant sections were never brought into force, and were eventually repealed by the incoming Labour government's Crime and Disorder Act 1998. This Act, and the subsequent Criminal Justice Act 2003, took the system of early release in rather different directions.

1999: Home Detention Curfew – Early Release Goes Electronic

Whereas Michael Howard had sought to reduce early release (thereby inevitably further increasing the prison population), New Labour began by taking a small but pioneering step towards letting some prisoners out even earlier. The Crime and Disorder Act 1998 introduced the home detention curfew (HDC) scheme which started operating in January 1999 (and is now governed by section 246 of the Criminal Justice Act 2003). It allows prisoners serving sentences of three months or over to be considered for release before the normal automatic release at the halfway point of the sentence. Those serving extended sentences for violent or sexual crimes are excluded from the scheme, and other sex offenders are only exceptionally to be released. Release is on licence, and the conditions include a home curfew for at least nine hours per day, enforced by electronic monitoring (or 'tagging'), as described in Chapter 5. The decision as to whether a prisoner is released on HDC is a discretionary one, with the discretion resting formally with the Secretary of State but in practice normally with the prison governor (not the Parole Board). The governor's decision is taken on the basis of a risk assessment carried out by prison and probation staff. A governor's decision to release can be overridden, as occurred in the high-profile case of Maxine Carr, the ex-girlfriend of the Soham child murderer Ian Huntley, who was imprisoned for conspiring to pervert the course of justice. Carr's release was blocked by Martin Narey, the Commissioner for Correctional Services, in February 2004 in the interests of Carr's own safety and on the grounds that her release could undermine public confidence in the HDC scheme.

This is not a scheme designed to maximize natural justice, but a flexible administrative arrangement intended to achieve the (Strategy B) practical, managerial goals of reducing prison numbers and hopefully achieving a smooth and safe transition from custody to freedom for many prisoners. The introduction of HDC and its subsequent expansion (see below) is a classic example of the government creating and adjusting early release mechanisms to use as an administrative 'safety valve' for the prison system. It also took the early release system in the reverse direction – further away from 'real-time sentencing', with release once again being possible before the halfway point in the sentence.

When the HDC scheme was first introduced in January 1999, prisoners could be released on HDC up to 60 days early. The scheme was originally expected to reduce the prison population by around 4,000, but in the event the reduction achieved in the first year of operation was only about half this amount. This was because – as with the early days of parole – governors were being deliberately cautious when assessing the risk of prisoners either reoffending or failing to comply with their release conditions.[13] Nevertheless, the introduction of HDC did succeed in engineering a slight decrease in the prison population in 1999 and 2000, but as prison numbers began to climb again thereafter, the period of early HDC release was increased to 90 days in 2002 and to 135 days (four and a half months) in 2003.[14] In 2002, 'presumptive' HDC was introduced for short-term prisoners: prison governors were instructed that HDC should normally be granted to prisoners serving less than 12 months (except for violent, sexual and serious drug offenders) unless there were compelling reasons not to. There have since been reports of the government considering a further extension of HDC to a maximum period of six months to combat further rises in the prison population (*Guardian*, 14 October 2005).

Home detention curfew's proponents can argue that it reduces the prison population (by about 3,500 currently), that it makes for a successful supervised transition from prison to liberty, and that only a tiny percentage of those released are convicted of further offences or recalled to prison while on HDC.[15] However, since many thousands of prisoners are released on HDC – a total of around 130,000 by October 2006 – the figures can be (and have been) presented in a more alarming manner. Much publicity was given in October 2006 to figures showing that 1,021 'serious offences' had been committed by offenders on HDC. Although it is doubtful just how 'serious' many of these crimes were,[16] they did include four cases of manslaughter and one high-profile murder.[17] HDC is also seen by some as eroding public confidence in the criminal justice system (Coulsfield, 2004: 55), because it breaches the 'what you get is what you serve' principle and can be perceived as undermining the sentence of the court and reducing public safety. It has been a particular target of the Conservative opposition, who have repeatedly pledged to abolish it when and if they regain power.

Home detention curfew was only the first New Labour amendment to the early release system. With the Criminal Justice Act 2003, whose complex provisions we detail in the next section, the government rewrote the early release rule book once again.

Early Release Today

The Criminal Justice Act 2003

8.5 The Criminal Justice Act 2003 introduced a significantly different system of early release. One notable feature of the Act was that – perhaps anticipating the day when a human rights court case would make this inevitable – it finally removed the power of the Home Secretary to veto the release of prisoners by the Parole Board (although notably not his similar power with regard to those recommended for release under home detention curfew by prison governors). However, as we shall see, the Secretary of State for Justice retains an important role in recalling released inmates to prison, and in setting the conditions upon which prisoners are released on licence.

The 2003 Act contained a variety of new sentences, some of which come with their own built-in provisions for early release. Thus, the new sentence of *custody plus* (if it ever comes into force)[18] – which is intended to replace sentences of imprisonment of less than 12 months – will consist of a minimum of two weeks and maximum of 13 weeks (three months) in prison, plus a compulsory period of at least 26 weeks (six months) on licence in the community, adding up to a maximum of 51 weeks. The court will specify what the periods of custody and licence shall be when it passes sentence. It will also specify what the conditions of the licence shall be: possible conditions are set out in a statutory 'menu' similar to but shorter than that for community orders (see Chapter 5), and may include supervision. Licence conditions can also include a variety of requirements such as curfews with electronic tagging, community service and treatment programmes; and the Justice Secretary will set out standard conditions which should normally be included in any 'custody plus' licence.[19] Unless and until 'custody plus' is brought in, however, the pre-existing arrangements apply to sentences of less than 12 months, namely that the prisoner is normally released without licence conditions after serving half the sentence.[20]

The early release provisions for those sentenced to *imprisonment for 12 months or more* (but not to life imprisonment, the new 'extended' sentences or 'imprisonment for public protection', which we discuss later) are as follows. Such prisoners are now normally released *automatically* halfway through their sentences (s. 244),[21] and remain on licence *for the rest of their sentences* (s. 249). In most cases this represents a significant increase in the licence period compared with the provisions of the 1991 Act, under which most licences came to an end at the three-quarters point.[22] Released prisoners are subject to licence conditions which are decided upon by the Justice Secretary and which include the 'standard conditions' mentioned earlier. Additionally, the court which originally sentences the offender can recommend particular conditions which it considers the Justice Secretary should include in the licence (ss. 250 and 238).

Home detention curfew (HDC: see above, section 8.4) continues to be available under section 246 of the 2003 Act. Prisoners can be released on HDC up to 135 days before the date on which they would normally have been released on licence (but not before serving at least four weeks, and at least a quarter of the full sentence in prison).[23] Thus, an offender sentenced to 12 months' imprisonment will normally be automatically released on licence after six months, but will be eligible for HDC after three months (a quarter), while a prisoner serving a four-year sentence may be eligible for HDC after one year and 230 days. As explained in section 8.4 above, the conditions of HDC must include a home curfew for at least nine hours per day, enforced by electronic monitoring, and the decision whether to release a prisoner on HDC is normally taken by the prison governor on the basis of a risk assessment.

The various times at which prisoners may be released early, whether automatically or under the discretionary HDC scheme, can still be delayed if 'additional days' are awarded against the prisoner for breaches of prison discipline (s. 257). As explained in Chapter 6 and section 8.2 above, up to 42 such additional days may now only be awarded by an independent adjudicator rather than a prison governor holding an internal disciplinary hearing.

Prisoners on licence (including HDC) are under a legal duty to abide by their licence conditions (s. 252). They can be recalled to prison by the Justice Secretary at any time (s. 254), and the Act does not restrict this power of the Justice Secretary to cases where the offender has breached the terms of the licence or reoffended. Thus released prisoners can be recalled, for example, simply because it is feared that they may be about to reoffend. However, recalled prisoners must be informed of the reasons for their recall, and their cases are then considered by the Parole Board, which can order their immediate re-release. The number of prisoners recalled from early release has more than trebled in the last few years, (over a period when the numbers of prisoners on licence increased by just 15 per cent: HM Inspectorate of Prisons, 2005c: 7), reflecting tougher enforcement practices by the probation service. In 2005/6 there were 9,296 recalls, of whom only 389 had committed a further offence (Parole Board, 2006: 11). The number of recalls looks likely to rise still further, partly because under the Criminal Justice Act 2003 many more prisoners will be on licence at any one time,[24] and partly as a reaction to the massive publicity recently devoted to serious offences committed by prisoners released early (see below). All this naturally adds to the inflationary pressure on prison numbers: recalled prisoners now make up 11 per cent of the population of local prisons (HM Inspectorate of Prisons, 2005c: 5).

Other than their – increasingly important – role in considering the cases of prisoners recalled by the Justice Secretary, the Parole Board will in future no longer[25] be involved in release decisions unless the offender is subject to certain types of sentence: extended sentences, sentences of imprisonment for public protection and sentences of life imprisonment.

Extended sentences of imprisonment were introduced by the Criminal Justice Act 2003. An extended sentence must be passed on offenders who have committed certain specified violent or sexual offences whenever the court considers that there is 'a significant risk to the public of serious harm' because they are likely to commit similar offences again.[26] The court specifies an 'appropriate custodial term' (of at least 12 months) equivalent to what would be a normal overall sentence for the offence[27] *plus* an extended period to be served on licence thereafter, 'of such length as the court considers necessary' to protect the public – up to a maximum of five years for a violent offence and eight years for a sexual offence. Extended sentence prisoners are not eligible for release under home detention curfew, and are not automatically released after half their 'appropriate custodial term'. Instead, they are merely *eligible* at this halfway point to be considered for discretionary release by the Parole Board, which may not release unless satisfied that continued detention is no longer necessary for the protection of the public (s. 247). If not paroled, the offender will serve the full custodial term, followed by the extended licence originally specified by the court.

An even more drastic innovation for offenders who are thought to be dangerous is *imprisonment for public protection*, a new indeterminate sentence introduced by section 225 of the 2003 Act.[28] Courts are required by the Act to impose this on offenders who are convicted of specified serious offences provided (again) that the court believes there is 'a significant risk to the public of serious harm' from the offender committing further crimes – even if the crimes committed are not punishable by life imprisonment, and whether or not the seriousness of the offence justifies such a sentence. When passing such a sentence, the court must specify a 'tariff' period – a minimum period which must be served in prison before release on parole can even be considered – in a similar manner as for life imprisonment sentences (see below). When this tariff period has expired, the prisoner can then apply to the Parole Board for release, but if the Board considers that the prisoner might still be dangerous if released, the prisoner can be kept in custody indefinitely.[29]

We saw in Chapter 4 (section 4.5) that senior judges have expressed deep concerns about these new sentences which the courts are now not merely allowed, but in some cases required to pass on offenders who are reckoned to be dangerous. What such sentences mean is that some offenders are being imprisoned and kept in prison on the basis of what it is (speculatively) feared they might do in the future rather than what they have been proved to have done in the past. There are profound and long-standing objections to such measures, not only on the moral ground that they obviously violate the principles of 'just deserts' (punishment should be what is deserved on the basis of what the offender has done wrong), but also on practical and empirical grounds. Practically, it has been estimated that imprisonment for public protection will increase the prison population to the tune of 3,500 (*Guardian*, 10 January 2007). Moreover it is well established that techniques for assessing dangerousness are inherently (indeed, inevitably) inaccurate, and in particular that future violent behaviour always tends to be 'overpredicted' (see e.g. Bottoms, 1977; Monahan, 1981; Cavadino, 1989: 99–100), so that in practice the use of such measures is likely to mean that many 'safe' individuals are detained for every one who would pose a genuine danger. Moreover, the 2003 Act does not even require sentencers to consider those predictive techniques which do currently exist (and which might help them make fewer false assessments) before passing these sentences. Section 229 does require the court to take into account all the information available to it when trying to assess dangerousness, but remarkably it also requires the court to *assume* that an adult who has committed one of the specified offences is dangerous unless it decides 'that it would be unreasonable to conclude that there is such a risk' (s. 229(3)).

These new sentences now exist in addition to the long-standing sentence of imprisonment for life, to which we now turn.

Life Imprisonment

There are more inmates serving sentences of imprisonment for life in England and Wales that there are in all the rest of the European Union put together, and three times more than any other individual EU country.[30] The number of 'lifers' in England has grown rapidly over the years: on 31 December 2005 there were 6,431 such prisoners representing 8.6 per cent of the total prison population, compared with 3,000 in 1992, 1,535 in 1980, 730 in 1970 (2 per cent of the prison population) and only 140 in 1957. (NOMS, 2005e: Table 1; Penal Affairs Consortium, 1994: 2).[31]

One reason why England has so many 'lifers' is that life imprisonment is the *maximum* sentence for a remarkably large number of offences in English law (about 70), for which judges can pass a *'discretionary* life' sentence. Another is that this is one of the few countries with a *mandatory* sentence of life imprisonment for any murder.[32] The judiciary and the overwhelming majority of commentators over the years (for example, Nathan, 1989; Lane, 1993; Blom-Cooper and Morris, 2004) have called for the abolition of the mandatory life sentence, on the grounds that there are many different kinds of murder ranging from 'mercy killings' to terrorist bombings. As a wide range of degrees of blameworthiness attaches to those responsible, the judge should – as with other crimes – decide (assisted by guidelines) what sentence is just and appropriate in each individual case. However, successive governments have taken the position that murder is a uniquely serious offence which needs to be marked with the mandatory imposition of the most severe sentence and special arrangements to guard against premature release from prison. Until very recently the mandatory life sentence (which politicians favour) also meant that some of those same politicians had the power to make the final decision as to when lifers were released. (Although, as we shall see, the sentence of 'life imprisonment' can mean that the offender is never released, this is the exception.) This situation always sat badly with the constitutional doctrine of the 'separation of powers' (since members of the executive – the government – were performing the judicial task of deciding on the punishment of individual offenders), and also clashed with Article 6 of the European Convention on Human Rights, which establishes the right to fair trial before an independent and impartial tribunal in criminal matters. It was accordingly perhaps inevitable that the position of lifers would gradually become 'judicialized' with politicians losing their powers to determine their release dates; but lifers remain subject to a complex and peculiar set of rules and procedures.

All offenders sentenced to life imprisonment have a *tariff* period set for them.[33] This tariff is the *minimum* amount of time they must spend in prison, and is based on the seriousness of the offence. Once this tariff period has expired, the prisoner is eligible for parole at the discretion of the authorities. If paroled, the lifer will be on a 'life licence' which will never come to an end (unless the lifer is subsequently recalled to prison). If not paroled, the lifer will stay in prison indefinitely. Over the years there has been a long drawn-out process of successive alterations to the way in which the tariff periods have been set and the way in which it is decided whether a lifer whose tariff has expired should be released. At this point we need to digress from describing the current system to sketch the history of this process of change (for fuller details see Shute, 2004).

Originally the decision to release lifers on licence was entirely at the discretion of the Home Secretary, although when capital punishment was abolished he acquired an obligation to consult the judiciary before releasing a murderer. When the Parole Board was created in 1967, the Board made recommendations for the release of lifers, but the Home Secretary retained the final say. In 1983 the government adopted (without any legislation) the tariff system, whereby lifers would not be considered for release unless and until the Home Secretary decided that they had served the minimum period required to meet 'the requirements of *retribution and deterrence*'. The judiciary (in the shape of the Lord Chief Justice and trial judge) were consulted on what the tariff should be, but it was then fixed by the Home Secretary. Once a tariff expired, the Parole Board could then consider whether the lifer should be released, with the Board's primary consideration being the consequent *risk to the public*. A decision by the Parole Board that the lifer was safe to release was not final, for the Home Secretary retained the last word and could still veto the release. Thus – in breach of such principles as the separation of powers and the rights enshrined in the European Convention on Human Rights – a politician (the Home Secretary, or often in practice a junior Home Office minister) was in a position to overrule the judiciary about how long a lifer had to stay in prison as a minimum; and Home Secretaries made frequent use of this power.[34] The Home Secretary could also overrule the independent Parole Board and require that an individual prisoner should not be released. Indeed, politicians could decide that certain individuals should never be released. In 1988 Home Secretary Douglas Hurd imposed the first 'whole life tariff', creating a category of prisoners[35] who were doomed to die in prison at the behest of politicians whose decisions might be influenced by considerations of electoral advantage.

These arrangements were contested in a long series of court challenges over the years, both in the English courts and in the European Court of Human Rights in Strasbourg. Successive court decisions had the effect of whittling away the Home Secretary's powers both to set tariffs and to veto release, first for 'discretionary lifers' (for whom special provision was made in the Criminal Justice Act 1991);

then for minors; and finally for adult murderers. The process was all but completed by two cases in 2002. In *Dennis Stafford v United Kingdom*,[36] the European Court of Human Rights held that the Home Secretary's power to veto Parole Board decisions to release murderers was a breach of human rights. Subsequently, in the case of *Anderson*,[37] the House of Lords (applying the Human Rights Act) ruled that the Home Secretary's power to set murderers' tariffs was incompatible with the European Convention on Human Rights.

The New Labour government (in the shape of Home Secretary David Blunkett) responded by very reluctantly accepting that henceforth it would have to be judges rather than politicians who set minimum terms, and the Parole Board rather than the Home Secretary who then made the final decision on release. And this is what the Criminal Justice Act 2003 provided.[38] When someone is convicted of murder, the sentence must still be 'imprisonment for life'. But both in these mandatory cases and in cases where the judge passes a discretionary life sentence, the trial judge must then proceed to impose such 'minimum term order' (tariff) as seems appropriate, taking into account the seriousness of the particular crime. After the tariff has elapsed, the Parole Board alone is responsible for deciding whether or not the prisoner is released on licence, based on the perceived risk to the public, with the total abolition of the Home Secretary's veto on Parole Board recommendations for release. However, in the case of murderers, the politicians were not prepared to let the matter rest wholly in the hands of judges and the Parole Board. The Criminal Justice Act 2003 (Schedule 21) contains *statutory guidelines*[39] for the setting of tariffs for murderers, with certain particularly serious types of murder (including terrorist murders) being liable to attract 'whole life orders', meaning that they will never be considered for release. The guidelines also provide 'starting points' for murders falling into other categories, which can be adjusted upwards or downwards depending on the aggravating and mitigating circumstances of the individual case. Thus for example, the starting point for the murder of a police officer is a tariff of 30 years, and for 'normal' murders by adults it is 15 years. These guidelines are for many cases substantially more severe than ones previously issued by the Lord Chief Justice for trial judges recommending tariffs under the previous system,[40] so are likely to significantly increase the amount of time many murderers will spend in prison. This increase will come on top of previous increases, for already many lifers spend much longer in prison than they used to. Whereas 35 per cent of murderers who went to prison between 1965 and 1972 were released within ten years, this figure had been reduced to 8 per cent for those sentenced between 1981 and 1991 (Shute, 2004: 894). The average time spent in prison by a mandatory lifer released in 2005 was 14 years (RDS NOMS, 2006b: 124), compared with around nine years in 1965 (*Guardian*, 17 June 2006).

The Parole Board and Its Procedures

The Parole Board is an independent body[41] whose membership includes judges, psychiatrists, probation officers and criminologists. Since under the Criminal Justice Act 2003 most prisoners will henceforth be *automatically* released from their sentences at some stage, if not released under home detention curfew by prison governors, the Board will in future only consider the discretionary release of offenders who receive extended sentences, life imprisonment and imprisonment for public protection;[42] as well as considering the cases of prisoners released on licence who are subsequently recalled by the Justice Secretary. However, many prisoners currently eligible for parole were originally sentenced under the Criminal Justice Act 1991 and many of those who are now receiving the new sentences will not become eligible for parole for a while. Hence, for the time being, much of the Board's workload still concerns inmates serving determinate sentences of four years or more. The great majority of release decisions relating to these prisoners are made 'on paper' (by 'paper panels' of three Parole Board members without an oral hearing). Indeed, in 2004 the Parole Board (reluctantly, and for financial reasons) abolished the automatic practice of having a Board member interview every applicant, which had been introduced in 1992.[43]

In respect of life sentence prisoners, the Board's procedure has changed radically in recent years. As we saw previously (in sections 8.3 and 8.4), the Board's procedures were originally highly secretive and open to objection on grounds of natural justice, but over the years its procedures have become increasingly 'judicialized'. The Parole Board Rules 2004 (made by the Home Secretary under statutory powers) contain a full procedure which applies to lifers and will also be increasingly applied to prisoners serving extended sentences and imprisonment for public protection under the Criminal Justice Act 2003.[44] Under this system, prisoners are entitled to a full oral hearing with many 'natural justice' features. When prisoners apply for parole, their case is first considered (or 'sifted') by a single member of the Parole Board (without a hearing at this stage). This member may decide either that the case should be considered at an oral hearing; or (provisionally) that the prisoner should or should not be paroled. Prisoners may appeal against such a provisional decision not to release; if they do, the case goes to an oral hearing, but if they do not, then the provisional decision becomes final. Provisional decisions in favour of release go to a three-member paper panel of the Board, who then decide (still without a hearing) either that the prisoner should be released, or that the case should be heard by a three-member oral panel. Oral hearings are held in private by a three-member panel chaired by a judge or lawyer. Prisoners are entitled to attend the hearing, may be represented by a lawyer or other person, and can give evidence to the hearing, call and question witnesses and argue for their release. The Board must give written reasons for all decisions.[45]

However, even in this greatly 'judicialized' process there is still no right of appeal from the Board's refusal to grant parole; nor is there always an absolute right to know all the information that the Board uses to make its decisions. Normally the prisoner can hear and see all the evidence (including reports on the prisoner made within the prison system and by probation officers etc.). But the 2004 Rules allow the Justice Secretary to withhold certain information from both prisoners and their representatives and divulge it only to the Parole Board on the grounds that disclosing it 'would adversely affect national security, the prevention of disorder or crime or the health or welfare of the prisoner'. In 2005[46] the House of Lords held that it was lawful for information to be withheld from the prisoner in this way and disclosed only to a 'special advocate' who was appointed to make representations on the prisoner's behalf concerning the secret information, but who was bound not to communicate the information to the prisoner or his or her representative.

The Parole Board is bound to apply set criteria when making its decisions. The Carlisle Committee recommended in 1988 that the parole decision should henceforth simply be based upon an evaluation of the *risk of the prisoner committing a serious offence* while on parole (Carlisle, 1988: para. 321). Thus, the parole authorities should not engage in 'resentencing' offenders for their original offences,[47] but purely look towards the future in judging whether they were a 'good risk' to release. The 'release directions' issued by the Secretary of State to the Parole Board (under powers first granted by the Criminal Justice Act 1991) do state that the Board should focus primarily on the risk of future reoffending,[48] balanced against the benefits of supervised early release to both the offender and the community. However, the criteria are framed in such a way as to make any possible risk bear almost paramount importance: the Board is directed to 'take into account that safeguarding the public may often outweigh the benefits to the offender of early release'. In the case of lifers, the Board must not grant parole if 'the lifer's level of risk to the life and limb of others is considered to be more than minimal'. Following the introduction of these criteria, there was a steep decline in the rate of parole. We have already seen that lifers are spending longer in prison than previously (Shute, 2004: 894). Of determinate sentence prisoners who were considered for parole in 1996/97, 36 per cent were granted it, compared with 53 per cent in 1991 (and 62 per cent in 1984). Of all such prisoners eligible for parole whose cases were reviewed between 1992 and 1995, about 70 per cent were paroled at some point in their sentence; under the post-1991 scheme this figure dropped to 48 per cent at the end of the 1990s (Hood and Shute, 2000: x). The following years saw further fluctuations in the parole rates of these determinate sentence prisoners. The proportion of those considered who received parole rose again to 53 per cent in 2002/3 before a renewed caution led to another decline (to 49 per cent in 2005/6).

There are concerns about some of the other (formal and informal) criteria used by the Parole Board when assessing applications for release. The formal release directions include 'whether the prisoner has shown by his attitude and behaviour in custody that he is willing to address his offending behaviour … and has made positive effort and progress in doing so'.[49] Clearly, such a criterion is both vague and subjective, leaving the prisoner's liberty largely at the mercy of the possibly arbitrary assessments and reports of Prison Service staff and the interpretations put on them by Parole Board panel members. There is also a specific problem concerning those prisoners who continue to deny that they were ever guilty of the offence for which they were convicted. Although there is no blanket Parole Board policy against granting parole to 'offence deniers' (which would be unlawful),[50] denial is often a potent factor working against prisoners since it is seen as an indication of poor attitude and unwillingness to address their offending behaviour (Hood and Shute, 2000: 29–30; Samuels, 2003). In 2003, 51 per cent of all applicants were granted parole, but only 24 per cent of those who maintained their innocence (Parole Board, 2005). Lifers who are 'in denial of murder' seem to have particular difficulty in obtaining release: it is believed that only one person to date has been released on life licence despite proclaiming her innocence of the murder for which she was convicted.[51] This, of course, places genuinely innocent prisoners in a cruel 'Catch-22' dilemma – should they continue to honestly deny the offence and jeopardize their parole chances, or lie and admit the offence, crushing their chances of ever having their miscarriage of justice righted? Given the number of such miscarriages which have come to light in recent years and the likelihood that many more have not, there is no saying how many people, wrongly in prison to start with, have been kept in because they honestly assert their innocence.[52]

2006: Scandal and Panic

In 2006, early release and the post-release supervision of offenders on licence became the subject of much concern and discussion thanks to a spate of high-profile cases in which released offenders committed serious crimes, including the murders of London financier John Monckton in 2004 and of Naomi Bryant in Winchester in 2005. Official inquiries into these two cases (HM Inspectorate of Probation, 2006a, 2006b) found that there had been a range of deficiencies in the management of the released offenders, but also found that the Parole Board's decisions to release them were defensible on the basis of the information available to the Board at the time. The inquiry into the case of Anthony Rice (who killed Naomi Bryant) concluded that consideration of public protection had been undermined by consideration of the prisoner's human rights – in our view a dubious conclusion for which little evidence can be found in the inquiry report (HM Inspectorate of Probation, 2006b), which paints a picture of sloppy rather than over-liberal management.

The government responded with a flurry of initiatives and proposals whose eventual outcome is presently unclear,[53] but whose general tenor was of an attempt to tighten up and toughen up procedures for early release decisions and post-release management. At the same time, however, the government seemed to come within an ace of creating a new extension of early release to deal with a prison population rapidly approaching 80,000 and the prison system's 'bust limit'. In August 2006 it was confidently reported that Home Secretary John Reid was about to introduce a scheme called 'transitional home leave', under which up to 30,000 inmates per year could be released up to ten days early, freeing up to 500 prison places. At the last minute the plan seemed to be vetoed by the Prime Minister's office, fearing that it would damage the government's reputation on law and order (*Guardian* and *Times Online*, 17 August 2006). But then in June 2007 over 1,000 prisoners were released on license up to 18 days early in a classic 'safety value' response to prison numbers now exceeding 81,000.

Conclusion: Early Release Evaluated

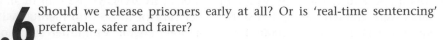

Should we release prisoners early at all? Or is 'real-time sentencing' preferable, safer and fairer?

There is certainly a case against early release. Any such system is likely to lead to a variety of unfairnesses and discontents which reduce the legitimacy of the system. On the one hand, discretionary procedures can lead to a sense of injustice on the part of those denied release; on the other hand, judges and members of the public can be dismayed to find that the sentence served sometimes bears a fairly tenuous relationship to the one passed in court. Sentencing courts are now directed[54] not only to pronounce the 'headline' term of the prison sentences they pass (which expresses the total period of the sentence including any time spent on early release), but also to explain the (increasingly complex) full effect, including when early release may occur, but this attempt at making sentences 'transparent' has its limitations. It also seems likely that the development of early release provisions (and indeed this 'transparency') has had the undesirable effect of encouraging courts to pass longer overall sentences to compensate, deciding first how long the offender should stay in prison and then calculating what overall sentence would achieve this (Coulsfield, 2004: 29). If so, early release will not actually be succeeding in reducing the prison population, merely ensuring that offenders are subject to onerous supervision conditions on release on top of serving time in prison. Again, increasing media attention on the *minimum* terms to be spent in custody rather than the headline terms ('X could be freed in as little as Y years') may well have had the effect of undermining the legitimacy of sentences.

What is to be said on the other side? Broadly speaking, three arguments are put forward for releasing prisoners early, and in our opinion they do each provide valid reasons for retaining an early release system of some kind. First, early release is advocated as a way of dealing with deficiencies elsewhere in the criminal justice system, in particular[55] the overuse of custody by sentencers and the excessive length of many custodial sentences, which creates the prison numbers crisis. Ideally, this should be tackled at source, at the sentencing stage; nevertheless it would probably be politically impractical in the foreseeable future to engineer the massive reduction in overall sentence lengths that would be required to compensate for a complete abolition of early release.[56] So even if progressive moves in the direction of 'real-time sentencing' might be generally desirable in the long run, there is a strong case for retaining some kind of early release in the interests of humanity and of limiting prison numbers in a manner that is both practical and publicly acceptable. In this respect, although we remain somewhat sceptical about the real benefits of electronic monitoring of offenders (see Chapter 5 and Cavadino et al., 1999: 19–20, 210), it might be worth accepting in the context of rendering early release more palatable to the public.

A second argument for early release stems from the remarkable fact that parole is one of the relatively few penal measures which has actually been shown to 'work' to a modest but significant extent in the sense of reducing reoffending rates for those who receive it. Research has shown (Nuttall, 1977; Ward, 1987; Carlisle, 1988: para. 48; Hann et al., 1991; Ellis and Marshall, 1998) that reconviction rates are significantly lower for those who are released on parole than for those who have been refused it. For example, one study found that parolees were 12 per cent less likely to commit a violent offence than might have been predicted from their histories of offending (Ellis and Marshall, 1998); another found that 8 per cent of paroled prisoners were reconvicted within 6 months of release compared with 29 per cent of non-parolees (Nuttall, 1977). It is true that 'better risk' offenders do tend to be selected for discretionary parole to start with; but even taking account of risk factors, parolees still seem to do better (Hann et al., 1991: 68–73). It is possible that parolees' better results may be due partly to the deleterious consequences of the 'knock-back' received by prisoners who are refused discretionary parole (Hann, 1991: 73–4). However, the likeliest explanation is that the combination of supervision and the threat of being returned to prison does serve to reduce the rate of reoffending after release.[57] And it seems at least intuitively likely that a degree of support and supervision in the months following release from prison could well be of genuine assistance to many prisoners who would otherwise be left completely to their own devices as soon as they found themselves outside the prison walls. If this is the case, it argues for a system of *automatic* early release (with compulsory supervision), so that as many prisoners as possible receive its benefits, rather than a discretionary system, especially one that denies potential parolees many of the rights of natural justice.[58]

A third argument – and one that, conversely, argues for *discretionary* early release, at least in certain cases – is that a parole system enables the length of a prison sentence to be modified in the light of developments after the time it is passed. Perhaps most importantly, parole allows an offender to be released when (and not until) the degree of risk to the public is thought to have diminished to an acceptable level. And indeed, even the most radical penal reformers (such as 'abolitionists' – see Sim, 1992: 296) envisage some continuing need for at least a few exceptionally dangerous offenders to be detained on an indeterminate basis for purposes of incapacitation. (This is also true of our own vision for the future of the penal system which we outline in Chapter 11.) So long as this is the case, there will obviously have to be some means for determining when they are sufficiently safe to be released. However, the systems of highly discretionary early release which have predominated in the past represent a poor method of doing this. The oral hearings which now deal with lifers are a distinct improvement in terms of procedure, but still do not provide a fully fair system. There should be a full judicial hearing with a right to publicly funded legal representation and an unrestricted right of appeal, and certainly no political veto on releases. Bearing in mind all the difficulties associated with the assessment of dangerousness and the well-established tendency for dangerousness to be officially 'overpredicted' (Bottoms, 1977; Monahan, 1981; Cavadino, 1989: 99–100), decisions should as far as possible not be based on the impressions, guesses and hunches even of experienced experts, since these are known to be unreliable and to give rise to the risk of unconscious prejudices swaying release decisions. They ought instead to be based on precise criteria that have an established and valid bearing on the genuine likelihood of the prisoner posing a serious risk if released. Nor should release criteria be framed (as they currently are) to encourage excessive caution in releasing.

So in our opinion, a morally defensible penal system would include provision for early release, although under a system different from the existing one. And this would need to form part of a more comprehensive reform package containing measures to reduce levels of custodial sentencing, which remains the crux of the crisis. The Carlisle Committee (1988: para. 236) was quite right to say that bailing out water from the boat is futile without repairing the hole in its bottom. On the other hand, to abolish or restrict early release without at the same time effectively tackling sentencing practice would be to court disaster on an epic scale.

Notes

1 An ex-prisoner wrote in the 1970s that 'parole and the people running it are to blame for much of the tension in prisons today' (Stratton, 1973: 44).
2 An important factor in this 'judicialization' has been the growing impact of the European Convention on Human Rights on the reform of English law, even before the implementation of the Human Rights Act 1998. Note, however, that the advent of home detention curfew (see section 8.4) represents a move back towards a more administrative system of determining release dates.
3 This section and its predecessors are used to release prisoners in the last stages of terminal illness; for example, the power was used by Home Secretary Jack Straw in 2000 to release the gangster Reggie Kray a few weeks before his death from cancer.
4 In October 2005 it was reported that the government had specifically ruled out using executive release to ease the prison overcrowding crisis (*Guardian*, 14 October 2005). By contrast, many other countries (such as France) make extensive use of 'amnesties' to reduce their prison populations periodically.
5 A more detailed historical account of the first 25 years of parole is contained in Cavadino and Dignan (1992: ch. 6).
6 This was during the 'Hurd era' (see Chapter 11), and coincided with the announcement of Lord Carlisle's review of early release (see below). The immediate effect of the 1987 increase in remission was a reduction in the prison population by approximately 3,500.
7 *Ezeh and Connors v. United Kingdom* (2002) 35 EHRR 28 and (2004) 39 EHRR 1, in which the court ruled that such hearings amounted to criminal proceedings and therefore prisoners had the right to a fair trial under Article 6 of the European Convention on Human Rights. Consequently it was a breach of the convention to deny prisoners legal representation where an award of additional days was at stake. Article 6 also specifically requires a hearing before 'an independent and impartial tribunal'.
8 Prison (Amendment) Rules 2002 (S.I. 2116).
9 It seems likely that at least two serious prison disturbances in Scotland (at Peterhead in 1986 and Perth in 1987) were directly linked with these changes in parole, which also applied to Scotland (Scraton et al., 1991: 25, 104).
10 *Practice Direction (Crime: Sentencing)* [1992] 1 WLR 948.
11 See Chapter 4, section 4.4, p. 101.
12 Similar proposals were also contained in the Conservative manifesto for the 2005 General Election.
13 Only 31 per cent of eligible prisoners were granted release by governors in the first year, compared with an expected rate of around 50 per cent.
14 HDC was originally available to prisoners sentenced to less than four years, but the Criminal Justice Act 2003 removed this limitation. For further details of the current provisions, see section 8.5 below.
15 Dodgson et al. (2001) found that only 2 per cent were convicted of further offences while on HDC and only 5 per cent were recalled to prison before the end of their HDC

period (although 61 per cent had 'experienced a curfew violation', two-thirds of them claiming that this was due to equipment malfunction rather than their own misbehaviour). Of those released on HDC in 2005, 15 per cent were recalled, mostly for breaches of licence conditions; just 2 per cent of all releasees being recalled for a fresh offence (RDS NOMS, 2006b: 125). At 31 October 2005, of the 119,000 offenders released on HDC since the beginning of the scheme, just 3.4 per cent had been convicted or cautioned or were awaiting prosecution (F. Mactaggart in a Parliamentary Written Answer on 19 January 2006).

16 The 1,021 'serious offences' included 562 minor assaults, 145 assaults on a police officer, 100 offences of obstructing or resisting an officer and 100 possessions of offensive weapons (House of Commons Public Accounts Committee, 2006b).

17 This case involved a young tagged offender called Peter Williams, who was convicted of assisting the 2003 murder of Nottingham jeweller Marian Bates. It was found that Williams had repeatedly breached his curfew order and removed his tag, but little was done to control him (*Guardian,* 19 September 2005).

18 The relevant sections of the Criminal Justice Act 2003 (ss. 181–2) were expected to come into force in late 2006, but were shelved indefinitely in July 2006. See further Chapters 4 and 5.

19 Criminal Justice Act 2003, section 250.

20 Criminal Justice Act 1991, s. 33, as partially retained by SI 2005/950 Sch. 2 para. 14.

21 In November 2006 the government put forward for consultation a proposal that prisoners serving ordinary determinate sentences could lose their right to automatic release at the halfway point if they were subsequently assessed as dangerous and referred via a High Court judge to the Parole Board (Home Office, 2006d: 13–14).

22 Prior to the 1991 Act, licences normally expired after two-thirds of the sentence.

23 Prisoners on 'custody plus' sentences (if and when this is introduced: see note 18 above) must have served at least half of the custodial period ordered by the court.

24 Because long-term prisoners will henceforth be on licence for the whole of the rest of their sentence (rather than until the three-quarters point as previously), and new sentences such as imprisonment for public protection involve long licence periods.

25 Except that most prisoners *currently* eligible for parole were originally sentenced under the Criminal Justice Act 1991; hence for the time being, most of the Board's workload still relates to inmates serving determinate sentences of four years or more.

26 Criminal Justice Act 2003, s. 227 (offenders aged 18 or over). Section 228 provides for similar extended sentences of detention for younger offenders.

27 I.e., 'the shortest term commensurate with the seriousness of the offence' (s. 153(2), but rounded up to 12 months if necessary (s. 227(3)(b)).

28 Section 225 applies to adult offenders; section 226 provides for a similar sentence of 'detention for public protection' for offenders under 18.

29 If such prisoners are paroled, it is possible for the Parole Board eventually to discharge them from their licences, but only when they have been on licence for at least ten years and the Board is satisfied that keeping the offender on licence is no longer necessary (s. 31A, Crime (Sentences) Act 1997, inserted by the Criminal Justice Act 2003, Sch. 18). Otherwise, the licence will last for the whole of the offender's life.

30 At the end of 2002 there were 5,268 lifers in England and Wales and 5,046 in the rest of the EU (Solomon, 2004a).

31 By 31 October 2006 there were 7,959 prisoners serving indeterminate sentences (life and imprisonment for public protection) (NOMS, 2006d: Table 1).

32 Another reason is that the definition of murder in English law is particularly wide, probably much wider than is generally realized. Murder does not require premeditation or even an intention to kill, merely to inflict 'serious harm'. Recent reform proposals by the

Law Commission (2006) would create 'first degree' and 'second degree' classes of murder, of which only 'first degree' murders would attract an automatic life sentence. Killing with an intention to cause serious injury would only be first degree murder if the killer was aware there was a serious risk of causing death; otherwise it would be second degree murder. However, if the sentence of imprisonment for public protection were to continue in its present form, it seems likely that many second degree murderers would receive such a sentence – with similar effect to a life sentence.

33 Criminal Justice Act 2003, s. 269 and Sch. 18 (adult mandatory lifers); Powers of Criminal Courts (Sentencing) Act 2000, s. 82A (inserted by Criminal Justice and Court Services Act 2000, s. 60 and amended by Criminal Justice Act 2003 (discretionary lifers, murderers under the age of 18 and those sentenced to imprisonment for public protection).

34 Between August 1990 and July 1993, the Home Secretary increased the tariffs recommended by the judges in 112 mandatory life cases out of 806 and reduced them in only three (Shute, 2004: 885). According to James (2004), it was not uncommon for the Home Secretary to double the tariffs recommended by trial judges, and clear reasons for doing so were never provided.

35 In 2004 there were 20 prisoners with 'whole life tariffs'. The best known prisoner of this kind was the 'Moors murderer' Myra Hindley, who waged a long campaign to be freed but died in prison in November 2002 after 36 years in prison.

36 (2002) 35 EHRR 32.

37 *R. (on the application of Anderson) v. Secretary of State for the Home Department* [2002] UKHL 46; [2003] 1 AC 837.

38 Sections 269 and 275 (amending s. 28 of the Crime (Sentences) Act 1997). See also section 82A of the Powers of Criminal Courts (Sentencing) Act 2000 (as amended) for the fixing of tariffs in non-mandatory life cases.

39 These statutory guidelines are not as open to objection on constitutional grounds as the previous powers of the Home Secretary, since Parliament (as opposed to the government) can make what laws it likes; and judges remain free to depart from the guidelines where the merits of the individual case seem to require it. However, the Act (s. 269(6)) also gives the Secretary of State the power to amend the guidelines by order; before doing so the Justice Secretary must consult the Sentencing Guidelines Council, but need not take their advice.

40 *Practice Direction: Minimum Periods of Imprisonment* [2003] 1 Cr App R (S) 16.

41 A 'body corporate', according to section 239 of the Criminal Justice Act 2003.

42 Along with the juvenile versions of the latter two sentences, known as 'detention during Her Majesty's pleasure' and 'detention for public protection'.

43 This was because the government had withdrawn 90 per cent of the funding for these interviews in 2004. In 2006 the Board committed itself to re-introducing, from April 2007, such interviews for selected offenders (Parole Board, 2006: 9).

44 Parolees who are recalled to prison by the Justice Secretary also now receive an oral hearing (from a single legally qualified member of the Parole Board), following the case of *R. (on the application of Smith) v. Parole Board and R. (on the application of West) v. Parole Board* [2005] UKHL 1.

45 If a three-member panel is divided over a release decision, until now it has been the majority view which prevails. The government in July 2006 announced that the Parole Board should move to a system requiring unanimity before a prisoner can be paroled (Home Office, 2006c: 33–4).

46 *Roberts v. Parole Board and the Secretary of State for the Home Department* [2005] UKHL 45; [2005] 2 AC 738. The case concerned the application for parole of Harry Roberts, who was serving life sentences for the murders of three policemen in 1966.

47 One criticism of the old system of parole (for example, Hood, 1974: 8; Ashworth, 1983: 368) was that it amounted to a form of 'executive resentencing', since the criteria included not only factors relating to the risk of future offending, but also those relating to the seriousness of the offence. This would have the effect that any aggravating and mitigating circumstances would be 'double weighted', since they would be influential both in setting the original sentence and in the decision about whether (and if so, when) to release early.

48 This does not fully eliminate the problem of 'double weighting' (see previous note), as factors increasing risk include past offending and the seriousness of the current offence, both of which will have largely determined the sentence originally passed. Indeed, in assessing risk the Board is required to take into account the 'nature and circumstances' of the offence, including its impact on the victim. (The release directions are available on the Parole Board's website at http://www.paroleboard.gov.uk.)

49 This quotation is from the release direction for determinate sentence prisoners; the direction for lifers similarly requires the Board to consider 'whether the lifer has made positive and successful attempts to address the attitudes and behavioural problems' which led to the offence.

50 *R. v. Secretary of State for the Home Department ex p. Zulfikar* (*The Times*, 26 July 1995).

51 Susan May, released in 2005 following 12 years in prison for the murder of her aunt (*Guardian*, 23 April 2005).

52 Harold Williams may have been one of these innocent victims. In August 2000 his murder conviction was referred to the Court of Appeal as a possible miscarriage of justice by the Criminal Cases Review Commission. He was convicted in 1977 and would have been paroled in 1988 had he admitted his guilt. In October 2000, Williams died in prison.

53 See e.g. Home Office (2006d) mentioned in the following note.

54 By a 1998 Practice Direction issued to courts by the Lord Chief Justice (*Practice Direction (Custodial Sentences: Explanation)* (1998) 1 Cr App R 397; see also (2004) 2 Cr App R 391). A consultation paper in November 2006 (Home Office, 2006d: 10–12) put forward as one option that sentences should henceforth be described in American-style phraseology such as 'six years to life'.

55 It is sometimes also argued that early release systems can be used to rectify the shortcomings of the criminal appeals system and disparities in sentence lengths. However, there are serious objections in principle to the use of early release rather than judicial mechanisms to, in effect, pardon and resentence offenders.

56 History suggests as much: the 1991 reforms represented a move towards 'real-time sentencing', for which sentencers were supposed to compensate by reducing sentence lengths (see note 10 above). The following years instead saw an *increase* in sentence lengths. We are not optimistic that the Sentencing Guidelines Council's direction that following the implementation of the Criminal Justice Act 2003 sentencers should scale down prison sentences by 15 per cent (see Chapter 4, section 4.5) will be any more effective; so far it has certainly not been.

57 This would fit in with the finding that certain supervisory non-custodial sentences appear able to exert a 'holding effect' on supervisees and at least delay reoffending while the supervision lasts: see Ashworth (1983: 32); Raynor (1988: 111).

58 A contrary view would be taken by anyone who believed that it is the 'demonstration of trust' placed in the prisoner (Hann et al., 1991: 73) which generates the beneficial effect, and that this demonstration would be lost in automatic early release. We find this implausible.

9 Young Offenders: Systems Management or System Disaster?

Children in Trouble or Troubled Children?

9.1 There is a curious ambivalence in what Durkheim (see Chapter 3) would have called our 'collective sentiments' about young offenders.[1] On the one hand, the image of the 'young thug' is a perennial focus for fear, hatred and periodic 'moral panics' (Pearson, 1983; Cohen, 1980),[2] and this sometimes leads to particularly repressive measures being devised for young offenders. On the other hand, our attitudes towards 'children in trouble' can also be infected with the sentimentality evoked by children more generally in our culture, particularly where they are mistreated, and this can lead to less harsh measures being countenanced for them. Perhaps because of this ambivalence, the history of the penal treatment of young offenders has been especially chequered and contradictory.

Experience in England and Wales in the last few decades shows this particularly well. An Act of Parliament (the Children and Young Persons Act 1969), which was intended to create a radically new and more lenient system for dealing with juvenile offenders, led paradoxically to a massive increase in the incarceration of young people in the 1970s. In the 1980s, despite an apparently discouraging political climate, developments in juvenile justice were hailed as highly successful in reducing the custody rate for young people and as showing the way forward for more general reform of the criminal justice system. But these approaches to youthful offending were in turn to fall out of favour with the government in the 1990s, as the pendulum swung against the young offender once more. Currently, the trend towards harsher treatment for youthful offenders shows little sign of abating; but at the same time there are some developments pointing in a more humane direction.

Young People, Crime and the Penal Crisis

9.2 There hardly seems to have been a time, at least since the early nineteenth century, when the criminal activity of young people has not been a cause of major public concern. We seem to be repeatedly told, not least by the media, that crime among young people is a serious and ever-worsening problem, often in contrast to a previous golden age – perhaps about 50 years ago – when youth posed no great threat to public order and safety. If we check the historical record, however, we find that at the time of the supposed golden age people were saying exactly the same things (Pearson, 1983).

It is true that adolescents do appear to commit a disproportionate number of crimes compared with their elders.[3] In 2004, 38 per cent of people found guilty of or cautioned[4] for an indictable offence in England and Wales were under 21. The rate of known offending for males between the ages of 15 and 20 was almost five times the rate of known offending for adult males, and the peak age for committing a detected offence was 17 for boys and 15 for girls. But little of this was serious crime, especially for offenders under 18, whose commonest detected crime is shoplifting.[5] The vast majority of really serious crime is committed by adults.

As the above figures suggest, offending by young people is in the great majority of cases a transient phenomenon of adolescence. Research studies (see, for example, Belson, 1975; West, 1982; Graham and Bowling, 1995) suggest that most young people commit at least some minor offences, which in the main go undetected, while even the ones who are repeatedly caught offending in their teens typically 'grow out of crime' as they progress to adulthood (Osborn and West, 1980; Rutherford, 1992: ch. 2; Flood-Page et al., 2000: 18–19). To complete this comparatively unthreatening picture of young people's crime, the official statistics suggest that – far from a youth crime wave being upon us – offending by young people has been *decreasing* in recent years. The number of people under 21 who were proceeded against for indictable offences in 2004 was down by 17 per cent on the figure for 2001, and was the lowest since 1994. The number of young adults (those aged 18 and over but under 21) proceeded against for indictable offences in 2004 was 14 per cent down on the previous year and 25 per cent down on the figure for 1994.

And yet young people continue to contribute substantially to the 'numbers crisis' in the custodial system. In December 2005 offenders under the age of 21 accounted for 14 per cent of the prison population (which includes custodial institutions for young offenders).[6] Hardly any other Western European countries lock up as many young people proportionately (NACRO, 2003; see also Cavadino and Dignan, 2006: 300–1), despite research results suggesting that young English people commit fewer offences than their counterparts in other Western European countries.[7]

The way we deal with young offenders also affects the penal system's 'crisis of legitimacy'. The most commonly voiced concerns – apart, of course, from the usual perennial complaints about alleged 'softness' – relate to the conditions and regimes of the custodial institutions which contain so many young people, many of whom are officially classified as 'vulnerable'.[8] Custodial institutions for young offenders – and certain ones in particular – have repeatedly been the focus of serious concern. In 1999 the Chief Inspector of Prisons described conditions at Feltham Young Offender Institution as 'unacceptable in a civilised country'. In March 2000 he was similarly scathing about Portland YOI, describing conditions there as a 'moral outrage' (HM Chief Inspector of Prisons, 1999e, 2000a); there have also been serious allegations about brutal staff behaviour in Portland over many years, culminating in the dismissal of two members of staff in 2002. Recent reports by the Chief Inspector of Prisons voicing concerns about bullying, staff intimidation and the use of inappropriate control and restraint techniques at a number of other young offender institutions including Stoke Heath, Brinsford and Onley suggest that these are far from being isolated incidents (see also Amnesty International, 2002). Following the death in 2004 of 15-year-old Gareth Myatt at Rainsbrook Secure Training Centre while being restrained by staff, the Howard League for Penal Reform commissioned an independent inquiry into the restraint, strip searching and seclusion of children in secure training centres and secure children's homes. Lord Carlile (2006), who conducted the inquiry, found that children were being subjected to painful restraint methods and forcible strip searching, while hundreds were being held in solitary confinement, often for weeks at a time. Another concern is that young people who are sentenced to detention are often housed many miles from home, which makes it extremely difficult for them to maintain contact with their families.

Perhaps the most disturbing single recent incident concerning young offenders was the brutal murder of 19-year-old Zahid Mubarek at Feltham in 2000. Mubarek, serving a short sentence for minor property offences, was battered to death by his cellmate, a known violent racist. A public inquiry (Keith, 2006) found that 186 separate individual and systemic failures had led to the murder, and that prison staff possibly did at times (as had been alleged) deliberately put unsuitable inmates together in cells (although not on this occasion). The young offender institution had been overstretched, under-resourced and blighted by racism, both institutional and at times overt.

Not surprisingly, perhaps, there is a disturbingly high level of suicide and self-harm within custodial institutions for young offenders: no fewer than 29 young people under the age of 17 are known to have committed suicide between 1990 and 2005 (see also Goldson and Coles, 2005). In August 2004, 14-year-old Adam Rickwood became the youngest person to commit suicide in a British penal institution when he took his own life in Hassockfield Secure Training Centre. Finally, the stubbornly high reoffending rates – over 80 per cent of males under 18 who left custody in 2001 were reconvicted within two years (RDS NOMS, 2004: Figure 11.1) – bluntly calls into question the effectiveness of locking up young people as we do.

In general, young offenders represent a crucial facet of the penal crisis. For while, on the one hand, concern about young offenders has helped to fuel the ideology of law and order, thereby worsening the crisis, the youth justice system has also provided examples of successful ways of dealing with young offenders that suggest ways of defusing the crisis if the right lessons could be learned and applied.

Responding to Youth Crime: Models of Youth Justice

9.3 The history of the English 'youth justice' (or 'juvenile justice') system[9] has been turbulent, complex and frequently paradoxical. In particular, the pace and scale of the changes that have been made since 1998 are so great that the current system is now often referred to as 'the New Youth Justice' (e.g. Goldson, 2000). We shall present a detailed account of the current youth justice system later in the chapter. First, however, we provide an overview of five distinct approaches that have influenced youth justice policy-making over the years (see also Cavadino and Dignan, 2006: 200)[10] the *welfare, justice, minimum intervention, restorative justice* and *neo-correctionalist* approaches. They are in approximate chronological order in the sense that the successive models have enjoyed their greatest popularity with British governments roughly in the order in which we discuss them,[11] but none of these approaches has ever been pursued to the total exclusion of all the others. In practice policy is always a mixture of models, which can often give rise to tensions and contradictions.

The Welfare Model

The emergence, in the nineteenth century, of a juvenile justice system that was distinct from its adult counterpart owed much to the influence of the 'welfare model'. This approach incorporates the positivistic assumption that juvenile wrongdoing is the product of social or environmental factors over which the young person has little or no control, and maintains that young offenders should, accordingly, be helped rather than punished. The influence of the welfare model on the English youth justice system has in general been much less pervasive than in many other countries (see Cavadino and Dignan, 2006 for details). Nevertheless, it was reflected in the imposition of a long-standing statutory duty requiring all courts to 'have regard to the welfare of the child' in making its decisions and to ensure that 'proper provision is made for his education and training' (Children and Young Persons Act, 1933 s. 44(1)). Although still in force, the impact of this stipulation has been greatly diminished by the fact that it has not consistently been reflected in subsequent youth justice policy and legislation. A very radical attempt to reform the juvenile justice system in line with the welfare model was introduced in 1969 with the passing of the Children and Young Persons Act (CYPA) by the Labour government of the day. This aimed to promote a much more positivistic approach, in which the young person's welfare would be the prime consideration and almost all children who offended under the age of 14 would be dealt with by means of civil care proceedings rather than prosecution. The Act also intended to phase out criminal proceedings for all but the most serious juvenile offenders over the age of 14 and to ensure that even those who were convicted would be placed in care rather than punitive custody.

This radical reform agenda never came to pass, however,[12] for a change of government in 1970 meant that the CYPA was only partially implemented and, as a result, the traditional function and custodial sentencing powers of the juvenile court remained largely unscathed. Although the intention of the CYPA was that juveniles who offended should be helped rather than punished and that they should be dealt with in the community rather than sent to custody, the actual result was, spectacularly, the reverse. There was a distinct decline in the use of community-based disposals for juvenile offenders coupled with a massive rise in the use of custody, from 3,000 custodial sentences in 1970 to over 7,000 in 1978. The most telling figures are for males between the ages of 14 and 16 inclusive. Only 6 per cent of sentenced offenders in this category were sent to custodial institutions in 1970 (the last year before the CYPA came into force). By 1978 the proportion had doubled to 12 per cent.[13]

The Justice Model

In contrast to the positivism of the welfare model, the 'justice model' espouses a more 'classicist' punishment-oriented approach, which treats young offenders as reasoning agents who are responsible for their actions. Accordingly, it places more emphasis on the deeds and deserts of the child rather than their welfare needs. It also seeks to reduce official discretion in the system; to ensure that like cases are treated alike according to the offenders' 'just deserts'; and to ensure that suspects' rights of 'due process' are upheld (Morris et al., 1980; Taylor et al., 1979). The strong influence of justice model thinking is reflected in the fact that the English youth court has essentially remained a 'junior criminal court' with only minor modifications from its adult counterpart as opposed to the welfare tribunal, which has become established in a number of other jurisdictions.[14] It was also reflected in the replacement, in 1983, of a semi-indeterminate, treatment-oriented form of custody known as 'borstal training' with a determinate, more explicitly punitive, custodial sentence known as 'youth custody' (now 'detention and training orders').[15] A variety of procedural reforms during the final quarter of the twentieth century – including the growth of state-aided legal representation for defendants and advance disclosure of the prosecution case – was likewise consistent with a justice model approach. However, these reforms also resulted in increased delay and expenditure, which fuelled concerns about the efficiency and effectiveness of the youth justice system. These were to come to a head in the 1990s with a hard-hitting review by the politically independent Audit Commission (1996: 26–9). It complained that a preoccupation with procedural reforms had slowed down procedures, increased the number of court appearances before a young defendant was finally dealt with, and added greatly to the expense of the system.

Justice model thinking also strongly influenced a fundamental change in the orientation and structure of the English youth justice system that came into force in 1991. Hitherto, the English juvenile court had incorporated two distinct jurisdictional strands, for it was responsible for dealing both with young offenders and with vulnerable young people who were considered to be 'in need of care and protection'. These two strands were disaggregated, however, by the Children Act 1989. Since then, responsibility for children who are in need of care and protection has been vested in a separate care jurisdiction that is administered by lower civil courts known as 'family proceedings courts'. Here, the welfare of the child continues to be the paramount consideration save in exceptional circumstances (s. 1(1) Children Act 1989). This left the juvenile court – soon to be renamed the youth court[16] – to deal exclusively with criminal cases. This reform was politically uncontentious at the time, having been the subject of extensive consultation. Indeed, it was welcomed by many leading child law experts for removing such cases from 'the criminal overtones associated with the juvenile court' (Bainham, 1990: 181–2).

Subsequently, this rigid institutional separation between the civil care jurisdiction and the criminal jurisdiction has been retained throughout the many turbulent changes that have since been visited upon the youth justice system. One very important consequence, however, has been to further attenuate the influence of welfare considerations when dealing with young offenders, even though the youth court remains bound by the long-standing statutory duty[17] to have regard to the welfare of the child' in making its decisions. This can cause particular problems for those young people with acute welfare needs who also break the law, since they now find themselves subject to two separate sets of agencies, courts and operational philosophies. Many commentators see it as a matter of growing concern that such troubled young people, when prosecuted in the youth court with its unambiguous criminal orientation, may be dealt with without proper regard to their welfare needs (see, for example, Ball, 2004: 37; Bottoms and Dignan, 2004: 124–7).

Minimum Intervention and Systems Management

A third approach that exerted a considerable influence over youth justice policy-making and (more particularly) youth justice practice during the 1980s and early 1990s is characterized by a philosophy of 'minimum intervention'.[18] One of its conceptual roots derived from Rutherford's influential thesis that – as we noted earlier – the great majority of young offenders simply 'grow out of crime' (Rutherford, 1986a). A second root – strongly influenced by criminological 'labelling theory' (see Chapter 2, above) – derives from the belief that formally processing offenders by catching and punishing them is harmful and can make matters worse by increasing the likelihood of reoffending. The minimum intervention strategy itself is linked with a number of specific policies with regard to young offenders:

- **'Decriminalization'**, whereby certain offences – particularly so-called 'status offences' that involve wayward of dissolute behaviour on the part of young people, such as truancy, under-age drinking and illicit sexual behaviour – no longer carry the threat of prosecution and punishment;
- **Diversion from prosecution** by cautioning or warning young offenders instead;
- **Avoiding 'net widening'** (see Chapter 5) by trying to ensure that alternatives to prosecution such as cautioning are used only for those who would otherwise have been prosecuted;
- **Diversion from custody** by encouraging sentencers to make use wherever possible of community-based alternatives;
- **'Depenalization'** by removing some or all young offenders from the criminal jurisdiction entirely and dealing with them instead by means of civil proceedings involving the use of 'child sensitive' institutions or tribunals.

This minimum intervention philosophy was enthusiastically embraced by a remarkably influential coalition of academics (all of whom were experienced former juvenile justice workers) and practitioners who collectively became known as the 'Juvenile Justice Movement' (and later, the 'Youth Justice Movement'). The movement was led by the Lancaster Group,[19] which not only engaged in research and published influential writings (most notably, *Out of Care* by Thorpe et al., 1980) but also pioneered a highly effective strategy for promoting and implementing a minimum intervention approach. The strategy was based on the development and systematic application of a new approach to youth justice known as *systems management*, which seeks to harness managerialist techniques associated with a Strategy B approach to criminal justice, though with the ultimate aim in this instance of achieving humanitarian (Strategy C) goals.

The systems management approach starts with systems *analysis*: a rigorous attempt to elucidate how the criminal or youth justice systems and their constituent parts interact and interconnect, why they function in the way that they do, and what this means for suspects and defendants as they pass through the system. Armed with this knowledge, it may then be possible to devise and facilitate systems *interventions* in order to modify the process to achieve specific desired outcomes, such as a decrease in the numbers of young people being prosecuted or ending up in custody. Various techniques were developed in order to pursue minimum interventionist policies such as decarceration, diversion from prosecution and custody and the avoidance of net-widening. These techniques included: the targeting of offenders known to be 'at risk' of formal processing; developing gatekeeping mechanisms to divert[20] young suspects and offenders away from prosecution and custody; and fostering inter-agency cooperation and monitoring to ensure that the interventions were having the desired effect.

In terms of its impact on the youth justice system, this kind of systems management could claim a substantial degree of success during the 1980s and early 1990s, including dramatic reductions in the rates of prosecution and custody.[21] One of the factors contributing to this success[22] was that – at least for a time and albeit for largely pragmatic reasons – it gained the interest and active support of the Conservative government of the day. Despite that government's enthusiastic espousal of 'law and order' rhetoric generally, it encouraged the use of police cautioning as an alternative to prosecution and invested heavily in diversionary alternatives to custody. Ultimately, however, this uneasy alliance between ideological opponents foundered during the early 1990s when John Major's Conservative government responded to a growing moral panic over various youth crime issues by reverting to a more characteristic 'law and order' approach that castigated any attempts to limit punishment.

Restorative Justice Model

A fourth approach which, as we shall see, is becoming increasingly influential in the youth justice sphere is the 'restorative justice' approach. This advocates a more participatory decision-making process, in which those with an interest in a particular offence – offenders, victims and other interested parties – have the opportunity to deliberate together and seek agreement on the most appropriate way of responding to it (see also Chapters 2, 5 and 11). In terms of youth justice policies and processes, the restorative justice model shares the minimum intervention model's preference for diverting many, if not most, offenders from prosecution, since the conventional criminal trial process is seen as an inappropriate forum for collective decision-making. Strategies aimed at decarceration are likewise favoured for most offenders who continue to be tried and sentenced in the conventional manner, on the ground that custodial penalties often make it very difficult to secure restorative outcomes. Penalties that contain elements of reparation (such as compensation orders, reparation orders and community service) are preferred where possible.

Many restorative justice advocates also share the minimum intervention model's view that formal responses to offending are potentially harmful, though not simply because of their stigmatizing effect on offenders. An additional weakness in their view is that they are typically insensitive to the needs of victims and deaf to the concerns of the wider community. Other restorative justice advocates are more optimistic about the compatibility of restorative justice and criminal justice values and processes and view the former as a valuable means of reforming and ameliorating the latter. Restorative justice advocates do not favour a minimum intervention approach, however, since this does nothing to address the needs and concerns of any of the key protagonists. It fails to provide help, where needed, for offenders – or to hold them accountable for their actions; it does nothing to facilitate reparation and support for victims; and it fails to provide a forum in which the views and concerns of the relevant 'community of interest' might be addressed.

The adoption of a 'full-blown' restorative justice model would restrict the role of the youth court to determining issues of guilt and innocence in contested cases and to providing a back-up in cases where a restorative justice approach would be unsuitable. No jurisdiction has gone quite this far,[23] and the English youth justice system is a long way from it. Indeed, before 1997 there was no specific legal basis or framework within which restorative justice initiatives might operate and, consequently, these were confined for the most part to small-scale, local, ad hoc experimental projects. Most of these were not in any way integrated within the mainstream criminal justice system but co-existed, often rather precariously, on its margins, though some did enjoy short-term Home Office funding linked to an evaluation study (Marshall and Merry, 1990). Most projects operating during this period were either based on the process of victim/offender mediation (see sections 2.4 and 5.3 above) or relied on indirect mediation to negotiate reparation agreements between victims and offenders. Many were also linked to diversionary initiatives that were inspired by the systems management approach and, perhaps as a result, several were criticized for being more concerned with avoiding prosecution or custody for offenders than with meeting the needs of victims.[24]

Since 1997, as we shall see, certain aspects of a restorative justice approach have been incorporated as part of the regular mainstream response to youth offending in England and Wales, though this has been done on a rather piecemeal basis that supplements rather than supplants the existing youth justice system. Consequently, the strength and direction of this particular current within the overall post-1997 reform programme remain rather weak and uncertain, largely due to the overwhelming influence exerted by the neo-correctionalist approach which we discuss next.[25]

Neo-correctionalism

The 'neo-correctionalist' approach has much in common with the punishment-oriented Strategy A, 'law and order' ideology (see the Introduction) which flourished most notably in the period of the Conservatives' 'law and order counter-reformation' between 1992 and 1997. However, neo-correctionalism has a much larger and more ambitious agenda than simply ensuring that offenders are dealt with as harshly and punitively as possible at every stage of the criminal justice system. Indeed, in certain other respects, it has more in common with some of the other approaches we have been examining.

Among the law and order inspired policy precursors of neo-correctionalism, three early developments merit a brief mention. The first is associated with the 'short sharp shock' initiative of the early 1980s, in which the regimes in certain detention centres[26] were experimentally modified to incorporate a greater emphasis on physical education, physical work and military style drills and inspections. Government hopes that the new regimes would be more effective than the ones they replaced, however, were dashed by negative research findings (Home Office, 1984b). Remarkably, though by no means uniquely, the government's response to this failed experiment was not to abandon the initiative, but to extend the same approach to all detention centres, only to find that sentencers did not share their enthusiasm for the measure, which was abolished in 1988.

The other two policy precursors were both products of a growing moral panic during the early 1990s over the perceived prevalence and seriousness of youth offending,[27] linked to a perception in much media and political discourse that official responses to young offenders were inadequate and ineffective. One response took the form of an initial backlash against the minimum intervention philosophy of the 1980s, and was reflected in a withdrawal of the presumption in favour of cautioning juvenile offenders. The second was linked to a revival of interest in a militaristic shock intervention known as the *'boot camp'* or 'high intensity training' concept (Cavadino and Dignan, 1997a: 265) that was imported from America in the mid-1980s.[28] As we shall see, the thinking that lay behind these precursors continues to resurface periodically, even though the overall philosophical context has changed considerably.

The main aim of the neo-correctionalist approach is the prevention of offending and reoffending rather than imposing punishment for its own sake, and all other aims are subordinated to this overriding objective. However, the type of behaviour that a neo-correctionalist approach aims to prevent is not confined to purely criminal behaviour but extends to acts of 'pre-delinquency', including truancy and other forms of rowdy or anti-social behaviour, which is reminiscent of early welfare approaches.[29] This much broader focus reflects a far more ambitious agenda for the entire criminal justice system, which is no longer restricted to responding to crime per se, but is also concerned about the preservation of 'community safety' and public order in general. Moreover, the techniques that are used to combat such behaviour likewise draw on a wider armoury of measures comprising diversionary, civil and quasi-criminal interventions as well as more traditional criminal penalties.

Within a more traditional youth justice context, neo-correctionalism explicitly rejects the 'don't make matters worse' philosophy of the minimum intervention approach in favour of a policy of *'zero tolerance'* (see Cavadino et al., 1999: 28–30). This requires offending behaviour to be 'nipped in the bud' even if it is petty or first-time offending. With regard to more serious or persistent young offenders, the neo-correctionalist approach seeks to intervene 'progressively' – with increasing intensiveness with each successive offence – rather than making the severity of the punishment fit the seriousness of the offence as the justice model demands. As for the nature of the intervention, the neo-correctionalist approach is interested in measures that are considered likely, in the light of known evidence, to succeed in preventing a recurrence of the problem rather than simply imposing punishment for its own sake. But in contrast to the welfare model, with its holistic emphasis on the personal rehabilitation of convicted offenders, the neo-correctionalist approach seeks to address a relatively limited range of 'risk factors' – for example, truancy, poor parenting or dysfunctional peer relationships – that are known to be predictive of offending behaviour.

This ostensibly 'evidence-led' approach[30] underscores another important aim of the neo-correctionalist model: to improve the effectiveness and efficiency of the youth justice system by coordinating the activities of the relevant agencies, targeting interventions according to the perceived degree of risk, and by speeding up youth justice processes. In this respect, the neo-correctionalist approach shares with the minimum intervention model an enthusiasm for applying 'systems management' techniques, though in this case the main goal is the reduction of crime rather than the diversion of young offenders from court and custody. Thus, as in other spheres of penal policy-making, the neo-correctionalist agenda has likewise been strongly influenced by the managerialism that is associated with a Strategy B approach to criminal justice (see Chapter 1, section 1.4).

Although the origins of the neo-correctionalist approach can be traced back to the 1990s and beyond, as we shall see in the next section the approach itself has come to epitomize the youth justice policies of the New Labour government that was elected in 1997.

New Labour: 'New Youth Justice'

9.4 When a new Labour government was elected in 1997 after a period of 18 years in opposition, the influence of three major youth justice approaches – welfare, justice and minimum intervention – had already been eclipsed by its predecessor's adoption of a more strident law and order approach.[31] Further radical reform of the English youth justice system had been signalled as a major priority by the new administration in a series of policy documents, the earliest of which pre-dated the General Election (Straw and Michael, 1996; Home Office, 1997a). Two major pieces of legislation – the Crime and Disorder Act 1998 and the Youth Justice and Criminal Evidence Act 1999 – were implemented during the government's first term in office. The 'new' youth justice system that they ushered in was indelibly stamped by neo-correctionalist hallmarks, though it also incorporated important elements of restorative justice thinking and a systems management approach. These influences are reflected in five key principles that have guided the government's youth justice reform programme: the primacy of offending prevention; responsibilization; reparation; early, effective and progressive intervention; and efficiency. We examine each of these below.

The primacy of offending prevention

The Crime and Disorder Act 1998 adopted as the principal aim of the youth justice system 'to prevent offending by children and young persons' (s. 37). Although the Act did not repeal the various earlier provisions imposing different obligations, such as the duty of the youth court to have regard to the welfare of children and young people,[32] it did nevertheless represent an important symbolic change of emphasis away from the principles of the welfare, justice and minimum intervention models. As we shall see, this change of direction was reflected in the introduction of a range of new and often controversial preventive measures for dealing with pre-delinquent offenders, including some who are under the age of criminal responsibility (currently age of 10).

Responsibilization

This rather inelegant neologism was appropriated by Muncie (1999: 169)[33] in order to draw attention to another important feature of the new youth justice system: its insistence on making people accountable for their actions (or, in some instances, for their omissions). 'Responsibilization' means, first, that young offenders are expected to accept responsibility for their own actions instead of being absolved on account of their age or a belief that they will 'grow out of crime'. One early manifestation of this principle was New Labour's abolition of the traditional legal doctrine of *doli incapax,* whereby children aged 10 to 13 were presumed to be incapable of committing a crime unless they could be shown to appreciate the difference between right and wrong (see section 9.6 below). Second, responsibilization also means that *parents* may be held responsible for the offending behaviour of their children, and the Crime and Disorder Act 1998 introduced parenting orders[34] which permit courts to require parents of misbehaving children to attend counselling and guidance sessions and comply with other conditions.

Reparation

In addition to – but explicitly subordinate to – the new primary aim of preventing offending, the new youth justice system also encourages the principle of reparation. Reparation has been made to serve a double purpose in the new youth justice. First, it is proclaimed as a tangible manifestation of an offender's willingness to take responsibility for an offence, so it is seen as a suitable response for relatively minor offenders who might in the past have been 'let off' with a caution. In addition, the introduction of a range of penalties including the reparation order (see below) that require offenders to make amends for the harm they have caused to victims or the community also serves to demonstrate the government's oft-voiced commitment to prioritize the needs of victims. Another innovation to be explained shortly– the referral order for young offenders who are being prosecuted for the first time – can also contain reparative elements. Reparation constitutes one element of the wider 'restorative justice' approach, but as we shall see shortly, these new measures in practice only embody restorative justice in a very partial and watered-down way.

Early, effective and progressive intervention

In pursuit of its overriding aim of preventing offending – and in line with the notion of 'zero tolerance' – the new youth justice strategy is based on the principle of early intervention with first-time offenders in order to 'nip offending in the bud' (Straw and Michael, 1996: 18) instead of diverting them or 'making excuses for them'.[35] This shift marked a decisive break with the 'minimum intervention' philosophy of the youth justice movement. This was reflected in the adoption of a new statutory pre-trial diversion process that was set up in place of the old system of juvenile cautioning which was inextricably associated with that movement. As we shall see, the new procedure entails a *graduated* response in which young offenders who carry on offending can expect to receive progressively more intensive and intrusive interventions, the aim of which is to confront them with their behaviour, investigate its causes and take action to address it. The same approach also underpinned the introduction from 2001 of community-based Intensive Supervision and Surveillance Programmes (ISSPs), which are intended for persistent young offenders either as an alternative to custody or as part of the post-release supervisory arrangements for those given detention and training orders.

Efficiency

Shortly before the 1997 election, the 'old' youth justice system was lambasted by the politically independent Audit Commission (1996) for being expensive, inefficient, inconsistent and ineffective and for devoting too much time, effort and resources to processing young offenders rather than taking effective remedial action with them. This conclusion chimed in with the Labour Party's own analysis and it sought to improve the efficiency of the system through a combination of measures intended to speed up the processing of youth justice cases[36] and a radical programme of institutional reform, to which we now turn.

New Youth Justice: New Institutions

9.5 In order to pursue its reform agenda, one of New Labour's first priorities was to reconfigure the organizational framework that had developed in the era of minimum interventionism, while relying on similar managerialist techniques involving inter-agency work and system monitoring. Table 9.1 provides a schematic overview of the institutional structure that underpins the new youth justice system.[37]

Table 9.1 Institutions of the 'new youth justice'

Function	Criminal jurisdiction	Care jurisdiction
Policy-making	Home Office Juvenile Offenders Unit	Department for Education and Skills Children, Young Persons and Families Directorate
Strategic implementation	Youth Justice Board Crime and disorder reduction partnerships (at local level)	Pathfinder Children's Trusts and Regional Change Advisers
Operational delivery	Multi-agency Youth Offending Teams (YOTs) comprising social workers, police, probation, education and health workers	Multi-agency Children's Trusts comprising representatives from local education authority, children's social services departments, community and acute health services
Quasi-judicial	Youth Offender Panels	
Judicial	Youth Court	Family Proceedings Court

As previously noted, ever since the Children Act came into force in 1991, there have been two quite distinct jurisdictions catering respectively for children who may have committed criminal deeds and those with welfare needs, each of which has its own separate organizational structure. Within the 'criminal jurisdiction', the new youth justice reforms have brought about a much clearer division of responsibilities between different institutions than existed under the old system. Responsibility for policy-making remains with central government and mostly falls within the remit of the *Juvenile Offenders' Unit* in the Home Office.[38] Responsibility for overseeing the strategic development, direction, implementation and monitoring of youth justice policy, however, is now vested in a separate national body known as the *Youth Justice Board* (YJB).[39] This is a non-departmental public body (or 'quango') whose members are appointed by the Home Secretary. Its responsibilities include advising the Home Secretary on how the principal aim of the youth justice system (preventing offending) might most effectively be pursued, setting national standards, promoting good practice,[40] overseeing the provision of youth justice services and monitoring the operation of the system. It is also responsible for commissioning and managing 'the juvenile secure estate', i.e. all custodial and other secure facilities for young people under the age of 18.

Local authorities have also been given significant additional responsibilities relating to crime prevention and for formulating (in consultation with other agencies) annual youth justice plans to ensure the delivery of comprehensive youth justice services within their localities.[41] However, the primary operational responsibility for delivering those local services has been assigned to multi-agency *Youth Offending Teams* (or 'YOTs', as they have become colloquially known), which local authorities have also been required to establish.[42] The composition of each YOT is partially prescribed by statute: it must include representatives from the police, probation service, local education and health services and local authority social service departments, though it can also include other occupational groups.

In addition to their general task of preventing juvenile offending, Youth Offending Teams spend much of their time preparing reports for and generally servicing the *youth court*, a specialized version of the magistrates' court where offenders under 18 are prosecuted and, if convicted, sentenced. (Until 1992, this court was known as the 'juvenile court', and dealt only with offenders who had not reached the age of 17.) Youth court magistrates are drawn from a special panel of local magistrates who have particular experience of, or interest in, work with young people. Unlike adult magistrates' proceedings, youth courts are not open to the public, though in most other respects their procedures are broadly similar to their adult counterparts. Steps have been taken, however, to 'open up' the youth court by encouraging greater communication between youth court magistrates and young offenders and their families and making them more accessible to victims also (Allen et al., 2000; Home Office and Lord Chancellor's Department, 2001). The sentencing powers of the youth court have always included punitive measures (see below), notwithstanding the continuing statutory duty to 'have regard to the welfare of the child', though youth has traditionally been seen as a mitigating factor in sentencing.[43]

The establishment of YOTs and the wider institutional changes with which they are associated are a good example of the government's much-vaunted commitment to a more coordinated and integrated – or 'joined up' in the approved jargon[44] – approach to policy-making and service delivery. Radical though this reform programme was in many respects, it did nothing to disturb the marked institutional separation between the criminal jurisdiction dealing with the criminal needs of young offenders and the care jurisdiction dealing with the welfare needs of vulnerable young people.

Turning more briefly, now, to the care jurisdiction, this has also experienced further upheavals since 1989. A major catalyst for change has been the succession of damning reports following inquiries that have been set up to investigate the deaths of vulnerable children who have been let down by the care and protection authorities (e.g. Laming, 2003). This has prompted a succession of policy documents[45] and legislative guidance under the Children Act 2004, which set out a comprehensive programme of local and national action designed to bring about a transformation of children's services and the way they are delivered. The ongoing reform programme draws in many respects upon the experience gained in overhauling the 'offence jurisdiction', though with some significant differences.

As Table 9.1 (on p. 324) indicates, responsibility for policy-making with regard to the 'care jurisdiction' is now vested in the Children, Young Persons and Families Directorate located within the Department for Education and Skills. There is no overarching agency equivalent to the Youth Justice Board that is responsible for the strategic implementation of the programme. Instead, the government is relying on 35 'Pathfinder' Children's Trusts that were established in 2003 in order to pioneer and develop its preferred model[46] for achieving the closer integration and coordination of children's services within each local area. However, it has also appointed a number of Regional Change Advisers based in key government departments to supplement their role and work with local authorities and their partners in setting up Children's Trust arrangements. Children's Trusts are intended to operate on a multi-agency basis, coordinating the activities of local education authorities, children's social services departments[47] and also community and acute health services. They will be expected to operate on the basis of multi-disciplinary teams, joint training arrangements, better information-sharing procedures and a common assessment framework across all services. The government hopes that most local authorities will have Children's Trusts in place by 2006 and expects all to have done so by 2008. Judicial responsibility for the conduct of 'care and protection' litigation is unchanged and remains in the hands of the lower civil courts known as 'family proceedings courts'.

Whatever impact the reform programme may have on the level of coordination between children's service agencies, it will do little to bridge the sharp divide between their activities and those of the YOTs. For the foreseeable future, therefore, young people who offend will continue to be dealt with in criminal courts principally on the basis of their offending behaviour and largely irrespective of any welfare needs they might have. Taken as a whole, the government's reforms may conceivably bring about a greater degree of *'vertical'* coordination and integration within each jurisdiction, but they do little or nothing to promote *'horizontal'* coordination across the two jurisdictions. This would require a more holistic approach to be taken, in which account is taken of the welfare needs of young offenders as well as any criminal deeds that they may have committed.[48] Things could be managed differently. Scotland's unique system of children's hearings deals with both offence and care and protection cases within a civil procedure that combines a welfare approach with a strong diversionary commitment, and offers one accessible model of how such a system might operate (see Bottoms and Dignan, 2004 for details).

Putting 'Prevention' into Practice: Extending the Net of Social Control

9.6 The government has sought to pursue its aim of preventing juvenile offending by means of four key strategies:

1 Lowering or circumventing the minimum age thresholds for prosecution;
2 Extending the range of pre-emptive interventions;
3 Strengthening the array of reactive measures for dealing with young offenders; and
4 Broadening the category of unacceptable and punishable behaviour.

The *age of criminal responsibility* in England and Wales is 10, which is one of the lowest in Western Europe.[49] Before 1998, the effect of this low threshold was mitigated to some extent by the doctrine of *doli incapax*,[50] whereby children between the ages of 10 and 13 could only be convicted of an offence if the prosecution could establish that they knew the difference between right and wrong. However, this doctrine was abolished by section 34 of the Crime and Disorder Act 1998, as a result of which all children of 10 or over are now liable to prosecution. Moreover, even children below this age are increasingly exposed to the risk of formal intervention by a range of criminal justice and other agencies, as we shall see shortly.

In pursuit of its preventive agenda, the New Labour government introduced a variety of purely *pre-emptive initiatives* directed at 'pre-delinquent' young people: those who are considered likely to engage in criminal, disruptive or anti-social behaviour. Their aim has been to divert them in other directions and to encourage their 'social inclusion' into the law-abiding community. They include play schemes known as 'Splash',[51] which seek to engage 13 to 17-year-olds living in deprived areas who are considered to be at risk of offending by providing them with a range of purposeful activities during school holidays. Youth Inclusion Programmes (YIPs) are somewhat similar but operate throughout the year in some of the most deprived neighbourhoods in England and Wales,[52] where they seek to engage and work with those most at risk of offending, including those who fail to regularly attend school. A further variation on a broadly similar theme involves the establishment of multi-agency teams known as Youth Inclusion and Support Panels (YISPs) in areas with high levels of street crime. Their task is to identify and offer support to young children aged between 8 and 13 (and also their parents) whose anti-social or problematic behaviour is considered to put them at high risk of offending. Ninety-two local authorities had set up YISPs by the end of 2004, and the government had pledged to increase the number by 50 per cent by 2008 (Home Office, 2004c).[53]

In addition to these schemes, some of which seek to provide positive alternatives to criminal activity as 'carrots' to discourage misbehaviour, the government also created a number of new 'sticks' – sanctions and coercive measures intended to 'nip in the bud' incipient criminality in a 'zero tolerance' fashion. The Crime and Disorder Act 1998 and later legislation empowered local authorities to introduce local *child curfews* banning children under the age of 10 – later raised to 16 – from streets and other public places at night unless supervised by a responsible adult.[54] Powers have also been introduced enabling police officers to issue *dispersal orders* against groups of two or more young people under the age of 16 in designated areas, requiring them to disperse and, if after 9 p.m., to return home.[55]

As well as these 'preventive' initiatives, the government has also introduced an extensive array of '*reactive* measures', several of which have proved highly controversial. One such measure involves a quasi-criminal procedure known as a *child safety order*. This is imposed by a civil court (the magistrates' family proceedings court) on the application of a local authority social services department. Child safety orders may be imposed on children under the age of 10 who have committed (or are thought to be at risk of committing) an act for which they could have been prosecuted if over the age of 10, or who have behaved in an 'anti-social' manner. The effect of a child safety order is to place the child under the supervision of a social worker or youth justice worker[56] subject to whatever specific requirements may be imposed by the court. For example, the court may seek to ensure that the child receives appropriate care, protection and support and is subject to proper control; or to prevent any repetition of the behaviour that gave rise to the order. Very little use has been made of this power as yet, however, and only 12 such orders had been imposed in the 21-month period following their introduction.[57]

The most contentious of the reactive measures is another quasi-criminal intervention known as the *anti-social behaviour order* (ASBO; in operation since 1999).[58] ASBOs are technically civil orders, but they can have severe consequences in the event of non-compliance. The orders may be issued against any person aged 10 or over who has acted 'in an anti-social manner', defined as behaviour 'that caused or was likely to cause harassment, alarm or distress to one of more persons not of the same household'. Although it was originally expected that ASBOs would chiefly be used against adults (Home Office, 1998a), between 40 and 60 per cent of ASBOs have been imposed on persons aged 10–17.[59] In response to pressure from the Youth Justice Board, young people who are subject to an ASBO may now also be assigned to a YOT-based 'responsible officer' with the power to issue directions to them for a period of six months.[60]

ASBOs may be made in civil proceedings by a magistrates' court following an application by the local council, chief police officer or a registered social landlord including Housing Action Trusts; or they may be made by a criminal court following a conviction.[61] If the proceedings are civil, the rules of evidence and standard of proof are less rigorous, since the past anti-social behaviour only has to be proved 'on the balance of probabilities' rather than beyond reasonable doubt. This is one of the reasons why the order has proved to be so controversial in practice (see Gardner et al., 1998). Critics are also alarmed at the vagueness of the term 'anti-social behaviour' and the fact that only 1 per cent of applications were refused in the first five years in which they were available.[62] All ASBO applications in civil proceedings are heard in the adult magistrates' court, regardless of the age of the person against whom it is sought. This has also proved to be a contentious issue, not least because the reporting restrictions that normally apply in the youth court do not routinely operate in a magistrates' court. As a result, ASBO proceedings are often reported in the press with the youngsters involved being named, although this would not be possible if they were convicted of an actual crime in the youth court.

The order itself may contain any kind of prohibition which the court feels is necessary to prevent further anti-social behaviour from the recipient of the order. Failure to comply with an ASBO is an offence. For juveniles aged 10 to 17 the maximum sentence is a 24-month detention and training order (see section 9.7 below).[63] Just under half (47 per cent) of ASBOs issued to persons aged 10–17 during the period 1 June 2000 to 31 December 2003 were breached,[64] and a YJB study shows that 43 per cent of young people under the age of 18 who breach them receive an immediate custodial term (Brogan, 2005: 18). This has fuelled concerns that ASBOs are increasingly accelerating young people into custody, thereby escalating the juvenile prison population and adding to the accommodation pressures experienced by the juvenile secure estate. The use of ASBOs on young people has been strongly criticized by, among others, the former Head of the prison and correctional services Martin Narey and Rod Morgan, former Director of the Youth Justice Board. Mr Narey has said that the overuse of ASBOs was 'unnecessarily catapulting children into a custodial system which has so many children in it that the chances of rehabilitation are extremely slim and the chances of deeper criminalization very likely'. Professor Morgan has warned that children were being 'demonized' and labelled with 'the mark of Cain', and that 'we are sucking into the criminal justice system behaviour which should be capable, and used to be capable, of being dealt with by informal, non-criminal means'.[65] Doubts about the effectiveness of ASBOs in curbing anti-social behaviour have been buttressed by research suggesting that they are regarded by many offending teenagers and their parents as 'badges of honour' (Youth Justice Board, 2006).

Prior to 1998, criminal justice commentators (e.g. Moynihan, 1992; Garland, 1996) had spoken of a tendency for criminal justice agencies to moderate their ambitions by 'defining deviance down' and only invoking formal interventions in respect of the more serious forms of criminal wrongdoing. As the title of the 1998 Crime and Disorder Act makes clear, however, this process has been dramatically reversed and *the category of unacceptable and punishable behaviour has been broadened*. It is no longer restricted to actual crime, but also encompasses a wide and ill-defined range of 'disorderly' and 'anti-social' conduct.

The government's approach to anti-social behaviour is based on a 'zero tolerance' mentality, though the phrase itself is no longer used. Its preference for summary justice that is administered with scant regard for traditional legal safeguards[66] betrays an increasingly authoritarian attitude towards young people whose behaviour may be deemed unacceptable even though it falls a long way short of what would have been considered criminal in the past. As for those who do go on to offend, or reoffend, the prevailing principle that underpins the operation of the 'new youth justice' system itself is one of 'progressive interventionism', whereby increasingly intrusive measures are taken with each successive transgression.

Responding to Youth Crime: The Youth Justice System in Operation

9.7 The youth justice system, which deals with young offenders between their tenth and eighteenth birthdays,[67] is summarized diagrammatically in Figure 9.1 and differs in certain respects from the equivalent scheme for adults shown in Figure I.1 in the Introduction. The police and Crown Prosecution Service (CPS) have a number of 'diversionary' options available to them when dealing with young offenders, which provide an alternative to prosecution (see boxes 2–5). Where the offence is very trivial or there is insufficient evidence linking it to a suspected offender, the police may decide to take no further action (NFA), which effectively means that the case is dropped (box 2). Alternatively, they may decide to issue an informal warning (box 3), which means that no formal record is made and the incident cannot be mentioned in court in the event of future proceedings. Since 1998, however, this practice has been discouraged by the Home Office, which has

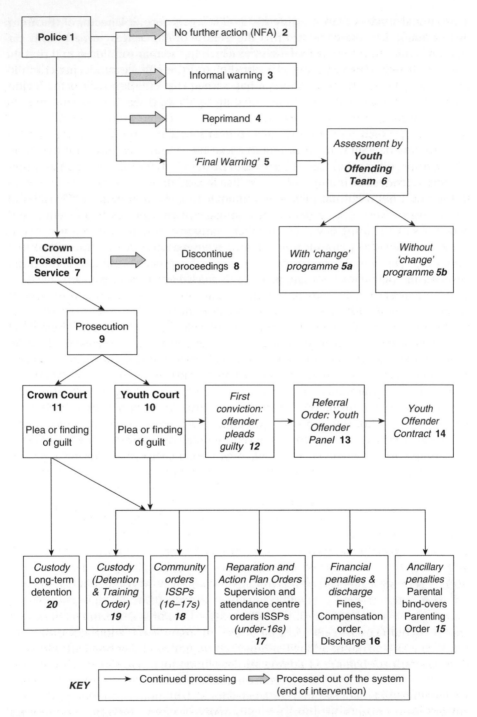

Figure 9.1 *The English youth justice system (for under 1-18s)*

been keen to hold offenders accountable for any wrongdoing. Consequently, the approach that is now favoured relies on a graded system of formal warnings leading up to a prosecution in the event of reoffending.

Under the new statutory regime that was introduced by the Crime and Disorder Act 1998,[68] the appropriate response for a young offender committing a minor offence for the first time is for the police to issue a *reprimand* (box 4), which is a formal warning that is recorded. If a further minor offence is committed, this is liable to be dealt with by means of a *'final warning'* (the statutory name for which is simply 'warning'; box 5), which is intended as a 'last chance' measure after which any further offending is almost certain to result in prosecution. When a young person is issued with a final warning, the police are also required to refer the case to the local Youth Offending Team (box 6), which should then undertake an assessment to identify the factors that may have been responsible for the offending behaviour. If some form of intervention is thought appropriate in order to address such problems, the young person will be required to participate in a 'change programme' (the statutory name for which is a 'rehabilitation programme'; box 5a), and the Home Office has made it clear that it expects this to be the norm.[69] The system of reprimands and final warnings is thus intended to operate on a progressive 'three strikes and you're out' basis, culminating almost inevitably in a prosecution if there is a third minor offence. However, if any of the previous offences are felt to be sufficiently serious, the police and CPS are expected to move straight to a prosecution rather than proceeding down the diversionary route.

Decisions on whether suspected offenders should be charged and prosecuted are now taken by the CPS (box 7) rather than the police. The CPS can also decide to discontinue prosecution proceedings at a later stage (box 8). Discontinuation may occur because the CPS considers either that the available evidence is insufficiently strong or that it is not in the public interest to prosecute.

When young offenders under the age of 18 are prosecuted, their cases are normally dealt with by the youth court (box 10), though exceptionally in more serious cases they may be tried and sentenced instead by the adult Crown Court (box 11).[70] Where a young offender is being prosecuted for the first time and decides to plead guilty, the youth court is normally obliged to deal with such cases by passing a sentence known as a 'referral order', which is a special procedure that was introduced in April 2002 (box 12).[71] This order requires the young offender to attend a meeting of the Youth Offender Panel or 'YOP' (box 13).

The YOP is convened by the local Youth Offending Team (YOT), which also provides one member of the three-person YOP panel, the other two being lay members drawn from an approved list of volunteers. The YOP procedure was inspired in part by restorative justice thinking (see above, section 9.3) and, consequently, the victim of an offence may be invited to attend, in addition to the young offender and his or her parents. The purpose of the panel meeting is to provide a forum in which the offence can be discussed with the victim, if present, and to devise an appropriate 'youth offender contract' (box 14) containing one or more elements that are intended to prevent further offending (with reparation also featuring prominently). The duration of the order (between 3 and 12 months) is determined by the youth court on the basis of the seriousness of the offence, though the terms of the contract are a matter for negotiation within the panel. If no agreement can be reached, however, or the offender fails to comply with the agreement, the young offender will be returned to the court to be sentenced for the original offence.

For offenders who are prosecuted and sentenced in the normal way, a wide range of disposals is available. These can be divided into three main categories: custodial penalties; community sentences; and other penalties including financial penalties, warnings and certain ancillary measures.

Prior to 1998, among the lower-level disposals (box 16), the principal penalty for dealing with young offenders appearing in the youth court for the first time for less serious offences was the conditional discharge (see Chapter 5, section 5.2). However, statute now discourages its use for most such offenders,[72] and it has declined sharply. Other lower-level disposals include fines and compensation orders, both of which may be imposed either on young offenders themselves or their parents.

Since 1998, a new penalty has been available for less serious offenders aged under 18 in the form of the reparation order (box 17).[73] Such orders require young offenders to make reparation either to the victim of the offence (provided the victim consents to this) or to the community at large (for example, by doing unpaid work). Although the court is supposed to specify the nature of the reparation that is to be undertaken, in practice the YOT has an important part to play in assessing and advising what may be appropriate, and also in facilitating and monitoring it. The reparation that is imposed must be proportionate to the seriousness of the offence, and may not exceed 24 hours in total while the reparation order itself lasts for a maximum of three months. Although the courts are required to give reasons for not imposing such an order where they have the power to do so, in practice its usage appears to have been largely eclipsed by the introduction of the referral order.[74]

Another relatively recent measure that has been available to the courts since 1998 is the 'action plan order'[75] (box 17 in Fig 9.1). This is designed to provide a short (three months) but intensive and individually tailored intervention in a young person's life, focused on addressing the factors that are felt to be responsible for the offence. As with the reparation order, YOTs are also actively engaged in advising the Youth Court about the possible content of the order, coordinating arrangements and also supervising offenders while completing it.

Other community sentences are also available for offenders under 16, including the supervision order and attendance centre order (box 17 in Fig 9.1), both of which pre-date the introduction of the action plan order. Offenders aged 16 to 17 are now liable to be dealt with by means of the new generic community order that we described in Chapter 5, section 5.2.

In addition, since 2001, new community-based Intensive Supervision and Surveillance Programmes (ISSPs)[76] have been introduced, which can be attached to supervision orders, community orders or bail supervision packages. (ISSPs may also form part of the post-custodial supervision arrangements for those given detention and training orders (see below).) They were originally intended to be 'targeted' on persistent offenders who have been charged or warned at least four times within a 12-month period, and who have previously been subject to a custodial sentence or community service order. The criteria were later extended to include offenders who were less persistent but who had committed more serious offences, or who had a history of repeat offending while on bail. ISSPs involve intensive monitoring of the young offender's movements and whereabouts by means such as electronic monitoring and telephone monitoring using voice verification technology. They also include highly structured individually tailored packages of measures that are intended to address the young person's offending behaviour (for example, training and education programmes lasting up to five hours per day) and they, too, are intended to encourage the performance of reparation.

A study of the original pilot trial, when ISSPs were introduced in selected areas only, found that just under half the ISSPs were completed successfully, with 31 per cent of those who breached the requirements being sent to custody. Ninety-one per cent of youngsters given ISSPs were reconvicted at least once in the following two years; but this was hardly surprising since they had committed an average of 11.6 offences in the previous two years. In fact, both the frequency and seriousness of offending was reduced, as was the use of custody for young offenders in the ISSP areas. However, these changes were probably not attributable to the ISSPs themselves, since similar results were also reported from comparison areas without ISSPs (Gray et al., 2005).

So far the sentences that we have mentioned are imposed on the young offenders themselves (although parents can be ordered to pay their fines and compensation orders). However, there are also various orders which can be imposed on the parents of young offenders (box 15 in Figure 9.1), some of which have been around for a considerable time. One such measure is the parental bind-over, a common law power that enables the court to require any person to 'be of good behaviour and keep the peace' on forfeit of a specified sum of money. Since 1998 the courts can also issue a 'parenting order' against the parents or guardians of young offenders or those who are guilty of 'anti-social behaviour' (Crime and Disorder Act 1998, s. 8). The parenting order consists of two main elements. The first requires parents to attend counselling or guidance sessions, which can last for up to three months and which are intended to improve their parenting skills. The second may require parents to exercise a measure of control over their child (for example, by ensuring that they attend school, or avoid certain people or places) for a period of up to 12 months. Failure to comply with the order (which is supervised by YOT workers) constitutes a criminal offence punishable with a fine of up to £1,000.

With regard to custodial options (box 19 in Figure 9.1), young offenders between the ages of 12 and 18 may be given a detention and training order (DTO) for a period of between 4 and 24 months if certain criteria are satisfied.[77] The first half of a DTO is served in custody, while the second half is served under supervision in the community. Offenders aged 18 to 20 presently may receive a sentence of 'detention in a young offender institution' (YOI),[78] although the government plans in future to make this age group liable to receive adult sentences of imprisonment.[79] Finally, with regard to those young offenders who are, exceptionally, dealt with by the Crown Court (box 11), additional custodial options are also available (box 20). If the offence is murder, the penalty will be a mandatory indeterminate sentence of long-term detention known as 'detention at Her Majesty's pleasure'.[80] For other serious offences, a specified period of long-term detention may be imposed. This 'long-term detention' is subject to the same maximum lengths as in the case of adult offenders.

Young offenders who are sentenced to custody may be held in one of three main types of facilities, which together comprise the *'juvenile secure estate'*. Younger children (up to the age of 16) may be kept in *secure children's homes* run by local authorities (accounting for 235 places in April 2005); privately run *secure training centres* (STCs) house boys aged 12 to 15 and girls between 12 and 17 (274 places); while *young offender institutions* (YOIs) account for 84 per cent (2,700 places) of the estate. These young offender institutions, which are run by the Prison Service, cater for offenders aged 15 to 20. Even though they are physically separate from adult prisons, the facilities and regimes in young offender institutions are not that different from those catering for adult inmates, although the long-term objective is to deal with under-18s entirely separately from all older offenders in the future.

The government has set out its agenda for further reform of the youth justice system over the next few years, though it is clear that no major change of approach is envisaged.[81] It proposes to enact that the sentencing of juveniles should have a single purpose – to prevent offending. This would represent a further erosion of the welfare principle and would arguably put Britain in breach of its international treaty obligations under the United Nations Convention on the Rights of the Child (see also Ball, 2004: 34). It also plans to simplify the range of juvenile sentences by replacing the existing non-custodial measures for offenders under 16 with a single, more flexible order[82] lasting between one and 12 months that would incorporate two or possibly three interventions from a comprehensive menu of options. The referral order would continue to operate as at present, although it could in future be made available as an option for the court on a second or subsequent court appearance, which is not currently allowed.

With regard to custody, the government proposes to augment the existing detention and training order with an Intensive Supervision or Detention Order for serious and repeat offenders. This would provide two standard options: either six months of intensive programmes followed by six months' normal supervision or a period spent in custody followed by an equivalent period under intensive supervision (along the lines of the current detention and training order). This would be available for offenders as young as 12–14 years old, though the maximum duration for this age group would be 12 months as opposed to 24 months for 15–17 year olds.

The government also favours the development of new-style custodial units nearer to major population centres. At the time of writing, however, these remained statements of intent. So too did the Youth Justice Board's target of reducing the number of under-18s in custody by 10 per cent between March 2005 and March 2008. More recently, former Home Secretary John Reid had expressed renewed interest in getting the army involved in the delivery of punishment for young offenders in order to 'provide structure' in their lives (*Guardian*, 22 July 2006). Although the proposal was couched in terms of 'thinking outside the box', it represents a retrograde step in the direction of previous militaristic interventions such as the 'short sharp shock' and 'boot camps' that have been tried and have failed in the past.

Concluding Assessment: No More Excuses?

9.8 The flurry of developments since 1998 generally fits the 'neo-correctionalist' model well, although it represents something of a mixture of approaches. The Strategy A 'law and order' inclinations of the previous Conservative government retain a presence, for example in the 'finality' of the final warning (where previously further cautioning might have been an option).[83] Other examples include the lowering of the minimum age for curfews with electronic tagging to 16, not to mention the 1997 White Paper's title *No More Excuses* and much of the government's rhetoric. One particular strain of Strategy A which is well in evidence here – though less openly acknowledged than in the past – is the notion of 'zero tolerance', which underpins the government's continuing preoccupation with tackling anti-social behaviour. On the other hand, measures such as the final warning, reparation, action plan and referral orders also contain a welcome – if overly eclectic – element of restorative justice. There is in addition a great deal of managerial Strategy B in the neo-correctional mix. This is reflected in measures to produce a more 'joined-up' youth justice system; to speed up the prosecution process, overhaul the culture of youth justice; and to drive up standards nationally by means of the Youth Justice Board.

Managerialism, combined with a laudable desire to protect offenders in the younger age ranges, is also evident in the government's policy towards *custody* for young offenders. In 1997 a 'Thematic Review' by Chief Inspector of Prisons Sir David Ramsbotham recommended that children under 18 should be dealt with separately from those of 18 and over, and that the Prison Service should lose all responsibility for them (HM Inspectorate of Prisons, 1997c). Since 2000, the Youth Justice Board has been responsible for the commissioning of places and for regime standards in the juvenile secure estate. It remains to be seen whether significant improvements can be achieved over the lamentably poor conditions, regimes and training programmes uncovered by the Chief Inspector in his 1997 Thematic Review and in many inspections of individual institutions before and since. Even if things do improve for those under 18 who find themselves in custody, this is unlikely to be the case with 'young adults' aged 18 to 20, who will in future be given adult sentences of imprisonment and serve them in adult prisons (see also Lyon, 2003).

But of equal importance to the way young people are treated when in custody is the prior question of how many young offenders find their way into custody – and for how long – in the first place. Here, as with adult offenders, the overall trend in the early 2000s is still significantly upwards. The number of people under 21 in custody under sentence almost doubled from 5,319 in 1994 to 10,351 in 2005.[84] Once again, as with adults, this is driven by court sentencing decisions. In 1994, 17,200 people under 21 received custodial sentences; in 2004 the figure was 20,961, an increase of 22 per cent, though it had been as high as 25,855 (an increase of 50 per cent) in 2000.[85]

Similarly, the number of 15 to 17-year-olds in prison more than doubled over the same period from 840 in 1994 to 1,836 in 2005 (NOMS, 2005f; 2006d). Despite the welcome reduction in the number of 10 to 17-year-old offenders sentenced to custody since the all-time high recorded in 1999 (RDS NOMS, 2005b: Table 2.3), the average length of custodial sentence imposed on 10 to 17-year-old offenders at both magistrates' court and Crown Court has been relentlessly upwards. In the Crown Court the average length of sentence imposed on this age group for indictable offences was 23.3 months in 2004 compared with 16.6 months a decade earlier, an increase of 40 per cent.[86] Sentence lengths for older age groups also increased over the same period, but less dramatically: 35 per cent in the case of 18 to 20-year-old offenders and 31 per cent in the case of adult offenders. In the magistrates' court the disparity was even starker, for average sentence lengths for 10 to 17-year-olds increased from 3.8 months in 1994 to 7.2 months a decade later, an increase of 89.5 per cent, whereas they declined slightly in respect of both young adults and adult offenders.[87] By October 2006, youth justice was heading for a 'system disaster' to parallel the crisis in the adult penal system as the Youth Justice Board warned that the secure estate 'faced meltdown' with only a handful of beds left available as the number of incarcerated under-18s exceeded 3,350 (*Guardian Unlimited*, 24 October 2006).

We continue, therefore, to incarcerate large numbers of young people, despite the abiding truism that 'prison doesn't work' to reform young offenders. Certain kinds of intervention – such as 'cognitive behavioural' training to try to alter attitudes towards crime – may well help to reduce offending. This is more likely to happen, however, where the young person is not locked up in custody (McGuire, 1995; Vennard et al., 1997; Andrews et al., 1990: 382; Lipsey, 1992: 138). Yet the government remains reluctant to take effective steps to substantially reduce the use of custody for young people.

We think this is a mistake. Essentially there are two opposing views about young offenders: the 'zero tolerance' view (Strategy A) and the Strategy C approach which combines an inclination to 'minimum intervention' with a preference for restorative and rehabilitative measures where intervention is warranted. The government continues to reject the view that young offenders simply grow out of crime – although in general it seems that they do (Cavadino et al., 1999: 182–4; Flood-Page et al., 2000: 18–19) – and that tough early intervention is needed to nip offending in the bud. Even if some of this 'tough early intervention' takes positive forms such as reparation or programmes to confront offending behaviour, getting tough earlier simply increases the likelihood that young offenders will suffer the adverse effects of stigmatizing 'labelling'. These effects include accelerating young people 'up the tariff' into overcrowded and damaging custodial institutions before they have a chance to grow out of crime.

The government's current approach borrows extensively from the pioneering work done by the proponents of systems management from the 1980s onwards, for example in its emphasis on system-wide thinking and coordination and cooperation between agencies. Unfortunately, however, its quest for a joined-up approach has failed to devise a coherent strategy for dealing with the many young people with acute welfare needs who also get in trouble with the law. Likewise, its aspirations to prevent young people offending concentrate for the most part on addressing a narrow range of 'criminogenic factors' (such as faulty parenting and petty anti-social behaviour) rather than the underlying social problems that give rise to them. We think the government should be more realistic, and accept that, whatever exactly it does with young offenders, the potential of the criminal justice system to prevent juvenile offending is strictly limited. There are no quick fixes to juvenile crime. Accepting this, it would make sense for the government to borrow more from systems management, adopting its humanitarian (Strategy C) goals and its minimum-intervention bias[88] as well as its managerial (Strategy B) techniques while simultaneously increasing the emphasis on restorative justice and other constructive approaches. Such techniques may or may not have a serious impact on the level of juvenile crime, but at least they could help us to avoid damaging young lives – in particular by the excessive use of penal custody – to the extent we currently do.

Notes

1   Public attitudes with regard to youth justice and restorative justice are explored more fully in Hough and Roberts (2005).
2   A recent study suggests that in comparison with other European citizens, Britons are more likely to express concern about anti-social behaviour on the part of young people and, conversely, less likely to challenge such behaviour themselves for fear of reprisals (ADT Europe, 2006).
3   It is also the case, but often overlooked, that children and young people are more than twice as likely as any other age group to be *victims* of crime (Wood, 2003; Evans, K., 2005).
4   For offenders under 18, 'cautions' now include 'reprimands' and 'warnings' – explained later in this chapter and in the Introduction – which were introduced under the Crime and Disorder Act 1998.
5   In 2004, male offenders under 18 were mainly found guilty or cautioned for theft and handling stolen goods (37.5 per cent), whereas the corresponding figure for males over the age of 21 was 31 per cent. (These figures and those in the text are taken or calculated from Home Office, 2005). Likewise in a recent large-scale, self-report survey almost eight in ten of the incidents reported to the survey were described as being of a less serious nature. The most numerous were non-injury assaults (28 per cent of all incidents measured); the selling of non-Class A substances (19 per cent); and thefts from either workplace or school (16 per cent) (Budd et al., 2005).
6   Calculated from the prison statistics published by NOMS (2005e: Table 1).
7   An international self-report study found that 44 per cent of young people in England and Wales admitted to delinquent behaviour in the previous year compared with between 57 and 72 per cent in Portugal, Spain, the Netherlands and Switzerland (Junger-Tas et al., 1994).
8   A survey conducted by the Howard League for Penal Reform (2006b) revealed that on 12 May 2006 nearly one-third (709) of the 2,351 children in custody had been assessed as vulnerable by their Youth Offending Team.
9   The former term is now used more generally following the establishment of the 'youth court' in place of the 'juvenile court' by the Criminal Justice Act 1991. However, the term 'juvenile' is still useful to refer (since 1992) to the age range 10 to 17 inclusive.
10 See the previous edition of this book (Cavadino and Dignan, 2002) for a fuller chronological account of these developments.

11 With the exception of the last two models. Although the origins of the restorative justice model can be traced back to the mid-1980s, it is only since 1997 that it has begun to exert a serious influence on youth justice policy-making. Since then, however, the influence of the neo-correctionalist model has been predominant, which is why we leave it until the end.

12 Though an equally radical reform of the Scottish juvenile justice system was implemented at around the same time by the Social Work (Scotland) Act 1968. This has prevailed largely intact despite the discrediting of the rehabilitative ideal in the adult sphere during the 1970s (Martin and Murray, 1982; Pratt, 1986; Bottoms and Dignan, 2004).

13 Figures abstracted and calculated from Home Office (1981a: Table 7.7).

14 Including Scotland and also the Scandinavian countries; see Cavadino and Dignan (2006: ch. 15).

15 The influence of justice model thinking can also be discerned in the introduction (in 1982) of 'gatekeeping' criteria that had to be met before juvenile courts were authorized to impose a custodial sentence.

16 Criminal Justice Act 1991 (s. 70), which came into force in 1992.

17 Imposed by section 44(1) Children and Young Persons Act 1933 (see above).

18 See also Schur (1973), who propounded a somewhat similar 'radical non-intervention' strategy as the best way of dealing with young offenders. Elsewhere the approach is often referred to as the 'juvenile diversion movement'.

19 So called because of their association with Lancaster University's Centre of Youth, Crime and Community.

20 Figure 9.1 (presented later in this chapter) illustrates the various diversionary routes at different stages throughout the contemporary process. Many of the mechanisms that were developed or invoked by the Lancaster group systems analysis exponents have been superseded by more recent reforms that we describe below. Former mechanisms included the use of multi-agency 'cautioning panels' (replaced by a new statutory framework for reprimands and final warnings and multi-agency youth offending teams) and also 'intermediate treatment' which was once a pivotal diversionary, non-custodial penalty for young offenders. See previous editions of this book for a more detailed account of their operations and impact.

21 By 1992, 82 per cent of known indictable offenders under the age of 17 were being cautioned, compared with just 49 per cent in 1980 (calculated from Home Office, 1990b and 1993: Table 5.22). As for diversion from custody, the percentage of custodial sentences imposed on prosecuted male offenders aged between 14 and 16 declined from a peak of 12 per cent in the years 1979 to 1985 to 7 per cent in 1990, though it had increased to 9 per cent by 1992. In some parts of the country the impact of systems management was so marked that particular localities declared themselves 'custody-free zones' for juveniles under 17.

22 Notwithstanding its influence on youth justice policy and practice, systems management doctrine is open to objection from classicist adherents of the justice model on the grounds that decisions relating to detected offenders should be based on rules applied by courts of law rather than out-of-court discretion. Moreover, welfare model advocates may object to it on the grounds that diversion alone will do nothing to address a suspect's welfare needs. Others (e.g. Pitts, 1986, 1988) have criticized it on theoretical and political grounds.

23 The New Zealand youth justice system has gone further then most in implementing such an approach; see Morris, A. (2004). Closer to home, however, recent reforms to the Northern Ireland youth justice system have also been very heavily influenced by restorative justice thinking; see Dignan (2006).

24 See, for example, Davis et al. (1988, 1989). This did not apply to all such schemes, however; see Dignan (1991, 1992).

25 The restorative justice approach has also been criticized by justice model adherents (see in particular Ashworth (2002) and von Hirsch et al. (2003) who distrust its lack of formalism and rejection of rule-based outcomes), on the grounds that it fails to address their concerns about the need for proportionality and consistency.

26 Detention centres had initially been established by the Criminal Justice Act 1948 to provide a brisker, more militaristic, deterrence-based alternative to the reform-oriented borstal system, but apart from the length of sentence differentials, the distinctions between the two had become increasingly blurred over the years. See previous editions of this book for a fuller account of the measure and its shortcomings.

27 The moral panic was fuelled in part by claims made by various interest groups (notably police organizations) about the supposed extent of juvenile crime and partly by the public response to the shocking murder of 2-year-old James Bulger by two 10-year-old boys in Liverpool in February 1993. See Cavadino and Dignan (2002) for further details.

28 The name 'boot camp' was applied somewhat indiscriminately. One based at Colchester in which young offenders were dealt with alongside military offenders in the Ministry of Defence's military corrective training centre more closely resembled the typical American boot camp. However, the first English institution to bear this name – at Thorn Cross in Cheshire, which opened in 1996 – was less tough, less militaristic and more constructive than its American namesakes.

29 In many welfare-oriented youth justice systems, the jurisdiction of the juvenile court has encompassed not just conventional criminal offences but also so-called 'status offences' where the behaviour in question (for example, truancy, drinking alcohol and sexual behaviour) was only criminalized if engaged in by juveniles.

30 In practice the government has not always waited for the evidence to become available before pressing ahead with its youth justice reform programme. The decision to 'roll out' Youth Offending Teams nationally, for example, was taken before the findings of the pilot evaluation were known.

31 See previous editions (Cavadino and Dignan, 1997 and 2002) for a more detailed analysis of youth justice under the previous Conservative government.

32 Children and Young Persons Act 1933 (s. 44(1)). Also left in place was the duty of sentencers to impose sentences commensurate with the seriousness of the offence (for which see now Criminal Justice Act 2003, ss. 148, 152–3).

33 The term has also been used in a very different sense by Garland (1996: 452), to mean the increasing tendency for the modern state to devolve responsibility for crime prevention and other responses to crime onto other agencies, private organizations and individuals.

34 Crime and Disorder Act 1998 (s. 8). Parenting orders may be imposed in a variety of contexts, including where a child has committed an offence, acted anti-socially or is made subject to a child safety order or a referral order.

35 This new approach was reflected in the title – *No More Excuses* – of the official policy paper that preceded the Crime and Disorder Act 1998, and also in a hard-hitting preface from the then Home Secretary, Jack Straw (Home Office, 1997a).

36 One of five key pledges in the Labour Party's 1997 manifesto was to halve the average time taken to bring persistent young offenders to court from 142 to 71 days (Labour Party, 1997). This was achieved by August 2001 (Audit Commission, 2004: 28).

37 Table 9.1 and the accompanying text need to be read in the light of the important departmental restructuring that took place just as the book was going to press in the early summer of 2007. Please note in particular the creation of a separate Ministry of Justice that has assumed many of the responsibilities previously undertaken by the Home Office, and also the replacement of the Department for Education and Skills by the Department for Children, Schools and Families. Under the new arrangements the Ministry of Justice will sponsor the Youth Justice Board, but both departments will share

responsibility for youth justice policy-making. In addition, a new directorate for young people has been established within the Department for Children, Schools and Families to help co-ordinate youth policy across Whitehall. Whether these changes are ultimately successful in achieving the kind of 'horizontal co-ordination' across the hitherto segmented 'criminal' and 'care' jurisdictions that we advocate in this section remains to be seen, but they could be viewed as an important step in the right direction.

38 The government itself, of course, retains the final say on policy-making. For example, responsibility for developing the recent 'Respect Agenda' was vested in a cross-government team comprising the Deputy Prime Minister, Treasury and Home Office, with Prime Minister Tony Blair himself clearly being actively involved in setting the agenda and driving the initiative forward.

39 Set up by the Crime and Disorder Act 1998 (s. 41). On 3 April 2006 it announced that it would formally become known simply by its acronym as the YJB.

40 The YJB also has grant-making powers to promote the development and evaluation of innovative practices, which it has used, inter alia, to fund projects to develop restorative justice initiatives and also mentoring and cognitive behavioural programmes.

41 The 1998 Crime and Disorder Act set up Crime and Disorder Reduction Partnerships to bring together key players such as local authorities, the police, probation service, health authorities, the voluntary sector, businesses and local residents. Their function is to audit levels of crime and disorder in their areas, consult with the local population and devise local strategies to tackle those problems identified locally as priorities. See also Table 9.1.

42 Crime and Disorder Act 1998 (ss. 38–40). The composition, powers and early development of Youth Offending Teams is described more fully in Holdaway et al. (2001).

43 In general young offenders tend to be sentenced less harshly than adults who have committed similar offences (see, for exampe, for example, Flood-Page and Mackie, 1998: 123–4).

44 Geoff Mulgan (1998), special advisor to the Prime Minister, is credited with coining the epithet.

45 See, for example, the Green Paper *Every Child Matters* (Chief Secretary to the Treasury, 2003); see also HM Government (2004) and the other papers referred to on the government website: http://www.everychildmatters.gov.uk/publications/

46 Unlike YOTs, there is no statutory obligation to set up a Children's Trust, though the Children's Act 2004 does impose a duty on children's service agencies to cooperate and gives them power to pool their budgets as also happens with YOTs.

47 Who are responsible for 'looked after' children, as children 'in care', are now called.

48 Dame Butler-Sloss, who retired as President of the High Court's Family Division in 2005, has recently proposed that young offenders with welfare needs should be diverted from the criminal courts and dealt with through the care system instead (*Guardian*, 12 December 2005).

49 See Cavadino and Dignan (2006: 298). It is eight in Scotland. In 2005, the European Social Rights Committee declared the UK to be in breach of Article 17 of the European Social Charter because the age of criminal responsibility is 'manifestly too low' (Children's Rights Alliance, 2005).

50 'Incapable of evil intent'.

51 Subsequently renamed as 'Positive Activities for Young People'.

52 There were 72 such programmes in 2005.

53 More recently the government has proposed intervening *even before a potential young offender is born*, by identifying familial risk factors and providing a range of interventions, some of them compulsory (*Guardian*, 1 and 6 September 2006).

54 Crime and Disorder Act 1998 (s. 14); Criminal Justice and Police Act 2001 (s. 48). The power was successfully challenged by a 15-year-old boy who persuaded the court that

the police were not authorized to enforce such a measure where no criminal offence had been committed (*R (W) v. Commissioner of Police of the Metropolis and Another* [2005] EWHC 1586 (Admin); (2005) 3 All ER 749.)

55 Anti-Social Behaviour Act 2003 (s. 30). These powers are available when a local authority has designated an area in response to an application by a police superintendent who is satisfied that people in the area have been affected by anti-social behaviour on the part of groups in the locality. In the first nine months following their introduction, dispersal orders were authorized in over 400 localities, covering approximately half of all crime and disorder reduction partnership areas (Hazel Blears, H.C. Deb. 20 December 2004 (pt 1), col. 1894).

56 The effect is much the same as might be achieved under the auspices of the 1989 Children Act by imposing a supervision order designed to safeguard the child's welfare, apart from the fact that the ground for invoking the order is specifically offence-related. Moreover, the normal 'paramountcy of the child' principle that is set out in the Children Act does not apply to such orders.

57 April 2000 to December 2001: House of Commons Hansard Written Answers for 1 May 2002.

58 The measure was originally introduced under the Crime and Disorder Act 1998 (s. 1); the powers it conferred were considerably strengthened by the Anti-Social Behaviour Act 2003. The ASBO went on to form the cornerstone of the 'Respect Agenda', a centrepiece of New Labour's third term programme (2005 onwards; see especially Home Office, 2006a).

59 The proportion fluctuates from year to year; in 2004 40 per cent of ASBOs were imposed on young persons aged 10–17, though it had been as high as 59 per cent in 2002. Of the 6,497 ASBOs issued to the end of June 2005, 43 per cent were imposed on young people (Home Office ASBO statistics for the period April 1999–June 2005, available at: http://www.crimereduction.gov.uk/asbos2.htm.)

60 This was done by inserting into the legislative framework that regulates ASBOs a new power to impose an 'individual support order' (Criminal Justice Act 2003, s. 292).

61 Crime and Disorder Act 1998, ss. 1 and 1C (s. 1C added by the Police Reform Act 2002).

62 Home Office ASBO statistics for the period April 1999–June 2005, available at: http://www.crimereduction.gov.uk/asbos2.htm.

63 In the case of an adult, the maximum penalty for breach of an ASBO is six months' imprisonment if tried in a magistrates' court, or five years if tried in the Crown Court.

64 Hazel Blears, House of Commons Hansard Written Answers for 24 January 2006.

65 *Guardian*, 30 March 2006; *Independent on Sunday*, 23 April 2006.

66 Exemplified not only by ASBOs, but also by the expanding use of 'fixed penalty notices' (see Introduction) rather than traditional court proceedings.

67 These form a distinct legal category and are still known as 'juvenile' offenders.

68 Sections 65–6. This statutory system has replaced the previous non-statutory system of formal police cautions, though only with regard to young offenders under the age of 18.

69 In 2003/4, 77 per cent of all final warnings were accompanied by this type of intervention (Youth Justice Board, 2004).

70 The rules as to remand in custody prior to trial also differ for young suspects (under the age of 17). If not left at liberty or conditionally free on bail, young offenders may be remanded to live in local authority accommodation, which may be a secure children's home if certain criteria are met.

71 Under Part III of the Powers of Criminal Courts (Sentencing) Act 2000; originally introduced by the Youth Justice and Criminal Evidence Act 1999, sections 1–15. This is a semi-mandatory procedure with relatively few exceptions; however, it does not apply if, for example, the court decides that the case could be dealt with by means of an

absolute discharge, or that it warrants a custodial sentence. Both these disposals are relatively rare in the case of young offenders.

72 Under section 66 of the Crime and Disorder Act 1998 the conditional discharge is not available when a young offender has received a final warning within the previous two years unless, there are exceptional circumstances relating either to the offender or the offence.

73 Powers of Criminal Courts (Sentencing) Act 2000 (s. 73).

74 In 2003/4 over 27,000 referral orders were imposed, accounting for 25 per cent of all Youth Court disposals, compared with under 4,000 reparation orders (3.5 per cent of the total) (Youth Justice Board, 2004).

75 Powers of Criminal Courts (Sentencing) Act 2000 (s. 69).

76 Broadly similar Intensive Change and Control Programmes, aimed at 18 to 20-year-old offenders, were introduced in April 2003.

77 First, as with offenders of any age, the court must be of the opinion that the offence was 'so serious that neither a fine alone nor a community sentence can be justified for the offence' (Criminal Justice Act 2003, s. 152(2); see Chapter 4). Additionally, offenders under 15 may only receive a DTO if the court believes they are 'persistent' offenders (not further defined) (Powers of Criminal Courts (Sentencing) Act 2000, s. 100).

78 Powers of Criminal Courts (Sentencing) Act 2000 (s. 96).

79 Criminal Justice and Court Services Act 2000 (s. 61) (not yet implemented as we write).

80 Powers of Criminal Courts (Sentencing) Act 2000 (s. 90).

81 See in particular Home Office (2003c; 2004d; 2006b).

82 On 25 June 2007 the Criminal Justice and Immigration Bill was published which, inter alia, will introduce a new single community order for juveniles, which will be known as a 'youth rehabilitation order'.

83 Not that this seems to have been very common under the pre-existing system of juvenile cautioning: Evans (1994: 69) found that young offenders were usually prosecuted after their second caution, and that the proportion receiving three or more cautions was less than 4 per cent.

84 Calculated from Cullen and Minchin (2000b: Table 1) and NOMS (2005e: Table 1). At the same time the number of young offenders aged 15 and 16 remanded to custody continues to increase even more dramatically and was 22 per cent higher in December 2005 than a year earlier (NOMS 2005e: Table 1).

85 Calculated from NOMS (2005a: Table 2.9).

86 Calculated from NOMS (2005b: Table 2.15).

87 From 3.3 months to 2.8 months and from 3.1 months to 2.6 months respectively.

88 Our own view is that minimum intervention is appropriate provided it does not prejudice the needs and interests of victims. There may be a balance to be struck here, as for instance if minimum intervention with offenders meant that victims were deprived of their right to reparation. However, there are ways of achieving a satisfactory balance, including providing flexible ways of encouraging reparation outside the mainstream criminal justice system.

10 Bias in the Criminal Justice System

Introductory

10.1 In Chapter 2 (section 2.3), we referred to the fundamental principle of justice which states that 'like cases should be treated alike'. If two people have committed crimes of similar gravity, then justice demands that they should normally be equally liable to punishment, unless there is some important relevant difference between the two cases or some other strong justification for departing from equal treatment. We have already seen in Chapter 4 how the arrangements for sentencing in England and Wales fail to ensure even rough equality of treatment for similar offenders – on the contrary, the wide discretion granted to sentencers ensures that there are enormous disparities, geographical and otherwise. Such disparities can, and doubtless often do, operate in a more or less arbitrary manner, so that the punishment an offender suffers bears little relation either to the offence or to the characteristics of the offender, being more a result of factors such as the local sentencing culture or the whims of the particular sentencers. In this chapter, however, we concentrate on *biases* within the criminal justice system – injustices that are related to certain characteristics of the offender. We consider three such characteristics: social class, race and gender.

As we shall see, these biases do not only – or indeed, primarily – occur at the sentencing stage, or even within the *penal* system, as opposed to the wider criminal justice system. Bias can operate at any or every stage of the criminal process, stages which include investigation and charge by the police, prosecution decisions by the Crown Prosecution Service, bail decisions, court verdicts and sentencing decisions (see Figure I.1 in the Introduction). Further possibilities for bias arise after sentence, in official decisions concerning *inter alia* allocation to different prisons and early release. The penal system cannot be viewed in isolation when considering the issue of bias. Suppose, for example, that the sentencing practices of the courts were unbiased, but the prior actions of the police ensured that members of an oppressed group were prosecuted to an unfair extent. In that case the sentencing system viewed on its own would seem fair, but would have the effect of reproducing the bias created in a previous stage of the process. Consequently, this chapter deals with the entire criminal justice system.

At any stage, bias can occur for a variety of reasons. It often results, not from deliberate discrimination (though this may also happen), but from unconscious prejudices and stereotypes (fixed preconceptions that some kinds of people are more criminal than others) and even as an unintended consequence of prima facie reasonable attitudes, practices and decisions. But whatever the causes, such biases add weight to radical critiques that claim that the penal system functions to reinforce the position of powerful sections of society over the less powerful (see Chapter 3, section 3.2). They also – yet again – suggest that the penal system's crisis of legitimacy may be largely self-inflicted: the system is perceived as unjust because it really is unjust.

The issue of bias in the criminal justice system has received a measure of official recognition, one example[1] being section 95 of the Criminal Justice Act 1991. This requires the Secretary of State every year

> to publish such information as he considers expedient for the purpose of ... facilitating the performance by [persons engaged in the administration of criminal justice] of their duty to avoid discriminating against any persons on the ground of race or sex or any other improper ground.

This provision has prompted the issuing of a regular series of publications (for the most recent examples, see Home Office, 2006e, 2006f) containing the results of research and monitoring. To some extent this has helped in the identification of biases within the system. But so far there is little sign that it has brought about any diminution in the actual occurrence of bias.

Class

10.2 Although the regular official series of criminal and penal statistics do not provide data on social class or occupation, it is clear that the penal system's subjects are overwhelmingly working class, and that unskilled and unemployed people are particularly over-represented in the penal population. The 1991 National Prison Survey found that 6 per cent of prisoners aged 17 or over had never had a job. Of the rest, 82 per cent had had manual occupations (compared with 56 per cent of the general population), and 41 per cent were unskilled (compared with 19 per cent generally) (Walmsley et al., 1992: 10–11, 21). Just prior to imprisonment, two-thirds of prisoners were unemployed (Social Exclusion Unit, 2002: 20). Similarly, Harris and Webb (1987: 115–16) found that almost all of a sample of 971 boys on supervision orders were working class, and fewer than 8 per cent had a parent in a 'white-collar' job. Several surveys of defendants in criminal courts have yielded similar results. Bottoms and McClean (1976: 75), for example, found that only 5 per cent of defendants in Sheffield in 1971 and 1972 (excluding motoring cases) were from social classes I and II, compared with 35 per cent of the general population. (In similar vein, a study of four magistrates' courts in the North of England in 1993 found that between 75 and 91 per cent of defendants sampled were unemployed (Crow et al., 1995: 46; cf. Crow and Simon, 1987).

This does not in itself demonstrate that there is a class bias operating in the criminal justice system to produce these results, for they could occur without bias if a similar proportion of crimes were committed by members of the working class. But 'self-report' research studies (in which respondents are asked in confidence what offences they have committed) suggest that this is not the case. It seems that there is a greater tendency for people from lower socio-economic groups to commit offences, or at least the kind of offences which tend to be dealt with by means of the normal criminal justice system. (This is not perhaps surprising when – just to mention the most obvious line of explanation – the vast majority of recorded crime is against property, which is exactly what poorer people lack.) But the class differential in commission of crimes as measured by self-report studies is much smaller than the class differential in officially processed offenders (see, for example,

Rutter and Giller, 1983: 132–7; Hood and Sparks, 1970: ch. 2). Gold's (1966: 44) American findings were fairly typical: 'About five times more lowest than highest status boys appear in the official records; if records were complete and unselective we estimate that the ratio should be closer to 1.5:1.' Somehow, between the commission of offences and the official responses of prosecution and punishment, the difference between the classes gets vastly magnified.

Such magnification could occur for a variety of reasons, not all of them necessarily connected with bias. Perhaps some misdeeds of middle-class offenders are relatively invisible and hence unlikely to come to official notice. This is probably true of embezzlement and tax evasion compared to burglary and robbery, for example. But there could also be biases operating at the various stages of the criminal process[2] which ensure that middle-class offenders are dealt with more leniently. At many of these stages, there is little research evidence to confirm or deny the existence of class bias in the system. But there are some straws in the wind.

A classic study in the United States in the 1960s by Piliavin and Briar (1964) indicates one way in which unintended class bias could occur at the police stage. The authors found that police officers who came across juveniles committing offences were expected to exercise discretion as to whether to arrest or reprimand the juvenile. The result was that, for nearly all minor violators and for some serious delinquents, it was the police's *assessment of the youth's character* which was the prime determinant of the officers' decisions. Officers decided whether the young person was basically law-abiding and 'salvageable', or an incorrigible 'punk', and made their decisions accordingly. This assessment of 'character' was, however, based on the very limited information available to the officers, notably 'cues' such as the youths' race, dress and – most importantly – their *demeanour*. Those who failed to show the police what was considered to be sufficient respect received negative character assessments and harsher treatment. Since attitudes towards the police vary across socio-economic groups,[3] such a criterion is extremely likely to result in effective class discrimination. It could also be that a 'rougher' demeanour not intended to convey disrespect could be misinterpreted, again to the disadvantage of the suspect from the lower socio-economic group.

Such a bias could occur at a very early stage in the criminal process, before the police have even discovered or decided that an offence has been committed. When police officers encounter members of the public, they often have to decide – perhaps instantly – whether this person is a potential criminal or not. There is usually little to go on in making this decision except by using stereotypical 'cues' which mark people as either 'rough' or 'respectable', yet a snap decision of this kind may condition the entire ensuing interaction (Cain, 1971: 81–4; Bottomley, 1973: ch. 2). This suggests that the police may be much less likely to suspect or investigate middle-class people – or, probably equally importantly, people who give the impression of belonging to the stably employed; 'respectable working class'. Indeed, studies have found that unemployed[4] people are significantly more likely to be stopped by the police than those who have a job (Clancy et al., 2001: 56, 65). As a result, the police will be likely to detect or recognize a higher proportion of offences committed by those in lower socio-economic groups.

Subsequent to detection of a possible offence comes the decision whether or not to prosecute or caution. In England, Bennett (1979) found that middle-class juvenile offenders in London were more likely than their working-class counterparts to be cautioned instead of being prosecuted for minor offences. There could be several factors influencing the police decision which have the effect of creating a class bias. Farrington and Bennett (1981) demonstrated that a juvenile's perceived 'bad attitude' is a potent determining factor of the police decision in London as well as in the USA; other studies have found that the offenders' *parents'* perceived attitudes are influential (Bennett, 1979; Fisher and Mawby, 1982; Gold, 1966). And Landau and Nathan (1983), again in London, found that the police were more inclined to prosecute 'latch-key children', a practice likely to work against low-income families.

It is also the case that, at the investigation and prosecution stages, typically middle-class offences can be dealt with in a radically different manner from 'ordinary crime', often by agencies other than the police. For example, breaches of factory health and safety regulations, including those that threaten or cause serious accidents,[6] are policed by an agency (the Health and Safety Executive) that prefers to warn rather than prosecute. Carson (1971) found that in the 1960s the HSE's predecessor, the Inspectorate of Factories, prosecuted a mere 1.5 per cent of detected offences. However, when a firm was detected offending three or more times, the rate of prosecution increased – to 3.5 per cent! Even disregarding cases where the Inspectorate took no formal action at all, this made an overall 'cautioning rate' of 98 per cent. This rate later declined, standing at 86 per cent in 2005/6,[6] but it still puts the police's cautioning rate of 38 per cent in the shade. (See further Sanders, 1985; Sanders and Young, 2000: 365–8.) Similarly, the Inland Revenue very rarely prosecutes tax fraud offenders, although the authorities are much more likely to prosecute those people (from lower socio-economic groups) who defraud the benefits system, typically of much smaller amounts[7] (NACRO, 1986a: ch. 10; Cook, 1989: ch. 7).

There is a distinct lack of studies at the sentencing stage which directly compare the sentences received by working-class and middle-class offenders *for the same offences*,[8] although it is (for example) highly plausible that sentencers might perceive a middle-class offender as less incorrigible and therefore deserving of a lesser sentence. Again, sentencers (themselves overwhelmingly middle-class) might well feel that a middle-class offender has already suffered enough through the disgrace of conviction, and sentence leniently as a result. Or richer defendants may be able to afford better lawyers who are more adept at representing their clients' circumstances as mitigating their culpability. There is plenty of anecdotal evidence of apparent leniency towards middle-class offenders, especially those convicted of typical 'white-collar' offences. Examples include the £3 million fraudsters in the 1960s whose prison sentences were a fraction of those imposed on the £2 million Great Train Robbers (Morris, 1980: 92); the non-custodial sentences passed on insider dealer Geoffrey Collier in 1987 and fraudulent trader Roger Levitt in 1993; and the halving of 'Guinness trial' defendant Ernest Saunders' sentence to two and a half years by the Court of Appeal in 1991 following evidence that he was suffering from pre-senile dementia (which went into remission after his release).

Research seems to have confirmed that the courts are often much more punitive towards the relatively poor people who fraudulently draw too much social security than towards the relatively well-off people who defraud the Inland Revenue of what may be much greater sums (Cook, 1989: 160–5). Again, this is not the result of intentional class bias, but the effect of the prevailing (Marxists might say 'bourgeois') ideology which holds that the latter method of defrauding the public purse is less reprehensible than the former.

Unemployed people can again get a particularly raw deal at the sentencing stage. Traditionally, the fact that an offender has a job and a steady work record has been regarded as counting in his or her favour, whereas unemployment has been seen as reflecting negatively on the offender's character. Again, sentencers may sometimes decide to pass non-custodial sentences on employed offenders so that they do not lose their jobs although they would imprison a similar but unemployed offender. (An analogous effect can occur when the court decides whether to grant bail or remand in custody.) Finally, unemployment can restrict the sentencing options the court perceives itself as having. In particular, the court may be reluctant to impose a fine or other financial penalty on an unemployed offender. This might be because the sum imposed would seem (to the relatively affluent sentencer) ridiculously small if related to the offender's means, or because it is felt that the offender cannot or will not pay up. Research studies have confirmed that unemployed offenders are significantly less likely to be fined than those who are employed. Although some of the unemployed who might otherwise have been fined are given discharges or probation orders, others receive custodial sentences.[9]

Following a sentence of imprisonment, white-collar offenders are much more likely to be allocated to open prisons, where the conditions and regime may be distinctly preferable (Jones et al., 1977: 66–70). This fact was highlighted in August 1990, when three businessmen found guilty of dishonesty offences involving millions of pounds in the 'Guinness affair' were transferred instantly from the slum conditions of Brixton Prison to the relatively salubrious Ford Open Prison. It is also possible that white-collar offenders get parole more easily (Levi, 1989: 102–5). Certainly this was suggested by the experience of jockey Lester Piggott, who in 1988 was paroled at the earliest opportunity from his (relatively speaking, hardly draconian) three-year prison sentence imposed for evading over £3 million in taxes.

None of this will come as any surprise to Marxists, who as we saw in Chapter 3 (section 3.2) view the penal system as an instrument of class power. The particular injustices suffered by the unemployed can be explained by a sophisticated Marxism which sees the role of the criminal justice system (and especially the historic role of the police) as imposing order on the 'rough' rather than 'respectable' sections of the working class (for example, Cohen, 1981). (It can also be maintained that the roles of criminal justice agencies have recently been shifting towards a greater emphasis on controlling an emerging 'underclass' of the impoverished and permanently unemployed – a perception by no means confined to Marxists.) However, traditional Marxism has more difficulty in providing explanations for the injustices we now proceed to investigate, concerning race and gender.

Race

10.3 According to official estimates, around 9 per cent of the population of England and Wales is of non-white ethnic origin. Yet in June 2005, 25 per cent of prisoners (and 28 per cent of female prisoners) were non-white. These figures are partly due to the large number of foreign inmates in English prisons.[10] In 2005, 14 per cent of all prisoners (and 38 per cent of non-white prisoners) were not of UK nationality.[11] But this is only part of the explanation. When non-UK nationals are excluded from the figures, 18 per cent of male and 17 per cent of female prisoners are of ethnic minority origin. (All figures taken or calculated from Home Office, 2006e: 86–7.)

The most dramatic racial disparity in these prison figures concerns 'black' (or 'Afro-Caribbean') people,[12] who account for around 3 per cent of people aged 10 and over in England and Wales, but comprised 14 per cent of the male and 19 per cent of the female prison population in 2005. It has been estimated that at this rate nearly one in ten young black men will have received a custodial sentence before their 21st birthdays, double the proportion of their white peers (*New Law Journal*, 30 March 1990; *Guardian*, 27 February 1989). Why do such disproportionately large numbers of black people find their way into custody?

One obvious hypothesis would be that black people are more likely to commit offences than white people. Since racial discrimination (conscious and unconscious, direct and indirect) results in black people being disproportionately materially deprived in the realms of employment, housing and education, it might not be surprising if this led to higher levels of offending. However, there is little evidence that this is the case. When it has been claimed – notoriously, by the Metropolitan Police in 1982 and again by the Metropolitan Police Commissioner in 1995 – that black people are disproportionately involved in crime, the statistics produced to back up these claims have been rightly criticized as unreliable and misleading (Smith, S., 1982; Crow, 1987: 305). The 2000 British Crime Survey found that, for crimes where the victim could identify the race of the offender, 5 per cent of offenders were black; but we need to take into account that most offenders are under 30 and that ethnic minority populations are significantly younger than the population as a whole.[13] Home Office research has found that *young* Afro-Caribbeans have very similar rates of offending to white youths (Graham and Bowling, 1995; Flood-Page et al., 2000: 20).

However, it is clear from a plethora of research studies over the years that Afro-Caribbean people are disproportionately the object of police attention and suspicion. The manifestation of this to attract the most attention is the use of police powers to *stop and search* people on the street. A national study using British Crime Survey data from 1996 found that 23 per cent of black respondents had been stopped by the police during the previous year compared with 16 per cent of whites and 15 per cent of Asians.[14] Black people are also more likely to be stopped several times in a year, and to be searched by the police following a stop. Overall, black people are, according to official figures, six times more likely to be stopped *and searched* by the police on the streets than white people.[15] Currently, Asian people are twice as likely to be stopped and searched as white people.

These results may be related to what the Policy Studies Institute (PSI) found when they researched the work of the Metropolitan Police in the early 1980s, that 'racialist language and racial prejudice were prominent and pervasive and that many individual officers and also whole groups were preoccupied with ethnic differences'. (Only 3.7 per cent of police officers are from ethnic minorities: Clegg and Kirwan, 2006: 5.) Although this racism did not usually manifest itself on the street, the PSI specifically noted that 'one criterion that police officers use for stopping people (especially in areas of *low* ethnic concentration) is that they are black' (Smith and Gray, 1983: 109–10). It seems that many police officers hold inaccurate, stereotyped views of black people, automatically placing them in the 'rough' (potentially criminal) category, especially when they are seen in areas where they 'don't belong'.[16] Research has found instances of police officers acting on the basis of stereotypes such as 'the assumption that West Indians running or carrying a bag are up to no good' (Southgate and Ekblom, 1986: 11).

The issue of police racism, and of their use of stop and search powers in particular, came to the fore in Lord Scarman's inquiry into the Brixton riots of 1981 (Scarman, 1986) and again on the publication of the Policy Studies Institute research on the Metropolitan Police in 1983. But little seemed to have changed by the time the Macpherson Report was published in February 1999. This was the report of an official inquiry into the case of Stephen Lawrence, a black student who was murdered by a gang of white youths at a South East London bus stop in April 1993. Macpherson concluded that the bungled police investigation into the murder, as a result of which none of the murderers were brought to justice, was affected by the '*institutional racism*' evident in the Metropolitan Police.[17] This institutional racism, Macpherson thought, was for the most part unintentional and unconscious, but the police were nevertheless infected by 'processes, attitudes and behaviour which amount to discrimination through unwitting prejudice, ignorance, thoughtlessness, and racist stereotyping which disadvantage minority ethnic people' (Macpherson, 1999: para. 6.34). Macpherson identified stop and search practices as a particular cause of ill-feeling between the police and the black community, and declared: 'we are clear that the perception and experience of the minority communities that discrimination is a major element in the stop and search problem is correct' (1999: para. 45.8).

Although police practices may have improved in some respects since the Macpherson Report (Foster et al., 2005) – and despite claims in some quarters that after Macpherson the police became afraid to use their stop and search powers on black people in particular[18] – there is no evidence that much has changed for the better in relation to the use of stop and search powers on members of ethnic minorities. There is now official ethnic monitoring of stops and searches (following a Macpherson recommendation), and police codes of practice were altered between 2003 and 2005 to require stops and searches (and the reasons for them) to be recorded, and copies of the records to be immediately handed to the person stopped. There have been claims that police use of stop and search is now more 'targeted' and 'intelligence-led' (O'Connor, 2000), but there are suspicions that this often involves the targeting of searches on people fitting 'profiles' of likely criminals which include racial characteristics; arguably this is just a new and officially endorsed form of stereotyping.

There has been particular concern in the last few years about the disproportionate use of stop and search powers against people of Asian appearance, especially those extra search powers provided by the Terrorism Act 2000, which dispense with the normal legal requirement for the police officer to have 'reasonable suspicion' that the person searched is carrying some specific type of unlawful goods or objects (such as stolen goods, illegal weapons or drugs). In 2004/5 Asians were three times more likely to be stopped and searched under these powers than their numbers in the general population would suggest.[19] The situation may well have worsened since the London bombings of 7 July 2005. Unpublished figures from the British Transport Police in the following two months reportedly show a sevenfold increase in the use of these powers, with Asians being five times more likely to be searched than white people (*Guardian*, 17 August 2005). Metropolitan Police figures also indicate a large and disproportionate increase in searches of Asian and Afro-Caribbean people following the bombings (*Guardian*, 24 December 2005). Both the Chief Constable of the British Transport Police (*Mail on Sunday*, 31 July 2005) and the Home Office minister Hazel Blears (*Guardian*, 2 March 2005) have said explicitly that Asians will inevitably be disproportionately stopped and searched in the post-9/11 climate – although, confusingly, Ms Blears also said (*Guardian*, 3 August 2005) that she did not endorse 'racial profiling' in the use of stop and search.

Black people[20] are *arrested* more often than their numbers in the general population would lead one to expect – over three times as often as white people in 2004/5 (Home Office, 2006e: 36). Some of this difference may be explained by the fact that many arrests result from stops, which as we have just seen happen more often to black people.[21] It is also the case that black people are arrested particularly often for offences 'in which there is considerable scope for selective perception of potential or actual offenders' (Stevens and Willis, 1979: 41). Phillips and Brown (1998: 44–5) found that the evidence against arrested black and Asian suspects was less often sufficient to charge them than in cases with white suspects.

There is also evidence that race can make a difference to the police's decision whether to *caution* offenders or proceed to prosecution. In 2004/5, 13 per cent of arrested black suspects were cautioned, compared with 17.5 per cent of white and 16 per cent of Asian suspects (Home Office, 2006e: 47). Landau and Nathan (1983) found in London that white juveniles were significantly more likely to be cautioned than their black counterparts, and a white juvenile with previous convictions was over four times more likely to be cautioned than a similar black youth.[22] Some other studies have found that black defendants are more likely to have been brought to court for offences that caused no loss, damage or injury (Stevens and Willis, 1979: 37; Crow and Cove, 1984), raising the possibility that similar white offenders might not have been prosecuted. This could, however, be partly due to the actions of victims rather than the police: perhaps similar offences by white people might have gone unreported to the police in the first place (see Shah and Pease, 1992).

Interestingly, research has found that ethnic minority defendants (both black and Asian) are more likely to have the prosecutions against them dropped after being charged by the police,[23] that black defendants are more likely to plead not guilty, and that black and Asian defendants who plead not guilty are more likely to be acquitted in court (Home Office, 2000b: 37; 2005b: 53; Phillips and Brown, 1998). This suggests that the police may often charge ethnic minority suspects on the basis of a lesser amount of solid evidence than they might require in the case of a white suspect.

Ethnic minority defendants are more likely than whites to be *committed for Crown Court trial*, according to a number of studies (Fitzgerald, 1993: 19–21; Home Office, 2006e: 54) and, as we saw in Chapter 4, defendants who are tried in the Crown Court are likely to receive harsher sentences than those tried by magistrates. The higher committal rate seems to be partly the result of ethnic minority defendants more often electing to be tried at the Crown Court, but it is at least as often due to magistrates declining jurisdiction. Moreover, black Crown Court defendants are *remanded in custody*, instead of being granted bail, more often than whites: one study found 26 per cent of sentenced black defendants had been remanded in custody compared with 20 per cent of whites and 18 per cent of Asians (Hood, 1992: 146–7). The fact that black defendants who are remanded in custody are much more likely than their white counterparts to be acquitted or not proceeded against (Fitzgerald, 1993: 22) suggests that they may often be wrongly denied bail.

There is good evidence that race can also play an important part in *sentencing*. Several studies in the United States indicate that black defendants tend to receive more severe sentences (including more custodial sentences and more death sentences; see, for example, Spohn et al., 1981–2; Baldus et al., 1989; Lambie, 2002; see also Cavadino and Dignan, 2006: 59), but the evidence from the USA is not entirely consistent (Pruitt and Wilson, 1983). Nor is it consistent in England, where several studies (for example, McConville and Baldwin, 1982; Crow and Cove, 1984; Moxon, 1988: 59) have found no evidence of racial bias in sentencing, but a variety of others (for example, NACRO, 1986b: ch. 3; Walker, M., 1988; Hudson, 1989) have found that black defendants are more likely to receive custodial sentences than are comparable white defendants.

The largest and most rigorous study of this question – Roger Hood's *Race and Sentencing* (1992) – provides the best evidence to date of a race effect in sentencing. Hood carefully examined sentencing at five Crown Courts in the West Midlands in 1989, and found that 57 per cent of black male defendants were sentenced to custody compared with 48 per cent of the white men; for women the figures were 29 per cent and 23 per cent. Taking into account all other relevant variables such as the offence charged and the offender's previous record, black men were 5 per cent more likely than white men to be sent to prison (Hood, 1992: 75–9; 163).[24] At one court (Dudley Crown Court), black defendants were 23 per cent more likely to receive custody. Adult black and Asian males also received longer average sentences of imprisonment, and were particularly likely to receive sentences of over three years.

Several studies have found that, although black offenders are to be found disproportionately in prisons, they are *under*-represented in other sectors of the penal system. Notably, black offenders have been found to receive proportionately fewer probation orders; and there have also been claims that young black offenders have been under-represented on non-custodial programmes (Taylor, 1981; NACRO, 1986b: ch. 4; Moxon, 1988; Pitts, 1986: 133). These phenomena could well be related: for some reason black offenders are deemed unsuitable for non-custodial supervisory sentences and, as a result, find their way into custody relatively quickly. This raises questions not only about sentencers, but also about the provision of suitable non-custodial programmes for ethnic minority offenders (see Kemshall et al., 2004) and about the role of the probation officers and youth justice workers who assess offenders' suitability for these disposals and relay their assessments to the courts in pre-sentence reports (PSRs).

Some studies have indeed suggested that PSRs serve to disadvantage black defendants. For example, de la Motta (1984) found that reports on young black defendants in Nottingham were three times as likely as those on whites to make no recommendation as to sentence – usually interpreted by the sentencing court to amount to a veiled recommendation for custody. It has been suggested that 'probation officers may well make fewer recommendations for supervision in the community because they lack the confidence to carry this out successfully' (NACRO, 1986b: 16). However, other studies have found no such differences between recommendations in reports on black and white defendants (Mair, 1986; Moxon, 1988; Hood, 1992: 150–60) – but still fewer black defendants received probation orders than whites. One factor seems to be that PSRs are prepared less often on black defendants (for example, Hood, 1992: 150–1; Flood-Page and Mackie, 1998: 117), which is partly (but only partly) because reports are usually prepared in advance only on defendants pleading guilty, and black defendants are more likely to plead not guilty.[25]

The overall situation may have altered since some of this research was carried out. A study of sentencing in the mid-1990s found no difference in custody rates between black and white defendants whether or not other factors were taken into account, although Asian men received more custodial sentences than would have been expected on this basis (Flood-Page and Mackie, 1998: 115–20; see also Home Office, 2005b: 53–4). However, concerns remain about both sentencing and the quality of treatment ethnic minority offenders receive from the probation service. HM Inspectorate of Probation (2000) found that the quality of pre-sentence reports on white offenders was significantly higher than those prepared for offenders from ethnic minorities. The quality of supervision given to African and Afro-Caribbean probationers also raised significant concerns with regard to risk assessments, the level of contact received and enforcement practice.

Bias against black people in the criminal justice system does not by any means cease at the point of sentence. Black prisoners are less likely than whites to be allocated to open prisons (NACRO, 1986b: 20). Elaine Genders and Elaine Player (1989) have provided substantial evidence of racial discrimination within prisons, finding for example that the best jobs were regularly allocated to white prisoners.

Again, inaccurate racial stereotypes (this time held by prison officers) had a lot to answer for. Prison officers (only 2 per cent of whom are black: Home Office, 2006e: 102) believed that Afro-Caribbean prisoners were arrogant, lazy and anti-authority, had 'chips on their shoulders' and tended to stick together. Although these stereotypes were demonstrably false, they led prison staff to perceive black prisoners as unsuitable for the most desirable jobs.

Genders and Player's (1989) findings were perfectly exemplified by the case of John Alexander. The courts found in 1987 that the Home Office had unlawfully discriminated against Mr Alexander, a black prisoner whose application to work in the kitchen at Parkhurst was refused on the basis of an assessment report which stated that 'he displays the usual traits associated with his ethnic background, being arrogant, suspicious of staff, anti-authority, devious and possessing a very large chip on his shoulder'. The Prison Service has had a formal race relations policy since 1983 and has made repeated statements in recent years opposing any discrimination or display of prejudice by prison staff or by prisoners against each other, but racism is of course not so easily eradicated. This was reflected in the findings of the 1991 National Prison Survey (Walmsley et al., 1992: 38) that only 29 per cent of black Caribbean prisoners felt that prison officers treated them well, compared with 43 per cent of white prisoners. Another study (Burnett and Farrell, 1994) found that nearly half of black prisoners reported having been racially victimized by prison staff and over half thought they had been discriminated against over access to facilities and activities. In 2001, Prison Service Director General Martin Narey reported receiving hate mail following his own admissions that institutional racism and indeed 'pockets of malicious racism' exist within the Prison Service (*Guardian*, 14 February 2001).

Even more disturbing was the murder of Zahid Mubarek in March 2000 by his rabidly racist cellmate in Feltham Young Offender Institution. Inquiries into this incident discovered that ethnic minority staff and inmates at Feltham were subjected to both overt racist abuse and less explicit discrimination from prison officers (*Guardian*, 22 January 2001, 18 December 2004, 6 October 2005; Keith, 2006: 644). A public judicial inquiry into the Mubarek case by Mr Justice Keith (2006) took it to be an established and uncontested fact that both Feltham and the Prison Service generally suffered from institutional racism (and also proposed the adoption of a parallel concept of 'institutional religious intolerance'). The Mubarek murder also led to an investigation into the Prison Service by the Commission for Racial Equality (2003), which found 14 areas of failure and made 17 findings of unlawful discrimination against the service. Currently the Prison Service and Commission for Racial Equality are working together on a five-year action plan, including carrying out race equality reviews in all establishments. However, a survey by HM Inspectorate of Prisons (2005a) again found that ethnic minority prisoners were significantly more likely to feel that they were treated badly, felt they were treated with less respect and felt less safe than white prisoners, with 30 per cent saying that they had been victimized by members of staff (see also Edgar and Martin, 2004). Racism and racial discrimination remain a potent and undeniable reality in English prisons.

There is little evidence, however, of any relationship between race and the *parole* decision. A recent Home Office study (Moorthy et al., 2004; cf. Home Office, 1994a) found that the release rates for ethnic minority prisoners were actually higher than for white prisoners; these variations could be explained by other factors that influenced the parole decision (such as type of offence and length of sentence).

To sum up: it may not be true to say that there is bias working consistently against black people throughout the entire criminal justice system. Nevertheless, it seems that a black person who comes into contact with the criminal justice system has a good chance of being seriously disadvantaged compared with a white person, and may be particularly likely to end up in prison. There may be some cause for hope, if not necessarily optimism, in the fact that the race issue in criminal justice has become increasingly recognized as one of the most pressing issues in criminal justice, especially since the Macpherson Report of 1999. Steps have been taken, for example, to ensure that sentencers receive racial awareness training and that ethnic monitoring is introduced and improved throughout the criminal justice system, and the legal duty not to discriminate on grounds of race has been extended to the police by the Race Relations (Amendment) Act 2000. Race is clearly now seen as a potential source of serious illegitimacy – and rightly, since studies have repeatedly shown not only that black people have considerably less confidence in criminal justice than white people (see, for example, BBC, 2002; Dholakia and Sumner, 1993: 34–5; Skogan, 1990: 55), but also that large proportions of white as well as black people believe that justice is biased against black people (for example, Smellie and Crow, 1991: 20; Flood-Page et al., 2000: 54). Hopeful signs were detectable in a 2003 study in magistrates' and Crown Courts (Hood et al., 2003), which found fewer ethnic minority defendants feeling that they had been unfairly treated because of their race. Some things may be changing; and there is no reason to doubt the genuine concern of many people within the criminal justice system about the issue of racial discrimination. But – especially with regard to the police and the Prison Service – there is clearly still a long way to go.

Gender

10.4 Within the criminal justice system, the dimension of gender differs in one crucial respect from those of class and race: in this case, members of the oppressed group (women) are distinctly *under*-represented in the criminal statistics. Women and girls accounted for a mere 6 per cent of the prison population on 31 October 2006[26] despite comprising just over half of the general population. (Nevertheless, there are currently more women prisoners than almost ever before – 4,447 in October 2006 – and in recent years their numbers have been rising even faster than men's, having nearly trebled since 1993.) Women are also under-represented at previous stages of the criminal justice system, though to lesser extents. In 2005 15 per cent of those found guilty of indictable offences and 20 per cent of those found guilty or cautioned were female,[27] while only 17 per cent of those arrested in 2004/5 were female (Ayres and Murray, 2005).

Again the question arises as to whether this difference is due to a real difference in offending behaviour between the two sections of the population (in this case, males and females). With very rare exceptions,[28] commentators agree that females do, in fact, commit fewer offences than do males, although the difference may be much smaller than the official figures suggest.[29] Moreover, female offenders generally commit less serious offences than their male counterparts, and have committed fewer offences previously: the typical detected female offender is 'a young girl, a first offender charged with shoplifting' (Heidensohn, 1985: 11). Explanations for this state of affairs vary. Positivistic explanations exist which claim that differing male and female biologies are the cause: girls may not literally be made out of sugar and spice and all things nice, but their hormones lead them to be more law-abiding. More plausible in our opinion are theories that emphasize the different social experiences of males and females. Girls have traditionally been socialized to be more passive and conformist than boys, and throughout their lives girls and women may find themselves subject to greater informal social controls; they may also have less opportunity to commit certain types of crime (Smart, 1976: 66–70; Heidensohn, 1985: ch. 9).

Whatever the explanation, if we accept that women and girls do in fact commit fewer (and generally less serious) offences than men and boys, then the bare statistics say nothing about whether there is any bias operating in the criminal justice system either in favour of women or against them. Perhaps there would be even fewer women in prison if they were treated the same as comparable male offenders; or perhaps there would be more. There have traditionally been two rival schools of thought on this issue, one holding that female offenders are dealt with more leniently than males and one asserting the reverse.

The first view – the 'chivalry theory' – claims that chivalry leads police and sentencers (who are predominantly male)[30] to afford women less harsh treatment. It is easy to point to incidents which appear to bear this out. Our personal favourite is a case reported in the *Daily Mirror* in 1978: '*Judge frees "inhuman" mum*. A mother who flogged her eight-year-old son with a belt, gave him cold baths and forced him to stand naked for hours at night … was saved from prison *because she has another child to care for*' (cited by Heidensohn 1985: 51; our italics). Were the chivalry theory to be correct, this would not of course mean that there is no sexist bias in the criminal justice system, but that the sexism takes the form of a patronizing 'chivalry' which may benefit some female offenders but is hardly likely to advance the general cause of female social equality. (It is, however, the kind of view often propounded by anti-feminists of the 'women should stop moaning because they get the better deal as things are' ilk.)

The opposing view, put forward in particular by feminist commentators, has been termed the 'evil woman' theory (Nagel and Hagan, 1983). It asserts that women who offend will receive *harsher* treatment from the criminal justice system. This is because women who commit crimes are seen as 'doubly deviant': they have offended not only against the law, but also against deeply ingrained social norms about how women should be, so they are perceived as being particularly depraved. Rebellious anti-social behaviour on the part of a young man may be reprehensible, but it is less disturbing because such behaviour is after all masculine – 'boys will be boys'. Similar conduct on the part of a young woman is far more unsettling because it is unfeminine. Moreover, there is a tendency for female criminality to be 'sexualized' in a way that male offending is not. Female offenders are assumed to be sexually deviant, or their sexuality is regarded as associated with their offending, assumptions which are not generally made with male offenders. The result is that women's crime evokes an especially punitive response. This punitiveness may be overt, or it may be disguised as paternalistic concern for the woman's welfare. The woman's disturbing deviance may be rationalized away as 'sickness', leading to a positivistic 'treatment' measure which could be more intrusive than the sentence a male offender would receive for a similar offence. (See generally Heidensohn, 1985: ch. 3.)

These theories can be tested against the evidence that exists concerning the different stages of the criminal process. At the first stages of initial contact between the police and possible female suspects, one clearly established fact is that the police stop and search men much more often than women.[31] A national survey of boys and girls aged 14 and 15, carried out by Home Office researchers in 1983 (Riley and Shaw, 1985; Riley, 1986) casts some light on the phenomenon. Boys were more than twice as likely to have been stopped by the police than girls of the same age (29 per cent compared with 13 per cent in the preceding 12 months). Boys were more likely to be stopped if they and their friends were delinquent, but this was not true for girls. Girls were more likely to be stopped if their lifestyles were 'unfeminine' – if they went around in mixed-sex groups, were relatively more involved with drugs and alcohol, spent more time with their friends and were subject to less parental supervision. These findings do not show that the police treat girls worse than boys, but they do lend some support to the feminist claim that females are dealt with by criminal justice agencies according to different criteria from those applied to males, criteria related to traditional female gender-roles, with the result that their femininity is being policed as much as their offending. This is a theme that will recur as we progress through the criminal process.

Moving on to the decision whether to *arrest* a suspect, while there is little directly relevant British research evidence, a study of drug arrests in Chicago between 1942 and 1970 (de Fleur, 1975: 101) found 'a tendency not to arrest females as often as males if they behaved in expected, stereotypic ways. During drugs raids females often cried, claimed to have been led astray by men, or expressed concern about the fate of their children. These behaviors usually were successful.' However, females who were more aggressive and hostile were arrested more often than those who behaved in more traditionally feminine ways.

There is no doubt that detected female offenders are *cautioned* much more often than males. In 2005, 54 per cent of females found guilty of or cautioned for an indictable offence received a caution, compared with 34 per cent of males (Home Office, 2006g: Table 3.3). Claims have been made that such figures show chivalry operating in women's favour (Walker, 1968: 299–300), and also that they show the reverse (Smart, 1976: 137–8).[32] It is, of course, necessary to take into account the type of offences involved and the offenders' previous records in deciding whether any bias goes into the creation of the statistical difference between the sexes. Ideally, one should also allow for other variables which may affect the decision whether to caution or prosecute, such as social class and race. Landau and Nathan's (1983) study of juvenile cautioning in London found that, when such other variables were controlled for, the sex of the offender made no significant difference to the decision of the police (see also Landau, 1981; cf. Home Office, 2004b: 9). (However, Gelsthorpe (1989: 106) found evidence that girls were more likely than boys to be cautioned for offences of similar seriousness.) Again, although girls are not overall dealt with more harshly than boys, it may be that they are judged by different, gender-role-related criteria. It has been suggested that police again act more leniently towards female offenders who act in stereotypically feminine ways, such as showing remorse by crying or apologizing (Gelsthorpe, 1985: 3, 1989: 105).[33]

Women are *remanded in custody* less often than men, apparently because they commit less serious offences, have fewer previous convictions and are less likely to have breached bail in the past or to be of no fixed abode (Home Office, 2004b: 15; Flood-Page and Mackie, 1998: 121). When women are remanded in custody, they are less likely than remanded males to be subsequently sentenced to custody by the court (41 per cent of female and 50 per cent of male remandees in 1999 – Home Office, 2004b: 15). This could mean that some women are being remanded in custody when comparable male offenders are not;[34] certainly it means that many women offenders are being sent to prison before trial, although their actual offence is subsequently not deemed serious enough to warrant deprivation of liberty. 43 per cent of women who are remanded in custody are charged with theft or handling rather than more serious or violent offences (Home Office, 2004b: 16).

The 'chivalry' and 'evil woman' theories have both been put forward in respect of *sentencing*. The bare statistics show, as one would expect, that women and girls sentenced for indictable offences on the whole receive less severe sentences than males. In 2004, 15 per cent of females' sentences were custodial compared with 27 per cent of males' (RDS NOMS, 2005b: Table 2.10). Sentencing patterns differ in some other respects as well: women are more likely than males to receive supervisory court orders and discharges, and less likely to be fined.[35] Do these figures indicate bias – and if so, in what direction?

Pat Carlen (1983) argues that sexist bias enters into the sentencing decision to the disadvantage of women who offend against the norms of traditional femininity. From her interviews with sheriffs (Scottish judges), she concludes that when sentencers are 'faced with a sentencing dilemma in a case where the offender is female, they mainly decide their sentence on the basis of their assessment of the woman as mother' (1983: 63). All the sheriffs she interviewed said (chivalrously) that they particularly hated sending women to prison. Nevertheless, they admitted that they sometimes imprisoned women in circumstances when they would have fined a man, because women were normally financially dependent on their husbands and often could not afford to pay a fine appropriate to the offence. They would be particularly inclined to send a woman to prison if her children were in care. Carlen quotes sheriffs as commenting: 'If she's a good mother we don't want to take her away. If she's not a good mother it doesn't really matter', and 'One often finds out, when inquiries are made, that the women have left their husbands and their children are already in care. In those cases it may seem a very good idea to send them to prison for three months to sort themselves out' (1983: 67).

Carlen's claim that sentencers make their decisions in this manner receives some support from surveys of women in prison, a disproportionate number of whom seem to have unconventional family backgrounds. Of Carlen's own sample of 20 Scottish women prisoners, only one was currently married and living with her husband (1983: 38). In another Scottish sample, 65 per cent of the women prisoners had children under 18, but only half of these had been looking after them immediately prior to being imprisoned (Dobash et al., 1986: 193). In England, Genders and Player (1986: 360) found that half of their sample of women prisoners over the age of 30 had a non-conventional background; fewer than half of those with dependent children lived within a 'traditional nuclear family setting' (in which they included living with a long-term cohabitee). The findings of the 1991 National Prison Survey (Walmsley et al., 1992: 17) differed only slightly from this: 49 per cent of female prisoners of 18 or over had been living with a spouse or partner prior to their imprisonment, and nearly half of those with dependent children were unmarried. Further support for Carlen's thesis comes from a study of magistrates' sentencing in Cambridge by Farrington and Morris. They found that women who were divorced or separated or had a 'deviant family background' were more likely to receive a relatively severe sentence, but these factors made no difference to the kind of sentences which male offenders received (Farrington and Morris, 1983: 244–5). (In the United States, Nagel (1981) reported similar findings.)

Overall, Farrington and Morris found that the sentences received by female defendants at the Cambridge City magistrates' court were not significantly heavier or lighter than those passed on men when the relevant factors of offence type and offender's previous record were controlled for. In combination with their findings about the effects of 'deviant family backgrounds', this suggests the possibility that there could be sexist biases in sentencing operating *in both directions* (and, in this study, cancelling each other out). Women who are married and looking after their children may be the beneficiaries of chivalry and receive a lighter sentence than a man, but women who are less acceptably feminine – who are perceived as 'evil women' because they are not good wives and mothers[36] – may be treated more harshly.

However, the same cancelling out of biases was not apparent in two studies of Crown Court sentencing practice (Moxon, 1988; Hood, 1992: ch. 11); chivalry seemed to predominate. (Nagel (1981) has also found this to be true in the USA.) After allowing for factors such as offence and criminal record, women were significantly less likely than men to receive a custodial sentence. For example, Moxon (1988: 54) found that male first offenders charged with theft or fraud were almost twice as likely to receive unsuspended custody as were comparable women. Similarly, Hedderman and Hough (1994) found that in 1992 female first offenders were only half as likely to receive a sentence of immediate imprisonment than were male first offenders, and the pattern was similar for specific offences such as theft and for offenders with one, two or three previous convictions. Flood-Page and Mackie (1998: 121–3) found much the same picture emerging in the mid-1990s.

Dowds and Hedderman (1997) found a more mixed picture when they examined a large sample of male and female adult offenders sentenced in 1991 for shoplifting, violence and drugs offences. Taking other factors into account, female shoplifters were less likely than comparable males to receive a prison sentence. Men and women were equally likely to be imprisoned for their first conviction for violence or a repeat drug offence – but women were less likely to receive custody for a *first* drug conviction or *repeated* violent offence.[37] Thus the general picture is that results often show women receiving lighter sentences than comparable males, but never show them being sentenced more harshly.

It is often claimed (for example, by Mawby, 1977) that women must be sentenced more harshly because a greater proportion of women who receive prison sentences have no previous convictions compared with imprisoned men: this was true of 37 per cent of women serving prison sentences in 2002 but only 15 per cent of male prisoners (RDS NOMS, 2004: 8.24). (Similarly, a much smaller proportion of female than male prisoners have been found guilty of a violent offence.)[38] This argument looks convincing at first sight, but it is fallacious. For these kinds of percentages are just what we should expect to find given that the great majority of female offenders have no or few previous convictions, and the figures are perfectly compatible with women receiving sentences that are similar to or more lenient than those passed on comparable male offenders (Walker, 1981). The correct comparison – of how female and male offenders with similar records are actually dealt with at the sentencing stage – was made in the studies we mentioned in the previous two paragraphs.

There seems to be a certain reluctance on the part of sentencing courts to impose *fines* on women. This could be partly – though probably not entirely – due to sentencers taking into account the fact that women are less likely to have their own income and more likely to have childcare responsibilities (Dowds and Hedderman, 1997; Gelsthorpe and Loucks, 1997). The result of this seems to be that (like unemployed offenders, whom courts are also reluctant to fine) a woman may end up receiving a less severe sentence than a male offender (such as a discharge rather than a fine) but may also sometimes receive a more intrusive sentence such as probation supervision.

However, the preponderance of research evidence reviewed above suggests that women who offend are not on the whole sentenced more severely than comparable males, and that they sometimes receive more lenient sentences, including escaping custody where a male would not. What we do not know, however, is to what extent this could be accounted for by arguably *relevant differences*[39] in the situations of male and female offenders. One such difference that often exists concerns childcare responsibilities. Perhaps a woman with a child to look after does not herself deserve to escape imprisonment any more than an otherwise comparable male offender without such a responsibility, but does the child deserve to lose its mother? It may well be that such considerations – perhaps rightly – account for the differences between men and women as regards whether they receive custodial sentences. The possibility also remains that some women – perhaps those who are perceived as especially deviant because of their lifestyles or their particular crimes – come off worse than comparable male offenders because of their gender. As Chris Tchaikovsky of the organization Women in Prison once aptly put it:

> Judges tell me all the time that they never send women to prison. The truth is that the woman in the neat white blouse who is sorry and depressed is acceptable, but the girl in the leather jacket with the Mohican haircut and the drug problem is treated very badly. (*Guardian*, 9 February 1994)

Much attention has been focused over the years on the position of women who kill their violent male partners. The best-known example is Sara Thornton, whose murder conviction was quashed by the Court of Appeal in December 1995. It is argued that the legal defence of 'provocation' (which can reduce a charge of murder to manslaughter, with consequent possibilities of a lesser sentence than the mandatory life imprisonment sentence for murder) serves to prejudice women in comparison with men, because it requires a sudden loss of self-control. Men may be more able to avail themselves of this defence because they are more likely to kill women using methods such as strangulation, which they can claim resulted from a sudden burst of anger, whereas women's methods of killing their partner may look more premeditated. Moreover, the law was slow to recognize the effects of 'cumulative provocation' consisting of recurrent violence over a long period (Nicolson and Sanghvi, 1995). These arguments may well be correct, despite the fact that women seem to succeed in pleading provocation in a higher proportion of domestic homicides than do men (Hedderman and Hough, 1994). For it seems very likely that women in such cases are typically subjected to much higher degrees of provocation (and especially of violence) from their partners than the men are. The law of provocation was significantly reinterpreted by the Court of Appeal in the 1990s,[40] giving greater recognition to 'cumulative provocation' but still requiring 'loss of self control' to establish the provocation defence. It cannot of course be assumed that homicide – one of the rarest of offences – provides a typical picture of the way the legal and penal systems deal routinely with the great bulk of non-violent female offending.

If courts do indeed have a general tendency to be relatively lenient with female offenders, especially as regards custody, it could be a leniency bought by exploiting stereotyped notions about women and their crimes, at the price of reinforcing these stereotypes. Defence lawyers' pleas in mitigation and pre-sentence reports might encourage leniency by playing on the positivistic idea that women who offend are sick, or 'mad rather than bad', or by portraying the woman as weak and led astray by a dominant man. In thus arguing that the women cannot help their actions, lawyers and probation officers could be helping to perpetuate the sexist ideology that holds that women are in general weaker, less rational than men and more driven by their emotions. Mary Eaton (1986) makes the wider claim that mitigation pleas and pre-sentence reports reinforce prevailing ideologies about women's rightful roles within the family by stressing either the normality of the woman's domestic behaviour (and therefore her essential goodness) or else its abnormality (as either a cause or a symptom of the pathology that has led her to offend).

It is doubtless the perception of women who offend as 'mad rather than bad' and in need of help (perhaps combined in some cases with reluctance to impose a fine) which leads to the tendency for female offenders to receive more supervisory orders than males.[41] Such paternalism could have the effect of moving some female offenders with comparatively trivial offending records 'up the tariff', leading to an increased danger of a more severe sentence if they reoffend subsequently.

When women are sentenced to custody, how does their treatment compare to that of men? At first sight it might seem that they are treated better, since penal establishments for females are on the whole (superficially at least, and with some notable exceptions) physically less unpleasant places than those for males. But in some respects women prisoners are worse off. For example, because women comprise such a small percentage of the prison population, currently only 15 out of the 142 prisons in England and Wales accommodate females;[42] this means that women are often held at enormous distances from their homes, in remote locations, which makes visiting a particular problem. Again, it is probably the case that, for a variety of social and psychological reasons, women find the experience of imprisonment much more traumatic than men do (Heidensohn, 1985: 75–9), leading to a higher incidence of flare-ups and self-mutilation in women's prisons.[43]

It can be argued that women prisoners *should* be treated differently from men because their circumstances and needs are different. After all, women generally pose less risk to the public than do men, and are less likely to abscond (di Lustro, 2004: 6). Most of them have children under 16, of whom only a quarter are being cared for by the child's father or a spouse or partner.[44] Many women prisoners are vulnerable, in a variety of ways:[45] female inmates are more likely to be dependent on opiate drugs, and nearly half report having been physically and/or sexually abused (HM Chief Inspector of Prisons, 1997b). A large-scale survey in 1997 (Singleton et al., 1998) assessed two-thirds of women prisoners as suffering from neurotic disorders,[46] while 44 per cent of female remandees and 37 per cent of sentenced prisoners had attempted suicide at some stage.[47] And indeed women prisoners *are* treated differently from men, although how far these differences are appropriate to their needs is another question. Traditionally, the training of female prisoners is directed towards equipping them to perform the work they are thought most likely to do when they are released, namely housework. The general picture has not changed much: the work that women do in prison is still dominated by domestic-type tasks such as cleaning, sewing and cooking, which also figure prominently in the training provided for female prisoners, along with training for traditionally female jobs such as typing, catering and hairdressing (Hamlyn and Lewis, 2000: chs 4 and 5). Genders and Player, who studied female youth custody centres (now called young offender institutions), found this stereotyping of women's work to be combined with psychological rehabilitation theory:

> an important part of the treatment and training of young women serving youth custody relates to the building of self-confidence and self-esteem, the lack of which is deemed responsible for much of the attention- and approval-seeking which causes many girls to come into conflict with the law. The skills which are taught in youth custody centres,

however, continue to permit success mainly within the boundaries of stereotypical female roles. The concentration upon personal hygiene and appearance, through training in beauty care and hairdressing, and the development of domestic skills, such as cleaning, cooking and household budgeting, makes clear those areas in which delinquent young women are expected to develop feelings of self-worth. (Genders and Player, 1986: 368)

The positivistic stereotype which sees female offenders (but not males) as invariably being 'mad not bad'[48] has had a particular historical influence on prison regimes for women. An official Home Office publication once stated that 'most of the women in prison wish to conform with society but for various reasons are unable to do so. For example, many are in need of medical or psychiatric treatment' (Home Office, 1977: 101). In 1968 – roughly at the zenith of the 'rehabilitative ideal' – it was announced that Holloway (by far the largest women's penal establishment in England) was to be redesigned and rebuilt as, in essence, a secure psychiatric hospital. The new design turned out to be disastrous, and in 1981 the prison was given a 'modified brief' by the Home Office, abandoning the notion that all its inmates should be treated according to a medical model. This did not prevent the rebuilt Holloway from suffering severe problems, including overcrowding and low staff morale, compounded by a public scandal which blew up in 1984 about the prisoners' living conditions, especially (and ironically) in the psychiatric unit. The scandal resulted in a Home Office inquiry, following which the prison improved significantly (HM Chief Inspector of Prisons, 1992). Subsequently, however, conditions deteriorated again, provoking an unprecedented walkout by Chief Inspector of Prisons Sir David Ramsbotham in December 1995 after inspectors had reportedly found squalid conditions and a heavy-handed, over-zealous security regime in place at Holloway (Ramsbotham, 2005: chs 1 and 11). This was again followed by an apparent improvement in conditions, but Holloway's problems seem to recur on a regular basis, with a recent inspection finding squalid conditions (including mice-infested cells), and high levels of bullying and self-harm among inmates (*Guardian*, 30 March 2005; HM Inspectorate of Prisons, 2005b).

In recent years, female prisoners seem to have suffered at least as much as male inmates from the 'security first' atmosphere engendered by the Woodcock (1994) and Learmont (1995) reports into prison security, despite the fact that women generally pose much less of a threat to security. One manifestation of this was a policy introduced in 1995 that women prisoners (including those in advanced stages of pregnancy) should be handcuffed or chained when being treated in hospitals outside prisons. The outcry which followed a TV news report of a prisoner chained to a prison officer hours before and after giving birth led to a modification of the policy in 1996, but only to exempt women arriving at hospital to give birth (and most of those attending ante-natal checks) from being cuffed or chained while in the hospital.

Overall, though, it appears that female offenders do not in general receive harsher treatment than their opposite numbers of the opposite sex; and sometimes they may receive more lenient treatment, perhaps especially as regards the decision to impose custodial sentences. However, it also seems very likely that *some* women are effectively punished for deviating from conventional feminine norms, and that the system tends to react to female offenders in a manner which is, one way or another, imbued with sexism. To use Althusser's terminology, the penal system can be seen both as part of the 'Repressive State Apparatus' visiting deviant women with punitive sanctions and as an 'Ideological State Apparatus' communicating and reproducing the sexist ideology which structures patriarchal society (Eaton, 1986: 88–9; also see above, Chapter 3, section 3.2). Or, as a Durkheimian might put it, our social culture is still permeated with sexism, which is bound to find expression in our punitive practices.

Currently, women offenders are being punished increasingly harshly for their deviance. Indeed, the female prison population has recently been increasing much more rapidly than the numbers of male prisoners. Between 1993 and October 2006 the male prison population increased by a massive 75 per cent, but the numbers of female prisoners nearly *trebled*, from 1,560 to 4,447.[49] This disproportionate rise is not because women are now being sentenced more harshly than men, nor does it seem to result from an increase in the seriousness of female offending (Home Office, 2004b: 21). Rather, it seems to be because the increase in sentence severity since 1993 has in particular meant that a great many more relatively petty offenders have been sent to prison, or sent there for longer. And since, as we have seen, most female offenders are relatively petty criminals, this shift has affected women disproportionately (see also Hedderman, 2002).

We should stress that, although we accept the possibility that women offenders sometimes escape custody where men would not, we are emphatically *not* advocating that more women should be sent to prison. On the contrary, since women in prison are predominantly relatively petty, non-violent offenders with few previous convictions, a large proportion of them could probably be decarcerated or diverted from custody with comparatively little difficulty, if there were the will to do so. As long ago as 1986 (when there were far fewer women in prison) Nancy Seear and Elaine Player (1986: 12) were surprised to find near-unanimous agreement from prison governors, prison officers, educationalists and ex-offenders that very many women in prison should not be there at all, and proposed a plausible programme for reducing the female prison population to tiny proportions (see also Carlen, 1990). In a penal system that was generally fair and did not exercise the massive 'overkill' of punishment we exposed in Chapter 2, this could be achieved without any need to exercise 'chivalry'. But at present, of course, the trend is very much in the opposite direction.

There have been some recent attempts on the part of both government and senior judiciary to restrain the ever-increasing imprisonment of women. In the 2002 case of *R. v. Mills*,[50] Lord Chief Justice Lord Woolf referred to what he described as the recent remarkable and undesirable rise in the female prison population, and stated that courts should avoid imprisoning women who were the sole carers for young children, especially in cases that did not involve violence where the woman was of previous good character. For its part, the government has sought to encourage the use of non-custodial penalties for female offenders. A strategy for women offenders was first published in 2000, and in March 2004 the government launched the Women's Offending Reduction Programme, aimed at improving community-based provision for women offenders, tailoring it to meet their needs (with particular emphasis on mental health and substance abuse), in the hope that courts would be encouraged to make greater use of these improved community disposals as a result.[51] So far – and it is early days – there have been some limited signs[52] of such initiatives putting the brakes on the rising female prison population. Most recently, a government-commissioned review by Baroness Corston (2007) has put forward radical proposals for reducing and reforming custody for women, including closing all existing women's prisons within 10 years and replacing them with small local secure units. But for now it is still very much the case that, while there may not be an overall bias against female offenders, they nevertheless continue to suffer in the current punitive climate.

Notes

1 Another has been the introduction as from April 2007 of a new duty imposed on all 'public authorities' (including private organizations providing public services) to eliminate gender discrimination (Equality Act 2006).
2 Including the legislative phase. As we noted in Chapter 6 (section 6.2), Thomas Mathiesen (1974: 78) has suggested that even serious wrongdoing may be less likely to be defined and punished as criminal behaviour when committed by powerful individuals and classes. The lengthy and still ongoing campaign to establish an offence of 'corporate manslaughter' (see note 5 below) provides one example of the selective attitude of the criminal law towards socially harmful behaviour depending on the status and role of the wrongdoer.
3 The Policy Studies Institute (Smith, 1983: 247) found that Londoners in the professional and managerial occupational groups were more critical of the police than others; but it also seemed that unemployed people were significantly more likely to be critical of the police than people in employment. Similarly, results from the national British Crime Survey have shown manual workers, inner-city residents and people who are unemployed and less educated (Skogan, 1990: 13–14; 1995) to be less happy with the police than others. See also more generally Roberts and Hough (2005: ch. 3).
4 It does not, however, seem to be consistently the case that *employed working-class* people are stopped more often than middle-class people. In fact, if stops in cars are included, professionals and higher earners may be more likely to be stopped, because they are more likely to drive cars (Skogan, 1990: 28–9; 61).
5 For evidence that deaths at work which are caused by managers' culpable carelessness are dealt with very differently from other deaths caused by fault, see Bergman (1991). A Bill to create a new offence of 'corporate manslaughter' for which *companies* could be prosecuted was introduced into Parliament in late 2006, but this would not affect the criminal liability of the *individual* managers who might be at fault. In several high-profile cases in recent years, including major fatal rail crashes (at Southall in 1997, Paddington in 1999, Hatfield in 2000 and Potters Bar in 2002), no individuals have been convicted of crimes, although some have been prosecuted for manslaughter and acquitted, and in the Hatfield case record fines of £10 million and £3.5 million were imposed on culpable *firms* in 2005.
6 Calculated from HSE enforcement statistics available at http://www.hse.gov.uk/statistics/enforce/index.htm.

7   According to government estimates, the public purse currently loses about £900 million per year because of benefit fraud compared with between £97 and £150 *billion* to tax evasion (*Guardian*, 10 January 2007).

8   For an article attempting the tricky task of comparing the treatment of white-collar and other offenders, see Levi (1989). See also Nelken (2002, especially pp. 863–9).

9   Softley (1978); Crow et al. (1989). In both the magistrates' court and the Crown Court, unemployed offenders are significantly less likely to be fined and more likely to be imprisoned (Halliday, 2001: 82; Flood-Page and Mackie, 1998: 144, 165).

10   Foreign prisoners were the focus of a major panic in 2006, when it emerged that over 1,000 had been set free at the end of their sentences or on their normal release dates (see Chapter 8) rather than being considered for deportation, a failure which cost Home Secretary Charles Clarke his job in May 2006.

11   Drug couriers – who tend to receive harsh sentences as a supposed deterrent – account for some of this disparity, especially among females. (Around 75 per cent of foreign female prisoners are serving sentences for drugs offences.)

12   In this book, we use the term 'black' to refer to people of African or Caribbean ethnic origin only. This chapter mostly concentrates on the most obvious and most disturbing statistical differences between the races in the criminal justice system, which are between 'white' people on the one hand and 'black' people on the other. Comparisons between whites and people of 'Asian' (Indian, Pakistani or Bangladeshi) ethnic origin often yield different results. For example, most research over the years suggests that Asian people are *under*-represented in both recorded and unrecorded offending (e.g. Stevens and Willis, 1979: 2; Graham and Bowling, 1995). Hood (1992: 75–9) found that, unlike black defendants, Asian Crown Court defendants were slightly less likely than whites to be sentenced to custody, although Asians are now slightly over-represented in the prison population, accounting for 5.4 per cent of prisoners as opposed to 4.7 per cent of the general population. Genders and Player (1989) found that, within prisons, Asians were regarded stereotypically by staff as 'model prisoners', in stark contrast to Afro-Caribbeans. Again, studies that distinguish between people of Indian origin and those of Pakistani and Bangladeshi origin can find significant differences between these groups (Clancy et al., 2001).

13   Clancy et al. (2001: 15–17). Similarly, although the survey found black over-representation among muggers, this was largely accounted for by a concentration of mugging offences in London (2001: 18–19).

14   Bucke (1997); figures include stops on foot and in cars. See also Flood-Page et al. (2000: 49–50); Skogan (1990: 27–9; 1994: 25–6, 73); Willis (1983: 14). The British Crime Survey 2000 found that 12 per cent of white and Indian people were stopped in cars in 1999, as were 15 per cent of those of Afro-Caribbean, Pakistani and Bangladeshi origins. The figures for stops on foot were 3 per cent for whites, 2 per cent for Asians and 4 per cent for black people. On the basis of these figures, Clancy et al. (2001: 59–66) found (taking other factors into account) that ethnic origin did not in that year make a difference to someone's chances of being stopped on foot, but that black people and those of Pakistani and Bangladeshi origins were more likely to be stopped in cars.

15   Home Office (2006e: 23); 2004/5 figures. These numbers may not be as bad as they seem when different social, demographic and lifestyle characteristics of different ethnic groups are taken into account. The average black person may be more likely to be found on the city streets than the average white person, and the racial differences in stop and search rates sometimes disappear when these factors are controlled for (MVA and Miller, 2000; Waddington et al., 2004). Nevertheless it seems unlikely that a ratio as great as 6 to 1 can be satisfactorily explained away entirely in this way.

16   'Demeanour' could also be important here. Either stereotyping by the police, or the fact that black people tend to be more critical of the police than whites (Field, 1984: ch. 7;

Flood-Page et al., 2000: 54; Mirrlees-Black, 2001; Sims and Myhill, 2001; Clancy et al., 2001: ch. 6), or both, could lead to the police perceiving black people as having a bad attitude towards them and discriminating against them as a result.

17 While the Macpherson Inquiry was in session, 12 English police forces (but not the Metropolitan Police) admitted that they were institutionally racist. A finding of institutional racism was also made against the Crown Prosecution Service by the Denman Report of 2001.

18 See Cavadino and Dignan (2002: 315). Clancy et al. (2001: 65) did find some evidence that there could have been some 'Macpherson effect' immediately following the report, especially in London, since in 1999 living in London and being black no longer increased the likelihood of being stopped on foot; but it is not clear how durable any such effect may have been.

19 See Home Office (2006e: Tables A and 4.6), which shows that Asians (representing 4.7 per cent of the general population) constituted 15 per cent of those stopped and searched under these powers in 2004/5. (The figures for black people were 2.8 per cent and 11 per cent, making them even more over-represented than Asians.)

20 Asians are not over-represented among arrestees. However, figures for 2004/5 show a disproportionate increase in arrests of Asians compared with the previous year (3.9 per cent, as opposed to 1.8 per cent for black or white suspects: Home Office, 2006e: 35).

21 Eleven per cent of arrests of black people result from a stop and search, compared with 6 per cent for whites and 9 per cent for Asians (Home Office, 2006e: 36).

22 See further Cavadino and Dignan (2002: 330, n. 13).

23 An exception was a 2003 survey (with rather incomplete data) which found similar rates of discontinuance for black, white and Asian defendants (Home Office, 2005b: 53).

24 This difference was not statistically significant at the 0.05 level conventionally used by statisticians, and in theory there is a 7 per cent chance that it could be attributable to chance. However, in the light of other evidence about the effects of race in criminal justice and the fact that the difference is in the 'expected' direction, Hood (1992: 80–1; 1995) is doubtless justified in taking it as evidence of a genuine 'race effect' in sentencing.

25 Since it appears that more black than white defendants are *acquitted*, or have their cases dismissed by the court for lack of evidence (Walker, M., 1988; Phillips and Brown, 1998; Home Office, 2000b: 37), it may be that black defendants deny guilt more often simply because black people are more often wrongly arrested and wrongly prosecuted.

26 Calculated from NOMS (2006d: 2).

27 Calculated from Home Office (2006g: Tables 3.6 and 3.9).

28 One outstanding (and notoriously sexist) exception was Otto Pollak (1961), who claimed that women are responsible for vast amounts of crime which go undetected because of women's more deceitful nature and because chivalrous men do not want to see women prosecuted or punished (see Heidensohn, 1985: 118–21).

29 A recent 'self-report' study found that males aged 12–30 were two and a half times more likely than females to admit (in confidence, to researchers) having committed a crime in the last year (26 per cent compared with 11 per cent: see Home Office, 2004b: 3); this would mean that 30 per cent of all offenders were female.

30 Some 78 per cent of police officers are male (Clegg and Kirwan, 2006: 5), as are 88 per cent of Crown Court judges and 51 per cent of magistrates (Home Office, 2004b: ch. 10). Some research suggests that women magistrates deal more severely with female defendants (Farrington and Morris, 1983: 245), which may fit in with the 'chivalry theory'. On the other hand, it could mean that 'good', law-abiding women tend to come down even harder on 'evil', law-breaking women than men do.

31 For example, the 1992 British Crime Survey found that 28 per cent of males and 16 per cent of females had been stopped over a 12-month period (Skogan, 1994: 73). See also Flood-Page et al. (2000: 48–9); Clancy et al. (2001: ch. 5).

32   Walker's claim was based on unrefined statistics which took no account of the serious-ness of the offence or the offender's previous record; on the other hand, Smart's claim was based on a statistical fallacy which Walker later refuted (Walker, 1981: 380–1).

33   However, it is not clear that the police are acting in a *directly* sexist manner at this point. Gelsthorpe suggests that boys who showed remorse (which they did less often than girls) were also more likely to be cautioned.

34   It is possible that many sentencers pass a non-custodial sentence rather than a short prison sentence on a woman who has been remanded in custody, reasoning that she has already had 'a taste of custody'. If so, the fact that women's prison sentences are on average much shorter than men's (because their offences are less serious) could explain the gender difference pointed out in the text.

35   In 2004, 17.5 per cent of females sentenced for indictable offences were placed on community rehabilitation (probation) or supervision orders, 7.6 per cent given com-munity punishment (community service) orders and 16 per cent were fined. The corre-sponding figures for male offenders were 11.5, 8.8 and 20 per cent (calculated from RDS NOMS, 2005b: Tables 3.11 and 4.1). Whereas in previous years, women were less likely to receive community service orders, the differentials here (and indeed in respect of imprisonment and probation/supervision) have narrowed recently. In 2002, 23 per cent of women convicted of indictable offences received an absolute or conditional discharge compared with 13 per cent of males (Home Office, 2004b: 22).

36   The case of *Susan Jones* (1992) 13 Cr. App. R. (S.) 275 is interesting in this context. Her four-year prison sentence for robbing seven building societies was quashed by the Court of Appeal in 1991 and a probation order with a condition of psychiatric treatment was substituted. The trial judge had referred to her 'wicked crimes', but the Court of Appeal judges stated that she was *'not a wicked woman'* and had only robbed because she had become desperate about her family's debts and was concerned about her twin children but 'did not want to worry her husband'.

37   It is not entirely clear how or whether these findings can be reconciled with those of Farrington and Morris (1983). But it is noticeable that Farrington and Morris divided sentences into two categories, 'relatively lenient' and 'relatively severe', the latter including probation, community service and suspended sentences, whereas the other studies divided sentences into unsuspended custody and non-custodial sentences. Farrington and Morris's finding could therefore be explained by the known tendency for courts to sentence women disproportionately to probation, while the other studies sug-gest that – as Carlen's sheriffs claimed – courts may often be fairly loath to sentence women (especially mothers) to custody.

38   In October 2006, only 29 per cent of female sentenced prisoners were in prison for sexual or violent offences (including robbery), compared with 49 per cent of male prisoners. (Calculated from NOMS, 2006d: Table 2).

39   Brenda Hale (2006) argues cogently that the situations and experiences of male and female offenders are typically so different that it would not generally be fair to treat female offend-ers as severely as male offenders even if they are legally and formally similar.

40   In the cases of *R. v. Ahluwalia* [1992] 4 All ER 889 and *R. v. Humphries* [1995] 4 All ER 1008. Guidelines issued by the Sentencing Guidelines Council in November 2005 are intended to improve the fairness of the sentencing of men and women who kill their partners and are found guilty of manslaughter by reason of provocation. The proposals of the Law Commission (2006) regarding the law of murder could also alter the situa-tion if they are implemented.

41   See above, note 35.

42   Indeed, the current trend is for female prisons to be 're-roled', i.e. converted into male prisons, as has happened to Buckley Hall and Edmunds Hill and is due to happen to Brockhill as we write.

43 Women prisoners are punished for offences against prison discipline much more often than men: in 2001 there were 224 offences per 100 female prisoners compared with 160 per 100 males (Home Office, 2005b: 38). Part of the reason for this seems to be that, although the governing Prison Rules do not vary, there are generally more unnecessary restrictions placed on women prisoners and the rules are more rigorously enforced against them (NACRO, 1992; Morris, A., 1987: 121–4).

44 There are currently seven mother and baby units within women's prisons with places for over 80 women and their babies, who can stay with their mothers up to the age of 18 months. It is a controversial question whether this is the right approach to the needs of mothers and their children, as opposed to ensuring that as few mothers as possible are in prison in the first place.

45 Vulnerable women in the criminal justice system were the focus of the Corston Report (2007), mentioned at the end of this chapter.

46 Studies have yielded different results as to how prevalent different types of mental disorder are among women prisoners, but while they have typically only found a small percentage of women prisoners suffering from psychoses such as schizophrenia (see note 48 below), the prevalence of neurotic disorders, depression and 'personality disorders' has been high. Singleton et al. (1998) found that women prisoners were less likely than males to exhibit 'personality disorders', but significantly more likely to suffer from psychoses and neurotic symptoms. Female prisoners are certainly *treated as* mentally ill more often than males: in the same survey half of women prisoners were receiving psychotropic medication compared with one-fifth of males.

47 For males, the figures for attempted suicide were 27 per cent (remand) and 20 per cent (sentenced). Some women offenders attempt suicide while in prison; some succeed. No fewer than six women committed suicide in Styal Prison in a 12-month period between 2002 and 2003.

48 If 'mad' means suffering from psychoses such as schizophrenia, then this is hardly the case for the vast majority of prisoners, male or female. Singleton et al. (1998) rated 14 per cent of female prisoners as 'probably having a psychotic disorder' compared with 10 per cent of male remandees and 7 per cent of male sentenced prisoners; but did find considerably more symptoms of less extreme neurotic disorders among females (see note 46 above).

49 Slightly reduced from 4,595 in June 2003, prior to which the female prison population had risen year on year for an entire decade (NOMS, 2006d; RDS NOMS, 2006b. 97).

50 [2002] EWCA Crim 26; (2002) 2 Cr App R (S) 52.

51 The Women's Offending Reduction Programme is part of a broader initiative launched by the Women and Equality Unit at the Department for Trade and Industry, which published a report, 'Delivering on Gender Equality', in June 2003. See the Home Office Women's Policy Team (2003) for further details concerning both sets of initiatives.

52 The slight reduction in the numbers of female prisoners between 2003 and 2006 (see above, note 49) may offer some faint glimmerings of hope.

11 Solving the Crisis?

A Grim Fairy Tale

11.1

There was once a land where all the people firmly believed that sacrificing animals to the gods was certain to bring prosperity and good fortune to the nation. Whenever there was bad weather, or a poor harvest, or a military setback, the people would all go clamouring to the emperor, demanding that even more animals should be sacrificed. As we now know, all this achieved was an ever-increasing amount of pointless suffering.

One day an enlightened emperor declared that animal sacrifice was wrong, and banned the practice. He was immediately killed by an angry mob, and replaced by a more popular ruler who promised to double the numbers of animals sacrificed. Over time, more and more of the country's resources were devoted to devising new and increasingly cruel methods of sacrifice. Eventually the civilization died out when there were no animals left to provide milk and eggs, no horses to pull the carts and no oxen to draw the ploughs.

Fortunately, no modern society would ever be so foolish and primitive ...

****

Throughout this book we have seen how wide, deep and persistent the penal crisis is. It pervades every area and aspect of the penal system, manifesting itself in both a running malaise and periodic dramatic eruptions. In this final chapter we trace the recent history of strategies to solve the penal crisis and assess the likely (and in our view grim) future for the penal system if current policies are continued. We go on to expound our own ideas of the kind of short-, medium- and long-term measures and programmes which should be adopted to tackle the crisis, and discuss the prospects of this type of approach being adopted.

Responses to the Crisis, 1970–2006

From Positivism to 'Law and Order' with Bifurcation: 1970–1987

11.2

In the heyday of the 'rehabilitative ideal' in the 1960s, penal strategies on the whole moved fairly straightforwardly in a single, seemingly progressive direction. New penal measures (such as parole) were introduced for avowedly rehabilitative purposes, with the double advantage that they were not only ideologically attractive but also promised to reduce the prison population and hence ease the penal system's resource problems. In the 1970s, however, the penal system's ideological and resource difficulties both worsened as the legitimating ideology of the rehabilitative ideal collapsed and the penal population threatened to spiral out of control.

The response to this by both Conservative and Labour governments in the 1970s was predominantly pragmatic. Efforts were made to restrain the prison population by exhorting sentencers to use custody less extensively and for shorter periods, while providing them with a greater variety of non-custodial penalties to use as alternatives (the *'strategy of encouragement'*: see Chapters 4 and 5). At the same time, an increasing number of prisoners were released before the ends of their sentences (see Chapter 8, section 8.3). The discrediting of rehabilitation led to a shift towards 'law and order ideology' (Hall, 1979), and Tony Bottoms made his first perceptive sighting of the trend towards *'bifurcation'* in penal policy (Bottoms, 1977) as measures to increase the punishment inflicted on more serious criminals were combined with attempts to deal more leniently with some lesser offenders. The overall strategy for the prison population was to attempt to achieve a *'standstill'*, keeping the lid on prison numbers but not trying to reduce it substantially. But 'by the end of the 1970s standstill policy was near to collapse' (Rutherford, 1986b: 56).

It was at this stage – in 1979 – that the Conservative government of Margaret Thatcher came to power. The Conservative Party has usually portrayed itself as being 'tougher on crime' than its Labour opponents, and has more often than not been rewarded by general public approval for this stance. However, law and order had never been such a prominent election campaign theme as it was in 1979, when the Conservatives committed themselves to increase the resources of the criminal justice system (especially the police), to introduce a 'short sharp shock' regime into detention centres for young offenders, and to increase the sentencing powers of the courts. Although Home Secretary William Whitelaw tried to inject an element of liberal pragmatism by introducing earlier automatic release for short-term prisoners, this proposal was defeated by the combined opposition of the judges and the Conservative Party Conference (see Chapter 8, section 8.3). In March 1982, Mr Whitelaw effectively announced the end of the 'standstill policy' by telling Parliament: 'We are determined to ensure that there will be room in the prison system for every person whom the judges and magistrates decide should go there, and we will continue to do whatever is necessary for that purpose' (HC Deb., 25 March 1982; Rutherford, 1986b: 56–7). This heralded the birth of the most extensive programme of prison building of the twentieth century.

This did not, however, mean that the Thatcher government's penal policies in the early 1980s were entirely determined by law and order ideology. Pragmatic considerations still led to some attempts to limit the rise in the prison population, and the government continued to encourage diversion from court and custody and shorter sentences for many 'run-of-the-mill' offenders. Thus, for example, the same White Paper that introduced the 'short sharp shock' detention centre (see Chapter 9, section 9.3) also approved the practice of cautioning juvenile offenders, an approval later extended to older less serious offenders.[1] The Government also lent support to the use of alternatives to custody such as community service orders, and supported attempts by the Lord Chief Justice to reduce the length of custodial sentences for non-violent petty offenders. But these measures were to apply only to supposedly 'less serious offenders'. Bifurcation was not only alive and well but taking on a new lease of life, with less harsh measures still being advocated for petty offenders while the full force of law and order rhetoric and treatment was focused on the more serious 'violent criminals and thugs' (as the 1979 Conservative Manifesto called them). Notable in this context were some classically bifurcatory alterations to the parole system in 1983, which increased parole eligibility for shorter-term prisoners while simultaneously reducing it for some more serious offenders (see Chapter 8, section 8.3).

Overall, it could hardly be claimed that the penal strategy of the early 1980s proved an outstanding success. The prison population continued to rise throughout the 1980s, while outbreaks of riots and disorder within prisons were still a regular occurrence. The 'short, sharp shock' proved a disappointment, recorded crime rose almost every year, and Britain's inner cities were hit by serious rioting in the summers of 1981 and 1985. The magazine *Punch* once memorably observed that Mrs Thatcher's bark might be dogmatic but her bite was pragmatic, and so it proved now. In the second half of the 1980s, the Conservative government altered course.

'Just Deserts' and Punishment in the Community: 1987–1992

A profound change in the government's approach to criminal justice took place following the Conservative victory in the General Election of 1987. The shift occurred first under Douglas Hurd (Home Secretary from 1985 to 1989), but the new policies continued to be pursued under his successors David Waddington and Kenneth Baker. One symbolic moment was a meeting of Home Office ministers and civil servants at Leeds Castle in Kent in September 1987, two months after the prison population had reached a then record high of 50,979. When presented with statistical projections of an increase in the prison population to over 60,000 in the foreseeable future, possibly reaching 70,000 by the year 2000, ministers resolved that this should not be allowed to happen (Windlesham, 1993: 237–9).

The resulting new 'Hurd approach' (as we like to call it) represented a shift towards eclectic pragmatism. In terms of the typology of penal strategies we sketched out in the Introduction, it was a predominantly managerial, Strategy B approach, although it also contained some elements of the humanitarian Strategy C, and retained echoes of the harshly punitive Strategy A. The volume of 'law and order' rhetoric emanating from government was significantly toned down, and was combined with other themes and approaches to crime and punishment such as privatization and crime prevention. Prominent in this new pragmatic mix was *managerialism* (see Chapter 1), with the government continuing to favour the systems management approach to criminal justice (see Chapter 9), and in particular the expanded use of cautioning for adult offenders as well as juveniles. Above all, there was the 'just deserts' package of reforms contained in the Criminal Justice Act of 1991.

These reforms were based on the notion (expressed in the Green and White Papers which preceded the 1991 Act) that 'imprisonment is not the most effective punishment for most crime', and indeed (in a famous phrase) 'can be an expensive way of making bad people worse'. Consequently, 'custody should be reserved for very serious offences, especially when the offender is violent and a continuing risk to the public' (Home Office, 1988a: para. 1.8; 1990a: para. 2.7), with many more offenders than hitherto being dealt with by means of community penalties instead. Philosophically, this package of reforms was heavily influenced by the 'justice model' (see Chapter 2). The legislative framework for sentencing contained in the 1991 Act was based on the 'just deserts' notion of proportionality between the seriousness of the current offence and the severity of the sentence. But this was heavily qualified by exceptions for violent and sexual offenders, who were liable to get more than their just deserts if this was thought necessary to protect the public.

The Act embodied the *bifurcation* approach, for although less serious offenders were to be diverted from custody, at the same time violent and sexual offenders were to be treated more harshly. Moreover, it was what we call *punitive bifurcation* – meaning that it was punitive not only towards the more serious offenders, but also towards the less serious. True, the intention was to deal with them in the community rather than in custody; but the influence of law and order ideology lingered on in the insistence that the non-custodial measures were to be tough and punitive in nature, rather than being primarily intended to rehabilitate offenders or to make them perform reparation for victims. Nevertheless, the 'just deserts' package was a serious attempt to tackle not only the material crisis of resources (by reducing the prison population) but also the general ideological crisis of legitimacy by putting forward 'just deserts' as a legitimating ideology for punishment.

Another strand of the government's strategy around this time was its response to the Woolf Report on the 1990 disturbances in Strangeways and other prisons (Woolf and Tumim, 1991). As we saw in Chapters 1 and 6, Woolf implicitly diagnosed the major cause of prison disorder as being a lack of justice in prisons leading to a crisis of legitimacy, and produced a set of recommendations aimed at improving conditions and regimes within prisons and alleviating prisoners' sense of injustice, with particular emphasis on improving grievance and disciplinary procedures. The government accepted the main thrust of the Woolf Report and implemented a number of its recommendations (see Chapter 6), including a programme to abolish 'slopping out', some relaxations of restrictions on prisoners' contact with their families and the outside world, and the creation of the Prisons Ombudsman. Until the autumn of 1992, the government held to this strategy based upon the Criminal Justice Act 1991, acceptance of the Woolf Report and a generally managerial approach to criminal justice. This more liberal and pragmatic strategy for criminal justice started showing some signs of success. In the first months following the implementation of the Criminal Justice Act 1991 in October 1992, sentencing became less harsh,[2] and the prison population fell from 45,835 in September to 40,606 in December 1992.[3] But it was not to last.

Law and Order Reinvigorated: 1993–1997

The extraordinary U-turn of John Major's Conservative government on criminal justice policy – the 'law and order counter-reformation' – is difficult to explain without reference to the general political situation and party political electoral calculations. The government, in deep trouble and with desperately low opinion poll ratings, seemed to make a deliberate strategic decision to try to regain popularity by 'playing the law and order card'. This strategy, which had served them well in the past, was to be further encouraged by events such as the murder of 2-year-old James Bulger by two 10-year-olds in February 1993. October 1992 saw the implementation of the Criminal Justice Act 1991, followed rapidly by a backlash from sections of the media and the judiciary against its perceived 'softness'. Instead of defending the policy package which had been put together over five years by successive Conservative Home Secretaries, the government increasingly came to assume the remarkable role of criticizing and reversing its own policies and legislation. Key components of its 'Hurd era' strategy – the attempt to reduce the prison population by means of the 1991 legislation, the positive response to the Woolf Report, and the encouragement of systems management – were all abandoned between 1993 and 1995. In May 1993 Home Secretary Kenneth Clarke announced the swift repeal of two significant provisions of the Criminal Justice Act 1991: the unit fines system (see Chapter 5, section 5.3); and a section which had restricted the ability of courts to take previous convictions into account when sentencing offenders (see Chapter 4, section 4.5).[4]

In May 1993 the office of Home Secretary passed to Michael Howard (later to be Conservative opposition leader between 2003 and 2005), a right-winger with a profound attachment to the rhetoric and ideology of law and order, who was put in charge of implementing the government's 'crusade against crime'. At the Conservative Party Conference of October 1993, he famously proclaimed that *'prison works'* (see Chapter 2, section 2.2) and said of his package of proposals to toughen up the criminal justice system: 'This may mean that more people will go to prison. I do not flinch from that. We shall no longer judge the success of our system of justice by a fall in the prison population.' A retreat from Woolf's strategy for prisons was also evident, with Mr Howard proclaiming that conditions in prisons should be 'decent but austere', a remark which was given substance by moves to increase disciplinary powers for prison governors and reduce home leave for prisoners. Subsequently, the government moved even further in the direction of Strategy A, introducing legislation to provide for mandatory 'two or three strikes and you're out' sentences for certain categories of repeat offenders (see Chapter 4) and proposing massive cutbacks to the system of early release (see Chapter 8). The effects of this atmosphere of 'law and order' were predictable. Sentencers responded to the encouragement to make more punitive decisions from early 1993 onwards. The prison population rose immediately from its low point of 40,600 in December 1992 and by 1995 was breaking all previous records. By 1997 the daily average prison population was 61,114 – a spectacular 51 per cent above the December 1992 figure.

But the Conservatives failed to reap the reward in terms of popularity with the electorate which they must have hoped for. Although opinion polls had always favoured the Conservatives as having the best policies on crime, the Labour Party took a lead on this issue from 1993 onwards. This shift was facilitated by the efforts of Tony Blair (Shadow Home Secretary from 1992 to 1994 and Labour leader from 1994 to 2007), whose much-reiterated slogan – 'tough on crime and tough on the causes of crime' – did much to shed Labour's public image of being 'soft on crime'. The phrase 'tough on the causes of crime' evoked the Labour Party's more traditional concerns with what it saw as the social roots of crime such as unemployment. However, the slogan as a whole (and Labour's general rhetoric from 1992 onwards) was calculated to appeal to populist sentiments by fostering the impression that Labour wanted to deal severely with offenders. By the time of the General Election in May 1997 the two main parties were bidding against each other for who could sound 'toughest' on law and order.

'Tough on Crime, Tough on the Causes of Crime': New Labour, 1997 Onwards

The General Election of May 1997 resulted in a landslide victory for Tony Blair's 'New Labour' party. For all their recurrent use of the word 'tough', it would have been difficult for Labour to incline more towards Strategy A than Michael Howard had. And indeed the approach of Labour Home Secretaries Jack Straw (1997–2001), David Blunkett (2001–4) and Charles Clarke (2004–6) proved to be a mixture of Strategies A, B and C, well summed up by the term 'neo-correctionalism' (see especially Chapter 9, section 9.3). Soon after taking office, Mr. Straw declared that he had 'no interest in chanting a simplistic mantra that prison works'.[5] Yet Strategy A rhetoric lived on in talk of 'toughness' and 'zero tolerance' (see Cavadino et al., 1999: 28–30): the title of Mr Straw's 1997 White Paper on young offenders (*No More Excuses*, Home Office, 1997a) was typical. John Reid, who was Home Secretary from 2006 to 2007, sought to portray an even tougher image.

Overtly, the New Labour strategy has been one of rational, *'evidence-based'* crime control: finding out 'what works' to combat crime and then firmly implementing effective policies: a managerial, Strategy B approach. (One prominent strand in this has been an increasing emphasis on the use of *'risk assessment'* techniques and procedures in order to apply the appropriate management to offenders according to the level and nature of the risk they pose – see, for example, Robinson, 1999; 2002.) Much about the government's approach has been both sensible and welcome, including an increased emphasis on funding and implementing measures which have been shown to be effective in preventing the commission of crimes in the first place. But the clear subtext has always been a determination not to give the Conservatives political ammunition on law and order issues by appearing to be 'soft on crime'. For example, in the summer of 1997 the new Labour government took a deliberate decision to commit extra resources to prisons and to reverse the party's policy on privatized prisons (see further Chapter 7) in preference to taking action to cut the size of the prison population, moves which were explicitly defended in terms of the government's need not to seem 'soft on crime' (Cavadino et al., 1999: 53).

This is of course a considerable constraint on the kind of policies that can be pursued, since it means they can never stray too far away from a 'Strategy A' agenda. Even though the evidence as to 'what works' shows that prison doesn't work, the government feels it has to act as if the reverse were true. The overall effect is very largely the *'neo-correctionalist'* approach we delineated in Chapter 9 in relation to young offenders; or to use a different phrase, it is not far removed from the kind of combination of Strategies A and B we have termed *'punitive managerialism'* (Cavadino et al., 1999: 54.) Elements of Strategy C – such as 'restorative justice'-type measures like reparation orders for young offenders – have their place in the overall approach, but a very limited one. Such measures are for the most part justified by the government on the basis that they are *effective* ways of reducing crime (and in some instances helpful to victims), rather than that they are humane or needed to give effect to the rights of offenders.

This kind of mixed strategy is – yet again – a variant of *bifurcation*, with government policy going in more than one direction at once. On the one hand, for example, some prisoners now have access to television in their cells and the opportunity to be released on home detention curfew. And, as we shall see, there have been some attempts by the government to encourage the use of 'tough and rigorous' non-custodial alternatives to short prison sentences, in a manner reminiscent of Hurd-era 'punitive bifurcation'. On the other hand, there has so far been no sustained or concerted attempt to limit the numbers going to prison or the lengths of their sentences. Indeed, measures such as the implementation of 'three strikes and you're out' and other minimum sentences and tougher enforcement of community penalties have been deliberately aimed at putting more people into prison. Similarly, the government's introduction of new mandatory and indeterminate sentences and its insistence on longer 'tariff' periods for those convicted of murder (see Chapter 8, section 8.5) are designed to keep some offenders in for longer.

One aspect of the government's strategy has been a *concentration on the persistent offender*, with recidivists being singled out for particularly tough measures. This marks a sharp contrast with the Hurd era and the 'just deserts' philosophy of the 1991 Criminal Justice Act. Under that previous 'punitive bifurcation' approach, it was only serious (and dangerous) violent and sexual offenders who were singled out in this way, with petty persistent offenders being largely left to receive what might be termed (relatively) petty persistent punishment, commensurate with the 'just deserts' for their latest offence. Although the tough approach to serious and allegedly dangerous offenders is still in place, New Labour has also targeted petty persistent offenders, with little or no regard to their just deserts. Thus, as we saw in Chapter 4 (section 4.5), the Criminal Justice Act 2003 provides that in determining the 'seriousness' of the offence – which still largely dictates the severity of sentences – courts should have regard to the offender's previous record as well as the actual gravity of the current offence. Thus the Act provides for a progressive 'offender-based tariff' with harsher and harsher punishments the more an individual persists in reoffending, which could mean imprisonment even for relatively trivial crimes if the offender were persistent enough. Similarly, highly intrusive measures including intensive supervision and surveillance in the community have been and are being developed for persistent offenders of all ages: ISSPs (Intensive Supervision and Surveillance Programmes) for offenders aged under 18, ICCPs (Intensive Change and Control Programmes) for 18 to 20-year-olds, and ISMs (Intensive Supervision and Monitoring Programmes, now renamed Prolific and other Priority Offender Schemes) for persistent adult offenders.

On the one hand, this concentration on persistence is defended (*à la* Strategy B) as being based on evidence about what is likely to be effective in reducing crime. It is claimed that there are 100,000 offenders who are responsible for half of all crime[6] and that special measures targeted on them can be effective in significantly reducing crime rates. On the other hand, such a tough approach towards a bunch of unpopular social nuisances has obvious Strategy A appeal. The approach conspicuous by its absence is of course Strategy C, whose advocates would tend to regard such disproportionately intrusive responses to petty crimes – even a succession of petty crimes – as an infringement of human rights.

There is plenty of reason to doubt the likely effectiveness of such an approach even from a Strategy B point of view. Even if the claims about the 100,000 most persistent offenders are correct (and for doubts on this front, see Garside, 2004), it should be borne in mind that as many as 20,000 (one in five) will drop out of this Premier League of offending next year in any event (Home Office, 2001: 116). So our efforts on them are likely to be wasted. Again, 50,000 of them are under 21, and even the most persistent young offenders usually grow out of offending, or at least out of persistent offending (Hagell and Newburn, 1994). Moreover, the history of penology is littered with failed attempts to tackle the problem of persistent offenders by introducing new sentences (see, for example, Ashworth, 2005: 182–4). It may make sense to target *reformative* measures on recidivists – preferably in the community – if we want them to have the maximum effect in terms of crime reduction.[7] But trusting to custody as an effective treatment for recidivism looks like folly. Furthermore, it seems all too likely that any new measures for persistent offenders will in practice be targeted only vaguely at those who are judged to be 'persistent' with no particular criterion for deciding who qualifies for this description.[8] The result could well be a very large number of petty offenders sent to custody to no good long-term effect.

Another major theme of New Labour's approach to law and order has been the *Respect Agenda,* promoted tirelessly by Tony Blair personally since the General Election of 2005 (see especially Home Office, 2006a). According to Home Secretary Charles Clarke, the Respect Agenda 'is about nurturing and where needed, enforcing a modern culture of respect' (Home Office, 2006h). Its aim is to 'eradicate the scourge of anti-social behaviour', reasoning that the latter is caused by a breakdown in respect in a society where 'the self-reinforcing bonds of traditional community life do not exist in the same way'.[9] As well as attempting to promote this elusive social ethos of respect, where it is lacking and anti-social behaviour results, the approach is reminiscent of the 'zero tolerance' approach to minor crime and low-level disorder. It sees the traditional criminal process as exemplified by the criminal courts with their due process and legal safeguards as 'simply too cumbersome, too remote from reality, to be effective' in dealing with modern criminal and anti-social behaviour. Thus the agenda encompasses new and extended powers for dealing with such behaviour, such as anti-social behaviour orders (ASBOs, discussed in Chapter 9, section 9.6), and fixed penalty notices imposed by the police (see Introduction), which 'bluntly, reverse the burden of proof', alongside the traditional criminal process. Other novel measures – such as parenting classes and parenting orders (see Chapter 9, section 9.7) – seek to deal with 'problem families' and their delinquent offspring. The deliberate intention is to draw a greater range of less serious behaviour into the ambit of formal social control, often without traditional safeguards. The ASBO in particular carries with it the potential to increase the number of people sent to custody as a result of breaches of the orders imposed for relatively petty misbehaviour.

Paradoxically, at the same time as pursuing policies and employing rhetoric whose natural tendencies are to ensure that more petty offenders find themselves inside prison, the government has also made (it could be said, relatively half-hearted) attempts to divert some less serious offenders away from the prison gate. For example, David Blunkett (Home Secretary 2001–4) made several calls to the courts not to overload the prison system and to use 'tough community sentences' rather than short-term prison sentences for lesser, non-violent offences, joining Lord Woolf (the then Lord Chief Justice) in his similar pleas.[10] However, such statements tended to be drowned out by the roar of Mr Blunkett's higher-profile statements in which he insisted on longer 'tariff' periods for murderers,[11] and lambasted judges for not living 'in the same real world as the rest of us' (*Guardian*, 15 May 2003). At times he criticized Lord Woolf himself (*Guardian*, 14 January 2003). Mr Blunkett was not perhaps being strictly inconsistent: his policy was one of punitive bifurcation, favouring harsher prison terms for more serious offenders but (tough) community sentences rather than custody for many lesser offenders. However, the second, more *sotto voce* part of the message got lost thanks to the more strident rhetoric surrounding the first part. This was highlighted in surreal manner when civil servants resorted to showing judges and magistrates video clips of Mr Blunkett's Commons statements to try to convince the 'dumbfounded' sentencers that the Home Secretary really did want them to use non-custodial penalties for lesser offenders (*Guardian*, 17 November 2004).

There have been moments in the history of the New Labour government when it seemed possible that there might be a determined shift towards a less punitive policy and a serious attempt to reduce the prison population. But so far they have all proved to be false omens, inevitably followed by a reversion to a harsher stance. One such moment was in 1998, when Home Secretary Jack Straw gave an enthusiastic welcome to a major Home Office research report which expressed scepticism about the effectiveness of punitive measures such as custody in controlling crime. Conversely, it pointed out that targeted anti-burglary crime prevention methods were likely to be ten times more cost-effective than locking up burglars (Goldblatt and Lewis, 1998: 98, 135). But although in succeeding years the government did expand crime prevention initiatives, it did not follow the parallel logic and reduce the rate of imprisonment.

In 2004 David Blunkett's acceptance of the Carter Report also seemed a potential harbinger of a positive change in direction (see further Chapter 4, section 4.5; Carter, 2003; Blunkett, 2004). Although (in our opinion) Carter's recommendation for combining the prison and probation services in the form of the National Offender Management Service (see Chapter 5) is unlikely to prove beneficial, Carter to his credit recognized and stressed that sentencing had become noticeably harsher in recent years, and to no good purpose. Moreover, Carter's proposals to ratchet sentencing levels back down by using guidelines from the Sentencing Guidelines Council to 'target' the right level of sentence on offenders and to aim to prevent the prison population rising above 80,000 pointed towards a valid, maybe even realistic strategy for tackling the penal crisis. For its part, the Sentencing Guidelines Council duly set to its laborious task of forging comprehensive guidelines to give effect to this strategy (see Chapter 4).

In the meantime, however, numbers of prisoners were still rising. Michael Howard had bequeathed Labour a daily average prison population of 61,114 in 1997; in 1998 it was 65,298. Following a slight and temporary dip in 1999–2000 (brought about by the introduction of home detention curfew: see Chapter 8, section 8.4), the numbers rose again, to new all-time records. By the end of October 2006 the figure had topped 80,000, already exceeding Carter's ceiling of 80,000, and with the prison system's 'bust limit' (see Chapters 1 and 6) just a few hundred inmates away. Charles Clarke, who had succeeded David Blunkett as Home Secretary in 2004, had already dropped the aspiration to hold the line at 80,000 (*Guardian*, 19 September 2005), which was giving unwanted ammunition to political opponents and was in any event unlikely to be achieved.

However, Mr Clarke's own plans had again contained elements of a positive strategy to contain prison numbers. A 'Five Year Strategy' published in February 2006 stated that 'overall … prison should be used for the most dangerous, violent and seriously persistent offenders, and that others are usually best punished in the community' (Home Office, 2006b: para. 3.26). The strategy sought to reassure the public that they were being securely protected while simultaneously seeking to reduce the numbers of lesser offenders in prison. Central to this plan was community service (or 'unpaid work'), which was to be rebranded as 'Community Payback'. The intention was to double the hours of unpaid work performed as punishment from 5 million in 2005 to 10 million in 2011, to replace time in custody for many offenders. The context of this was the planned replacement of prison sentences of less than 12 months with the new sentence of 'custody plus' (Criminal Justice Act 2003, ss. 181–2) and the introduction of the new 'generic' community order (Criminal Justice Act 2003, ss.177–80) (see further Chapters 4 and 5). The government hoped that many offenders who might previously have received short prison terms would in future receive tough community orders in which unpaid work would figure strongly. (Especially since the 2003 Act had increased the maximum number of hours' work which can be ordered from 240 to 300.) Interestingly – in a partial reversal of previous New Labour policy – this was to include many petty persistent offenders (Home Office, 2006b: para. 3.21). It was also hoped that for many other offenders – a figure of 60,000 was mentioned in press reports (*Guardian* 21 July 2006) – the new custody plus sentences would mean a shorter 'taste of prison' followed by a period in the community subject to requirements which would again include work under the Community Payback scheme.

Whether this would have worked to control the prison population we may never know. Following a fiasco surrounding the failure of foreign prisoners to be considered for deportation (see Chapter 10, note 10), Mr Clarke lost his job in a Cabinet reshuffle in May 2006. His replacement as Home Secretary was John Reid, a man with a tough image and corresponding rhetoric (who famously declared on taking over that the Home Office was 'not fit for purpose'). The planned introduction of custody plus sentences in November 2006 was shelved indefinitely pending a review 'given the need to prioritise prison and probation resources on more serious offenders' (Home Office, 2006c: 34). This announcement came amid rumours that the probation service did not have sufficient resources to expand the unpaid work element of 'custody plus' and conflicting messages from Dr Reid over whether he approved of Mr Clarke's vision for how the new sentence should be used (*Guardian*, 21 July 2006; *Guardian Unlimited*, 3 August 2006). Dr Reid issued an apparently hastily compiled 'Criminal Justice Review' in July 2006 (Home Office, 2006c) which repeated a recurring New Labour promise (see, for example, Home Office, 2002a) to 'rebalance' the criminal justice system in favour of victims and law-abiding communities. This 'rebalancing' was largely to be achieved by a varied package of 'tough' proposals, several of which would have the effect of increasing sentences and restricting the granting of parole for certain prisoners (see Chapters 4 and 8). The only one of these to address the pressing problem of prison numbers was a pledge to create 8,000 more prison places. However, the target date for providing these 8,000 places was 2012, and the 'crunch point' was to arrive in the autumn of 2006. One symptom of the system's disarray was a plan to reduce the prison population by 500 by releasing large numbers of short-term prisoners ten days early on 'transitional home leave'. Dr Reid was reportedly due to announce this scheme on 17 August 2006, but the announcement was blocked by the Prime Minister's office, which feared it could damage Labour's tough image. In October 2006 Dr Reid announced a number of emergency measures to cope with the acute numbers crisis, including reviving the practice (not regularly employed since 1995) of housing prison inmates in cells in police stations (see Chapter 6, 6.5). Even this was insufficient. By January 2007 prisoners were also being kept in cells in court basements (*Guardian*, 18 January 2007), and the Home Secretary, Lord Chancellor and Attorney General were pleading with judges and magistrates to imprison only the most dangerous and persistent criminals (*BBC News Online*, 24 January 2007).

It is at this interesting point in history – with the penal system bearing an alarming resemblance to a badly driven vehicle crammed full of passengers careering wildly towards a cliff edge – that we write. The outcome is unclear (not least because we do not know what penal policies a post-Tony Blair government might pursue) but it seems fair to say – with perhaps a measure of understatement – that the penal crisis has not yet been solved. And if the immediate future for the penal system looks none too healthy, the long-term prospects could be even worse. Unless, that is, a new and different approach is taken to the penal system and the penal crisis.

How to Solve the Crisis

Approaches to the Penal Crisis

11.3 In the Introduction, we briefly set out three broad strategies for criminal justice: the highly punitive Strategy A (allied to the 'new punitiveness' discussed in Chapter 3, section 3.6), the managerial

Strategy B (associated with the 'new penology', for which also see Chapter 3) and the humanitarian, rights-based Strategy C.[12] Government penal strategies in recent years have combined elements of all three approaches, but it is fair to say that the first two have tended to dominate. Strategy A rhetoric and ideology reached its zenith under Michael Howard between 1993 and 1997. As we have seen, New Labour's 'neo-correctionalist' approach has been more mixed but has much more of Strategies A and B than C in the mixture. John Reid as Home Secretary mostly seemed to be tilting the balance further in the direction of Strategy A, his policies even being described (with perhaps – and hopefully – some degree of exaggeration) as marking 'a clear return for Labour to the "prison works" policy of Michael Howard' (*Guardian*, 21 July 2006).

Strategies A and B have both failed to solve the penal crisis to date, and indeed the enduring effects of Strategy A have exacerbated the crisis to an unprecedented degree. As we have argued more fully elsewhere (Cavadino et al., 1999: ch. 2), Strategy A is both ineffective and inefficient in controlling crime, while its immorality (in inflicting excessive punishment) inevitably creates crises of legitimacy. Strategy B, on the other hand, is morally empty and hence equally incapable of providing legitimacy to punishment, unless its managerial techniques are wedded to – and placed in the service of – a valid moral ideology based on human rights. So, although the difficulties involved are immense, we are firmly of the opinion that only an approach based on Strategy C has any chance of providing a real, long-term solution to the crisis. For only a systematic strategy of affording a consistent respect for human rights can effectively create the legitimacy whose lack is the key to the crisis. And on a more practical note, only a principled drive to avoid unnecessary human suffering by restricting incarceration to cases where it is genuinely necessary is likely to limit the numbers in prison to suitably manageable and affordable levels. We proceed to discuss what such a strategy would entail, and what chance it might have of being deployed in the foreseeable future.

Measures to Solve the Crisis

The penal crisis is a pressing political and moral problem that requires drastic action. It cannot await a detailed blueprint for radical reform. On the other hand, it is also a deep-seated, long-running problem which requires the wholesale reform of the system along principled lines. If the crisis is to be solved, we need an evolutionary approach, combining short-term measures and medium- and long-term reform in the context of a coherent overall strategy.

Any such strategy needs to commence from the recognition of the unpopular truth that *the penal system can do very little to control crime*. As we saw in Chapter 2 (section 2.2), alleged reductive mechanisms such as deterrence, incapacitation, denunciation and reform can at best only have very limited effects in reducing the amount of crime. No doubt the ways in which we treat offenders could be made more effective than they currently are, and we certainly favour attempts to pursue rehabilitation and investigate 'what works' to reform offenders. But even if such efforts were highly successful, they could still have little effect on overall crime rates given the fact that only about two offences in every hundred committed result in a conviction, with another one in a hundred attracting a police caution (Home Office, 1999a: 29). Consequently it is foolish, as well as inhumane, to look to punitive policies to solve the problems of crime. Crime levels have much more to do with social factors (such as the fragmentation of communities and the lack of legitimate opportunities for young people) and economic trends (see, for example, Field, 1990) than with punishment. Consequently, they would be better tackled by concentrating on the social causes of crime and on crime prevention strategies (see Pease, 2002) than by looking to punishment for a solution.

The only really plausible theory put forward in recent years linking national crime rates with punishment methods – John Braithwaite's theory of 'reintegrative shaming' (see Chapter 2, section 2.4) – provides a prescription not for greater punitiveness but for much *less* harsh levels of punishment than we currently indulge in, together with a shift towards a different approach. Such an approach fits well with our preference for a much greater employment of reparation and other 'restorative justice' measures among our responses to crime (Dignan, 1994). (We shall expand on our own vision for a much more restorative approach to crime later in this chapter.) If we are right about this, then it follows that the interests of victims and potential victims of crime do not demand harsh punishment for offenders. (Hence it is wrong to talk glibly, as the current government often has, of 'rebalancing' criminal justice in favour of victims by making it harsher for offenders and suspects.) On the contrary, a less punitive strategy could not only be more beneficial to the public generally (and considerably less expensive), but could also be more victim-friendly, while running little risk of creating more victims. Indeed, the strategy we advocate could well be said to fit the New Labour motto of being 'tough on crime and tough on the causes of crime'. It is tough in the sense of being hard-headed about implementing an effective (and cost-effective) system of responding to crime, whereas to be excessively tough *on criminals* may be hard-*hearted* (which holds attraction for some people); but in terms of effectiveness and cost it is actually soft-*headed* (see further Cavadino et al., 1999: 53–5).

The most urgent priority in tackling the penal crisis is the pressing need to tackle the crisis of resources by reducing prison numbers as quickly as possible. In the short term, there is much to be said for implementing emergency measures to relieve the pressure on the prison system. This could be achieved relatively easily by using the Justice Secretary's existing powers (under section 32 of the Criminal Justice Act 1982) to order that whole categories of prisoners should be released a few months early. (Such 'amnesties' are common in some other countries such as France.) In the slightly longer term, it would be perfectly possible to instruct prison governors to use their powers of temporary release and home leave as soon as a prison became full to ensure that no prison exceeded its Certified Normal Accommodation (Crook, 1991), or even to place non-violent offenders on a waiting list to enter prison, as used to occur in the Netherlands. A variety of other measures – such as a determined expansion of bail information schemes (see Chapter 4, section 4.2) – could also make significant inroads into the numbers of people in prison. Above all, perhaps, government could assist the numbers crisis by ceasing to encourage harsher court decisions with law and order rhetoric.

But numbers and material resources are only part of the problem. If we are right in identifying the crisis of legitimacy as the key to the crisis, and in our further claim that the widespread sense of injustice surrounding the penal system is mainly due to the fact that it really is deeply unjust, then the inference is clear. It is as true as ever that, as the Woolf Report suggested in 1991, more than anything, the penal system needs a massive injection of genuine justice. We would go further and submit that in the long term – but as soon as is humanly possible – *the penal system needs to be reconstructed around the principle of respect for human rights*. We are fortified in this (Strategy C) conclusion by the evidence we cited in Chapter 6, from both British research (Bottoms et al., 1990: 91; Sparks and Bottoms, 1995; Cooke 1989, 1991) and from experience elsewhere demonstrating that, while it may not be easy to create genuine improvements in justice, there are nevertheless hopeful signs that when these are achieved, they do indeed foster legitimacy.

Adopting a human rights approach in the present penal situation means recognizing that it is morally and practically imperative both to provide those resources that will improve conditions for penal subjects from their present state and increasingly to deny those resources (notably places within prisons) that worsen them. This kind of approach also requires a consistent and principled approach to the question of *prisoners' rights*. If human beings have fundamental rights (such as the equal right to maximum positive freedom we proposed in Chapter 2, section 2.7), then it follows that prisoners have a great many more specific rights – that is, strong moral entitlements which should be guaranteed by law and that they do not automatically lose by virtue of having transgressed the law.[13] These include rights to certain decent minimum standards of living conditions, the right to fair and independent channels for pursuing grievances against others who infringe their rights, the right to an equally fair disciplinary procedures before their liberties are further infringed, and so on. A minimum code of standards for prison conditions should become legally enforceable as soon as possible and prisoners should be able to feel that they can get a genuinely fair hearing in disciplinary and grievance procedures.

Vital as they undoubtedly are, however, neither better physical conditions nor improved grievance and discipline procedures are sufficient in themselves. One of the most important rights that prisoners should have is the preservation of as much autonomy and personal responsibility as is compatible with their inevitable loss of liberty. This is of central importance both in providing constructive and successful prison regimes, and in securing legitimacy for the prison system as a whole by those who are most directly and immediately affected by it.[14] If we are to make a reality of this right to inmate autonomy, there are important implications for prison regimes and, crucially, for the relationship between staff and inmates. As we saw in Chapter 6, staff – prisoner relationships within the English penal system generally leave much to be desired, although a great deal could still be learned from positive examples such as Grendon Underwood, Blantyre House and the erstwhile Barlinnie Special Unit in Scotland.

Of equal importance to the rights of those who are imprisoned is the justice of imprisonment itself, which leads to the issue of the *justice of sentencing* (and indeed, the justice of other decisions made within the criminal justice system, such as remand and parole decisions). This can be divided into two further questions, the first relating to consistency (or fairness between different offenders), and the second relating to the general severity of punishment and, in particular, the extent to which it takes the form of incarceration. We saw in Chapter 4 (section 4.4) that there is much inconsistency in sentencing, and in Chapter 10 that some sections of the population can rightly claim that they are the subject of bias at various stages of the criminal and penal process. We also noted in Chapter 2 that it is a principle of justice that like cases should be treated alike, and that there is something to be said for trying to achieve at least a rough proportionality between severity of punishment and gravity of offence (sections 2.3 and 2.7). These considerations lead us to support the 'guidelines' approach to sentencing, with guidelines being issued to courts to bring about both a greater measure of consistency and a more suitable degree of proportionality in sentencing. Consequently we welcome the introduction of the Sentencing Guidelines Council (see Chapter 4, section 4.4).

However, inconsistency is not the worst possible evil of a penal system. There would be little to recommend a system that was perfectly consistent but appallingly vicious, and indeed it could be said from recent experience in the United States that over-emphasizing consistency (especially in an ideological climate of law and order) can have just this kind of result (Hudson, 1987; but see von Hirsch, 1993: ch. 10). From a human rights point of view, the worst fault of our penal system is not inconsistency but excess of punishment: every single day that an individual is imprisoned unnecessarily represents not only a shamefully extravagant waste of resources but, more importantly, a grave infringement of human rights. For this reason, the system of sentencing guidelines should be explicitly and strongly geared to reducing general levels of punishment as well as to pursuing consistency. (As we saw in Chapter 4, the Sentencing Guidelines Council has made some attempts to frame its guidelines in such a way as to reduce the amount of time many offenders spend in custody, but it remains to be seen whether these guidelines will even survive in the current political climate, and if they do whether they will be effective. The danger is that guidelines could even have the unwanted effect of increasing prison numbers.)

A similar approach, involving guidelines aimed at not only consistency but also reduction of punishment by the encouragement of cautions and other methods of diversion, should also be applied to the decision whether to prosecute alleged offenders. The role of the Crown Prosecution Service could well prove to be just as crucial as that of the courts if a substantial reduction of the prison population is to be secured and sustained. This has certainly been the experience elsewhere in Europe, for example in the Netherlands and West Germany at different times (Cavadino and Dignan, 2006: chs 7 and 8).

In the short to medium term, therefore, we would advocate the following specific measures – many of them explained and canvassed in the preceding chapters – for tackling the penal crisis. We favour:

- Emergency steps to reduce the prison population by means of executive powers;
- A rapid expansion of bail hostels, bail information and bail support schemes;
- Restrictions on the use of custodial remands;
- Immediate abandonment of such misguided initiatives as mandatory and minimum sentences, including the mandatory life imprisonment sentence for murder;
- A return to a 'just deserts' sentencing framework such as that contained in the Criminal Justice Act 1991 – with only a small degree of 'progression' for more persistent offenders – strengthening it by abolishing disproportionately long incapacitatory sentences, including the new sentence of 'imprisonment for public protection';
- Giving the Sentencing Advisory Panel and Sentencing Guidelines Council an explicit remit to produce comprehensive guidelines for all offences (including murder) aimed at achieving a reduction in the use of custody as well as consistency in sentencing. Such guidelines should insist that offenders who do not pose a serious risk to the public should be punished in the community rather than in prison;
- Reintroducing[15] a requirement for mandatory pre-sentence reports before the passing of any custodial sentence or community order;
- Introduction of the 'custody plus' sentence, using guidelines and monitoring to ensure that its implementation effects a reduction in custody;
- Reintroducing unit fines (or 'day fines');
- Allocation of more resources for the treatment of drug offenders in the community, linked to the introduction of drug courts with a rehabilitative and restorative ethos;
- Ensuring the continued existence of a probation service (whether or not as part of NOMS) with its own identity and national presence, without the threat of partial abolition via privatization;
- Guidelines for probation officers to promote the use of positive methods to encourage compliance with community orders and licences and to ensure that offenders are not recalled to prison for mere technical breaches of their licences;
- Transfer of prisoners who are profoundly mentally ill to appropriate hospitals, and diversion of less serious offenders with mental illnesses from the criminal justice system to appropriate community treatment;
- Enforceable ceilings on the numbers in individual prisons;
- Implementation of Woolf's scheme for 'community prisons';
- A legally enforceable code of minimum standards for prison conditions together with a short and rigid timetable for implementation and the allocation of sufficient resources to make this possible;
- Implementation within prisons of the humanistic approach which proved so successful at the Barlinnie Special Unit and at Blantyre House;
- An expansion of home leave and visiting rights for prisoners;
- Extension of the remit and resources of the Prisons Ombudsman to enable prisoners to take their grievances directly to him;
- An end to further privatization in the prison system with the ultimate aim of abandoning the policy altogether;
- Reform of discretionary early release to make the procedures fairer;
- Encouragement and application of 'systems management' techniques to the criminal justice system, including:

  — New guidelines to encourage higher rates of cautioning; and
  — The expansion of schemes aimed at diverting offenders from prosecution and from custody.

On the last of these points, while we favour continuing efforts to combine diversion and the rehabilitation of offenders,[16] we would particularly advocate diversionary schemes which embody the *'restorative justice'* approach, whereby offenders perform reparation for victims and the community and attempts are made to bring about the 'reintegrative shaming' of the offender. This would be an *inclusive* approach (see Chapter 2, section 2.6), aiming to keep offenders within the mainstream community (or bring them back in) rather than excluding them by punitive measures such as custody or other types of stigmatizing punishment. We have explained in Chapter 2 why we think the restorative approach is appropriate within a system based upon human rights (and see also Cavadino and Dignan, 1997b; Dignan, 2003). Indeed, as we have outlined elsewhere (Dignan, 1994; Dignan and Cavadino, 1996; Cavadino and Dignan, 1997b), they could point the way forward – in the long term – to a radically different and radically more just penal system in which reparative and restorative measures constituted the normal response to offending, with punitive measures being very much the exception.

It is possible to envisage a perfectly workable future criminal justice system which makes minimal use of imprisonment.[17] Most offences could be dealt with by a local mediation service (or youth offending team for juvenile offenders; YOTs already do some work similar to this). A suitable 'restorative package' could be agreed between the offender and the victim[18] and arranged by the local mediation service, with the Crown Prosecution Service certifying that the overall package was an appropriate resolution of the case, bearing in mind the public interest and maintaining at least a rough proportionality between the seriousness of the offence and the severity of the sanction. However, a more serious case could still go to court if no suitable agreement was reached, if mediation was inappropriate, if either party refused mediation, or if the alleged offender denied guilt.

The most serious crimes would normally still go to court in any event. But even in those cases that reached court, the usual outcome would be that the offender would be ordered to make reparation either to the victim or to the community generally, perhaps combined with some measures aimed at the reformation of the offender. Many existing forms of non-custodial punishment (for example the fine, unpaid work and even probation supervision) could readily be reformulated to serve restorative justice rather than purely retributive or reformative ends (see Cavadino et al., 1999; Dignan, 2003). Thus, even in cases for which informal diversionary restorative justice processes are inappropriate, inapplicable or inadequate by themselves, it is possible to envisage a range of court-imposed punishments that could be adapted to promote restorative justice outcomes. There is potential, in other words, for restorative justice to change the terms of reference within which we discuss and think about punishment (to provide a 'replacement discourse': Ashworth, 1997: 14–15) so that in future we concentrate on seeking the reintegration and inclusion of offenders rather than automatically thinking in terms of their punitive exclusion by way of imprisonment. Custody would only be used where this was necessary to incapacitate genuinely dangerous offenders from committing serious offences (or perhaps, very exceptionally, as a true 'last resort' sanction for failure to comply with court orders when all other sanctions had failed). Even then, the custodial regime should be geared towards respecting the prisoner's rights, encouraging reparative work, facilitating the voluntary rehabilitation of the offender, and securing the earliest possible release from custody. In this way, society and its criminal justice system could finally end their 'love affair with custody' (Travis, 2003).

The prospects

This kind of model for a penal system seems a long way from where we are now, and it will probably strike many readers as incredible that it could ever be implemented successfully, or that public opinion would ever allow it to be. For it is usually assumed that public opinion is irredeemably wedded to the punitive attitude of 'law and order' and will not tolerate much of a shift in the direction of leniency. However, while accepting that public opinion would hardly take kindly to the immediate introduction of a model such as the one we have sketched, it is also the case that governments can often succeed with measures which go against the current state of public opinion. A classic example is the abolition of capital punishment in 1965: even today opinion polls in this country regularly demonstrate that substantial majorities of the public would like to see capital punishment restored, yet this is perhaps the least of the penal system's legitimacy problems. Progressive measures can be 'acceptable' in the sense that the public will put up with them even if they are not what the public will tell opinion pollsters they want. We are not naïve enough to believe that the utopia of a just and minimalist penal system can be rapidly achieved, but there is no reason why moves in that direction could not be pursued and given every encouragement by an enlightened government. In the longer term, however, it will be necessary to involve the public and assemble public support for a different kind of punishment if it is ever to become a reality.

Fortunately, there is a great deal of evidence that the public, although apparently at present more punitive in Britain than in most other countries (see, for example, Mayhew and van Kesteren, 2002: 87–9), is by no means as closed-minded as is often supposed. It seems, for example, that although most people when asked say they think sentences should be tougher than they are, this is because they underestimate the harshness of the sentences that courts typically pass at present (Hough and Roberts, 1998; Mattinson and Mirrlees-Black, 2000; Roberts and Hough, 2005: ch. 4). Compensation, community service and restorative justice find great favour with the public (Hough and Mayhew, 1985: ch. 6; van Dijk and Mayhew, 1992: 46; Roberts and Hough, 2005: ch. 7), including many victims of crime (Mattinson and Mirrlees-Black, 2000: ch. 6). Only 18 per cent of people agree that it is right to 'build more prisons and pay for them by raising taxes or cutting spending in other areas' (Hough and Roberts, 1998: 35).[19] These findings suggest that what the public really wants to see is an *adequate* response to crime, but they do not necessarily demand a punitive one, let alone an inhumane one. Nor do they wish vast quantities of public money to be spent on keeping offenders locked up. Another encouraging finding is that the more informed members of the public become about criminal justice, the less punitive they typically become (Roberts and Hough, 2005: 153–60), suggesting that those who seek progressive penal reform should favour involving the public in informed debate rather than trying to exclude them (see also Cavadino and Dignan, 2006: 341–2).

Apart from public opinion, another obstacle to progressive reforms could well be the opposition of certain occupational groups within the criminal justice system with vested interests in retaining the status quo, perhaps most notably prison officers and the judiciary. Most criminal justice agencies contain only a small minority of individuals who already espouse a human rights approach: Rutherford (1993: 7) found that such people constituted 'a rather small and distinct minority' among the upper echelons of the criminal justice system. In the past the judiciary in particular has made its political weight felt to destructive effect in the penal realm, for example, in helping to scupper proposed reforms of the parole system in 1981 (see Chapter 8, section 8.3) and in enfeebling the Criminal Justice Act 1991 (see Chapter 4, section 4.5). Joanna Shapland (1988) has perceptively suggested that one of the reasons for this kind of resistance stems from the tendency towards stasis that results from the existence of a largely decentralized collection of relatively autonomous agencies which she likens to feudal 'fiefdoms', each jealously guarding its own independence and methods of working.[20] In such circumstances, she suggests that change is difficult, since the 'fiefs' are hard either to persuade or to coerce successfully. However, a strategy for change is possible if it combines a measure of both coercion (via legislation imposing some legally enforceable duties on the fiefs) and persuasion following 'round table' consultation and negotiation with the fiefdoms.

Nor is it necessarily the case that the interests of the 'fiefdoms' invariably lead them to favour illiberal policies. For example, judicial criticisms of government penal policy have in the past gone in both directions. The judiciary tend to favour arrangements that maximize their own power and oppose those that *confine* (limit) their discretion or negate their decisions: hence their hostility to mandatory and minimum sentences and to the Home Secretary's erstwhile role in the early release process (see Chapter 8). On the other hand, they are less concerned about the *structuring* (guidance) of their discretion by means of guidelines. Again, some senior members of the judiciary – most notably Lord Woolf, who was Lord Chief Justice from 2000 to 2005 and who reportedly clashed with Home Secretaries on several occasions[21] – strongly favour a reduction in prison numbers. In the circumstances, the chances would be good for a round table agreement between government and judiciary for a guideline system aimed at reducing the use of custody from its present level. Whether this would lead to more junior, frontline sentencers genuinely using prison as a last resort and keeping sentence lengths to a minimum is less certain. But currently it looks to be the government, not the judges, which poses the greater barrier to such a development.

Similarly, it should be borne in mind that prison officers actively support some progressive reforms, such as the introduction of minimum standards for physical conditions within prisons, for the very good reason that they perceive such measures to be in their own best interests as well as those of the prisoners. They tend, however, to oppose measures that would improve standards of justice for prisoners in potential disputes with prison officers, such as giving prisoners the right to legal representation in disciplinary hearings (see Wozniak and McAllister, 1991). However, given that governments have in recent years had little compunction about confronting prison officers over pay, conditions, trade union rights and privatization, it is hard to see why they could not be brought onside by a committed government using a shrewd combination of reason and power. Persuasive techniques could include, for example the provision of appropriate financial and career incentives for cooperation with the government's strategy.

There is also the possibility – to return to the feudal metaphor – of change being forced by revolt among the peasants. So far peasants' revolts – in the shape of prison riots – have been contained, albeit with difficulty. But they would potentially strengthen the hand of a government that had the will to use its power to bring about change from above. Is this likely to happen?

The immediate political situation is clearly not encouraging for the kind of penal programme we wish to see. We would like to see a concerted drive to reduce the prison population; the government is unwilling to pursue this, and this failure combined with its obsession with appearing 'tough on crime' seems almost certain to bring about further increases. We would like to return to the 'just deserts' orientation of the Criminal Justice Act 1991; the government still seems determined that persistent offenders should get decidedly more than their just deserts. We want a major reorientation of penality towards restorative justice; there have merely been some tentative steps in this direction, mainly for young offenders[22] (see Chapters 5 and 9). Above all, we wish to see a demotion of 'toughness' towards criminals as the benchmark of policy and the hallmark of political rhetoric, whereas the government is still wedded to both.

Nevertheless, the prospects for penal improvement are not all hopeless. It has usually proved to be the case in Britain that law and order ideology can only prevail in penal policy for a limited time before its effects in exacerbating the crisis brings government into a rude collision with very concrete material realities. In a highly competitive political situation, long-term penal and financial consequences can be ignored by political parties for the sake of hoped-for electoral advantage. And individual politicians with instincts that lead them to favour 'tough' rhetoric and policies – in the case of New Labour, instincts that were formed during and after many years of frustrating opposition seen as the result of being 'out of touch' with the electorate – can also play their part. But will such a situation endure forever? We have seen occasions (such as at Leeds Castle in 1987) when fiscal and other pragmatic considerations have overridden powerful ideological pressures to pursue punitive policies. Perhaps the best hope for the penal system is that this will happen again.

There have been occasional suggestions that 'hyper-incarceration', even on the American scale, could actually be functional to the economy, at least in the short term, by providing jobs and at the same time disguising the true rate of unemployment (Downes, 1997, 2001; Western and Beckett, 1999; Cavadino and Dignan, 2006: 58). But such a strategy is surely unsustainable over a longer time frame. Quite apart from the problems of dealing with the kind of acute numbers crisis that we are seeing in 2006–7, the longer we go on consigning more and more offenders to prison for longer and longer periods, the more the expense will soar. The rapidly escalating cost is just taxpayers' money down the drain. For every pound that is spent on keeping inmates wastefully and counterproductively under lock and key is a pound that is not available for other pressing needs such as investing in education, health care or tackling poverty or climate change – or even to be left in citizens' pockets to spend on themselves. Such a waste of the nation's economic resources should hardly be a recipe for political success.

There is a Chinese word for 'crisis' which literally translates into English as 'danger-opportunity'. The penal crisis is indeed a situation of great danger, but if the danger is recognized it could provide the opportunity and incentive for making bold and far-sighted moves in a progressive direction. In the long run, we have to make a choice between a morally and financially bankrupt, permanently crisis-ridden and inexorably deteriorating penal system and one worthy of a modern and civilized society. We said at the end of Chapter 1 that we need to change people's minds about punishment. There is a long way to go, and the way looks much longer than it did 15 years ago, but the task is not impossible. We saw in Chapter 2 that ideas about punishment have changed radically in the past when the times and conditions were right. Perhaps – just perhaps – the time for another such change is not quite as far off as it now seems.

Notes

1   By Home Office Circulars and the 1986 Code for Crown Prosecutors (Home Office et al., 1980: para. 38; Home Office, 1985b, 1990d; Director of Public Prosecutions, 1986).
2   The proportion of custodial sentences passed on indictable offenders dropped, from 16 per cent in the period January – September 1992 to 12 per cent in the last quarter of 1992 (Home Office, 1993: para. 7.11).
3   These are actual figures. Using seasonally adjusted figures which allow for the usual drop in the prison population at the end of the year, the population still declined very significantly from 45,400 to 42,300 (Home Office, 1994c: Tables 1.2 and 1.3).
4   These repeals were achieved by the Criminal Justice Act 1993.
5   Quoted in *Prison Report*, no. 41, Winter 1997, p. 3.
6   'Tackling Persistent Offenders is Key to Improving Effectiveness in the Criminal Justice System', Home Office Press Release, 31 January 2001; Home Office (2001: Annex B).
7   Although research to date on the effects of intensive supervision schemes for persistent offenders has yielded some disappointing results: see Homes et al. (2005: 3–4). There is also the constant danger that these specially intrusive measures may serve to 'widen the net' and 'thin the mesh' for many offenders (see Chapter 5, section 5.6), thereby 'setting them up to fail', so that when they breach the over-demanding requirements of their supervision, they are 'catapulted into custody' rather than being diverted from custody and from crime.
8   As is the case for young offenders aged from 12 to 14, who may currently only receive a detention and training order if the court simply decides they are 'persistent' (Powers of Criminal Courts (Sentencing) Act 2000, s. 100). See Chapter 9, note 76.
9   This and the following quotations are taken from Tony Blair's 'Respect Action Plan' launch speech of 10 January 2006.
10 See for example, *Guardian*, 2 March 2002; Lord Chancellor's Department (2002).

11 A stance which led to the statutory guidelines for these tariffs contained in the Criminal Justice Act 2003 (see Chapter 8, section 8.5).

12 See further Cavadino et al. (1999), especially chapter 2. This typology of criminal justice strategies is not exhaustive. It is also possible, for example, to hold to a Marxist or an 'abolitionist' approach (see, for example, Sim, 1994). We will concentrate on Strategies A, B and C because although, for example, abolitionists have at times achieved real success campaigning on various issues (see Sim, 1992), their views are unlikely to be adopted wholesale by anyone close to governmental power in the foreseeable future.

13 This has been cogently argued by Genevra Richardson (1985: 23–4), who concludes that 'whatever view of imprisonment prevails ... imprisonment justifies only that degree of interference required to achieve separation from the rest of the community: all remaining rights should be safeguarded.'

14 A valuable symbolic step that could usefully be implemented without delay would be to restore to prisoners the right of vote, in accordance with the European Court of Human Rights decision in *R v Secretary of State for the Home Department, ex parte (1) Pearson; (2) Martinez; Hirst v. HM Attorney-General* [2001] EWHC Admin 239.

15 The Criminal Justice Act 1991 contained such a requirement, but it was watered down substantially by the Criminal Justice and Public Order Act 1994 (see Cavadino and Dignan, 2002: 92–3).

16 For example, in the shape of youth offender panels and contracts; 'change programmes' attached to warnings for young offenders; action plan orders and other training programmes based in the community; and conditional cautions for adults.

17 Cf.Blom-Cooper (1988: ch. 3). Such a vision has some affinities with the 'abolitionist' position of critics such as Joe Sim (1992, 1994), who does not in fact call for the total abolition of confinement but merely of the institution of prison as we know it. See also Dignan (2003).

18 Provided the victim is willing to take part. Not all crimes have identifiable individual victims, of course (although mediation can work very well when the victim is a corporate entity such as a business, even a large one: see Dignan, 1991). However, in 'victimless' cases, or those in which the victim is unwilling, an appropriate body representing the whole community – possibly the Crown Prosecution Service – could take on the role of the victim in the process, seeking to ensure that adequate reparation is made to the general public. Restorative packages could also include measures aimed at reforming offenders, for example, by 'confronting their offending behaviour', treatment for drug addiction, etc.

19 Similarly, a 2001 MORI opinion poll found that only 8 per cent of the public chose imprisonment when asked what would do most to reduce crime in Britain, while 53 per cent agreed that most people come out of prison worse than when they went in (MORI, 2001a, 2001b).

20 We explained in Chapter 3 (section 3.5) how these 'fiefdoms' fit into our general 'radical pluralist' analysis of penality.

21 In what the press called a 'clash' with Jack Straw, Lord Woolf was outspoken in calling overcrowding 'the AIDS virus of the prison system' and advocating a decrease both in the prison population and in the volume of 'tough talk' from politicians on law and order (*Guardian*, 28 December 2000 and 1 February 2001). He subsequently had more 'clashes' with David Blunkett over the sentencing of burglars and murderers.

22 However, the government has funded a major series of experimental restorative justice initiatives aimed at adult offenders, including those who have committed more serious offences such as those involving violence. An evaluation of these initiatives is currently under way, and a final report is expected to be published in 2007. Two interim reports have been published to date; see Shapland et al. (2004 and 2006).

A Self-study Guide to Electronic Sources Available on the Internet

We have tried to describe the English penal system as it was in January 2007. However, the pace of change is so fast (and appears to be increasing) that events will inevitably have moved on by the time this book appears in print. Fortunately, there is now a growing number of electronic websites that make it very much easier to follow events and keep pace with the latest penal developments as they occur. We have included references to electronic sources, where available, in the bibliography, but for convenience we present a selection of some of the more useful websites below, together with brief annotations that will hopefully make it easier for readers to keep themselves up to date until the next edition appears. They should also enable readers to consult the original sources if they wish to investigate topics in greater depth than we have been able to cover in the book.

1. Legislation

http://www.opsi.gov.uk/legislation/uk.htm
Provides access to Acts of the United Kingdom Parliament and also explanatory notes which summarize their main provisions.

http://www.parliament.the-stationery-office.co.uk/pa/pabills.htm
Provides access to the titles and full text of Bills that are currently before Parliament.

http://www.legislation.hmso.gov.uk/stat.htm
Provides access to the full text of recent (and also draft) statutory instruments.

2. Official Parliamentary Reports on Penal Matters

http://www.parliament.the-stationery-office.co.uk/pa/cm/cmhaff.htm
Contains reports published by the House of Commons Home Affairs Committee.

3. Information produced by the Ministry of Justice and the Home Office

http://www.justice.gov.uk
The Ministry of Justice is now responsible for courts, prisons, probation, criminal law and sentencing and provides access to a wide range of information and statistics on all these topics published since its creation on 9 May 2007. Follow the links to 'publications', 'statistics' and 'research'.

The web-site also provides a link to the Home Office website (see below), which is where material that was published before 9 May 2007 can still be found

http://www.homeoffice.gov.uk
The Home Office's home page. Provides access to a wide range of information about the criminal justice system and government policies covering the period prior to 9 May 2007.

The Science, Research and Statistics Directorate produces a wide range of helpful statistics and other publications and can be accessed via the following link.
http://scienceandresearch.homeoffice.gov.uk/
Follow the 'publications' link, which provides access to a variety of publications produced by the Research and Statistics Directorate. The most important of these are listed below:

Home Office Statistical Bulletins
Home Office Research Studies
Research Findings

One of the most important and useful statistical publications now is the Offender Management Caseload Statistics, published by RDS, which contains a wide range of statistics relating to offenders who are in prison or who have been dealt with by means of a Community Order. The latest version can be accessed at:
http://www. homeoffice.gov.uk/rds/hosbpubs1.html

Monthly figures on the population in custody may be accessed on:
http://www.homeoffice.gov.uk/rds/prisons1.html

Miscellaneous publications including occasional papers produced by the Home Office include:
http://www.homeoffice.gov.uk/rds/digest41.html
Provides access to Digest 4, which contains information on the Criminal Justice System in England and Wales. Although the most recent version, Digest 4 was published in 2000.

4. Major Penal Agencies and Organizations

Prison Service website

http://www.hmprisonservice.gov.uk/

Contains some statistics (e.g. relating to staffing levels, and also a daily prison population briefing) plus news (which includes an archive service), copy of the Prison Rules, Prison Orders and corporate information. The latter includes the Annual Report, Framework Document, Business Plan and information relating to privately managed prisons (see Contracts and Competitions Group).

Scottish Prison Service

http://www.sps.gov.uk/
Contains annual reports, research, publications and statistics relating to the Scottish Prison Service.

HM Chief Inspector of Prisons

http://inspectorates.homeoffice.gov.uk/hmiprisons/
Contains information about the inspectorate, the inspection programme, and a full list of inspection reports (including thematic reports) published on the website.

Prisons Ombudsman

http://www.ppo.gov.uk/
Provides access to annual reports.

Parole Board website

http://www.paroleboard.gov.uk/
Contains annual report and other publications plus news section and press releases.

The National Probation Service website

http://www.probation.homeoffice.gov.uk/output/Page1.asp

HM Inspectorate of Probation

http://inspectorates.homeoffice.gov.uk/hmiprobation/
Contains references to a variety of publications relating to the probation service, plus details of inspection reports.

Judicial Studies Board

http://www.jsboard.co.uk/

Magistrates' Association

http://www.magistrates-association.org.uk/

National Offender Management Service

http://www.noms.homeoffice.gov.uk/

Sentencing Advisory Panel

http://www.sentencing-guidelines.gov.uk/about/sap/

Contains annual reports and advice to the Sentencing Guidelines Council.

Sentencing Guidelines Council

http://www.sentencing-guidelines.gov.uk/about/sgc/index.html

Information about the SGC Guidelines (including draft guidelines and consultation documentation).

Youth Justice Board (now known as the YJB)

http://www.yjb.gov.uk/

Contains information about the Board's policies, aims and responsibilities, guidance manuals and information relating to Youth Offending Teams.

5. Penal Reform Organizations

CLINKS (supporting voluntary organizations that work with offenders and their families)

http://www.clinks.org/(S(dhdw4s45ow34a2bzfyk2cx45))/index.aspx

Crime and Society Foundation

http://www.crimeandsociety.org.uk/

Howard League

http://www.howardleague.org/

Inquest

http://www.inquest.org.uk/

National Association for the Care and Resettlement of Offenders

http://www.nacro.org.uk/

Prison Privatisation Report International

http://www.psiru.org/ppricurrent.asp

Prison Reform Trust

http://www.prisonreformtrust.org.uk/main.html

Rethinking Crime and Punishment

http://www.rethinking.org.uk

Victim Support

http://www.victimsupport.org.uk/vs_england_wales/index.php

6. Law Reform Organizations and Ongoing Reviews

The Law Commission

http://www.lawcom.gov.uk/

Criminal Courts Review by Lord Justice Auld

http://www.criminal-courts-review.org.uk/index.htm

7. Other Relevant Government Departments Referred to in the Text

General access portal for government websites

http://www.open.gov.uk/lcd/

Also contains links to Department for Constitutional Affairs, Human Rights legislation and regulations, etc.

8. Useful Academic Sites

Centre for Criminal Justice Studies at King's College London

http://www.kcl.ac.uk/depsta/rel/ccjs/

9. Other Useful Sites

CrimLinks – excellent general portal providing access to a wide range of key online source materials and sites

http://www.crimlinks.com/

Restorative Justice Online – useful first port of call for restorative justice matters

http://www.restorativejustice.org/

Glossary of Key Terms

Words and phrases *in italics* have their own entry in this glossary.

Abolitionism   A penal reform movement that seeks to abolish all or part of the *penal system*, particularly its most coercive practices such as the use of capital punishment and *imprisonment*.

Action Plan Order   A *community sentence* for young offenders (10–17) consisting of a short (3 months) intensive intervention programme that seeks to address their offending behaviour.

Age of Criminal Responsibility   The age at which it becomes possible to *prosecute* an offender (10 in *England* and Wales).

Agency Status   A term used to describe the relationship between the Prison Service and senior policy-makers, whereby responsibility for 'operational' matters is vested in the former while responsibility for strategic policy-making is vested in the latter.

Anti-social Behaviour Orders ('ASBOs')   A court order that prohibits behaviour deemed to be 'anti-social'. Breach of an ASBO is a criminal offence punishable by a fine or imprisonment up to five years (in the case of adult offenders).

Attorney General   The government law officer responsible for the *Crown Prosecution Service*.

Bail   Conditional freedom granted to a suspect, normally during police investigations or pending trial.

Bifurcation   A dual-edged (or 'twin-track') approach to punishment which distinguishes between 'ordinary' offenders with whom less severe measures can be taken, and on the other hand 'serious' or 'dangerous' offenders who are subjected to much tougher measures.

Bifurcation, Punitive   A term we use to describe the policy underlying the Criminal Justice Act 1991, which combined *bifurcation* with a concern to make *non-custodial penalties* more *punitive*. See also *punishment in the community*.

Bind-overs   Akin to a suspended *fine*. A sum of money is forfeited unless the person bound over complies with an undertaking to be of good behaviour and keep the peace.

Boot Camps   *Custodial* institutions for young offenders with a military-style training regime. See also *'short, sharp shock'*.

Breach   Failure to comply with the terms of a court order. The term is also used to refer to the proceedings whereby an offender who has not complied with an order is returned to court to be sanctioned for the breach.

'Bust Limit'   An informal term for the total 'usable operational capacity' of the prison system, or the total number of prisoners that the system can safely hold.

Caution   A formal disposal of a criminal case, consisting of a warning administered to an offender by a police officer. The measure is an alternative to *prosecution* and therefore does not involve either *prosecution* or the courts. Since 1998 cautions have been replaced for offenders under the age of 18 by a new system comprising a single *reprimand*, followed by a ('final') *warning* and then *prosecution*. See also *conditional caution'*.

Certified Normal Accommodation (or 'CNA')   The officially prescribed capacity of a prison indicating the number of inmates for whom it has adequate space.

Charge   The first step in the *prosecution* process. Normally the police charge a suspect on the advice of the *Crown Prosecution Service*.

Chief Inspector of Prisons   A government-appointed official who heads an independent inspectorate responsible for monitoring and reporting on conditions in prisons.

Chivalry Theory   The theory that female offenders are treated more leniently than males due to the 'chivalry' (courteousness) of criminal justice practitioners.

Classicism   The school of penal thought that holds that offenders should be held responsible for their actions and punished in proportion to their wrongdoing. See also *just deserts/justice model; proportionality, principle of*.

Cognitive Behavioural Treatment   A form of treatment focusing on the way offenders think about themselves, their offending behaviour and its consequences.

Combination Order   A *community sentence* combining *community service* with *probation* supervision. Known between 2001 and 2005 as the 'community punishment and rehabilitation order'. Superseded by the *community order*.

Community Order   A court order, introduced by the Criminal Justice Act 2003, which may contain one or more of twelve different requirements, including *unpaid work, probation supervision* or a *curfew* enforced by *electronic monitoring*.

Community Payback   The name given by the government to *community service* when 'rebranding' the scheme in 2006.

Community Prisons   A multi-purpose prison housing different kinds of prisoners close to their homes.

Community Punishment Order   The official name for a *community service* order between 2001 and 2005.

Community Rehabilitation Order   The official name for a *probation order* between 2001 and 2005.

Community Sentence   A category of sentences which include the *community order* and also various measures for *young offenders*.

Community Service   Work for the benefit of the community carried out by offenders as a requirement of their *punishment*. This may be under an *unpaid work* requirement in a *community order*, or under some other court order. See also *community payback, community punishment order*.

Comparative Penology   The study of penal systems and penal policies in different countries, their similarities and differences and the factors that may account for them.

Compensation   Financial redress provided for *victims* of crime. A court sentencing an offender can pass a compensation order requiring the offender to pay compensation to the *victim*.

Conditional Caution   A *caution* combined with additional conditions.

Containment, Crisis of   See *crisis of containment*.

Control, Crisis of   See *crisis of control*.

Corporatism   (Or 'conservative corporatism'): a term used to describe countries such as Germany, where important national interest groups are integrated with the national state and are expected to act in accordance with the national interest.

CPS   See *Crown Prosecution Service*.

Criminal Justice System   A collective term encompassing the various agencies responsible for enforcing the criminal law and administering criminal justice, including the police, the *prosecuting* authorities, the criminal courts and the prison and *probation* services.

Crisis   See *penal crisis*.

Crisis of Containment   An aspect of the wider *penal crisis* that relates to concerns over prison escapes and *security* matters in general.

Crisis of Control   An aspect of the wider *penal crisis* that relates to the problem of maintaining order within prisons.

Crisis of Legitimacy   An aspect of the *penal crisis* consisting of the *penal system*'s lack of *legitimacy* with, among others, (a) the general public; (b) 'penal subjects' such as prisoners; and (c) practitioners working within the *penal system*.

Crisis of Resources   An aspect of the wider *penal crisis* that relates to the scarcity of material resources – including staff, money, buildings and equipment – needed for punishing offenders, whether in prison or in the community.

Crisis of Visibility   An aspect of the *penal crisis* which relates to the existence, and dispelling, of secrecy surrounding what happens within prisons.

Crown Court   The court which tries the more important criminal cases in *England* and Wales, hearing both *indictable* and *triable either way* cases.

Crown Prosecution Service (CPS)   The state agency with responsibility for conducting the great majority of *prosecutions* in *England* and Wales.

Culture   The collective beliefs, norms, feelings and practices of a society, or organisation.

Curfew   A form of punishment in which restrictions are imposed on the hours during which an offender is free to leave home, usually enforced by *electronic monitoring*. *Community orders* may include curfew requirements.

Custody   Confinement in a prison or similar institution.

Custody Plus   A penalty that consists of a short period in *custody* followed by a longer period during which an offender is punished in the community. [Not yet in force]

Day Fine   A system of relating fines to the means of the offender, similar to the *unit fine* system. The day fine system exists in some other countries, and its introduction in *England* and Wales was recommended by the Carter Report in 2003.

'DCMF' Contracts   A form of prison privatization in which a private sector operator is contracted to design, construct, manage and finance a prison in return for daily payments per prisoner from the government once the prison begins to admit prisoners. The normal duration of such contracts is 25 years.

Decarceration   A policy of attempting to reduce or abolish the use of *custodial* and other institutional methods of dealing with offenders and other *deviants*. Can also mean the widespread closure of *custodial* and other institutions housing *deviants*.

Denunciation   The theory that *punishment* is justified because it expresses the community's condemnation of the crime.

Detention Centres   *Custodial* institutions for *juvenile* and *young adult* offenders, abolished in 1988.

Detention and Training Order   A *custodial penalty* for young offenders (aged 12 to 18), part of which is served in custody and part under supervision in the community.

Determinate Sentence   A *sentence* with a fixed end point, such as a specific number of years' imprisonment.

Determinism   See *positivism*.

Deterrence   The prevention of crime by inducing potential offenders to fear that they will be punished.

Deviants   A term encompassing offenders and others who 'deviate' from the norms of society.

Discharge   The most lenient penalty available to the court. An absolute discharge requires nothing from an offender and imposes no obligations on future conduct. A conditional discharge requires an offender not to commit a further offence during a specified period on pain of being further punished for the original offence.

Discipline   A term used by Foucault (1977) to refer to a technique of social control that involves the use of constant surveillance and the imposition of a highly regulated physical routine often involving repetitive forced labour.

Dispersal Prison   See *high security prison*.

Diversion   Dealing with offenders by means other than either *prosecution* or *custody*.

Doli Incapax   A legal doctrine whereby it was presumed that children aged 10 to 13 were incapable of committing a crime unless they could be shown to appreciate the difference between right and wrong. Abolished by the Crime and Disorder Act 1988.

Due Process   A system of legal safeguards designed to prevent the conviction of the innocent or other wrongful *punishment*. Due process safeguards include the right to a fair trial and the presumption of innocence.

Early Release   The release of a prisoner before the end of the *sentence*, whether automatically or by a discretionary process. See also *parole* and *remission*.

Economic Determinism   The idea (associated with some forms of Marxism) that economics determines everything, that the 'superstructure' of law, politics and ideology merely reflects the state of the economic 'base'.

England   In this book we normally use the words 'England' and 'English' to refer to the legal and penal systems of England and Wales.

Either Way Offences   Offences which can be tried in either the *Crown Court* or the *magistrates' court*.

Electronic Monitoring   (Or *'tagging'*) The use of electronic surveillance techniques (such as a 'tag' fastened around the wrist or ankle) to monitor an offender's compliance with the terms of a court order or *licence*.

Evil Woman Theory   The theory that female offenders are treated more harshly than males due to being seen as 'doubly *deviant*' because they flout the social norms of femininity as well as breaking the law.

Exclusionary Approach   An approach to dealing with offenders or other *deviants* by excluding them from the life of mainstream society, for example by imprisonment. See also *inclusionary approach*.

Exclusion Requirement   A restriction that may be imposed as part of a *community order*, which prohibits the offender from entering a specified place.

'Fiefdoms'   Fiefdoms were semi-autonomous realms within feudal society. Shapland (1988) likened both non-state groups and state agencies within the *criminal justice system* (such as the police and the courts) to 'fiefdoms'.

Final Warning   See *caution*.

Fine   A *punishment* which consists of the offender being required to pay a sum of money to the state.

Fixed Penalty Notice   (Or 'spot fine'.) A financial *penalty* which can be imposed by police officers and other specified officials for a variety of minor offences.

Freedom   See *positive freedom*.

Gatekeeping   A term which refers to the power of agencies such as the police or *Crown Prosecution Service* to determine who is admitted to the formal *criminal justice system* by being *prosecuted* and who is *diverted* from it.

'Great Transformation'   A major shift in the nature of punishment from 'corporal' to 'carceral', which took place during the late eighteenth and early nineteenth centuries.

Green Paper   A term sometimes used for a Government discussion or consultation document. See also *White Paper*.

Guidelines   See *sentencing guidelines*.

High Security Prison   Maximum-security prisons capable of housing high-risk inmates whose escape would be dangerous. Formerly known as 'dispersal prisons'.

Home Detention Curfew   A type of *early release* which includes a *curfew* enforced by *electronic monitoring*.

Home Office   The government department responsible until May 2007 for prisons, *probation* and the formulation of *criminal justice policy*. Still responsible for the police, crime, anti-social behaviour, drugs policy, anti-terrorism and immigration.

Home Secretary   The Secretary of State (i.e. the senior minister) in charge of the *Home Office*.

Honesty in Sentencing   See *truth in sentencing*.

House of Lords   (1) The 'Upper House' of Parliament, forming (with the House of Commons) the supreme legislature of the United Kingdom. (2) The highest court in the United Kingdom. Under the Constitutional Reform Act 2005, it is to become the Supreme Court.

Human Rights   See *Human Rights Act 1998; rights theory*.

Human Rights Act 1998   The Act by which the European Convention on Human Rights was incorporated into English law.

'Hurd Era'   The period between 1987–1992, when a reform agenda influenced by *just deserts* culminated in the 1991 Criminal Justice Act. Douglas Hurd was Home Secretary for part of this period (1985–99).

Ideology   We use this word to refer to the entire realm of ideas, including philosophies, which may affect people's attitudes and practices. (This is wider than the classic Marxist concept which sees ideologies as ideas which function in the interests of particular social classes.)

Imprisonment for Public Protection   A new *indeterminate* sentence introduced by the Criminal Justice Act 2003 and imposed on offenders who have committed a serious violent or sexual offence and are considered dangerous, but who do not qualify for a *life imprisonment sentence*.

Imprisonment Rate   A measure of *'punitiveness'* based on the number of prisoners in a country expressed as a proportion of its total population (usually per 100,000).

Incapacitation   The prevention of crime by making it impossible for a person to offend, for example by means of execution, imprisonment or disqualification.

Inclusionary (or 'Inclusive') Approach   An approach to dealing with offenders or other *deviants* by seeking to keep them included in the life of mainstream society, or by reintegrating them into society. See also *exclusionary approach, Strategy C*.

Indeterminate Sentence   A *sentence* with no fixed end point, such as *life imprisonment*.

Indictable offences   Offences which can be tried in the *Crown Court*. Statistics presented in this book typically refer to 'indictable offences' meaning both 'indictable only' offences (triable only in the *Crown Court*) and offences *triable either way* (i.e. in either the *Crown* or *magistrates' courts*).

Intensive Supervision and Surveillance Programmes ('ISSPs')   Community programmes for serious and persistent *young offenders* which may be attached to *community orders, supervision orders, licences* or *bail* supervision. They involve intensive monitoring of the young offender's movements (including *electronic monitoring*) and training and education programmes lasting up to five hours per day.

Inter-agency Approach   See *multi-agency approach*

Intermittent Custody   A *sentence* of imprisonment which may be served at intervals, for example at weekends. Introduced on an experimental basis by the Criminal Justice Act 2003, but subsequently abandoned.

Judicial Independence, Doctrine of   A constitutional doctrine which holds that the executive (i.e. government) should not interfere with the decisions of courts.

Judicialization   A process whereby decision-making procedures (such as those for *early release*) become progressively more like court procedures, in particular incorporating *due process* safeguards.

Just Deserts/Justice Model   A doctrine and movement which advocates that the amount of *punishment* imposed on an offender should be proportionate to the seriousness of the offence that has been committed. Allied to the *retributivist* theory of punishment. See also *proportionality, principle of*.

Juvenile Justice   See *youth justice*.

Key Performance Indicators   A *managerialist* technique involving the setting of targets for an organization and regular monitoring of its performance.

Labelling Theory   The idea that catching and punishing offenders 'labels' and stigmatizes them as criminals, which makes it harder for them to lead a law-abiding life in future. See also *minimum intervention*.

Law and Order Counter-Reformation   A term we use to refer to the abandonment of the sentencing reform strategy pursued during the *Hurd era* and the adoption of harsh *Strategy A*-inspired policies during the period 1993–7.

Law and Order Ideology   A set of attitudes including the beliefs that people must be strictly disciplined by restrictive rules, and that they should be harshly punished if they break the rules. See also *Strategy A, populist punitiveness*.

Legitimacy   The perception that power (as exercised by, e.g., government or the *penal system*) is morally acceptable.

Licence   Conditional freedom at the end of a *custodial sentence* as part of *early release*. Licences may contain requirements regarding, e.g., residence or supervision.

Life Imprisonment   An *indeterminate* prison *sentence* that is potentially lifelong, from which an offender will only be released when the *Parole Board* is satisfied that there is no longer an unacceptable risk of serious reoffending.

Local Prison A prison used mainly for housing lower security inmates on *remand* and serving short prison *sentences*.

Lord Chancellor The government minister who has responsibility for the administration of justice and is also the Secretary of State for Justice Affairs. See *Ministry of Justice*.

Lord Chief Justice The head of the judiciary in *England* and Wales, and also of the Court of Appeal (Criminal Division). Chairs the *Sentencing Guidelines Council*.

Magistrates' Court The court in which around 95 per cent of criminal cases are tried in *England* and Wales, presided over by 'lay' magistrates and district judges, and hearing both *summary* and *triable either way* cases.

Managerialism An approach based on the notion that modern managerial techniques can be successfully applied to the problems of crime and punishment, both to control crime and to deploy penal resources effectively and efficiently. It is the basis of the *Strategy B* approach to criminal justice.

Mediation An informal dispute resolution process involving the parties who are directly involved and an independent mediator who facilitates the process. See also *restorative justice*.

Minimum Intervention The belief that formal responses to crime involving prosecution and punishment can increase the likelihood of re-offending and that the best approach is one based on *diversion* from *prosecution* and *custody*. See also *labelling theory*, and contrast *zero tolerance*.

Ministry of Justice Ministry created in May 2007, replacing the Department for Constitutional Affairs and assuming responsibility for *NOMS*, criminal justice policy and *youth justice* (formerly the responsibility of the *Home Office*). Also responsible for courts, civil law and legal aid.

Modality We use this term to refer to various types of *punishment* (*probation* supervision, *community service*, the *fine*, etc.), the forms that *punishment* takes (e.g. *supervision*, surveillance, the levying of *penalties* on the offender's money or time) and the methods by which it is delivered (e.g. by state agency or by the private or voluntary sectors).

Mode of Trial Whether a criminal case is tried in the *Crown Court* or *magistrates' court*.

Multi-agency (or 'Inter-agency') Approach The policy of promoting closer collaboration between *criminal justice* agencies in pursuit of a common set of objectives. See also *youth offending teams*.

National Offender Management Service (NOMS) An organization set up in 2004 combining the prison and *probation* services.

Neo-classicism A school of *penal* thought associated with Jeremy Bentham among others, sharing some characteristics of the *classicist* approach but also concerned to achieve the *reform* of offenders.

Neo-correctionalism An approach associated with the current *New Labour* government that combines the *punitiveness* of *Strategy A* with an illiberal approach towards those who behave in an anti-social manner, a willingness to adopt pre-emptive strategies for 'pre-delinquent' young people and a measure of *managerialism*. See also *zero tolerance*.

Neo-liberalism   Free-market capitalism, as exemplified by the United States.

Net-widening   The process whereby *'diversionary'* measures result in those who might otherwise have been dealt with informally end up receiving a more formal intervention, thus 'widening the net' of the *criminal justice system*.

New Labour   The Labour Party as led by Tony Blair between 1994 and June 2007 and by Gordon Brown from June 2007 onwards.

New Penology   A *managerial* approach which is 'concerned with techniques to identify, classify, and manage groupings sorted by dangerousness' (Feeley and Simon, 1992), including 'risk assessments' of offenders.

New Punitiveness   An international trend, on the rise since the 1970s, for increased harshness of *punishment* associated with *Strategy A* policies and *law and order ideology*.

NOMS   See *National Offender Management Service*.

Non-custodial Penalty   Any *punishment* that does not involve *custody*.

Normalization   A term associated with Foucault (1977), referring to a process whereby offenders are schooled into conformity (for example, by *discipline*). The term is also used to refer to attempts to approximate prison life more closely to life on the outside.

'Nothing Works'   The idea, associated with Martinson (1974), that no method of treating offenders will make any difference to their propensity to reoffend.

Numbers Crisis   An aspect of the wider *penal crisis* that relates specifically to the fact that the number of prisoners exceeds the amount of suitable accommodation that is available.

Open Prisons   Prisons designed for relatively low-risk inmates who can safely be housed in less secure establishments.

Orthodox Account (of the *penal crisis*)   An account which explains the *penal crisis* as the natural outcome of a combination of factors including the *numbers crisis*, prison overcrowding and poor conditions, staff unrest, poor *security* and a *toxic mix* of prisoners.

Panopticon   A prison designed by Jeremy Bentham (but never built) in which inmates were to be kept under constant surveillance by warders in a central observation tower.

Parenting Orders   Court orders that require parents of misbehaving children to attend counselling and guidance sessions and comply with other conditions.

Parole   *Early release* granted at the discretion of the *Parole Board*.

Parole Board   An independent body which decides on the granting of *parole*.

Parsimony, Principle of   The principle that punishments, and especially imprisonment, should be used as sparingly as possible.

Penal Crisis   The parlous state of affairs affecting the *penal system*.

Penal System   The system that exists to *punish* and otherwise deal with those who have been convicted of criminal offences.

Penality   This word includes ideas about *punishment* as well as concrete penal practices (cf. Garland and Young, 1983a; Garland, 1990b.)

Penalty   Any *punishment* or *sentence* imposed for an offence.

Penology   The study of *punishment*.

Plea Before Venue   A system introduced in 1997 whereby defendants are asked to indicate whether they will be pleading guilty or not guilty before a decision is taken as to their *mode of trial*.

Pluralism   The sociological theory which holds that power in society is distributed between a number of competing interest groups. See also *radical pluralism*.

Populism, Penal   Defined by Roberts et al. (2003: 5) as 'allowing the electoral advantage of a policy to take precedence over its penal effectiveness'. See also *populist punitiveness*.

Populist Punitiveness   A near-synonym for *'law and order ideology'* coined by Bottoms (1995a). See also *populism, penal*.

Positive Freedom   Freedom defined as the ability of people to make effective choices about their lives. (As opposed to 'negative freedom', defined as the absence of constraint and coercion imposed by other people.)

Positivism   The theory that crime, together with all other natural and social phenomena, is caused by factors and processes that can be discovered by scientific investigation. It is a *'deterministic'* approach, i.e. one which denies that human actions such as crime are the result of an exercise of free will, and hence also denies that offenders are responsible for their crimes. Associated with the *treatment model*, *welfare model* and *rehabilitative ideal*.

Post-Marxism   Theories which continue the Marxist tradition but depart from Marxism in certain fundamental respects, for example by abandoning a belief in an 'economic base' ultimately determining all social phenomena (see *economic determinism*).

Post-modernism   A range of theories which depart from modernism by abandoning the search for general ('totalizing') theories and (in some cases) rejecting any notion of universal reason.

Post-structuralism   A school of social theory which continues the tradition of *structuralism*, but sees the structures of society and thought as constantly changing.

Pragmatism, Penological   The tendency of governments to respond to penal developments and attempt to manage the *crisis of resources* 'with no clear or coherent philosophical or other theoretical basis' (Bottoms, 1980: 4).

Pre-sentence Report (PSR)   A report compiled by a *probation* officer or *youth offending team* officer that provides sentencers with information about an offender and usually includes a proposal for how the offender might be *sentenced*.

Prison Officers' Association   A trade union representing the interests of prison officers.

Prisons Ombudsman   An independent official who is responsible for investigating complaints about the way prisoners have been treated, including disciplinary decisions, but excluding complaints about convictions, *sentence* lengths and release dates. His remit now also includes the *probation* service and deaths in prison.

Private Finance Initiative (PFI)   A self-imposed Treasury rule forbidding any public expenditure on new projects unless the use of private finance has first been considered.

Privatization   A policy of promoting greater private sector involvement in the operation of the prison system (including the construction and management of prisons) and also in the delivery of *non-custodial penalties*.

Probation   The name given to the penal supervision of offenders. For many years this was undertaken almost exclusively by members of the probation service.

Probation Order   A court order requiring the offender to be supervised by a *probation* officer. Known as a *'community rehabilitation order'* between 2001 and 2005; replaced by supervision requirements in *community orders* since the Criminal Justice Act 2003.

Proportionality, Principle of   The principle that the severity of an offender's *punishment* should be proportionate to the seriousness of the offence. See also *just deserts*, *retributivism*.

Prosecution   The process whereby a suspected offender is taken to court and tried for the alleged offence.

Punishment   We use this term to refer to any measure that is imposed on an offender in response to an offence, regardless of whether it is *punitive*.

Punishment in the Community   The name given to *non-custodial penalties* that impose restrictions on the liberty of an offender. Also refers to a policy (associated with the *Hurd era*) of making *non-custodial penalties* more *punitive* in the hope of encouraging sentencers to use them more often in preference to imprisonment. See also *strategy of encouragement*.

Punitive   We use this word to refer to *punishments* which are intended to make the offender suffer, for purposes such as *retribution* or *deterrence*. Also refers to the mindset we call *law and order ideology*.

Punitive Bifurcation   See *bifurcation, punitive*.

Radical Pluralism   A theory which represents a compromise between *pluralism* and Marxism.

Recidivism   The repetition of criminal behaviour by an offender.

Reconviction Rate   One (imperfect) measure of *recidivism*, based on how many offenders subject to a *penalty* receive another conviction within a certain length of time (typically two years).

Reductivism   The theory that *punishment* can be justified by its effects in controlling crime, by means such as *deterrence, incapacitation* and *reform*.

Referral Order   An order imposed by a court on a young offender (aged 10 to 17) who pleads guilty and is convicted for the first time. The order consists of a referral to a *Youth Offender Panel*.

Reform/Rehabilitation   The prevention of crime by improving an offender's character or behaviour.

Rehabilitative Ideal   The notion that the aim of all *punishment* should be *rehabilitation*. See also *positivism, treatment model, welfare model*.

Reintegrative Shaming   A term coined by John Braithwaite (1989) and used to describe a process whereby an offender is shamed in the company of *victims* and 'significant others' for what they have done, while treating the offender with concern and respect, the aim being to strengthen the moral bonds between the offender, the offender's family and the wider community.

Remand   A court order specifying what is to happen to a defendant or convicted offender pending trial or *sentence*, which may be remand on *bail* or in *custody*.

Remand Centres/Remand Prisons   *Custodial* institutions housing prisoners on *remand*.

Remission   Automatic *early release*, forfeited only if the prisoner is judged to have misbehaved while in prison.

Reparation   Any action that is undertaken by an offender to help put right or 'repair' the wrong they have done, thereby acknowledging the wrongfulness of their actions. Reparation is an important component of *restorative justice*.

Reparation Order   A sentence which requires a young offender to perform *reparation* to the *victim* or to the community.

Reprimand   See *caution*.

Resources, Crisis of   See *crisis of resources*.

Responsibilization   The policy of requiring people (especially young offenders) to be accountable for their actions; or holding parents responsible for the actions of their children).

Restorative Justice   A term used to refer to a wide range of informal processes that seek to resolve offences by involving offenders, *victims* and others affected by the offence, with an emphasis on *reparation*. These processes include *mediation*.

Retribution   Punishing offenders because they are thought to deserve *punishment*.

Retributivism   The theory that wrongdoers may and should be *punished* because (and as much as) they deserve to be. See also *just deserts, proportionality, principle of*.

Rights Theory   (Or 'human rights theory'.) The theory that individuals possess certain fundamental moral entitlements.

SAP   See *Sentencing Advisory Panel*.

Seamless Sentences   Sentences that are served partly in custody and partly in the community with a smooth transition between the two.

Secure Children's Homes   Secure accommodation for younger children (up to the age of 16) run by local authorities.

Secure Training Centres   Privately run secure accommodation for *young offenders* (boys aged 12 to 15 and girls between 12 and 17) who are serving *custodial sentences*.

Security   A term variously used to mean (1) keeping prisoners *contained* within prisons (i.e. preventing escapes); (2) exercising appropriate *control* over prisoners; (3) keeping prisoners and staff safe while within the prison.

Sentence   A court order specifying the *punishment* to be imposed on a person who has been convicted of an offence.

Sentencing Advisory Panel (SAP)   An official body which advises the *Sentencing Guidelines Council*.

Sentencing Guidelines   Relatively imprecise rules which guide courts in making their *sentencing* decisions.

Sentencing Guidelines Council (SGC)   An official body chaired by the *Lord Chief Justice* which issues *sentencing guidelines* to the courts.

'Short, Sharp Shock'   A brisk militaristic regime that operated in certain *detention centres* in the 1980s, historical precursor to *boot camps*.

'Slopping Out'   The former daily prison routine of emptying chamber pots when most prison cells lacked integral sanitation.

Social Control   A term which encompasses all the methods whereby society keeps its members obedient to its rules.

Social Democracy   A political system (whose prime example is Sweden) which shares the consensual approach of conservative *corporatism*, but with a more generous and egalitarian welfare system.

Statute   An Act of Parliament.

Strategy A   A highly *punitive* approach to crime and *punishment*, embodying *law and order ideology* and an *exclusionary* approach to offenders.

Strategy B   A *managerialist* approach to crime and *punishment* which seeks to apply administrative and bureaucratic mechanisms to criminal justice in an attempt to make the system as smooth-running and cost-effective as possible.

Strategy C   An *inclusive* approach to crime and *punishment* which seeks to protect and uphold the human *rights* of offenders and *victims* of crime, to minimize punishment and to ensure fairness and humane treatment within the *criminal justice system*.

Strategy of Encouragement   A policy of encouraging, but not requiring, courts to make greater use of *non-custodial penalties* in preference to imprisonment. See also *punishment in the community*.

Structuralism   A type of social theory which regards the structure of the social system as central to the understanding of society.

Summary Offences   Offences which can only be tried in the *magistrates' court*.

Supervision Order A penalty for young offenders (under the age of 18) equivalent to the former *probation* order for adult offenders.

Suspended Sentence A sentence of imprisonment that is held in suspense for a specified period and not activated provided that no further offence is committed during this time. Under the 2003 Criminal Justice Act suspended sentences were replaced by the 'suspended sentence order', which enables a court to add one or more additional requirements (similar to those in *community orders*).

Systems Management An approach to criminal justice, especially influential in *juvenile justice* in the 1980s, which seeks to apply *managerialist* techniques to achieve goals such as a decrease in the use of *custody*. Systems management techniques include *decarceration, diversion*, and *inter-agency* co-operation.

Tagging See *curfews, electronic monitoring, exclusion orders, home detention curfew.*

Tariff A set of punishments of varying severity which are matched to crimes of differing seriousness ('offence-based tariff') or to offenders with different criminal records ('offender-based tariff'). Also denotes the minimum term which must be served in prison under an *indeterminate sentense.*

'Three Strikes and You're Out' Laws which prescribe mandatory or minimum prison *sentences* for a third offence.

'Tough on Crime and Tough on the Causes of Crime' A slogan associated with *New Labour*, and in particular with Tony Blair, first used in 1992.

'Toxic Mix' A combination of different types of difficult prisoners within a single institution, said by the *orthodox account* of the *penal crisis* to be an important factor in riots and disorder within prisons.

Treatment Model The notion that offenders should be 'treated' (as if they were ill) to *reform* them rather than dealing with them in a *punitive* manner. See also *positivism, rehabilitative ideal, welfare model.*

Triable Either Way See *either way offences.*

'Truth in Sentencing' (Also known as *honesty in sentencing*.) The notion that the *sentence* pronounced by the judge in court should denote the exact length of time the offender spends in prison, i.e. that there should be no *early release.*

Twin-track Strategy See *bifurcation.*

Unit Fines A system introduced into magistrates' courts by the Criminal Justice Act 1991 designed to relate *fines* to the offenders' means. Abolished by the Criminal Justice Act 1993. See also *day fines.*

Unpaid Work See *community service, community payback, community order.*

Utilitarianism The theory that moral actions are those which promote the 'greatest happiness of the greatest number' (Jeremy Bentham). Associated with *reductivism.*

Venue See *mode of trial.*

Victim Someone who is harmed by a criminal act.

Visibility, Crisis of See *crisis of visibility.*

Warning See *caution.*

Welfare Model The notion that criminal justice (and especially *youth justice*) should aim to promote the welfare of the offender above all. Associated with *positivism.* See also *rehabilitative ideal, treatment model.*

White Paper An official document setting out the Government's plans for new legislation or policy.

Young Adult Offenders Offenders aged between 18 and 20 inclusive.

Young Offender Institutions Secure institutions run by the Prison Service for *young offenders* serving custodial sentences.

Young Offenders Usually means offenders under the age of 18, sometimes includes *young adult offenders* aged 18 to 20.

Youth Court The court which tries *young offenders* under the age of 18.

Youth Justice The *criminal justice system* as it applies to *young offenders* under the age of 18.

Youth Justice Board (YJB) The Youth Justice Board, now known as the YJB, is a public body with strategic responsibility for the *youth justice* system as a whole, including the provision of *custodial* institutions for those aged under 18.

Youth Offender Panel A forum to which *young offenders* who receive a *referral order* are sent by the court. The panel meets the offender and seeks to agree a 'contract' aimed at *reparation* and tackling the causes of the young person's offending behaviour.

Youth Offending Teams *Multi-agency* teams (including representatives of the police, social services, *probation* service, local education and health authorities) that are responsible for delivering community-based interventions and supervision for *young offenders.*

Zero Tolerance The notion that there should always be a firm response to even minor offending and other anti-social behaviour. Contrast *minimum intervention.*

References

Abt Associates (1998) *Private Prisons in the United States: An Assessment of Current Practice,* Cambridge, MA: Abt Associates Inc.

Acheson, D. (1996) 'Review on the Effects on Health in the Special Secure Units at Full Sutton, Whitemoor and Bemarsh Prisons' (unpublished).

Adam Smith Institute (1984) *Justice Policy*. London: ASI Research.

Adams, R. (1994) *Prison Riots in Britain and the USA.* Basingstoke: Macmillan.

ADT Europe (2006) *Anti-social Behaviour Across Britain*, available online at: http://adt.pl/news/2006_06_01_Antisocial/cc4471AD.pdf

Advisory Council on the Penal System (1968) (chaired by Sir Leon Radzinowicz) *The Regime for Long-term Prisoners in Conditions of Maximum Security*. London: HMSO.

Advisory Council on the Penal System (1970) *Non-custodial and Semi-custodial Penalties*. London: HMSO.

Advisory Council on the Penal System (1977) *The Length of Prison Sentences*. London: HMSO.

Aertsen, I. and Peters, T. (1998) 'Mediation and Restorative Justice in Belgium', *European Journal on Criminal Policy and Research* 6: 507–25.

Allen, C., Crow, I. and Cavadino, M. (2000) *Evaluation of the Youth Court Demonstration Project*. Home Office Research Study No. 214. London: Home Office.

Althusser, L. (1969) *For Marx*. London: Allen Lane.

Althusser, L. (1971) *Lenin and Philosophy and Other Essays*. New York and London: Monthly Review Press.

American Friends Service Committee (1971) *Struggle for Justice*. New York: Hill & Wang.

Amnesty International (1997) *Special Security Units: Cruel, inhuman or degrading treatment*. London: Amnesty International. Also available online at: http://www.oil.ca/amnesty/ailib/aipub/1997/EUR/44500697.htm.

Amnesty International (2002) *United Kingdom: Failing Children and Young People in Detention – Concerns Regarding Young Offender Institutions*. Available online at: http://web.amnesty.org/library/Index/ENGEUR450042002.

Andrews, C. (2000) *Contracted and Publicly Managed Prisons: Cost and Staffing Comparisons 1997–8*. London: HM Prison Service.

Andrews, D.A. (2001) 'Principles of Effective Correctional Programming', in L. Motiuk and R. Serin (eds), *Compendium 2000 on Effective Correctional Programming*. Ottawa: Correctional Service of Canada, pp. 9–17.

Andrews, D.A., Zinger, I., Hodge, R.D., Bonta, J., Gendreau, P. and Cullen, F.T. (1990) 'Does Correctional Treatment Work? A Clinically Relevant and Psychologically Informed Meta-Analysis', *Criminology*, 28: 369–429.

Ashworth, A. (1983) *Sentencing and Penal Policy*. London: Weidenfeld & Nicolson.

Ashworth, A. (1997) 'Sentenced by the Media', *Criminal Justice Matters*, 29: 14–15.

Ashworth, A. (1998) *The Criminal Process: An Evaluative Study* (2nd edition). Oxford: Oxford University Press.

Ashworth, A. (2000) *Sentencing and Criminal Justice* (3rd edition). London: Butterworths.

Ashworth, A. (2002) 'Responsibilities, Rights and Restorative Justice', *British Journal of Criminology*, 42: 578–94.

Ashworth, A. (2005) *Sentencing and Criminal Justice* (4th edition). Cambridge: Cambridge University Press.

Ashworth, A. and Gibson, B. (1994) 'The Criminal Justice Act 1993: Altering the Sentencing Framework', [1994] *Criminal Law Review*: 101–9.

Ashworth, A. and Player, E. (2005) 'Criminal Justice Act 2003: The Sentencing Provisions', *The Modern Law Review*: 822–38.

Audit Commission (1996) *Misspent Youth: Young People and Crime*. London: Audit Commission.

Audit Commission (2004) *Youth Justice 2004: A Review of the Reformed Youth Justice System*. London: Audit Commission.

Auld, Sir Robin (2001) *A Review of the Criminal Courts of England and Wales*. London: The Stationery Office. Available online at: http://www.criminal-courts-review. org.uk

Austin, J. and Coventry, G. (2001) *Emerging Issues on Privatized Prisons*. National Council on Crime and Delinquency Bureau of Justice Assistance Monograph. Available online at: http://www.ncjrs.org/pdffiles1/bja/181249.pdf.

Ayres, M. and Murray, L. (2005) *Arrests for Notifiable Offences and the Operation of Certain Police Powers under PACE England and Wales, 2004/05*. Home Office Statistical Bulletin 21/05. London: Home Office. Available online at: http://www.homeoffice.gov.uk/rds/pubsstatistical.html

Bach, S.D. (2002) 'Public Sector Employment Relations Under Labour: Muddling through on Modernization', *British Journal of Industrial Relations*, 40 (2): 319–39.

Bainham, A. (1990) *Children – The New Law: The Children Act 1989*. Bristol: Jordan & Sons.

Baker, E. and Roberts, J.V. (2005) 'Globalisation and the New Punitiveness', in Pratt et al. (eds), *The New Punitiveness: Trends, Theories, Perspectives*. Cullompton: Willan, pp. 121–38.

Baldus, D.C., Woodworth, G.W. and Pulaski, C.A. Jr. (1989) *Equal Justice and the Death Penalty: A Legal and Empirical Analysis*. Boston: NorthEastern University Press.

Baldwin, J. (1976) 'Social Composition of the Magistracy', *British Journal of Criminology*, 16: 171–4.

Ball, C. (2004) 'Youth Justice? Half a Century of Responses to Youth Offending', [2004] *Criminal Law Review*: 28–41.

Barak-Glantz, I.L. (1981) 'Towards a Conceptual Schema of Prison Management Styles', *The Prison Journal*, 61(2): 42–60.

Barclay, G.C. and Tavares, C. (2000) *International Comparisons of Criminal Justice Statistics 1998*. Home Office Statistical Bulletin 04/00. London: Home Office.

Barclay, G.C., Tavares, C. and Prout, A. (eds) (1995) *Digest 3: Information on the Criminal Justice System in England and Wales*. London: Home Office Research and Statistics Department.

Baxter, R. and Nuttall, C. (1975) 'Severe Sentences: No Deterrent to Crime?', *New Society*, 2 January: 11–13.

BBC (2002) *BBC Race Survey*. Available online at: http://news.bbc.co.uk/hi/english/static/in_depth/uk/2002/race/survey.stm#Justice

Bean, P. (1981) *Punishment: A Philosophical and Criminological Inquiry*. Oxford: Martin Robertson.

Bean, P. (1996) 'America's Drug Courts: A New Development in Criminal Justice', [1996] *Criminal Law Review*: 718–21.

Beccaria, C. (1963) *On Crimes and Punishments*. Indianapolis: Bobbs-Merrill.

Beckett, K. and Western, B. (2001) 'Governing Social Marginality: Welfare, Incarceration, and the Transformation of State Policy', *Punishment & Society*, 3: 43–59.

Belson, W.A. (1975) *Juvenile Theft: The Causal Factors*. London: Harper & Row.

Bennett, J. and Hartley, A. (2006) 'High Reliability Organisations and High Security Prisons', *Prison Service Journal*, 166.

Bennett, T. (1979) 'The Social Distribution of Criminal Labels', *British Journal of Criminology*, 19: 134–45.

Bennett, T. and Wright, R. (1984) *Burglars on Burglary*. Aldershot: Gower.

Bentham, J. (1970) *An Introduction to the Principles of Morals and Legislation*. London: Methuen.

Bergman, D. (1991) *Deaths at Work: Accidents or Corporate Crime?* London: Workers' Educational Association.

Beyleveld, D. (1980) *A Bibliography on General Deterrence Research*. Westmead: Saxon House.

Bianchi, H. (1994) *Justice as Sanctuary: Towards a New System of Social Control*. Bloomington, IN: Indiana University Press.

Blair, T. (1993) 'The Future of the Prison Service'. Perrie lecture, March 1993. *Prison Service Journal*, 90: 19–25.

Blom-Cooper, L. (1988) *The Penalty of Imprisonment*. London: Prison Reform Trust.

Blom-Cooper, Sir L. and Morris, T. (2004) *With Malice Aforethought: A Study of the Crime and Punishment for Homicide*. Oxford: Hart Publishing.

Blunkett, D. (2004) *Reducing Crime, Changing Lives*. London: Home Office. Available online at: http://www.homeoffice.gov.uk/documents/reducing-crime-changing-lives?version=1

Boag, D. (1988) 'The Special Unit at Lincoln Prison: Descriptive Account of the First Six Months', unpublished report to the Home Office.

Boag, D. (1989) 'The Lincoln Special Unit: 30 November 1987 to 25 July 1988: the Second Descriptive Account', unpublished report to the Home Office.

Bottomley, A.K. (1973) *Decisions in the Penal Process*. London: Martin Robertson.

Bottomley, A.K. (1980) 'The "Justice Model" in America and Britain: Development and Analysis', in A.E. Bottoms and R.H. Preston (eds), *The Coming Penal Crisis*. Edinburgh: Scottish Academic Press, pp. 25–52.

Bottomley, A.K. (1984) 'Dilemmas of Parole in a Penal Crisis', *Howard Journal of Criminal Justice*, 23: 24–40.

Bottomley, A.K. (1990) 'Lincoln Special Unit', unpublished report to the Home Office.

Bottomley, A.K. and Hay, W. (eds) (1991) *Special Units for Difficult Prisoners*. Hull: University of Hull.

Bottomley, A.K., James, A., Clare, E. and Liebling, A. (1996) *Wolds Remand Prison: An Evaluation,* Home Office Research Findings No. 32. London: HMSO.

Bottomley, A.K., Liebling, A. and Sparks, R. (1994) *An Evaluation of Barlinnie and Shotts Units.* Scottish Prison Service Occasioned Papers No. 7. Edinburgh: Scottish Prison Service.

Bottoms, A.E. (1977) 'Reflections on the Renaissance of Dangerousness', *Howard Journal of Criminal Justice,* 16: 70–96.

Bottoms, A.E. (1980) 'An Introduction to "The Coming Crisis"', in A.E. Bottoms and R.H. Preston (eds) *The Coming Penal Crisis.* Edinburgh: Scottish Academic Press, pp. 1–24.

Bottoms, A.E. (1981) 'The Suspended Sentence', *British Journal of Criminology,* 21: 1–26.

Bottoms, A.E. (1983) 'Neglected Features of Contemporary Penal Systems', in D. Garland and P. Young (eds), *The Power to Punish.* London: Heinemann, pp. 166–202.

Bottoms, A.E. (1987) 'Limiting Prison Use: Experience in England and Wales', *Howard Journal of Criminal Justice,* 26: 177–202.

Bottoms, A.E. (1995a) 'The Philosophy and Politics of Punishment and Sentencing', in C. Clarkson and R. Morgan (eds), *The Politics of Sentencing Reform.* Oxford: Clarendon Press, pp. 17–49.

Bottoms, A.E. (1995b) *Intensive Community Supervision for Young Offenders: Outcomes, Process and Cost.* Cambridge: Institute of Criminology.

Bottoms, A.E. (2000) Oral contribution in the course of a conference on 'Restorative Justice: Exploring the Aims and Determining the Limits', Institute of Criminology, Cambridge, 6–8 October.

Bottoms, A.E. (2001) 'Compliance and Community Penalties', ch. 5 in A.E. Bottoms, L. Gelsthorpe and S. Rex (eds), *Community Penalties: Change and Challenges.* Cullompton: Willan Publishing.

Bottoms, A. (2004) 'Empirical Research Relevant to Sentencing Frameworks', in A. Bottoms, S. Rex and G. Robinson (eds), *Alternatives to Prison: Options for an Insecure Society.* Cullompton: Willan Publishing, pp. 59–82.

Bottoms, A.E. and Brownsword, R. (1983) 'Dangerousness and Rights', in J.W. Hinton (ed.), *Dangerousness: Problems of Assessment and Prediction.* London: George Allen & Unwin, pp. 9–22.

Bottoms, A.E. and Dignan, J. (2004) 'Youth Justice in Great Britain', in M. Tonry and A.N. Doob (eds), *Crime and Justice: A Review of Research,* vol. 31. Chicago: University of Chicago Press, pp. 21–183.

Bottoms, A.E. and McClean, J.D. (1976) *Defendants in the Criminal Process.* London: Routledge & Kegan Paul.

Bottoms, A.E. and Preston, R.H. (eds) (1980) *The Coming Penal Crisis: A Criminological and Theological Exploration.* Edinburgh: Scottish Academic Press.

Bottoms, A.E. and Stevenson, S. (1992) '"What Went Wrong?": Criminal Justice Policy in England and Wales, 1945–70', in D. Downes (ed.), *Unravelling Criminal Justice.* Basingstoke: Macmillan Press, pp. 1–45.

Bottoms, A. and Wilson, A. (2004) 'Attitudes to Punishment in Two High Crime Communities', ch. 15 in A. Bottoms, S. Rex and G. Robinson (eds), *Alternatives to Prison: Options for an Insecure Society.* Cullompton: Willan Publishing.

Bottoms, A.E., Hay, W. and Sparks, J.R. (1990) 'Situational and Social Approaches to the Prevention of Disorder in Long-term Prisons', *The Prison Journal* (Journal of the Pennsylvania Prison Society), 70: 83–95.

Bottoms, A., Rex, S. and Robinson, G. (eds) (2004) *Alternatives to Prison: Options for an Insecure Society.* Cullompton: Willan Publishing.

Bowden, J. (1995) 'Barlinnie Special Unit: the End of an Experiment', *Prison Report*, 30: 24–5.

Boyle, J. (1977) *A Sense of Freedom.* London: Pan Books.

Braggins, J. and Talbot, J. (2003) *Time to Learn: Prisoners' Views on Prison Education.* London: Prison Reform Trust.

Braithwaite, J. (1989) *Crime, Shame and Reintegration.* Cambridge: Cambridge University Press.

Briggs, D. (1975) *In Place of Prison.* London: Temple Smith.

Brody, S.R. (1976), *The Effectiveness of Sentencing*, Home Office Research Study No. 35. London: HMSO.

Brody, S.R. and Tarling, R. (1980) *Taking Offenders out of Circulation*, Home Office Research Study No. 64. London: HMSO.

Brogan, D. (2005) *Anti-social Behaviour: An Assessment of Current Management of Information Systems and the Scale of Anti-social Behaviour Order Breaking Resulting in Custody.* London: Youth Justice Board.

Bronstein, A.J. (1993/4) 'More Prison Less Crime?', *Criminal Justice Matters,* 14: 8–9.

Brown, D. (1998) *Offending on Bail and Police Use of Conditional Bail.* Home Office Research Findings No. 72. London: Home Office Research and Statistics Directorate.

Bucke, T. (1997) *Ethnicity and Contacts with the Police: Findings from the British Crime Survey.* Home Office Research Findings No. 59. London: Home Office.

Budd, T., Sharp, C., Weir, G., Wilson, D. and Owen, N. (2005) *Young People and Crime: Findings from the 2004 Offending, Crime and Justice Survey.* Home Office Statistical Bulletin 20/05. London: Home Office.

Burnett, R. and Farrell, G. (1994) *Reported and Unreported Racial Incidents in Prison.* Oxford: University of Oxford Centre for Criminological Research Occasional Paper No. 14.

Burney, E. (1979) *JP, Magistrate, Court and Community.* London: Hutchinson.

Burns, J. (2004) 'Prison Officers Threaten Summer Strikes', *Financial Times*, 26 May.

Burton, M. (1983) 'Understanding Mental Health Services: Theory and Practice', *Critical Social Policy*, 3: 54–74.

Cain, M. (1971) 'On the Beat: Interactions and Relations in Rural and Urban Police Forces', in S. Cohen (ed.), *Images of Deviance.* Harmondsworth: Penguin.

Campbell, S. (2002) *A Review of Anti-Social Behaviour Orders.* Home Office Research Study No. 236. London: Home Office Research, Development and Statistics Directorate.

Carlen, P. (1983) *Women's Imprisonment: A Study in Social Control.* London: Routledge & Kegan Paul.

Carlen, P. (1990) *Alternatives to Women's Imprisonment.* Milton Keynes: Open University Press.

Carlen, P. (2006) 'The Nonsense of the Therapunitive Prison for Women and Men', *The Howard League Magazine,* 24(3): 6.

Carlile, A. (2006) *The Carlile Inquiry.* London: Howard League for Penal Reform.

Carlisle, M. (1988) *The Parole System in England and Wales: Report of the Review Committee*, Cm 532. London: HMSO.

Carlsson, K. (2003) 'Intensive Supervision with Electronic Monitoring in Sweden', in M. Mayer, R. Haverkamp and R. Levy (eds), *Will Electronic Monitoring Have a Future in Europe?'* Freiburg: Max Planck Institute.

Carson, W.G. (1971) 'White Collar Crime and the Enforcement of Factory Legislation', in W.G. Carson and P. Wiles (eds), *Crime and Delinquency in Britain*. London: Martin Robertson, pp. 192–206.

Carter, P. (2002) *Review of PFI and Market Testing in the Prison Service*. London: HM Prison Service. Extracts from the executive summary are available online at: http://www.hmprisonservice.gov.uk/library/dynpage.asp?Page=964

Carter, P. (2003) *Managing Offenders, Reducing Crime*. London: Home Office. Available online at: http://www.cabinetoffice.gov.uk/strategy/downloads/files/managingoffenders.pdf

Cavadino, M. (1983) 'An Examination and Evaluation of English Mental Health Law'. Unpublished PhD thesis, University of Sheffield.

Cavadino, M. (1989) *Mental Health Law in Context: Doctors' Orders?* Aldershot: Dartmouth.

Cavadino, M. (1992) 'Theorising the Penal Crisis', in K. Bottomley, D. Farrington, T. Fowles, R. Reiner and S. Walklate (eds), *Criminal Justice: Theory and Practice*. London: British Society of Criminology, pp. 1–22.

Cavadino, M. (1994) Review of M W McMahon, *The Persistent Prison? Rethinking Decarceration and Penal Reform*, in *Social and Legal Studies*, 3: 554–5.

Cavadino, M. (1997a) 'A Vindication of the Rights of Psychiatric Patients', *Journal of Law and Society*, 24: 235–51.

Cavadino, M. (1997b) *The Law of Gravity: Offence Seriousness and Criminal Justice*. Sheffield: Joint Unit for Social Services Research.

Cavadino, M. (2002) 'New Mental Health Law for Old: Safety-Plus Equals Human Rights Minus', *Child and Family Law Quarterly*, 14: 175–89.

Cavadino, M. and Dignan, J. (1992) *The Penal System: An Introduction*. London: Sage.

Cavadino, M. and Dignan, J. (1997a) *The Penal System: An Introduction* (2nd edition). London: Sage Publications.

Cavadino, M. and Dignan, J. (1997b) 'Reparation, Retribution and Rights', *International Review of Victimology*, 4: 233–53.

Cavadino, M. and Dignan, J. (2002) *The Penal System: An Introduction* (3rd edition). London: Sage Publications.

Cavadino, M. and Dignan, J. (with others) (2006) *Penal Systems: A Comparative Approach*. London: Sage Publications.

Cavadino, M., Crow, I. and Dignan, J. (1999) *Criminal Justice 2000*. Winchester: Waterside Press.

Central Statistical Office (1991) *The CSO Blue Book*, ed. D. Ruffles. UK National Accounts. London: HMSO.

Centre for Public Services (2002) *Privatizing Justice: the Impact of the Private Finance Initiative in the Criminal Justice System*. Sheffield: Centre for Public Services. Available online at: http://www.centre.public.org.uk/briefings.

Chapman, L. (1978) *Your Disobedient Servant*. London: Chatto & Windus.

Charles, N., Whittaker, C. and Ball, C. (1997) *Sentencing without a Pre-Sentence Report*. Home Office Research Findings No. 47. London: Home Office Research and Statistics Directorate.

Charman, E., Gibson, B., Honess, T. and Morgan, R. (1996) *Fine Impositions and Enforcement Following the Criminal Justice Act 1993*, Home Office Research Findings 36. London: Home Office.

Chief Secretary to the Treasury (2003) *Every Child Matters*. Cm. 5860. Also available online at: http://www.everychildmatters.gov.uk/publications/

Children's Rights Alliance (2005) *State of Children's Rights 2005*. London: Children's Rights Alliance.

Christiansen, K.O. (1975) 'On General Prevention from an Empirical Viewpoint', in National Swedish Council for Crime Prevention, *General Deterrence: A Conference on Current Research and Standpoints, June 2–4, 1975*. Stockholm: National Swedish Council for Crime Prevention, pp. 60–74.

Christie, N. (1978) 'Conflicts as Property', *British Journal of Criminology*, 17: 1–15.

Christie, N. (1981) *Limits to Pain*. London: Routledge.

Clancy, A., Hough, M., Aust, R. and Kershaw, C. (2001) *Crime, Policing and Justice: The Experience of Ethnic Minorities*. Home Office Research Study No. 223. London: Home Office. Available online at: http://www.homeoffice.gov.uk/rds/pubsintro1.html

Clare, E. and Bottomley, K. (eds) (2001) *Evaluation of Close Supervision Centres*. Home Office Research Study No. 136. London: Home Office Research, Development and Statistics Directorate.

Clegg, M. and Kirwan, S. (2006) *Police Service Strength, England and Wales, 31 March 2005*. Home Office Statistical Bulletin 13/06. Available online at: http://www.homeoffice.gov.uk/rds/pubsstatistical.html

Codd, H. (1998) 'Prisoners' Families: the "Forgotten Victims"', *Probation Journal*, 45: 148–54.

Coggan, G. and Walker, M. (1982) *Frightened for My Life*. London: Fontana.

Cohen, P. (1981) 'Policing the Working Class City', in M. Fitzgerald, G. McLennan and J. Pawson (eds), *Crime and Society: Readings in History and Theory*. London: Routledge & Kegan Paul, pp. 116–33.

Cohen, S. (1979) 'The Punitive City: Notes on the Dispersal of Social Control', *Contemporary Crises*, 3: 339–63.

Cohen, S. (1980) *Folk Devils and Moral Panics: The Creation of the Mods and Rockers*. Oxford: Martin Robertson.

Cohen, S. (1985) *Visions of Social Control*. Cambridge: Polity Press.

Cohen, S. and Taylor, L. (1978) *Prison Secrets*. London: National Council for Civil Liberties/Radical Alternatives to Prison.

Commission for Racial Equality (2003) *Race Equality in Prisons*. London: Commission for Racial Equality. Available online at: http://www.cre.gov.uk/downloads/race_equality_in_prisons.pdf

Committee of Public Accounts (2002) *Reducing Prisoner Re-offending*. Fifty-third Report of Session 2001–02, (HC 619), para 8.

Confederation of British Industry (2003) 'Competition: a Catalyst for Change in the Prison Service'. London: Confederation of British Industry.

Cook, D. (1989) *Rich Law, Poor Law: Differential Response to Tax and Supplementary Benefit Fraud*. Milton Keynes: Open University Press.

Cooke, D.J. (1989) 'Containing Violent Prisoners: An Analysis of the Barlinnie Special Unit', *British Journal of Criminology*, 29: 129–43.

Cooke, D.J. (1991) 'Violence in Prisons: The Influence of Regime Factors', *Howard Journal of Criminal Justice*, 30: 95–109.

Corre, N. and Wolchover, D. (1999) *Bail in Criminal Proceedings*. London: Blackstone Press.

Corston, J. (2007) *A Report by Baroness Jean Corston of a Review of Women With Particular Vulnerabilities in the Criminal Justice System*, London: Home Office, March 2007. Available online at: http://www.homeoffice.gov.uk/documents/corston-report/

Coulsfield, L. (2004) *Crime, Courts and Confidence: Report of an Inquiry Into Alternatives to Prison*. London: The Stationery Office.

Coyle, A. (2005a) *Understanding Prisons: Key Issues in Policy and Practice*. Cullompton: Willan Publishing.

Coyle, A. (2005b) 'Imprisonment: The Four Blair Principles', Perrie lecture 2005. *Prison Service Journal*, 161: 25–32. Also available online at: http://www.hmprisonservice.gov.uk/assets/documents/100011E6524_perrie_lecture_andrew_coyle.doc

Coyle, A., Campbell, A. and Neufield, R. (2003) *Capitalist Punishment: Prison Privatization and Human Rights*. London: Zed Books.

Crabbe, T. (1993) 'Private Profits in the Public Sector', *International Union Rights* (Journal of the International Centre for Trade Union Rights), 1 (4): 34–5.

Creighton, S. and King, V. (2000) *Prisoners and the Law* (2nd edition). London: Butterworths.

Crighton, D. and Towl, G. (1997) 'Self-inflicted Deaths in England and Wales: An Analysis of the Data for 1988–90 and 1994–5', in Suicide and Self-Injury in Prisons, *Issues in Criminological and Legal Psychology*, 28.

Crook, F. (1991) 'Shut the Door and Let Them Out', *Guardian*, 4 September.

Crow, I. (1987) 'Black People and Criminal Justice in the UK', *Howard Journal of Criminal Justice*, 26: 303–14.

Crow, I. and Cove, J. (1984) 'Ethnic Minorities and the Courts', [1984] *Criminal Law Review*: 413–17.

Crow, I. and Simon, F. (1987) *Unemployment and Magistrates' Courts*. London: NACRO.

Crow, I., Cavadino, M., Dignan, J., Johnston, V. and Walker, M. (1995) *The Impact of the Criminal Justice Act 1991 in Four Areas in the North of England*. Sheffield: University of Sheffield.

Crow, I., Richardson, P., Riddington, C. and Simon, F. (1989) *Unemployment, Crime and Offenders*. London: Routledge.

Cullen and Minchin (2000) *The Prison Population in 1999: A Statistical Review*, Home Office Research Findings No. 118. London: Home Office Research and Statistics Directorate.

Dahl, R.A. (1961) *Who Governs?* New Haven, CT: Yale University Press.

Dahl, R.A. (1985) *A Preface to Economic Democracy*. Cambridge: Polity Press.

Darbyshire, P. (1999) 'A Comment on the Powers of Magistrates' Clerks', [1999] *Criminal Law Review*: 377–86.

Davis, G., Boucherat, J. and Watson, D. (1988) 'Reparation in the Service of Diversion: The Subordination of a Good Idea', *Howard Journal of Criminal Justice*, 27: 127–262.

Davis, G., Boucherat, J. and Watson, D. (1989) 'Pre-court Decision-making in Juvenile Justice', *British Journal of Criminology*, 29: 219–35.

Davis, K.C. (1969) *Discretionary Justice: A Preliminary Inquiry*. Baton Rouge: Louisiana State University Press.

Debidin, M. and Lovbakke, J. (2005) 'Offending Behaviour Programmes in Prison and Probation', in G. Harper and C. Chitty (eds), *The Impact of Corrections on Re-offending: A Review of 'What Works'* (3rd edition). Home Office Research Study No. 291. London: Home Office Research, Development and Statistics Directorate.

Denman, S. (2001) *Race Discrimination in the Crown Prosecution Service – Final Report*. London: Crown Prosecution Service.

Department for Christian Responsibility and Citizenship (2004) *A Place of Redemption: A Christian Approach to Punishment and Prison*, Catholic Bishops' Conference of England and Wales. London: Burns and Oates.

Dholakia, N. and Sumner, M. (1993) 'Research, Policy and Racial Justice', in D. Cook and B. Hudson (eds), *Racism and Criminology*. London: Sage, pp. 28–44.

Dignan, J. (1991) *Repairing the Damage: An Evaluation of an Experimental Adult Reparation Scheme in Kettering, Northamptonshire*. Sheffield: University of Sheffield, Centre for Criminological and Legal Research.

Dignan, J. (1992) 'Repairing the Damage: Can Reparation Be Made to Work in the Service of Diversion?', *British Journal of Criminology*, 32: 453–72.

Dignan, J. (1994) 'Reintegration through Reparation: A Way Forward for Restorative Justice?', in A. Duff, S. Marshall, R.E. Dobash and R.P. Dobash (eds), *Penal Theory and Penal Practice: Tradition and Innovation in Criminal Justice*. Manchester: Manchester University Press, pp. 231–44.

Dignan, J. (2002) 'Restorative Justice and the Law: The Case for an Integrated, Systemic Approach', ch. 9 in L. Walgrave (ed.), *Restorative Justice and the Law*. Cullompton: Willan Publishing.

Dignan, J. (2003) 'Towards a Systemic Model of Restorative Justice' in A. von Hirsch, J. Roberts, A.E. Bottoms, K. Roach and M. Schiff (eds), *Restorative Justice and Criminal Justice: Competing or Reconcilable Paradigms?* Oxford: Hart Publishing, pp. 135–56.

Dignan, J. (2005a) *Understanding Victims and Restorative Justice*. Maidenhead: Open University Press.

Dignan, J. (2005b) 'Alternatives to the Prosecution of Unruly Children and Young Persons: The Position in England and Wales', ch. 3 in T. Wing Lo, D. Wong and G. Maxwell (eds) *Alternatives to Prosecution: Rehabilitative and Restorative Models of Youth Justice*. Singapore: Marshall Cavendish Academic.

Dignan, J. (2006) 'Restorative Justice in Juvenile Justice and Criminal Court Settings', in G. Johnstone and D.W. van Ness (eds), *Handbook of Restorative Justice*. Cullompton: Willan Publishing, pp. 269–91.

Dignan, J. and Cavadino, M. (1996) 'Towards a Framework for Conceptualising and Evaluating Models of Criminal Justice from a Victim's Perspective', *International Review of Victimology*, 4: 153–82.

Dignan, J. and Wynne, A. (1997) 'A Microcosm of the Local Community?', *British Journal of Criminology*, 37: 184–97.

van Dijk, J. J. M. and Mayhew, P. (1992) *Criminal Victimization in the Industrialized World: Key Findings of the 1989 and 1992 International Crime Surveys*. The Hague: Directorate for Crime Prevention, Ministry of Justice.

Director of Public Prosecutions (1986) 'Code for Crown Prosecutors', *Law Society Gazette*, 23 July.

Ditchfield, J. (1990) *Control in Prisons: A Review of the Literature*. Home Office Research Study No. 118. London: HMSO.

DLA MCG Consulting (2003) *Privately Managed Custodial Services*. Liverpool: DLA MCG Consulting.

DLA MGC Consulting (2005) *Privately Managed Custodial Services*. Liverpool: DLA MGC Consulting.

Dobash, R.P., Dobash, R.E. and Gutteridge, S. (1986) *The Imprisonment of Women*. Oxford: Basil Blackwell.

Dodgson, K., Goodwin, P., Howard, P., Llewellyn-Thomas, S., Mortimer, E., Russell, N. and Weiner, M. (2001) *Electronic Monitoring of Prisoners: An Evaluation of the*

Home Detention Curfew Scheme. Home Office Research Study No. 222. London: Home Office Research, Development and Statistics Directorate.

Dowds, L. and Hedderman, C. (1997), 'The Sentencing of Men and Women', in C. Hedderman and L. Gelsthorpe (eds), *Understanding the Sentencing of Women*. Home Office Research Study No. 170. London: Home Office, pp. 9–22.

Downes, D. (1988) *Contrasts in Tolerance: Post-War Penal Policy in The Netherlands and England and Wales*. Oxford: Oxford University Press.

Downes, D. (1997) 'Prison Does Wonders for the Jobless Figures', *Guardian*, 25 November.

Downes, D. (2001) 'The *Macho* Penal Economy: Mass Incarceration in the United States – A European Perspective', *Punishment & Society*, 3: 61–80.

Duff, A., Marshall, S., Dobash, R.E. and Dobash, R.P. (eds) (1994) *Penal Theory and Penal Practice: Tradition and Innovation in Criminal Justice*. Manchester: Manchester University Press.

Duff, R.A. (1986) *Trials and Punishments*. Cambridge: Cambridge University Press.

Duff, R.A. (2001) *Punishment, Communication and Community*. Oxford: Oxford University Press.

Durkheim, E. (1960) *The Division of Labor in Society*. Glencoe, IL: Free Press.

Durkheim, E. (1973) 'Two Laws of Penal Evolution', *Economy and Society*, 2: 285–308.

Dworkin, R. (1978) *Taking Rights Seriously* (new impression). London: Gerald Duckworth.

Eaton, M. (1986) *Justice for Women? Family, Court and Social Control*. Milton Keynes: Open University Press.

Edgar, K. and Martin, C. (2004) *Perceptions of Race and Conflict: Perspectives of Minority Ethnic Prisoners and of Prison Officers*. Home Office Online Report, 11/04. Available online at: http://www.homeoffice.gov.uk/rds/onlinepubs1.html

Edgar, K., O'Donnell, I. and Martin, C. (2003) *Prison Violence: The Dynamics of Conflict, Fear and Power*. Cullompton: Willan Publishing.

Edwards, A. (2002) *No Truth No Justice*. Hook, Hampshire: Waterside Press.

Edwards, I. (2002) 'The Place of Victims' Preferences in the Sentencing of "Their" Offenders', [2002] *Criminal Law Review*: 689–702.

Eley, S., Malloch, M., McIvor, G., Yates, R. and Brown, A. (2002) *Glasgow's Pilot Drug Court in Action: The First Six Months*. Edinburgh: Scottish Executive Social Research.

Ellis, T. and Marshall, P. (1998) 'Does Parole Work?', *Home Office Research Bulletin*, 39: 43–50.

Ellis, T., Hedderman, C. and Mortimer, E. (1996) *Enforcing Community Sentences'*, Home Office Research Study No. 158. London: Home Office.

Esping-Andersen, G. (1990) *The Three Worlds of Welfare Capitalism*. Cambridge: Polity Press.

Estes, R. (1996) *Tyranny of the Bottom Line: Why Corporations Make Good People Do Bad Things*. San Francisco: Berrett-Koehler.

European Committee for the Prevention of Torture (1991) *Report to the United Kingdom Government on the Visit to United Kingdom Carried out by the CPT from 29 July 1990 to 10 August 1990*. Council of Europe, CPT/INF series. Also available online at: http://www.cpt.coe.int.

European Committee for the Prevention of Torture and Inhuman and Degrading Treatment (2002) *Report to the Government of the United Kingdom on the Visit to the United Kingdom, 4 to 16 February 2001*. Strasbourg: CPT.

European Committee for the Prevention of Torture and Inhuman and Degrading Treatment (2005) *Report to the Government of the United Kingdom.* CPT/ Inf (2005) 1. Strasbourg: CPT.

European Committee for the Prevention of Torture and Inhuman and Degrading Treatment (2006) *Report to the United Kingdom Government on the Visit to the United Kingdom carried out by the European Committee for the Prevention of Torture and Inhuman or Degrading Treatment or Punishment (CPT) from 20 to 25 November 2005.* CPT/Inf (2006) 28. Strasbourg: CPT. Also available online at: http://www.cpt.coe.int/en/ states/gbr. htm

Evans, K. (2005) 'Young People in the Media: A Dangerous and Anti-Social Obsession', *Criminal Justice Matters*, 60 (Spring): 14–15.

Evans, R. (1994) 'Cautioning: Counting the Cost of Retrenchment', *Criminal Law Review*: 566–77.

Eves, K. (2005) *Juveniles in Custody 2003–4: An Analysis of Children's Experiences of Prison.* London: HM Inspectorate of Prisons and Youth Justice Board.

Fabelo, T. (2000) '"Technocorrections": The Promises, the Uncertain Threats', available online at the National Institute of Justice website: http://www.ncjrs. gov/txtfiles1/nij/189106-2a.txt

Fagan, J. (2005) *Deterrence and the Death Penalty: A Critical Review of New Evidence.* Testimony to the New York State Assembly Standing Committee on Codes, Assembly Standing Committee on Judiciary and Assembly Standing Committee on Correction Hearings on the Future of Capital Punishment in the State of New York. Available online at: http://www.deathpenaltyinfo.org/FaganTestimony.pdf

Farrington, D.P. and Bennett, T. (1981) 'Police Cautioning of Juveniles in London', *British Journal of Criminology*, 21: 123–35.

Farrington, D.P. and Morris, A.M. (1983) 'Sex, Sentencing and Reconviction', *British Journal of Criminology*, 23: 229–48.

Faulkner, D. (2005) 'Parties, Politics and Punishment', *Criminal Justice Matters*, 60: 6–7, 39.

Faulkner, D. (2006) 'A Modern Service, Fit For Purpose?', ch. 7 in M. Hough, R. Allen and U. Padel (eds), *Reshaping Probation and Prisons: The New Offender Management Framework.* Bristol: Policy Press.

Fazel, S., Benning, R. and Danesh, J. (2005) 'Suicides in Male Prisoners in England and Wales, 1978–2003', *The Lancet,* 36: 1242–4.

Feeley, M. and Simon, J. (1992) 'The New Penology', *Criminology*, 39: 449–74.

Feeney, F. (1985) 'Interdependence as a Working Concept', in D. Moxon (ed.), *Managing Criminal Justice: A Collection of Papers.* London: HMSO, pp. 8–17.

Feest, J. (1988) *Reducing the Prison Population: Lessons from the West German Experience?* London: NACRO.

Field, S. (1984) *The Attitudes of Ethnic Minorities*, Home Office Research Study No. 80. London: HMSO.

Field, S. (1990) *Trends in Crime and their Interpretation: A Study of Recorded Crime in Post War England and Wales*, Home Office Research Study No. 119. London: HMSO.

Fisher, C.J. and Mawby, R.L. (1982) 'Juvenile Delinquency and Police Discretion in an Inner City Area', *British Journal of Criminology*, 22: 63–75.

Fitzgerald, M. (1993) *Ethnic Minorities and the Criminal Justice System.* The Royal Commission on Criminal Justice, Research Study No. 20. London: HMSO.

Fitzgerald, M. and Sim, J. (1980) 'Legitimating the Prison Crisis: A Critical Review of the May Report', *Howard Journal of Criminal Justice*, 19: 73–84.

Fitzgerald, M. and Sim, J. (1982) *British Prisons* (2nd edition). Oxford: Basil Blackwell.

de Fleur, L.B. (1975) 'Bias Influences on Drug Arrest Records: Implications for Deviance Research', *American Sociological Review*, 40: 88–103.

Flood-Page, C. and Mackie, A. (1998) *Sentencing Practice: An Examination of Decisions in Magistrates' Courts and the Crown Court in the Mid-1990's*. Home Office Research Study No. 180. London: Home Office.

Flood-Page, C., Campbell, S., Harrington, V. and Miller, J. (2000) *Youth Crime: Findings from the 1998/99 Youth Lifestyles Survey*. Home Office Research Study No. 209. London: Home Office.

Flynn, N. (1995) 'Germany's Crime Backlash', *Prison Report* 30 (Spring): 8–9.

Foster, J., Newburn, T. and Souhami, A. (2005) *Assessing the Impact of the Stephen Lawrence Inquiry*, Home Office Research Study No. 294. London: Home Office. Available online at: http://www.homeoffice.gov.uk/rds/pubsintro1.html

Foucault, M. (1967) *Madness and Civilization*. London: Tavistock.

Foucault, M. (1977) *Discipline and Punish: The Birth of the Prison*. London: Allen Lane.

Foucault, M. (1980) 'Prison Talk', in *Michel Foucault: Power/Knowledge, Selected Interviews and Other Writings 1972–1977*, ed. C. Gordon. Brighton: Harvester Press.

Fox, L.W. (1934) *The Modern English Prison*. London: Routledge & Kegan Paul.

Franko Aas, L. (2005) *Sentencing in the Age of Information: From Faust to Macintosh*. London: Glasshouse Press.

Gaes, G., Camp, S.D., Nelson, J.B. and Saylor, W.G. (2004) *Measuring Prison Performance: Government Privatization and Accountability*. Walnut Creek, CA and Oxford: Altamira Press.

Gardner, J., von Hirsch, A., Smith, A.H., Morgan, R., Ashworth, A. and Wasik, M. (1998) 'Clause I – the Hybrid from Hell?', *Criminal Justice Matters*, 31 (Spring): 25–7.

Garland, D. (1985) *Punishment and Welfare: A History of Penal Strategies*. Aldershot: Gower.

Garland, D. (1990a) *Punishment and Modern Society: A Study in Social Theory*. Oxford: Clarendon Press.

Garland, D. (1990b) 'Frameworks of Inquiry in the Sociology of Punishment', *British Journal of Sociology*, 41: 1–15.

Garland, D. (1995a) 'Penal Modernism and Postmodernism', in T. Blomberg and S. Cohen (eds), *Punishment and Social Control: Essays in Honour of Sheldon Messinger*. New York: Aldine de Gruyter, pp. 181–209.

Garland, D. (1995b) 'Panopticon Days: Surveillance and Society', *Criminal Justice Matters*, 20: 3–4.

Garland, D. (1996) 'The Limits of the Sovereign State: Strategies of Crime Control in Contemporary Society', *British Journal of Criminology*, 36: 445–71.

Garland, D. (2001) *The Culture of Control: Crime and Social Order in Contemporary Society*. Oxford: Oxford University Press.

Garland, D. and Young, P. (eds) (1983a) *The Power to Punish: Contemporary Penality and Social Analysis*. London: Heinemann.

Garland, D. and Young, P. (1983b) 'Towards a Social Analysis of Penality', in D. Garland and P. Young (eds), *The Power to Punish: Contemporary Penality and Social Analysis*. London: Heinemann, pp. 1–36.

Garside, R. (2004) *Crime, Persistent Offenders and the Justice Gap*. London: Crime and Society Foundation. Available online at: http://www.crimeandsociety.org.uk/briefings/jgap.html?search_string=garside

Geis, G. (1987) 'The Privatization of Prisons: Panacea or Placebo?', in B.J. Carroll, R.W. Conant and T.A. Easton (eds), *Private Means, Public Ends: Private Business in Social Service Delivery*. New York: Praeger, pp. 76–97.

Gelsthorpe, L. (1985) 'Girls and Juvenile Justice', *Youth and Policy*, 11: 1–5.

Gelsthorpe, L. (1989) *Sexism and the Female Offender: An Organizational Analysis*. Aldershot: Gower.

Gelsthorpe, L. and Loucks, N. (1997) 'Magistrates' Explanations of Sentencing Decisions', in C. Hedderman and L. Gelsthorpe (eds), *Understanding the Sentencing of Women*. Home Office Research Study No. 170. London: Home Office.

Genders, E. and Player, E. (1986) 'Women's Imprisonment: The Effects of Youth Custody', *British Journal of Criminology*, 26: 357–71.

Genders, E. and Player, E. (1989) *Race Relations in Prisons*. Oxford: Clarendon Press.

Genders, E. and Player, E. (1995) *Grendon: A Study of a Therapeutic Prison*. London: Clarendon Press.

Gewirth, A. (1978) *Reason and Morality*. Chicago: University of Chicago Press.

Gibson, B. (1987) 'Why Bournemouth?', *Justice of the Peace*, 151: 520–1.

Gill, M. (2000) *Commercial Robbery*. London: Blackstone Press.

Gold, M. (1966) 'Undetected Delinquent Activity', *Journal of Research in Crime and Delinquency*, 3: 27–46.

Goldblatt, P. and Lewis, C. (eds) (1998) *Reducing Offending: An Assessment of Research Evidence on Ways of Dealing with Offending Behaviour*. Home Office Research Study No. 187. London: HMSO.

Goldson, B. (2000) *The New Youth Justice*. Lyme Regis: Russell.

Goldson, B. and Coles, D. (2005) *In the Care of the State: Child Deaths in Penal Custody in England and Wales*. London: Inquest.

Goodhart, C.A.E. (1984) *Monetary Theory and Practice: The UK Experience*. London: Macmillan.

Gowers, E. (1953) *Report of the Royal Commission on Capital Punishment*, Cmd 8932. London: HMSO.

Graham, C. (2004) 'Custody or Community: An Interview with Paul Goggins', *Criminal Justice Management,* July: 4–7.

Graham, J. and Bowling, B. (1995) *Young People and Crime*. Home Office Research Study No. 145. London: HMSO.

Gramsci, A. (1971) *Selections from the Prison Notebooks of Antonio Gramsci* (eds Q. Hoare and G. Nowell-Smith). London: Lawrence & Wishart.

Gray, E., Taylor, E., Merrington, S. and Roberts, C. (2005) *ISSP: The Final Report*. Oxford Centre for Criminology/Youth Justice Board.

Green, D.G., Grove, E. and Martin, N. (2005) *Crime and Civil Society: Can We Become a More Law Abiding People?* London: Civitas.

Green, P. (1989) *Private Sector Involvement in the Immigrant Detention Centres*. London: Howard League for Penal Reform.

Greenberg, D. (1999) 'Punishment, Division of Labor, and Social Solidarity', in W.S. Laufer and F. Adler (eds), *The Criminology of Criminal Law,* Advances in Criminological Theory, vol. 8. New Brunswick, NJ: Transaction Books, pp. 283–361.

Griffith, J.A.G. (1997) *The Politics of the Judiciary* (5th edition). London: Fontana.

Gunn, J., Maden, T. and Swinton, M. (1991) *Mentally Disordered Prisoners*. London: Home Office.

de Haan, W. (1990) *The Politics of Redress: Crime, Abolition and Penal Abolition*. London: Unwin Hyman.

Habermas, J. (1976) *Legitimation Crisis*. London: Heinemann.

Hagell, A. and Newburn, T. (1994) *Persistent Young Offenders*. London: Policy Studies Institute.

Haggarty, K.D. and Ericson, R.V. (2000) 'The Surveillant Assemblage', *British Journal of Sociology*, 51 (4): 605–22.

Haggerty, K.D. (2004) 'Displaced Expertise: Three Constraints on the Policy Relevance of Criminological Thought', *Theoretical Criminology*, 8: 211–31.

Hale, B. (2006) *The Sinners and the Sinned Against: Women in the Criminal Justice System*, 4th Longford Lecture. Available online at: http://www.fawcettsociety.org.uk/documents/longford%20lecture.pdf

Hall, S. (1979) 'The Great Moving Right Show', *Marxism Today*, 23: 14–20.

Hall, S. (1980) *Drifting into a Law and Order Society*. London: Cobden Trust.

Hall, S., Clarke, J., Critcher, C., Jefferson, T. and Roberts, B. (1978) *Policing the Crisis*. London: Macmillan.

Halliday, J. (2001) *Making Punishments Work: Report of a Review of the Sentencing Framework for England and Wales*. London: Home Office Communication Directorate. Available online at: http://www.homeoffice.gov.uk/documents/halliday-report-sppu/

Hamlyn, B. and Lewis, D. (2000) *Women Prisoners: A Survey of Their Work and Training Experiences in Custody and on Release*. Home Office Research Study No. 208. London: Home Office.

Hann, R., Harman, R. and Pease, K. (1991) 'Does Parole Reduce the Risk of Reconviction?', *Howard Journal of Criminal Justice*, 30: 66–75.

Harding, R. (1997) *Private Prisons and Public Accountability*. New Brunswick, NJ: Transaction Publishing.

Harris, R. and Webb, D. (1987) *Welfare, Power and Juvenile Justice*. London: Tavistock.

Hart, H.L.A. (1968) *Punishment and Responsibility*. Oxford: Oxford University Press.

Hayward, D. and Aspin, R. (2001) 'Contracting Out: Time for a Policy Rethink?' Available online at: http://www.sisr.net

Health and Safety Executive (2005) 'Enforcement'. Available online at: http://www.hse.gov.uk/statistics/enforce/index.htm.

Hearnden, I. and Millie, A. (2003) *Investigation Links between Probation Enforcement and Reconviction*, Home Office Online Report 41/03. London: Home Office. Also available online at: www.homeoffice.gov.uk/rds/pdfs2/rdsolr4103.pdf

Hedderman, C. (2002) 'Going Up', *Prison Report*, 59: 23.

Hedderman, C. (2003) 'Enforcing Supervision and Encouraging Compliance' in W.-H. Chui and M. Nellis (eds), *Moving Probation Forward: Evidence, Arguments and Practice*. Harlow: Pearson Education, pp. 181–94.

Hedderman, C. and Gelsthorpe, L. (eds) (1997) *Understanding the Sentencing of Women*. Home Office Research Study No. 170. London: Home Office.

Hedderman, C. and Hough, M. (1994) *Does the Criminal Justice System Treat Men and Women Differently?* Home Office Research and Statistics Department Research Findings No. 10. London: Home Office.

Hedderman, C. and Hough, M. (2000) 'Tightening Up Probation: a Step Too Far?', *Criminal Justice Matters*, 39: 5.

Hedderman, C. and Hough, M. (2004) 'Getting Tough or Being Effective: What Matters?' in G. Mair (ed.), *What Matters in Probation.* Cullompton: Willan Publishing, pp. 146–69.

Hedderman, C. and Moxon, D. (1992) *Magistrates' Court or Crown Court? Mode of Trial Decisions and Sentencing.* Home Office Research Study No. 125. London: HMSO.

Heidensohn, F. (1985) *Women and Crime.* Basingstoke: Macmillan.

Hennessy, J. (1987) *Report of an Inquiry by Her Majesty's Chief Inspector of Prisons for England and Wales into the Disturbances in Prison Service Establishments in England between 29 April–2 May 1986.* London: HMSO.

Herbert, A. (2003) 'Mode of Trial and Magistrates' Sentencing Powers: Will Increased Powers Inevitably Lead to a Reduction in the Committal Rate?', [2003] *Criminal Law Review*: 314–25.

Herbert, A. (2004) 'Mode of Trial and the Influence of Local Justice', *Howard Journal of Criminal Justice*, 43: 65–78.

von Hirsch, A. (1976) *Doing Justice: The Choice of Punishments* (Report of the Committee for the Study of Incarceration). New York: Hill & Wang.

von Hirsch, A. (1986) *Past or Future Crimes: Deservedness and Dangerousness in the Sentencing of Criminals.* Manchester: Manchester University Press.

von Hirsch, A. (1987) 'Guidance by Numbers or by Words? Numerical Versus Narrative Guidelines for Sentencers', in K. Pease and M. Wasik (eds), *Sentencing Reform: Guidance or Guidelines?* Manchester: Manchester University Press, pp. 46–69.

von Hirsch, A. (1993) *Censure and Sanctions.* Oxford: Clarendon Press.

von Hirsch, A., Bottoms, A.E., Burney, E. and Wikström, P.-O. (1999) *Criminal Deterrence and Sentence Severity: An Analysis of Recent Research.* Oxford: Hart Publishing.

von Hirsch, A., Ashworth, A. and Shearing, C. (2003) 'Specifying Aims and Limits for Restorative Justice: A 'Making Amends Model?, ch. 2 in A. von Hirsch, J. Roberts, A.E. Bottoms, K. Roach and M. Schiff (eds), *Restorative Justice and Penal Justice: Competing or Reconcilable Paradigms?* Oxford: Hart Publishing.

HM Chief Inspector of Prisons (1987) *A Review of Prisoners' Complaints.* London: HMSO.

HM Chief Inspector of Prisons (1990a) *Report of a Review by Her Majesty's Chief Inspector of Prisons for England and Wales of Suicide and Self-harm in Prison Service Establishments in England and Wales.* London: HMSO.

HM Chief Inspector of Prisons (1990b) *Report of HM Chief Inspector of Prisons, 1989.* London: HMSO.

HM Chief Inspector of Prisons (1992) *HMP Holloway: Report by HM Chief Inspector of Prisons.* London: Home Office.

HM Chief Inspector of Prisons (1993) *Report on Wolds Remand Prison.* London: HMSO.

HM Chief Inspector of Prisons (1994) *Report of HM Chief Inspector of Prisons, April 1993-March 1994.* London: HMSO.

HM Chief Inspector of Prisons (1995) *HM Prison, Blakenhurst: A Report by HM Chief Inspector of Prisons.* London: Home Office.

HM Chief Inspector of Prisons (1997a) *HM Prison Whitemoor: Report of an Unannounced Short Inspection, 19 June 1997.* London: HMSO.

HM Chief Inspector of Prisons (1997b) *Women in Prison: A Thematic Review by HM Chief Inspector of Prisons.* London: Home Office.

HM Chief Inspector of Prisons (1997c) *Young Prisoners: A Thematic Review*. London: Home Office.

HM Chief Inspector of Prisons (1998) *Report on HM Prisons Grendon and Springhill, February 1998*. London: Home Office. Also available online at: http://www.penlex.org.uk/pages/cigrend.html

HM Chief Inspector of Prisons (1999a) *Report of an Unannounced Inspection of HM Prison Wormwood Scrubs, 8–12 March, 1999*. London: Home Office.

HM Chief Inspector of Prisons (1999b) *Suicide Is Everyone's Concern: A Thematic Review by Her Majesty's Chief Inspector of Prisons*. London: The Stationery Office. Also available online at: http://www.penlex.org.uk/pages/cisuic03.html#8

HM Chief Inspector of Prisons (1999c) *1998–9 Annual Report of Chief Inspector of Prisons*. London: Home Office.

HM Chief Inspector of Prisons (1999d) *Inspection of Close Supervision Centres: A Thematic Inspection by Her Majesty's Chief Inspector of Prisons*. London: Home Office. Also available online at: http://www.penlex.org.uk/pages/cicsc00.html#8

HM Chief Inspector of Prisons (1999e) *HMYOI and Remand Centre Feltham, Report of an Unannounced Full Inspection 30 November–4 December 1998*. London: Home Office.

HM Chief Inspector of Prisons (2000a) *Unjust Deserts: A Thematic Review by Her Majesty's Chief Inspector of Prisons of the Treatment and Conditions of Unsentenced Prisoners in England and Wales*. London: Home Office. Available online at: http://inspectorates.homeoffice.gov.uk/hmiprisons/thematic-reports1/unjust.pdf

HM Chief Inspector of Prisons (2000b) *Inspection Report on a Full Announced Inspection of HMYOI Portland, 24 October–3 November 1999*. London: Home Office.

HM Chief Inspector of Prisons (2002) *Report on a Full Announced Inspection of HMP and YOI Ashfield, 1–5 July 2002*.

HM Chief Inspector of Prisons (2003) *Report on a Full Announced Inspection of HMP Wealstun, 27–31 October 2003*. London: Home Office.

HM Chief Inspector of Prisons (2004) *Report of an Unannounced Inspection of HMYOI Portland, 12–16 July 2004*. London: Home Office.

HM Chief Inspector of Prisons (2005a) *Report on an Unannounced Inspection of HMP Doncaster, 14–18 November 2005*. London: Home Office.

HM Chief Inspector of Prisons (2005b) *Report on an Unannounced Inspection of HMP Rye Hill, 11–15 April 2005*. London: Home Office.

HM Chief Inspector of Prisons (2005c) *Report on an Unannounced Full Follow-Up Inspection of HMP Leeds, 22–26 August 2005*. London: Home Office.

HM Chief Inspector of Prisons (2005d) *Report on an Announced Inspection of HMP Kirkham, 5–10 December 2004*. London: HM Inspectorate of Prisons. Available online at: http://inspectorates.homeoffice.gov.uk/hmiprisons/inspect_reports/hmp-yoi-inspections.html/KIRKHAM_FINAL_edit_8.3.05.pdf

HM Chief Inspector of Prisons (2006) *Report on an Unannounced Full Follow-up Inspection of HMP Pentonville, 7–16 June 2006*. London: Home office.

HM Government (2004) *Every Child Matters: Change for Children*. Available online at: http://www.everychildmatters.gov.uk/publications/

HM Inspectorate of Prisons (2005a) *Parallel Worlds: A Thematic Review of Race Relations in Prisons*. London: HM Inspectorate of Prisons. Available online at: http://inspectorates.homeoffice.gov.uk/hmiprisons/thematic-reports1/parallelworlds.pdf?view=Binary

HM Inspectorate of Prisons (2005b) *Report on a Full Unannounced Inspection of HM Prison/Young Offenders Institution Holloway, October 2004*. London: HM

Inspectorate of Prisons. Available online at: http://inspectorates.homeoffice. gov.uk/hmiprisons/inspect_reports/hmp-yoi-inspections.html/hmp-holloway1.pdf?version=1

HM Inspectorate of Prisons (2005c) *Recalled Prisoners.* London: HM Inspectorate of Prisons. Available online at: http://inspectorates.homeoffice.gov.uk/hmiprisons/thematic-reports1/recalledprisoners.pdf?view=Binary

HM Inspectorate of Probation (2000) *Towards Race Equality.* Thematic Inspection Report. London: Home Office. Available online at: www.homeoffice.gov.uk/newindexs/index_probation.htm

HM Inspectorate of Probation (2006a) *An Independent Review of a Serious Further Offence Case: Damien Hanson and Elliot White.* London: HM Inspectorate of Probation. Available online at: http://inspectorates.homeoffice.gov.uk/hmiprobation/inspect_reports/serious-further-offences/HansonandWhiteReview.pdf

HM Inspectorate of Probation (2006b) *An Independent Review of a Serious Further Offence Case: Anthony Rice.* London: HM Inspectorate of Probation. Available online at: http://www.inspectorates.homeoffice.gov.uk/hmiprobation/inspect_reports/serious-further-offences/AnthonyRiceReport.pdf?view=Binary

HM Inspectorate of Probation (2006c) *Working to Make Amends: An Inspection of Enhanced Community Punishment and Unpaid Work by the National Probation Service.* London: HM Inspectorate of Probation. Also available online at: http://inspectorates.homeoffice.gov.uk/hmiprobation/inspect_reports/thematic inspection1.html/ECPUPW.pdf

HM Prison Service (1993) 'Michael Howard Unveils Plans for More Private Sector Involvement in the Prison Service'. News release, 2 September 1993.

HM Prison Service (1996) *Management of Disruptive Prisoners: CRC Review Project Final Report* (The Spurr Report). London: HM Prison Service, unpublished report.

HM Prison Service (1999) *Framework Document.* London: The Stationery Office. Also available online at: http://www.hmprisonservice.gov.uk/filestore/33_38.pdf

HM Prison Service (2004) *Annual Report and Accounts April 2003–March 2004.* London: HM Prison Service.

HM Prison Service (2005a) *Annual Report and Accounts April 2004–March 2005.* HC 193. London: HM Prison Service.

HM Prison Service (2005b) *Business Plan 2005–2006.* London: National Offender Management Service.

HM Prison Service (2006a) *Annual Report and Accounts April 2005–March 2006,* HC 1291. London: The Stationery Office. Available online at: http://www.hmprisonservice. gov.uk/news/index.asp?id=5380,22,6,22,0,0.

HM Prison Service (2006b) *Business Plan 2006–2007.* London: National Offender Management Service.

Hogg, R. (1979) 'Imprisonment and Society under Early British Capitalism', in T. Platt and P. Takagi (eds), *Punishment and Penal Discipline: Essays on the Prison and the Prisoners' Movement.* Berkeley, CA: Crime and Social Justice Associates.

Holdaway, S., Davidson, N., Dignan, J., Hammersley, R., Hine, J. and Marsh, P. (2001) *New Strategies to Address Youth Offending: The National Evaluation of Pilot Youth Offending Teams.* RDS Occasional Paper No. 69. London: Home Office Research, Development and Statistics Directorate. Also available online at: http://www.homeoffice.gov.uk/rds/index.html

Hollin, C.R. (1990) *Cognitive-Behavioural Interventions with Young Offenders.* Elmsford: Pergamon Press.

Holt, P. (2000) *Case Management: Context for supervision,* Community and Criminal Justice Monograph 2. Leicester: De Montford University.

Home Office (1964) *The Sentence of the Court.* London: HMSO.

Home Office (1965) *The Adult Offender.* Cmnd 2852. London: HMSO.

Home Office (1966) *Report of the Inquiry into Prison Escapes and Security by Admiral of the Fleet, the Earl Mountbatten of Burma.* Cmnd 3175. London: HMSO.

Home Office (1977) *Prisons and the Prisoner: The Work of the Prison Service in England and Wales.* London: HMSO.

Home Office (1980) *Criminal Statistics, England and Wales 1979.* Cmnd 8098. London: HMSO.

Home Office (1981a) *Criminal Statistics, England and Wales 1980.* Cmnd 8668. London: HMSO.

Home Office (1981b) *Review of Parole in England and Wales.* London: HMSO.

Home Office (1984a) *Managing the Long Term Prison System: The Report of the Control Review Committee.* London: HMSO.

Home Office (1984b) *Tougher Regimes in Detention Centres: Report of an Evaluation by the Young Offender Psychology Unit.* London: HMSO.

Home Office (1984c) *Statement of National Objectives and Priorities for the Probation Service.* London: Home Office.

Home Office (1985a) *Staff Attitudes in the Prison Service.* London: HMSO.

Home Office (1985b) *The Cautioning of Offenders,* Home Office Circular 14/1985.

Home Office (1987) *Report of an Inquiry by HM Chief Inspector of Prisons for England and Wales into the Disturbances in Prison Service Establishments in England between 29 April–2 May, 1986.* London: HMSO.

Home Office (1988a) *Punishment, Custody and the Community.* Cm 424. London: HMSO.

Home Office (1988b) *Private Sector Involvement in the Remand System.* Cm 434. London: HMSO.

Home Office (1990a) *Crime, Justice and Protecting the Public: The Government's Proposals for Legislation.* Cm 965. London: HMSO.

Home Office (1990b) *Criminal Statistics, England and Wales 1989.* Cm 1322. London: HMSO.

Home Office (1990c) *Supervision and Punishment in the Community.* Cm 966. London: HMSO.

Home Office (1990d) *The Cautioning of Offenders,* Home Office Circular 59/1990. London: HMSO.

Home Office (1991) *Custody, Care and Justice: The Way Ahead for the Prison Service in England and Wales.* Cm 1647. London: HMSO.

Home Office (1993) *Criminal Statistics, England and Wales 1992.* Cm 2410. London: HMSO.

Home Office (1994a) *Parole Recommendations and Ethnic Origin, England and Wales 1990.* Home Office Statistical Bulletin 2/94. London: Home Office.

Home Office (1994b) *Monitoring of the Criminal Justice Acts 1991 and 1993 – Results from a Special Data Collection Exercise.* Home Office Statistical Bulletin 20/94, London: Home Office.

Home Office (1994c) *Prison Statistics, England and Wales 1992.* Cm 2581. London: HMSO.

Home Office (1995a) *Strengthening Punishment in the Community: A Consultation Document.* Cm 2780. London: HMSO.

Home Office (1995b) *Criminal Statistics, England and Wales 1994.* CM 3010. London: HMSO.

Home Office (1997a) *No More Excuses: A New Approach to Tackling Youth Crime in England and Wales.* Cm 3809. London: Stationery Office.

Home Office (1997b) *Tackling Delays in the Youth Justice System: A Consultation Paper.* London: Home Office.

Home Office (1998a) *Crime and Disorder Act 1998: Introductory Guide.* London: Home Office Communication Directorate.

Home Office (1998b) *Joining Forces to Protect the Public.* London: HMSO.

Home Office (1998c) *Prisons-Probation Review: Final Report.* London HMSO.

Home Office (1999a) *Digest 4: Information on the Criminal Justice System in England and Wales.* London: Home Office Research and Statistics Department.

Home Office (1999b) *Reconviction of Offenders Sentenced or Discharged from Prison in 1994, England and Wales.* Home Office Statistical Bulletin 5/99. London: Home Office.

Home Office (2000a) *Criminal Statistics, England and Wales 1999.* Cm 5001. London: The Stationery Office.

Home Office (2000b) *Statistics on Race and the Criminal Justice System 2000.* London: Home Office.

Home Office (2001) *Criminal Justice: The Way Ahead.* Cm 5074. London: The Stationery Office.

Home Office (2002a) *Justice for All.* Cm 5563. London: The Stationery Office. Available online at: http://www.cjsonline.gov.uk/publications/whitepaper_2002/cjs_white_paper.html

Home Office (2002b) *National Standards for the Supervision of Offenders in the Community.* London: Home Office.

Home Office (2002c) *Probation Statistics England and Wales 2001.* London: Home Office.

Home Office (2003a) *Prison Statistics 2002.* Cm 5996. London: The Stationery Office.

Home Office (2003b) *Restorative Justice: The Government's Strategy.* London: Home Office. Also available online at: http://www.homeoffice.gov.uk/docs2/restorativestrategy.pdf

Home Office (2003c) *Youth Justice: the Next Steps.* London: Home Office. Also available online at: http://www.everychildmatters.gov.uk/publications/

Home Office (2003d) 'Bind Overs – A Power for the 21st Century'. Archived consultation paper, May 2003. London: Home Office. Also available online at: http://www.magistrate.co.uk/reports/archived-consultations/bind-overs.htm

Home Office (2004a) *Criminal Statistics, England and Wales 2003.* Cm 6361. London: The Stationery Office.

Home Office (2004b) *Statistics on Women and the Criminal Justice System – 2003.* London: Home Office. Available online at: http://www.homeoffice.gov.uk/rds/index.htm

Home Office (2004c) *Confident Communities in a Secure Britain: The Home Office Strategic Plan 2004–2008.* London: Home Office.

Home Office (2004d) *Every Child Matters: Change for Children in the Criminal Justice System.* London: Home Office. Also available online at: http://www.everychildmatters.gov.uk/publications/

Home Office (2004e) *Reducing Crime – Changing Lives: the Government's Plans for Transforming the Management of Offenders.* London: Home Office. Available online at: http://www.homeoffice.gov.uk/docs2/changinglives.pdf

Home Office (2004f) *Probation Statistics, England and Wales, 2002*. London: Home Office.

Home Office (2004g) *National Offender Management Service – Next Steps: Summary of Responses to the Two Government Consultation Exercises*. London: Home Office.

Home Office (2005a) *Population in Custody, Monthly Tables April 2005, England and Wales*. Available online at: http://www.homeoffice.gov.uk/rds/pdfs05/pris-apr05.pdf

Home Office (2005b) *Statistics on Race and the Criminal Justice System – 2004*. London: Home Office. Available online at: http://www.homeoffice.gov.uk/rds/index.htm

Home Office (2005c) *Reoffending of Adults: Results from the 2002 Cohort*. Home Office Statistical Bulletin 25/05. London: Home Office.

Home Office (2005d) *Neighbourhood Policing Your Police: Your Community; Our Commitment*. London: Home Office. Also available online at: http://www.crimereduction.gov.uk/policing08.htm

Home Office (2005e) *Criminal Statistics 2004 England and Wales*. Home Office Statistical Bulletin 19/05. London: Home Office. Available online at: http://www.homeoffice.gov.uk/rds/pubsstatistical.html

Home Office (2005f) *Restructuring Probation to Reduce Re-offending*. London: NOMS.

Home Office (2006a) *Respect Action Plan*. London: Home Office. Available online at: http://www.respect.gov.uk/

Home Office (2006b) *A Five Year Strategy for Protecting the Public and Reducing Re-offending* (February 2006). Cm 6717. London: The Stationery Office. Available online at: http://www.homeoffice.gov.uk/documents/five-year-strategy?view=Binary

Home Office (2006c) *Rebalancing the Criminal Justice System in Favour of the Law-Abiding Majority: Cutting Crime, Reducing Reoffending and Protecting the Public*. (July 2006). London: Home Office. Available online at: http://www.crimereduction.gov.uk/criminaljusticesystem19.htm

Home Office (2006d) *Making Sentencing Clearer* (November 2006). London: Home Office. Available online at: http://www.noms.homeoffice.gov.uk/news-publications-vents/publications/consultations/Making_sentencing_clearer_consul

Home Office (2006e) *Statistics on Race and the Criminal Justice System – 2005*. Available online at: http://www.homeoffice.gov.uk/rds/index.htm

Home Office (2006f) *Statistics on Women and the Criminal Justice System – 2004/05*. Available online at: http://www.homeoffice.gov.uk/rds/index.htm

Home Office (2006g) *Criminal Statistics 2005 England and Wales*. Home Office Statistical Bulletin 19/06. London: Home Office. Available online at: http://www.homeoffice.gov.uk/rds/pubsstatistical.html

Home Office (2006h) 'Respect Drive Targets Troublesome Families'. Press release, 10 January.

Home Office and Lord Chancellor's Department (2001) *The Youth Court 2001: The Changing Culture of the Youth Court – Good Practice Guide*. London: Home Office.

Home Office, Welsh Office and Department of Health and Social Security (1980) *Young Offenders*. Cm 8045. London: HMSO.

Home Office, Lord Chancellor's Department and Attorney General's Office (2002) *Justice for All*, Cm 5563. London: Home Office, Lord Chancellor's Department and Attorney General's Office. Available online at: http://www.cjsonline.gov.uk/downloads/application/pdf/CJS%20White%20Paper%20-%20Justice%20For%20All.pdf

Home Office, Department of Constitutional Affairs and Attorney-General (2005) *Rebuilding Lives: Supporting Victims of Crime*. Cm 6705. London: The Stationery Office. Available online at: http://www.cjsonline.gov.uk/downloads/application. pdf/Rebuilding%20Lives%20-%20Supporting%20Victims%20of%20crime.pdf

Home Office, Department of Health and Welsh Office (2000) *National Standards for the Supervision of Offenders in the Community*. London: Home Office.

Home Office Women's Policy Team (2003) 'Women Offenders: The Case for a Distinct Response', *Criminal Justice Matters*, 53: 32–3.

Homes, A., Walmsley, R.K. and Debidin, M. (2005) *Intensive Supervision and Monitoring Schemes for Persistent Offenders: Staff and Offender Perceptions*. Home Office Development and Practice Report No. 41. London: Home Office. Available online at: http://www.homeoffice.gov.uk/rds/pdfs05/dpr41.pdf

Honderich, T. (1984) *Punishment: The Supposed Justifications*. Harmondsworth: Penguin.

Hood, C. (1991) 'A Public Management for all Seasons', *Public Administration*, 69: 3–19.

Hood, R. (1962) *Sentencing in Magistrates' Courts*. London: Stevens.

Hood, R. (1972) *Sentencing the Motoring Offender*. London: Heinemann.

Hood, R. (1974) 'Tolerance and the Tariff', in J. Baldwin and A.K. Bottomley (eds), *Criminal Justice: Selected Readings* (1978). London: Martin Robertson, pp. 296–307.

Hood, R. (with G. Cordovil) (1992) *Race and Sentencing: A Study in the Crown Court*. Oxford: Clarendon Press.

Hood, R. (1995) 'Race and Sentencing: A Reply', [1995] *Criminal Law Review*: 272–9.

Hood, R. and Shute, S. (1996) 'Parole Criteria, Parole Decisions and the Prison Population: Evaluating the Impact of the Criminal Justice Act 1991', [1996] *Criminal Law Review*: 77–87.

Hood, R. and Shute, S. (2000) *The Parole System at Work: A Study of Risk Based Decision-making*. Home Office Research Study No. 202. London: Home Office.

Hood, R. and Sparks, R. (1970) *Key Issues in Criminology*. London: Weidenfeld & Nicolson.

Hood, R., Shute, S. and Seemungal, F. (2003) *Ethnic Minorities in the Criminal Courts: Perceptions of Fairness and Equality of Treatment*. London: Department for Constitutional Affairs. Summary available online at: http://www.dca.gov.uk/ research/2003/2-03es.htm

Hope, T. (1995) 'Community Crime Prevention' in M. Tonry and D.P. Farrington (eds), *Building a Safer Society: Strategic Approaches to Crime Prevention*. Chicago: University of Chicago Press.

Hough, M. (2006) 'Introduction', in M. Hough, R. Allen and U. Padel (eds), *Reshaping Probation and Prisons: the New Offender Management Framework*. Bristol: Policy Press.

Hough, M. and Allen, R. (2005/6) 'Probation Work and NOMS', *Criminal Justice Matters*, 62: 31–1.

Hough, M. and Mayhew, P. (1985) *Taking Account of Crime: Key Findings from the 1984 British Crime Survey*. Home Office Research Study No. 85. London: HMSO.

Hough, M. and Roberts, J. (1998) *Attitudes to Punishment: Findings from the British Crime Survey*. Home Office Research Study No. 179. London: Home Office.

Hough, M. and Roberts, J. (2005) *Understanding Public Attitudes to Crime and Justice*. Maidenhead: Open University Press.

Hough, M., Allen, R. and Padel, U. (eds) (2006) *Reshaping Probation and Prisons: the New Offender Management Framework*. Bristol: Policy Press.

Hough, M., Jacobson, J. and Millie, A. (2003) *The Decision to Imprison: Sentencing and the Prison Population*. London: Prison Reform Trust.

House of Commons Education and Skills Committee (2005) *Prison Education*. Seventh Report of Session 2004–2005. London: HMSO.

House of Commons Home Affairs Committee (1987) *Contract Provision of Prisons*. Fourth Report, Session 1986/7, HC 291. London: HMSO.

House of Commons Home Affairs Committee (1995) *Judicial Appointments*. London: HMSO.

House of Commons Home Affairs Committee (1997) *The Management of the Prison Service (Public and Private), Vol. 1, 19 March 1997*. Second Report, Session 1996–7, HC 57–1. London: HMSO.

House of Commons Home Affairs Committee (1998) *Third Report. Alternatives to Prison Sentences*, Vol. 1. London: HMSO.

House of Commons Home Affairs Committee (2000) *Fourth Report. Blantyre House Prison*. Session 1999–2000. London: The Stationery Office. The whole report is also available online at: http://www.parliament.the-stationery-office.co.uk/pa/cm199900/cmselect/cmhaff/904/90403.htm

House of Commons Home Affairs Committee (2005) *First Report*. Session 2004–2005. Also available online at: http://www.publications.parliament.uk/pa/cm200405/cmselect/cmhaff/193/19305.htm#n22

House of Commons Public Accounts Committee (2006a) *National Offender Management Service: Dealing with Increased Numbers in Custody*. Forty-fourth Report of Session 2005–2006. House of Commons papers 788 2005–06.

House of Commons Public Accounts Committee (2006b) *Sixty-Second Report*. Available online at: http://www.publications.parliament.uk/pa/cm200506/cmselect/cmpubacc/997/99702.htm

Howard League for Penal Reform (2002) *Suicide and Self-Harm Prevention Following Release From Prison*. London: Howard League.

Howard League for Penal Reform (2005) 'Shocking New Suicide Figures Expose the Prison Death Toll'. Press release, 5 July.

Howard League for Penal Reform (2006a) ' "Gulag Britain" Presaged by New Home Office Projections'. Press release, 27 July. See also http://www.howardleague.org/fileadmin/howard_league/user/pdf/Gulag_Britain_27_July_2006.pdf

Howard League for Penal Reform (2006b) 'Howard League for Penal Reform Fears over Enforced Cell-sharing for Children in Prison'. Press release, 15 August.

Hucklesby, A. (1997) 'Court Culture: An Explanation of Variations in the Use of Bail in Magistrates' Courts', *Howard Journal of Criminal Justice*, 36: 129–45.

Hudson, B. (1984) 'The Rising Use of Imprisonment: The Impact of "Decarceration" Policies', *Critical Social Policy*, 11: 46–59.

Hudson, B. (1987) *Justice Through Punishment: A Critique of the 'Justice Model' of Corrections*. London: Macmillan Education.

Hudson, B. (1989) 'Discrimination and Disparity: The Influence of Race on Sentencing', *New Community*, 16: 23–34.

Hughes, R. (1987) *The Fatal Shore: A History of Transportation of Convicts to Australia, 1187–1868,* London: Collins Harvill.

Hulsman, L.H.C. (1991) 'The Abolitionist Case: Alternative Crime Policies', *Israel Law Review*, 25 (3–4): 681–709.

Humphry, D. and May, D. (1977) 'Why the Prisons Could Explode', *Sunday Times*, 23 January.

Hutto, T.D. (1990) 'The Privatization of Prisons' in J.W. Murphy and J.E. Dison (eds), *Are Prisons Any Better? Twenty Years of Correctional Reform*. Newbury Park, CA: Sage, pp. 111–27.

Ignatieff, M. (1978) *A Just Measure of Pain: The Penitentiary in the Industrial Revolution 1750–1850*. New York: Columbia University Press.

Ignatieff, M. (1981) 'State, Civil Society, and Total Institution: A Critique of Recent Social Histories of Punishment', in M. Tonry and N. Morris (eds), *Crime and Justice*, vol. 3. Chicago: University of Chicago Press, pp. 153–92.

International Bar Association (1990) 'Sentencing Questionnaire' (2nd edition). Unpublished; presented at the 23rd biennial conference of the International Bar Association, 19–23 September.

Jago, R. and Thompson, E. (1999) 'Privatisation of Prisons', in M. Leech and D. Cheney (eds), *The Prisons Handbook* (4th edition). Winchester: Waterside Press, pp. 229–31.

James, A. and Bottomley, K. (1998) 'Prison Privatisation and the Remand Population: Principle versus Pragmatism?', *Howard Journal of Criminal Justice*, 37: 223–33.

James, A.L., Bottomley, A.K., Liebling, A. and Clare, E. (1997) *Privatizing Prisons: Rhetoric and Reality*. London: Sage.

James, E. (2004) ' "Long-term Prison is Animalising" ', *Guardian*, 22 September.

Jenkins, S. (1995) 'Another Fine Mess of Porage', *The Times*, 18 October.

Jewkes, Y. (2004/5) 'High-Tech Solutions to Low-Tech Crimes? Crime and Terror in the Surveillance Assemblage', *Criminal Justice Matters*, 58: 6–7.

Joint Council for the Welfare of Immigrants (1988) *Annual Report 1988*. London: Joint Council for the Welfare of Immigrants.

Jones, H., Cornes, P. and Stackford, R. (1977) *Open Prisons*. London: Routledge & Kegan Paul.

Jones, T. and Newburn, T. (2005) 'Comparative Criminal Justice Policymaking in the United States and the United Kingdom', *British Journal of Criminology*, 45: 58–80.

Junger-Tas, J., Terlouw, G.-J. and Klein, M.W. (1994) *Delinquent Behaviour among Young People in the Western World: First Results of the International Self-Report Delinquency Study*. Amsterdam: Kugler.

Justices' Clerks' Society (1982) 'A Case for Summary Trial: Proposals for a Redistribution of Criminal Business'. Unpublished.

Kamenka, E. and Tay, A.E.-S. (1975) 'Beyond Bourgeois Individualism: The Contemporary Crisis in Law and Legal Ideology', in E. Kamenka and R.S. Neale (eds), *Feudalism, Capitalism and Beyond*. London: Edward Arnold, pp. 126–44.

Kamerman, S.B. and Kahn, A.J. (eds) (1989) *Privatization and the Welfare State*. Princeton, NJ: Princeton University Press.

Keith, B. (2006) *Report of the Zahid Mubarek Inquiry*, HC 1082. London: The Stationery Office. Available online at: http://www.zahidmubarekinquiry.org.uk/category.asp?c=509

Kellner, P. and Crowther-Hunt, N. (1980) *The Civil Servants: An Inquiry into Britain's Ruling Class*. London: Macdonald Futura.

Kemshall, H., Canton, R. and Bailey, R. (2004) 'Dimensions of Difference', in A. Bottoms, S. Rex and G. Robinson (eds), *Alternatives to Prison: Options for an Insecure Society*. Cullompton: Willan Publishing, pp. 341–65.

Kershaw, C. (1999) *Reconviction of Offenders Sentenced or Discharged from Prison in 1994*. Home Office Statistical Bulletin 05/99. London: Home Office.

Kershaw, C., Goodman, J. and White, S. (1999) *Reconvictions of Offenders Sentenced or Discharged from Prison in 1995, England and Wales*. Home Office Statistical Bulletin 19/99. London: Home Office.

Kesteren, J. van, Mayhew, P. and Nieuwbeerta, P. (2001) *Criminal Victimisation in Seventeen Industrialised Countries: Key Findings from the 2000 International Crime Victims Survey*. The Hague: WODC.

Killias, M., Aebi, M. and Ribeaud, D. (2000) 'Does Community Service Rehabilitate Better than Short-term Imprisonment? Results of a Controlled Experiment'. *Howard Journal of Criminal Justice*, 39 (1): 40–57.

King, R.D. (1985) 'Control in Prison', in M. Maguire, J. Vagg and R. Morgan (eds), *Accountability and Prisons: Opening up a Closed World*. London: Tavistock.

King, R.D. and Elliott, K.W. (1977) *Albany: Birth of a Prison – End of an Era*. London: Routledge & Kegan Paul.

King, R.D. and McDermott, K. (1989) 'British Prisons 1970–1987: The Ever-Deepening Crisis', *British Journal of Criminology*, 29: 107–28.

King, R.D. and Morgan, R. (1980) *The Future of the Prison System*. Farnborough: Gower.

Kochan, N. (2002) 'Is the PFI About to Hit the Buffers?' *The Banker*, 2 August 2002. Available online at: http://www.thebanker.com/news/fullstory.php/aid/224/Is_the_PFI_about_to_hit_the_buffers_.html

Kovandzic, T.V., Sloan, J.J. and Vieraitis, L.M. (2004) '"Striking Out" as Crime Reduction Policy: The Impact of "Three Strikes" Laws on Crime Rates in U.S. Cities', *Justice Quarterly*, 21: 207–39.

Kuhn, T.S. (1962) *The Structure of Scientific Revolutions*. Chicago: University of Chicago Press.

Labour Party (1997) *New Labour: Because Britain Deserves Better* (General Election Manifesto). London: Labour Party.

Lacey, N. (1988) *State Punishment: Political Principles and Community Values*. London: Routledge.

Lambie, A. (2002) 'When Colour Is an Issue', *Howard League Magazine*, 20 (1): 14.

Laming Lord (2000) *Modernising the Management of the Prison Service: An Independent Report by the Targeted Performance Initiative Working Group*, London: HM Prison Service. Also available online at: http://www.hmprisonservice.gov.uk/filestore/263_281.pdf

Laming, Lord (2003) *The Victoria Climbié Inquiry*. Available online at: http://www.victoria-climbie-inquiry.org.uk/finreport/introduction.htm

Landau, S.F. (1981) 'Juveniles and the Police: Who Is Charged Immediately and Who Is Referred to the Juvenile Bureau?', *British Journal of Criminology*, 21: 27–46.

Landau, S.F. and Nathan, G. (1983) 'Selecting Delinquents for Cautioning in the London Metropolitan Area', *British Journal of Criminology*, 23: 128–49.

Lane, Lord (1993) *Report of the Committee on the Penalty for Homicide*. London: Prison Reform Trust.

Lash, S. and Urry, J. (1987) *The End of Organised Capitalism*. Cambridge: Polity.

Lash, S. and Urry, J. (1994) *Economies of Signs and Space*. London: Sage.

Law Commission (1994) *Binding Over*. Cm 2439. London: HMSO.

Law Commission (1999) *Bail and the Human Rights Act 1998*. Consultation Paper No. 157. London: Law Commission. Available online at: http://www.lawcom.gov.uk/docs/cp157.pdf

Law Commission (2001) *Bail and the Human Rights Act 1998.* Law Com No. 269. London: Law Commission. Available online at: http://www.lawcom.gov.uk/docs/lc269.pdf

Law Commission (2005) *A New Homicide Act for England and Wales?* Consultation Paper No. 177. London: Law Commission. Available online at: http://www.lawcom.gov.uk/docs/cp177_web.pdf

Law Commission (2006) *Murder, Manslaughter and Infanticide.* Law Com No. 304. London: Law Commission. Available online at: http://www.lawcom.gov.uk/docs/lc304.pdf

Lawrence, D.M. (1986) 'Private Exercise of Governmental Power', *Indiana Law Journal*, 61: 647–95.

Learmont, J. (1995) *Review of Prison Service Security in England and Wales and the Escape from Parkhurst Prison on Tuesday 3 January 1995.* Cm 3020. London: HMSO.

Leech, M. (1995) *The Prisoners' Handbook.* Oxford: Oxford University Press.

Leech, M. and Cheney, D. (1999) *The Prisons Handbook 2000* (4th edition). Winchester: Waterside Press.

Leech, M. and Cheney, D. (2001) *The Prisons Handbook 2001* (5th edition). Winchester: Waterside Press.

Lennon, J. (2003) 'Penal Case Law' in M. Leech and J. Shepherd (eds), *Prisons Handbook 2003–4.* Manchester: MLA Press.

Levi, M. (1989) 'Fraudulent Justice? Sentencing the Business Criminal', in P. Carlen and D. Cook (eds), *Paying for Crime.* Milton Keynes: Open University Press, pp. 86–108.

Lewis, D. (1996) 'Prisons: the Case for Constitutional Reform', *Prison Report, vol.* 35. London: Prison Reform Trust, pp. 10–11.

Lewis, D. (1997) *Hidden Agendas: Politics, Law and Disorder.* London and New York: Hamish Hamilton.

Liebling, A. (1992) *Suicides in Prison.* London: Routledge.

Liebling, A. (1997) 'Risk and Prison Suicide', in H. Kemshall and J. Pritchard (eds), *Good Practice in Risk Assessment and Risk Management.* London: Jessica Kingsley.

Liebling, A. (2001) 'Policy and Practice in the Management of Disruptive Prisoners: Incentives and Earned Privileges, the Spurr Report and Close Supervision Centres', in E. Clare and K. Bottomley (eds), *Evaluation of Close Supervision Centres.* Home Office Research Study No. 136. London: Home Office Research, Development and Statistics Directorate.

Liebling, A. (2006) 'Lessons from Prison Privatisation for Probation', ch. 6 in M. Hough, R. Allen and U. Padel (eds), *Reshaping Probation and Prisons.* Bristol: Policy Press.

Liebling, A. and Arnold, H. (2002) 'Measuring the Quality of Prison Life'. Home Office Research Findings No. 174. London: Home Office.

Liebling, A. and Arnold, H. (2004) *Prisons and their Moral Performance: A Study of the Values, Quality and Prison Life.* Oxford: Oxford University Press.

Liebling, A. and Krarup, H. (1993) *Suicide Attempts and Self-Injury in Male Prisons.* Cambridge: Institute of Criminology.

Liebling, A. and Maruna, S. (2005) *The Effects of Imprisonment.* Cullompton: Willan Publishing.

Liebling, A., Muir, G., Rose, G. and Bottoms, A. (1999) *Incentives and Earned Privileges for Prisoners – An Evaluation.* Home Office Research Findings No. 87. London: Home Office Research and Statistics Directorate.

Lilly, J.R. and Knepper, P. (1990) 'The Corrections-industrial Complex', *Prison Service Journal*, 87: 43–52.

Lilly, J.R. and Knepper, P. (1992) 'An International Perspective on the Privatization of Corrections', *Howard Journal of Criminal Justice*, 31: 174–91.

Lipsey, M.W. (1992) 'The Effect of Treatment on Juvenile Delinquents: Results from Meta-Analysis', in F. Lösel, D. Bender and T. Bliesener (eds), *Psychology and Law: International Perspectives*. Berlin: Walter de Gruyter, pp. 131–43.

Lipsey, M.W., (1995) 'What Do We Learn from 400 Research Studies on the Effectiveness of Treatment with Juvenile Delinquents?', in J. McGuire (ed.), *What Works: Reducing Reoffending – Guidelines from Research and Practice*. London: Wiley, pp. 63–78.

Lipton, D., Martinson, R. and Wilks, J. (1975) *Effectiveness of Treatment Evaluation Studies*. New York: Praeger.

Livingstone, S. and Owen, T. (1993) *Prison Law*. Oxford: Oxford University Press.

Livingstone, S. and Owen, T. (1999) *Prison Law*. Oxford: Oxford University Press.

Livingstone, S., Owen, T. and Macdonald, A. (2003) *Prison Law* (3rd edition). Oxford: Oxford University Press.

Lloyd, C., Mair, G. and Hough, M. (1995) *Explaining Reconviction Rates: A Critical Analysis*. Home Office Research Study No. 136. London: HMSO.

Lodge, G. and Rogers, B. (2006) *Whitehall's Black Box: Accountability and Performance in the Senior Civil Service*. London: The Institute for Public Policy Reform.

Logan, C. (1990) *Private Prisons: Cons and Pros*. Oxford: Oxford University Press.

Lombroso, C. (1876) *L'Uomo Delinquente*. Milan: Hoepli.

Lord Chancellor's Department (2002) 'Home Secretary and Lord Chancellor: Clear Message on Sentencing', Press Notice 194/02, 14 June.

Lukes, S. (1975) *Émile Durkheim: His Life and Work*. Harmondsworth: Penguin.

di Lustro, M. (2004) 'Containment at the Expense of Care?', *Howard League Magazine*, 22(4): 6.

Lygo, R. (1991) *Management of the Prison Service: A Report*. London: Home Office.

Lynn, J. and Jay, A. (eds) (1981) *Yes Minister: The Diaries of a Cabinet Minister by the Rt. Hon. James Hacker MP*. London: British Broadcasting Corporation.

Lyon, J. (2003) 'The Cost of a Broken Promise', *Criminal Justice Matters*, 54 (Winter): 28–9.

Machover, D. (2002) 'Compensation for the Innocent', *Prison Report*, 57: 5.

Macpherson, W. (1999) *The Stephen Lawrence Inquiry: Report of an Inquiry by Sir William Macpherson*, Cm 4262–I. London: The Stationery Office.

MacRae, D.G. (1974) *Weber*. Glasgow: Fontana/Collins.

Maghan, J. (1991) 'Privatization of Corrections: Anticipating the Unanticipated', in R.J. Kelly and D.E.J. Macnamara (eds), *Perspectives on Deviance: Dominance, Degradation and Denigration*. Cincinnati: Anderson Publishing, pp. 135–96.

Maguire, M. (with T. Bennett) (1982) *Burglary in a Dwelling: The Offence, the Offender and the Victim*. London: Heinemann.

Maguire, M. and Pointing, J. (eds) (1988) *Victims of Crime: A New Deal*. Milton Keynes and Philadelphia: Open University Press.

Maguire, M., Morgan, R. and Reiner, R. (eds) (2002) *The Oxford Handbook of Criminology* (3rd edition). Oxford: Oxford University Press.

Maguire, M., Vagg J., and Morgan R. (eds) (1985) *Accountability and Prisons: Opening Up a Closed World*. London: Tavistock.

Mair, G. (1986) 'Ethnic Minorities, Probation and the Magistrates' Courts', *British Journal of Criminology*, 26: 147–55.

Mair, G. (1997) 'Community Penalties and the Probation Service', in M. Maguire, R. Morgan and R. Reiner (eds), *The Oxford Handbook of Criminology* (2nd edition). Oxford: Oxford University Press, pp. 1195–1232.

Mair, G. (2004) 'Diversionary and Non-supervisory Approaches to Dealing with Offenders', in A. Bottoms, S. Rex and G. Robinson (eds), *Alternatives to Prison: Options for an Insecure Society*. Cullompton: Willan Publishing, pp. 135–61.

Maltz, M. (1984) *Recidivism*. London: Academic Press.

Marshall, S. (1997) *Control in Category C Prisons*. Home Office Research Findings No. 54. London: Home Office Research and Statistics Directorate.

Marshall, T.F. (1985) *Alternatives to Criminal Courts: the Potential for Non-judicial Settlement*. Aldershot: Gower.

Marshall, T.F. (1999) *Restorative Justice: An Overview*. London: Home Office Research Development and Statistics Directorate.

Marshall, T.F. and Merry, S. (1990) *Crime and Accountability: Victim/Offender Mediation in Practice*. London: HMSO.

Martin, F.M. and Murray, K. (eds) (1982) *The Scottish Juvenile Justice System*. Edinburgh: Scottish Academic Press.

Martin, J.P. (1991) 'Parkhurst Special Unit: Some Aspects of Management', in R. Walmsley (ed.), *Managing Difficult Prisoners: The Parkhurst Special Unit*. Home Office Research Study No. 122. London: HMSO.

Martinson, R. (1974) 'What Works? – Questions and Answers about Prison Reform', *The Public Interest*, 35 (Spring): 22–54.

Martinson, R. (1979) 'New Findings, New Views: A Note of Caution Regarding Sentencing Reform', *Hofstra Law Review*, 7: 243–58.

Maruna, S. and King, A. (2004) 'Public Opinion and Community Penalties', in A. Bottoms, S. Rex and G. Robinson (eds), *Alternatives to Prison: Options for an Insecure Society*. Cullompton: Willan Publishing, pp. 83–112.

Marx, K. (1977) *Selected Writings*, ed. D. McLellan. Oxford: Oxford University Press.

Mathiesen, T. (1974) *The Politics of Abolition: Essays in Political Action Theory*. Oxford: Martin Robertson.

Mathiesen, T. (1983) 'The Future of Control Systems – the Case of Norway' in D. Garland, and P. Young (eds), *The Power to Punish: Contemporary Penality and Social Analysis*. London: Heinemann, pp. 130–45.

Mathiesen, T. (1990) *Prison on Trial*. London: Sage.

Mathiesen, T. (2000) *Prison on Trial*. Winchester: Waterside Press.

Matthews, R. (1979) 'Decarceration and the Fiscal Crisis' in B. Fine et al. (eds), *Capitalism and the Rule of Law: From Deviancy Theory to Marxism*. London: Hutchinson, pp. 100–17.

Matthews, R. (ed.) (1989) *Privatizing Criminal Justice*. London: Sage Publications.

Matthews, R. (1999) *Doing Time: An Introduction to the Sociology of Imprisonment*. Basingstoke: Macmillan.

Mattinson, J. and Mirrlees-Black, C. (2000) *Attitudes to Crime and Criminal Justice: Findings from the 1998 British Crime Survey*. Home Office Research Study No. 200. London: Home Office.

Mawby, R. (1977) 'Sexual Discrimination and the Law', *Probation Journal*, 24: 38–43.

Mawby, R.I. (1989) 'The Voluntary Sector's Role in a Mixed Economy of Criminal Justice', in R. Matthews (ed.), *Privatizing Criminal Justice*. London: Sage Publications, pp. 135–54.

May, C. (1999) *Exploring Reconviction Following Community Sentences: The Role of Social Factors*. Home Office Research Study No. 192. London: Home Office.

May, C. and Wadwell, J. (2001) *Enforcing Community Penalties: the Relationship between Enforcement and Reconviction*. Home Office Research Findings No. 155. London: Home Office.

May, J. (1979) *Committee of Inquiry into the United Kingdom Prison Services: Report*. Cm 7673. London: HMSO.

Mayhew, P. (1994) *Findings from the International Crime Survey*. Home Office Research Findings No. 8. London: Home Office.

Mayhew, P. and van Kesteren, J. (2002) 'Cross-National Attitudes to Punishment', in J.V. Roberts and M. Hough (eds), *Changing Attitudes to Punishment: Public Opinion, Crime and Justice*. Cullompton: Willan, pp. 63–92.

McConville, M. and Baldwin, J. (1982) 'The Influence of Race on Sentencing in England', [1982] *Criminal Law Review*: 652–8.

McConville, S. (1981) *A History of English Prison Administration Volume 1, 1760–1877*. London: Routledge & Kegan Paul.

McConville, S. and Williams, J.E. (1985) *Crime and Punishment: A Radical Rethink*. London: Tawney Society.

McDonald, D.C. (1990) *Private Prisons and the Public Interest*. New Brunswick, NJ: Rutgers University Press.

McDonald, D.C. (1994) 'Public Imprisonment by Private Means: The Re-emergence of Private Prisons in the United States, the United Kingdom and Australia', *British Journal of Criminology*, 34: 29–48.

McElrea, F.W. (1994) 'Justice in the Community: The New Zealand Experience', in J. Burnside and N. Baker (eds), *Relational Justice: Repairing the Breach*. Winchester: Waterside Press.

McEvoy, K. (2001) *Paramilitary Imprisonment in Northern Ireland: Resistance, Management and Release*. Oxford: Oxford University Press.

McGuire, J. (ed.) (1995) *What Works: Reducing Re-offending – Guidelines from Research and Practice*. London: Wiley.

McGuire, J. (2002) 'Criminal Sanctions Versus Psychologically-Based Interventions with Offenders: A Comparative Empirical Analysis', *Psychology, Crime and Law*, 8: 183–208.

McGuire, J. and Priestley, P. (1995) 'Reviewing "What Works": Past, Present and Future', in J. McGuire (ed.), *What Works: Reducing Offending*. Chichester: Wiley, pp. 3–34.

McIvor, G. (1992) *Sentenced to Serve*. Aldershot: Avebury.

McIvor, G. (1998) 'Pro-social Modeling and Legitimacy: Lessons from a Study of Community Service' in *Pro-social Modeling and Legitimacy: The Clarke Hall Day Conference*. Cambridge: University of Cambridge.

McIvor, G. (2004) 'Reparative and Restorative Approaches', in A. Bottoms, S. Rex and G. Robinson (eds), *Alternatives to Prison: Options for an Insecure Society*. Cullompton: Willan Publishing, pp. 162–94.

McLaughlin, E., Muncie, J. and Hughes, G. (2001) 'The Permanent Revolution: New Labour, New Public Management and the Modernization of Criminal Justice', *Criminal Justice*, 1: 301–18.

McLennan, G. (1989) *Marxism, Pluralism and Beyond*. Cambridge: Polity Press.

McMahon, M.W. (1992) *The Persistent Prison? Rethinking Decarceration and Penal Reform*. Toronto: University of Toronto Press.

McWilliams, W. (1981) 'The Probation Officer at Court: From Friend to Acquaintance', *Howard Journal of Criminal Justice*, 20: 97–116.

McWilliams, W. (1983) 'The Mission to the English Police Courts 1876–1936', *Howard Journal,* 22: 129–47.

McWilliams, W. (1985) 'The Mission Transformed: Professionalisation of Probation Between the Wars', *Howard Journal,* 24: 257–74.

McWilliams, W. (1986) 'The English Probation System and the Diagnostic Ideal', *Howard Journal,* 25: 241–60.

McWilliams, W. (1987) 'Probation, Pragmatism and Policy', *Howard Journal,* 26: 97–121.

Meichenbaum, D. (1977) *Cognitive-Bahavior Modification: An Integrative Approach.* New York: Plenum.

Merton, R.K. (1968) *Social Theory and Social Structure.* New York: Free Press.

Mirrlees-Black, C. (2001) *Confidence in the Criminal Justice System: Findings from the 2000 British Crime Survey.* Home Office Research Findings No. 137. London: Home Office.

Monahan, J. (1981) *Predicting Violent Behavior: An Assessment of Clinical Techniques.* London: Sage.

Monbiot, G. (2002) 'Public Fraud Initiative', *Guardian,* 18 June.

Moore, R. (2003) 'The Use of Financial Penalties and the Amounts Imposed: The Need for a New Approach', *Criminal Law Review*: 13–27.

Moorthy, U., Cahalin, K. and Howard, P. (2004) *Ethnicity and Parole.* Home Office Research Findings No. 222. London: Home Office. Available online at: http://www.homeoffice.gov.uk/rds/pubsintro1.html

Morgan, N. (1983) 'The Shaping of Parole in England and Wales', [1983] *Criminal Law Review*: 137–51.

Morgan, R. (1985) 'Her Majesty's Inspectorate of Prisons' in M. Maguire, J. Vagg and R. Morgan (eds), *Accountability and Prisons: Opening up a Closed World.* London: Tavistock.

Morgan, R. (1995) 'Prison', in M. Walker (ed.), *Interpreting Crime Statistics.* Oxford: Clarendon Press, pp. 91–110.

Morgan, R. (2003) 'Thinking about the Demand for Probation Services', *Probation Journal,* 50: 7.

Morgan, R. (2004) 'Thinking About the Future of Probation Inspection', *Howard Journal of Criminal Justice',* 43: 79–82.

MORI (2001a) *Public Attitudes to Prison: An Analysis of MORI Trend Data.*

MORI (2001b) *Public Attitudes Towards Prisons: A Review of the Evidence.*

MORI (2003) *Magistrates' Perceptions of the Probation Service.* Available online at: http://www.probation.homeoffice.gov.uk/files/pdf/Morifinalreport2003.pdf

Morris, A. (1987) *Women, Crime and Criminal Justice.* Oxford: Basil Blackwell.

Morris, A. (2004) 'Youth Justice in New Zealand', in M. Tonry and A.N. Doob (eds), *Crime and Justice: A Review of Research.* Chicago. University of Chicago Press, pp. 243–92.

Morris, A., Giller, H., Szwed, E. and Geach, H. (1980) *Justice for Children.* London: Macmillan.

Morris, A., Maxwell, G.M., and Robertson, J.P. (1993) 'Giving Victims a Voice: A New Zealand Experiment', *Howard Journal of Criminal Justice,* 32: 304–21.

Morris, N. (1974) *The Future of Imprisonment.* London: University of Chicago Press.

Morris, T. (1980) 'Penology and the Crimes of the Powerful', in A.E. Bottoms and R.H. Preston (eds), *The Coming Penal Crisis.* Edinburgh: Scottish Academic Press, pp. 84–108.

Morris, T. (1989) *Crime and Criminal Justice since 1945.* Oxford: Basil Blackwell.

Mortimer, E. and May, C. (1997) *Electronic Monitoring in Practice: The Second Year of the Trials of Curfew Orders*. Home Office Research Study No. 177. London: Home Office.

de la Motta, K. (1984) 'Blacks in the Criminal Justice System'. Unpublished MSc thesis, Aston University.

Moxon, D. (1988) *Sentencing Practice in the Crown Court*. Home Office Research Study No. 103. London: HMSO.

Moynihan, D.P. (1992) 'Defining Deviance Down', *The American Scholar*. Autumn.

Mulgan, G. (1998) 'Social Exclusion: Joined Up Solutions to Joined Up Problems' in C. Oppenheim (ed.), *An Inclusive Society: Strategies for Tackling Poverty*. London: Institute for Public Policy Research.

Mulgan, R. (2000) '"Accountability": An Ever-Expanding Concept?', *Public Administration*, 78(3): 555–73.

Muncie, J. (1999) 'Institutionalized Intolerance: Youth Justice and the 1998 Crime and Disorder Act', *Critical Social Policy* 19: 147–75.

Murphy, J. (1979) *Retribution, Justice and Therapy: Essays in the Philosophy of Law*. London: D. Reidel Publishing.

Murphy, J. (1992) *Retribution Reconsidered*. Dordrecht: Kluwer Academic Publishers.

MVA and Miller, J. (2000) *Profiling Populations Available for Stops and Searches*. Police Research Series, Paper 131. London: Home Office.

NACRO (1986a) *Enforcement of the Law Relating to Social Security: Report of a NACRO Working Party*. London: NACRO.

NACRO (1986b) *Black People and the Criminal Justice System*. London: NACRO.

NACRO (1988) 'The Electronic Monitoring of Offenders', Briefing Paper.

NACRO (1992) 'Offences against Discipline in Women's Prisons', Briefing Paper.

NACRO (1995) 'The Cost of Penal Measures', Briefing Paper.

NACRO (1998) *Contrasting Judgements: Report on Two International Sentencing Seminars*. London: NACRO.

NACRO (2003) *A Failure of Justice: Reducing Child Imprisonment*. London: NACRO.

Nagel, I. (1981) 'Sex Differences in the Processing of Criminal Defendants', in A. Morris and L. Gelsthorpe (eds), *Women and Crime*. Cambridge: Institute of Criminology, pp. 104–24.

Nagel, I.H. and Hagan, J. (1983) 'Gender and Crime: Offence Patterns and Criminal Court Sanctions', in M. Tonry and N. Morris (eds), *Crime and Justice*, vol. 4. Chicago: University of Chicago Press, pp. 91–144.

Narey, M. (1997) 'Review of Delay in the Criminal Justice System'. London: Home Office. Available online at: http://www.homeoffice.gov.uk/docs/crimrev.html

Narey, M. (1999) Speech to the Prison Service Conference at Harrogate, February.

Narey, M. (2001) Speech to the Prison Service Conference at Nottingham, 5 February. Also available online at: http://www.hmprisonservice.gov.uk/news/newstext.asp?201

Nathan, H.L., Baron Nathan of Churt (Chairman) (1989) *Report of the Select Committee on Murder and Life Imprisonment*, HL Paper 78, Session 1988-9, vol. 1.

Nathan, S. (1993a) 'Privatisation Factfile 1', *Prison Report* 22: 12–14.

Nathan, S. (1993b) 'Privatisation Factfile 2', *Prison Report* 22: 12–13.

Nathan, S. (1993c) 'Privatisation Factfile 3', *Prison Report* 24: 11–18.

Nathan, S. (1994) 'Privatisation Factfile 7', *Prison Report* 28: 11–18.

Nathan, S. (1995a) 'Privatisation Factfile 9', *Prison Report* 30: 13–20.

Nathan, S. (1995b) 'Privatisation Factfile 10', *Prison Report* 31: 13–20.

Nathan, S. (1999) 'Privatisation Factfile 28', *Prison Report* 44: 13–16.

Nathan, S. (2000) 'Privatisation Factfile 32', *Prison Report* 53: 13–16.

National Association of Probation Officers (2005) 'Electronically Monitored Curfew Orders: Time for a Review'. A Briefing Paper. April 2005. BRF08-05. Available online at: http://www.napo.org.uk/cgi-bin/dbman/db.cgi?db=default&uid= default&ID=111&viewrecords=1&ww=1

National Audit Office (1994) *Wolds Remand Prison: A Report by the Comptroller and Auditor General.* London: HMSO.

National Audit Office (1997) *The PFI contracts for Bridgend and Fazakerley Prisons: Report by the Comptroller and Auditor General.* HC 253 1997/8; and Press Notice, 31 October.

National Audit Office (2003) *The Operational Performance of PFI Prisons: Report by the Comptroller and Auditor General.* HC Session 2002–3: 18 June 2003. London: HMSO.

National Probation Service (2001) *A New Choreography: An Integrated Strategy for the National Probation Service.* London: Home Office.

Nelken, D. (2002) 'White Collar Crime', in M. Maguire, R. Morgan and R. Reiner (eds), *Accountability and Prisons: Opening up a Closed World.* London: Tavistock, pp. 844–77.

Nellis, M. (1989) 'Juvenile Justice and the Voluntary Sector' in R. Matthews (ed.), *Privatizing Criminal Justice.* London: Sage Publications, pp. 155–77.

Nellis, M. (2003) 'Electronic Monitoring and the Future of Probation', ch. 15 in W.-H. Chui and M. Nellis (eds), *Moving Probation Forward: Evidence, Arguments and Practice.* Harlow: Longman.

Nellis, M. (2004) 'Electronic Monitoring and the Community Supervision of Offenders', in A. Bottoms, S. Rex and G. Robinson (eds), *Alternatives to Prison: Options for an Insecure Society.* Cullompton: Willan Publishing, pp. 224–47.

Nellis, M. (2005) 'Out of this World: The Advent of Satellite Tracking of Offenders in England and Wales', *Howard Journal of Criminal Justice*, 44 (2): 125–50.

Nellis, M. (2006) 'NOMS, Contestability and the Process of Technocratic Innovation', ch. 5 in M. Hough, R. Allen and U. Padel (eds), *Reshaping Probation and Prisons: The New Offender Management Framework.* Bristol: Policy Press.

Nellis, M. and Gelsthorpe, L. (2003) 'Human Rights and the Probation Values Debate', ch. 14 in W.-H. Chui and M. Nellis (eds), *Moving Probation Forward: Evidence, Arguments and Practice.* Harlow: Longman.

Nicholas, S., Povey, D., Walker, A. and Kershaw, C. (2005) *Crime In England and Wales 2004/2005.* Home Office Statistical Bulletin 11/05. London: Home Office. Available online at: http://www.homeoffice.gov.uk/rds/pubsstatistical.html

Nicolson, D. and Sanghvi, R. (1995) 'More Justice for Battered Women', *New Law Journal*, 28 July: 1122–4.

NOMS (2005a) *Sentencing Statistics Quarterly Brief England and Wales, April to June 2005.* Available online at: http://www.homeoffice.gov.uk/rds/spnd.html

NOMS (2005b) *Population in Custody: Quarterly Brief, April to June 2005, England and Wales.* Available online at: http://www.homeoffice.gov.uk/rds/omcs.html

NOMS (2005c) *Population in Custody: Monthly Tables, April 2005, England and Wales.* Available online at: http://www.homeoffice.gov.uk/rds/omcs.html

NOMS (2005d) *Population in Custody: Monthly Tables, October 2005, England and Wales.* Available online at: http://www.homeoffice.gov.uk/rds/omcs.html

NOMS (2005e) *Population in Custody: Monthly Tables, December 2005, England and Wales.* London: Home Office/National Offender Management Service.

NOMS (2005f) *Offender Management Caseload Statistics, 2004.* Home Office Statistical Bulletin 17/05. London: Home Office/National Offender Management Service.

NOMS (2006) 'Prison Population and Accommodation Briefing for 22 September 2006. Available online at: http://www.hmprisonservice.gov.uk/assets/documents/1000218520060922PSWEBREPORT.doc

NOMS (2006a) *Population in Custody: Monthly Tables, June 2006, England and Wales.* London: NOMS.

NOMS (2006b) *Offender Management Caseload Statistics: Quarterly Brief October to December 2005 England and Wales.* Available online at: http://www.homeoffice.gov.uk/rds/pdfs06/omcsq405.pdf

NOMS (2006c) *Offender Management Caseload Statistics Quarterly Brief, July to September 2005.* Available online at: http://www.homeoffice.gov.uk/rds/omcs.html

NOMS (2006d) *Population in Custody: Monthly Tables October 2006 England and Wales.* Available online at: http://www.homeoffice.gov.uk/rds/pdfs06/prisoct06.pdf

Norris, C. (1995) 'Video Charts: Algorithmic Surveillance', *Criminal Justice Matters*, 20: 7–8.

Norris, C. (2003) 'From Personal to Digital: CCTV, the Panopticon and the Technological Mediation of Suspicion and Social Control', in D. Lyon (ed.), *Surveillance and Social Sorting: Privacy, Risk and Digital Discrimination,* London: Routledge, pp. 249–81.

Nuttall, C.P. (1977) *Parole in England and Wales.* Home Office Research Study No. 38. London: HMSO.

O'Connor, D. (2000) 'Stop and Think', *Guardian Society*, 19 January.

O'Donnell, I. and Edgar, K. (1996a) 'Routine Victimisation in Prisons', *Howard Journal,* 37: 266–79.

O'Donnell, I. and Edgar, K. (1996b) *Victimisation in Prisons.* Home Office Research Findings No. 37. London: Home Office Research and Statistics Directorate.

Office for National Statistics (2001) *Census 2001.* London: HMSO.

Oldfield, M. (1998) 'Case Management: Developing Theory and Practice', *Vista,* 4: 21–36.

Olkiewicz, E. (2003) 'The Evaluation of a Three Year Project on Electronic Monitoring in Sweden' in M. Mayer, R. Haverkamp and R. Levy (eds), *Will Electronic Monitoring Have a Future in Europe?'.* Freiburg: Max Planck Institute.

Osborn, S.G. and West, D.J. (1980) 'Do Young Delinquents Really Reform?', *Journal of Adolescence,* 3: 99–114.

PA Consultancy Group and MORI (2005) *Action Research Study of the Implementation of the National Offender Management Model in the North West Pathfinder.* London: Home Office.

Palmer, T. (1975) 'Martinson Revisited', *Journal for Research in Crime and Delinquency*, 12: 133–52.

Palumbo, D.J. (1986) 'Privatization and Corrections Policy', *Policy Studies Review* 5: 598–605.

Park, I. (2000) *Review of Comparative Costs and Performance of Privately and Publicly Operated Prisons, 1998–9.* Home Office Statistical Bulletin, 6/00. London: Home Office.

Parker, H., Sumner, M. and Jarvis, G. (1989) *Unmasking the Magistrates: The 'Custody or Not' Decision in Sentencing Young Offenders.* Milton Keynes: Open University Press.

Parole Board (2005) 'Denial of Guilt and the Parole Board'. Available online at: http://www.paroleboard.gov.uk/newsPage.asp?id+18.

Parole Board (2006) *Annual Report and Accounts of the Parole Board for England and Wales, 2005–06.* HC 1661. London: The Stationery Office. Available online at: http://www.paroleboard.gov.uk.

Parsons, T. (1937) *The Structure of Social Action.* New York: McGraw-Hill.

Parsons, T. (1951) *The Social System.* New York: Free Press.

Paternoster, R., Saltzman, L.E., Waldo, G.P. and Chiricos, T.G. (1983) 'Perceived Risk and Social Control: Do Sanctions Really Deter?', *Law and Society Review*, 17: 457–79.

Pearson, G. (1983) *Hooligan: A History of Respectable Fears.* London: Macmillan.

Pease, K. (1985) 'Community Service Orders' in N. Morris and M. Tonry (eds), *Criminal Justice: An Annual Review of Research,* vol. 6. Chicago: University of Chicago Press, pp. 51–94.

Pease, K. (1992) 'Punitiveness and Prison Populations', *Justice of the Peace*, 156: 405–8.

Pease, K. (1994) 'Cross-national Imprisonment Rates: Limitations of Method and Possible Conclusions', *British Journal of Criminology,* 34: 116–30.

Pease, K. (1999) 'The Probation Career of Al Truism', *Howard Journal of Criminal Justice*, 38: 2–15.

Pease, K. (2002) 'Crime Reduction', in M. Maguire, R. Morgan and R. Reiner (eds), 3rd edition, *The Oxford Handbook of Criminology* (3rd edition). Oxford: Oxford University Press, pp. 947–79.

Pease, K. and Wasik, M. (eds) (1987) *Sentencing Reform: Guidance or Guidelines?* Manchester: Manchester University Press.

Penal Affairs Consortium (1994) *The Mandatory Life Sentence.* London: Penal Affairs Consortium.

Penal Affairs Consortium (1995a) *Sentencing and Early Release: The Home Secretary's Proposals.* London: Penal Affairs Consortium.

Penal Affairs Consortium (1995b) *The 'Supermax' Option.* London: Penal Affairs Consortium.

Penal Affairs Consortium (2000) *A Joint Manifesto for Penal Reform 2000.* London: Penal Affairs Consortium.

Phillips, C. and Brown, D. (1998) *Entry into the Criminal Justice System: A Survey of Police Arrests and Their Outcomes.* Home Office Research Study No. 185. London: Home Office.

Piliavin, I. and Briar, S. (1964) 'Police Encounters with Juveniles', *American Journal of Sociology*, 70: 206–14.

Pilling, J. (1992) 'Back to Basics: Relationships in the Prison Service'. Eve Saville Memorial Lecture to the Institute for the Study and Treatment of Delinquency, reprinted in *Perspectives on Prison: A Collection of Views on Prison Life,* supplement to the annual report of the Prison Service for 1991–2. London: HMSO.

Pitts, J. (1986) 'Black Young People and Juvenile Crime: Some Unanswered Questions', in R. Matthews and J. Young (eds), *Confronting Crime.* London: Sage, pp. 118–44.

Pitts, J. (1988) *The Politics of Juvenile Crime.* London: Sage.

Pollak, O. (1961) *The Criminality of Women.* New York: A.S. Barnes.

Porter, R.G. (1990) 'The Privatization of Prisons in the United States: A Policy that Britain Should Not Emulate', *Howard Journal of Criminal Justice*, 29: 65–81.

Posen, D. (2003) 'Managing a Correctional Market Place: Prison Privatization in the United States and the United Kingdom', *Journal of Law and Ethics*, XIX: 253–84.

Pratt, J. (1986) 'A Comparative Analysis of Two Different Systems of Juvenile Justice: Some Implications for England and Wales', *Howard Journal of Criminal Justice*, 25: 33–51.

Pratt, J. (2000) 'The Return of the Wheelbarrow Men: Or, The Arrival of Postmodern Penality', *British Journal of Criminology*, 40: 127–45.

Pratt, J., Brown, D., Hallsworth, S., Brown, M. and Morrison, W. (eds) (2005) *The New Punitiveness: Trends, Theories, Perspectives*. Cullompton: Willan Publishing.

Pratt, T.C. and Maahs, J. (1999) 'Are Private Prisons More Cost Effective than Public Prisons? A Meta Analysis of Evaluation Research Studies', *Crime and Delinquency*, 45 (3): 358–71.

Prior, P.J. (1985) *Report of the Committee on the Prison Disciplinary System*. Cm 9641–I. London: HMSO.

Prison Industries Review Team (2003) *Prison Industries: An Internal Review of the Strategic Oversight and Management of Public Sector Prison Industries in England and Wales. Report by the Prison Industries Review Team.*

Prison Reform Trust (1991) *Management and Structure of the Prison Service: Woolf Briefing Paper No. 2*. London: Prison Reform Trust.

Prison Reform Trust (1996) 'Act of Immunity'. *Prison Report*, 36: 3.

Prison Reform Trust (1997a) *Sentencing: A Geographical Lottery*. London: Prison Reform Trust.

Prison Reform Trust (1997b) *The Rising Toll of Prison Suicides*. London: Prison Reform Trust. Also available online at: http://www.penlex.org.uk/pages/prtsuic.html.

Prison Reform Trust (1998a) 'Boards of Visitors: Whistle-blowers or Governors' Patsies?', *Prison Report*, 44: 6–7.

Prison Reform Trust (1998b) *Prison Privatization Report International*, Vol. 21.

Prison Reform Trust (1999a) *Prison Report*, 46: 3.

Prison Reform Trust (1999b) *Prison Privatization Report International*, Vol. 27.

Prison Reform Trust (2000) *A Hard Act to Follow? Prison and the Human Rights Act*. London: Prison Reform Trust.

Prison Reform Trust (2005a) 'Five Ways to Stem Prison Overcrowding'. Press release, October.

Prison Reform Trust (2005b) *Private Punishment: Who Profits?* London: Prison Reform Trust.

Prison Reform Trust (2005c) 'Jail Breaches Safe Limits.' Press release, 5 August.

Prison Reform Trust (2006a) 'Prisons Face Renewed Crowding Crisis'. Prison Facts briefing 4, April 2006. Also available online at: http://www.howardleague.org/fileadmin/howard_league/user/pdf/Gulag_Britain_27_July_2006.pdf

Prison Reform Trust (2006b) *Bromley Briefings, Prison Factfile*, November 2006. London: Prison Reform Trust.

Prisons Ombudsman (1995) *Prisons Ombudsman: A Six Month Review*. London: Prisons Ombudsman.

Prisons Ombudsman (2000) *Prisons Ombudsman: Annual Report 1999–2000*. London: Prisons Ombudsman.

Prisons and Probation Ombudsman (2006) *Annual Report, 2005-6*. Cm 6873. London: Prisons Ombudsman. Also available online at: http://www.ppo.gov.uk/annureps.htm

Pruitt, C.R. and Wilson, J.Q. (1983) 'A Longitudinal Study of the Effect of Race on Sentencing', *Law and Society Review*, 17: 613–35.

Public Services International Research Unit (PSIRU) (2004) *Prison Privatization Report International*, Vol. 65.

Public Services International Research Unit (PSIRU) (2005a) *Prison Privatization Report International*, Vol. 68.

Public Services International Research Unit (PSIRU) (2005b) *Prison Privatization Report International*, Vol. 69.

Public Services International Research Unit (PSIRU) (2005c) *Prison Privatization Report International*, Vol. 70.

Public Services International Research Unit (PSIRU) (2006) *Prison Privatization Report International*, vol. 71/22.

Pugh, R.B. (1968) *Imprisonment in Medieval England*. Cambridge: Cambridge University Press.

Quinn, P.M. (1993) 'Adjudications in Prison: Custody, Care and a Little Less Justice', *Howard Journal of Criminal Justice,* 32: 191–202.

Quinn, P.M. (1995) 'Adjudications in Prison: Custody, Care and a Little Less Justice', in M. Leech (ed.), *The Prisoners' Handbook 1995*. Oxford: Oxford University Press, pp. 320–7.

Quinney, R. (1977) *Class, State and Crime: on the Theory and Practice of Criminal Justice*. New York: David McKay.

Radzinowicz, L. (ed.) (1958) *The Results of Probation*. A Report of the Cambridge Department of Criminal Science. London: Macmillan.

Radzinowicz, L. (1988) Letter to *The Times,* 22 September.

Raher, S. (2002) 'Private Prisons and Public Money: Hidden Costs borne by Colorado's Taxpayers'. Available online at http://www.ccjrc.org

Raine, J.W. (1989) *Local Justice – Ideals and Realities*. Edinburgh: Clark.

Raine, J.W. (2006) 'NOMS and its Relationship to Crime Reduction', ch. 2 in M. Hough, R. Allen and U. Padel (eds), *Reshaping Probation and Prisons: the New Offender Management Framework*. Bristol: Policy Press.

Ramsbotham, D. (2005) *Prisongate: The Shocking State of Britain's Prisons and the Need for Visionary Change*. London: The Free Press.

Raynor, P. (1988) *Probation as an Alternative to Custody: A Case Study*. Aldershot: Avebury.

Raynor, P. (1993) *Social Work, Justice and Control*. Oxford: Blackwell.

Raynor, P. (2002) 'Community Penalties: Probation, Punishment and "What Works"', in M. Maguire, R. Morgan and R. Reiner (eds), *The Oxford Handbook of Criminology* (3rd edition). Oxford: Oxford University Press, pp. 1168–1205.

Raynor, P. (2004) 'Rehabilitative and Reintegrative Approaches', ch. 8 in A. Bottoms, S. Rex and G. Robinson (eds), *Alternative to Prison: Options for an Inseucre Society*. Cullompton: Willan.

Raynor, P. and Maguire, M. (2006) 'End-to-end or End in Tears? Prospects for the Effectiveness of the National Offender Management Model', ch. 3 in M. Hough, R. Allen and U. Padel (eds), *Reshaping Probation and Prisons: The New Offender Management Framework*. Bristol: Policy Press.

RDS NOMS (2004) *Offender Management Caseload Statistics 2003*. Available online at: http://www.homeoffice.gov.uk/rds/pdfs04/hosb1504.pdf

RDS NOMS (2005a) *Sentencing Statistics 2003 England and Wales*. Home Office Statistical Bulletin 05/05. London: Home Office. Available online at: http://www.homeoffice.gov.uk/rds/spnd.html

RDS NOMS (2005b) *Sentencing Statistics 2004 England and Wales*. Home Office Statistical Bulletin 15/05. London: Home Office. Available online at: http://www.homeoffice.gov.uk/rds/spnd.html

RDS NOMS (2006a) *Offender Management Caseload Statistics Quarterly Brief October to December 2005*. London: Home Office. Available online at: http://www.homeoffice.gov.uk/rds/omcs.html

RDS NOMS (2006b) *Offender Management Caseload Statistics 2005*. Home Office Statistical Bulletin 18/06. London: Home Office. Available online at: http://www.homeoffice.gov.uk/rds/omcs.html

Reed, J. and Lyne, M. (2000) 'Inpatient Care of Mentally Ill Prisoners: Results of a Year's Programme of Semistructured Inspections', *British Medical Journal*, 320: 1031–4.

Richardson, G. (1985) 'The Case for Prisoners' Rights', in M. Maguire, J. Vagg and R. Morgan (eds), *Accountability and Prisons: Opening Up a Closed World*. London: Tavistock Publications.

Riley, D. (1986) 'Sex Differences in Teenage Crime: The Role of Lifestyle', *Home Office Research Bulletin*, 20: 34–8.

Riley, D. and Shaw, M. (1985) *Parental Supervision and Juvenile Delinquency*, Home Office Research Study No. 83. London: HMSO.

Riley, D. and Vennard, J. (1988) *Triable Either Way Cases: Crown Court or Magistrates' Courts*. Home Office Research Study No. 98. London: HMSO.

Ritchie, J.H. (1994) *Report of the Inquiry into the Care and Treatment of Christopher Clunis*. London: HMSO.

Roberts, C. (2004) *Evaluation of the Community Sentences and Withdrawal of Benefits Pilots*, National Centre for Social Research and Department of Work and Pensions. Available online at: http://www.dwp.gov.uk/asd/asd5/rports2003-2004/rrep198.asp

Roberts, J. (2002) 'Public Opinion and the Nature of Community Penalties: International Findings', in J. Roberts and M. Hough (eds), *Changing Attitudes to Punishment: Public Opinion, Crime and Justice*. Cullompton: Willan Publishing, pp. 33–62.

Roberts, J. (2003) 'Evaluating the Pluses and Minuses of Custody: Sentencing Reform in England and Wales', *Howard Journal of Criminal Justice*, 42: 229–47.

Roberts, J. (2004) *The Virtual Prison*. Cambridge: Cambridge University Press.

Roberts, J. and Hough, M. (2005) *Understanding Public Attitudes to Criminal Justice*. Maidenhead: Open University Press.

Roberts, J., Stalans, L., Indermaur, D. and Hough, M. (2003), *Penal Populism and Public Opinion: Lessons from Five Countries*. Oxford: Oxford University Press.

Robinson, G. (1999) 'Risk-management and Rehabilitation in the Probation Service: Collision and Collusion', *Howard Journal of Criminal Justice*, 38 (4): 421–33.

Robinson, G. (2002) 'Exploring Risk Management in Probation Practice: Contemporary Developments in England and Wales', *Punishment & Society*, 4: 5–25.

Robinson, G. and Burnett, R. (forthcoming) 'The Elephant in the Room: Frontline Probation Perspectives on the Transition to a National Offender Management Service', *Criminology and Criminal Justice*.

Robinson, G. and Dignan, J. (2004) 'Sentence Management', in A. Bottoms, S. Rex and G. Robinson (eds), *Alternatives to Prison: Options for an Insecure Society*. Cullompton: Willan, pp. 313–40.

Ross, R.R., Fabiano, E.A. and Ewles, C.D. (1989) *Reasoning and Rehabilitation: A Handbook for Teaching Cognitive Skills*. Ottawa: The Cognitive Centre.

Rothman, D.J. (1971) *The Discovery of the Asylum*. Boston and Toronto: Little, Brown.

Rottman, D. and Casey, P. (1999) 'Therapeutic Jurisprudence and the Emergence of Problem-Solving Courts', *National Institution of Justice Journal*, 240: 12–19.

Royal Commission on Criminal Justice (1993) *Report*, Cm 2263. London: HMSO.

Ruggles-Brise, E. (1921) *The English Prison System*. London: Macmillan.

Rumgay, J. (2005) 'Counterblast: NOMS bombs?', *Howard Journal of Criminal Justice*, 44 (2): 207–8.

Rusche, G. and Kirchheimer, O. (1939) *Punishment and Social Structure*. New York: Columbia University Press.

Rutherford, A. (1985) 'The New Generation of Prisons', *New Society*, 73: 408–10.

Rutherford, A. (1986a) *Growing out of Crime*. Harmondsworth: Penguin.

Rutherford, A. (1986b) *Prisons and the Process of Justice*. Oxford: Oxford University Press.

Rutherford, A. (1988) 'The English Penal Crisis: Paradox and Possibilities', [1988] *Current Legal Problems*, pp. 93–113.

Rutherford, A. (1990) 'British Penal Policy and the Idea of Prison Privatization' in D.C. McDonald (ed.), *Private Prisons and the Public Interest*. New Brunswick, NJ: Rutgers University Press, pp. 42–65.

Rutherford, A. (1992) *Growing out of Crime: The New Era*. Winchester: Waterside Press.

Rutherford, A. (1993) *Criminal Justice and the Pursuit of Decency*. Oxford: Oxford University Press.

Rutter, M. and Giller, H. (1983) *Juvenile Delinquency: Trends and Perspectives*. Harmondsworth: Penguin.

Ryan, M. (1978) *The Acceptable Pressure Group*. Farnborough: Saxon House.

Ryan, M. (1993) Review of first edition of M. Cavadino and J. Dignan, *The Penal System: An Introduction*, in *International Journal of the Sociology of Law*, 21: 399–401.

Ryan, M. (1994) 'Some Arguments against the Use of Private Prisons', in C. Martin (ed.), *Contracts to Punish: Private or Public?*. Report of a Conference organized by the Institute for the Study and Treatment of Delinquency, held in Manchester on 24 November.

Ryan, M. and Ward, T. (1989a) *Privatization and the Penal System: The American Experience and the Debate in Britain*. Milton Keynes: Open University Press.

Ryan, M. and Ward, T. (1989b) 'Privatization and Penal Politics' in R. Matthews (ed.) (1989), *Privatizing Criminal Justice*. London: Sage Publications, pp. 53–73.

Sachdev, S. (2004) *Paying the Cost? Public Private Partnerships and the Public Sector Workforce*. A Catalyst Working Paper. London: Catalyst.

Samuels, A. (2003) 'In Denial of Murder: No Parole', *Howard Journal of Criminal Justice*, 42: 176–80.

Sanders, A. (1985) 'Class Bias in Prosecutions', *Howard Journal of Criminal Justice*, 24: 176–97.

Sanders, A. and Young, R. (2000) *Criminal Justice* (2nd edition). London: Butterworths.

Scarman, L. (1986) *The Scarman Report*. Harmondsworth: Penguin.

Schur, E.M. (1973) *Radical Nonintervention: Rethinking the Delinquency Problem*. Englewood Cliffs, NJ: Prentice-Hall.

Scottish Prison Service (2000) *The Scottish Prison Service Annual Report and Accounts 1999-2000*. Edinburgh: Scottish Prison Service. Also available online at: http://www.sps.gov.uk/Annual%20report%202000/sps0-00.htm

Scraton, P., Sim, J. and Skidmore, P. (1991) *Prisons Under Protest*. Milton Keynes: Open University Press.

Scull, A. (1977) *Decarceration: Community Treatment and the Deviant – A Radical View*. Englewood Cliffs, NJ: Prentice-Hall.

Scull, A. (1983) 'Community Corrections: Panacea, Progress or Pretence?' in D. Garland and P. Young (eds), *The Power to Punish: Contemporary Penality and Social Analysis*. London: Heinemann, pp. 146–65.

Scull, A. (1984) *Decarceration: Community Treatment and the Deviant – A Radical View* (2nd edition). Cambridge: Polity Press.

Seear, N. and Player, E. (1986) *Women in the Penal System*. London: Howard League for Penal Reform.

Sennett, R. (1998) *The Corrosion of Character: The Personal Consequences of Work in the New Capitalism*. New York: W.W. Norton.

Sentencing Guidelines Council (SGC) (2004) *New Sentences, Criminal Justice Act 2003*. Available online at: http://www.sentencing-guidelines.gov.uk

Sentencing Guidelines Council and Sentencing Advisory Panel (2006) *Annual Report 2005/06*. Available online at: http://www.sentencing-guidelines.gov.uk/docs

Shah, R. and Pease, K. (1992) 'Crime, Race and Reporting to the Police', *Howard Journal of Criminal Justice*, 31: 192–9.

Shapland, J. (1984) 'The Victim, the Criminal Justice System and Compensation', *British Journal of Criminology*, 24: 131–49.

Shapland, J. (1988) 'Fiefs and Peasants: Accomplishing Change for Victims in the Criminal Justice System', in M. Maguire and J. Pointing (eds), *Victims of Crime: A New Deal*. Milton Keynes and Philadelphia: Open University Press, pp. 187–94.

Shapland, J., Willmore, J. and Duff, P. (1985) *Victims in the Criminal Justice System*. Aldershot: Gower.

Shapland, J., Atkinson, A., Atkinson, H., Chapman, B., Colledge, E., Dignan, J., Howes, M., Johnstone, J., Robinson, G. and Sorsby, A. (2006) *Restorative Justice in Practice: The Second Report from the Evaluation of Three Schemes*. Sheffield: Centre for Criminological Research. Available online at: http://www.shef.ac.uk/ccr/

Shapland, J., Atkinson, A., Colledge, E., Dignan, J., Howes, M., Johnstone, J., Pennant, R., Robinson, G. and Sorsby, A. (2004) *Implementing Restorative Justice Schemes (Crime Reduction Programme). A Report on the First Year*. Home Office Online Report 32/04. London: Home Office.

Shaw, A. (1966) *Convicts and the Colonies*. London: Faber.

Shaw, S. (1980) *Paying the Penalty: An Analysis of the Cost of Penal Sanctions*. London: NACRO.

Shaw, S. (1989) 'A Bull Market for Prisons', ch. 4 in P. Carter, T. Jeffs, and M. Smith (eds), *Social Work and Social Welfare Yearbook 1*. Milton Keynes: Open University Press.

Shaw, S. (1992a) 'Prisons' in E. Stockdale and S. Casale (eds), *Criminal Justice under Stress*. London: Blackstone, pp. 160–78.

Shaw, S. (1992b) 'The Short History of Prison Privatization', *Prison Service Journal*, 87: 30–2.

Shaw, S. (1998) 'Desolation Row', *Prison Report*, 44: 10–11.

Shaw, S. (1999a) 'Desolation Row Revisited', *Prison Report*, 47: 8–9.

Shaw, S. (1999b) 'Home Detention Curfew – a Geographical Lottery', *Prison Report*, 48: 10.

Shepherd, A. and Whiting, E. (2006) *Re-offending of Adults: Results from the 2003 Cohort*. Home Office Statistical Bulletin 20/06. London: Home Office. Available online at: http://www.homeoffice.gov.uk/rds/pubsstatistical.html

Sheridan, A. (1980) *Michel Foucault: The Will to Truth*. London: Tavistock.

Shichor, D. (1995) *Prisons for Profit: Private Prisons/Public Concerns*. Thousand Oaks, CA: Sage.

Shute, S. (2004) '50th Anniversary Article: Punishing Murderers: Release Procedures and the "Tariff" 1952–2004' [2004] *Criminal Law Review*. 873–95.

de Silva, N., Cowell, P., Chow, T. and Worthington, P. (2006) *Prison Population Projections 2006–2013*. Home Office Statistical Bulletin 11/06. London: Home Office. Available online at: http://www.homeoffice.gov.uk/rds/pubsstatistical.html

Sim, J. (1992) '"When You Ain't Got Nothing You Got Nothing to Lose": The Peterhead Rebellion, the State and the Case for Prison Abolition', in K. Bottomley, T. Fowles and R. Reiner (eds), *Criminal Justice: Theory and Practice*. London: British Society of Criminology, pp. 273–300.

Sim, J. (1994) 'The Abolitionist Approach: A British Perspective', in A. Duff, S. Marshall, R.E. Dobash, and R.P. Dobash (eds), *Penal Theory and Penal Practice*. Manchester: Manchester University Press, pp. 263–84.

Simon, J. (1993) *Poor Discipline: Parole and the Social Control of the Underclass, 1890–1990*. Chicago: University of Chicago Press.

Sims, L. and Myhill, A. (2001) *Policing and the Public: Findings from the 2000 British Crime Survey*. Home Office Research Findings No. 136. London: Home Office.

Singleton, N., Meltzer, H. and Gatward, R. with Coid, J. and Deasy, D. (1998) *Psychiatric Morbidity among Prisoners in England and Wales*. London: The Stationery Office. Available online at: http://www.dh.gov.uk/PublicationsAndStatistics/Publications/PublicationsStatistics/PublicationsStatisticsArticle/fs/en?CONTENT_ID=4007132&chk=/NKemU

Skogan, W.G. (1990) *The Police and Public in England and Wales: A British Crime Survey Report*. Home Office Research Study No. 117. London: HMSO.

Skogan, W.G. (1994) *Contacts between Police and Public: Findings from the 1992 British Crime Survey*. Home Office Research Study No. 134. London: HMSO.

Skogan, W.G. (1995) *Policing and the Public in England and Wales: Findings from the 1994 British Crime Survey*. Home Office Research Findings No. 28. London: Home Office.

Smart, C. (1976) *Women, Crime and Criminology: A Feminist Critique*. London: Routledge & Kegan Paul.

Smellie, E. and Crow, I. (1991) *Black People's Experience of Criminal Justice*. London: NACRO.

Smith, D.J. (1983) *Police and People in London. I: A Survey of Londoners*. London: Policy Studies Institute.

Smith, D.J. and Gray, J. (1983) *Police and People in London. IV: The Police in Action*. London: Policy Studies Institute.

Smith, S. (1982) *Race and Crime Statistics*. London: Board for Social Responsibility, Church of England.

Social Exclusion Unit (2002) *Reducing Re-offending by Ex-prisoners*. London: Social Exclusion Unit.

Softley, P. (1978) *Fines in Magistrates' Courts*, Home Office Research Study No. 46. London: HMSO.

Solomon, E. (2004a) 'Jail Capital of Western Europe', *Prison Report* 63, March 2003: 8–9.

Solomon, E. (2004b) *A Measure of Success: An Analysis of the Prison Service's Performance against its Key Performance Indicators 2003–04.* London: Prison Report Trust, August.

Solomon, E. (2005), 'Returning to Punishment: Prison Recalls', *Criminal Justice Matters* 60.

Southgate, P. and Ekblom, P. (1986) Police–Public Encounters, Home Office Research Study No. 90. London: HMSO.

Sparks, J.R. and Bottoms, A.E.B. (1995) 'Legitimacy and Order in Prisons', *British Journal of Sociology*, 46: 45–62.

Sparks, J.R., Bottoms, A.E.B. and Hay, W. (1996) *Prisons and the Problem of Order.* Oxford: Clarendon Press.

Sparks, R. (1994) 'Can Prisons Be Legitimate? Penal Politics, Privatization, and the Timeliness of an Old Idea', *British Journal of Criminology*, 34: 14–28.

Sparks, R. (2001) 'The Special Handling of Difficult Prisoners in Comparative Context: a Note on Research Resources and Research Needs', in E. Clare and K. Bottomley (eds), *Evaluation of Close Supervision Centres.* Home Office Research Study No. 136. London: Home Office Research, Development and Statistics Directorate.

Spohn, C., Gruhl, J. and Welch, S. (1981–2) 'The Effect of Race on Sentencing: A Re-examination of an Unsettled Question', *Law and Society Review*, 16: 71–88.

Stafford, E. and Hill, J. (1987) 'The Tariff, Social Inquiry Reports and the Sentencing of Juveniles', *British Journal of Criminology*, 27: 411–20.

Statewatch Bulletin (2003) 'Prison Crisis', *Statewatch Bulletin*,14 (2).

Stern, V. (1993) *Bricks of Shame: Britain's Prisons* (2nd edition). London: Penguin.

Stern, V. (2005) *Prisons and their Communities: Testing a New Approach: An Account of the Restorative Prison Project 2000–2004.* London: International Centre for Prison Studies.

Stevens, J. (2002) Address to the Leicester Graduates' Association and the Haldane Society, 6 March. Available online at: http://www.guardian.co.uk/crime/article/0,2763,664344,00.html

Stevens, P. and Willis, C.F. (1979) *Race, Crime and Arrests.* Home Office Research Study No. 58. London: HMSO.

Stolzenberg, L. and D'Alessio, S.J. (1997) '"Three Strikes and You're Out". The Impact of California's New Mandatory Sentencing Law on Serious Crime Rates', *Crime and Delinquency*, 43: 457–69.

Stratton, B. (1973) *Who Guards the Guards?* London: North London Group of PROP (Preservation of the Rights of Prisoners).

Straw, J. (1996) 'Honesty, Consistency and Progression in Sentencing'. Paper for the PLP Home Affairs Committee.

Straw, J. and Michael, A. (1996) *Tackling Youth Crime, Reforming Youth Justice: A Consultation Paper on an Agenda for Change.* London: Labour Party.

Sutherland, E.H. (1956) 'Crime of Corporations' in A. Cohen, A. Lindesmith and K. Schuessler (eds), *The Sutherland Papers.* Bloomington, IN: Indiana University Press, pp. 78–96.

Tarling, R. (1993) *Analysing Offending: Data, Models and Interpretations.* London: HMSO.

Tarling, R. (2006) 'Sentencing Practice in Magistrates' Courts Revisited', *Howard Journal of Criminal Justice*, 45: 29–41

Tarling, R., Moxon, D. and Jones, P. (1985) 'Sentencing of Adults and Juveniles in Magistrates' Courts', in D. Moxon (ed.), *Managing Criminal Justice*. London: HMSO.

Taylor, I., Walton, P. and Young, J. (1973) *The New Criminology: For a Social Theory of Deviance*. London: Routledge and Kegan Paul.

Taylor, L., Lacey, R. and Bracken, D. (1979) *In Whose Best Interests? The Unjust Treatment of Children in Courts and Institutions*. London: Cobden Trust/MIND.

Taylor, M. and Pease, K. (1989) 'Private Prisons and Penal Purpose' in R. Matthews (ed.), *Privatizing Criminal Justice*. London: Sage Publications, pp.178–94.

Taylor, R. (2000) *A Seven-Year Reconviction Study of HMP Grendon Therapeutic Community*. Home Office Research Findings No. 115. London: Home Office Research and Statistics Directorate.

Taylor, W. (1981) *Probation and After-Care in a Multi-Racial Society*. London: Commission for Racial Equality.

Thomas, J.E. (1972) *The English Prison Officer since 1850*. London: Routledge and Kegan Paul.

Thomas, J.E. and Pooley, R. (1980) *The Exploding Prison: Prison Riots and the Case of Hull*. London: Junction Books.

Thompson, E.P. (1977) *Whigs and Hunters: The Origin of the Black Act*. Harmondsworth: Penguin.

Thompson, E.P. (1978) *The Poverty of Theory and Other Essays*. London: Merlin Press.

Thorpe, D.H., Smith, D., Green, C.J. and Paley, J.G. (1980) *Out of Care: The Community Support of Juvenile Offenders*. London: George Allen & Unwin.

Tonry, M. (2004) *Punishment and Politics: Evidence and Emulation in the Making of English Crime Control Policy*. Cullompton: Willan Publishing.

Tonry, M. and Farrington, D.P. (eds) (1995) *Building a Safer Society: Strategic Approaches to Crime Prevention*. Chicago: University of Chicago Press.

Törnudd, P. (1993) *Fifteen Years of Decreasing Prisoner Rates in Finland*. Helsinki: National Research Institute of Legal Policy.

Travis, A. (1993) 'Ministers' Tough Rhetoric to Blame for Overcrowding, Say Prison Reformers', *Guardian,* 8 September.

Travis, A. (2003) 'Courts Send Record Numbers to Prison', *Guardian*, 29 December.

Travis, A. (2005) 'Probation Hurtles Towards Labour's Big Market Test', *Guardian,* 19 October 2005.

Tremblay, R.E. and Craig, W.M. (1995) 'Developmental Crime Prevention' in M. Tonry and D.P. Farrington (eds), *Building a Safer Society: Strategic Approaches to Crime Prevention*. Chicago: University of Chicago Press, pp. 151–234.

Tyler, T.R. (1990) *Why People Obey the Law*. New Haven CT: Yale University Press.

Underdown, A. (1998) *Strategies for Effective Offender Supervision: Report of the HMIP What Works Project*. London: Home Office.

Underdown, A. (2001) 'Making "What Works" Work: Challenges In the Delivery of Community Penalties' in A.E. Bottoms, L. Gelsthorpe and S. Rex (eds), *Community Penalties: Change and Challenges*. Cullompton: Willan Publishing.

United States General Accounting Office (1991) *Private Prisons*. Washington DC: US Government Printing Office.

United States General Accounting Office (1996) *Private and Public Prisons: Studies Comparing Operational Costs and/or Quality of Service*. Reference Number GAO/GGD-96-198. Gaithersburg, MD: US General Accounting Office.

Vagg, J. (1991) 'Correcting Manifest Wrongs: Prison Grievance and Inspection Procedures in England and Wales, France, Germany and the Netherlands' in J. Muncie and R. Sparks (eds), *Imprisonment: European Perspectives*, Hemel Hempstead: Harvester Wheatsheaf, pp. 146–65.

Vennard, J. (1985) 'The Outcome of Contested Trials', in D. Moxon (ed.), *Managing Criminal Justice*. London: HMSO, pp. 126–51.

Vennard, J., Sugg, D. and Hedderman, C. (1997) *Changing Offenders' Attitudes and Behaviour: What Works?* Home Office Research Study No. 171. London: Home Office.

Voltaire (1947) *Candide*. Harmondsworth: Penguin.

Waddington, P.A., Stenson, K. and Don, D. (2004) 'In Proportion: Race and Police Stop and Search', *British Journal of Criminology*, 44: 889–914.

Walgrave, L. (1999) 'Community Service as a Cornerstone of a Systemic Restorative Response to (Juvenile) Crime' in G. Bazemore and L. Walgrave (eds), *Restorative Juvenile Justice: Repairing the Harm of Youth Crime*. Monsey, NY: Criminal Justice Press.

Walker, M. (1988) 'The Court Disposal of Young Males, by Race, in London in 1983', *British Journal of Criminology*, 28: 441–60.

Walker, N. (1968) *Crime and Punishment in Britain*. Edinburgh: University of Edinburgh Press.

Walker, N. (1972) *Sentencing in a Rational Society*. Harmondsworth: Penguin.

Walker, N. (1981) 'Feminists' Extravaganzas', [1981] *Criminal Law Review*: 379–86.

Walker, N. and Marsh, C. (1984) 'Do Sentences Affect Public Disapproval?', *British Journal of Criminology*, 24: 27–48.

Walmsley, R, (2005) *World Prison Population List* (6th edition). London: International Centre for Prison Studies, King's College London. Also available online at: http://www.prisonstudies.org.

Walmsley, R., Howard, L. and White, S. (1992) *The National Prison Survey 1991: Main Findings*. Home Office Research Study No. 128. London: HMSO.

Walters, I. (2002) *Evaluation of the National Roll-Out of Curfew Orders*. Home Office Online Report 15/02. Available at: http://www.crimereduction.gov.uk/working offenders38.htm

Ward, D. (1987) *The Validity of The Reconviction Prediction Score*. Home Office Research Study No. 94. London: HMSO.

Wasik, M. (2004a) 'What Guides Sentencing Decisions?', in A. Bottoms, S. Rex and G. Robinson (eds), *Alternatives to Prison: Options for an Insecure Society*. Cullompton: Willan Publishing, pp. 290–312.

Wasik, M. (2004b) 'Sentencing Guidelines: Past, Present and Future', in M. Freeman (ed.), *Current Legal Problems 2003*. Oxford: Oxford University Press, pp. 239–64.

Watkins, M., (2003) *The Sentence of the Court* (4th edition). Winchester: Waterside Press.

Watson, D., Boucherat, J. and Davis, G. (1989) 'Reparation for Retributivists' in M. Wright and B. Galaway (eds), *Mediation and Criminal Justice: Victims, Offenders an Community*. London: Sage.

Weber, M. (1930) *The Protestant Ethic and the Spirit of Capitalism*. London: George Allen & Unwin.

Weber, M. (1968) *Economy and Society*. New York: Bedminster Press.

West, D.J. (1982) *Delinquency: Its Roots, Careers and Prospects*. London: Heinemann.

Western, B. and Beckett, K. (1999), 'How Unregulated is the US Labor Market? The Penal System as Labor Market Institution', *American Journal of Sociology*, 104: 1030–60.

Whatmore, P.B. (1987) 'Barlinnie Special Unit: An Insider's View', in A.E. Bottoms and R. Light (eds), *Problems of Long-Term Imprisonment*, Aldershot: Gower, pp. 249–60.

Wilcox, A., Young, R. and Hoyle, C. (2004) *Two-year Resanctioning Study: A Comparison of Restorative and Traditional Cautions*. Home Office Online Report No. 57/04, available online at: http://www.homeoffice.gov.uk/rds/

Willcock, H.D. and Stokes, J. (1968) *Deterrents and Incentives to Crime Among Boys and Young Men Aged 15–21 Years*. London: HMSO.

Willis, C.F. (1983) *The Use, Effectiveness and Impact of Police Stop and Search Powers*. London: Home Office.

Wilson, D. (2006) 'The Case for Penal Abolition in England and Wales'. Lecture delivered to the Public Management and Policy Association on 17 February.

Windlesham, D. (1993) *Responses to Crime, Volume 2: Penal Policy in the Making*. Oxford: Clarendon Press.

Wolds Board of Visitors (1995) *Annual Report to the Secretary of State for the Home Department, Year Ending 31 December 1994*, BoV, HMP Wolds.

Wood, M. (2003) *Victimisation of Young People: Findings from Crime and Justice Survey 2003*. Home Office Research Findings No. 246. London: Home Office.

Woodbridge, J. (1999) *Review of Comparative Costs and Performance of Privately and Publicly Operated Prisons, 1997–8*. Home Office Statistical Bulletin, 13/99.

Woodcock, J. (1994) *The Escape from Whitemoor Prison on Friday 9th September 1994 (The Woodcock Enquiry)*, Cm 2741. London: HMSO.

Woolf, H. and Tumim, S. (1991) *Prison Disturbances April 1990*, Cm 1456. London: HMSO.

Worrall, A. and Pease, K. (1986) 'The Prison Population in 1985', *British Journal of Criminology*, 26: 184–7.

Wozniak, E. and McAllister, D. (1991) 'Facilities, Standards and Change in the Scottish Prison Service: The Prison Survey 1990/91'. Paper presented at the British Criminology Conference, University of York, July.

Wynne, J. (1996) 'Leeds Mediation and Reparation Service: Ten Years' Experience with Victim–Offender Mediation', ch. 26 in B. Galaway and J. Hudson (eds) *Restorative Justice: International Perspectives*. Monsey, NY: Criminal Justice Press and Amsterdam: Kugler Publications.

Young, P. (1987) *The Prison Cell*. London: Adam Smith Institute.

Youth Justice Board (2004) *Annual Statistics 2003/4*. London: Youth Justice Board.

Youth Justice Board (2006) *Anti-Social Behaviour Orders*. London: Youth Justice Board. Summary available online at: http://www.yjb.gov.uk/publications/Scripts/prodView.asp?idproduct=309&eP=

Zehr, H. (1985) *Retributive Justice, Restorative Justice*. Elkhart, IN: Mennonite Central Committee, US Office of Criminal Justice.

Zimring, F.E., Hawkins, G. and Kamin, S. (2001) *Punishment and Democracy: Three Strikes and You're Out in California*. Oxford: Oxford University Press.

Index